Lecture Notes in Computer Science   **9358**

Commenced Publication in 1973
Founding and Former Series Editors:
Gerhard Goos, Juris Hartmanis, and Jan van Leeuwen

More information about this series at http://www.springer.com/series/7412

Juergen Gall · Peter Gehler
Bastian Leibe (Eds.)

Pattern Recognition

37th German Conference, GCPR 2015
Aachen, Germany, October 7–10, 2015
Proceedings

 Springer

Editors
Juergen Gall
Institute of Computer Science III
University of Bonn
Bonn
Germany

Peter Gehler
MPI for Intelligent Systems
University of Tübingen
Tübingen
Germany

Bastian Leibe
Computer Vision Group
Visual Computing Institute
RWTH Aachen
Aachen
Germany

ISSN 0302-9743 ISSN 1611-3349 (electronic)
Lecture Notes in Computer Science
ISBN 978-3-319-24946-9 ISBN 978-3-319-24947-6 (eBook)
DOI 10.1007/978-3-319-24947-6

Library of Congress Control Number: 2015949444

LNCS Sublibrary: SL6 – Image Processing, Computer Vision, Pattern Recognition, and Graphics

Printed on acid-free paper

Springer International Publishing AG Switzerland is part of Springer Science+Business Media
(www.springer.com)

Preface

It was a pleasure to organize the 37th German Conference on Pattern Recognition (GCPR), which was held in Aachen during October 7–10, 2015. This time, GCPR was co-located with the 20th International Symposium on Vision, Modeling and Visualization (VMV).

For GCPR 2015, we received 108 submissions from institutions of 28 countries. Each paper underwent a rigorous double-blind reviewing procedure by at least three Program Committee (PC) members, sometimes with support from additional experts. Afterward, one of the involved PC members served as moderator for a discussion among the reviewers and prepared a consolidation report that was also forwarded to the authors in addition to the reviews. The final decision was made during a PC meeting held in Aachen based on all reviews, discussions, and, if necessary, additional reviewing. As a result of this rigorous reviewing procedure, 45 of the 108 submissions were accepted, which corresponds to an acceptance rate of 42 %. Finally, these accepted papers were presented either as oral talks (18) or posters (27) in a single-track program. All accepted papers are published in these proceedings and cover the entire spectrum of pattern recognition, machine learning, image processing, and computer vision. Following the tradition of this conference series, GCPR 2015 also featured a Young Researchers Forum to promote scientific interaction between excellent young researchers and our community. From eight submissions, five works were selected for a poster presentation and one was additionally included as a short paper in the proceedings.

In addition, we were very happy to have three internationally renowned researchers as our invited speakers to present their work in three fascinating areas: Andrew Blake (Microsoft Research Cambridge, UK), Niloy J. Mitra (University College London, UK), and Max Welling (University of Amsterdam, The Netherlands and University of California Irvine, USA). The technical program was complemented by one workshop and one tutorial. The Workshop on New Challenges in Neural Computation (NC2) was organized by Barbara Hammer (Bielefeld University), Thomas Martinetz (University of Lübeck), and Thomas Villmann (University of Applied Sciences Mittweida). The Tutorial on Causality was held by Jonas Peters (Max Planck Institute for Intelligent Systems).

The success of GCPR 2015 would not have been possible without the support of many institutions and people. First of all, we would like to thank all authors of the submitted papers and the invited speakers for their contributions. All PC members and additional reviewers deserve great thanks for their timely and competent reviews. We are grateful to our sponsors for their support as well. Finally, special thanks go to the

Proceedings and Website Chairs and the Local Organizing Committee. We would like to thank Springer for giving us the opportunity of continuing to publish GCPR proceedings in the LNCS series.

October 2015

Juergen Gall
Peter Gehler
Bastian Leibe

Organization

General Chair

Bastian Leibe   RWTH Aachen University, Germany

Program Chairs

Juergen Gall   University of Bonn, Germany
Peter Gehler   University of Tübingen and MPI for Intelligent Systems, Germany

Program Committee

Christian Bauckhage	Fraunhofer IAIS, Germany
Horst Bischof	Graz University of Technology, Austria
Thomas Brox	University of Freiburg, Germany
Andrés Bruhn	University of Stuttgart, Germany
Joachim Buhmann	ETH Zürich, Switzerland
Daniel Cremers	TU Munich, Germany
Andreas Dengel	DFKI and TU Kaiserslautern, Germany
Joachim Denzler	University of Jena, Germany
Paolo Favaro	University of Bern, Switzerland
Michael Felsberg	Linköping University, Sweden
Gernot A. Fink	TU Dortmund, Germany
Boris Flach	Czech TU in Prague, Czech Republic
Jan-Michael Frahm	University of North Carolina, USA
Uwe Franke	Daimler AG, Germany
Simone Frintrop	University of Bonn, Germany
Mario Fritz	MPI for Informatics and Saarland University, Germany
Andreas Geiger	MPI for Intelligent Systems, Germany
Michael Goesele	TU Darmstadt, Germany
Bastian Goldlücke	University of Konstanz, Germany
Olaf Hellwich	TU Berlin, Germany
Slobodan Ilic	TU Munich, Germany
Stefanie Jegelka	Massachusetts Institute of Technology, USA
Xiaoyi Jiang	Münster University, Germany
Reinhard Klette	University of Auckland, New Zealand
Reinhard Koch	Kiel University, Germany
Ullrich Köthe	University of Heidelberg, Germany
Walter G. Kropatsch	Vienna University of Technology, Austria
Christoph H. Lampert	IST Austria

Hendrik Lensch	University of Tübingen, Germany
Andreas Maier	University of Erlangen-Nürnberg, Germany
Helmut Mayer	Bundeswehr University Munich, Germany
Rudolf Mester	University of Frankfurt, Germany
Sebastian Nowozin	Microsoft Research, Cambridge, UK
Björn Ommer	University of Heidelberg, Germany
Josef Pauli	University of Duisburg-Essen, Germany
Dietrich Paulus	University of Koblenz-Landau, Germany
Thomas Pock	Graz University of Technology, Austria
Olaf Ronneberger	University of Freiburg, Germany
Bodo Rosenhahn	University of Hannover, Germany
Stefan Roth	TU Darmstadt, Germany
Volker Roth	University of Basel, Switzerland
Carsten Rother	TU Dresden, Germany
Hanno Scharr	Jülich Research Centre, Germany
Daniel Scharstein	Middlebury College, USA
Bernt Schiele	MPI for Informatics and Saarland University, Germany
Konrad Schindler	ETH Zürich, Switzerland
Christoph Schnörr	University of Heidelberg, Germany
Carsten Steger	MVTec Software GmbH, Germany
Rainer Stiefelhagen	Karlsruhe Institute of Technology, Germany
Peter Sturm	Inria Grenoble - Rhône-Alpes, France
Björn Schuller	University of Passau, Germany
Joachim Weickert	Saarland University, Germany
Martin Welk	UMIT Hall, Austria
Angela Yao	University of Bonn, Germany

Additional Reviewers

H. Ackermann	F. Engelmann	A. Krull
S. Ahmed	S. Esquivel	A. Kuznetsova
Z. Al-Halah	T. Falk	C. Lanaras
M. Barnada	N. Fanani	L. Leal-Taixe
V. Belagiannis	P. Fischer	D. Liu
R. Bensch	O. Fleischmann	O. Müller
T. Birdal	J. Gast	L. Ma
J. Brünger	H. Geng	D. Mai
E. Brachmann	V. Golkov	R. Maier
S. Breuers	R. Grzeszick	S. Majumder
H.-J. Chien	T. Hackel	D. Maurer
Ö. Cicek	D. Hafner	G. Meneghetti
M. Danelljan	V. Haltakov	F. Miletari
J. Deng	S. Hoffmann	E.-D. Mousa
B. Dong	Y.-C. Ju	S. Nagaraja
B. Drayer	M. Kiefel	M. Ochs

K. Öfjäll	L. Rothacker	M. Stoll
A. Osep	S. Sarfraz	S. Sudholt
N. Persch	S. Schaeffer	J. Tao
P. Peter	T. Scharwächter	M. Tapaswi
S. Poelsterl	M. Schmidt	V. Usenko
S. Reinhold	A. Schwarz	S. Volz
F. Ringeval	N. Sedaghat	T. von Marcard
A. Robinson	M. Souiai	D. Wolters

Proceedings Chair

Esther Horbert

Website Chairs

Anne Kathrein
Michael Kramp
Isaak Lim

Local Organizing Committee

Silke van Betteray
Monika Maszynkiewicz
Claudia Prast

Awards 2014

Deutscher Mustererkennungspreis 2014

The "Deutscher Mustererkennungspreis 2014" was awarded to

Prof. Dr. Juergen Gall

for his outstanding work on interacting particle systems and random forests with applications to human pose estimation, object detection, and action recognition.

GCPR 2014

Best Paper Award

Daniel Scharstein, Heiko Hirschmüller, York Kitajima, Greg Krathwohl, Nera Nesic, Xi Wang, and Porter Westling:
High-Resolution Stereo Datasets with Subpixel-Accurate Ground Truth

Honorable Mention

Dmitry Laptev and Joachim M. Buhman:
Convolutional Decision Trees for Feature Learning and Segmentation

Rene Ranftl and Thomas Pock:
A Deep Variational Model for Image Segmentation

Young Researchers Forum

Ilya Kostrikov, RWTH Aachen University:
Random Forests for 3D Pose Estimation from 2D Images

Christian Rupprecht, TU Munich:
Image Segmentation in Twenty Questions

Miroslava Slavcheva, TU Munich:
Implicit-to-Implicit Registration for Real-Time 3D Reconstruction from RGB-D Data

David Stutz, RWTH Aachen University:
Superpixel Segmentation: An Evaluation

Felix Widmaier, University of Tübingen:
Robot Arm Tracking with Random Decision Forests

Contents

Young Researchers Forum

Motion and Reconstruction

Road Condition Estimation Based on Spatio-Temporal Reflection Models

Manuel Amthor[1]([✉]), Bernd Hartmann[2], and Joachim Denzler[1]

[1] Computer Vision Group, Friedrich Schiller University Jena,
Jena, Germany
`manuel.amthor@uni-jena.de`
[2] Advanced Engineering, Continental Teves AG & Co. oHG,
Frankfurt a.M., Germany

Abstract. Automated road condition estimation is a crucial basis for Advanced Driver Assistance Systems (ADAS) and even more for highly and fully automated driving functions in future. In order to improve vehicle safety relevant vehicle dynamics parameters, *e.g. last-point-to-brake* (LPB), *last-point-to-steer* (LPS), or *vehicle curve speed* should be adapted depending on the current weather-related road surface conditions. As vision-based systems are already integrated in many of today's vehicles they constitute a beneficial resource for such a task. As a first contribution, we present a novel approach for reflection modeling which is a reliable and robust indicator for wet road surface conditions. We then extend our method by texture description features since local structures enable for the distinction of snow-covered and bare road surfaces. Based on a large real-life dataset we evaluate the performance of our approach and achieve results which clearly outperform other established vision-based methods while ensuring real-time capability.

1 Introduction

The continuous improvement of road safety is an important field of research and development in the automotive industry. Considerable efforts have been made to reduce the number of road fatalities, damages and the consequences of accidents, *e.g.* by automated emergency brake systems [10], road detection for lane departure warning [2], or vulnerability prediction [18]. Advanced Driver Assistance Systems (ADAS) which warn and support the driver in normal driving and especially in hazard situations form an important contribution towards "vision zero" [6]. As for example to assess a critical driving situation properly the understanding of the present road condition is of vital importance. Nowadays, this information is determined manually by the driver but is intended to be estimated automatically to serve as input for higher automated vehicle safety systems. Based on this valuable information the effectiveness of current assistance systems can be increased considerably, *e.g.* by adapting system thresholds such as *last-point-to-brake* (LPB) for automated emergency brake systems. Furthermore, it is desired to obtain the current road condition automatically for the purpose of highly and fully automated driving in the future.

© Springer International Publishing Switzerland 2015
J. Gall et al. (Eds.): GCPR 2015, LNCS 9358, pp. 3–15, 2015.
DOI: 10.1007/978-3-319-24947-6_1

Recent advances in road condition estimation based on on-board surrounding sensors, as for example rain, humidity, or laser sensors, have proven to be the key element for the task at hand. Another potential resource are visual sensors which have the advantage of being already integrated in many of today's vehicles. Additionally, cameras allow for hazard prediction as they asses the area directly in front of the moving vehicle. Thereby, the most difficult task is the recognition of wet and icy areas, being some of the most dangerous situations. By using stereo vision systems this challenge can be addressed by utilizing polarization filters [7] to obtain information about the presence of reflections as a typical indicator for those conditions. However, since the market penetration of stereo camera systems is very low compared to mono camera systems, road condition estimation has to be performed on monocular image data which renders the task very challenging.

In this paper, our goal is to overcome limitations of road condition estimation based on single cameras in order to distinguish between dry, wet and snow-covered road surface conditions. In particular, we apply enhanced spatio-temporal reflection models combined with strong texture description features. Furthermore, our proposed method is very robust to occurring disturbances and achieves real-time capability.

In Sect. 2 we give an overview of related work and motivate our approach. Section 3 presents our novel method in detail based on previously introduced standard techniques for reflection modeling. In Sect. 4 the actual road condition estimation framework is explained which is currently implemented in a first demonstration vehicle. A comprehensive evaluation on a large real-life dataset is finally presented in Sect. 5.

2   Related Work

In the past decades several approaches have been developed for the challenging task of road condition estimation. There are mainly two approaches to provide weather-related information for individual vehicles. On the first hand, so-called road side units [16] collect data in a specific region by a variety of sensors. Afterwards, these statistics are processed and distributed to individual vehicles as presented in [13]. On the other hand, this network can be supported by each particular vehicle as well by utilizing on-board surrounding sensors for rain [8], air humidity [21], acoustics [1,12], and surface roughness [5].

In the area of pure computer vision, the most challenging task is to detect wet road surface conditions. Usually, this problem can be addressed by using a stereo camera setup utilized with polarization filters [7]. To be able to distinguish between dry, wet and snowy conditions, polarization characteristics are combined with additional image feature types like *gray level co-occurrence matrices* [17,24] or *wavelet packet transforms* [25].

However, in the absence of a stereo camera system, as it is commonly the case for most of the today's vehicles, more elaborate features based on single cameras have to be developed. As for example in [19,20] sole texture description followed by a dimensionality reduction technique is applied for stationary road condition estimation. Examples for on-board systems are presented in [9,22] where texture characterization based on *gray level co-occurrence matrices* is the key element. In the work of [9] texture description is extended by additional block-wise RGB ratios to obtain color and luminance features. Another interesting method presented in [15] applies block-wise RGB histograms combined with edge histograms considering the entire lower image region in order to cover additional information.

In the case of monocular image analysis it is still difficult to detect wet areas due to the high variability of the appearance of those regions caused by mirrored environmental objects. To overcome these difficulties certain road conditions can be determined by modeling different reflection types based on spatio-temporal information, *i.e.* taking an image sequence into account. In the course of this, typical reflections for wet situations, namely *specular reflections*, are modeled by investigating appearance variations of individual road surface regions as presented in [23]. The major drawback of this approach is the required time-consuming registration of individual regions which is also prone to unregistered movements of the vehicle.

Therefore, in this work we present a novel approach to model reflection types by not considering individual regions directly but by evaluating the paths those regions pass. By assuming an almost linear motion of the vehicle together with an appropriate image transformation, considered regions will pass the scene through individual image columns which then provide all relevant information of potential appearance changes. This enables us to avoid expensive and unstable registration techniques in contrast to other works. We then combine our novel reflection features with strong texture description to obtain a robust and fast approach for the challenging task of road condition estimation.

3   Fast and Robust Reflection Modeling

The most difficult part of road condition estimation is the recognition of wet areas on the road surface. Due to the high variability of the appearance of wet regions particularly caused by unpredictable mirrored environmental objects, features such as texture description, color information, statistical moments, etc. turned out to be not very discriminative. However, exactly those mirrored objects are considered as key elements for wet surface recognition in our paper. The main issue is to not only consider one single frame but to evaluate a sequence of consecutive images. With the help of this spatio-temporal modeling the nature of different reflection types can be revealed. This allows for the recognition of wet surfaces in a very general way. Thus, in the following sections different reflection types together with their properties are introduced in detail. Afterwards, a basic approach for the detection of a specific reflection type indicating wet conditions–namely *specular reflections*–is presented. Motivated by serious shortcomings of this basic technique a novel method for the recognition of reflection types is introduced in Subsect. 3.3.

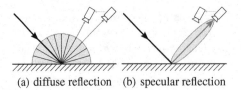

(a) diffuse reflection   (b) specular reflection

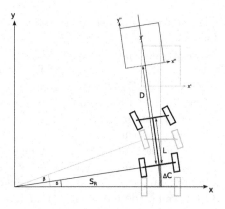

Fig. 1. Scheme of different reflection types. In (a) diffuse reflection is shown where the incident light is equally scattered in all directions. A change of the viewpoint has no visual effect on the observed surface point. In (b) a specular reflection is depicted and the reflected light is focused into one single direction. An altered perspective would lead to an appearance shift of the observed surface, since the particular reflected ray would no longer meet the camera.

Fig. 2. Schematic representation of recovering individual regions on the road in consecutive frames based on the one-track-model.

3.1   Diffuse and Specular Reflections

As mentioned above our main assumption is that identifying surface reflection types allows for the distinction between the underlying road condition. In Fig. 1(a) and (b) the difference between diffuse and specular reflections is depicted. In the case of dry asphalt as well as snow coverage fine-grained structures on the surface reflect incident light in all directions equally. Thus, a change of the perspective would lead to the same visual appearance of the focused region. In contrast, a surface covered by water is very smooth which has the properties of a mirror and thus the incident light is theoretically reflected in exactly one direction. If the perspective changes, this reflection will no longer encounter the observer's view and the region seems to change its appearance.

To decide about the presence of specular reflections and thus the occurrence of wet road conditions, potential appearance changes of individual regions have to be evaluated. This can be realized by comparing identical regions on the road between several consecutive frames. In the following section a basic method is presented which allows for the examination of particular regions with respect to the presence of specular reflections given a sequence of images.

3.2   Physical Model

To decide about the present reflection type it is required to evaluate the change of appearance of individual regions on the surface along consecutive frames. Therefore, corresponding pixel values of those regions have to be considered. To be able to align such regions over different frames it is beneficial to project the original image into a top view image based on an estimated homography. Hence, potential transformations are reduced to simple translation and rotation. To obtain the geometric transition between two consecutive frames *vehicle dynamics parameters* have to be taken into account. Those parameters–available from the vehicle's system–provide the current steering angle as well as the actual velocity and thus the distance traveled during two acquired images. In Fig. 2 the geometric relationship between two frames is shown exemplarily. As can be seen an individual point (x', y') placed in the top view image of frame f' can be recovered as (x'', y'') in the subsequent frame f''. The corresponding transformation between these points can be expressed in general by

$$x'' = (x' + S_R) \cdot \cos\left(\frac{\Delta C}{S_R}\right) + (y' + D) \cdot \sin\left(\frac{\Delta C}{S_R}\right) - S_R$$

$$y'' = -(x' + S_R) \cdot \sin\left(\frac{\Delta C}{S_R}\right) + (y' + D) \cdot \cos\left(\frac{\Delta C}{S_R}\right) - D, \qquad (1)$$

where S_R is the pole distance, ΔC is the distance traveled, and D is the offset between rear axle and the region of interest. Additionally, the pole distance can be obtained by $S_R = \frac{L}{\tan(\beta)}$ where L denotes the distance between rear and front axle. However, β increases proportionally with the current steering angle for which the relationship has to be estimated in advance. As can be seen $\delta = \frac{\Delta C}{S_R}$ is basically the angle of the rotation matrix for the required image transformation.

Once all frames are registered and related regions are aligned the evaluation of potential appearance changes can be applied. The most intuitive way is to determine the gray value variances of corresponding pixels along the time axis which can be enhanced by considering grid cells instead of single pixels to avoid misalignments caused by small transformation errors. The result of this procedure is an image containing the variance over time at each pixel location and thus an indication of the present reflection type. However, under real world conditions, serious problems arise due to the technical setup as well as the simple assumptions. At first, erroneous transformations between two frames can be obtained due to the fixed homography in combination with common vertical movements of the car. Those errors increase drastically for regions which are far away from the observer. In order to rectify the biased transformation it is possible to adapt the homography for each frame individually based on ground-plane estimation. However, the estimation over several frames leads to cumulative errors in terms of sub-pixel accuracy caused by the coarse discrete scale of the *vehicle dynamics parameters*, e.g. the steering angle. To resolve these problems, in the following, we propose a novel fast and robust reflection modeling approach which can easily deal with inaccurate motion estimation.

3.3 A Novel Approach: Specular Reflection Maps

The idea we suggest in our paper is to evaluate paths of individual regions instead of regions themselves. This approach allows for accurate detections of different reflection types even during severe unregistered movements of the car. Note, that the following method is based on the introduced top view transformation (*cf.* Subsect. 3.2).

Let us assume an almost linear motion of the vehicle. Then, an individual point on the surface will pass the region of interest through a single image column of the transformed top view image. Hence, potential appearance variations can be detected not by tracking the region directly but by assessing the path of the region, *i.e.* the same image column of consecutive frames. To obtain one image including those temporal information an average image $\bar{I}_t$ is computed by

$$\bar{I}_t = \alpha \cdot \bar{I}_{t-1} + (1 - \alpha) \cdot I_t. \tag{2}$$

To be able to emphasize recent events we make use of the moving average controlled by the parameter α. Furthermore, only one single image has to be kept in memory which is of great benefit regarding embedded systems. By subtracting the column average from each point of the average image $\bar{I}_t$ reflection types can be distinguished by the resulting *specular reflection map* given by

$$SRM_t(x,y) = \bar{I}_t(x,y) - \frac{1}{K} \sum_{k=0}^{K} \left(\bar{I}_t(x,k) \right). \tag{3}$$

The idea is that diffuse reflections, *i.e.* without appearance variations, have similar values along the corresponding image column in $\bar{I}_t$. Thus, subtracting the column average leads to small values for most of the surface points. In contrast, specular reflections provide severe appearance changes and the related image column of $\bar{I}_t$ yields high variance resulting in high values for SRM_t. In Fig. 3 the different stages of our approach can be seen for two examples showing dry and

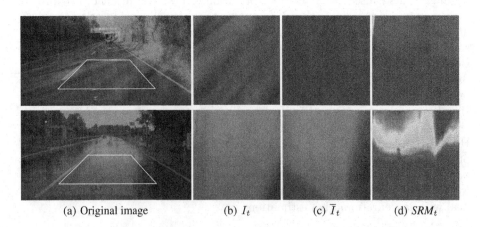

(a) Original image   (b) I_t (c) $\bar{I}_t$ (d) SRM_t

Fig. 3. Examples for reflection modeling based on *specular reflection maps*. The first row shows an example taken from a dry road. In the second row an instance of a wet road is presented. The pipeline for reflection detection is depicted for an image (a) which was transformed into a top view (b). The averaged frame (c) is computed based on previous frames which results finally in the corresponding refection map (d).

wet asphalt. The resulting reflection maps clearly show the indication for the described reflection types and in consequence the different road conditions.

To finally obtain features based on the computed *specular reflection map* (SRM_t) several methods can be applied. As presented later (*cf.* Subsect. 4.2) we use texture description based on *Local Binary Patterns* (*LBPs*) [14] in order to extract discriminative features for dry and wet road conditions.

The major advantage of our proposed method is that no expensive tracking of individual regions or an image registration technique is required. Furthermore, our method only needs to compute simple image averages and subsequent subtractions. Hence, results can be computed very efficiently while being robust against unregistered movements in contrast to the physical model described in Subsect. 3.2.

4 Road Condition Estimation Framework

Since the main goal of this work is to estimate the actual road condition, a common classification framework is utilized. The processing pipeline consists of three stages, namely the selection of a region of interest, the extraction of appropriate features, and finally the classification into road condition classes. In the following each of these essential steps is explained in detail.

4.1 Region of Interest

To obtain suitable feature vectors, describing a specific image region, the shape and size of this region has to be defined in advance. In [2] it was shown that road-only parts can be determined optimally by *semantic segmentation*. For our method, however, the region is limited to a simple and static geometric shape since we focus on feature extraction as well as the classification process. As already mentioned in Sect. 3, a favorable shape of this region would be a trapezoidal one, since the required rectangular top view image can be obtained based on an estimated homography. In our setup the homography is assumed to be fixed, although the ground-plane changes due to small vertical movements of the car.

4.2 Feature Extraction

Once the region of interest is defined, features can be obtained from the covered area to describe the underlying road condition. Several feature types have been investigated during the past and we found two very crucial feature types for the task at hand. In the first place, the novel *specular reflection maps* introduced in Subsect. 3.3 which aim to detect specular reflections are an essential resource to distinguish between dry and wet road conditions. Secondly, texture features have proven to be most suitable to describe characteristic structures caused by wheel tracks on wet asphalt or on snow-covered roads.

Specular Reflection Maps Based on a quantitative analysis–which is not presented in this paper due to the limited space–we found that texture description methods are most suitable to cover meaningful information provided by the *specular reflection map*. Thereby, unique patterns induced by the presence of wet areas can be recognized in a very robust manner. As shown in the next paragraph *LBPs* are a prominent approach for the task of texture description. For our scenario of reflection maps it is superior in terms of accuracy to other state-of-the-art approaches such as GLCMs [4]. Additionally, those descriptors can be computed very efficiently which is a crucial factor when implemented on embedded systems.

Texture Description Since sole reflection modeling is not sufficient to distinguish between dry and snow-covered areas, texture description on the original image became the second key element. Here, characteristic structures on the lane provide useful information about the present road condition. As already mentioned in the previous paragraph *LBPs* have proven to be the most suitable texture description approach for the task at hand. The reasons for that are twofold: On the one hand, *LBPs* can be computed very efficiently which is as beneficial as crucial while running on an embedded environment. On the other hand, it is highly discriminative in contrast to other fast texture recognition methods. As we are interested in the texture of the actual road surface, a cropped version of the original image is transformed into a top view image (*cf.* Sect. 3). We limit ourselves to the intensity channel of the HSI image representation, since color information is prone to color shifts (*e.g.* different colored windshields).

4.3 Classification

The final step in our framework is the classification into road condition classes, namely dry, wet, and snow-covered. We have decided for *Extremely Randomized Trees* [3] as a prominent non-linear classifier for two reasons. On the one hand, the implementation is highly memory efficient in contrast to comparable methods like Nearest-Neighbor classifier. Only some simple thresholds have to be kept in memory instead of entire highly dimensional feature vectors of some or even all training samples. On the other hand, the computation time during classification is very low based on only few and simple numerical comparisons. Both advantages make *Extremely Randomized Trees* highly preferable for our task.

5 Experiments

In the following, we present evaluations of our proposed method which are based on a huge real-life data collection acquired over the past 18 months. The dataset comprises a variety of environmental settings such as motorways as well as urban and suburban scenes at different locations from all over Germany as well as from Sweden. We use a total of ∼3,500 sequences resulting in ∼150,000 single images each with a resolution of 1076×648 pixels at a frame rate of 16 fps. Ground-truth data was provided for all sequences by an human expert during the acquisition including the unique labels *dry*, *wet*, and *snow-covered*. Additionally, intermediate labels are assigned to sequences which show mixed conditions and transition between unique classes which are not considered for this evaluation. The overall distribution of class labels is given by 60 % showing dry, 14 % showing wet, and 26 % showing snow-covered conditions. Example images for each road condition class can be seen in Fig. 4. For the evaluation we conduct a 10-fold cross validation where only 10 % of the data was used for training and the remaining 90 % for testing. Overall and average recognition rates were used in order to measure the classification performance sample-wise as well as in a class-wise manner. We compare our proposed method to state-of-the-art techniques and provide a simple baseline approach developed during a preliminary study of this work. It is shown that our method outperforms all other methods despite of challenges, *e.g.* color shifts, under- and overexposed images, severe reflections due to low sun, and even image artifacts caused by erroneous demosaicing [11]. In the course of a parameter evaluation–which is not presented in this paper due to the limited space–we found the most suitable setting given by $\alpha = 0.05$, $P = 8$, $R = 1, 2, 4$. Thereby, an increasing value of α would lead to erroneous estimations caused by short-term disturbances whereas smaller values would cause a delayed recognition of an actual change of the road condition. As presented in [14] the number of neighbors is set to $P = 8$ to ensure an efficient implementation by using an 8-bit data type. The corresponding radius R has been set to different distances to obtain a pyramidal representation. As suggested in [3] an ensemble size of 100 trees was selected for the classification.

5.1 Evaluation and Comparison

Since there is no commonly used dataset for the task of road condition estimation and sources of other methods are not publicly available, works of [9,15,22] have been reimplemented. This allows us to compare the performance of our proposed method with recent works in this field of research. Additionally, we present results produced by a baseline approach developed during a preliminary study.

Table 1. Comparison of various camera based methods for road condition estimation.

Method	dry	wet	snow	ARR	ORR
Baseline	82.71	75.22	64.24	74.06	77.33
Kawai *et al.* [9]	42.03	52.56	79.25	57.95	55.55
Sun *et al.* [22]	70.23	91.31	76.35	79.30	74.95
Omer *et al.* [15]	96.85	79.89	95.49	90.74	94.25
Ours	98.90	93.17	94.93	95.67	96.84
Ours + context	**99.44**	**93.50**	**97.84**	**96.79**	**98.09**

In Table 1 the recognition rates for our approach as well as for works of [9,15,22] are presented. As can be seen our method is superior regarding each condition class which results in a substantial increase of overall and average performances. The system of [22] which is solely based on GLCM texture modeling is capable of detecting wet conditions, but shows poor results for dry and snow-covered scenes. Our implementation of [9] provides rather poor results for all classes and has the additional disadvantage of high computational costs, *i.e.* 12 s per frame, which renders the method useless for real-time applications. In contrast to that, [15] provides high recognition rates for snow-covered and bare roads for which the method was initially designed. This strength can be explained by the fact, that they use context information from non-road parts by considering the entire lower image region. Additionally, the usage of color information is very useful as long as the setup does not change, *e.g.* by differently colored windshields or unexpected illumination changes. Although our method produces slightly worse results for snow-coverage compared to [15], it was possible to obtain superior overall as well as average recognition rates while still considering only-road parts without using color information. As a further improvement of our approach, the entire lower image region was considered to cover useful information about saturation and intensity variations between road and non-road parts. The idea is that snow-covered areas yield low variances in the saturation channel whereas bare road scenes show high variances caused by road-markings and grass verges. The resulting performance gain can be seen in the last row of Table 1.

The major advantages of our proposed approach is the ability to distinguish between all potential road conditions in a very robust manner without the sensitivity to color and illumination changes. Furthermore, the actual runtime, *e.g.* at least 16 fps, renders our method suitable for real-time applications. In Fig. 4 qualitative results are presented for each road surface condition class showing the advantages of our method.

Limitations of our approach appear when driving through narrow bends as the method assumes an almost linear motion. This drawback can be resolved by an adaptation of the static homography in terms of aligning the top view image in the direction of motion. Furthermore, disturbances on the windshield, *e.g.* contamination and reflections caused by the car's hood can result in erroneous estimations. In addition, varying exposure times of the camera can lead to changing appearance of individual regions which can be rectified by taking the corresponding value into account.

5.2 Computation Times

The presented road condition estimation framework was solely implemented in C/C++ using the OpenCV library 2.4.9. Similar to the computer setup of the demonstration vehicle an Intel® Core™ i7-2600 standard desktop computer @3.40 GHz was used for our experiments. The computation time for one single frame was approximately 50 ms which guarantees real-time capability of our approach, *i.e.* 16 frames per second.

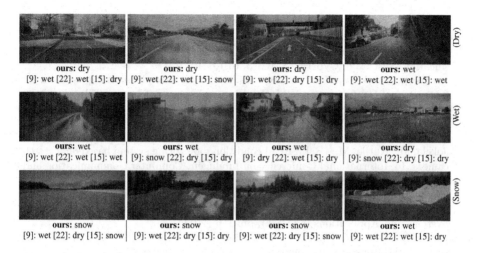

Fig. 4. Qualitative evaluation of our approach compared to Kawai *et al.* [9], Sun *et al.* [22], and Omer *et al.* [15]. Results are highlighted below each image (color figure online).

6   Conclusions

In this paper we presented a fast and robust approach for the task of road condition estimation based on a monocular camera. Motivated by a physical reflection model a transformation of the input image into a reflection map was proposed. Feature vectors were obtained by the extraction of texture features based on the reflection map as well as on the original image. Afterwards, a standard classifier was applied which meets the special requirements of embedded systems. Based on a large and challenging dataset it was possible to show that the proposed method clearly outperforms other vision-based state-of-the-art methods. The main advantages of our approach are the capability of running in real-time as well as the robustness against diverse disturbances in contrast to standard reflection modeling based on image registration and tracking.

Acknowledgements. The proposed method in this paper was developed in a joint research project funded by Continental Teves AG & Co. oHG.

References

1. Alonso, J., López, J.M., Pavón, I., Recuero, M., Asensio, C., Arcas, G., Bravo, A.: On-board wet road surface identification using tyre/road noise and support vector machines. Appl. Acoust. **76**, 407–415 (2014)
2. Brust, C.A., Sickert, S., Simon, M., Rodner, E., Denzler, J.: Convolutional patch networks with spatial prior for road detection and urban scene understanding. In: International Conference on Computer Vision Theory and Applications (VISAPP), pp. 510–517 (2015)

3. Geurts, P., Ernst, D., Wehenkel, L.: Extremely randomized trees. Mach. Learn. (ML) **36**, 3–42 (2006)
4. Haralick, R.M., Shanmugam, K., Dinstein, I.H.: Textural features for image classification. Syst. Man Cybern. (SMC) **3**, 610–621 (1973)
5. Irschik, D., Stork, W.: Road surface classification for extended floating car data. In: International Conference on Vehicular Electronics and Safety (ICVES), pp. 78–83 (2014)
6. Johansson, R.: Vision zero-implementing a policy for traffic safety. Saf. Sci. **47**, 826–831 (2009)
7. Jokela, M., Kutila, M., Le, L.: Road condition monitoring system based on a stereo camera. In: International Conference on Intelligent Computer Communication and Processing (ICCP), pp. 423–428 (2009)
8. Jonsson, P.: Classification of road conditions: From camera images and weather data. In: International Conference on Computational Intelligence for Measurement Systems and Applications (CIMSA), pp. 1–6 (2011)
9. Kawai, S., Takeuchi, K., Shibata, K., Horita, Y.: A method to distinguish road surface conditions for car-mounted camera images at night-time. In: International Conference on ITS Telecommunications (ITST), pp. 668–672 (2012)
10. Lüke, S., Rieth, P., Darms, M.: From brake assist to autonomous collision avoidance. In: FISITA World Automotive Congress (FISITA) (2008)
11. Malvar, H.S., He, L.-W., Cutler, R.: High-quality linear interpolation for demosaicing of bayer-patterned color images. In: International Conference on Acoustics, Speech, and Signal Processing (ICASSP), pp. 482–485 (2004)
12. McFall, K., Niittula, T.: Results of av winter road condition sensor prototype. In: International Road Weather Congress (SIRWEC) (2002)
13. Mondal, A., Sharma, A., Yadav, K., Tripathi, A., Singh, A., Piratla, N.: Roadeye: A system for personalized retrieval of dynamic road conditions. In: International Conference on Mobile Data Management (MDM), pp. 297–304 (2014)
14. Ojala, T., Pietikainen, M., Maenpaa, T.: Multiresolution gray-scale and rotation invariant texture classification with local binary patterns. Pattern Anal. Mach. Intell. (PAMI) **24**, 971–987 (2002)
15. Omer, R., Fu, L.: An automatic image recognition system for winter road surface condition classification. In: International Conference on Intelligent Transportation Systems (ITSC), pp. 1375–1379 (2010)
16. Pyykonen, P., Laitinen, J., Viitanen, J., Eloranta, P., Korhonen, T.: Iot for intelligent traffic system. In: International Conference on Intelligent Computer Communication and Processing (ICCP), pp. 175–179 (2013)
17. Rankin, A.L., Matthies, L.H., Huertas, A.: Daytime water detection by fusing multiple cues for autonomous off-road navigation (2004)
18. Rühle, J., Rodner, E., Denzler, J.: Beyond thinking in common categories: Predicting obstacle vulnerability using large random codebooks. In: Machine Vision Applications (MVA), pp. 198–201 (2015)
19. Shibata, K., Furukane, T., Kawai, S., Horita, Y.: Distinction of wet road surface condition at night using texture features. Electron. Commun. Jpn. (ECJ) **97**, 51–57 (2014)
20. Shibata, K., Takeuch, K., Kawai, S., Horita, Y.: Detection of road surface conditions in winter using road surveillance cameras at daytime, night-time and twilight. Int. J. Comput. Sci. Netw. Secur. (IJCSNS) **14**, 21–24 (2014)
21. Silion, S., Fosalau, C.: Wet road surfaces detection by measuring the air humidity in two points. In: International Conference and Exposition on Electrical and Power Engineering (EPE), pp. 744–747 (2014)

22. Sun, Z., Jia, K.: Road surface condition classification based on color and texture information. In: International Conference on Intelligent Information Hiding and Multimedia Signal Processing (IIHMSP), pp. 137–140 (2013)
23. Teshima, T., Saito, H., Shimizu, M., Taguchi, A.: Classification of wet/dry area based on the mahalanobis distance of feature from time space image analysis. In: International Conference on Machine Vision Applications (MVA), pp. 467–470 (2009)
24. Yamada, M., Ueda, K., Horiba, I., Sugie, N.: Discrimination of the road condition toward understanding of vehicle driving environments. Intell. Transp. Syst. (ITS) **2**, 26–31 (2001)
25. Yang, H.J., Jang, H., Kang, J.W., Jeong, D.S.: Classification algorithm for road surface condition. Int. J. Comput. Sci. Netw. Secur. (IJCSNS) **14**, 1–5 (2014)

Discrete Optimization for Optical Flow

Moritz Menze[1]([✉]), Christian Heipke[1], and Andreas Geiger[2]

[1] Leibniz Universität Hannover, Hanover, Germany
menze@ipi.uni-hannover.de
[2] Max Planck Institute for Intelligent Systems, Tübingen, Germany

Abstract. We propose to look at large-displacement optical flow from a discrete point of view. Motivated by the observation that sub-pixel accuracy is easily obtained given pixel-accurate optical flow, we conjecture that computing the integral part is the hardest piece of the problem. Consequently, we formulate optical flow estimation as a discrete inference problem in a conditional random field, followed by sub-pixel refinement. Naïve discretization of the 2D flow space, however, is intractable due to the resulting size of the label set. In this paper, we therefore investigate three different strategies, each able to reduce computation and memory demands by several orders of magnitude. Their combination allows us to estimate large-displacement optical flow both accurately and efficiently and demonstrates the potential of discrete optimization for optical flow. We obtain state-of-the-art performance on MPI Sintel and KITTI.

1   Introduction

Estimating dense optical flow is a fundamental problem in computer vision. Despite significant progress over the last decades, realistic scenes with displacements of several hundred pixels, strong changes in illumination and textureless or specular regions remain challenging to date [9,17]. Traditionally, dense optical flow estimation has been formulated as a *continuous* optimization problem [20,25], and many of today's most successful methods leverage elaborate variants of the original formulation, allowing for more robust penalties or improving optimization. As continuous methods typically require linearizing the highly non-convex data term, they only permit the estimation of very small displacements up to a few pixels. Thus, in order to handle large displacements in real-world videos, a simple heuristic is often employed: Optical flow is estimated in a coarse-to-fine manner, thereby guaranteeing an upper bound to the maximal displacement at each level of the image pyramid. Unfortunately, this strategy is highly susceptible to local minima as small structures and textural details vanish at coarse image resolutions, leading to oversmoothing artifacts in the estimated flow field.

In contrast to optical flow, the most successful approaches to stereo matching typically rely on *discrete* inference in graphical models. While such models are loopy by nature and thus lead to NP-hard optimization problems, good approximate solutions can often be efficiently computed using graph cuts, belief

© Springer International Publishing Switzerland 2015
J. Gall et al. (Eds.): GCPR 2015, LNCS 9358, pp. 16–28, 2015.
DOI: 10.1007/978-3-319-24947-6_2

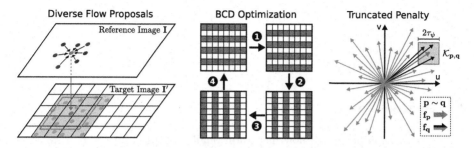

Fig. 1. Strategies for Efficient Discrete Optical Flow. Left: We create a large set of diverse flow proposals per pixel (red node) by combining nearest neighbors in feature space from a set of grid cells (green nodes) with winner-takes-all solutions from neighboring pixels (blue nodes). The red square indicates the search region. Middle: We apply block coordinate descent, iteratively optimizing all image rows and columns (red) conditioned on neighboring blocks (white) via dynamic programming. Right: Taking advantage of robust penalties, we reduce pairwise computation costs by pre-computing the set of non-truncated ($< \tau_\psi$) neighboring flow proposals (black) for each flow vector (red) (Color figure online).

propagation or mean field approximations. Importantly, no image pyramids are required as the full data cost volume is considered at the same time during inference. Unfortunately, the application of discrete methods to the problem of optical flow is not straightforward and hence there exists only relatively little work in this direction. The main reason for this is the huge size of the label space which needs to be considered for the 2D large-displacement optical flow problem as opposed to the 1D stereo problem.

In this paper, we propose three different strategies to make discrete inference in a pairwise conditional random field (CRF) applicable to the estimation of optical flow, see Fig. 1 for an illustration. First, we restrict the label set by considering only the L most likely matches per pixel which we obtain via approximate nearest neighbor search in feature space subject to non-maxima suppression constraints. To validate this restriction, we experimentally show that the oracle solution of the restricted set outperforms all existing optical flow techniques by a significant margin. Second, our inference scheme takes advantage of efficient convergent block coordinate descent (BCD) and iteratively updates all image rows and columns conditioned on the remaining variables via dynamic programming. Third, we exploit the special form of the pairwise potentials used by our formulation to further decrease computational complexity, thereby making very large unordered label sets with hundreds of labels tractable. Upon convergence, we remove outliers (e.g., in occluded regions) using strategies borrowed from the stereo literature. Finally, we regress a real-valued dense flow field from our semi-dense integer flow estimate using variational techniques [32,42]. We experimentally validate the proposed method on two challenging benchmarks: MPI Sintel [9] and KITTI [17]. Our experiments show that the proposed method attains state-of-the-art performance. Importantly, our results indicate that discrete optimization can be a powerful tool for solving optical flow problems - even when considering pairwise flow priors only. Our code and supplementary material are available from our project page: http://www.cvlibs.net/projects/discrete_flow.

2   Related Work

Global estimation of optical flow has traditionally been formulated as a continuous variational optimization problem with linearized data terms [4,20] and many of the most successful works still follow the same paradigm to date [8,12,30,34,35,37,40,43]. To estimate displacements larger than 1 pixel, as required by modern benchmarks [1,9,17] and for many applications, continuous methods typically rely on image pyramids [7]. Unfortunately, this heuristic is prone to local minima as texture details and fine structures vanish at small scales. As a consequence, methods leveraging sparse feature correspondences to guide the optimization process have been popularized [5,6,32,38,42], incorporating feature matches into initialization or as an additional data term. Our approach shares similarity with these methods in the sense that we also refine our integer-valued flow result to sub-pixel accuracy as proposed in [32,42]. However, in contrast to the above-mentioned works, our integral matches are obtained via discrete optimization with optical flow priors. This allows our algorithm to establish denser correspondences than possible with independently matched sparse features and, in combination with sub-pixel refinement, leads to better results.

Alternatively, optical flow can be viewed as a discrete optimization problem. In the absence of regularization constraints, this corresponds to a complete search of the discretized 2D flow space which has to be carried out for each pixel [2,47]. While local support windows [33] alleviate the effect of border bleeding, they generally cannot compete with methods that leverage global regularization. Incorporating smoothness constraints, however, is much more difficult for discrete optical flow than for the related stereo matching problem due to the extremely large label space of the discretized 2D flow field. To avoid this difficulty, a number of approaches formulate optical flow as a segmentation problem: Based on a small set of dense flow field proposals, the most likely flow field at each pixel subject to regularization constraints is approximated via quadratic pseudo-boolean optimization (QPBO) or belief propagation (BP) [11,23,44,45,48]. A reduced label set for all pixels is proposed by [28] restricting the method to scenes with little and non-complex motion. In contrast, here we pursue a more direct approach to discrete optical flow which does not rely on proposed flow fields or a global label set but allows for an arbitrary set of flow proposals *per pixel*. Compared to the approaches of Steinbrücker et al. [36] and Liu et al. [24], we neither require a complete search nor image pyramids [24]. Our approach is also related to particle-based methods such as particle BP [46] or Patch-Match BP [3,21]. In contrast to those methods, our algorithm is not restricted to a relatively small set of particles or local resampling which can lead to local minima. Instead, we maintain diverse distributions over much larger state spaces throughout the whole inference process.

Very recently, object recognition and feature learning have been exploited as a powerful source of information for optical flow. Notable examples are the data-driven flow transfer method of Wei et al. [41] and FlowNets based on deep neural networks by Fischer et al. [15]. In this paper our focus lies on a more generic model without the need for large annotated training sets. However, these ideas could be easily incorporated into the proposed model, e.g., via additional unary terms, promising further gains in performance in the future.

3   Model

Let us assume two input images $\mathbf{I}$ and $\mathbf{I}'$ of size $W \times H$. Our goal is to assign as many pixels as possible from the reference image $\mathbf{I}$ to pixels in the target image $\mathbf{I}'$. In other words, we aim for a semi-dense integer-valued flow field, establishing correspondences which are visible in both views. Flow vectors are selected from a diverse set of proposals (Sect. 3.1) based on a CRF model (Sect. 3.2) which is efficiently optimized (Sect. 3.3). Interpolation, extrapolation and sub-pixel refinement are then addressed in a subsequent post-processing step (Sect. 3.4).

3.1   Diverse Flow Proposals

Unfortunately, naïve pixel-wise discretization of all possible flow vectors would lead to an intractably large set of labels at each pixel. Consider for instance a flow range of ± 250 pixels in u- and v-direction. While this range is sufficiently large for the datasets tackled in this paper (see supplementary material), it leads to more than $60,000$ labels per pixel for which even the data term alone would be challenging to calculate and to store. In this section, we therefore propose a mechanism which extracts a subset of L flow proposals ($L = 500$ in our experiments) while maintaining a high recall of ground truth optical flow.

Towards this goal, we partition the target image into cells of equal size as illustrated in Fig. 1 (left). For each cell, we apply the randomized k-d tree algorithm [29] on the feature descriptors[1] of the pixels falling into that cell, yielding an efficient approximate search structure. Next, for each pixel in the reference image (red node in Fig. 1), we find all relevant cells in the target image according to the desired optical flow range (red shaded cells in Fig. 1) and concatenate all M flow vectors corresponding to the K nearest neighbor matches from the k-d tree of each cell (green nodes in Fig. 1). In contrast to a single search structure constructed for the entire target image, this strategy has two advantages: First, arbitrary optical flow search ranges can be implemented with little computational overhead by searching only in relevant cells. Second, the retrieved flow vectors respect an approximate non-maximal-suppression constraint, i.e., we obtain exactly K flow vectors per cell.

---

[1] As feature descriptor, we leverage DAISY [39] due to its computational efficiency and robustness against changes in illumination.

As neighboring pixels often exhibit similar optical flow, we additionally sample N random pixels (blue nodes in Fig. 1) from a local Gaussian distribution centered at the reference pixel and add the respective winner-takes-all solution (i.e., the flow vector corresponding to the best match at the sampled pixel) to the proposal set of the current pixel. In case it is already present in the proposal set, we proceed with the next best flow vector, ensuring that the final set of $L = M + N$ flow vectors is unique. In our experiments we use $M = 300$ nearest neighbors and $N = 200$ proposals from neighboring pixels.

3.2   Random Field Model

We associate a discrete label $l_{\mathbf{p}} \in \{1, \ldots, L\}$ with each pixel $\mathbf{p} = (x, y)$ in the reference image, corresponding to the (unique) integer-valued proposal flow vectors $\mathbf{f}_{\mathbf{p}}(l_{\mathbf{p}}) \in \mathbb{Z}^2$ described in Sect. 3.1. We consider optical flow estimation as MAP inference in a pairwise CRF. More specifically, we aim at minimizing

$$E(\mathbf{l}) = \lambda \sum_{\mathbf{p} \in \mathcal{P}} \underbrace{\varphi_{\mathbf{p}}(l_{\mathbf{p}})}_{\text{data}} + \sum_{\mathbf{p} \sim \mathbf{q}} \underbrace{\psi_{\mathbf{p},\mathbf{q}}(l_{\mathbf{p}}, l_{\mathbf{q}})}_{\text{smoothness}} \tag{1}$$

with respect to the set of image labels $\mathbf{l} = \{l_{\mathbf{p}} | \mathbf{p} \in \mathcal{P}\}$ where $\mathcal{P}$ denotes the set of pixels in image $\mathbf{I}$. Here, we have dropped the dependency on the input images $\mathbf{I}$ and $\mathbf{I}'$ for clarity and $\sim$ denotes all neighbors on a 4-connected image grid. The relative weight between the data term (measuring data fidelity) and the smoothness term (encouraging smooth flow fields) is defined by λ.

The data term $\varphi_{\mathbf{p}}(l_{\mathbf{p}})$ encodes the cost at pixel $\mathbf{p}$ given label $l_{\mathbf{p}}$. We model it as the truncated ℓ_1-penalty evaluating the difference between feature descriptors

$$\varphi_{\mathbf{p}}(l_{\mathbf{p}}) = \min \left(\|\mathbf{d}_{\mathbf{p}} - \mathbf{d}_{\mathbf{p}}'(l_{\mathbf{p}})\|_1, \tau_{\varphi} \right) \tag{2}$$

where $\mathbf{d}_{\mathbf{p}} \in \mathbb{R}^D$ denotes the feature descriptor at pixel $\mathbf{p}$ in the reference image, $\mathbf{d}_{\mathbf{p}}'(l_{\mathbf{p}}) \in \mathbb{R}^D$ denotes the feature descriptor associated with pixel $\mathbf{p}$ and label $l_{\mathbf{p}}$ in the target image, and τ_{φ} is the truncation threshold of the data term.

The second term in Eq. 1 encourages smooth flow fields and is modeled as the weighted truncated ℓ_1-distance of neighboring optical flow vectors

$$\psi_{\mathbf{p},\mathbf{q}}(l_{\mathbf{p}}, l_{\mathbf{q}}) = w_{\mathbf{p},\mathbf{q}} \min \left(\|\mathbf{f}_{\mathbf{p}}(l_{\mathbf{p}}) - \mathbf{f}_{\mathbf{q}}(l_{\mathbf{q}})\|_1, \tau_{\psi} \right) \tag{3}$$

where $\mathbf{f}_{\mathbf{p}}(l_{\mathbf{p}}) \in \mathbb{R}^2$ denotes the flow vector at pixel $\mathbf{p}$ associated with label $l_{\mathbf{p}}$ and τ_{ψ} is the truncation threshold of the smoothness term. We remark that a truncated penalty is not only robust against outliers and thus preferable from a statistical point of view [34], but it is also critical for tractable inference in our model as described in Sect. 3.3. Moreover, note that Eq. 3 is a generalization of the pairwise potential proposed for stereo matching by Hirschmüller [19] to arbitrary truncation thresholds τ_{ψ}. As we expect flow boundaries to coincide with image edges, we additionally weight the smoothness term by a weight factor $w_{\mathbf{p},\mathbf{q}} = \exp\left(-\alpha \kappa_{\mathbf{p},\mathbf{q}}^2\right)$. Here, $\kappa_{\mathbf{p},\mathbf{q}} \in [0, 1]$ measures the strength of the edge between pixel $\mathbf{p}$ and pixel $\mathbf{q}$. We calculate $\kappa_{\mathbf{p},\mathbf{q}}$ using structured edge detection [13].

3.3   Inference

Despite the simplicity of the model described in Sect. 3.2 and the label set of size $L = 500$, inference using max-product loopy BP is still prohibitively slow. To enable efficient inference, we therefore exploit two additional strategies. First, instead of loopy belief propagation, we perform block coordinate descent (BCD). More specifically, we follow [10] and iteratively update alternating image rows and columns conditioned on the MAP solution of the remaining variables as illustrated in Fig. 1 (middle). Second, we exploit the truncated form of the pairwise potentials in Eq. 3. This is illustrated in Fig. 1 (right). In combination, both steps reduce computational complexity by about four orders of magnitude.

Without loss of generality, consider the optimization of image row y. The naïve dynamic programming algorithm recursively fills the cumulative cost matrix $\mathbf{C}$ for each x from 1 to W using the following update equation:

$$\mathbf{C}(x, l) = \lambda\,\varphi_{(x,y)}(l) + \psi_{(x,y),(x,y-1)}(l, l^*_{x,y-1}) + \psi_{(x,y),(x,y+1)}(l, l^*_{x,y+1})$$
$$+ \min_{0 \leq k < L} \left(\psi_{(x,y),(x-1,y)}(l, k) + \mathbf{C}(x-1, k) \right) \tag{4}$$

Here, $l^*_{\mathbf{p}}$ denotes the assignment of the fixed variables, i.e., the variables outside row y. While the global problem is NP-hard and can be solved only approximately, each sub-problem corresponds to a chain MRF for which we obtain an optimal solution via dynamic programming (backtracking). This leads to the desirable property that this algorithm (unlike loopy BP) is guaranteed to converge.

In case of ordered label sets (e.g., in stereo matching [14] or depth reconstruction [10]) the efficient distance transform [14] can be employed to lower the complexity of this algorithm from $O(WL^2)$ to $O(WL)$ by calculating the expression in the last row of Eq. 4 in linear time. Unfortunately, in our case the flow vectors involved in $\psi_{(x,y),(x-1,y)}(l, k)$ are sparse and unordered, therefore prohibiting the application of this trick. However, we are still able to utilize the fact that our pairwise potentials ψ are truncated at τ_ψ: First, note that for practical truncation thresholds (i.e., $\tau_\psi < 15$), the majority of the L^2 pairwise terms evaluates to τ_ψ. We exploit this observation by partitioning the labels of each neighboring pixel pair $(\mathbf{p}, \mathbf{q})$ into sets

$$\mathcal{K}_{\mathbf{p},\mathbf{q},l} = \{k \in \{1, \ldots, L\} \mid \|\mathbf{f}_{\mathbf{p}}(l) - \mathbf{f}_{\mathbf{q}}(k)\|_1 < \tau_\psi\} \tag{5}$$

which contain all labels k at pixel $\mathbf{q}$ for which the flow $\mathbf{f}_{\mathbf{q}}(k)$ is within τ_ψ from the flow $\mathbf{f}_{\mathbf{p}}(l)$ associated with label l at pixel $\mathbf{p}$. Figure 1 (right) illustrates $\mathcal{K}_{\mathbf{p},\mathbf{q}}$ for a single flow vector at pixel $\mathbf{p}$ (shown in red) and a set of flow vectors at pixel $\mathbf{q}$ (black+gray). Given this definition, the last term in Eq. 4 can be written as

$$\min \left(\min_{k \in \mathcal{K}_{(x,y),(x-1,y),l}} \left(\psi_{(x,y),(x-1,y)}(l, k) + \mathbf{C}(x-1, k) \right), c \right) \tag{6}$$

where the constant c is given by

$$c = \min_{0 \leq k < L} \left(w_{(x,y),(x-1,y)} \tau_\psi + \mathbf{C}(x-1, k) \right) \tag{7}$$

Table 1. Pilot Study on MPI Sintel and KITTI Training Sets. See text.

	EPE (px)	Out (%)		EPE (px)	Out (%)
DM+DeepFlow [42]	2.85	10.22	DM+DeepFlow [42]	1.40	7.13
DM+EpicFlow [32]	**2.25**	8.63	DM+EpicFlow [32]	1.41	7.43
Ours+DeepFlow	2.64	9.14	Ours+DeepFlow	**1.17**	6.13
Ours+EpicFlow	**2.25**	**8.06**	Ours+EpicFlow	**1.17**	**5.64**
Ours+Oracle	0.85	3.97	Ours+Oracle	0.58	1.01

<table>
<tr><td>(a) MPI Sintel</td><td>(b) KITTI</td></tr>
</table>

As c does not depend on l and can be calculated in $O(L)$, Eq. 6 can be evaluated (for all l) in $O(\sum_l |\mathcal{K}_{\mathbf{p},\mathbf{q},l}|)$ instead of $O(L^2)$, where $|\mathcal{K}_{\mathbf{p},\mathbf{q},l}| \ll L$ in practice due to the diversity of the proposal set as evidenced by our experimental evaluation in Sect. 4. It is important to note that the sets $\mathcal{K}_{\mathbf{p},\mathbf{q},l}$ can be pre-computed and reused during all BCD iterations. In our implementation, we further accelerate this pre-computation step using hash maps for efficiently retrieving flow vectors.

3.4 Postprocessing

The inference algorithm described above solves the correspondence problem, i.e., it assigns each pixel in the reference image to a pixel in the target image. As we do not model occlusions explicitly, also occluded pixels and pixels leaving the image domain are assigned a label. We therefore remove outliers from our result, borrowing ideas from the stereo matching literature [19]. More specifically, we perform forward-backward consistency checking, i.e., we calculate the optical flow forwards and backwards in time and retain only flow vectors which are consistent. In addition, we remove small isolated segments which often correspond to wrong optical flow estimates using connected component labeling with a minimum segment size of 100 px and a flow consistency threshold of 10 px. Finally, in order to obtain sub-pixel flow values and to inter-/extrapolate into unmatched regions, we refine our results using the state-of-the-art flow refinement techniques of DeepFlow and EpicFlow.

4 Experimental Evaluation

We evaluate our approach on the challenging MPI Sintel [9] and KITTI [17] datasets. Our evaluation starts with a pilot study where we experimentally validate the claims from the introduction, followed by a quantitative and qualitative evaluation of our model. The parameters in our model are set via block coordinate descent on the respective training set (see supplementary material). To further increase efficiency we use a stride of 4 pixels. For subpixel interpolation of our results, we leverage the *interpolation stages* of Deep-Flow ("Ours+DeepFlow") and EpicFlow ("Ours+EpicFlow"). On average, our MATLAB/C++ implementation requires about 3 min for one 0.5 megapixel color image pair from the KITTI training set (10 % descriptor extraction, 40 % proposal generation, 35 % BCD, 15 % postprocessing and overhead).

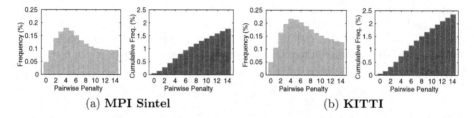

(a) **MPI Sintel**   (b) **KITTI**

Fig. 2. Frequency of Neighboring Flow Proposals wrt. Distance. This figure shows the frequency of neighboring flow proposal vectors with respect to their endpoint distance on MPI Sintel (a) and KITTI (b) in red. The blue plots depict the cumulative frequency corresponding to $|\mathcal{K}_{\mathbf{p},\mathbf{q},l}|/L$ over the distance threshold τ_ψ, respectively (Color figure online).

4.1 Pilot Study

Table 1 shows results on the non-occluded parts of the MPI Sintel and KITTI training sets in terms of endpoint error (EPE) and outliers (threshold: 3 px). We show (from top-to-bottom) the results of DeepFlow [42], EpicFlow [32], our results in combination with the refinement stages of DeepFlow [42] and EpicFlow [32], as well as an "Oracle" which refers to the flow map obtained by selecting the flow with the smallest EPE at each pixel from our proposal set. Note that our approach uses only the refinement stages of [32,42] and not the DeepMatches (DM) which form the foundation for [32,42]. As evidenced by this experiment, our method obtains state-of-the-art performance, outperforming [32,42] in most of the error metrics. Furthermore, our proposal set contains flow vectors close to the ground truth for most of the pixels while being diverse enough to avoid local minima and reduce the computational complexity of the pairwise terms. Figure 2 shows histograms of the frequency of neighboring flow proposals with respect to the distance of their endpoints for $L = 500$. While the pairwise term in Eq. 3 can take $L^2 = 250,000$ states in total, only 2 % of them fall below the

Table 2. Evaluation on MPI Sintel Test Set. This table lists the top 10 out of 44 ranked methods on the MPI Sintel flow benchmark in terms of endpoint error (EPE) in all, matched (Noc) and unmatched (Occ) regions. The results on the clean images are shown in (a). The results on the final set are shown in (b).

	EPE (px)				EPE (px)		
	All	Noc	Occ		All	Noc	Occ
Ours+EpicFlow	**3.567**	1.108	**23.626**	FlowFields	5.810	**2.621**	31.799
FlowFields	3.748	**1.056**	25.700	Ours+EpicFlow	6.077	2.937	**31.685**
DM+EpicFlow [32]	4.115	1.360	26.595	DM+EpicFlow [32]	6.285	3.060	32.564
PH-Flow [48]	4.388	1.714	26.202	TF+OFM [22]	6.727	3.388	33.929
AggregFlow [16]	4.754	1.694	29.685	Deep+R	6.769	2.996	37.494
TF+OFM [22]	4.917	1.874	29.735	SparseFlowFused [38]	7.189	3.286	38.977
Deep+R	5.041	1.481	34.047	DM+DeepFlow [42]	7.212	3.336	38.781
SPM-BP	5.202	1.815	32.839	FlowNetS+ft+v [15]	7.218	3.752	35.445
SparseFlowFused [38]	5.257	1.627	34.834	NNF-Local	7.249	2.973	42.088
DM+DeepFlow [42]	5.377	1.771	34.751	SPM-BP	7.325	3.493	38.561

(a) **Clean Set**   (b) **Final Set**

Table 3. Evaluation on KITTI Test Set. This table lists the top 15 out of 57 ranked methods on the KITTI optical flow benchmark in terms of outliers and endpoint error (EPE) in non-occluded and all regions. For comparability, only pure optical flow methods are shown, excluding motion stereo methods and techniques which use stereo information or more than two frames as input.

	Outliers (%)		EPE (px)			Outliers (%)		EPE (px)	
	Noc	All	Noc	All		Noc	All	Noc	All
PH-Flow [48]	**5.76**	**10.57**	**1.3**	2.9	Ours+EpicFlow	**3.89**	12.46	**1.3**	3.6
FlowFields	5.77	14.01	1.4	3.5	PH-Flow [48]	3.93	**7.72**	**1.3**	2.9
NLTGV-SC [30]	5.93	11.96	1.6	3.8	FlowFields	3.95	10.21	1.4	3.5
DDS-DF [41]	6.03	13.08	1.6	4.2	DDS-DF [41]	4.41	10.41	1.6	4.2
TGV2ADCSIFT [5]	6.20	15.15	1.5	4.5	NLTGV-SC [30]	4.50	9.42	1.6	3.8
Ours+EpicFlow	6.23	16.63	**1.3**	3.6	AnyFlow	4.51	12.55	1.5	4.3
AnyFlow	6.37	15.80	1.5	4.3	TGV2ADCSIFT [5]	4.60	12.17	1.5	4.5
BTF-ILLUM [12]	6.52	11.03	1.5	**2.8**	BTF-ILLUM [12]	4.64	8.11	1.5	**2.8**
DeepFlow2	6.61	17.35	1.4	5.3	DeepFlow2	4.73	14.19	1.4	5.3
CRT-TGV	6.71	12.09	2.0	3.9	CRT-TGV	5.01	8.97	2.0	3.9
Data-Flow [40]	7.11	14.57	1.9	5.5	TVL1-HOG [31]	5.26	15.45	2.0	6.1
DM+DeepFlow [42]	7.22	17.79	1.5	5.8	DM+DeepFlow [42]	5.31	14.69	1.5	5.8
RME	7.25	17.74	3.1	8.5	Data-Flow [40]	5.34	11.72	1.9	5.5
DM+EpicFlow [32]	7.88	17.08	1.5	3.8	DM+EpicFlow [32]	5.36	12.86	1.5	3.8
TVL1-HOG [31]	7.91	18.90	2.0	6.1	RME	5.49	14.70	3.1	8.5

(a) **Outlier Threshold: 3 px**   (b) **Outlier Threshold: 5 px**

truncation value of 15 px and need to be evaluated in Eq. 6. Thus, pre-calculating the partitions $\mathcal{K}_{\mathbf{p},\mathbf{q},l}$ saves almost two orders of magnitude in computation time.

4.2 Quantitative Results

We also compare our method to the state-of-the-art on the challenging held-out test data of MPI Sintel [9] and KITTI [17]. As requested by the evaluation protocol, we only submitted our strongest entry ("Ours+EpicFlow") for evaluation on the test set. Tables 2 and 3 compare our results to the state-of-the-art in two-frame optical flow. On MPI Sintel we obtain rank 1 on the "clean" set and rank 2 on the "final" set out of 44 ranked methods in total. On KITTI our method ranks 6th (out of 57 submitted results) for an outlier threshold of 3 pixels and 1st when using a threshold of 5 pixels. Note that we have excluded motion stereo methods and methods using additional information from Table 3 for a fair comparison. For full results, we refer to the online leaderboards[2].

4.3 Qualitative Results

Figure 3 depicts qualitative results of our method on a subset of MPI Sintel (top four images) and KITTI (bottom four images). As we require ground truth for visualizing the error maps we utilize the training sets for this purpose. We show the input image (left), our results in combination with EpicFlow postprocessing (middle) and the color-coded error map with respect to the ground truth flow

---

[2] http://sintel.is.tue.mpg.de.
   http://www.cvlibs.net/datasets/kitti.

Fig. 3. Qualitative Results on MPI Sintel and KITTI Training Sets. From left-to-right: Input image, "Ours+EpicFlow", inliers (blue)/outliers (red) (Color figure online).

field (right). At the top of each error map we specify the percentage of outliers and the endpoint error (EPE). The color coding visualizes outliers (> 3 px EPE) in red and inliers (< 3 px EPE) in blue on a logarithmic color scale. Pixels without ground truth value are shown in black. Note how our method is able to capture fine details in the optical flow. The last result of each dataset shows a failure case. For MPI Sintel, errors can be mostly attributed to homogeneous regions, occlusions and large changes in motion blur. On KITTI, we identified large perspective distortions, illumination artifacts and saturated or reflective regions as the primary sources of error.

5 Conclusions

We presented a discrete solution to the estimation of optical flow by exploiting three strategies which limit computational and memory requirements. Our experiments show that discrete optimization can lead to state-of-the-art optical flow results using a relatively simple prior model. In the future, we plan to integrate richer optical flow priors into our approach. In particular, we aim at jointly reasoning about several image scales and at incorporating semantic information [18,41] into optical flow estimation. Furthermore, we plan to extend our approach to the estimation of 3D scene flow [26,27].

References

1. Baker, S., Scharstein, D., Lewis, J., Roth, S., Black, M., Szeliski, R.: A database and evaluation methodology for optical flow. IJCV **92**, 1–31 (2011)
2. Bao, L., Yang, Q., Jin, H.: Fast edge-preserving PatchMatch for large displacement optical flow. In: CVPR (2014)
3. Besse, F., Rother, C., Fitzgibbon, A., Kautz, J.: PMBP: PatchMatch pelief propagation for correspondence field estimation. IJCV **110**(1), 2–13 (2014)
4. Black, M.J., Anandan, P.: A framework for the robust estimation of optical flow. In: ICCV (1993)
5. Braux-Zin, J., Dupont, R., Bartoli, A.: A general dense image matching framework combining direct and feature-based costs. In: ICCV (2013)
6. Brox, T., Malik, J.: Large displacement optical flow: descriptor matching in variational motion estimation. PAMI **33**, 500–513 (2011)
7. Brox, T., Bruhn, A., Papenberg, N., Weickert, J.: High Accuracy Optical Flow Estimation Based on a Theory for Warping. In: Pajdla, T., Matas, J.G. (eds.) ECCV 2004. LNCS, vol. 3024, pp. 25–36. Springer, Heidelberg (2004)
8. Bruhn, A., Weickert, J., Schnörr, C.: Lucas/Kanade meets Horn/Schunck: combining local and global optic flow methods. IJCV **61**(3), 211–231 (2005)
9. Butler, D.J., Wulff, J., Stanley, G.B., Black, M.J.: A naturalistic open source movie for optical flow evaluation. In: Fitzgibbon, A., Lazebnik, S., Perona, P., Sato, Y., Schmid, C. (eds.) ECCV 2012, Part VI. LNCS, vol. 7577, pp. 611–625. Springer, Heidelberg (2012)
10. Chen, Q., Koltun, V.: Fast MRF optimization with application to depth reconstruction. In: CVPR (2014)
11. Chen, Z., Jin, H., Lin, Z., Cohen, S., Wu, Y.: Large displacement optical flow from nearest neighbor fields. In: CVPR (2013)
12. Demetz, O., Stoll, M., Volz, S., Weickert, J., Bruhn, A.: Learning brightness transfer functions for the joint recovery of illumination changes and optical flow. In: Fleet, D., Pajdla, T., Schiele, B., Tuytelaars, T. (eds.) ECCV 2014, Part I. LNCS, vol. 8689, pp. 455–471. Springer, Heidelberg (2014)
13. Dollár, P., Zitnick, C.L.: Structured forests for fast edge detection. In: ICCV, pp. 1841–1848 (2013)
14. Felzenszwalb, P., Huttenlocher, D.: Efficient belief propagation for early vision. IJCV **70**(1), 41–54 (2006)
15. Fischer, P., Dosovitskiy, A., Ilg, E., Häusser, P., Hazirbas, C., Smagt, V.G.P., Cremers, D., Brox, T.: FlowNet: learning optical flow with convolutional networks (2015). arXiv.org 1504.06852

16. Fortun, D., Bouthemy, P., Kervrann, C.: Aggregation of local parametric candidates and exemplar-based occlusion handling for optical flow. arXiv.org 1407.5759 (2014)

17. Geiger, A., Lenz, P., Urtasun, R.: Are we ready for autonomous driving? The KITTI vision benchmark suite. In: CVPR (2012)

18. Güney, F., Geiger, A.: Displets: resolving stereo ambiguities using object knowledge. In: CVPR (2015)

19. Hirschmüller, H.: Stereo processing by semiglobal matching and mutual information. PAMI 30(2), 328–341 (2008)

20. Horn, B.K.P., Schunck, B.G.: Determining optical flow. AI 17(1–3), 185–203 (1980)

21. Hornáček, M., Besse, F., Kautz, J., Fitzgibbon, A., Rother, C.: Highly overparameterized optical flow using patchmatch belief propagation. In: Fleet, D., Pajdla, T., Schiele, B., Tuytelaars, T. (eds.) ECCV 2014, Part III. LNCS, vol. 8691, pp. 220–234. Springer, Heidelberg (2014)

22. Kennedy, R., Taylor, C.J.: Optical flow with geometric occlusion estimation and fusion of multiple frames. In: Tai, X.-C., Bae, E., Chan, T.F., Lysaker, M. (eds.) EMMCVPR 2015. LNCS, vol. 8932, pp. 364–377. Springer, Heidelberg (2015)

23. Lempitsky, V.S., Roth, S., Rother, C.: Fusionflow: Discrete-continuous optimization for optical flow estimation. In: CVPR (2008)

24. Liu, C., Yuen, J., Torralba, A.: SIFT flow: dense correspondence across scenes and its applications. PAMI 33(5), 978–994 (2011)

25. Lucas, B.D., Kanade, T.: An iterative image registration technique with an application to stereo vision. In: IJCAI (1981)

26. Menze, M., Geiger, A.: Object scene flow for autonomous vehicles. In: CVPR (2015)

27. Menze, M., Heipke, C., Geiger, A.: Joint 3d estimation of vehicles and scene flow. In: ISA (2015)

28. Mozerov, M.: Constrained optical flow estimation as a matching problem. TIP 22(5), 2044–2055 (2013)

29. Muja, M., Lowe, D.G.: Scalable nearest neighbor algorithms for high dimensional data. PAMI 36(11), 2227–2240 (2014)

30. Ranftl, R., Bredies, K., Pock, T.: Non-local total generalized variation for optical flow estimation. In: Fleet, D., Pajdla, T., Schiele, B., Tuytelaars, T. (eds.) ECCV 2014, Part I. LNCS, vol. 8689, pp. 439–454. Springer, Heidelberg (2014)

31. Rashwan, H.A., Mohamed, M.A., García, M.A., Mertsching, B., Puig, D.: Illumination robust optical flow model based on histogram of oriented gradients. In: Weickert, J., Hein, M., Schiele, B. (eds.) GCPR 2013. LNCS, vol. 8142, pp. 354–363. Springer, Heidelberg (2013)

32. Revaud, J., Weinzaepfel, P., Harchaoui, Z., Schmid, C.: EpicFlow: edge-preserving interpolation of correspondences for optical flow. In: CVPR (2015)

33. Rhemann, C., Hosni, A., Bleyer, M., Rother, C., Gelautz, M.: Fast cost-volume filtering for visual correspondence and beyond. In: CVPR (2011)

34. Roth, S., Black, M.J.: On the spatial statistics of optical flow. IJCV 74(1), 33–50 (2007)

35. Sevilla-Lara, L., Sun, D., Learned-Miller, E.G., Black, M.J.: Optical flow estimation with channel constancy. In: Fleet, D., Pajdla, T., Schiele, B., Tuytelaars, T. (eds.) ECCV 2014, Part I. LNCS, vol. 8689, pp. 423–438. Springer, Heidelberg (2014)

36. Steinbrücker, F., Pock, T., Cremers, D.: Large displacement optical flow computation without warping. In: ICCV, pp. 1609–1614 (2009)

37. Sun, D., Roth, S., Black, M.J.: A quantitative analysis of current practices in optical flow estimation and the principles behind them. IJCV 106(2), 115–137 (2013)

38. Timofte, R., Gool, L.V.: Sparse flow: Sparse matching for small to large displacement optical flow. In: WACV (2015)
39. Tola, E., Lepetit, V., Fua, P.: Daisy: an efficient dense descriptor applied to wide baseline stereo. PAMI **32**(5), 815–830 (2010)
40. Vogel, C., Roth, S., Schindler, K.: An evaluation of data costs for optical flow. In: Weickert, J., Hein, M., Schiele, B. (eds.) GCPR 2013. LNCS, vol. 8142, pp. 343–353. Springer, Heidelberg (2013)
41. Wei, D., Liu, C., Freeman, W.: A data-driven regularization model for stereo and flow. In: 3DV (2014)
42. Weinzaepfel, P., Revaud, J., Harchaoui, Z., Schmid, C.: DeepFlow: Large displacement optical flow with deep matching. In: ICCV (2013)
43. Werlberger, M., Trobin, W., Pock, T., Wedel, A., Cremers, D., Bischof, H.: Anisotropic Huber-L1 optical flow. In: BMVC (2009)
44. Wulff, J., Black, M.J.: Efficient sparse-to-dense optical flow estimation using a learned basis and layers. In: CVPR (2015)
45. Xu, L., Jia, J., Matsushita, Y.: Motion detail preserving optical flow estimation. PAMI **34**(9), 1744–1757 (2012)
46. Yamaguchi, K., McAllester, D., Urtasun, R.: Robust monocular epipolar flow estimation. In: CVPR (2013)
47. Yang, H., Lin, W., Lu, J.: DAISY filter flow: A generalized discrete approach to dense correspondences. In: CVPR (2014)
48. Yang, J., Li, H.: Dense, accurate optical flow estimation with piecewise parametric model. In: CVPR (2015)

Multi-Camera Structure from Motion with Eye-to-Eye Calibration

Sandro Esquivel$^{(\boxtimes)}$ and Reinhard Koch

Christian-Albrechts-University, Kiel, Germany
`esquivel@mip.informatik.uni-kiel.de`

Abstract. Imaging systems consisting of multiple conventional cameras are of increasing interest for computer vision applications such as Structure from Motion (SfM) due to their large combined field of view and high composite image resolution. In this work we present a SfM framework for multi-camera systems w/o overlapping camera views that integrates on-line extrinsic camera calibration, local scene reconstruction, and global optimization based on combining hand-eye calibration methods with standard SfM. For this purpose, we propose a novel method for extrinsic calibration based on rigid motion constraints that uses visual measurements directly instead of motion correspondences. Only a single calibration pattern visible within the view of one camera is needed to provide an accurate reconstruction with absolute scale.

1 Introduction

During the recent years, camera systems with large visual field coverage have proved useful to solve a variety of practical computer vision problems such as surveillance tasks, pose tracking, scene reconstruction, and Augmented Reality. Omnidirectional cameras with a 360° field of view in the horizontal plane are commonly used in robotics for visual odometry and simultaneous localization and mapping, e.g., for advanced driver assistant systems, autonomous vehicle navigation, and urban scenes modeling, while wide-angle fisheye lens cameras are often used for panorama imaging, edificial inspection, and site measuring.

While omnidirectional cameras made up from specific lenses or cameras imaging mirror surfaces are still very common for these tasks, rigs composed of multiple off-the-shelf cameras have gained popularity during the recent years. Major advantages of such devices are often lower costs, flexible configuration, less complex mathematical models and intrinsic calibration, and considerably higher resolution of the virtual composite field of view. In order to maximize the visual field it is beneficial to assemble the individual cameras so that their fields of view have minimal overlap. However, extrinsic camera calibration (i.e., determining the locations and orientations of all cameras within a common reference coordinate frame) is complicated by this setup since conventional calibration methods such as [26] rely on jointly observed patterns or objects with known geometry.

© Springer International Publishing Switzerland 2015
J. Gall et al. (Eds.): GCPR 2015, LNCS 9358, pp. 29–40, 2015.
DOI: 10.1007/978-3-319-24947-6_3

Previous Work. Common approaches for extrinsic multi-camera calibration without overlapping views require very specific calibration objects such as large patterns [15] or planar mirrors [11,13,21] to supply global image correspondences. Finding correspondences between cameras over time during motion of the rig [9] poses difficult matching problems. Also, all these methods can be impractical due to occlusions or large camera offsets. Attempts based on *per-camera* image or pose correspondences only were first proposed in [3] for cameras with coinciding projection centers and in [5] for general setups. In [7], a flexible method for extrinsic camera calibration from rigid motion constraints was described that utilizes simultaneous Structure from Motion (SfM) to estimate camera motion correspondences. This approach – denoted as *eye-to-eye calibration* here – is based on the classical hand-eye calibration problem from the robotics community [25], in particular on extended methods using SfM for camera localization [1]. Since publication, it has been developed further, most notably towards vehicle-based camera systems [20], and improved by global optimization using joint bundle adjustment [14] or including partial rigid motion constraints in the SfM step [6].

Our Contribution. In this paper we will propose a multi-camera SfM pipeline integrating the aforementioned approaches to provide a reconstruction with absolute scale from rigidly coupled cameras without overlapping views with known intrinsics but a priori unknown extrinsic parameters. Only a single calibration pattern visible for the first camera is needed. The eye-to-eye calibration problem is solved with a novel method minimizing image errors instead of motion differences and is further refined via the bundle adjustment approach from [14].

2   Rigidly Coupled Motion Constraints

Each *pose transformation* $\mathbf{T} \in \mathrm{SE}(3)$ is described by a rotation matrix $\mathbf{R} \in \mathrm{SO}(3)$ and translation vector $t \in \mathbb{R}^3$. Rotations with angle α around axis $r \in S^2$ are parametrized by unit quaternions $\mathbf{q} \in S^3$ in the following (see [24], Sect. 2.4):

$$\mathbf{q} = (\boldsymbol{q}, q) = (\sin(\tfrac{\alpha}{2})\boldsymbol{r}, \cos(\tfrac{\alpha}{2})) \quad \text{and} \quad \mathbf{R_q} = (q^2 + 1)\mathbf{I} + 2q[\boldsymbol{q}]_\times + 2[\boldsymbol{q}]_\times^2 \quad (1)$$

Given $n + 1$ rigidly coupled cameras at $m + 1$ different positions as illustrated in Fig. 1, the relative coordinate transformations $\mathbf{R}_k^i, t_k^i$ for the i-th camera at the k-th position with respect to the *reference pose* at $k = 0$ ("local" measurements) are given by some pose measuring process. Denoting the *reference camera* by $i = 0$, the *eye-to-eye transformations* $\Delta\mathbf{T}_i, \Delta\lambda_i$ describe the coordinate transfer from the i-th camera to the reference camera for each $i = 0, \ldots, n$. Due to the rigid coupling, for each $k = 0, \ldots, m$ holds:

$$\mathbf{R}_k^0\Delta\mathbf{R}_i = \Delta\mathbf{R}_i\mathbf{R}_k^i \quad \text{and} \quad \mathbf{R}_k^0\Delta t_i + t_k^0 = \Delta\lambda_i\Delta\mathbf{R}_i t_k^i + \Delta t_i \quad (2)$$

Each scalar $\Delta\lambda_i > 0$ describes an isometric scaling between the local coordinate frames of the i-th and the reference camera while $\Delta\mathbf{R}_i, \Delta t_i$ describe the pose of

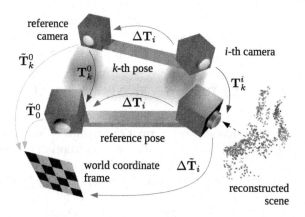

Fig. 1. Overview of coordinate frames and transformations for two rigidly coupled cameras at reference location and k-th location as used in eye-to-eye SfM.

camera i within its reference coordinate frame. Note that $\mathbf{R}_0^i = \mathbf{I}, t_0^i = \mathbf{0}$ for all $i = 0, \ldots, n$ and $\Delta\mathbf{R}_0 = \mathbf{I}, \Delta t_0 = \mathbf{0}, \Delta\lambda_0 = 1$ are fixed in (2).

If poses of the reference camera are measured within the world coordinate frame instead, a similar equation is derived:

$$\tilde{\mathbf{R}}_k^0 \Delta\mathbf{R}_i = \Delta\tilde{\mathbf{R}}_i \mathbf{R}_k^i \quad \text{and} \quad \tilde{\mathbf{R}}_k^0 \Delta t_i + \tilde{t}_k^0 = \Delta\lambda_i \Delta\tilde{\mathbf{R}}_i t_k^i + \Delta\tilde{t}_i \tag{3}$$

where $\Delta\tilde{\mathbf{T}}_i = \tilde{\mathbf{T}}_0^0 \Delta\mathbf{T}_i$ describes the *eye-to-world transformation* (in accordance to the *hand/eye and world/base calibration* problem from robotics). To distinguish local poses and 3d points from measurements within the world coordinate frame ("global" measurements), we will use a tilde for the latter.

Partial Rigid Motion Constraints. Following from (2), all rigidly coupled motions $\mathbf{R}_k^i, t_k^i$ with non-zero rotation have the same absolute rotation angle α_k^i and amount of translation along the rotation axis $p_k^i = r_k^{iT} t_k^i$ (see [4], Sect. 4.1). Using the latter constraint, the scaling $\Delta\lambda_i$ can be derived for non-planar motion as $\Delta\lambda_i = p_k^0 / p_k^i$ for any pose with $\mathbf{R} \neq \mathbf{I}$ and $p_k^i \neq 0$. Both constraints can be used to robustify simultaneous SfM for rigidly coupled cameras as described in [6].

Geometric Eye-to-Eye Calibration. Similar to hand-eye calibration where the reference camera is replaced by a robotic gripper providing absolute poses, (2) can be solved for the eye-to-eye transformation parameters from $m \geq 2$ motion correspondences with sufficient rotation and translation and distinct rotation axes. A standard approach is to solve the first part of (2) for $\Delta\mathbf{R}_i$ first, e.g., using the unit quaternion parametrization [7] (solved via SVD):

$$\min_{\Delta\mathbf{q}_i} \sum_{k=0}^{m} \|\mathbf{q}_k^0 \cdot \Delta\mathbf{q}_i - \Delta\mathbf{q}_i \cdot \mathbf{q}_k^i\|^2 \quad \text{s. t. } \|\Delta\mathbf{q}_i\| = 1 \tag{4}$$

Then solve the linear equation system resulting from the second part of (2) for $\Delta t_i, \Delta \lambda_i$ and refine all parameters jointly via nonlinear optimization [23] (using the reduced unit quaternion parametrization from [24] to avoid constraints):

$$\min_{\Delta \theta_i} \sum_{k=0}^{m} d_{\mathrm{rot}}(\mathbf{R}_k^0 \Delta \mathbf{R}_i, \Delta \mathbf{R}_i \mathbf{R}_k^i)^2 + d_{\mathrm{pos}}(\mathbf{R}_k^0 \Delta t_i + t_k^0, \Delta \lambda_i \Delta \mathbf{R}_i t_k^i + \Delta t_i)^2 \quad (5)$$

where $\Delta \theta_i$ are the eye-to-eye transformation parameters describing $\Delta \mathbf{R}_i$, $\Delta t_i, \Delta \lambda_i$ for the i-th camera, and $d_{\mathrm{rot}}, d_{\mathrm{pos}}$ are appropriately weighted error measures between rotations (e.g., quaternion distance or residual angle measure $d_\angle$) and translations (e.g., Euclidean distance). This approach is denoted as *geometric eye-to-eye calibration* (E2E-GEOM) in the following since the error function (5) describes differences between pose transformations. As pointed out in [23], weighting of the rotational and translational error terms has a crucial impact on the estimation results. The authors advise to use statistical weights derived from the input pose accuracy, accessed for instance via covariance propagation from the prior pose estimation process.

3   Integrating Eye-to-Eye Calibration into SfM

In the following we describe how to integrate eye-to-eye calibration into the classical SfM pipeline and provide an algorithm for incremental eye-to-eye calibration of multi-camera systems based on errors in the image domain, relieving the problem of weighting geometric error terms.

Pose Transfer. Given an estimate for the k-th pose of the reference camera $\mathbf{R}_k^0, t_k^0$ relative to the reference pose, the corresponding pose for the i-th camera within its reference frame is inferred from (2) as:

$$\mathbf{R}_k^i = \Delta \mathbf{R}_i^T \mathbf{R}_k^0 \Delta \mathbf{R}_i \quad \text{and} \quad t_k^i = \Delta \lambda_i^{-1} \Delta \mathbf{R}_i^T \left((\mathbf{R}_k^0 - \mathbf{I}) \Delta t_i + t_k^0 \right) \quad (6)$$

where $\mathbf{R}_0^0 = \mathbf{I}, t_0^0 = 0$ are fixed. The corresponding global pose given the initial global pose $\tilde{\mathbf{R}}_0^0, \tilde{t}_0^0$ of the reference camera is inferred by:

$$\tilde{\mathbf{R}}_k^i = \tilde{\mathbf{R}}_0^0 \mathbf{R}_k^0 \Delta \mathbf{R}_i \quad \text{and} \quad \tilde{t}_k^i = \tilde{\mathbf{R}}_0^0 (\mathbf{R}_k^0 \Delta t_i + t_k^0) + \tilde{t}_0^0 \quad (7)$$

Visual Eye-to-Eye Calibration. Given N_i 3d points for the i-th camera within its local coordinate frame and corresponding projections $x_{k,\ell}^i$ of the ℓ-th 3d point X_ℓ^i into the k-th image with known camera functions $\mathcal{K}_i$, the i-th eye-to-eye transformation is obtained by minimizing the reprojection error using the pose transfer function (6):

$$\min_{\Delta \theta_i} \sum_{k=0}^{m} \sum_{\ell=1}^{N_i} V_{k,\ell}^i \, d_i(x_{k,\ell}^i, \mathbf{R}_k^{i\,T}(X_\ell^i - t_k^i))^2 \quad (8)$$

where $V_{k,\ell}^i \in \{0,1\}$ describes the visibility of 3d point $\boldsymbol{X}_\ell^i$ in the k-th image. The reprojection error is described by a generic function $d_i : \mathbb{R}^2 \times \mathbb{R}^3 \to \mathbb{R}$ for the i-th camera which is commonly chosen as $d_i(\boldsymbol{x}, \boldsymbol{X}) = \|\boldsymbol{x} - \mathcal{K}_i(\boldsymbol{X})\|$ assuming that the camera function $\mathcal{K}_i$ is known (e.g., from previous intrinsic calibration). For 2d point observations $\boldsymbol{x}$ with non-isometric errors described by covariance matrices $\boldsymbol{\Sigma}_{\boldsymbol{x}}$, the Mahalanobis distance $\|\boldsymbol{x} - \mathcal{K}_i(\boldsymbol{X})\|_{\boldsymbol{\Sigma}_{\boldsymbol{x}}}$ can be used instead. This novel approach will be denoted as *visual eye-to-eye calibration* (E2E-VIS). Note that the scaling parameter $\Delta\lambda_i$ can be encoded implicitly in (8) by parametrizing the scaled rotation matrix $\Delta\lambda_i^{-1}\Delta\mathbf{R}_i$ used in the prediction function (6) with a non-unit quaternion $\Delta\mathbf{q}_i$, i.e. $\Delta\lambda_i^{-1}\Delta\mathbf{R}_i = \mathbf{R}_{\Delta\mathbf{q}_i}$ with $\Delta\lambda_i^{-1} = \|\Delta\mathbf{q}_i\|^2$ as defined in (1), leading to an unconstrained optimization problem.

Eye-to-Eye Bundle Adjustment. Including 3d points and reference camera poses within the world coordinate frame according to (7) as parameters provides the *eye-to-eye bundle adjustment* (E2E-BA) problem similar to [14]:

$$\min_{\substack{\Delta\theta_i, \tilde{\theta}_0, \ldots, \tilde{\theta}_m \\ \tilde{\chi}_1^i, \ldots, \tilde{\chi}_{N_i}^i}} \sum_{k=0}^{m} \sum_{j \in \{0,i\}} \sum_{\ell=1}^{N_j} V_{k,\ell}^j \, d_j(\boldsymbol{x}_{k,\ell}^j, \tilde{\mathbf{R}}_k^{jT}(\tilde{\boldsymbol{X}}_\ell^j - \tilde{\boldsymbol{t}}_k^j))^2 \tag{9}$$

where $\tilde{\theta}_k$ are the k-th global pose parameters for the reference camera and $\tilde{\chi}_\ell^i$ are the parameters of the ℓ-th 3d point $\tilde{\boldsymbol{X}}_\ell^i$ for the i-th camera transformed into the world coordinate frame, initialized by $\tilde{\boldsymbol{X}}_\ell^i = \tilde{\mathbf{R}}_0^0(\Delta\lambda_i\Delta\mathbf{R}_i\boldsymbol{X}_\ell^i + \Delta\boldsymbol{t}_i) + \tilde{\boldsymbol{t}}_0^0$. The scaling parameter $\Delta\lambda_i$ is dropped from $\Delta\theta_i$ since it is encoded by the 3d points. Note that 3d points for the reference camera are already expressed within the world coordinate frame associated with some calibration object here. Gauge freedoms are avoided since the 3d points of the reference camera are fixed. Depending on the given application, the E2E-BA error function can be modified in order to fix either all 3d points (calibration objects used for both cameras) or none (SfM used for both cameras). The first case is equivalent to adding the reference camera poses as parameters to E2E-VIS, in the latter case gauge freedoms must be taken care of (in general by fixing $\mathbf{T}_0^0 = \mathbf{I}$ and $\|\boldsymbol{t}_1^0\| = 1$).

Pairwise E2E-BA as defined in (9) can be extended to cover several coupled cameras at the same time in a straightforward way, leading to large-scale sparse optimization problems. Common sparse bundle adjustment implementations such as sba cannot be applied to solve (9) since the Jacobian matrix of the error function has not the distinct block structure needed to compute the Schur complement [17], due to the fact that $\Delta\theta_i$ appears in all residuals for the i-th camera. We use sparseLM instead, a sparse implementation of the Levenberg-Marquardt algorithm [16].

Eye-to-Eye Structure from Motion. The proposed algorithm for interactive online eye-to-eye calibration via SfM (E2E-SFM) is outlined as follows. First, camera functions $\mathcal{K}_1, \ldots, \mathcal{K}_n$ are obtained by individual intrinsic camera calibration (e.g., following [26]). A calibration object (e.g., a checkerboard pattern) is placed within viewing range of the reference camera. Images of the calibration pattern are captured with the reference camera during motion of the camera rig, and images for the i-th camera are captured simultaneously (start with $i := 1$):

- Add initial keyframe with poses $\mathbf{T}_0^0 = \mathbf{I}$ and $\mathbf{T}_0^i = \mathbf{I}$.
- Compute global reference pose $\tilde{\mathbf{T}}_0^0$ for reference camera from 2d/3d matches.
- Detect feature points in reference image of the i-th coupled camera.
- For each subsequently captured image:
  - Set $k :=$ number of keyframes for each camera.
  - Compute current global pose $\tilde{\mathbf{T}}_k^0$ for reference camera from 2d/3d matches.
  - Find feature matches from reference to current image of i-th camera.
  - If $k = 1$ ($\rightarrow$ *SfM initialization stage*):
    - If $\|\boldsymbol{t}_1^0\| = \|(\tilde{\mathbf{R}}_0^0)^T(\tilde{\boldsymbol{t}}_1^0 - \tilde{\boldsymbol{t}}_0^0)\| > t_{\min}$:
      - Estimate essential matrix $\mathbf{E}_i$ from 2d/2d correspondences and initialize SfM for i-th camera (see [10], Part II).
      - Refine and scale relative pose $\mathbf{T}_1^i$ derived from essential matrix $\mathbf{E}_i$ using partial rigid motion constraints as described in [6].
      - Add keyframe with poses $\mathbf{T}_1^0 = (\tilde{\mathbf{T}}_0^0)^{-1}\tilde{\mathbf{T}}_1^0$ and $\mathbf{T}_1^i$.
  - Else ($\rightarrow$ *SfM tracking stage*):
    - Estimate current pose $\mathbf{T}_k^i$ for i-th camera from 2d/3d matches.
    - Refine pose $\mathbf{T}_k^i$ using partial rigid motion constraints [6].
    - Triangulate new 3d points for i-th camera from 2d/2d matches.
    - If $d_\angle(\tilde{\mathbf{R}}_{k-1}^0, \tilde{\mathbf{R}}_k^0) > \alpha_{\min}$ and $\angle(\tilde{\boldsymbol{r}}_{k-1}^0, \tilde{\boldsymbol{r}}_k^0) > \beta_{\min}$:
      - Add keyframe with poses $\mathbf{T}_k^0 = (\tilde{\mathbf{T}}_0^0)^{-1}\tilde{\mathbf{T}}_k^0$ and $\mathbf{T}_k^i$.
      - Compute initial eye-to-eye transformation $\Delta\mathbf{T}_i$ from corresponding motions in keyframes via E2E-GEOM.
      - Refine eye-to-eye transformation $\Delta\mathbf{T}_i$ from 2d/3d matches in keyframes via E2E-VIS.
      - Compute E2E-BA with fixed 3d points for the reference camera.
  - If $k = k_{\max}$ (or other termination criterion holds):
    - Clear keyframes and start over with $i := i + 1$ unless $i = n$ holds.

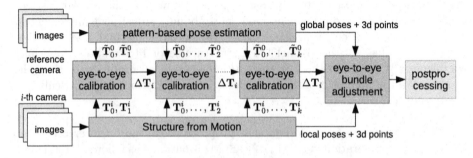

Fig. 2. Overview of eye-to-eye Structure from Motion pipeline.

The main pipeline is illustrated in Fig. 2. SfM requires some minimal initial translation defined by the threshold t_{min} (here: $t_{min} = 25\,cm$). Keyframes for eye-to-eye calibration are added according to the criteria suggested in [1] for on-line hand-eye calibration, i.e., sufficiently large rotation angle and rotation axis difference w. r. t. the previous keyframe pose using thresholds α_{min}, β_{min} (here: $\alpha_{min} = 10°$, $\beta_{min} = 15°$). The termination criterion can be based on the covariance matrix $\Sigma_{\Delta\theta_i}$ of the estimated eye-to-eye transformation parameters $\Delta\theta_i$ resulting from E2E-BA given some accuracy requirement for the solution, or maximal keyframe number k_{max}. Further details on the basic SfM algorithms can be found in [10]. E2E-BA can be computed in a separate thread for efficiency.

Post-processing. After all eye-to-eye transformations have been estimated, multi-camera SfM using all cameras jointly as described in [9] or [12] can be applied. The resulting reconstruction and extrinsic parameters can be optionally refined via E2E-BA using all coupled cameras at the same time.

4   Tests and Evaluation

4.1   Evaluation of Visual Eye-to-Eye Calibration

First, geometric and visual eye-to-eye calibration as described above were implemented in C/C++ (using MINPACK [18] and sparseLM [16]) in order to compare both methods with synthetic data. For each test case, N_i random 3d points with uniform distribution were created in front of 2 virtual cameras with random spatial arrangement set apart by $\Delta\alpha_1 = 60°$ and $\|\Delta t_1\| = 25\,cm$, image

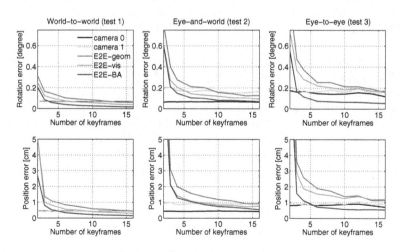

Fig. 3. Evaluation of pose estimation and eye-to-eye calibration accuracy with respect to number of keyframes m (left column: known 3d points for both cameras [test 1], middle column: known 3d points for reference camera [test 2], right: known 3d points for none [test 3]; upper row: rotation errors, lower row: position errors).

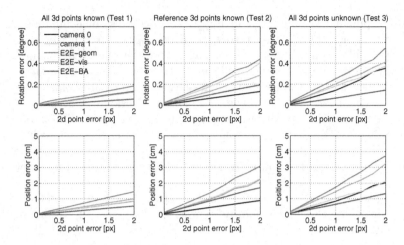

Fig. 4. Evaluation of pose estimation and eye-to-eye calibration accuracy with respect to 2d point error σ_x (see Fig. 3 for description).

size 800×600 px and $60° \times 46.8°$ field of view (FOV). m random poses of the reference camera with max. rotation angle $\alpha_{\max} = 30°$ and distance $d_{\max} = 1$ m w. r. t. the original location were created, providing up to N_i 2d projections into the virtual image of the i-th camera per keyframe. Zero-mean Gaussian noise with standard deviation σ_x was added to all 2d points prior to pose estimation.

In the first test, all 3d points are supposed to be known, resembling the case of using a calibration object for each camera. In the second test, only 3d points for the reference camera are known, corresponding to the proposed scenario. In the third test, all 3d points are assumed unknown (Δt_1 can only be recovered up to scale here). Camera poses are computed from 2d/3d matches for known 3d points (use $N_i = 100$), otherwise via SfM initialized with the first two keyframes and extended via triangulation for each subsequent keyframe (use $N_i = 1000$).

Methods E2E-GEOM, E2E-VIS, and E2E-BA were evaluated for 1000 random samples with respect to the number of keyframes m for fixed $\sigma_x = 1$ px resp. 2d point error σ_x with fixed $m = 8$. The resulting average pose estimation errors for both cameras and eye-to-eye calibration errors for all methods are shown in Figs. 3 and 4. In all cases, E2E-VIS is capable of improving the results from E2E-GEOM. This becomes most significant when SfM and absolute pose estimation from known 3d points are combined (2nd test). In general, calibration accuracy increases with rising number of keyframes and 2d point accuracy.

4.2   Eye-to-Eye Structure from Motion Application

The complete eye-to-eye SfM pipeline including image preprocessing, feature detection and matching (using methods from the OpenCV library [2]) was evaluated with rendered and real image sequences. In order to achieve robustness against erroneous feature point matches, RANSAC is used in the SfM initialization and

Fig. 5. Scene and example images of 4 cameras from virtual test dataset.

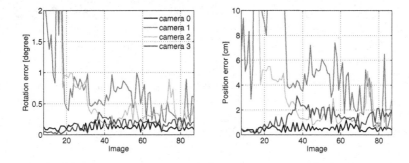

Fig. 6. Pose estimation errors for virtual test dataset (left: rotation, right: position).

tracking stages, and triangulated 3d points are pruned by evaluating their reprojection errors using the *X84* outlier rejection rule [8].

In the first test, a sequence consisting of 87 images (800×600 px) viewed by
a virtual rig composed of 4 cameras was rendered (see Fig. 5). The scene size is
$8 \times 8 \times 3$ m. Cameras $\mathcal{C}_1$ and $\mathcal{C}_2$ are yawed 81° left and right w. r. t. reference
camera $\mathcal{C}_0$, camera $\mathcal{C}_3$ is tilted 30° upwards. The distance to $\mathcal{C}_0$ is 57.4 cm for
$\mathcal{C}_{1/2}$ and 70.1 cm for $\mathcal{C}_3$. $\mathcal{C}_0$ has 60° $\times$ 46.8° FOV, the other cameras are limited
to 53.1° $\times$ 41.1°. SfM initialization succeeded after 8 images. For each camera,
10 keyframes were used for eye-to-eye calibration. The pose estimation errors for
each camera during eye-to-eye SfM are shown in Fig. 6. While the pattern-based
pose estimation for $\mathcal{C}_0$ has constant error, pose estimation errors of $\mathcal{C}_{1-3}$ via
SfM vary depending on the visible scene and motion. However, the plots show
that intermediate rigid motion constraint enforcement is capable of preventing
drift and reducing the average pose estimation error over time. The calibration
error is $< 0.3°$ in rotation and $1.1\% - 1.7\%$ in translation (Table 1), improving
comparable test results from [21] ($\Delta\alpha_{\mathrm{err}} \approx 0.8°$, $\Delta t_{\mathrm{err}} \approx 1.8\%$ for 10 views).

In the second test, a video sequence was captured with a real setup consisting of two *Point Grey Grasshopper*® (GRAS-20S4C-C) cameras equipped with
Schneider-Kreuznach Cinegon 1.8/4.8 lenses with 70° $\times$ 56° FOV. Camera $\mathcal{C}_1$
is mounted approx. 25 cm to the right of $\mathcal{C}_0$ and is rotated towards the upper

Table 1. Eye-to-eye parameters and calibration results for virtual test dataset INDOOR (rotation angles in XYZ order, symbols with * indicate ground truth values).

	$\Delta\alpha_x^*$	$\Delta\alpha_y^*$	$\Delta\alpha_z^*$	Δt_x^*	Δt_y^*	Δt_z^*	$\Delta\alpha_x$	$\Delta\alpha_y$	$\Delta\alpha_z$	Δt_x	Δt_y	Δt_z	$\Delta\alpha_{\mathrm{err}}$	Δt_{err}
$\mathcal{C}_1$	60°	60°	−5°	50	20	−20	60.1°	60.0°	−4.99°	49.9	20.8	−20.5	0.07°	1.0 cm
$\mathcal{C}_2$	60°	−60°	5°	−50	20	−20	59.8°	−60.1°	4.65°	−49.5	19.3	−20.4	0.21°	0.98 cm
$\mathcal{C}_3$	30°	0°	0°	0	−50	−50	30.0°	−0.01°	0.01°	0.03	−49.2	−49.9	0.03°	0.8 cm

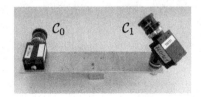 

Fig. 7. Camera setup and example images from real test dataset.

Table 2. Eye-to-eye parameters and calibration results for real test dataset BOXES (rotation angles in XYZ order, symbols with * indicate stereo calibration results).

	$\Delta\alpha_x^*$	$\Delta\alpha_y^*$	$\Delta\alpha_z^*$	Δt_x^*	Δt_y^*	Δt_z^*	$\Delta\alpha_x$	$\Delta\alpha_y$	$\Delta\alpha_z$	Δt_x	Δt_y	Δt_z	$\Delta\alpha_{\mathrm{err}}$	Δt_{err}
$\mathcal{C}_1$	38.5°	−36.2°	22.1°	24.8	−8.5	−7.4	38.4°	−35.9°	22.3°	24.6	−8.7	−7.2	0.42°	0.37 cm

left direction (Fig. 7). Note that the cameras have partially overlapping fields of view. However, this is used only for validation of the calibration results. An image sequence of 320 images (800 × 600 px) captured during handheld motion was used for the eye-to-eye SfM pipeline, providing 24 keyframes in total.

The calibration results are shown in Table 2. For comparison, the results from classical stereo calibration according to [26] were used instead of ground truth data. The translational part of $\Delta\mathbf{T}_1$ differs by 1.4 % which is slightly better than comparable results from [21] ($\Delta\alpha_{\mathrm{err}} \approx 0.7°$, $\Delta t_{\mathrm{err}} \approx 1.6\,\%$ for > 12 views).

5   Conclusion

In this paper we proposed a Structure from Motion framework with integrated eye-to-eye calibration that is capable of estimating the extrinsics of a multi-camera system with non-overlapping views stepwise for each camera with respect to a designated reference camera capturing images of a default calibration pattern. We proposed a novel method for eye-to-eye calibration (E2E-VIS) based on reprojection errors instead of pose-based error functions as used in existing methods (E2E-GEOM) adopted from hand-eye calibration. It was demonstrated that E2E-VIS improves the results from E2E-GEOM and can be used a preprocessing step for advanced optimization methods such as eye-to-eye bundle adjustment (E2E-BA). Accurate calibration results could be obtained in experiments with both synthetic data and real image sequences.

Future work. A remaining disadvantage of E2E-BA as final optimization step is the large problem size for systems consisting of several cameras. This problem could be solved by either pruning the resulting 3d point clouds prior to joint bundle adjustment or by removing explicit 3d point parameters from the error function entirely as proposed in [22] for monocular bundle adjustment. Furthermore, real-time processing of the proposed algorithm should be achieved by further parallelization and usage of GPU accelerated algorithms as present in more recent real-time SfM applications such as DTAM [19].

References

1. Andreff, N., Horaud, R., Espiau, B.: On-line hand-eye calibration. In: 2nd International Conference on 3D Digital Imaging and Modeling, pp. 430–436 (1999)
2. Bradski, G.: The OpenCV library. Dr. Dobb's J. Softw. Tools **25**(11), 120–126 (2000)
3. Caspi, Y., Irani, M.: Alignment of non-overlapping sequences. Int. J. Comput. Vision **48**(1), 39–51 (2002)
4. Chen, H.H.: A screw motion approach to uniqueness analysis of head-eye geometry. In: IEEE Conference on Computer Vision and Pattern Recognition, pp. 145–151 (1991)
5. Dornaika, F., Chung, R.: Stereo geometry from 3D ego-motion streams. IEEE Trans. Syst. Man Cybern. B Cybern. **33**(2), 308–323 (2003)
6. Esquivel, S., Koch, R.: Structure from motion using rigidly coupled cameras without overlapping views. In: Weickert, J., Hein, M., Schiele, B. (eds.) GCPR 2013. LNCS, vol. 8142, pp. 11–20. Springer, Heidelberg (2013)
7. Esquivel, S., Woelk, F., Koch, R.: Calibration of a multi-camera rig from non-overlapping views. In: Hamprecht, F.A., Schnörr, C., Jähne, B. (eds.) DAGM 2007. LNCS, vol. 4713, pp. 82–91. Springer, Heidelberg (2007)
8. Farenzena, M., Fusiello, A., Gherardi, R.: Structure-and-motion pipeline on a hierarchical cluster tree. In: IEEE International Conference on Computer Vision Workshops, pp. 1489–1496 (2009)
9. Frahm, J.-M., Köser, K., Koch, R.: Pose estimation for multi-camera systems. In: Rasmussen, C.E., Bülthoff, H.H., Schölkopf, B., Giese, M.A. (eds.) DAGM 2004. LNCS, vol. 3175, pp. 286–293. Springer, Heidelberg (2004)
10. Hartley, R.I., Zisserman, A.: Multiple View Geometry in Computer Vision, 2nd edn. Cambridge University Press, Cambridge (2004)
11. Hesch, J.A., Mourikis, A.I., Roumeliotis, S.I.: Mirror-based extrinsic camera calibration. In: Workshop on the Algorithmic Foundations of Robotics, pp. 285–299 (2008)
12. Kim, J.H., Chung, M.J.: Absolute motion and structure from stereo image sequences without stereo correspondence and analysis of degenerate cases. Pattern Recogn. **39**(9), 1649–1661 (2006)
13. Kumar, R.K., Ilie, A., Frahm, J.M., Pollefeys, M.: Simple calibration of non-overlapping cameras with a mirror. In: IEEE Conference on Computer Vision and Pattern Recognition, pp. 1–7 (2008)
14. Lébraly, P., Royer, E., Ait-Aider, O., Deymier, C., Dhome, M.: Fast calibration of embedded non-overlapping cameras. In: IEEE International Conference on Robotics and Automation, pp. 221–227 (2011)

15. Li, B., Heng, L., Köser, K., Pollefeys, M.: A multiple-camera system calibration toolbox using a feature descriptor-based calibration pattern. In: IEEE/RSJ International Conference on Intelligent Robots and Systems, pp. 1301–1307 (2013)

16. Lourakis, M.I.A.: Sparse non-linear least squares optimization for geometric vision. In: Daniilidis, K., Maragos, P., Paragios, N. (eds.) ECCV 2010, Part II. LNCS, vol. 6312, pp. 43–56. Springer, Heidelberg (2010)

17. Lourakis, M.I.A., Argyros, A.A.: The design and implementation of a generic sparse bundle adjustment software package based on the Levenberg-Marquardt algorithm. Technical report #340, Institute of Computer Science, Foundation for Research and Technology - Hellas (FORTH) (2004)

18. Moré, J.J., Garbow, B.S., Hillstrom, K.E.: User guide for MINPACK-1. Technical report ANL-80-74, Argonne National Laboratory (1980)

19. Newcombe, R.A., Lovegrove, S., Davison, A.J.: DTAM: Dense tracking and mapping in real-time. In: IEEE International Conference on Computer Vision, pp. 2320–2327 (2011)

20. Pagel, F.: Calibration of non-overlapping cameras in vehicles. In: IEEE Intelligent Vehicles Symposium, pp. 1178–1183 (2010)

21. Rodrigues, R., Barreto, J.P., Nunes, U.: Camera pose estimation using images of planar mirror reflections. In: Daniilidis, K., Maragos, P., Paragios, N. (eds.) ECCV 2010, Part IV. LNCS, vol. 6314, pp. 382–395. Springer, Heidelberg (2010)

22. Rodríguez, A.L., de Teruel, P.E.L., Ruiz, A.: GEA optimization for live structure-less motion estimation. In: IEEE International Conference on Computer Vision, pp. 715–718 (2011)

23. Strobl, K.H., Hirzinger, G.: Optimal hand-eye calibration. In: IEEE/RSJ International Conference on Intelligent Robots and Systems, pp. 4647–4653 (2006)

24. Terzakis, G., Culverhouse, P., Bugmann, G., Sharma, S., Sutton, R.: A recipe on the parameterization of rotation matrices for non-linear optimization using quaternions. Technical report MIDAS.SMSE.2012.TR.004, Marine and Industrial Dynamic Analysis School of Marine Science and Engineering, Plymouth University (2012)

25. Tsai, R.Y., Lenz, R.K.: A new technique for fully autonomous and efficient 3d robotics hand/eye calibration. IEEE Trans. Robot. Autom. **5**(3), 345–358 (1989)

26. Zhang, Z.: A flexible new technique for camera calibration. IEEE Transactions on Pattern Analysis and Machine Intelligence, 1330–1334 (2000)

Estimating Vehicle Ego-Motion and Piecewise Planar Scene Structure from Optical Flow in a Continuous Framework

Andreas Neufeld[✉], Johannes Berger, Florian Becker,
Frank Lenzen, and Christoph Schnörr

IPA and HCI, University of Heidelberg, Heidelberg, Germany
{neufeld,becker,schnoerr}@math.uni-heidelberg.de,
{johannes.berger,frank.lenzen}@iwr.uni-heidelberg.de

Abstract. We propose a variational approach for estimating egomotion and structure of a static scene from a pair of images recorded by a single moving camera. In our approach the scene structure is described by a set of 3D planar surfaces, which are linked to a SLIC superpixel decomposition of the image domain. The continuously parametrized planes are determined along with the extrinsic camera parameters by jointly minimizing a non-convex smooth objective function, that comprises a data term based on the pre-calculated optical flow between the input images and suitable priors on the scene variables. Our experiments demonstrate that our approach estimates egomotion and scene structure with a high quality, that reaches the accuracy of state-of-the-art stereo methods, but relies on a single sensor that is more cost-efficient for autonomous systems.

1 Introduction

1.1 Overview

For the scenario of a camera moving through a static scene, e.g. in an automotive environment, we present an approach for jointly estimating the scene structure and the camera egomotion. In a preprocessing step the optical flow between these two frames together with a confidence map is estimated, and serves as input data. Moreover, for one of the frames, a partition of the image domain into superpixels is determined. The main part (and main contribution) of our method consists of a variational approach with a non-convex smooth objective function, which includes suitable chosen priors on the scene depth and plane parameters to guarantee a consistent scene representation with only a sparse set of depth discontinuities. By minimizing this objective function we obtain an estimate of the egomotion in terms of rotation and translation together with a description of the scene by one 3D plane per superpixel. Figure 1 depicts a typical scene reconstruction. From the plane parameters both scene depth and surface normals can be determined directly.

We stress that, due to the *monocular* nature of the considered problem with a less favorable motion parallax, the task is more difficult than stereo setups

J. Gall et al. (Eds.): GCPR 2015, LNCS 9358, pp. 41–52, 2015.
DOI: 10.1007/978-3-319-24947-6_4

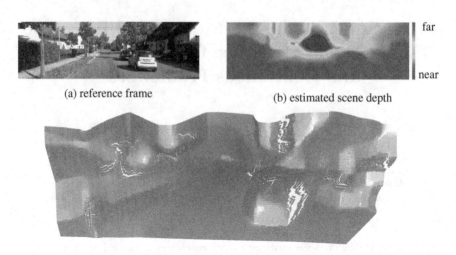

(a) reference frame   (b) estimated scene depth

(c) surface visualization of reconstructed scene

Fig. 1. *Best viewed in color.* (a) first frame of an image pair from the KITTI stereo benchmark; (b) depth map derived from the piecewise planar scene structures computed by our monocular approach jointly with the camera motion; (c) shaded visualization of the piecewise planar structure (Color figure online).

studied in this context. However, industry favors more cost- and energy-efficient sensor solutions.

1.2 Related Work

Scene reconstruction in the automotive context poses an important foundation for higher-level reasoning e.g. in advanced driver assistant systems. For vision based outdoor scene reconstruction stereo based systems currently dominate, as this well-posed problem setting with a known calibrated stereo camera setup leads to highly accurate results. This is substantiated by the enormous popularity of the KITTI benchmark [7].

In the recent years *monocular* scene reconstruction approaches became increasingly popular although they have to additionally determine the unknown relative camera position between two frames. This has been proved to be feasible also in real-time both for indoor [9, 12, 13, 15, 16] and the even more challenging task of outdoor setups, where a world map is aggregated over an entire image sequence (Simultaneous Localization And Mapping, SLAM) [5, 22]. Despite the higher computational effort compared to stereo setups, monocular camera systems feature reduced calibration effort which is interesting from the industrial point of view. Results presented e.g. in [3] demonstrate that depth accuracy comparable to stereo methods can be achieved even in an automotive context. Similar to the methods above we consider the case of a monocular camera setup, however, do not accumulate information over an image sequence but only resort to *two* consecutive image frames to estimate scene and egomotion. In [24,25] epipolar geometry is pre-computed and flow is restricted to fixed epipolar lines. We implement a *joint* estimation approach of egomotion and scene description, as is also done in [3,13].

A few algorithms rely on independent matches for scene reconstruction [18], but most algorithms incorporate a prior on the regularity of the depth map to cope with ambiguities and distortions in the data. Piecewise constant depth maps seem to be a reasonable assumption in connection with modeling shallow objects and occlusions present in indoor scenes. For street scenes however, slanted planes such as the street or house fronts dominate, and providing an accurate reconstruction is important for subsequent reasoning steps. Stereo methods [20,21,23,24] implementing this prior rank at top positions in the according KITTI benchmark. While the above methods work with a (partially) discretized parameter space, we consider continuous variables, which results in a differentiable objective function, for which established and soundly studied numerical method are available. The objective function enables us to perform a joint optimization in all variables.

Since our approach utilizes a scene description by piecewise planar surfaces, it closely relates to estimating multiple homographies explaining the optical flow induced by the motion of a camera relative to planar surfaces. The seminal works [14,26] showed that the set of homographies of any number of views is embedded in a four dimensional subspace which also carries a manifold structure [6]. Recent approaches [4,17] are based on inter-homography constraints and do not require camera calibration. In contrast, our method assumes the *intrinsic camera parameters* to be known. This requirement comes with the advantage, that the planes can be estimated physically correctly (up to a global scale).

The approach presented in this work builds upon an accurate estimation of the optical flow for which we can resort to existing and *publicly available* methods that have proven to be accurate in the considered scenario. We choose to the top ranked monocular optical flow method [19] in the KITTI benchmark with source code available.

2 Approach Overview

Preliminaries, Notation. Throughout this paper, we consider scenarios where a 3D scene is recorded by a projective camera from two different perspectives. We denote 3D points by $X \in \mathbb{R}^3$. W.l.o.g. we assume the first camera position to be $(0,0,0)^\top$ with viewing direction $(0,0,1)^\top$ and refer to the image recorded from this position by I_1. We denote the projection of a point X onto the first image plane by $x = \pi(X) \in \Omega$ with *image domain* $\Omega \subset \mathbb{R}^2$. Assuming the *intrinsic* camera parameter to be known we can w.l.o.g. utilize normalized image coordinates, i.e. $\pi(X) := X_3^{-1} \left(\begin{smallmatrix} X_1 \\ X_2 \end{smallmatrix} \right)$.

For the second recording, the camera is rotated with rotation matrix $R \in$ SO(3) and translated by vector $t \in S^2$. We refer to (R,t) as the *extrinsic* camera parameters. The translation is constrained to unit norm, since scene scale cannot be determined from monocular images. The projection of a point X onto the second image plane then is given as $x' := \pi(R^\top(X - t))$ and the acquired image is denoted by I_2.

We aim at representing the reconstructed scene by a number of space planes which we parametrize by $v \in \mathbb{R}^3$, such that any space point $X \in \mathbb{R}^3$ lying on the plane fulfills $\langle v, X \rangle = 1$. Assuming that the scene can be (locally) represented by plane parameters v, the apparent motion induced by the camera movement is described by

$$x' = \pi\left(H(R, t, v)\left(\begin{smallmatrix} x \\ 1 \end{smallmatrix}\right)\right), \tag{1}$$

with the homography $H(R, t, v) := R^\top(I - tv^\top)$ (cf. e.g. [10, Chap. 13]).

Finally, we estimate planes on a pre-computed connected partition $\{\Omega^i\}_i$ (superpixels) of the first image using the SLIC (Simple Linear Iterative Clustering) method [2]. We further define the common boundary of superpixel i and j by $\partial^{ij} := \overline{\Omega^i} \cap \overline{\Omega^j}$. The set of all neighboring superpixel pairs is denoted by $\mathcal{N}_\Omega := \{(i, j) | i, j \in \{1, \ldots, n\}, \partial^{ij} \neq \emptyset\}$. We *assume* that all space points $X \in \mathbb{R}^3$ projected to superpixel $i \in \{1, \ldots, n\}$, i.e. $\pi(X) \in \Omega^i$, lie on a plane parametrized by $v^i \in \mathbb{R}^3$, see Fig. 2 for an illustration. Using (1) we gain a low-parametric *model* for the optical flow

$$u(x; R, t, v) := x' - x = \pi(H(R, t, v)\left(\begin{smallmatrix} x \\ 1 \end{smallmatrix}\right)) - x. \tag{2}$$

Then, for an *observed* optical flow $\hat{u} : \Omega \mapsto \mathbb{R}^2$ which approximately transports I_1 to I_2 we formulate the inverse problem of determining the piecewise planar scene description $v := (v^1, \ldots, v^n) \in \mathbb{R}^{3n}$ and camera motion (R, t), which explains $\hat{u}$, as finding a solution to the problem

$$\min_{R \in \mathsf{SO}(3), t \in \mathsf{S}^2, v \in \mathbb{R}^{3n}} E(R, t, v). \tag{3}$$

The energy function $E(R, t, v)$ furthermore incorporates priors on the scene structure and is detailed in Sect. 3.

3   Variational Approach

Our energy function $E(R, t, v)$ decomposes into

$$E(R, t, v) = E_u(R, t, v) + \lambda_z E_z(v) + \lambda_v E_v(v) + \lambda_p E_p(v), \tag{4}$$

where E_u is the data fidelity term, E_z and E_v are priors on the depth and the plane parameters, respectively and E_p is a term penalizing negative depth values. We detail all four terms in Sects. 3.1, 3.2, 3.3 and 3.4. The terms are coupled via the positive weighting parameters λ_z, λ_v and λ_p. Our choice for these parameters is provided in the experimental section, cf. Sect. 4. Our numerical approach to minimize (4) is presented in Sect. 3.5.

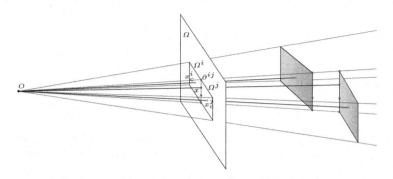

Fig. 2. *Best viewed in color.* Projective camera and discretization. Two rectangular superpixels Ω^i, Ω^j in the image domain Ω and two space planes parametrized by v^i, v^j and restricted to the cone defined by the camera origin O and the superpixel coverage. Regularity of depth is evaluated at all positions $x \in \partial^{ij}$ (blue dots) along common superpixel boundaries – see Sect. 3.2. The non-negativity prior on depth is evaluated on superpixel centers x_c^i, x_c^j (red dots) – see Sect. 3.4 (Color figure online).

3.1   Data Fidelity

The fidelity term $E_u(R, t, v)$ in our optimization problem is the deviation of an *observed* optical flow $\hat{u}(x)$ from our model (2) and is defined as

$$E_u(R, t, v) := \sum_{i=1}^{n} \sum_{x \in \Omega^i} w_{\hat{u}}(x) \| u(x; R, t, v^i) - \hat{u}(x) \|_2^2. \tag{5}$$

Here, $w_{\hat{u}}(x) \geq 0$ denotes a spatially varying weighting of the data term which is provided by a confidence measure of the optical flow algorithm as detailed next.

Optical Flow Estimation. The optical flow $\hat{u}$ between images I_1 and I_2 as required by the data term (5) is computed in a pre-processing step using the algorithm *Data-Flow* being the highest ranked publicly available monocular implementation (cf. [19]) in the KITTI optical flow challenge.

  We complement the output obtained from *Data-Flow* with a confidence map $w_{\hat{u}}(x)$, which avoids the influence of flow vectors which are considered incorrect. To this end we also estimate the *backward* flow between I_2 and I_1, providing an estimate $\hat{u}^{-1}(x)$ of the inverse mapping of $\hat{u}(x)$. Only points that are consistently mapped forth and back are considered correct and we define the confidence map as

$$w_{\hat{u}}(x) := \exp\left(-\tfrac{1}{2}\|x - (\hat{u}^{-1} \circ \hat{u})(x)\|_2^2 / \sigma_{\hat{u}}^2\right) \tag{6}$$

with value $\sigma_{\hat{u}} > 0$. Experimentally, we found the value $\sigma_{\hat{u}} = \frac{1}{2\sqrt{2}}$ to be suitable.

3.2   Smoothness Prior on Depth

In order to enforce that planes of neighboring superpixels form a seamlessly connected surface in most parts of the image, we introduce the prior $E_z(v)$ as follows. We consider points on the common boundary $x_\partial \in \partial^{ij}$ of superpixel i and j and penalize deviations of their inverse depth $z^{-1}(x_\partial, v) = x_\partial^\top v$ according to the two plane models v^i and v^j, see Fig. 2 for an illustration.

In order to encourage sharp depth edges we make use of the generalized Charbonnier functional

$$\rho_C(x) := (x^2 + \epsilon)^\alpha - \epsilon^\alpha. \tag{7}$$

We choose $\epsilon = 10^{-10}$ and $\alpha = 1/4$ throughout the work, so that $\rho_C^2(x)$ smoothly approximates $|x|$. Then the energy function for one boundary ∂^{ij} reads as

$$E_z^{ij}(v) := \sum_{x \in \partial^{ij}} \rho_C^2(x^\top v^i - x^\top v^j). \tag{8}$$

Note that we opted to compare *inverse* depth $z^{-1}(x, v)$ due to a superior numerical performance and reconstruction. Then the global smoothness term consists of a weighted sum of E_z^{ij} over all neighboring superpixels $(i, j) \in \mathcal{N}_\Omega$:

$$E_z(v) := \sum_{(i,j) \in \mathcal{N}_\Omega} w_\Omega^{ij} E_z^{ij}(v). \tag{9}$$

The weights $w_\Omega^{ij} \geq 0$ are computed based on appearance differences, i.e.

$$w_\Omega^{ij} := \exp\left(-\tfrac{1}{2}(m_i - m_j)^2/\sigma_\Omega^2\right), \tag{10}$$

where m_i and m_j are the mean gray values of frame I_1 in superpixel Ω^i and Ω^j, respectively. For parameter σ_Ω, we use a fixed value of 0.2.

3.3 Smoothness Prior on Plane Parameters

In addition to seamless surfaces on superpixel boundaries, we aim at plane parameters which up to a small set of discontinuities are constant over the image domain. This property encourages large connected planar structures.

For the plane smoothness prior we employ again the Charbonnier function ρ_C (see (7), here applied component-wise), and the boundary weights w_Ω^{ij} from (10):

$$E_v(v) = \sum_{(i,j) \in \mathcal{N}_\Omega} w_\Omega^{ij} \|\rho_C(v^i - v^j)\|_2^2. \tag{11}$$

3.4 Positive Depth Prior

As a further constraint, we require all observed space points to be in front of the camera. Thus, we introduce an additional prior E_p. We apply a soft hinge function

$$\rho_+(x) := \begin{cases} 1 - 2x & x \leq 0 \\ (1 - x)^2 & 0 < x \leq 1, \\ 0 & 1 < x \end{cases} \tag{12}$$

to the inverse depth given by $z^{-1}(x_c^i, v^i) = \left\langle \begin{pmatrix} x_c^i \\ 1 \end{pmatrix}, v^i \right\rangle$, evaluated at superpixel centers $x_c^i \in \Omega^i$, see Fig. 2. Summing over all superpixels, this leads to

$$E_p(v) = \sum_{i=1}^{n} \rho_+^2 (z^{-1}(x_c^i, v^i)). \tag{13}$$

3.5 Optimization

The considered optimization task (3) comprises a non-convex smooth energy function (4) and manifold constraints $R \in SO(3)$ and $t \in S^2$. In order to find a local minimum of $E(R, t, v)$, we choose the Levenberg-Marquardt method [11], which has been adapted to Riemannian manifolds in [1].

The proposed energy function $E(R, t, v)$ can be decomposed into a sum of m squared functions $f_j(R, t, v)$, where $m = 2|\Omega| + \sum_{(i,j) \in \mathcal{N}_\Omega} |\partial_{ij}| + 3|\mathcal{N}_\Omega| + n$, i.e.

$$E(R, t, v) = \sum_{j=1}^{m} (f_j(R, t, v))^2 = \|f(R, t, v)\|_2^2, \tag{14}$$

with $f(R, t, v) := (f_1(R, t, v), \dots, f_m(R, t, v))^\top \in \mathbb{R}^m$.

We combine the variables into a joint vector $Y := (R, t, v)$ and locally re-parametrize Y near (R^k, t^k, v^k) by parameters $\eta := (\omega, \delta t, \delta v)^\top \in \mathbb{R}^{3+3+3n}$ as

$$Y(\eta) := (R^k \operatorname{Exp}([\omega]_\times), \Pi_{S^2}(t^k + \delta_t), v^k + \delta_v). \tag{15}$$

Here, $\operatorname{Exp}(\cdot)$ is the matrix exponential function applied to the skew-symmetric matrix $[\omega]_\times := \begin{pmatrix} 0 & -\omega_3 & \omega_2 \\ \omega_3 & 0 & -\omega_1 \\ -\omega_2 & \omega_1 & 0 \end{pmatrix}$, which can be efficiently evaluated using the Rodrigues' rotation formula, c.f. [10]. Furthermore, $\Pi_{S^2}(t) := t/\|t\|_2$ denotes the orthogonal projection of t to S^2. Using first order Taylor expansion we obtain an approximation of $f(Y(\eta))$ in $Y = (R^k, t^k, v^k)$,

$$\tilde{f}^k(\eta) := f^k(0) + \left(J f^k(\eta) \big|_{\eta=0} \right) \eta, \tag{16}$$

with Jacobian $J f^k$ of f^k. The Jacobian is obtained for the rotation and translation by differentiating the function compositions $\frac{\partial}{\partial \omega}(f \circ \operatorname{Exp})(\omega)$ and $\frac{\partial}{\partial t}(f \circ \Pi_{S^2})(t)$, respectively. Substituting this approximation in (14) yields a model of the actual energy function $\tilde{E}^k(\eta)$. However, we augment this objective function by a step regularization term in order to cope with strongly non-linear terms:

$$\min_\eta \tilde{E}^k(\eta) + \mu^k \|\eta\|_2^2. \tag{17}$$

The resulting objective is quadratic in η and thus can be solved efficiently. The update rule for the damping parameter μ^k is described in [1]. A limit of 80 iterations was used as stopping criterion which was sufficient for most of the considered data. We again stress the fact that the minimization of $E(R, t, v)$ is performed jointly w.r.t. R, t, v.

4   Experiments

Evaluation Methodology. In the following we evaluate the quality of scene description and egomotion estimate separately, see paragraphs *Plane Parameter Evaluation* and *Camera Motion Evaluation* below. The KITTI benchmark database [7] provides a suitable image data source as it is annotated with accurate depth and egomotion estimates. As reference surface normal information is not available in these data sets and no *monocular* approach with publicly available code can be compared to, we resort to a state-of-the-art *stereo* method [24], which is highly ranked as *SPS-St* in the KITTI stereo benchmark. It provides scene depth as well as a surface normals and can be assumed to be very accurate due to the well-posed stereo setup.

The KITTI odometry benchmark contains reference camera poses for a small number of sequences. Based on this reference data, we compare the *odometry results* of our approach to those of the freely available monocular approach *VISO2-M* [8].

Parameter Choice. In order to reduce errors caused by optical flow vectors pointing outside the image area, we apply our method to an image pair in inverse temporal order. The camera motion is thus initialized by a trivial *backward* motion $R = I$, $t = (0, 0, -1)^\top$ and flat scene $v = (0, 0, 0.001)^\top$ everywhere. Furthermore, we chose $\lambda_z = 0.05$, $\lambda_v = 0.001$ and $\lambda_p = 0.1$ – see (4) – throughout the experiments.

Plane Parameter Evaluation. In contrast to stereo methods, the accuracy of *depth* estimates of monocular methods varies depending on the projected position in the image plane and camera motion. We adopt the error measure proposed in [3] between estimated depth $z(x)$ and reference depth $z_{\text{ref}}(x)$ which respects this varying sensitivity,

$$e(x) := F \frac{|z(x) - z_{\text{ref}}(x)|}{\sigma_g(z_{\text{ref}}(x), x)} \tag{18}$$

with F denoting the camera's focal length in pixels.

Estimating the global scale inherently unknown in a monocular setting allows a quantitative comparison to metric reference data. To this end we approximate

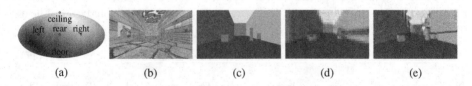

(a)   (b)   (c)   (d)   (e)

Fig. 3. *Best viewed in color.* (a) Approximate visually equidistant color scheme for plane normal visualization used throughout the work. (b) Exemplarily frame of a simple synthetic sequence and (c) ground truth normals, and normals as reconstructed by (d) *SPS-St* and (e) our method (Color figure online).

0 m ▬▬▬▬▬ 60 m   -10 m ▬▬▬▬ +10 m

(a) Depth color map (clipped)   (b) Depth difference color map (clipped)

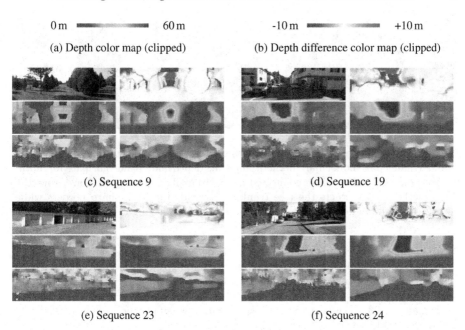

(c) Sequence 9   (d) Sequence 19

(e) Sequence 23   (f) Sequence 24

Fig. 4. *Best viewed in color.* Depth and plane normal comparison between our monocular and a reference stereo method [24]. From top to bottom, and left to right, each subfigure shows (top row) the reference frame and depth difference, (middle row) reference and estimated depth and (bottom row) reference and estimated normals. The depth values and depth differences are encoded as depicted in (a) and (b), respectively. The encoding of plane normals is illustrated in Fig. 3. Both depth and normal reconstructions mostly agree, but there is a loss in reconstruction detail near the epipole (near image center), see e.g. (d), which is an inherent problem of all monocular setups. Note that especially the ground surface is reconstructed well in most cases (Color figure online).

the scale as the median of the depth ratios $z(x)/z_{\mathrm{ref}}(x)$ on the most reliable 10 % according to sensibility prediction similar as done in [3].

Table 1 lists summarizing statistics of errors $e(x)$ computed over all pixels with reference depth z_{ref} (calculated from disparities) for 194 frames. A qualitative comparison against the stereo method *SPS-St* is given in Fig. 4.

Plane normal parameters are qualitatively compared to those obtained from [24] in Figs. 4 and 5. For a quantitative comparison, we use 240 frame pairs (each with 1280×720 pixels) from four simple ray-traced scenes but with known ground truth normals, see Fig. 3 for an example. Results for our method and *SPS-St* are presented in Table 2. We use the same parameters as on the KITTI dataset with both methods. We observe that despite the less favorable monocular setup the error of the plane normals estimated by the proposed method is smaller than the errors from SPS-St.

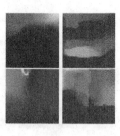

Fig. 5. *Best viewed in color.* Detailed views of scene reconstruction by (center) *SPS-St* and (right) our monocular method, showing depth and plane normals for both. Top row: our method uses less connected planes to explain the object. Lower row: the stereo method reconstructs the tree trunk overly wide but with sharp borders while our solution is more detailed but has smoother edges (Color figure online).

Table 1. Depth accuracy of our *monocular* method and *stereo* reference method *SPS-St*, evaluated on the KITTI stereo benchmark training data, distinguishing between areas without (*noc*) and with occluded areas (*occ*) as specified in the benchmark. Mean of depth error measurement $e(x)$ (see (18)) and percentage of pixels with error $e > 2$ px and $e > 3$ px, respectively. Our approach shows similar performance as *SPS-St* despite the less beneficial parallax and unknown camera position.

	noc			occ		
	Mean e [px]	p_{2px} [%]	p_{3px} [%]	Mean e [px]	p_{2px} [%]	p_{3px} [%]
Our method	4.09	12.9	8.63	4.88	13.6	9.17
SPS-St	3.15	12.6	7.46	9.12	13.8	8.57

Table 2. Plane normal errors for four synthetic sequences with known normals, see Fig. 3. The normal angle error w.r.t. ground truth is evaluated over 240 scene reconstructions. Note that we do not use a normalization scheme as in Eq. (18). Our method outperforms the stereo method despite the less favourable monocular setup.

	Mean [deg.]	$p_{1deg.}$ [%]	$p_{2deg.}$ [%]	$p_{5deg.}$ [%]	$p_{10deg.}$ [%]
Our method	11.5	58.4	45.5	31.1	22.7
SPS-St	14.8	79.4	66.6	46.4	33.4

Egomotion Evaluation. We evaluate the egomotion accuracy of the proposed method as well as a reference method [8] on the first 100 frames of the first 11 KITTI odometry sequences which all provide ground truth camera poses. We determine the *angle* error of the camera rotation and – due to the ambiguity in global scale – also between the translation vectors. Our method has an average rotational error of 0.057° and translation error of 3.86°, and performs better than the reference method *VISO2-M* [8] with errors 0.18° and 6.0°, respectively.

5 Conclusion and Further Work

We presented a variational method for estimating relative camera positions and planar scene structure from two views of a static scene. An objective function over egomotion and scene planes defined on superpixels was formulated and minimized continuously. We demonstrated that our *monocular* approach provides a scene reconstruction with reasonable accuracy in depth and plane normals compared to an approach in the less challenging *stereo* setup. Egomotion estimates also show a slightly better performance than a state-of-the-art odometry method. Future directions are extension to multiple frames, explicitly handling depth discontinuities and simultaneous estimation of flow and scene parameters.

References

1. Absil, P.A., Mahony, R., Sepulchre, R.: Optimization Algorithms on Matrix Manifolds. Princeton University Press, Princeton (2008)
2. Achanta, R., Shaji, A., Smith, K., Lucchi, A., Fua, P., Süsstrunk, S.: SLIC superpixels compared to state-of-the-art superpixel methods. IEEE Trans. Pattern Anal. Mach. Intell. **34**(11), 2274–2282 (2012)
3. Becker, F., Lenzen, F., Kappes, J.H., Schnörr, C.: Variational recursive joint estimation of dense scene structure and camera motion from monocular high speed traffic sequences. Int. J. Comput. Vis. **105**(3), 269–297 (2013)
4. Chojnacki, W., Szpak, Z.L., Brooks, M.J., van den Hengel, A.: Multiple homography estimation with full consistency constraints. In: DICTA (2010)
5. Engel, J., Schöps, T., Cremers, D.: LSD-SLAM: large-scale direct monocular SLAM. In: Fleet, D., Pajdla, T., Schiele, B., Tuytelaars, T. (eds.) ECCV 2014, Part II. LNCS, vol. 8690, pp. 834–849. Springer, Heidelberg (2014)
6. Eriksson, A., van den Hengel, A.: Optimization on the manifold of multiple homographies. In: ICCV (2009)
7. Geiger, A., Lenz, P., Stiller, C., Urtasun, R.: Vision meets robotics: the KITTI dataset. Int. J. Robot. Res. **32**, 1231–1237 (2013)
8. Geiger, A., Ziegler, J., Stiller, C.: Stereoscan: dense 3D reconstruction in real-time. In: IEEE Intelligent Vehicles Symposium, pp. 963–968 (2011)
9. Graber, G., Pock, T., Bischof, H.: Online 3D reconstruction using convex optimization. In: ICCV (2011)
10. Hartley, R.I., Zisserman, A.: Multiple View Geometry in Computer Vision, 2nd edn. Cambridge University Press, Cambridge (2004)
11. Moré, J.J.: The Levenberg-Marquardt algorithm: implementation and theory. In: Cleaveland, W.R. (ed.) CONCUR 1992. LNCS, vol. 630, pp. 105–116. Springer, Heidelberg (1992)
12. Newcombe, R.A., Davison, A.J.: Live dense reconstruction with a single moving camera. In: CVPR (2010)
13. Newcombe, R.A., Lovegrove, S.J., Davison, A.J.: DTAM: dense tracking and mapping in real-time. In: ICCV, pp. 2320–2327 (2011)
14. Shashua, A., Avidan, S.: The Rank 4 Constraint in Multiple ($\geq$3) View Geometry. In: Buxton, B.F., Cipolla, R. (eds.) ECCV 1996. LNCS, vol. 1065, pp. 196–206. Springer, Heidelberg (1996)
15. Stühmer, J., Gumhold, S., Cremers, D.: Parallel generalized thresholding scheme for live dense geometry from a handheld camera. In: CVGPU (2010)

16. Stühmer, J., Gumhold, S., Cremers, D.: Real-time dense geometry from a handheld camera. In: Goesele, M., Roth, S., Kuijper, A., Schiele, B., Schindler, K. (eds.) Pattern Recognition. LNCS, vol. 6376, pp. 11–20. Springer, Heidelberg (2010)
17. Szpak, Z.L., Chojnacki, W., Eriksson, A., van den Hengel, A.: Sampson distance based joint estimation of multiple homographies with uncalibrated cameras. Comput. Vis. Image Und. **125**, 200–213 (2014)
18. Tola, E., Strecha, C., Fua, P.: Efficient large-scale multi-view stereo for ultra high-resolution image sets. Mach. Vis. Appl. **23**(5), 903–920 (2012)
19. Vogel, C., Roth, S., Schindler, K.: An evaluation of data costs for optical flow. In: Weickert, J., Hein, M., Schiele, B. (eds.) GCPR 2013. LNCS, vol. 8142, pp. 343–353. Springer, Heidelberg (2013)
20. Vogel, C., Roth, S., Schindler, K.: View-consistent 3D scene flow estimation over multiple frames. In: Fleet, D., Pajdla, T., Schiele, B., Tuytelaars, T. (eds.) ECCV 2014, Part IV. LNCS, vol. 8692, pp. 263–278. Springer, Heidelberg (2014)
21. Vogel, C., Schindler, K., Roth, S.: Piecewise rigid scene flow. In: ICCV (2013)
22. Wendel, A., Maurer, M., Graber, G., Pock, T., Bischof, H.: Dense reconstruction on-the-fly. In: CVPR (2012)
23. Yamaguchi, K., Hazan, T., McAllester, D., Urtasun, R.: Continuous Markov random fields for robust stereo estimation. In: Fitzgibbon, A., Lazebnik, S., Perona, P., Sato, Y., Schmid, C. (eds.) ECCV 2012, Part V. LNCS, vol. 7576, pp. 45–58. Springer, Heidelberg (2012)
24. Yamaguchi, K., McAllester, D., Urtasun, R.: Efficient joint segmentation, occlusion labeling, stereo and flow estimation. In: Fleet, D., Pajdla, T., Schiele, B., Tuytelaars, T. (eds.) ECCV 2014, Part V. LNCS, vol. 8693, pp. 756–771. Springer, Heidelberg (2014)
25. Yamaguchi, K., McAllester, D.A., Urtasun, R.: Robust monocular epipolar flow estimation. In: CVPR (2013)
26. Zelnik-Manor, L., Irani, M.: Multi-view subspace constraints on homographies. In: ICCV (1999)

Efficient Two-View Geometry Classification

Johannes L. Schönberger$^{(\boxtimes)}$, Alexander C. Berg, and Jan-Michael Frahm

The University of North Carolina at Chapel Hill,
Chapel Hill, NC, USA
jsch@cs.unc.edu

Abstract. Typical Structure-from-Motion systems spend major computational effort on geometric verification. Geometric verification recovers the epipolar geometry of two views for a moving camera by estimating a fundamental or essential matrix. The essential matrix describes the relative geometry for two views up to an unknown scale. Two-view triangulation or multi-model estimation approaches can reveal the relative geometric configuration of two views, e.g., small or large baseline and forward or sideward motion. Information about the relative configuration is essential for many problems in Structure-from-Motion. However, essential matrix estimation and assessment of the relative geometric configuration are computationally expensive. In this paper, we propose a learning-based approach for efficient two-view geometry classification, leveraging the by-products of feature matching. Our approach can predict whether two views have scene overlap and for overlapping views it can assess the relative geometric configuration. Experiments on several datasets demonstrate the performance of the proposed approach and its utility for Structure-from-Motion.

1 Introduction

Over the last decade Structure-from-Motion (SfM) systems have seen tremendous evolution in terms of robustness and efficiency [1,8,13,31]. Incremental SfM systems (Fig. 2) typically start with feature extraction and detection (Stage 1), followed by matching (Stage 2) and geometric verification (Stage 3) of successfully matched pairs by the assessment of the relative viewing configuration. The major computational effort is spent on Stages 2 and 3. The incremental reconstruction seeds the model with a carefully selected initial two-view reconstruction. Next, the procedure incrementally registers new cameras from 2D–3D correspondences, triangulates new 3D features, and refines the reconstruction using a non-linear optimization, known as bundle-adjustment (Stage 4). The input to the incremental reconstruction procedure (Stage 4) is typically a graph of relative, pairwise epipolar transformations. Information about the relative geometric configuration, such as small or large baseline and forward or sideward motion, is essential for SfM, since the incremental reconstruction procedure is highly dependent on the order in which cameras are registered. A suitable initial image pair and similarly a suitable next-best-view during the incremental extension depends on the relative viewing geometry, i.e. uncertainty of 3D features

© Springer International Publishing Switzerland 2015
J. Gall et al. (Eds.): GCPR 2015, LNCS 9358, pp. 53–64, 2015.
DOI: 10.1007/978-3-319-24947-6_5

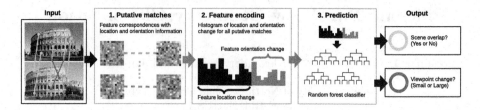

Fig. 1. The proposed framework for extracting PAIGE, and its application for scene overlap and viewpoint change prediction.

and camera parameters. However, assessment of the relative viewing geometry for every overlapping image pair in a dataset is computationally expensive. This paper presents a technique for efficiently recognizing image pairs that work well for incremental SfM – significantly improving efficiency for geometric verification as well as improving reconstruction robustness.

The relative geometric configuration of overlapping image pairs serves as the input to the incremental reconstruction procedure. Geometric verification attempts to estimate the relative viewing geometry for pairs of overlapping images. Usually, the majority of image pairs in large-scale, unordered photo-collections do not have scene overlap, and thus rejecting invalid pairs dominates execution time. Determining the relative viewing geometry for large image sets comes at significant computational expense, especially if the overlap between most images is sparse. However, it is a necessary step, as unfavorable initializations or an unfortunate order in camera registrations, e.g., pairs resulting in high camera and/or point uncertainty, can lead to failures in registration and bundle-adjustment due to weak geometry, local minima, degeneracies, etc.

The traditional procedure to assess the two-view geometry in geometric verification comprises fundamental or essential matrix estimation [20] followed by triangulation of 3D points [15], multi-model estimation strategies like GRIC [29], or extended RANSAC procedures for model selection such as QDEGSAC [12]. The essential matrix reveals the entire two-view geometry of calibrated cameras up to unknown scale. Triangulation of 3D points, GRIC, or QDEGSAC then determine the properties of the relative viewing geometry, e.g., the amount and direction of viewpoint change. However, while efficient on a per pair basis, these methods are computationally expensive for a large number of image pairs.

In this paper, we design an encoding of image characteristics and build a framework (Fig. 1) for the efficient recognition of image pairs with scene overlap and prediction of the stability of their two-view geometry, all without explicitly reconstructing the actual camera configuration using essential matrix estimation. The approach is based on the location and orientation properties of putative feature correspondences. In Sect. 6, we experimentally demonstrate the utility of the proposed framework for a variety of SfM modules, e.g. reducing the set of image pairs for which to perform geometric verification and efficient search for stable initial image pairs in large datasets.

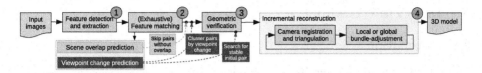

Fig. 2. The stages of a typical SfM pipeline, and applications of our proposed scene overlap and viewpoint change predictor in green and purple (Color figure online).

2 Related Work

Over the last years large-scale SfM systems have tremendously advanced in terms of increased robustness and reduced runtime. A variety of methods to reduce runtime in different stages of the SfM pipeline (Fig. 2) have been proposed. However, current state-of-the-art systems typically still spend major time in Stages 2 and 3. To reduce the number of image pairs in the exhaustive matching module (Stage 2), Frahm et al. [13] leverage iconic image selection through clustering of similar images, Agarwal et al. [1] employ image retrieval systems [21] to only match against similar images, Raguram et al. [26] use GPS tags to match images only to spatially nearby ones, and Wu [31] proposes a preemptive matching strategy. Recently, Hartmann et al. [16] proposed to predict the matchability of individual features (Stage 1) to reduce the number of feature comparisons during exhaustive matching (Stage 2). Most recently, Schönberger et al. [27] proposed a learning-based approach to predict scene overlap based on approximate feature correspondences. However, these techniques still yield a significant amount of image pairs that have no scene overlap, and the set of images contains many redundant viewpoints. Despite the variety of approaches, they all rely on elaborate two-view reconstructions on their potentially reduced set of images in the geometric verification stage. Apart from algorithmic advancements on estimation techniques [20,23], only Raguram et al. [25] tried to specifically improve runtime of Stage 3 using an online learning strategy. However, their approach suffers from a significant loss of image registrations.

Complementary to these previous efforts, we propose a new method to further improve the efficiency in SfM by significantly reducing the runtime of the geometric verification module (Stage 3). Our method can detect overlapping image pairs before geometric verification and for overlapping image pairs it can efficiently classify the geometric two-view configuration in terms of the amount of viewpoint change. We achieve this by extending the method of Schönberger et al. [27] who pose the problem of scene overlap detection as a classification task. Similar to their method, we exploit the observation that when images are taken from different viewpoints, corresponding features change in scale, location, and rotation in recognizable patterns. However, instead of approximate correspondences through histogram intersection, we leverage the more reliable feature correspondences from putative matching enabling a less noisy encoding and more accurate prediction. Even though our method builds on the idea of Schönberger et al. [27], both approaches can be used together as filters for feature matching and geometric verification in the same SfM pipeline.

3   Two-View Geometry

3.1   Estimation

Traditional techniques to derive the two-view geometry comprise feature matching (Stage 2), followed by robust essential matrix estimation (Stage 3). The essential matrix reveals the relative viewing geometry [15], but its estimation is computationally expensive [20] due to outliers and non-linearity. RANdom SAmple Consens (RANSAC) [10] or its more efficient variants [6,7,23,24] are usually used for robust estimation. RANSAC can deal with large fractions of outliers, but has exponential computational complexity in the number of model parameters s and the inlier ratio e. To sample at least one outlier-free set of measurements with confidence p, one must run at least

$$d = \log\left(1 - p\right) / \log\left(1 - e^s\right) \tag{1}$$

number of iterations. Hence, the complexity quickly rises for small inlier ratios which are commonly encountered in SfM from unordered photo collections [26] (see Sect. 5). Moreover, RANSAC becomes infinitely expensive for image pairs without overlap since those pairs have no inliers. Hence, traditionally a minimum inlier ratio e_{min} is assumed to set an upper bound for the number of RANSAC iterations. Efficiently detecting image pairs that do not have scene overlap prior to geometric verification can significantly reduce the runtime of Stage 3.

The essential matrix reveals the relative transformation between two views up to an unknown scale. To derive more information about the relative viewing geometry, such as the amount of viewpoint change or the type of motion, further processing is necessary. Scene reconstruction enables to determine the amount of viewpoint change through scene analysis such as triangulation angle calculation. Alternatively, decision criterions like GRIC [29] or an extend RANSAC procedure like QDEGSAC [12] can be used to avoid degenerate viewing configurations. These methods are computationally expensive. In this paper, we propose a more efficient method to classify the amount of viewpoint change without explicit reconstruction of the scene.

3.2   Uncertainty

In this section, we briefly describe the relevance of the two-view geometry for uncertainty estimation in 3D reconstruction, its relation to the baseline-length and the triangulation angles, and how this affects the search for an initial pair and the order of camera registrations in SfM. Uncertainty of the 3D feature and the camera parameter estimates in bundle-adjustment are determined by five main factors [9,11,17,18]: redundancy, reliability, uncertainty of measurements, viewing geometry, and gauge. These factors have important implications for the design of SfM systems w.r.t. the search for an optimal initial pair and a suitable next-best-view. On the one hand, for accurate reconstructions, we want to jointly maximize the number of image measurements (high redundancy and reliability) and the stability of the two-view geometry (large triangulation angles). On the other hand, we wish to achieve optimal results (uncertainty and model size) with minimal computational effort, i.e. with as few measurements and camera registrations as possible.

4 Feature Representation

Our proposed feature representation builds upon the PAIGE feature by Schönberger et al. [27]. In this section, we describe our adaptions and extensions to their method for the efficient prediction of the two-view geometry.

PAIGE takes the extracted features from Stage 1, performs approximate feature matching through histogram intersection, and predicts scene overlap for an image pair by exploiting statistics from corresponding feature properties. Only overlapping image pairs are then forwarded to the computationally expensive pairwise image matching module (Stage 2). Analogous to their approach, we exploit the fact that corresponding features change in scale, location x, and orientation o in recognizable patterns when images are taken at different viewpoints. However, our approach leverages the more precise feature correspondences produced by feature matching in Stage 2, which enables us to produce a less noisy encoding for more accurate prediction.

For each putative feature correspondence of a matched image pair a and b, we determine the normalized image coordinates $\mathbf{x}_a, \mathbf{x}_b$, such that $x_i \in [0,1]^2$. Normalization is necessary due to possibly different image resolutions of image a and b. Next, we calculate the displacement for each correspondence as

$$\Delta x = \|\mathbf{x}_a - \mathbf{x}_b\|_2 \tag{2}$$

We quantize the distribution of feature displacements in a $d_{\Delta x}$-dimensional histogram $\mathbf{h}_{\Delta x}$ with evenly spaced bins in the interval $[0,1]$. Analogously, for each feature correspondence, we calculate the change in feature orientation

$$\Delta o = |o_a - o_b| \mod 2\pi \tag{3}$$

and we quantize the distribution of orientation changes in an $d_{\Delta o}$-dimensional histogram $\mathbf{h}_o$ with evenly spaced bins in the interval $[0, 2\pi]$. We normalize each of the histograms

$$\bar{\mathbf{h}}_x = \frac{\mathbf{h}_x}{\|\mathbf{h}_x\|_2}, \quad \bar{\mathbf{h}}_o = \frac{\mathbf{h}_o}{\|\mathbf{h}_o\|_2} \tag{4}$$

for invariance w.r.t. the number of feature correspondences. Finally, we use the concatenation of the normalized histograms as our proposed encoding

$$\mathcal{P}(a,b) = [\bar{\mathbf{h}}_x \ \bar{\mathbf{h}}_o] \tag{5}$$

Similarly to PAIGE, we do not represent scale changes in the feature as it is a noisy measure. The next section describes a classification strategy leveraging this feature representation for scene overlap and triangulation angle prediction.

5   Classification

Based on the proposed encoding in Sect. 4, we now describe a classification strategy to answer the following two questions for any given image pair: *Is there scene overlap (C_A)?* and *Is there a stable two-view geometry (C_B)?*. We choose random forests [3] as a classification method as it gave best results in terms of accuracy and computational efficiency.

Table 1. Evaluation datasets with average inlier ratio for matched (e_{all}) and verified pairs (e_{geo}). Number of RANSAC iterations for geometric verification without classifiers C_A and C_B (d_0), after classifier C_A (d_1), and after classifiers C_A and C_B (d_2). d_0, d_1, d_2 for *Training & Test* only given for held-out test set.

	Total pairs	Matched pairs	Verified pairs	e_{all}	e_{geo}	d_0	d_1	d_2
Training & Test	73,542,704	1,602,996	449,207	47 %	70 %	2,357,586,073 (100 %)	295,230,950 (12.5 %)	194,851,427 (8.3 %)
Oxford	82,944	21,574	16,303	56 %	70 %	72,445,847 (100 %)	14,557,490 (20.0 %)	9,604,943 (13.2 %)
Louvre	693,889	252,798	4,539	27 %	65 %	613,625,401 (100 %)	72,898,480 (11.9 %)	48,212,996 (7.9 %)
Acropolis	8,767,521	439,609	16,492	29 %	78 %	1,139,606,104 (100 %)	117,886,481 (10.3 %)	77,105,077 (6.8 %)

5.1   Training

For training, we use an existing 3D reconstruction of an image collection and its feature correspondences. Then, we calculate the mean triangulation angle $\bar{a}_{ab}$ for each image pair $\{a, b\}$ with scene overlap as the dependent variable and extract the proposed feature $\mathcal{P}(a, b)$ as the independent variable.

Specifically, we use 3D reconstructions of 17 unordered Internet photo-collections from different locations across the world (Rome, Notre Dame, Stonehenge, etc.) and a set of temporally sequential image sequences acquired by video cameras (to account for the orientation bias of crowd-sourced images) to serve as a training and test dataset (Table 1). The dataset consists of 1,602,996 matched (≥ 30 putative feature correspondences) out of all 73,542,704 possible image pairs, of which 449,207 pairs have a geometrically verified overlap (≥ 15 inliers for essential matrix estimation). Table 1 lists the minimum number of RANSAC iterations (Sect. 3) for essential matrix estimation of all matched image pairs with confidence $p = 0.99$, sample size $s = 5$, and minimum inlier ratio $e_{min} = 0.28$. As a result of these parameters, RANSAC runs for a maximum of $d_{max} = 2674$ iterations for each image pair. The maximum number of iterations is reached for <5 % of the pairs, since >95 % of the pairs have an inlier ratio >28 %. We employ SIFT features and use the ratio test for robust matching [19]; note that SIFT could be replaced by any other feature that provides location and orientation properties. The quantization of the location and orientation histograms include all 110,587,256 putative feature matches for all image

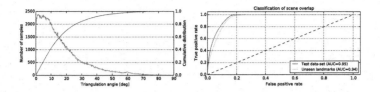

Fig. 3. *Left:* Triangulation angle distribution for geometrically verified image pairs. *Right:* Performance evaluation for scene overlap classification $\mathcal{C}_{\mathcal{A}}$.

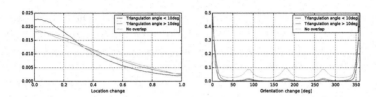

Fig. 4. Location and orientation change distributions of PAIGE for the entire dataset.

pairs, including 51,968,824 geometric inliers and 58,618,432 outliers, i.e. overall inlier ratio $e_{all} = 47\%$ and $e_{geo} = 70\%$ for geometrically verified pairs. We use a 172-dimensional feature vector $\mathcal{P}(a, b)$ with $d_{\Delta x} = 100$ and $d_{\Delta o} = 72$. Figure 3 visualizes the distribution of triangulation angles and Fig. 4 the average feature vector $\mathcal{P}(a, b)$ over all image pairs. We find a significant amount of pairs with only a small viewpoint change, caused by popular viewpoints of famous landmarks and less stable feature matching for large viewpoint changes. As expected, the overall location and orientation change is higher for wide than for small baselines, and the orientation change for images without overlap is significantly larger.

To answer the two binary classification problems $\mathcal{C}_{\mathcal{A}}$ and $\mathcal{C}_{\mathcal{B}}$, we divide the set of image pairs into three different categories: small and large mean triangulation angle (using an angle threshold), and no scene overlap (pairs with failed geometric verification). Next, the dataset is split in randomly permuted training (70%) and test samples (30%). Two random forests were trained on the training dataset, using 50 decision trees each, entropy as the splitting criterion, and considering $\sqrt{172} \approx 13$ features when looking for the best split at each node in the tree. A minimum number of three samples per leaf is enforced to avoid over-fitting. The parameters were determined with a 5-folded cross-validation on the training set. The trained random forests can efficiently decide on the two classification problems $\mathcal{C}_{\mathcal{A}}$ and $\mathcal{C}_{\mathcal{B}}$. An embedding of the proposed classifiers in a typical SfM pipeline is demonstrated in Sect. 6.

5.2 Performance Evaluation

On a conventional desktop computer the training time for both classifiers is approximately 5 min, and the classification frequency averages at around 200 K pairs per second including quantization and prediction, compared to around 20 K

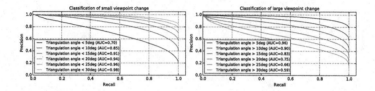

Fig. 5. Performance evaluation for triangulation angle classification C_B using different angle thresholds. Area under curve as AUC.

pairs per second for the PAIGE approach [27]. We evaluate the classification performance on the held-out test set (30 %), and three unordered photo-collections of completely unseen landmarks (see Table 1) at different geo-locations (Oxford, Louvre, Acropolis). Figure 5 demonstrates the performance for both classifiers C_A and C_B. For classifier C_A, we find minimal bias towards the trained landmarks, and we experience the same for classifier C_B. In a subsequent evaluation, the performance of classifier C_B is evaluated on the unseen landmarks w.r.t. different triangulation angle thresholds by only considering overlapping image pairs using C_A. Figure 5 shows that our method generalizes well. Next, we demonstrate the applicability of the two classifiers C_A and C_B within the context of SfM.

6   Efficient Structure-from-Motion

In the following, we show the embedding of the proposed method into a typical SfM system (Fig. 2) w.r.t. the datasets in Table 1. We demonstrate that the classifiers significantly improve the computational performance by reducing the set of images for the geometric verification module. Furthermore, we show the utility for the efficient search of stable initial image pairs in large datasets.

6.1   Scene Overlap Prediction

In Sect. 3, we have seen that the number of RANSAC iterations is exponentially dependent on the outlier ratio. Hence, we spend a majority of the runtime to evaluate pairs with no scene overlap. For these pairs RANSAC reaches the maximum number of iterations, leading to a significant computational burden. Our proposed method allows to filter these pairs prior to geometric verification, preventing the high computational effort for pairs that do not contribute to the final 3D model. Assuming we filtered all pairs with no scene overlap for the unseen landmarks (see Table 1) using a perfect classifier, and run RANSAC only for the remaining pairs, we can reduce the number of iterations by a factor of 35. For our classifier C_A, we enforce a precision of ≥ 0.99 for classifying pairs with no scene overlap using an appropriate prediction confidence, and hereby lower the recall to 81 %. This leads to the fact that our modified SfM pipeline only misses 1.7 % of actually overlapping pairs. Please note that the majority of those images are still contributing to the final model through other pairs. Using these parameters, we achieve a 7.8× speedup for the training & test-set, and overall an 8.9×

speedup for the unseen landmarks compared to the potential speedup of 35 using a perfect classifier. Since the computational effort for the classification is insignificant compared to geometric verification (3 to 4 orders of magnitudes faster), this speedup directly propagates to the overall geometric verification runtime. Note that the performance improves even more, if we verify very weak image pair connections, since we assume a minimum inlier ratio of 28 % ($d_{max} = 2674$). The reported runtimes are a vast improvement over previous efforts [25], which achieve a 70 % speedup but lose 26 % of image registrations, in contrast to our 9-fold speedup with 1.7 % loss. Due to the less noisy encoding based on putative feature matches, our approach misses significantly fewer image pairs than the PAIGE [27] approach, which loses 38–90 % of actually overlapping image pairs. Note that both approaches could be employed together, since PAIGE operates as a filter to feature matching and our approach as a filter to geometric verification. On average, we find that exhaustive matching and geometric verification spends 52 % in Stage 2 using a GPU SIFT implementation and 48 % in Stage 3 using a multi-threaded CPU RANSAC implementation. Ideally, the PAIGE approach [27] can eliminate the runtime of Stage 2 for sparsely connected image collections. Our proposed approach in this paper reduces the runtime of Stage 3 by a factor of 9. Combining the two approaches, we can effectively eliminate the original cost of Stages 2 and 3 compared to standard exhaustive matching.

6.2   Redundant Viewpoint Detection

In SfM systems, we achieve redundancy by tracking a 3D feature over multiple images. Corresponding features between two images cannot only be verified with direct pairwise geometric verification, but also by bridging the track using an intermediate image, that has the same point in common. Especially for small viewpoint changes, the continuation of tracks over multiple images is very likely. Beyond that, uncertainty and reliability of parameter estimates in bundle-adjustment only improve up to a certain redundancy [2,30], i.e. the resulting 3D models do not gain from high redundancy in the same way as we spend an unproportional amount of increased computational effort. For outlier-detection in SfM, it is typically critical to have at least 3–4 observations per 3D point. Leveraging these facts and classifier $\mathcal{C_B}$, we can detect clusters of images with small viewpoint change. Next, we select one iconic image in the cluster with the most points in common, and finally only perform geometric verification from the iconic image to the rest of the images in the cluster rather than exhaustive verification between all pairs. Moreover, for very large clusters, we can limit the number of images for geometric verification, and simply register the remaining images w.r.t. the final model using 2D-3D pose estimation [10]. In both datasets, we see 40 % of image pairs (282,387) with small viewpoint change ($\bar{\alpha} < 10°$). To find clusters, we build an undirected graph of all pairs with small viewpoint change using images as nodes and small viewpoint change as edges. In this graph, we find 6,404 disjoint maximal cliques [4,5,28] in the training & test-set. These cliques are similar to the clusters described by Frahm et al. [13], but our clusters are based on viewpoint change rather than GIST similarity [22].

By only considering edges from the iconic to the remaining images in a clique, we reduce the pairwise geometric verifications from 97,564 to 20,426. In addition, we further decrease this number to 14,469 by only considering images up to a maximum cluster size of 10, i.e. we improve geometric verification runtime by 30 % from 282,387 to 199,292 pairs. This technique is especially beneficial for very dense datasets, as often encountered in Internet photo-collections.

6.3   Search for Optimal Initial Pairs

Searching for a good initial pair as a seed for incremental reconstruction is computationally expensive, since it involves essential matrix estimation followed by triangulation of feature correspondences, and the calculation of triangulation angles or uncertainty estimates. With state-of-the-art essential matrix solvers [20] and linear triangulation [14, Chap. 12.2], around 10–50 two-view reconstructions can be computed per second [25] using the parameters as in Sect. 5. As opposed to the traditional approach, our classifier $\mathcal{C}_{\mathcal{B}}$ enables us to efficiently search for stable pairs through an entire dataset at significantly reduced computational cost. In the unseen landmarks, we find 14,886 stable pairs (out of 17,330 true stable pairs) with $\bar{\alpha} > 20°$, where 83 % of the reported pairs are actually stable. We use these pairs as initial seeds for the incremental reconstruction by ranking the reported stable pairs based on the number of putative feature matches to attain higher initial redundancy. On the one hand, our method leads to significantly faster search for initial pairs and, on the other hand, it allows us to search for optimal initial image pairs globally.

7   Conclusion

In this paper, we adapt the PAIGE feature for efficient two-view geometry classification to further improve the computational efficiency and robustness in SfM. Experiments demonstrate a speedup for geometric verification by an order of a magnitude over the traditional exhaustive approach, while only losing less than 1.7 % of the valid image pairs. Compared to PAIGE, our method provides an order of magnitude faster prediction performance, while achieving significantly better prediction accuracy. PAIGE and our approach are complementary methods that can both be integrated into the same SfM pipeline to speedup feature matching and geometric verification. Furthermore, the framework significantly reduces runtime for very dense photo-collections and we demonstrate the utility for the efficient, global search of optimal initial pairs.

Acknowledgment. This material is based upon work supported by the National Science Foundation under Grant No. IIS-1252921, IIS-1349074, IIS-1452851, CNS-1405847, and by the US Army Research, Development and Engineering Command Grant No. W911NF-14-1-0438.

References

1. Agarwal, S., Furukawa, Y., Snavely, N., Simon, I., Curless, B., Seitz, S., Szeliski, R.: Building rome in a day. In: ICCV (2009)
2. Baarda, W., Netherlands Geodetic Commission, et al.: Statistical concepts in geodesy, vol. 2(4). Rijkscommissie voor Geodesie (1967)
3. Breiman, L.: Random forests. Mach. Learn. **45**, 5–32 (2001)
4. Bron, C., Kerbosch, J.: Algorithm 457: finding all cliques of an undirected graph. ACM Commun. **16**, 48–50 (1973)
5. Cazals, F., Karande, C.: A note on the problem of reporting maximal cliques. Theoret. Comput. Sci. **407**(1), 564–568 (2008)
6. Chum, O., Matas, J.: Matching with prosac-progressive sample consensus (2005)
7. Chum, O., Matas, J., Obdrzalek, S.: Enhancing ransac by generalized model optimization. In: ACCV (2004)
8. Crandall, D., Owens, A., Snavely, N., Huttenlocher, D.P.: Discrete-continuous optimization for large-scale structure from motion. In: CVPR (2011)
9. Criminisi, A.: Accurate Visual Metrology from Single and Multiple Uncalibrated Images. Springer, London (2001)
10. Fischler, M.A., Bolles, R.C.: Random sample consensus: a paradigm for model fitting with applications to image analysis and automated cartography. ACM Commun. **24**(6), 381–395 (1981)
11. Förstner, W.: Uncertainty and projective geometry. In: Corrochano, E.B. (ed.) Handbook of Geometric Computing, pp. 493–534. Springer, Heidelberg (2005)
12. Frahm, J.M., Pollefeys, M.: RANSAC for (quasi-) degenerate data (QDEGSAC). In: CVPR (2006)
13. Frahm, J.-M., Fite-Georgel, P., Gallup, D., Johnson, T., Raguram, R., Wu, C., Jen, Y.-H.: Building rome on a cloudless day. In: Daniilidis, K., Maragos, P., Paragios, N. (eds.) ECCV 2010, Part IV. LNCS, vol. 6314, pp. 368–381. Springer, Heidelberg (2010)
14. Hartley, R., Schaffalitzky, F.: L_∞ minimization in geometric reconstruction problems. In: CVPR (2004)
15. Hartley, R., Zisserman, A.: Multiple View Geometry in Computer Vision. Cambridge University Press, Cambridge (2003)
16. Hartmann, W., Havlena, M., Schindler, K.: Predicting matchability. In: CVPR (2014)
17. Kanatani, K.: Statistical Optimization for Geometric Computation: Theory and Practice. Elsevier Science, Amsterdam (1996)
18. Kanatani, K., Morris, D.D.: Gauges and gauge transformations for uncertainty description of geometric structure with indeterminacy. IEEE Trans. Inf. Theor. **47**(5), 2017–2028 (2001)
19. Lowe, D.G.: Distinctive image features from scale-invariant keypoints. IJCV **60**(2), 91–110 (2004)
20. Nister, D.: An efficient solution to the five-point relative pose problem. In: CVPR (2003)
21. Nister, D., Stewenius, H.: Scalable recognition with a vocabulary tree. In: CVPR (2006)
22. Oliva, A., Torralba, A.: Modeling the shape of the scene: a holistic representation of the spatial envelope. IJCV **42**(3), 145–175 (2001)
23. Raguram, R., Chum, O., Pollefeys, M., Matas, J., Frahm, J.: Usac: a universal framework for random sample consensus. IEEE PAMI **35**(8), 2022–2038 (2013)

24. Raguram, R., Frahm, J.M., Pollefeys, M.: Arrsac: adaptive real-time random sample consensus. In: ECCV (2008)
25. Raguram, R., Tighe, J., Frahm, J.M.: Improved geometric verification for large scale landmark image collections. In: BMVC (2012)
26. Raguram, R., Wu, C., Frahm, J.M., Lazebnik, S.: Modeling and recognition of landmark image collections using iconic scene graphs. IJCV **95**(3), 213–239 (2011)
27. Schönberger, J.L., Berg, A.C., Frahm, J.M.: Paige: pairwise image geometry encoding for improved efficiency in structure-from-motion. In: CVPR (2015)
28. Tomita, E., Tanaka, A., Takahashi, H.: The worst-case time complexity for generating all maximal cliques and computational experiments. Theoret. Comput. Sci. **363**(1), 28–42 (2006)
29. Torr, P.H.: An assessment of information criteria for motion model selection. In: CVPR (1997)
30. Triggs, B., McLauchlan, P.F., Hartley, R.I., Fitzgibbon, A.W.: Bundle adjustment – a modern synthesis. In: Triggs, B., Zisserman, A., Szeliski, R. (eds.) ICCV-WS 1999. LNCS, vol. 1883, pp. 298–372. Springer, Heidelberg (2000)
31. Wu, C.: Towards linear-time incremental structure from motion. In: 3DV (2013)

Mathematical Foundations
and Image Processing

A Convex Relaxation Approach to the Affine Subspace Clustering Problem

Francesco Silvestri[1,2]([✉]), Gerhard Reinelt[1], and Christoph Schnörr[2]

[1] Discrete and Combinatorial Optimization Group, Heidelberg University,
Heidelberg, Germany
`francesco.silvestri@informatik.uni-heidelberg.de`
[2] IPA and HCI, Heidelberg University, Heidelberg, Germany

Abstract. Prototypical data clustering is known to suffer from poor initializations. Recently, a semidefinite relaxation has been proposed to overcome this issue and to enable the use of convex programming instead of ad-hoc procedures. Unfortunately, this relaxation does not extend to the more involved case where clusters are defined by parametric models, and where the computation of means has to be replaced by parametric regression. In this paper, we provide a novel convex relaxation approach to this more involved problem class that is relevant to many scenarios of unsupervised data analysis. Our approach applies, in particular, to data sets where assumptions of model recovery through sparse regularization, like the independent subspace model, do not hold. Our mathematical analysis enables to distinguish scenarios where the relaxation is tight enough and scenarios where the approach breaks down.

1 Introduction

Given data (measurement, pattern, observation, ...) vectors $b_i \in \mathbb{R}^d, i \in [n] := \{1, 2, \ldots, n\}$, the basic clustering problem amounts to jointly minimize the objective function

$$\min_{u,x} \sum_{i\in[n]} \sum_{j\in[k]} u_{ij} \|x_j - b_i\|^2 \tag{1}$$

with respect to *prototypes* $x_j \in \mathbb{R}^d, j \in [k]$, and *assignment variables* $u_{ij} \in \{0,1\}, i \in [n]$. The well-known k-means algorithm shows that, if either set of variables is fixed, then solving for the other set of variables is trivial. However, the task to *jointly* solve for *both* assignment variables and prototypes is inherently combinatorial. Accordingly, there exist a broad range of heuristic algorithms (k-means, mean-shift, etc.) that locally solve this chicken-and-egg problem in an EM-like alternating fashion and hence strongly depend on proper initializations. To overcome this shortcoming, combinatorial optimization techniques (e.g. [10]) have been applied, but they do not scale up to large data sets. Alternatively, semidefinite convex relaxations [11] have been suggested along with extensions to ensemble clustering [14], using the same relaxation.

In this paper, we adopt the latter focus on convex relaxation but study the more involved problem

© Springer International Publishing Switzerland 2015
J. Gall et al. (Eds.): GCPR 2015, LNCS 9358, pp. 67–78, 2015.
DOI: 10.1007/978-3-319-24947-6_6

$$\min_{u,x} \sum_{i \in [n]} \sum_{j \in [k]} u_{ij} \|A_i x_j - b_i\|^2 \tag{2}$$

with *given* data $(A_i, b_i) \in \mathbb{R}^{l \times d} \times \mathbb{R}^l, i \in [n]$, *unknown* model parameters $x_j \in \mathbb{R}^d, j \in [k]$, and *unknown* assignments $u_{ij} \in \{0,1\}$ of datum i to model j, to be determined by minimizing the objective (2). In comparison with (1), this approach extends the representation of data by *points* (prototypes, centroids) to *affine subspaces*, which is significant for many applications.

Regarding the fitting of such "union of subspaces" models to data, signifi-cant progress has been recently made by assuming the dimensions of these spaces to be *low relative* to the ambient space [3]. This enables to establish recovery guarantees based on sparsity priors and basic convex programming techniques [6] that are more convenient and robust than alternatives like, e.g., algebraic techniques [9]. *In this paper*, however, *we do not rely on such low-rank assump-tions*. A simple such problem, illustrated by Fig. 1, concerns the clustering of one-dimensional linear subspaces in $\mathbb{R}^2$, which clearly violates the "independent subspaces" assumption of [6, Sect. 4].

Fig. 1. *Left:* An unsupervised subspace clustering problem where recovery guaran-tees by sparse regularization fail. *Right:* Our approach jointly partitions the data and estimates the model parameter by solving a single convex optimization problem (relax-ation) followed by spectral clustering.

Another and equally important line of research concerns *pairwise, graph-based clustering* [8], where locally converging methods like mean-field annealing have been developed and also extended to piecewise regression problems [13]. To reduce the susceptibility to local initializations, spectral relaxation is commonly applied [4,17]. However, while Euclidean embeddings [1] of pairwise data pro-vide a connection to central clustering, working out the implications for our novel mathematical approach to solve problem (2) is beyond the scope of this paper.

Contribution, Organization. We sketch in Sect. 2 the semidefinite relaxation of the basic problem (1) and elucidate why this relaxation is specific to (1) and does *not* generalize to problem (2). As a consequence, we present in Sect. 3 our novel mathematical approach to the relaxation of the *joint* optimization problem (2). In Sect. 4, some properties of the approach are derived together with limitations that are inherent to any non-tight relaxation of a combinatorial problem. The approach is illustrated by few academical examples in Sect. 5. We point out that working out applications is beyond the scope of our theoretical work that has been motivated by the class of unsupervised learning problems (2).

2 Prototypical Clustering by Convex Programming

2.1 Problem, Convex Relaxation

Collecting the assignment variables into a matrix U, the basic clustering problem (1) reads

$$\min_{u,x} \sum_{i \in [n]} \sum_{j \in [k]} u_{ij} \|x_j - b_i\|^2 \quad \text{s. t.} \quad Ue = e, \quad U \in \{0,1\}^{n \times k}, \qquad (3)$$

where $e = (1, 1, \ldots, 1)^{\top}$. The derivation of a convex relaxation is based on the simple observation that, for any subset $S \subseteq [n]$ of data vectors $\{b_i\}_{i \in S}$, one has

$$\frac{1}{|S|} \sum_{i \in S} b_i \in \arg\min_x \sum_{i \in S} \|x - b_i\|^2. \qquad (4)$$

Thus, given a *fixed* assignment $\{u_{ij}\}$, one can express every x_j in terms of the respective u_{ij} variables by setting

$$x_j(U) = \frac{\sum_{i \in [n]} u_{ij} b_i}{\sum_{i \in [n]} u_{ij}}. \qquad (5)$$

Collecting all data vectors $b_i \in \mathbb{R}^d$, $i \in [n]$, as columns of a matrix $B \in \mathbb{R}^{d \times n}$, insertion of (5) into (3) yields after an elementary rearrangement

$$\min_U \langle B^{\top}B, I - U(U^{\top}U)^{-1}U^{\top} \rangle \quad \text{s. t.} \quad Ue = e, \quad U \in \{0,1\}^{n \times k}. \qquad (6)$$

Substituting $Z = U(U^{\top}U)^{-1}U^{\top}$ gives the equivalent [11] problem

$$\min_Z \langle B^{\top}B, I - Z \rangle \quad \text{s. t.} \quad Ze = e, \quad \langle Z, I \rangle = k, \quad Z^2 = Z, \quad Z \in \mathcal{S}^n \cap \mathbb{R}_+^{n \times n} \qquad (7)$$

where $\mathcal{S}^n$ denotes the linear space of symmetric $n \times n$ matrices.

Even though (7) looks much simpler than its original formulation (3), it is still intractable and nonconvex due to the constraint $Z^2 = Z$. However, this can be relaxed to $Z \in \mathcal{S}_+^n$ (semidefinite matrix cone) which yields a tractable *semidefinite program (SDP)*. In this context, $B^{\top}B$ plays the role of a similarity measure which is the only data-dependent information for the algorithm.

2.2   Why This Approach Does Not Generalize

A key property of (7) is dealing with the inherent symmetries of (3), which is necessary for any convex relaxation. To see why this is an issue, consider the convexified set $\mathcal{U}_{n,k} = \{U \in [0,1]^{n \times k} \,|\, Ue = e\}$. For any $U \in \mathcal{U}_{n,k}$ and for any $\pi \in \mathfrak{S}_k$ ($\mathfrak{S}_k$: symmetric group on $[k]$), let U_π be the result of permuting the columns of U according to π. Then $U_\pi \in \mathcal{U}_{n,k}$ and, by convexity, $\sum_{\pi \in \mathfrak{S}_k} U_\pi = \frac{1}{k}J \in \mathcal{U}_{n,k}$ where $J = ee^\top$ is the matrix of all ones. It follows for any symmetric convex function f ($f(U) = f(U_\pi)$ for all $\pi \in \mathfrak{S}_k$) that $\frac{1}{k}J$ is an optimal but useless solution, because every point can be assigned to every cluster at the same cost.

The two key properties of (7) are that the objective is asymmetric and that the feasible set can be easily convexified. Intuitively, the symmetry variant question of (3), "which points belong to which cluster", is reduced to a weighted version of the symmetry invariant question, "which points belong to the same cluster", since $u_{rj}u_{sj}$ in $Z_{rs} = \sum_{j \in [k]}(u_{rj}u_{sj})(\sum_{i \in [n]} u_{ij})^{-1}$ denotes whether r and s are in cluster j at the same time. This also allows to extract the clusters at the end.

Now consider generalizations of problem (1) of the form

$$\min_{u,x} \sum_{i \in [n]} \sum_{j \in [k]} u_{ij} \| f(x_j, A_i) - b_i \|^2 \quad \text{s. t.} \quad Ue = e, \quad U \in \{0,1\}^{n \times k} \qquad (8)$$

for some differentiable function f and data (A_i, b_i), $i \in [n]$. If one wants to generalize the approach of Sect. 2.1 accordingly, then the prototypes have to be eliminated and the objective has to be reduced to an asymmetric convex function in the remaining variables. Assume cluster j is indexed by $S \subseteq [n]$, that is the assignment variables are fixed and the constraints obsolete. Then, taking derivatives gives the optimality condition

$$0 = \sum_{i \in S} \langle \nabla_x f(x, A_i)|_{x=x_j}, f(x_j, A_i) - b_i \rangle. \qquad (9)$$

Depending on f, (9) is arbitrarily hard to solve for x_j in closed form. The simplest generalization takes the form (2), that is $f(x_j, A_i) = A_i x_j$. Then (9) becomes

$$x_j(U) = \Big(\sum_{i \in [n]} u_{ij} A_i^\top A_i \Big)^\dagger \Big(\sum_{i \in [n]} u_{ij} A_i^\top b_i \Big). \qquad (10)$$

Unfortunately, taking the pseudo-inverse $(\ldots)^\dagger$ of a linearly parametrized matrix is highly nonlinear. In particular, even if we could assume that the matrices $\sum_{i \in S} A_i^\top A_i$ admit an ordinary matrix inverse, then $x_j(U)$ in (10) would be a multivariate rational function in U whose coefficients strongly depend on the specific given data. Without further assumptions, there is neither an easy way to see the range of possible values for the coefficients of U after substituting x_j by (10) nor an easy way to estimate the approximation quality of the corresponding convex hull. These facts motivate our approach presented in the subsequent section.

3 Joint Approach to Clustering and Regression

3.1 Problem, Problem Reformulation

In this section, we consider problem (2) in the form

$$\min_{u,x} \sum_{i\in[n]} \sum_{j\in[k]} u_{ij}\|A_i x_j - b_i\|^2 \tag{11a}$$

$$\text{s.t. } Ue = e, \quad U \in \{0,1\}^{n\times k}, \quad \{x_j\}_{j\in[k]} \subseteq P \tag{11b}$$

where $P \subseteq \mathbb{R}^d$ is a polytope, $\{A_i\} \subseteq \mathbb{R}^{l\times d}$ and $\{b_i\} \subseteq \mathbb{R}^l$. This is equal to (2) if we know a polytope P containing the optimal solution. We will assume this for now, showing examples where we can construct P in closed form in Sect. 5.

Problem Reformulation. Since P is a polytope, $P = \text{conv}(\{v_s\}_{s\in[m]})$ for the columns v_s of some matrix $V \in \mathbb{R}^{d\times m}$. By Caratheodory's theorem [12, Theorem 2.29], we can thus assume that there is a $\lambda^j \in \mathbb{R}^m_+$ where $\langle \lambda^j, e \rangle = 1$ and $|\operatorname{supp}(\lambda^j)| \leq d+1$ such that $x_j = V\lambda^j$.
Using this substitution and applying that $1 = \langle \lambda^j, e \rangle$, one easily checks that

$$\|A_i x_j - b_i\|^2 = \sum_{r,s\in[m]} \lambda_r^j \lambda_s^j (v_r^\top A_i^\top A_i v_s - (b_i^\top A_i)(v_r + v_s) + \|b_i\|^2). \tag{12}$$

Setting W_i, $i \in [n]$, with $(W_i)_{rs} := (v_r^\top A_i^\top A_i v_s - (b_i^\top A_i)(v_r + v_s) + \|b_i\|^2)_{rs}$ and $\Lambda^j := \lambda_j \lambda_j^\top$, yields $\|A_i x_j - b_i\|^2 = \langle \Lambda^j, W_i \rangle := \text{tr}(\Lambda^j W_i)$ and the reformulation

$$\min_{u,\Lambda} \sum_{i\in[n]} \sum_{j\in[k]} u_{ij}\langle \Lambda^j, W_i \rangle \tag{13a}$$

$$\text{s.t. } Ue = e, \quad U \in \{0,1\}^{n\times k},$$

$$\langle \lambda^j, e \rangle = 1, \quad \lambda^j \geq 0, \quad \|\lambda^j\|_0 \leq d+1, \quad \Lambda^j = \lambda^j \lambda^{j\top}. \tag{13b}$$

The constraints (13b) can be equivalently expressed in terms of Λ^j by demanding

$$\langle \Lambda^j, J \rangle = 1, \quad \text{rank}(\Lambda^j) = 1, \quad \Lambda^j \in \mathcal{CP}^m, \quad \|\operatorname{diag}(\Lambda^j)\|_0 \leq d+1 \tag{14}$$

where $\mathcal{CP}^m := \{M \in \mathcal{S}^m : M = \sum \mu_i \mu_i^\top, \mu_i \in \mathbb{R}^m_+\}$ is the cone of completely positive matrices [2].

3.2 Convex Relaxation

In order to get a convex relaxation we have to convexify both the objective and the feasible set. We even go one step further and linearize the objective.

Linearizing the Objective. Setting $\Lambda_i(U) := \sum_{j\in[k]} u_{ij}\Lambda^j$, we get

$$\sum_{i\in[n]} \langle \sum_{j\in[k]} u_{ij}\Lambda^j, W_i \rangle = \sum_{i\in[n]} \langle \Lambda_i(U), W_i \rangle, \tag{15}$$

where the variables U model $\Lambda_i(U) \in \{\Lambda^j\}_{j \in [k]}$, which is invariant under permutations of $(\Lambda^1, \ldots, \Lambda^k)$. This implies that relaxing the condition $\Lambda_i(U) \in \{\Lambda^j\}_{j \in [k]}$ without introducing symmetry is a good first step to get a tractable relaxation with a linear objective.

To proceed, we derive some properties of $\{\Lambda^j\}_{j \in [k]}$. Consider the sets

$$\begin{aligned}
\mathcal{N}_{\nu,d}^m &:= \{\Lambda \in \mathcal{CP}^m : \langle \Lambda, J \rangle = \nu,\ \mathrm{rank}(\Lambda) \in [\nu],\ \|\,\mathrm{diag}(\Lambda)\|_0 \le \nu(d+1)\} \\
&= \nu \cdot \mathcal{N}_{1,d}^m
\end{aligned} \tag{16}$$

where $\nu \cdot \mathcal{N}_{1,d}^m$ denotes the Minkowski-sum of ν copies of $\mathcal{N}_{1,d}^m$. In particular, we have

$$\sum_{j \in S} \Lambda^j \in \mathcal{N}_{|S|,d}^m \quad \text{for all } S \subseteq [k]. \tag{17}$$

It follows that for every feasible, integral assignment U, we have

$$\Lambda_i(U) \in \mathcal{N}_{1,d}^m, \quad \Lambda^* := \sum_{j \in [k]} \Lambda^j \in \mathcal{N}_{k,d}^m \quad \text{and} \quad \Lambda^* - \Lambda_i(U) \in \mathcal{N}_{k-1,d}^m. \tag{18}$$

Thus, replacing $\Lambda_i(U)$ by a variable Λ_i defines an asymmetric linear objective function for the relaxation

$$\min_{\Lambda} \sum_{i \in [n]} \langle \Lambda_i, W_i \rangle \quad \text{s.t.} \quad \Lambda^* \in \mathcal{N}_{k,d}^m, \quad \Lambda_i \in \mathcal{N}_{1,d}^m, \quad \Lambda^* - \Lambda_i \in \mathcal{N}_{k-1,d}^m. \tag{19}$$

The only relaxation made so far concerns condition $\Lambda^* - \Lambda_i \in \mathcal{N}_{k-1,d}^m$ that cannot *strictly* enforce the set $\{\Lambda_i\}_{i \in [n]}$ to only have k distinct members. While some problem structure is lost, this is necessary to remove the symmetry.

Relaxing the Feasible Region. Optimizing over the set $\mathcal{N}_{\nu,d}^m$ is intractable. The rank-constraint as well as the bounded support make the problem non-convex and very hard in practice. Furthermore, even though $\mathcal{CP}^m$ is a convex cone, separation over $\mathcal{CP}^m$ is NP-hard [5], so this is intractable as well.

Since we are interested in a tractable convex relaxation, we apply standard relaxations for these conditions. To this end, define the sets

$$\mathcal{M}_{\nu,d}^m := \{\Lambda \in \mathcal{S}_+^m \cap \mathbb{R}_+^{m \times m} : \langle \Lambda, J \rangle = \nu, \mathrm{tr}(\Lambda) \ge \frac{\nu}{d+1}\} = \nu \cdot \mathcal{M}_{1,d}^m, \tag{20a}$$

$$\mathcal{K} := \mathcal{S}_+^m \cap \mathbb{R}_+^{m \times m}. \tag{20b}$$

Theorem 1. $\mathcal{M}_{\nu,d}^m$ *is convex, tractable and* $\mathcal{N}_{\nu,d}^m \subseteq \mathcal{M}_{\nu,d}^m$.

Proof. $\mathcal{CP}^m \subseteq \mathcal{K}$ follows from the definition. Furthermore, $\mathcal{N}_{\nu,d}^m \subseteq \mathcal{M}_{\nu,d}^m$ is implied by $\mathcal{N}_{1,d}^m \subseteq \mathcal{M}_{1,d}^m$, so consider $\nu = 1$. For $\Lambda \in \mathcal{N}_{1,d}^m$, by definition, there exists λ such that $\Lambda = \lambda\lambda^\top$, $\lambda \ge 0$, $\langle \lambda, e \rangle = 1$ and $\|\lambda\|_0 \le d+1$. We have $\mathrm{tr}(\Lambda) = \|\lambda\|_2^2$ and one can verify that under these constraints a minimizer of this term is given by any vector λ^* where $\|\lambda^*\|_0 = d+1$ and $\lambda_i^* = \frac{1}{d+1}$ for all $i \in \mathrm{supp}(\lambda^*)$. This gives the desired lowerbound on $\mathrm{tr}(\Lambda)$. $\square$

As a direct corollary, we get the *tractable, convex relaxation* of our problem

$$\min_{\Lambda} \sum_{i \in [n]} \langle \Lambda_i, W_i \rangle \quad \text{s.t.} \quad \Lambda^* \in \mathcal{M}^m_{k,d}, \ \Lambda_i \in \mathcal{M}^m_{1,d}, \ \Lambda^* - \Lambda_i \in \mathcal{M}^m_{k-1,d}. \quad (21)$$

Again, this relaxation loses some structure of the problem but is necessary to achieve tractability.

3.3 Extension to Disjunctive Programming

In (11), we required the prototypical model parameters to be contained in a polytope: $\{x_j\}_{j \in [k]} \subseteq P$. We can generalize P to a finite union of (not necessarily disjoint) polytopes $\mathcal{P} = \bigcup_{t \in T} P_t$ with some additional work. Let V_t be the matrix which has the vertices of P_t as columns. Then $x \in \mathcal{P}$ is equivalent to $x = \sum_{t \in T} V_t \lambda_t$ for a vector $\lambda^\top = (\lambda_1^\top, \ldots, \lambda_{|T|}^\top)$ such that

$$\langle \lambda, e \rangle = 1, \quad \lambda \geq 0, \quad \|\lambda\|_0 \leq d + 1, \quad \{(\lambda_r = 0) \vee (\lambda_s = 0)\}_{r,s \in T} \quad (22)$$

where $\vee$ denotes the logical *or*. Adding $\{(\lambda_r = 0) \vee (\lambda_s = 0)\}_{r,s \in T}$ to (13b) then results in a *disjunctive program* [7].

Now observe that $(\lambda_r = 0) \vee (\lambda_s = 0)$ implies $\lambda_r \lambda_s^\top = 0$ for any $r, s \in T$, so the matrix $\Lambda = \lambda \lambda^\top = (\lambda_r \lambda_s^\top)_{r,s \in T}$ is block diagonal. Since $\Lambda \geq 0$, this can be encoded by a 0/1-matrix Ω as a single linear constraint $\langle \Lambda, \Omega \rangle = 0$, where $J - \Omega$ shares the block structure of Λ.

Using the rank condition one can show that adding $\{(\lambda_r = 0) \vee (\lambda_s = 0)\}_{r,s \in T}$ to (13b) is equivalent to adding $\langle \Lambda^j, \Omega \rangle = 0$ to (14). Following Sect. 3.2 we can relax this constraint for (21) to $\langle \Lambda^*, \Omega \rangle = 0$, which implies $\langle \Lambda_i, \Omega \rangle = 0$ for all $i \in [n]$. Hence, we showed

Proposition 1. *Let $\Omega \in \{0,1\}^{m \times m}$ be symmetric and $\mathrm{tr}(\Omega) = 0$. Then adding $\langle \Lambda^*, \Omega \rangle = 0$ to (21) entails that the solution x_j of (11) can be written as a convex combination of $\{v_i\}_{i \in S_j}$ where $[m] \supseteq S_j \not\supseteq \{r, s\}$ for all $w_{rs} = 1$. In particular, if $J - \Omega$ is block diagonal, then $\langle \Lambda^*, \Omega \rangle = 0$ implies that $P = \bigcup_{t \in T} P_t$, where each P_t is the convex hull of columns V_t indexed by a diagonal block.*

Note that, while the relaxation in Λ is convex, the recovery of λ from Λ will in general not preserve convexity. Depending on how we recover λ, the relaxation does not necessarily model a convex space in the x variables, which makes this approach viable. Now observe, however, that for the objective function, convex combinations of rank-1 matrices are in general "bad" since, by linearity and for any convex combination $\Lambda = \sum_{i \in S} \mu_i \lambda_i \lambda_i^\top$, we have $\langle W, \Lambda \rangle = \sum_{i \in S} \mu_i \langle W, \lambda_i \lambda_i^\top \rangle \geq \min_{i \in S} \langle W, \lambda_i \lambda_i^\top \rangle$. Setting $w_{rs} = 1$ cuts off rank-1 matrices Λ corresponding to λ with $\lambda_r, \lambda_s > 0$. As a consequence, optimization will favor rank-1 matrices with either $\lambda_r = 0$ or $\lambda_s = 0$ instead of approximating the cut off matrix, which shows that Proposition 1 extends problem (11) and its relaxation in a reasonable way.

3.4   Algorithm

While the computation of (21) is straight forward using any SDP-solver, rounding the solution afterwards requires some care. The easiest way is to use spectral clustering. To this end, define a similarity matrix H by setting $H_{rs} = 1 - \langle \Lambda_r, \Lambda_s \rangle / (\|\Lambda_r\|_2 \cdot \|\Lambda_s\|_2)$, which yields a value in $[0, 1]$ corresponding to the angle between Λ_r and Λ_s in $\mathbb{R}^{m \times m}$.

Algorithm 1.1. k-Cluster Relaxation

Data: $\{(A_i, b_i)\}_{i \in [n]} \subseteq \mathbb{R}^{l \times d} \times \mathbb{R}^l, V \in \mathbb{R}^{d \times m}, k \in \mathbb{N}, \Omega \in \{0, 1\}^{m \times m}$
Result: assignments U and centroids $\{x_j\}_{j \in [k]}$
1 compute $W_i \leftarrow (v_r^\top A_i^\top A_i v_s - (b_i^\top A_i)(v_r + v_s) + \|b_i\|^2)_{rs}$ for $i \in [n]$;
2 solve (21) subject to $\langle \Lambda^*, \Omega \rangle = 0$ for $\{\Lambda_i\}_{i \in [n]}$;
3 compute similiarity matrix $H \leftarrow (1 - \langle \Lambda_r, \Lambda_s \rangle / (\|\Lambda_r\|_2 \cdot \|\Lambda_s\|_2))_{rs}$;
4 compute the assignment U by spectral clustering using H;
5 compute centroids $\{x_j\}_{j \in [k]}$ using U;
6 **return** $(U, \{x_j\}_{j \in [k]})$;

---

4   Analysis

Inspecting the relaxed problem formulation (21) reveals the following: The objective function is separable in terms of the variables Λ_i, and the right-most constraint that has to be satisfied *simultaneously* for all $\Lambda_i, i \in [n]$, fuses this local information. In this section we derive conditions that characterize when this latter condition is sufficiently weak so that the relaxation must fail. Conversely, the more these conditions are not satisfied, the more likely the relaxation will return a useful result. Our theoretical findings will be illustrated in Sect. 5.

Specifically, we derive values of (k, m, d) so that we can choose $\Lambda^* \in \mathcal{M}_{k,d}^m$ such that $\Lambda^* - \Lambda_i \in \mathcal{M}_{k-1,d}^m$ will be satisfied *for all* choices of $\Lambda_i \in \mathcal{M}_{1,d}^m$. Our corresponding main result is stated below as Theorem 2.

Condition $\Lambda^* - \Lambda_i \in \mathcal{M}_{k-1,d}^m$ is equivalent to

$$\text{tr}(\Lambda^*) - \text{tr}(\Lambda_i) \geq \frac{k-1}{d+1}, \qquad \Lambda^* - \Lambda_i \in \mathcal{K}. \tag{23}$$

Note that since $\text{tr}(\Lambda_i) \leq \langle \Lambda_i, J \rangle = 1$ is sharp, we infer that $\text{tr}(\Lambda^*) \geq \frac{d+k}{d+1}$ is necessary for the first condition to hold.

As for the second condition, let $A \leq_{\mathcal{K}} B$ denote the inclusion $B - A \in \mathcal{K}$. Then we need an upper bound of $\mathcal{M}_{1,d}^m$ with respect to the partial order $\leq_{\mathcal{K}}$, given by the following Lemma.

Lemma 1 ($\leq_{\mathcal{K}}$-Upper Bound of $\mathcal{M}_{1,d}^m$). $I + \frac{1}{4}J$ *is a* $\leq_{\mathcal{K}}$-*upper bound for* $\mathcal{M}_{1,d}^m$.

Our main result is

Theorem 2 (Decoupling Condition). *There is a matrix $\Lambda^* \in \mathcal{M}_{k,d}^m$ such that $(\Lambda^* - \Lambda) \in \mathcal{M}_{k-1,d}^m$ for all $\Lambda \in \mathcal{M}_{1,d}^m$ if there are $\alpha, \beta \in \mathbb{R}$ such that $k = \beta \cdot m^2 + \alpha \cdot m$, $\beta \geq \frac{1}{4}$ and*

$$\alpha \geq \max\{1, \frac{\beta}{d}(m - (d+1)) + \frac{1}{m}\}. \tag{24}$$

In particular, for fixed m, d there is a minimal value $k^*(m,d) \in \mathbb{N}$ that satisfies these conditions, and the conditions can be satisfied for all $k \geq k^*(m,d)$.

Proof. We fix m, d and derive conditions on k. By symmetry of $\mathcal{M}_{k,d}^m$ we can assume that $\Lambda^* = \alpha I + \beta J$ where $\beta \geq \frac{1}{4}$ and $\alpha \geq 1$ by Lemma 1. It follows that $k = \langle \Lambda^*, J \rangle = \beta \cdot m^2 + \alpha \cdot m$ and $\text{tr}(\Lambda^*) = (\alpha + \beta)m$.
Together with $\text{tr}(\Lambda^*) \geq \frac{d+k}{d+1}$ from (23), we have $(\alpha+\beta)m = \text{tr}(\Lambda^*) \geq \frac{d+k}{d+1} > \frac{k}{d+1}$, where we can substitute $k = \beta \cdot m^2 + \alpha \cdot m$ and rewrite it as $\alpha \geq \frac{\beta}{d}(m-(d+1)) + \frac{1}{m}$.
Since m, d is fixed, the inequalities bound α, β and thus k from below. Therefore a minimal value $k^*(m,d) \in \mathbb{N}$ that satisfies these conditions exists.   □

5   Experiments

All examples have been carried out in Matlab using the SDPT3 [15,16] package.

Euclidean Clustering. By choosing $A_i = I$ we recover (3), where (4) tells us to use $P \supseteq \text{conv}(\{b_i\}_{i\in[n]})$. Using any simplex containing all the points is a coarsest approximation, but yields in general bad results.
Figure 2 is tied to Theorem 2 - while k is fixed, $k^*(m,d)$ and the quality increase from top to bottom as a consequence of additional polytopes separating the local solutions: When Λ^r, Λ^s are optimal centroids, then (21) has $\langle J, \Lambda^r \wedge \Lambda^s \rangle$ excess weight to shift around in Λ^*, where $\wedge$ denotes the componentwise minimum. Refining P, $\Lambda^r \wedge \Lambda^s$ decreases, thus improving the quality. Given that the optimal solution is already covered, adding disjoint polytopes does not negatively impact the quality of the output, as can be seen in the bottom row of Fig. 2.

Hyperplane Clustering. By choosing $b_i = 0$ for all $i \in [n]$ and choosing $A_i = a_i$ as row vectors, problem (2) translates into finding normal vectors x_j of k hyperplanes such that every data point a_i lies on exactly one hyperplane. To exclude the degenerated solution 0 we need an appropriate P for (11).
Without loss of generality we can assume that the x_j are unit vectors belonging to the "upper" half-sphere $S^{d-1} \cap H$, where $H = \{x \in \mathbb{R}^d \mid x_1 \geq 0\}$. The coarsest polytope approximation P is then given by the union of the facets of C_d in H, where C_d is the cross polytope $C_d = \text{conv}\{\pm e_l \mid l \in [d]\}$ of dimension d. This yields $V = \begin{pmatrix} 0 & 1 & 0 \\ -I & 0 & I \end{pmatrix}$ and $\omega_{(e_l, -e_l)} = 1$ for all $1 \neq l \in [d]$.
Ideally, P corresponds to a disjoint union of polytopes each including one Λ^j. Figure 3 shows that one may need to use separate copies of the same vertices.

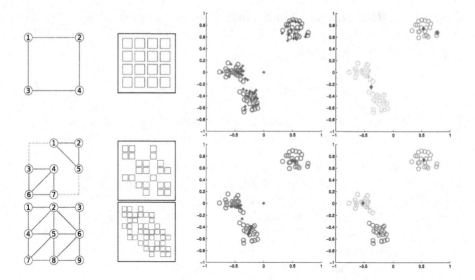

Fig. 2. Euclidean Clustering on data spread around three points in 2d, $k = 3$. *Left:* Partial cover of $[-1, 1]^2$ given by V and corresponding block structure of Λ^* given by Ω. *Middle:* Orange data points and blue centroids extracted from Λ_i. *Right:* Clustered data points and blue centroids given by our algorithm. *Top:* Naive cover by a single square where $\Omega = 0$. *Bottom:* Optimal choice of P and oversegmentation yield the same result (Color figure online).

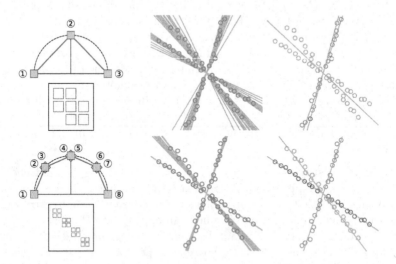

Fig. 3. Hyperplane Clustering on three Lines in 2d, $k = 3$. *Left:* Polytope approximation of $S^1 \cap H$ given by V and corresponding block structure of Λ^* given by Ω. *Middle:* Orange data points and grey centroids extracted from Λ_i. *Right:* Clustered data points and grey centroids given by our algorithm. *Top:* Coarsest approximation given by the facets of C_2 in H. *Bottom:* Oversegmentation where separate copies of the same vertices needed to be used to get the proper result (Color figure online).

6 Conclusion

We introduced a novel mathematical model to deal with the affine subspace clustering problem. Our analysis shows why it works reasonably well. Experiment show that it is attractive to use the algorithm with an oversegmentation of the set of feasible solutions, with the focus on separating local solutions. This cannot be achieved using sparsity regularization. Prior knowledge can be used to speed up the algorithm, but is not necessary. Automatically balancing this trade off based on the data in an efficient way is a subject for future work.

Acknowledgement. Authors gratefully acknowledge support by the DFG, grant GRK 1653.

References

1. Belkin, M., Niyogi, P.: Laplacian eigenmaps for dimensionality reduction and data representation. Neural Comput. **15**(6), 1373–1396 (2003)
2. Berman, A., Shaked-Monderer, N.: Completely Positive Matrices. World Scientific Publishing, New York (2003)
3. Carin, L., Baraniuk, R., Cevher, V., Dunson, V., Jordan, M., Sapiro, G., Wakin, M.: Learning low-dimensional signal models. IEEE Signal Proc. Mag. **28**(2), 39–51 (2011)
4. Chen, G., Lerman, G.: Foundations of a multi-way spectral clustering framework for hybrid linear modeling. Found. Comp. Math. **9**, 517–558 (2009)
5. Dickinson, P., Gijben, L.: On the computational complexity of membership problems for the completely positive cone and its dual. Comput. Optim. Appl. **57**(2), 403–415 (2014)
6. Elhamifar, E., Vidal, R.: Sparse subspace clustering: algorithm, theory, and applications. IEEE Trans. Patt. Anal. Mach. Intell. **35**(11), 2765–2781 (2013)
7. Grossmann, I.E., Lee, S.: Generalized convex disjunctive programming: nonlinear convex hull relaxation. Comput. Optim. Appl. **26**(1), 83–100 (2003)
8. Hofman, T., Buhmann, J.: Pairwise data clustering by deterministic annealing. IEEE Trans. Patt. Anal. Mach. Intell. **19**(1), 1–14 (1997)
9. Ma, Y., Yang, A., Derksen, H., Fossum, R.: Estimation of subspace arrangements with applications in modeling and segmenting mixed data. SIAM Rev. **50**(3), 413–458 (2008)
10. du Merle, O., Hansen, P., Jaumard, B., Mladenović, N.: An interior points algorithm for minimum sum-of-squares clustering. SIAM J. Sci. Comput. **21**(4), 1485–1505 (2000)
11. Peng, J., Wei, Y.: Approximating K-means-type clustering via semidefinite programming. SIAM J. Optim. **18**(1), 186–205 (2007)
12. Rockafellar, R., Wets, R.J.B.: Variational Analysis, 2nd edn. Springer, New York (2009)
13. Rose, K.: Deterministic annealing for clustering, compression, classification, regression, and related optimization problems. Proc. IEEE **86**(11), 2210–2239 (1998)
14. Singh, V., Mukherjee, L., Peng, J., Xu, J.: Ensemble clustering using semidefinite programming with applications. Mach. Learn. **79**(1–2), 177–200 (2010)

15. Toh, K.C., Todd, M.J., Tütüncü, R.H.: SDPT3 – a MATLAB software package for semidefinite programming, December 1996
16. Tütüncü, R.H., Toh, K.C., Todd, M.J.: Solving semidefinite-quadratic-linear programs using SDPT3. Math. Program. **95**(2), 189–217 (2003)
17. Xing, E., Jordan, M.: On Semidefinite relaxation for normalized k-cut and connections to spectral clustering. Technical report UCB/CSD-03-1265, EECS Department, University of California, Berkeley, June 2003

Introducing Maximal Anisotropy into Second Order Coupling Models

David Hafner$^{(\boxtimes)}$, Christopher Schroers, and Joachim Weickert

Mathematical Image Analysis Group, Faculty of Mathematics and Computer Science,
Saarland University, Campus E1.7, 66041 Saarbrücken, Germany
{hafner,schroers,weickert}@mia.uni-saarland.de

Abstract. On the one hand, anisotropic diffusion is a well-established concept that has improved numerous computer vision approaches by permitting direction-dependent smoothing. On the other hand, recent applications have uncovered the importance of second order regularisation. The goal of this work is to combine the benefits of both worlds. To this end, we propose a second order regulariser that allows to penalise both jumps and kinks in a direction-dependent way. We start with an isotropic coupling model, and systematically introduce anisotropic concepts from first order approaches. We demonstrate the benefits of our model by experiments, and apply it to improve an existing focus fusion method.

1 Introduction

Second order regularisation has become a powerful tool in a number of applications. For example, it is well-suited for the estimation of depth maps, because many real-world scenes are composed of piecewise planar surfaces. In a variational context, there are three popular approaches to model such a second order smoothness assumption: (*i*) The most intuitive one is to directly penalise second order derivatives, e.g. the Laplacian or the entries of the Hessian [6,8,16,18,28,30]. However, this direct approach only allows to model discontinuities in the second derivative that correspond to kinks in the solution. It does not give access to the first derivative which is required to model jumps. (*ii*) Thus, researchers came up with indirect higher order regularisation techniques; see e.g. [4,13,15] and related infimal convolution approaches [5]. Such indirect approaches can be interpreted in the sense of a *coupling model* that, in the second order case, consists of two terms: One term couples the gradient of the unknown with some auxiliary vector field, while the other one enforces smoothness of this vector field. Contrary to a direct second order penalisation, such coupling models allow to treat both jumps and kinks in the solution explicitly. (*iii*) A related idea is to locally parameterise the unknown by an affine function, and to optimise for the introduced parameters with a suitable smoothness constraint; see e.g. [21]. However, this does not allow such an explicit access to jumps and kinks [30].

© Springer International Publishing Switzerland 2015
J. Gall et al. (Eds.): GCPR 2015, LNCS 9358, pp. 79–90, 2015.
DOI: 10.1007/978-3-319-24947-6_7

Concerning first order regularisation, several approaches have demonstrated the benefits of incorporating anisotropy in the smoothness term; see e.g. [3,12,19,24,29,34]. Thus, it seems to be a fruitful idea to also apply anisotropic concepts in second order regularisation. For instance, Lenzen et al. [16] incorporate directional information into a direct second order approach. Unfortunately, as discussed, such a direct approach constrains the degree of freedom in the modelling. Also the nonlocal coupling model of Ranftl et al. [26] can be seen as related. However, in this work we aim at a fully local model that allows a natural definition of the anisotropy in terms of image and depth derivatives. In this way, we can provide a natural transition from anisotropic first to anisotropic second order approaches. In a local framework, Ranftl et al. [27] and Ferstl et al. [9] propose a coupling model that incorporates directional image information, but the anisotropy is restricted to the coupling term. To summarise, first steps to include anisotropy into second order models have been done. However, existing approaches do not exploit successful anisotropic ideas to the full extent.

Contributions. The goal of our work is to systematically incorporate well-established anisotropic ideas from first order approaches into second order coupling models. We make maximal use of directional information by introducing anisotropy both into the coupling as well as into the smoothness term. In addition, we propose a joint image- and depth-driven technique that allows a different amount of coupling and smoothing along and across image structures. Contrary to previous work, we apply a direction-dependent penalisation that is important for good inpainting results. Last but not least, we demonstrate the performance of our anisotropic second order technique in the context of focus fusion.

Paper Organisation. Starting with a discussion of related work, we present our variational framework for focus fusion in Sect. 2. In Sect. 3, we introduce our anisotropic second order regulariser and explain the minimisation of the full model in Sect. 4. We evaluate our approach and compare it to related baseline methods in Sect. 5. Section 6 illustrates the performance of our method on focus fusion. Finally, we summarise our work and give an outlook in Sect. 7.

2   Variational Model for Focus Fusion

Especially in macro photography, a typical problem is the limited depth of field of common cameras. Due to this, it is often not possible to capture a single entirely sharp image. A common remedy is to take several photographs while varying the focal plane. In this context, *focus fusion* describes the task of combining the acquired image stack to an all-in-focus composite that is sharp everywhere. Most previous focus fusion approaches rely on (multi-scale) transformations of the input images and combine them in the particular transform domain; see e.g. [1,10,17,22,25]. However, this may introduce undesirable artefacts. Inspired by [14,20], Boshtayeva et al. [3] recently demonstrated that it is preferable to approach focus fusion by regularising the underlying depth map. Afterwards, the fusion of the focal stack images to the all-in-focus image is done in a straightforward way by combining the pixels from the input images that correspond to the computed depth values. Related to this method are so-called *depth from defocus* approaches that also compute a sharp image in combination with a depth map; see e.g. [23]. However, they are computationally more demanding and require more assumptions such as the knowledge of the point spread function of the acquisition system. Hence, we do not consider them here.

The work of Boshtayeva et al. [3] motivates us to apply focus fusion as testbed for our novel anisotropic second order regularisation technique. More specifically, we start with an initial depth map d that is computed in the same way as in [3]: Based on some sharpness measure we determine the image where a pixel is in-focus. Then, we interpret the corresponding focal plane distance as depth value. This depth map d is equipped with a sparse confidence function w that indicates meaningful depth values. Next, we jointly regularise and fill-in the initial depth with the following variational approach:

$$E(u) = \frac{1}{2} \int_\Omega w(\boldsymbol{x}) \cdot \Psi\Big((u(\boldsymbol{x}) - d(\boldsymbol{x}))^2\Big) \, \mathrm{d}\boldsymbol{x} \; + \; \alpha \cdot R(u), \qquad (1)$$

where $\Omega \subset \mathbb{R}^2$ describes the rectangular image domain, and α is a positive regularisation parameter. Furthermore, we apply the penalisation function $\Psi(s^2) = \sqrt{s^2 + \varepsilon^2}$ with $\varepsilon > 0$ to handle outliers in the input. The regularisation term $R(u)$ provides smooth depth maps and fills in missing information. We propose and discuss different choices of $R(u)$ in Sect. 3.

3 Coupling Model for Second Order Regularisation

3.1 Isotropic Coupling Model

Compared to direct implementations of higher order regularisation, coupled formulations as in [4,13] offer several advantages: First they do not require the explicit estimation and implementation of higher order derivatives. Second and even more importantly, they allow to individually model discontinuities for each derivative order. This is not possible with direct higher order models. Hence, we base our anisotropic second order regulariser on the following isotropic coupling model that replaces a direct second order smoothness term of u by

$$R_\mathrm{I}(u) = \inf_{\boldsymbol{v}} \left\{ \frac{1}{2} \int_\Omega \Big(\Psi(|\boldsymbol{\nabla} u - \boldsymbol{v}|^2) + \beta \cdot \Psi(|\boldsymbol{\mathcal{J}v}|_\mathrm{F}^2) \Big) \, \mathrm{d}\boldsymbol{x} \right\}, \qquad (2)$$

where $\Psi(s^2) = \sqrt{s^2 + \varepsilon^2}$ is a subquadratic function with a small positive constant ε, $|\cdot|$ denotes the Euclidean norm, and $|\cdot|_\mathrm{F}$ the Frobenius norm. Furthermore, the vector field $\boldsymbol{v} = (v_1, v_2)^\top$ can be seen as an approximation of the gradient $\boldsymbol{\nabla} u$, and $\boldsymbol{\mathcal{J}v}$ is the Jacobian of this vector field. Since the first term in (2) inherently couples $\boldsymbol{\nabla} u$ to $\boldsymbol{v}$, we refer to it as *coupling term*. The second term provides smoothness of the vector field v. Hence, we refer to it as *smoothness term*. Here, the parameter $\beta > 0$ allows to steer the importance of both terms.

Let us discuss the meaning and interplay of both terms: With the nonlinear function Ψ, the smoothness term implements a first order penalisation of v that favours piecewise constant vector fields. For didactic reasons, let us first assume a hard coupling such that v is identical to ∇u. Then, piecewise constant v are equivalent to piecewise constant first order derivatives of u. This way, one can see that the smoothness term is responsible for modelling kinks in the solution. With that in mind, let us now consider the behaviour of the nonlinear coupling term. With $\varepsilon \to 0$, it allows sparse deviations of the vector field v from the gradient of u, i.e. sparse peaks of the coupling term energy. Regarding v as an approximation of ∇v, this shows that the coupling term allows to model peaks in the first derivative of u which correspond to jumps in the solution. Summing up, the discussed coupling model provides direct access to both jumps and kinks of the unknown function u by the coupling and smoothness term, respectively. For small ε, the coupling model in (2) resembles *total generalised variation* (TGV) of second order [4]. In many image processing and computer vision applications, such isotropic coupling models have led to high quality results. However, they do not make use of any directional information which is important for a variety of applications such as the one that we consider in this work.

3.2 Extracting Directional Information

As for instance demonstrated by Nagel and Enkelmann [19] in the context of optic flow estimation, it is highly beneficial to use the structure of a given input image to regularise the unknown flow in an anisotropic way. This allows to apply a different kind of smoothing along and across image structures. In this work, we extend this successful concept from first to second order regularisation, and in particular to the discussed coupling model. To this end, let us first determine a way to identify the structures of an image or more specifically the directions across and along them. Let f denote a given guidance image. In the case of focus fusion we take the evolving all-in-focus image as guidance. Then, we calculate those directions r_1 and r_2 as the normalised eigenvectors of the structure tensor [11]

$$G_\rho * \big(\nabla(G_\sigma * f) \nabla(G_\sigma * f)^\mathsf{T} \big), \tag{3}$$

where $*$ describes a convolution, and G_σ and G_ρ are Gaussians with standard deviation σ and ρ, respectively. The computed eigenvectors form an orthonormal system where the vector r_1, which belongs to the dominant eigenvalue, points across image structures and r_2 along them.

3.3 Anisotropic Modification of Coupling Term

Let us now incorporate this directional information into the isotropic coupling model. To this end, we first consider the isotropic coupling term from (2):

$$C_{\mathrm{I}}(u, v) = \Psi\big(|\nabla u - v|^2\big) = \Psi\Big(\sum_{\ell=1}^{2} \big(e_\ell^\mathsf{T}(\nabla u - v)\big)^2 \Big), \tag{4}$$

where $e_1 = (1,0)^\mathsf{T}$ and $e_2 = (0,1)^\mathsf{T}$. This reformulation of the coupling term in terms of the unit vectors e_1 and e_2 allows to incorporate the directional information as follows: First, we exchange e_1 and e_2 in Eq. (4) with the eigenvectors r_1 and r_2 of the structure tensor. Second, we penalise both directional components differently to introduce an anisotropic behaviour, i.e. we exchange the position of the penalisation function Ψ and the summation $\sum_{\ell=1}^{2}$. This results in the anisotropic coupling term

$$C_\mathrm{A}(u,v) = \sum_{\ell=1}^{2} \Psi_\ell\Big((r_\ell^\mathsf{T}(\nabla u - v))^2\Big). \tag{5}$$

Here, we apply different penalisation functions Ψ_ℓ along and across image structures. This allows for instance to enforce a full coupling along edges by setting the corresponding $\Psi_2(s^2) = s^2$, and to relax the coupling constraint in the orthogonal direction with $\Psi_1(s^2) = 2\varepsilon\sqrt{s^2 + \varepsilon^2}$ such that $\Psi_1'(s^2)$ is the Charbonnier diffusivity [7]. To analyse the introduced anisotropy in a better way, let us take a look at the resulting gradient descent of (5) w.r.t. u and v:

$$\partial_t u = \mathrm{div}\left(D(\nabla u - v)\right), \tag{6}$$
$$\partial_t v = D(\nabla u - v), \tag{7}$$

where div is the divergence operator, and ∂_t denotes an artificial time derivative to model an evolution of u and v, respectively. Equation (6) describes an evolution that occurs within gradient domain methods. However, here the tensor

$$D = \sum_{\ell=1}^{2} \Psi_\ell'\Big((r_\ell^\mathsf{T}(\nabla u - v))^2\Big) \cdot r_\ell r_\ell^\mathsf{T} \tag{8}$$

steers this process in an anisotropic way. Moreover, this equation shows a nice feature of our model: When fixing the coupling variable v to 0, our second order coupling model comes down to a first order anisotropic diffusion process on the unknown u; see e.g. Weickert [31] and references therein. Please note that for $v = 0$ the smoothness term vanishes since in this trivial case $|Jv|_\mathrm{F}^2$ is equal to 0. The right hand side of Eq. (7) is a reaction term that models the similarity of v and ∇u. Here, this similarity is enforced along edges (r_2) while it is relaxed across them (r_1). This becomes obvious by considering the tensor D in (8) that adapts the amount of similarity in a directional dependent way. This is achieved by a solution-driven scaling of the eigenvalues of D, where its eigenvectors are given by r_1 and r_2.

3.4 Anisotropic Modification of Smoothness Term

Let us now introduce anisotropy into the smoothness term in a similar way. To this end, we first rewrite it by means of the unit vectors e_1 and e_2:

$$S_\mathrm{I}(v) = \Psi\big(|Jv|_\mathrm{F}^2\big) = \Psi\Big(\sum_{\ell=1}^{2}\sum_{k=1}^{2}(e_k^\mathsf{T} Jv\, e_\ell)^2\Big), \tag{9}$$

where the term $e_k^\top \mathcal{J}v\, e_\ell$ can be seen as an equivalent of the second order directional derivative $\partial_{e_k e_\ell} u = e_k^\top \mathcal{H}u\, e_\ell$ with $\mathcal{H}u$ representing the Hessian of u. Our goal is to penalise this term differently along and across image structures. Hence, similarly to the anisotropic modification of the coupling term, we modify Eq. (9) by exchanging e_1 and e_2 with r_1 and r_2, and swapping the positions of the penalisation function Ψ and the summation $\sum_{\ell=1}^{2}$:

$$S_A(v) = \sum_{\ell=1}^{2} \Psi_\ell \Big(\sum_{k=1}^{2} (r_k^\top \mathcal{J}v\, r_\ell)^2 \Big), \tag{10}$$

where we again apply different penalisations Ψ_ℓ in both directions. Also here, let us shed light on the introduced anisotropy by analysing the associated gradient descent of (10):

$$\partial_t v = \mathbf{div}(\mathcal{J}v\, T) = \begin{pmatrix} \mathrm{div}(T\, \nabla v_1) \\ \mathrm{div}(T\, \nabla v_2) \end{pmatrix}, \tag{11}$$

where $\mathbf{div}$ applies the standard divergence operator div to the rows of a matrix-valued function (common definition), and thus yields a column vector with two components. Equation (11) can be seen as an anisotropic diffusion of the coupling variable v. Here the diffusion tensor

$$T = \sum_{\ell=1}^{2} \Psi_\ell' \Big(\sum_{k=1}^{2} (r_k^\top \mathcal{J}v\, r_\ell)^2 \Big) \cdot r_\ell r_\ell^\top \tag{12}$$

describes this anisotropic behaviour: We smooth the coupling variable v differently across and along image structures, where the amount of smoothness is determined by the eigenvalues of T.

3.5 Anisotropic Coupling Model

With the proposed coupling (5) and smoothness term (10), our fully anisotropic coupled regulariser is given by

$$R_A(u) = \inf_v \Big\{ \frac{1}{2} \int_\Omega \big(C_A(u, v) + \beta \cdot S_A(v) \big)\, d\boldsymbol{x} \Big\}. \tag{13}$$

As in the isotropic case (2), the coupling term $C_A(u, v)$ is responsible for handling jumps whereas the smoothness term $S_A(v)$ is responsible for handling kinks. However, contrary to the isotropic model our new anisotropic model now effectively incorporates directional information to steer this coupling and smoothing.

Furthermore, for scenarios where jumps or kinks of the unknown function highly correlate with edges of the guidance image, it is beneficial to include also the strength of an image edge in addition to its direction. To this end, we scale both summands of the coupling term (5) and of the smoothness term (10) with $g_\ell((r_\ell^\top \nabla f_\sigma)^2)$, where $g_\ell(s^2)$ is a decreasing function with $g_\ell(0) = 1$, and $f_\sigma = G_\sigma * f$ a smoothed version of the guidance image f. This further reduces coupling and smoothing across image edges while enforcing it along them. Referring to

Table 1. Overview of regularisers covered by our model. Note that D and T degenerate to the identity matrix I if $\Psi_\ell(s^2) = s^2$ and $g_\ell(s^2) = 1$, $\ell \in \{1, 2\}$.

Regularisation model			v	D	T
(FI)	First order	Isotropic	Fixed to 0	I	I
(FA)	First order	Anisotropic	Fixed to 0	Eq. (8)	Eq. (12)
(CI)	Coupled	Isotropic	Optimised	I	I
(CA)	Coupled	Anisotropic	Optimised	Eq. (8)	Eq. (12)

Sects. 3.3 and 3.4, this solely causes an additional scaling of the eigenvalues of the tensors D and T in Eqs. (8) and (12). In Table 1 we summarise different regularisation terms that result from our model with specific parameter choices. We will evaluate those regularisers in Sect. 5.

4   Minimisation

Minimising the convex energy (1) with the proposed convex regularisation term comes down to solving the following system of Euler-Lagrange equations:

$$\delta_u M(u) - \alpha \cdot \operatorname{div}(D(\nabla u - v)) = 0, \tag{14}$$

$$D(v - \nabla u) - \beta \cdot \mathbf{div}(\boldsymbol{Jv}\, T) = \mathbf{0}, \tag{15}$$

where

$$\delta_u M(u) = w(\boldsymbol{x}) \cdot \Psi'\left(\left(u(\boldsymbol{x}) - d(\boldsymbol{x})\right)^2\right) \cdot \left(u(\boldsymbol{x}) - d(\boldsymbol{x})\right) \tag{16}$$

is the functional derivative of the data term in (1) w.r.t. u. With n as outer normal vector on the image boundary $\partial\Omega$, the corresponding boundary conditions read $(\nabla u - v)^\top D n = 0$ and $\boldsymbol{Jv}\, T n = \mathbf{0}$.

We discretise the Euler-Lagrange Eqs. (14) and (15) on a uniform rectangular grid, and approximate the derivatives at intermediate grid points. Accordingly, we appropriately discretise the divergence expressions with the approach of Weickert et al. [33] using the parameters $\alpha = 0.4$ and $\gamma = 1$. Furthermore, we apply a lagged nonlinearity method where we solve the occurring linear systems of equations with a so-called *Fast Jacobi* solver [32].

5   Evaluation

In this section we evaluate the proposed regularisation model and compare it to the baseline methods from Table 1. To this end, we consider a synthetic data set where ground truth is available. Figure 1 (*top*) depicts the input guidance image, the ground truth depth map that consists of two segments with a linear slope in vertical direction, a noisy depth map, and a sparse version of it. The last one serves as input for our evaluation. More specifically, we generate the input depth map d in the following way: First we add Gaussian noise of standard deviation

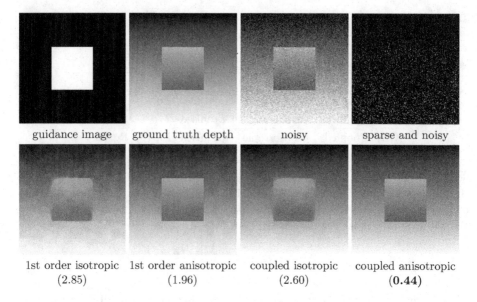

| guidance image | ground truth depth | noisy | sparse and noisy |

| 1st order isotropic | 1st order anisotropic | coupled isotropic | coupled anisotropic |
| (2.85) | (1.96) | (2.60) | **(0.44)** |

Fig. 1. Synthetic experiment. *Top*: Guidance image, ground truth depth map, noisy version, sparse and noisy version that serves as input depth map. *Bottom*: Computed depth maps. We state the root mean square error between the computed and the ground truth depth map in brackets under the corresponding results ($\times 10^{-2}$).

0.1 to the ground truth depth map, where the initial depth values range from 0 to 1. Next we randomly select 10 % of this noisy version to obtain the final sparse and noisy input depth map.

Figure 1 (*bottom*) shows the resulting depth maps that are computed with *first order isotropic* (FI), *first order anisotropic* (FA), *coupled isotropic* (CI), and *coupled anisotropic* (CA) regularisation; cf. Table 1. For each approach the regularisation parameters α and β are optimised w.r.t. the *root mean square error* (RMSE). These resulting RMSEs between the ground truth and the computed depth maps are listed right below the corresponding results in Fig. 1. First, this experiment demonstrates that incorporating directional information from the guidance image is highly beneficial. Both first and coupled anisotropic regularisers outperform their isotropic counterparts. With anisotropic regularisation the edges of the computed depth maps are desirably sharp, while the isotropic variants cannot provide this quality. Second, the assumption of piecewise affine functions is much more suited than assuming piecewise constant depth maps in this case. Accordingly, both second order coupling models yield better results than their corresponding first order variants. It is clearly visible that the latter ones lead to piecewise constant patches, which is not desirable in the considered scenario. Last but not least, the proposed coupled anisotropic regulariser provides the best results, both visually and in terms of the RMSE.

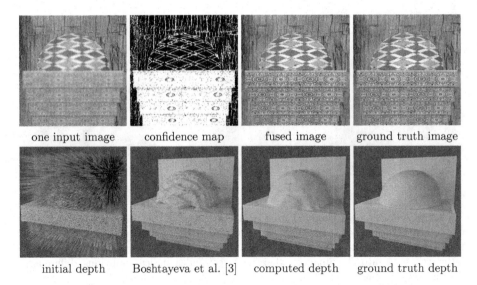

| one input image | confidence map | fused image | ground truth image |

| initial depth | Boshtayeva et al. [3] | computed depth | ground truth depth |

Fig. 2. Synthetic set from [3]. *Top*: One of the thirteen unsharp input images, confidence map, our fused image, and ground truth image. *Bottom*: Rendered depth maps.

6 Application to Focus Fusion

In this section, we demonstrate the performance of our technique with the application to focus fusion. To this end, we first consider a synthetic data set from [3]. It contains a ground truth all-in-focus image that allows a comparison in terms of the *mean square error* (MSE). Figure 2 (*top left*) depicts one of thirteen focal stack images and the confidence map w from [3]. In Fig. 2 (*bottom*), we compare the initial depth d, the result of Boshtayeva et al. [3], and our computed depth to the ground truth. We see that both approaches are able to improve the initial depth map effectively. However, our depth map shows less staircase artefacts than the first order smoothness approach of Boshtayeva et al., and is closer to the ground truth. Also our fused image resembles the ground truth all-in-focus image; cf. Fig. 2 (*top right*). This is underlined by Table 2, where we compare our result in terms of the MSE between the fused image and its ground truth. Using the initial depth map to fuse the images gives an error of 10.55. This is improved by [3] to obtain a MSE of 3.47. Exchanging their first order regularisation technique by our novel anisotropic second order approach yields an improvement with a MSE of 3.08. The comparison to further state-of-the-art approaches shows the usefulness of our technique for the task of focus fusion.

Table 2. Mean square error (MSE) between computed and ground truth image.

Forster et al. [10]	Agarwala et al. [1]	Aguet et al. [2]	Boshtayeva et al. [3]	Our
152.12	135.97	113.73	3.47	**3.08**

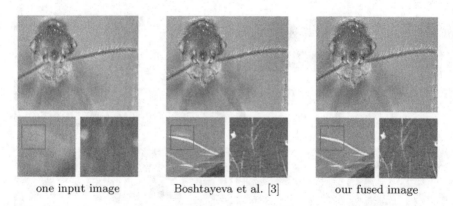

one input image   Boshtayeva et al. [3]   our fused image

Fig. 3. Real-world focal stack of an insect consisting of thirteen images with size 1344 × 1201 (available at grail.cs.washington.edu/projects/photomontage). *Top*: One of the unsharp input images, fused image of Boshtayeva et al. [3], and our fused image. *Bottom*: Zooms into the images, where red rectangles indicate obvious differences (Colour figure online).

In Fig. 3, we demonstrate the quality of our approach by an additional real-world experiment with a focus set of an insect. Since no ground truth is available, we have to restrict ourselves to a visual comparison. To this end, we depict one unsharp input image of the focal stack and the resulting fused images obtained with the approach of Boshtayeva et al. [3], and our method. Especially the zooms in the *bottom* illustrate that our fused image contains less errors and more small scale details than the first order approach of Boshtayeva et al. [3].

7   Conclusions

On the one hand, it is known that anisotropic techniques allow to obtain results of highest quality when using first order regularisation. On the other hand, recent developments have rendered higher order regularisation very attractive. In this paper, we build a bridge between both approaches and systematically combine such anisotropic ideas and higher order regularisation. As a result, our novel anisotropic second order regulariser allows to steer the preferred direction of jumps and kinks based on image structures. To achieve this, we have introduced a direction-dependent behaviour both in the coupling and the smoothness term. We have experimentally shown that this yields superior results compared to first order anisotropic and second order isotropic approaches. Moreover, we have demonstrated the usefulness of the proposed regularisation technique for the task of focus fusion. In this regard, we plan to show the benefits of our novel anisotropic second order smoothness term for further computer vision applications such as stereo or optic flow computation in future work.

Acknowledgments. Our research has been partially funded by the Deutsche Forschungsgemeinschaft (DFG) through a Gottfried Wilhelm Leibniz Prize for Joachim Weickert. This is gratefully acknowledged.

References

1. Agarwala, A., Dontcheva, M., Agrawala, M., Drucker, S., Colburn, A., Curless, B., Salesin, D., Cohen, M.: Interactive digital photomontage. ACM Trans. Graph. **23**(3), 294–302 (2004)
2. Aguet, F., Van De Ville, D., Unser, M.: Model-based 2.5-D deconvolution for extended depth of field in brightfield microscopy. IEEE Trans. Image Process. **17**(7), 1144–1153 (2008)
3. Boshtayeva, M., Hafner, D., Weickert, J.: A focus fusion framework with anisotropic depth map smoothing. Pattern Recogn. **48**(11), 3310–3323 (2015)
4. Bredies, K., Kunisch, K., Pock, T.: Total generalized variation. SIAM J. Imaging Sci. **3**(3), 492–526 (2010)
5. Chambolle, A., Lions, P.L.: Image recovery via total variation minimization and related problems. Numerische Mathematik **76**(2), 167–188 (1997)
6. Chan, T.F., Marquina, A., Mulet, P.: High-order total variation-based image restoration. SIAM J. Sci. Comput. **22**(2), 503–516 (2000)
7. Charbonnier, P., Blanc-Féraud, L., Aubert, G., Barlaud, M.: Two deterministic half-quadratic regularization algorithms for computed imaging. In: Proceedings of IEEE International Conference on Image Processing, Austin, TX, vol. 2, pp. 168–172, November 1994
8. Didas, S., Weickert, J., Burgeth, B.: Properties of higher order nonlinear diffusion filtering. J. Math. Imaging Vis. **35**(3), 208–226 (2009)
9. Ferstl, D., Reinbacher, C., Ranftl, R., Rüther, M., Bischof, H.: Image guided depth upsampling using anisotropic total generalized variation. In: Proceedings of International Conference on Computer Vision, Sydney, Australia, pp. 993–1000, December 2013
10. Forster, B., Van De Ville, D., Berent, J., Sage, D., Unser, M.: Complex wavelets for extended depth-of-field: a new method for the fusion of multichannel microscopy images. Microsc. Res. Tech. **65**(1–2), 33–42 (2004)
11. Förstner, W., Gülch, E.: A fast operator for detection and precise location of distinct points, corners and centres of circular features. In: Proceedings of ISPRS Intercommission Conference on Fast Processing of Photogrammetric Data, Interlaken, Switzerland, pp. 281–305, June 1987
12. Hafner, D., Demetz, O., Weickert, J.: Simultaneous HDR and optic flow computation. In: Proceedings of International Conference on Pattern Recognition, Stockholm, Sweden, pp. 2065–2070, August 2014
13. Hewer, A., Weickert, J., Scheffer, T., Seibert, H., Diebels, S.: Lagrangian strain tensor computation with higher order variational models. In: Burghardt, T., Damen, D., Mayol-Cuevas, W., Mirmehdi, M. (eds.) Proceedings of British Machine Vision Conference. BMVA Press, Bristol, September 2013
14. Horn, B.K.P.: Focusing. Tech. Rep. Memo No. 160, MIT Artificial Intelligence Laboratory, Cambridge, MA, May 1968
15. Horn, B.K.P.: Height and gradient from shading. Int. J. Comput. Vis. **5**(1), 37–75 (1990)
16. Lenzen, F., Becker, F., Lellmann, J.: Adaptive second-order total variation: an approach aware of slope discontinuities. In: Kuijper, A., Bredies, K., Pock, T., Bischof, H. (eds.) SSVM 2013. LNCS, vol. 7893, pp. 61–73. Springer, Heidelberg (2013)
17. Li, H., Manjunath, B., Mitra, S.: Multisensor image fusion using the wavelet transform. Graph. Models Image Process. **57**(3), 235–245 (1995)

18. Lysaker, M., Lundervold, A., Tai, X.C.: Noise removal using fourth-order partial differential equation with applications to medical magnetic resonance images in space and time. IEEE Trans. Image Process. **12**(12), 1579–1590 (2003)

19. Nagel, H.H., Enkelmann, W.: An investigation of smoothness constraints for the estimation of displacement vector fields from image sequences. IEEE Trans. Pattern Anal. Mach. Intell. **8**(5), 565–593 (1986)

20. Nayar, S.K., Nakagawa, Y.: Shape from focus. IEEE Trans. Pattern Anal. Mach. Intell. **16**(8), 824–831 (1994)

21. Nir, T., Bruckstein, A.M., Kimmel, R.: Over-parameterized variational optical flow. Int. J. Comput. Vis. **76**(2), 205–216 (2008)

22. Ogden, J., Adelson, E., Bergen, J., Burt, P.: Pyramid-based computer graphics. RCA Eng. **30**(5), 4–15 (1985)

23. Persch, N., Schroers, C., Setzer, S., Weickert, J.: Introducing more physics into variational depth–from–defocus. In: Jiang, X., Hornegger, J., Koch, R. (eds.) GCPR 2014. LNCS, vol. 8753, pp. 15–27. Springer, Heidelberg (2014)

24. Peter, P., Weickert, J., Munk, A., Krivobokova, T., Li, H.: Justifying tensor-driven diffusion from structure-adaptive statistics of natural images. In: Tai, X.-C., Bae, E., Chan, T.F., Lysaker, M. (eds.) EMMCVPR 2015. LNCS, vol. 8932, pp. 263–277. Springer, Heidelberg (2015)

25. Petrovic, V., Xydeas, C.: Gradient-based multiresolution image fusion. IEEE Trans. Image Process. **13**(2), 228–237 (2004)

26. Ranftl, R., Bredies, K., Pock, T.: Non-local total generalized variation for optical flow estimation. In: Fleet, D., Pajdla, T., Schiele, B., Tuytelaars, T. (eds.) ECCV 2014, Part I. LNCS, vol. 8689, pp. 439–454. Springer, Heidelberg (2014)

27. Ranftl, R., Gehrig, S., Pock, T., Bischof, H.: Pushing the limits of stereo using variational stereo estimation. In: Proceedings of IEEE Intelligent Vehicles Symposium, Alcalá de Henares, Spain, pp. 401–407, June 2012

28. Scherzer, O.: Denoising with higher order derivatives of bounded variation and an application to parameter estimation. Computing **60**(1), 1–27 (1998)

29. Schroers, C., Zimmer, H., Valgaerts, L., Bruhn, A., Demetz, O., Weickert, J.: Anisotropic range image integration. In: Pinz, A., Pock, T., Bischof, H., Leberl, F. (eds.) DAGM and OAGM 2012. LNCS, vol. 7476, pp. 73–82. Springer, Heidelberg (2012)

30. Trobin, W., Pock, T., Cremers, D., Bischof, H.: An unbiased second-order prior for high-accuracy motion estimation. In: Rigoll, G. (ed.) DAGM 2008. LNCS, vol. 5096, pp. 396–405. Springer, Heidelberg (2008)

31. Weickert, J.: Anisotropic Diffusion in Image Processing. Teubner, Stuttgart (1998)

32. Weickert, J., Grewenig, S., Schroers, C., Bruhn, A.: Cyclic schemes for PDE-based image analysis. Tech. Rep. 327 (revised), Department of Mathematics, Saarland University, Saarbrücken, German, April 2015

33. Weickert, J., Welk, M., Wickert, M.: L^2-stable nonstandard finite differences for anisotropic diffusion. In: Kuijper, A., Bredies, K., Pock, T., Bischof, H. (eds.) SSVM 2013. LNCS, vol. 7893, pp. 380–391. Springer, Heidelberg (2013)

34. Zimmer, H., Bruhn, A., Weickert, J.: Optic flow in harmony. Int. J. Compu. Vis. **93**(3), 368–388 (2011)

Binarization Driven Blind Deconvolution for Document Image Restoration

Thomas Köhler[1,2]([✉]), Andreas Maier[1,2], and Vincent Christlein[1]

[1] Pattern Recognition Lab, Friedrich-Alexander-Universität Erlangen-Nürnberg,
Erlangen, Germany
[2] Erlangen Graduate School in Advanced Optical Technologies (SAOT),
Erlangen, Germany
{thomas.koehler,andreas.maier,vincent.christlein}@fau.de

Abstract. Blind deconvolution is a common method for restoration of blurred text images, while binarization is employed to analyze and interpret the text semantics. In literature, these tasks are typically treated independently. This paper introduces a novel binarization driven blind deconvolution approach to couple both tasks in a common framework. The proposed method is derived as an energy minimization problem regularized by a novel consistency term to exploit text binarization as a prior for blind deconvolution. The binarization to establish our consistency term is inferred by spatially regularized soft clustering based on a set of discriminative features. Our algorithm is formulated by the alternating direction method of multipliers and iteratively refines blind deconvolution and binarization. In our experimental evaluation, we show that our joint framework is superior to treating binarization and deconvolution as independent subproblems. We also demonstrate the application of our method for the restoration and binarization of historic document images, where it improves the visual recognition of handwritten text.

1 Introduction

The automatic analysis of text images has become an essential tool within a wide range of applications in industry, forensics or historical research. Some of the most frequently required tasks for text image analysis include optical character recognition (OCR) or handwritten text recognition (HTR) [8], writer identification and verification [6] as well as structural document segmentation [9]. Hereby, most methods rely on the existence of accurate features extracted from document images, e.g., keypoints [6,9]. Another essential feature widely used for OCR and HTR is *binarization*, i.e., the segmentation of text images into character and background regions. The reliability of such features strongly depends on the quality of the underlying text images. To address this requirement, image enhancement and restoration techniques are commonly used for preprocessing prior to text analysis [8]. In this context, text image restoration by means of

This work is partly supported by the German Federal Ministry of Education and Research (BMBF), grant-nr. 01UG1236a

J. Gall et al. (Eds.): GCPR 2015, LNCS 9358, pp. 91–102, 2015.
DOI: 10.1007/978-3-319-24947-6_8

deconvolution is a technique to recover a sharp image from a blurred acquisition. Reasons for blurring can be motion blur, i.e., blur induced by moving the camera or a movement of the scene. Another reason that is relevant for document images acquired under a controlled environment, e.g., digital scanning, are limitations of optics and sensors. We consider the extraction of text features and image deconvolution as complementary problems that can be, however, strongly coupled in order to enhance both of them. In particular, this is the case for deconvolution and binarization. If a sharp text image obtained by image deconvolution is available, this serves as a reliable input for text binarization. Conversely, an accurate text binarization can be utilized as a strong prior for image deconvolution.

Text Image Binarization. Most methods for automatic binarization of text images can be categorized into two groups. The most basic *global* thresholding techniques estimate a single threshold, e.g., using Otsu's method [18], to discriminate characters and background in two-tone images. This approach is computationally efficient but is sensitive to global illumination changes, which is a common issue in large document images. As a complementary approach, *local* thresholding techniques estimate a threshold per image patch or even per pixel to make binarization spatially adaptive [1,20].

Text Image Restoration. Document image restoration can be approached from a natural scene statistics or a text-specific point of view. Most general-purpose methods exploit natural scene statistics and make use of the fact that natural images are sparse in the gradient domain. This can be modeled by total variation [2,17] or heavy tailed priors [15]. A variety of algorithms has been proposed to solve image deconvolution as a *non-blind* problem [5] or as *blind* estimation [14] in which the blur characteristics are estimated simultaneously with the deblurred image. Despite their success, natural image statistics typically fail to model the characteristics of text images [4] since they provide a too weak prior. For this reason, various blind deconvolution approaches have been proposed which exploit the properties of text images. One class of methods utilizes the two-tone property of document images for blur kernel estimation and deblurring [3,16]. A different strategy has been proposed by Zhang [23] that directly restores a binarization from a blurred two-tone image. However, this method does not provide a deblurred intensity image. The use of more comprehensive text-specific properties in addition to the intensity has been examined in the work of Cho et al. [4]. These properties guide the image deconvolution and include contrast, color-uniformity and gradient statistics of characters and background, respectively. However, the success of this algorithm relies on the stroke width transform (SWT) [7] that is used to describe text-specific properties. For this reason, a complementary approach has been proposed by Pan et al. [19]. In their method, text deblurring is formulated via an L_0 norm regularized energy function using intensity and gradient information. Deblurring yields outstanding results in presence of severe motion blur for both pure text images as well as natural images containing text. However, it yields only a deblurred image with the associated blur kernel estimate without considering binarization.

Proposed Binarization Driven Blind Deconvolution. This work faces document image restoration from a different point of view. Similar to prior work [3,16,23], we exploit properties of two-tone text images. In doing so, we consider blind deconvolution and binarization as coupled problems and aggregate them in a novel energy minimization framework. The proposed algorithm gradually refines text binarization that is exploited as a prior for blind deconvolution. The advantage of this novel strategy is twofold: (1) deconvolution is guided by binarization as a strong prior compared to priors derived from natural image statistics, and (2) text binarization benefits from deconvolution and is incrementally refined in our optimization. In detail, our contributions are:

- a novel energy minimization formulation for blind deconvolution that exploits text binarization as guidance,
- a binarization method using a soft clustering algorithm as inner optimization loop in the proposed framework,
- demonstration of the impact of our method in a comprehensive evaluation for document restoration on synthetic data as well as real historic text images.

2 Image Deconvolution Model

We examine blind deconvolution of single-channel images linearized to a vector $y \in \mathbb{R}^n$ with $y_i \in [0; 1]$. Our method is derived from the image formation model $y = h * x + \epsilon$, where $x \in \mathbb{R}^n$ denotes the unknown deblurred image, $h \in \mathbb{R}^m$ denotes a linear, space invariant blur kernel in vector notation and $*$ is the discrete convolution operator. The signal $\epsilon \in \mathbb{R}^n$ models additive noise.

In the proposed model, for x there exists a corresponding binarization s describing the partitioning of x into characters and background, respectively. This binarization is encoded by a probability map $s \in [0; 1]^n$, where s_i is the probability that the i-th pixel belongs to the background. The image x and its binarization s can be considered as coupled variables. If one knows an ideal image x, s could be determined accurately by means of image binarization. Conversely, if an ideal binarization s would be known, blind deconvolution could be guided by s. Hence, we formulate blind deconvolution as the joint energy function:

$$\mathcal{E}(x, h, s) = \mathcal{D}(x, h) + \lambda_x \mathcal{R}(x) + \lambda_h \mathcal{H}(h) + \lambda_c \mathcal{C}(x, s), \quad (1)$$

where $\mathcal{D}(x, h)$ and $\mathcal{R}(x)$ with weight $\lambda_x \geq 0$ denote the data fidelity and regularization term for image deconvolution, respectively. $\mathcal{H}(h)$ with weight $\lambda_h \geq 0$ denotes a regularizer for the blur kernel h. $\mathcal{C}(x, s)$ with weight $\lambda_c \geq 0$ describes a consistency term that couples the image x with the associated binarization s. We define the data fidelity term as:

$$\mathcal{D}(x, h) = ||Hx - y||_2^2, \quad (2)$$

where $H \in \mathbb{R}^{n \times n}$ denotes the blur kernel h in matrix notation. Mathematically, $\mathcal{D}(x, h)$ provides a maximum likelihood estimate under additive, zero-mean Gaussian noise. The regularization term for the deblurred image is given

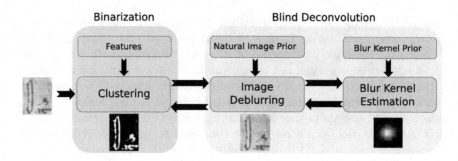

Fig. 1. Flowchart of the proposed binarization driven blind deconvolution method.

by a Hyper-Laplacian prior [14] derived from natural image statistics:

$$\mathcal{R}(\boldsymbol{x}) = \sum_{i=1}^{n} \left([\nabla_h \boldsymbol{x}]_i^2 + [\nabla_v \boldsymbol{x}_i^2]\right)^{\frac{p}{2}}, \tag{3}$$

where $0 \leq p \leq 1$, and ∇_h and ∇_v denote the gradient of $\boldsymbol{x}$ in horizontal and vertical direction (computed pixel-wise). This term exploits sparsity of $\boldsymbol{x}$ in the gradient domain for the regularization of image deconvolution. For the blur kernel estimation, we enforce non-negativity of its elements h_i [14] according to:

$$\mathcal{H}(\boldsymbol{h}) = \sum_{i=1}^{m} \mathcal{H}(h_i) \quad \text{where } \mathcal{H}(h) = \begin{cases} h & h \geq 0 \\ \infty & h < 0 \end{cases}. \tag{4}$$

In order to guide the estimation of $\boldsymbol{x}$, we propose a new consistency term to couple deconvolution with the associated binarization $\boldsymbol{s}$. In doing so, we exploit the fact that discontinuities in $\boldsymbol{x}$ and $\boldsymbol{s}$ should be aligned. Although this is not completely true for natural images, it is a reasonable assumption for document images. For instance, a discontinuity in $\boldsymbol{s}$ associated with the boundary of a character corresponds to a discontinuity of the intensities in $\boldsymbol{x}$ and the gradients $\nabla \boldsymbol{s}$ and $\nabla \boldsymbol{x}$ are equal up to scale. In background regions, one can even assume equal gradients $\nabla \boldsymbol{s}$ and $\nabla \boldsymbol{x}$. We enforce this consistency in the gradient domain by the term:

$$\mathcal{C}(\boldsymbol{x}, \boldsymbol{s}) = ||\nabla_h \boldsymbol{x} - \nabla_h \boldsymbol{s}||_2^2 + ||\nabla_v \boldsymbol{x} - \nabla_v \boldsymbol{s}||_2^2, \tag{5}$$

where we construct $\boldsymbol{s}$ such that its gradient $\nabla \boldsymbol{s}$ has a consistent direction with the gradient $\nabla \boldsymbol{x}$. For this purpose, a character at the i-th pixel in $\boldsymbol{x}$ associated with a low intensity x_i corresponds to a low probability s_i in the binarization $\boldsymbol{s}$.

3   Binarization Driven Deconvolution Algorithm

The proposed method is based on the minimization of the energy function in Eq. 1 and requires knowledge of the binarization $\boldsymbol{s}$ to exploit the consistency $\mathcal{C}(\boldsymbol{x}, \boldsymbol{s})$. However, in practice $\boldsymbol{s}$ is unknown and it would be error-prone to obtain it from the blurred image directly using standard image binarization techniques. For this reason, one strategy would be a formulation as joint energy minimization w. r. t. the deblurred image, the latent blur kernel and the binarization. Unfortunately, this approach is only computationally tractable with simplified models of image binarization. In the proposed method, we solve Eq. 1 w. r. t. x and h while the binarization s is gradually refined over $t \geq 1$ iterations. The outline of our approach as depicted in Fig. 1 is as follows: First, we obtain the binarization $s^{(t)}$ using soft clustering in an inner optimization as proposed in Sect. 3.1. Then, we minimize Eq. 1 w. r. t. x and h by exploiting the binarization $s^{(t)}$ as shown in Sects. 3.2 and 3.3 according to:

$$\left(x^{(t)}, h^{(t)}\right) = \arg\min_{x,h} \mathcal{E}\left(x, h, s^{(t)}\right). \tag{6}$$

These stages are solved alternately, where $(x^{(t-1)}, h^{(t-1)}, s^{(t-1)})$ is propagated from iteration $t-1$ to obtain refined estimates at iteration t. For an efficient implementation that avoids local minimums, iterations are performed in a coarse-to-fine scheme [14,19]. Starting at the coarsest level that is obtained by downsampling the input image and the support of the blur kernel, we gradually estimate the deblurred image and the blur kernel over different scales without using the consistency term in a first pass. Then, the blur kernel and the deblurred image with its binarization are refined on the finest scale using the full model with our consistency term in a second pass. Finally, we propose a further refinement of the deblurred image $\tilde{x}$ by means of guided filtering [12] that exploits the binarization $\tilde{s}$ to remove remaining deblurring artifacts, e. g. ringing [19]. We compute this refinement as the average image $x = \frac{1}{2}(\text{GF}(\tilde{x}, \tilde{s}) + \text{GF}(\tilde{x}, \tilde{x}))$, where $\text{GF}(p, q)$ denotes the guided filter with input image p and guidance image q.

3.1 Text-Specific Binarization

We formulate text binarization as a soft clustering problem using $c = 2$ clusters corresponding to characters and background. Each cluster is described in a feature space by the center $\mu_j \in \mathbb{R}^d$ with $j \in \{1, 2\}$. To take the property of text into account that adjacent pixels should be assigned to similar clusters, we incorporate spatially regularized Fuzzy C-means clustering [22] to the proposed text binarization. Based on the features f_x that are pixel-wise extracted as $f_{x,i} \in \mathbb{R}^d$ at the i-th pixel in the image x, the binarization is obtained by:

$$\left(\mu^{(t)}, s^{(t)}\right) = \arg\min_{\mu,s} \sum_{i=1}^{n} \sum_{j=1}^{c} s_{ij}^{q} \left|\left| f_{x,i} - \mu_j \right|\right|_2^2 + \alpha \sum_{i=1}^{n} \sum_{j=1}^{c} \sum_{k=1}^{n} w_{ik} s_{ij}^{q} (1 - s_{kj})^q, \tag{7}$$

where $q > 1$ is a weighting parameter for the fuzzy cluster membership $s_{ij} \in [0; 1]$ of the i-th feature vector to the j-th cluster. The weights w_{ik} are set to $w_{ik} = 1$ if the i-th and the k-th pixel are adjacent in an 8-neighborhood and $w_{ik} = 0$, otherwise. The data fidelity term of soft clustering and the regularization term for adjacent pixels in Eq. 7 are weighted to each other by $\alpha \geq 0$.

To define the feature set $\boldsymbol{f_x}$, we perform a scale space analysis over $d \geq 1$ scales on the image $\boldsymbol{x}^{(t-1)}$. The features associated with the i-th pixel are assembled as $\boldsymbol{f}_{x,i} = \left(Q_i\big(\boldsymbol{x}^{(t-1)}, \omega_1\big)\ Q_i\big(\boldsymbol{x}^{(t-1)}, \omega_2\big) \ldots Q_i\big(\boldsymbol{x}^{(t-1)}, \omega_d\big)\right)^{\top} \in \mathbb{R}^d$, where $Q_i(\boldsymbol{x}^{(t-1)}, \omega_j)$ is the i-th pixel of a filtered version of $\boldsymbol{x}^{(t-1)}$ using the filter size ω_j. In this work, we implement the discrete filter Q_i via 2-D median filtering. This provides edge preserving filtering and enables character analysis over various scales in soft clustering. Once the features $\boldsymbol{f_x}$ are extracted, the cluster centers and the binarization map $\boldsymbol{s}$ are computed as the zero-crossings of Eq. 7. Soft clustering is obtained by alternating computation of:

$$\boldsymbol{\mu_j} = \frac{\sum_{i=1}^n s_{ij}^q \boldsymbol{f}_{x,i}}{\sum_{i=1}^n s_{ij}^q} \tag{8}$$

$$s_{ij} = \left(\sum_{k=1}^c \frac{||\boldsymbol{f}_{x,i} - \boldsymbol{\mu_j}||_2^2 + \alpha \sum_{l=1}^n (1-s_{li})^q w_{jk)}}{||\boldsymbol{f}_{x,i} - \boldsymbol{\mu_k}||_2^2 + \alpha \sum_{l=1}^n (1-s_{lk})^q w_{jk}}\right)^{-\frac{1}{q-1}}, \tag{9}$$

until convergence of the clustering procedure using $\boldsymbol{s}^{(t-1)}$ obtained at the previous iteration as initialization. Finally, the refined binarization $\boldsymbol{s}^{(t)}$ is assembled from the cluster membership degrees s_{ij} associated with the background.

3.2   Estimation of the Deblurred Image

In order to estimate the deblurred image $\boldsymbol{x}^{(t)}$ at the current iteration, we solve Eq. 6 w. r. t. $\boldsymbol{x}$ while keeping the blur kernel fixed as $\boldsymbol{h}^{(t-1)}$. Using the consistency term $\mathcal{C}(\boldsymbol{x}, \boldsymbol{s}^{(t)})$ that couples the image $\boldsymbol{x}$ with the binarization map $\boldsymbol{s}^{(t)}$, the deblurred image is obtained by the energy minimization problem:

$$\boldsymbol{x}^{(t)} = \arg\min_{\boldsymbol{x}} \left\{ \mathcal{D}\big(\boldsymbol{x}, \boldsymbol{h}^{(t-1)}\big) + \lambda_x \mathcal{R}(\boldsymbol{x}) + \lambda_c \mathcal{C}\big(\boldsymbol{x}, \boldsymbol{s}^{(t)}\big) \right\}. \tag{10}$$

This unconstrained problem is solved by the alternating direction method of multipliers (ADMM) using Split Bregman iterations [11]. For this purpose, we derive a constrained problem that is equivalent to Eq. 10:

$$\arg\min_{\boldsymbol{x}, \boldsymbol{v}_h, \boldsymbol{v}_v} \Big\{ ||\boldsymbol{H}^{(t-1)}\boldsymbol{x} - \boldsymbol{y}||_2^2 + \lambda_c \big(||\boldsymbol{v}_h - \nabla_h \boldsymbol{s}^{(t)}||_2^2 + ||\boldsymbol{v}_v - \nabla_v \boldsymbol{s}^{(t)}||_2^2\big)$$

$$+ \lambda_x \sum_{i=1}^n \left([\boldsymbol{v}_h]_i^2 + [\boldsymbol{v}_v]_i^2\right)^{\frac{p}{2}} \Big\} \quad \text{s.t.}\ \boldsymbol{v}_h = \nabla_h \boldsymbol{x}, \boldsymbol{v}_v = \nabla_v \boldsymbol{x}, \tag{11}$$

where $\boldsymbol{v}_h$ and $\boldsymbol{v}_v$ are auxiliary variables and $\boldsymbol{H}^{(t-1)}$ is constructed from the kernel estimate $\boldsymbol{h}^{(t-1)}$. This provides a decoupling of the data fidelity term $\mathcal{D}(\boldsymbol{x}, \boldsymbol{h})$ from the regularizer $\mathcal{R}(\boldsymbol{x})$ and our consistency term $\mathcal{C}(\boldsymbol{x}, \boldsymbol{s})$. For numerical optimization, Eq. 11 is re-formulated to the unconstrained minimization problem:

$$\arg\min_{\boldsymbol{x}, \boldsymbol{v}_h, \boldsymbol{v}_v} \Big\{ ||\boldsymbol{H}^{(t-1)}\boldsymbol{x} - \boldsymbol{y}||_2^2 + \lambda_v \big(||\boldsymbol{v}_h - \nabla_h \boldsymbol{x} - \boldsymbol{b}_h||_2^2 + ||\boldsymbol{v}_v - \nabla_v \boldsymbol{x} - \boldsymbol{b}_v||_2^2\big)$$

$$+ \lambda_x \sum_{i=1}^n \left([\boldsymbol{v}_h]_i^2 + [\boldsymbol{v}_v]_i^2\right)^{\frac{p}{2}} + \lambda_c \big(||\boldsymbol{v}_h - \nabla_h \boldsymbol{s}^{(t)}||_2^2 + ||\boldsymbol{v}_v - \nabla_v \boldsymbol{s}^{(t)}||_2^2\big) \Big\}, \tag{12}$$

where λ_v is a Lagrangian multiplier that weights the quadratic penalty terms derived from the constraints in Eq. 11, and b_h and b_v denote the Bregman variables. We solve this minimization problem by coordinate descent for x, v_h and v_v, where b_h and b_v are chosen per Bregman iteration. Similar to [14], the optimization of Eq. 12 is performed in the Fourier domain.

3.3   Estimation of the Blur Kernel

The estimation of the blur kernel h can be done in a similar way. For blur estimation, we minimize Eq. 6 w.r.t. h and keep the deblurred image given by $x^{(t)}$ fixed. Hence, we can omit the consistency term and optimize only the deconvolution term. Similar to prior work [14,19], the kernel is estimated in the gradient domain resulting in the energy minimization problem:

$$h^{(t)} = \arg\min_{h} \left\{ \mathcal{D}(\nabla x^{(t)}, h) + \lambda_h \mathcal{H}(h) \right\}. \tag{13}$$

Then, we use ADMM and introduce the auxiliary variable g to substitute the blur kernel h in the regularizer $\mathcal{H}(h)$, the associated Bregman variable b_g, and the Lagrange multiplier λ_g. This yields the unconstrained problem:

$$\arg\min_{h,g} \left\{ \|\nabla X^{(t)} h - \nabla y\|_2^2 + \lambda_h \mathcal{H}(g) + \lambda_g \|h - g - b_g\|_2^2 \right\}, \tag{14}$$

where we reformulated $Hx^{(t)}$ as $X^{(t)}h$. Minimization is performed by coordinate descent for h and g in the Fourier domain with a re-centering of the kernel after each iteration [14]. The non-negativity constraint according to Eq. 4 is enforced at each iteration using thresholding of the kernel elements h_i.

4   Experiments and Results

We evaluated our algorithm on artificial and real document images. For a quantitative evaluation, we used an artificial dataset consisting of 18 images of sizes between 120×120 and 240×240 pixel that were simulated by blurring ground truth images with a 15×15 Gaussian kernel of standard deviation $\sigma_b = 2.5$, see Fig. 2. Moreover, images were disturbed by adding zero-mean Gaussian noise with varying standard deviation σ_n. To demonstrate the performance of our approach in terms of binarization, we used 19 excerpts of real historical documents with manually generated ground truth text binarizations. Our method was compared with the general-purpose deconvolution approach of Kotera et al. [14] and the method of Pan et al. [19] that has been recently proposed for text images. The F1 measure was used to assess the reliability of text binarization. For artificial data with known ground truth grayscale images, we also measured the peak-signal-to-noise ratio (PSNR) as well as structural similarity (SSIM).

Deconvolution Results. For a quantitative evaluation, the Gaussian noise standard deviation to simulate artificial text images was first set to $\sigma_n = 0.01$.

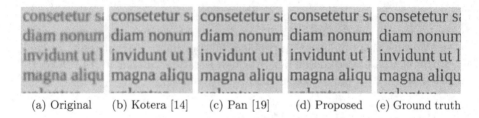

(a) Original   (b) Kotera [14]   (c) Pan [19]   (d) Proposed   (e) Ground truth

Fig. 2. Blind deconvolution results on simulated data with known ground truth.

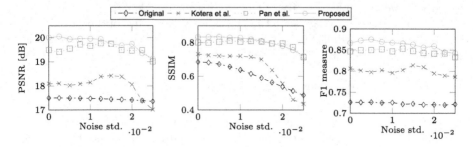

Fig. 3. Influence of Gaussian noise with standard deviation σ_n to blind deconvolution and the binarization obtained from the deblurred images. We evaluated the median of all quality measures over 18 simulated images with ground truth data.

Then, we adjusted the regularization weights of all compared deconvolution methods on one single training image taken from our simulated data by optimizing the PSNR of the deblurred image. In addition to pure blind deconvolution, we applied blind deconvolution and binarization as a two-stage approach using the methods of Kotera et al. [14] and Pan et al. [19] followed by hard thresholding using Otsu's method [18]. To assess binarization achieved by our method, we employ the binarization provided in the final pass of our coarse-to-fine optimization. For this setup, Table 1 compares the blind deconvolution methods on the simulated dataset using the PSNR and SSIM measures on grayscale images and the F1 measure to assess the binarizations. In terms of all measurements, our method consistently outperformed the methods of Kotera et al. [14] and Pan et al. [19].

Another experiment was conducted to analyze the noise robustness of the different algorithms. Therefore, we varied the noise standard deviation of the simulated images and compared the different deconvolution methods. Figure 3 shows the median of different quality measures over 18 simulated images. Binarization driven blind deconvolution consistently outperformed the approach of Kotera et al. [14] and achieved higher robustness with respect to image noise. For small noise levels, it also achieved higher quality measures compared to blind deconvolution of Pan et al. [19] with competitive results in case of severe noise.

For qualitative results on real data, we tested our method with excerpts of document images, cf. Fig. 4. As samples we used scans of historical handwritten

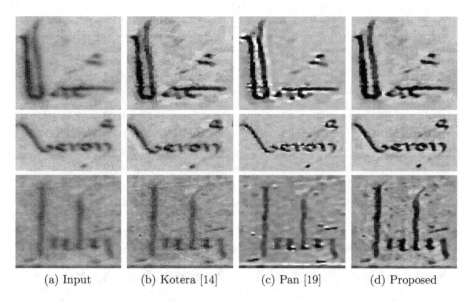

(a) Input   (b) Kotera [14]   (c) Pan [19]   (d) Proposed

Fig. 4. Results of the different blind deconvolution methods applied on scanned hand-written documents (source: Göttingen Academy of Sciences & Humanities).

Table 1. Mean and standard deviation of all quality measures for blind deconvolution on simulated images (noise level $\sigma_n = 0.01$). Binarizations for [14, 19] were obtained by applying Otsu's method [18] on the deblurred images.

	PSNR (in dB)	SSIM	F1 measure
Original	17.57 ± 0.42	0.64 ± 0.02	0.72 ± 0.01
Kotera et al. [14]	18.30 ± 0.54	0.73 ± 0.03	0.79 ± 0.02
Pan et al. [19]	19.79 ± 0.49	0.81 ± 0.02	0.85 ± 0.02
Proposed	$\mathbf{20.08 \pm 0.61}$	$\mathbf{0.83 \pm 0.02}$	$\mathbf{0.87 \pm 0.02}$

documents. The images are of low quality and are affected by image noise. Compared to the results of Kotera et al. [14], binarization driven blind deconvolution was able to reconstruct sharper boundaries of characters with accurate denoising in the background.

Binarization Results. Although the main target of our method is image blind deconvolution, we show that it provides also binarization results comparable to the state of the art. To investigate the performance of the binarization routine of our framework, we used the same artificial dataset as in the previous experiments as well as the handwritten dataset with manually generated ground truth binarization. Table 2 shows the results of our binarization in contrast to other local [1, 20, 21] and global binarization methods [18] applied to the original images. Moreover, we evaluated the deconvolution methods of Kotera et al. [14] and Pan et al. [19] by applying the method of Bradley and Roth [1] on the deblurred images.

Table 2. Mean and standard deviation of F1 measure on binarizations obtained from the artificial and handwritten documents as well as the merged dataset. The best and second best measures per dataset are highlighted.

	Artificial	Handwritten	Merged
Otsu [18]	0.72 ± 0.01	0.75 ± 0.15	0.73 ± 0.11
Sauvola and Pietikäinen [20]	0.79 ± 0.04	$\mathbf{0.78 \pm 0.07}$	0.79 ± 0.06
Bradley and Roth [1]	$\mathbf{0.85 \pm 0.01}$	$\mathbf{0.78 \pm 0.08}$	$\mathbf{0.82 \pm 0.07}$
Su et al. [21]	0.80 ± 0.01	$\mathbf{0.79 \pm 0.09}$	0.80 ± 0.07
Kotera et al. [14] + Bradley and Roth [1]	0.82 ± 0.01	0.71 ± 0.10	0.76 ± 0.09
Pan et al. [19] + Bradley and Roth [1]	0.85 ± 0.02	0.73 ± 0.09	0.79 ± 0.09
Proposed	$\mathbf{0.87 \pm 0.02}$	0.76 ± 0.11	$\mathbf{0.81 \pm 0.10}$

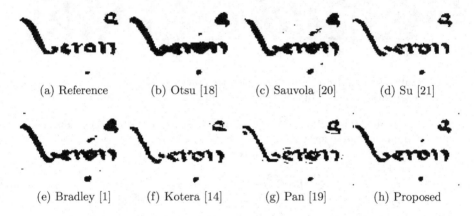

(a) Reference   (b) Otsu [18]   (c) Sauvola [20]   (d) Su [21]

(e) Bradley [1]   (f) Kotera [14]   (g) Pan [19]   (h) Proposed

Fig. 5. Binarization results on a scanned handwritten document image.

Binarization driven deconvolution outperformed all other binarization methods on the artificial dataset. On the historical dataset our method performed worse than local thresholding, but substantially outperformed global thresholding. The proposed method also achieved higher results than the the other deconvolution methods. Overall the method of Bradley and Roth [1] achieved slightly better results. A visual comparison between all methods is shown in Fig. 5.

5   Conclusions

In this work, we presented a new method for image blind deconvolution. Our algorithm explicitly incorporates text binarization as guidance. For this purpose, a novel consistency term serves as regularizer that couples deconvolution and binarization. Compared to existing blind deconvolution algorithms, our method provides more accurate deblurred intensity images as demonstrated for simulated and handwritten documents. In addition, our method provides a binarization as a by-product that is comparable to state-of-the-art text binarization techniques.

In our future work, we would like to incorporate our method as preprocessing step for successive processes like HTR or paleographic analysis. From an algorithmic point of view, our soft clustering procedure could benefit from the use of text-specific features like the stroke width transform [7]. By incorporating text-specific segmentation methods, we could extend our method to text images in the wild, i.e., non document texts. Finally, other domains like super-resolution [10,13] could benefit from our concept of a binarization driven deconvolution.

References

1. Bradley, D., Roth, G.: Adaptive thresholding using the integral image. J. Graph. GPU Game Tools **12**(2), 13–21 (2007)
2. Chan, T.F., Wong, C.K.: Total variation blind deconvolution. IEEE Trans. Image Process. **7**(3), 370–375 (1998)
3. Chen, X., He, X., Yang, J., Wu, Q.: An effective document image deblurring algorithm. In: 2011 IEEE Conference on Computer Vision and Pattern Recognition (CVPR), pp. 369–376. IEEE, June 2011
4. Cho, H., Wang, J., Lee, S.: Text image deblurring using text-specific properties. In: Fitzgibbon, A., Lazebnik, S., Perona, P., Sato, Y., Schmid, C. (eds.) ECCV 2012, Part V. LNCS, vol. 7576, pp. 524–537. Springer, Heidelberg (2012)
5. Cho, S., Wang, J., Lee, S.: Handling outliers in non-blind image deconvolution. In: IEEE International Conference on Computer Vision (ICCV), pp. 495–502 (2011)
6. Christlein, V., Bernecker, D., Hönig, F., Angelopoulou, E.: Writer identification and verification using GMM supervectors. In: IEEE Winter Conference on Applications of Computer Vision, pp. 998–1005 (2014)
7. Epshtein, B., Ofek, E., Wexler, Y.: Detecting text in natural scenes with stroke width transform. In: 2010 IEEE Conference on Computer Vision and Pattern Recognition (CVPR), pp. 2963–2970. IEEE, June 2010
8. Espana-Boquera, S., Castro-Bleda, M., Gorbe-Moya, J., Zamora-Martinez, F.: Improving offline handwritten text recognition with hybrid HMM/ANN models. IEEE Trans. Pattern Anal. Mach. Intell. **33**(4), 767–779 (2011)
9. Garz, A., Diem, M., Sablatnig, R.: Detecting text areas and decorative elements in ancient manuscripts. In: 2010 International Conference on Frontiers in Handwriting Recognition (ICFHR), pp. 176–181, November 2010
10. Ghesu, F.C., Köhler, T., Haase, S., Hornegger, J.: Guided image super-resolution: a new technique for photogeometric super-resolution in hybrid 3-D range imaging. In: Jiang, X., Hornegger, J., Koch, R. (eds.) GCPR 2014. LNCS, vol. 8753, pp. 227–238. Springer, Heidelberg (2014)
11. Goldstein, T., Osher, S.: The split Bregman method for L1-regularized problems. SIAM J. Imaging Sci. **2**(2), 323–343 (2009)
12. He, K., Sun, J., Tang, X.: Guided image filtering. IEEE Trans. Pattern Anal. Mach. Intell. **35**(6), 1397–1409 (2013)
13. Köhler, T., Jordan, J., Maier, A., Hornegger, J.: A unified bayesian approach to multi-frame super-resolution and single-image upsampling in multi-sensor imaging. In: Xie, X., Jones, M.W., Tam, G.K.L. (eds.) Proceedings of the British Machine Vision Conference (BMVC), pp. 143.1–143.12. BMVA Press (2015)

14. Kotera, J., Šroubek, F., Milanfar, P.: Blind deconvolution using alternating maximum a posteriori estimation with heavy-tailed priors. In: Wilson, R., Hancock, E., Bors, A., Smith, W. (eds.) CAIP 2013, Part II. LNCS, vol. 8048, pp. 59–66. Springer, Heidelberg (2013)
15. Levin, A., Weiss, Y., Durand, F., Freeman, W.: Understanding and evaluating blind deconvolution algorithms. In: 2009 IEEE Conference on Computer Vision and Pattern Recognition (CVPR), pp. 1964–1971. IEEE, June 2009
16. Li, T.H., Lii, K.S.: A joint estimation approach for two-tone image deblurring by blind deconvolution. IEEE Trans. Image Process. **11**(8), 847–858 (2002)
17. Oliveira, J.P., Bioucas-Dias, J.M., Figueiredo, M.A.: Adaptive total variation image deblurring: a majorization-minimization approach. Signal Process. **89**(9), 1683–1693 (2009)
18. Otsu, N.: A threshold selection method from gray-level histograms. IEEE Trans. Syst. Man Cybern. **9**(1), 62–66 (1979)
19. Pan, J., Hu, Z., Su, Z., Yang, M.H.: Deblurring text images via L0-regularized intensity and gradient prior. In: 2014 IEEE Conference on Computer Vision and Pattern Recognition (CVPR), pp. 2901–2908, June 2014
20. Sauvola, J., Pietikäinen, M.: Adaptive document image binarization. Pattern Recognit. **33**(2), 225–236 (2000)
21. Su, B., Lu, S., Tan, C.L.: Binarization of historical document images using the local maximum and minimum. In: 9th IAPR International Workshop on Document Analysis Systems, Boston, MA, pp. 159–165, June 2010
22. Yang, Y., Huang, S.: Image segmentation by fuzzy C-means clustering algorithm with a novel penalty term. Comput. Inf. **26**(1), 17–31 (2012)
23. Zhang, J.: An alternating minimization algorithm for binary image restoration. IEEE Trans. Image Process. **21**(2), 883–888 (2012)

Biomedical Image Analysis
and Applications

Unsupervised and Accurate Extraction of Primitive Unit Cells from Crystal Images

Niklas Mevenkamp[(✉)] and Benjamin Berkels

AICES Graduate School, RWTH Aachen University, Aachen, Germany
{mevenkamp,berkels}@aices.rwth-aachen.de

Abstract. We present a novel method for the unsupervised estimation of a primitive unit cell, i.e. a unit cell that can't be further simplified, from a crystal image. Significant peaks of the projective standard deviations of the image serve as candidate lattice vector angles. Corresponding fundamental periods are determined by clustering local minima of a periodicity energy. Robust unsupervised selection of the number of clusters is obtained from the likelihoods of multi-variance cluster models induced by the Akaike information criterion. Initial estimates for lattice angles and periods obtained in this manner are refined jointly using non-linear optimization. Results on both synthetic and experimental images show that the method is able to estimate complex primitive unit cells with sub-pixel accuracy, despite high levels of noise.

1 Introduction

The analysis and classification of the symmetry of crystalline structures is a fundamental necessity in various scientific fields, such as biology, chemistry and materials science [7,12,13,20]. Experimental analyses are often based on diffraction patterns, e.g. from X-rays [15] or electrons [21]. The most common technique for symmetry extraction from crystalline images is the classification of the Bragg reflections [3], i.e. relating the positions of image peaks in Fourier space with the lattice vectors of the crystal. This direct relation is the foundation for a variety of image processing techniques aimed at analyzing crystals or removing artifacts from corresponding images [14].

Recently, real-space methods have proven to be very powerful for a wide range of processing tasks on crystal images, such as grain segmentation [2], crystal defect localization [10], noise reduction [16] and sample drift correction [19]. All of these methods have in common that they exploit the (average) crystal symmetry in some way or another. Thus, they require prior knowledge on the geometry of the corresponding (perfect) crystals. Typically, the necessary crystal lattice parameters are estimated either manually or using Fourier-based techniques, which often also requires manual assessment in order to correct errors due to image distortion, noise and ambiguities. Thus, an entirely unsupervised use of these otherwise automated processing methods is usually not possible.

In [19], Sang and LeBeau proposed a new real-space method for lattice angle estimation based on *projective standard deviations* (PSD). While the method

© Springer International Publishing Switzerland 2015
J. Gall et al. (Eds.): GCPR 2015, LNCS 9358, pp. 105–116, 2015.
DOI: 10.1007/978-3-319-24947-6_9

outperforms Fourier methods in accuracy and robustness to noise, it still needs manual input to relate PSD peaks with the corresponding lattice directions.

The goal of this paper is to overcome the necessity for manual input in crystal lattice extraction from images. To this end, we propose a novel unsupervised real-space method to estimate primitive unit cells from crystal images. In particular, we show how fundamental periods can be estimated robustly from 1D signals.

2   Methods

A crystal can be characterized by the positions and types of its elements, i.e. $\mathscr{C} \subset \mathbb{R}^d \times \mathbb{R}$. In case $d = 3$, the elements are typically atoms and their type is given by the atomic number. An important property of crystals is their symmetry. It allows for a decomposition of $\mathscr{C}$ into a *unit cell* $U = \{v_1, \ldots, v_d\} \subset \mathbb{R}^d$, which defines the repeating pattern of the crystal, and the corresponding *motif* $M = M_\mathscr{C}(U) = \{(m_1, c_1), \ldots, (m_{n_U}, c_{n_U})\} \subset \mathbb{R}^d \times \mathbb{R}$, which defines the relative positions and types of the $n_U \in \mathbb{N}$ elements within the unit cell U. This results in the following representation of the crystal:

$$\mathscr{C}(U, M) = \left\{ \left(m_j + \sum_{i=1}^{d} z_i v_i, c_j \right) \,\Big|\, z_i \in \mathbb{Z} \text{ for } 1 \leq i \leq d,\ 1 \leq j \leq n_U \right\}. \quad (1)$$

Note that this decomposition is not unique. For any given crystal $\mathscr{C}$,

$$\mathcal{U}_\mathscr{C} = \{U \subset \mathbb{R}^d \,|\, \#(U) = d \wedge \exists M \subset \mathbb{R}^d \times \mathbb{R} : \#(M) < \infty \wedge \mathscr{C}(U, M) = \mathscr{C}\} \quad (2)$$

denotes the set of all of its unit cells. Then

$$\mathcal{U}_\mathscr{C}^p = \{U \in \mathcal{U} \,|\, \#(M_\mathscr{C}(U)) = \min_{U' \in \mathcal{U}_\mathscr{C}} \#(M_\mathscr{C}(U'))\} \quad (3)$$

is the set of *primitive* unit cells. The Bravais lattice

$$V_\mathscr{C} = \left\{ \sum_{i=1}^{d} z_i v_i \,\Big|\, \{v_1, \ldots, v_d\} \in \mathcal{U}_\mathscr{C}^p, z_1, \ldots, z_d \in \mathbb{Z} \right\} \quad (4)$$

is called *crystal lattice*, i.e. its elements are lattice points. Since $0 \in V_\mathscr{C}$, any $v \in V_\mathscr{C}$ can be interpreted as a vector connecting two lattice points. Such a vector is called *lattice vector*. For an introduction to this terminology from a mineral science point of view, we refer to [18]; for an illustration see Fig. 1.

$\mathcal{U}_\mathscr{C}$ can also be characterized by

$$\mathcal{U}_\mathscr{C} = \{\{v_1, \ldots, v_d\} \subset V_\mathscr{C} \,|\, v_1, \ldots, v_d \text{ linear independent}\}. \quad (5)$$

Furthermore, $\{v_1, \ldots, v_d\} \in \mathcal{U}_\mathscr{C}$ is primitive if and only if the parallelepiped (or a parallelogram in two dimensions) spanned by $v_1, \ldots, v_d$ contains no lattice point $v \in V_\mathscr{C}$ other than its corner points.

In this paper, we discuss how to extract a primitive unit cell from a two-dimensional experimental image of a projected crystal. The original crystal is three dimensional and during acquisition its orientation is manually refined until

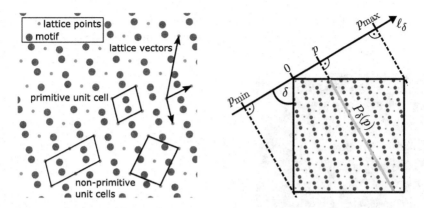

Fig. 1. Left: crystal lattice (red dots) with a minimal motif of size two (pairs of blue dots); Right: illustration of the points $P_\delta(p)$ in the image projected onto the line ℓ_p (Color figure online)

the desired projection - orthogonal to one of its unit cell vectors - is retrieved. This results in a crystal $\mathscr{C} \subset \mathbb{R}^2 \times \mathbb{R}$. In the following, we assume that the projection and the modality of the crystal image retain a unique identification of the elements in the crystal $\mathscr{C}$ and a unique relation to the image intensities.

Then, in an ideal setting, such an image $f : \Omega = (0,1)^2 \to \mathbb{R}$ fulfills

$$f(x + z_1 v_1 + z_2 v_2) = f(x) \ \forall x \in \Omega \ \forall z_1, z_2 \in \mathbb{Z} : x + z_1 v_1 + z_2 v_2 \in \Omega \qquad (6)$$

for any two lattice vectors $v_1, v_2 \in V_{\mathscr{C}}$. Thus, lattice vectors are minimizers (in the ideal setting also roots) of the following energy:

$$E(v_1, v_2) = \sum_{(z_1, z_2) \in \mathcal{Z}} \int_{x \in \tilde{\Omega}} (f(x) - f(x + z_1 v_1 + z_2 v_2))^2 \ dx, \qquad (7)$$

where $\mathcal{Z} = \{(1,0), (0,1), (1,1)\}$ and $\tilde{\Omega} \subset \Omega$ has to be chosen in a suitable way for the desired lattice vectors, which will be addressed later. In other words, $v_1, v_2 \in V_{\mathscr{C}} \Leftrightarrow E(v_1, v_2) = 0$. Moreover, the following non-parallel lattice vectors

$$(v_1, v_2) \in \operatorname*{arg\,min}_{(u_1, u_2) \in \{E=0\} \cap \{u_1 \times u_2 \neq 0\}} |u_1| + |u_2| \qquad (8)$$

form a primitive unit cell, since the parallelogram spanned by two shortest lattice vectors cannot contain any lattice points other than its corner points.

While obtaining a primitive unit cell may seem trivial at this point, it turns out to be very challenging in practice without manual input. Noise, image distortions and crystal defects result in the energy E being non-zero except for $v_1, v_2 = 0$ or $|v_1|, |v_2| > \operatorname{diam}\Omega$. Nevertheless, due to the regularity imposed by the integration, $\{v_1, v_2\} \in \mathcal{U}_{\mathscr{C}}$ still implies $\nabla E(v_1, v_2) = 0$. However, the reverse implication is not true in general. Figure 2 illustrates one potential pitfall. There are two types of local minima. The one with larger energy corresponds to the spacing between diagonally neighboring atoms, but the actual lattice points skip one row and belong to twice the spacing, i.e. the minima with smaller energy.

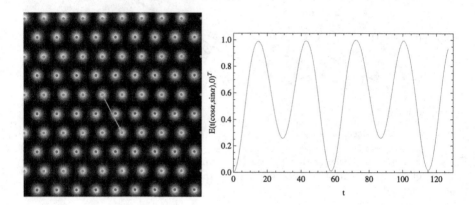

Fig. 2. Left: artificial crystal lattice (magenta dots) with a motif of size two (a magenta/blue dot pair is a motif copy). Right: normalized energy (7) for $v_1 = t(\cos\alpha, \sin\alpha)^T, v_2 = 0$ as a function of t with $\alpha = -61.95°$ (green vector) (Color figure online)

Furthermore, $\nabla E(v_1, v_2) = 0$ implies $\nabla E(n_1 v_1, n_2 v_2) = 0$ for all $n_1, n_2 \in \mathbb{Z}$. Thus, it is likely that minimization of E converges to a local minimum that either does not correspond to a unit cell at all, or not to a primitive one.

In the following, we will discuss a method that allows for an efficient estimation of primitive lattice vectors from E based on a sophisticated strategy for finding the desired local minima. The strategy is split into three parts: approximation of (1) *lattice vector angles* and (2) *fundamental periods*, and (3) refinement of the resulting approximate primitive unit cell.

2.1   Real-Space Analysis of Lattice Vector Angles

Any $\alpha \in [0, 2\pi]$ such that there is a $t \in (0, \infty)$ with $te_\alpha = t(\cos\alpha, \sin\alpha)^T \in V_{\mathscr{C}}$ is called *lattice vector angle*. In the following, we briefly recall a recent real-space method to estimate lattice vector angles by Sang and LeBeau [19]. Let $\pi_\delta(x) = (x_1 \cos\delta + x_2 \sin\delta)\, e_\delta$ be the projection of a point $x \in \Omega$ onto the line $\ell_\delta(p) = p e_\delta$ and $P_\delta(p) = \pi_\delta^{-1}(p)$ the points in Ω that are projected onto $\ell_\delta(p)$ (see Fig. 1). Then, the average intensity of the image projected onto $\ell_\delta(p)$ is

$$A_\delta(p) = \fint_{P_\delta(p)} f \, \mathrm{d}x \text{ for } |P_\delta(p)| > 0 \text{ and zero else .} \tag{9}$$

Here, for $B \subset \mathbb{R}^d$, $\fint_B f \, \mathrm{d}x = \frac{1}{|B|} \int_B f \, \mathrm{d}x$ is the integral mean. Let $x_1^c = (0,0)^T$, $x_2^c = (0,0)^T$, $x_3^c = (1,0)^T$, $x_4^c = (1,1)^T$ denote the corners of $\Omega = (0,1)^2$ and $p_{\min} = \min_{i=1,\dots,4} \pi(x_i^c)$, $p_{\max} = \max_{i=1,\dots,4} \pi(x_i^c)$ the lower and upper bounds of their projections onto ℓ_δ. Then, using the interval $[p_{\min}, p_{\max}]$ as a bound for the support of A_δ, we define the *projective standard deviation* as (cf. [19])

$$\mathrm{psd}(\delta) = \sqrt{\int_{p_{\min}}^{p_{\max}} (A_\delta(p) - \mu_\delta)^2 \, \mathrm{d}p}, \quad \mu_\delta = \int_{p_{\min}}^{p_{\max}} A_\delta(p) \, \mathrm{d}p. \tag{10}$$

Significant peaks $(\delta_1, \ldots, \delta_n)$ of the signal psd : $[0, 2\pi] \to \mathbb{R}_{\geq 0}$ are indicators that the image f is periodic along the perpendicular directions, i.e. $\alpha_i = \delta_i + \frac{\pi}{2}$, $i = 1, \ldots, n$ are lattice vector angles: As in the 3D case, projecting a 2D crystal along any of its lattice vectors, i.e. onto a line perpendicular to the lattice vector, yields a periodic signal, which is of high standard deviation.

Let us point out that the psd alone does not suffice to select two lattice vector angles. Consider the example shown in Fig. 3. Selecting the two highest peaks yields the lattice vector angles $\alpha_1 = 180°$ (green vector) and $\alpha_2 = 116.5°$ (blue vector) or $\alpha_2 = 243°$ (cyan vector). Lattice vectors pointing in these directions cannot form a primitive unit cell. Possible pairs resulting in primitive unit cells in this case are the blue & purple, purple & green, green & red, red & cyan and purple & red vectors, while only the latter results in a primitive unit cell satisfying (8). Since Sang and LeBeau [19] do not address this issue, we propose to select a suitable pair of lattice vector angles in an unsupervised fashion by finding one that satisfies (8). However, this requires knowledge of the corresponding fundamental periods.

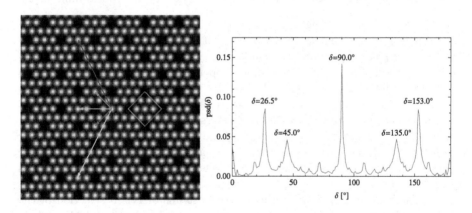

Fig. 3. Left: hex lattice with vacancies, vectors $T_{\alpha_i} e_{\alpha_i}$, $i = 1, \ldots, 5$ (blue, purple, green, red, cyan), primitive unit cell (purple/red box); Right: psd for $\delta \in [0, \pi]$ (Color figure online)

2.2 Real-Space Analysis of Fundamental Periods

For any lattice vector angle α, let $\mathcal{T}_\alpha = \{t \in (0, \infty) \,|\, t e_\alpha \in V_\mathscr{C}\}$. Then, the *fundamental period* is $T_\alpha = \min \mathcal{T}_\alpha$. In the following, we props a method to estimate T_α from an image f of the corresponding crystal $\mathscr{C}$.

We consider the one-dimensional energy

$$E_\alpha(t) = \fint_{\Omega_\alpha(t)} (f(x + t e_\alpha) - f(x))^2 \, dx, \tag{11}$$

where $\Omega_\alpha(t) = \{x \in \Omega \,|\, x + t e_\alpha \in \Omega\}$. Assuming that f is exactly periodic along the direction e_α yields $T_\alpha = E_\alpha^{-1}(0) \setminus \{0\}$. Thus, in an ideal situation, we have $T_\alpha = \min(E_\alpha^{-1}(0) \setminus \{0\})$. In practice, however, distortions and noise in the image f, as well as errors in the angle α prohibit such a classification of the fundamental period. Still, elements of T_α should be local minimizers of E_α. Let

$$S_\alpha = \{t \in (0, \infty) \,|\, \exists \delta > 0 \,\forall s \in [t - \delta, t + \delta] \setminus \{t\} : E_\alpha(t) < E_\alpha(s)\} \tag{12}$$

denote the set of isolated local minima of E_α except for $t = 0$. Unfortunately, as illustrated in Fig. 2, possibly $(\min S_\alpha) e_\alpha \notin V_{\mathscr{C}}$. Thus, we need a robust way to select the desired local minimum from S_α.

Let us assume that all errors (image noise, distortions, discretization) are small enough that the energy E_α at least fulfills the following properties:

I   The (numerical) fundamental period of the signal E_α is close to T_α
II Multiples of T_α lie near local minimizers of E_α
III The local minimizer with smallest energy is roughly a multiple of T_α
IV Distances between energies of local minimizers close to multiples of T_α are smaller than those between them and the energies of other local minimizers.

Note that in an ideal setting, these properties are a consequence of (6).

Property I implies that $E_\alpha(S_\alpha)$ may be split in $k \leq \#(\{t \in S_\alpha \,|\, t \leq T_\alpha\})$ clusters $C_1, \ldots, C_k$ corresponding to the different types of local minima in each fundamental period of E_α. Moreover, due to Properties II–IV, the cluster containing $\min E_\alpha(S_\alpha)$ also contains $E_\alpha(T_\alpha)$, but no $E_\alpha(t)$ with $t \notin T_\alpha$. Thus, T_α can be estimated as $\hat{T}_\alpha = \min(E^{-1}(C_i) \cap S_\alpha)$, where $1 \leq i \leq k$ with $\min E_\alpha(S_\alpha) \in C_i$.

The proper choice of the number of clusters is crucial in this context: on the one hand, if k is chosen too small, one risks that a local minimum corresponding to a period $t < T_\alpha$ ends up in the same cluster as $E(T_\alpha)$, which implies $\hat{T}_\alpha \neq T_\alpha$; on the other hand, if k is chosen too large, one risks that $E_\alpha(T_\alpha)$ does not end up in the same cluster as $\min E_\alpha(S_\alpha)$, also resulting in $\hat{T}_\alpha \neq T_\alpha$.

To this end, we propose a method for robust unsupervised selection of the number of clusters k. Our approach is based on work by Pelleg and Moore [17]. They use a Bayesian information criterion (BIC) under an identical spherical Gaussian assumption on the cluster formation to formulate an unsupervised variant of k-means, known as X-means. Note that G-means [11], which has been shown to outperform X-means, especially in higher dimensions, is not suitable for our setting, because the total number of data points $\#(S_\alpha)$ is very small.

We base our analysis on the Akaike information criterion $AIC_k = -2\hat{L}_k + 2p_k$ [1], where $\hat{L}_k = \hat{L}_k(S) = \max_\theta L_k(S|M_k(\theta))$ is the maximum of the log-likelihood

$$L_k(S|M_k(\theta)) = \log \prod_{j=1}^n P(x_j|M_k(\theta)) = \sum_{j=1}^n \log P(x_j|M_k(\theta)) \tag{13}$$

of the data $S = \{x_1, \ldots, x_n\}$ given a model $M_k(\theta)$ of the data, which induces point probabilities $P(x_j | M_k(\theta))$. As pointed out in [6], AIC has theoretical and practical advantages over BIC. For instance, it allows for the evaluation of actual model likelihoods, allowing for more sophisticated strategies to select a proper k than simply minimizing the value of the criterion, as is usually done with BIC.

In our setting, let $M_k(\theta)$ model the set $S_\alpha = \{x_1, \ldots, x_n\}$ as k one-dimensional Gaussian distributions with means $\mu_1, \ldots, \mu_k$, $\mu_i \neq \mu_l$, $i \neq l$, variances $\sigma_1^2, \ldots, \sigma_k^2$, and relative frequencies $\frac{n_1}{n}, \ldots, \frac{n_k}{n}$. Then

$$P(x_j | M_k(\theta)) = \frac{n_{(j)}}{n} \left(2\pi\sigma_{(j)}^2\right)^{-1/2} \exp\left\{-|x_j - \mu_{(j)}|^2 / (2\sigma_{(j)}^2)\right\}. \tag{14}$$

Here, $(j) = \min\{i \in \{1, \ldots, k\} \mid |x_j - \mu_i|^2 \leq |x_j - \mu_l|^2 \ \forall l \neq i\}$. Usually, there is only one such i. Since $n_k = n - \sum_{i=1}^{k-1} n_i$, the set of free model parameters is $\theta = (n_1, \ldots, n_{k-1}, \mu_1, \ldots, \mu_k, \sigma_1, \ldots, \sigma_k)$. The maximum-likelihood estimator $\hat{\mu}_i = \frac{1}{n_i} \sum_{x \in C_i} x$ is obtained as a result from the k-means clustering for each cluster C_i. The maximum-likelihood estimator of the variance is $\hat{\sigma}_i^2 = \frac{1}{n_i} \sum_{x \in C_i} (x - \hat{\mu}_i)^2$. This leads to the following expression for the maximum log-likelihood of S:

$$\hat{L}_k(S) = \sum_{i=1}^{k} \left[n_i \log \frac{n_i}{n} - \frac{1}{2} n_i \left(\log\left(2\pi\hat{\sigma}_i^2\right) + 1\right)\right]. \tag{15}$$

In this setting, the number of free parameters is $p_k = 3k - 1$.

As pointed out by Akaike, the likelihood of the model M_k given the data S is $\mathcal{L}(M_k | S) = \exp\{(AIC_{k_{\min}} - AIC_k)/2\}$, where $k_{\min} = \arg\min_k AIC_k$. Note that $\mathcal{L}(M_{k_{\min}} | S) = 1$. Models with a likelihood not significantly less than 1 cannot be discarded with confidence. In case two or more models cannot be discarded, we suggest to prefer models assuming fewer clusters in order to increase the probability that the desired local minimum $E_\alpha(T_\alpha)$ is assigned to the same cluster as the global minimum $\min E_\alpha(S_\alpha)$. Thus we suggest to choose the optimal number of clusters as

$$k^* = \min\{k \mid \mathcal{L}(M_k | S) > \tau\}. \tag{16}$$

We used the threshold $\tau = 0.1$ for all presented experiments and found that in the regarded cases the result was not sensitive to this particular choice.

Using the unsupervised k-means clustering described above, we can assign a fundamental period T_α to any given lattice vector angle α. Let $\alpha_1, \ldots, \alpha_n$ be candidate lattice vector angles estimated as described in Sect. 2.1 and $V^* = \{T_{\alpha_1} e_{\alpha_1}, \ldots, T_{\alpha_n} e_{\alpha_n}\} \subset V_{\mathscr{C}}$. Finally, in accordance with (8), we estimate the primitive unit cell by

$$U = \{v_1, v_2\}, \quad v_1 = \arg\min_{u \in V^*} \tfrac{1}{2} |u|^2, \quad v_2 = \arg\min_{u \in V^* \setminus \{v_1\}} \tfrac{1}{2} |u|^2. \tag{17}$$

2.3   Local Refinement of Lattice Vectors

The methods described above yield a good approximation of a primitive unit cell $U = \{v_1, v_2\} \in \mathcal{U}_{\mathscr{C}}^p$. However, by first estimating the angles of the desired lattice vectors followed by an estimation of their magnitudes, errors in the angles α_1, α_2 amplify the error in the magnitudes $|v_1|, |v_2|$. Nevertheless, the initial guess v_1, v_2 is expected to yield local convergence of iterative minimization of (7) to the desired local minimum. This minimization can be performed efficiently in practice, since the discretization of (7) is a sum of squares, which allows for Gauss-Newton type algorithms to be used for numerical minimization. Finally, $\tilde{\Omega} = \{x \in \Omega \mid \text{dist}(x, \partial\Omega) > \max\{|v_1|, |v_2|, |v_1 + v_2|\} + \epsilon\}$ can be used as the admissible set, with a fairly small ϵ (e.g. three times the pixels size), since the solution is not expected to be more than a few pixels away from the initial guess.

3   Results and Discussion

Here, we show unsupervised analyses of exemplary crystal structures, using both artificially created images, as well as electron micrographs acquired by scanning transmission electron microscopy (STEM) [4]. In the following figures, the *origin* of any crystal lattice is aligned manually with one of the atoms in the unit cell. Also, motif recognition is not part of the proposed method and was done manually to illustrate the full geometry of the crystals. The lattice and the motive is only overlayed in the lower half of each image to facilitate a visual confirmation of the correctness of the estimated lattice parameters.

Figure 4 shows an artificial rectangular crystal lattice with three 2D Gaussian bells of similar intensity in each primitive unit cell, placed along the horizontal lattice direction. The proposed estimator for the number of clusters yields the correct result ($k = 3$) for E_α with $\alpha = 0$, even though the absolute values of the local minima are extremely close to each other.

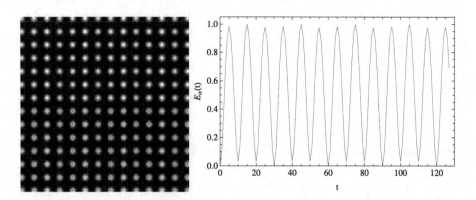

Fig. 4. Left: rectangular crystal lattice (magenta dots) with a motif of three very similar Gaussian bells placed along the horizontal lattice direction (magenta/blue/green dot triples); Right: $E_\alpha(t)$ (11) for $\alpha = 0$, i.e. the horizontal lattice direction (Color figure online)

The accuracy of the proposed method is assessed on four artificially created crystal lattices (cf. Fig. 5) with known parameters and varying levels of

Gaussian noise. The resulting absolute errors in Table 1 show sub-pixel accuracy in all cases except for the "Bumps3" image in Fig. 5 with 50 % noise standard deviation. In this case, the combination of strong noise and low contrast between local minima constitutes a violation of Property IV, resulting in a third of the period to be estimated - hence the large error. Note that a classical Fourier analysis, e.g. selecting the two brightest non-collinear peaks in Fourier space, does not yield useful results for the images shown in Fig. 5.

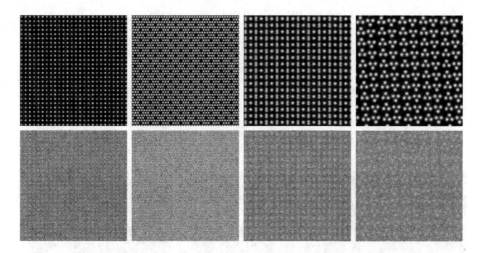

Fig. 5. Artificial crystal lattice images; top row: ideal crystals (from left to right: "Bumps3", "HexVacancy", "SingleDouble", "Triples2"); bottom row: same images plus Gaussian noise with a standard deviation of 50 % of the maximum intensity

Figure 6 shows experimental crystal images acquired using STEM. These images exhibit all artifacts inherent to this particular acquisition technique, namely intensity noise, small scale distortions and large scale sample drift. In the left image, along the roughly diagonal ($\alpha \approx -60°$) and vertical lattice directions, there is a horizontal offset between neighboring atoms (slight in the former and more apparent in the latter case). The proposed estimator (17) correctly identifies this and chooses the horizontal and vertical lattice vectors - the latter with a period that skips each second row of atoms (leaving the atoms in the other rows as part of the motif). In the right image, a similar difficulty is tackled, where a translation along the diagonal direction leads to high-auto correlation.

In [16], we recently proposed a method to denoise crystal images by non-local averaging over periodic lattices. This method showed a substantial performance increase over non-local averaging techniques [5,8] without such prior information. However, the accuracy of our previously proposed approach to unsupervised lattice vector estimation is limited due to its Fourier space lattice angle estimation and likely unable to cope with complex motifs due to the employed period estimation via real-space sine fitting. Experiments performed for a selection of

Table 1. Errors in the lattice vectors detected by our method for the images from Fig. 5. $\sigma/\max f$ is the noise standard deviation relative to the maximal image intensity

Crystal	$\sigma/\max f$	$\lvert v_1^* - v_1 \rvert$	$\lvert v_2^* - v_2 \rvert$
Bumps3	0	2.60×10^{-8}	4.13×10^{-8}
Bumps3	10 %	0.136	0.0670
Bumps3	50 %	0.425	22.3
HexVacancy	0	3.61×10^{-8}	1.50×10^{-7}
HexVacancy	10 %	0.218	0.408
HexVacancy	50 %	0.292	0.153
SingleDouble	0	2.20×10^{-10}	1.30×10^{-9}
SingleDouble	10 %	0.0937	0.0830
SingleDouble	50 %	0.360	0.306
Triples2	0	2.12×10^{-9}	8.84×10^{-9}
Triples2	10 %	0.0129	0.0240
Triples2	50 %	0.0172	0.00900

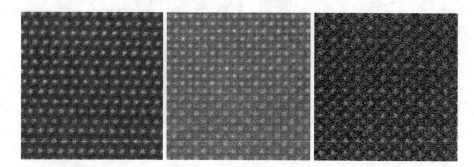

Fig. 6. Experimentally acquired STEM images and estimated crystal lattices (magenta dots) and motifs (magenta/blue dot pairs); STEM images courtesy of P.M. Voyles (Color figure online)

images from [16] indicate that the peak signal-to-noise ratio (PSNR) of the denoised image can be increased by more than 1 dB just by using the proposed real-space lattice vector estimation within the non-local denoising framework.

4   Conclusions

We have proposed a method for the unsupervised extraction of primitive unit cells from crystal images. It involves the selection of desired local minima of a periodicity energy by means of unsupervised clustering. Building on X-means [17], an improved strategy for the unsupervised selection of the number of clusters was proposed, using an extended data model considering clusters of different variances, and based on true model likelihoods derived from AIC.

Results on synthetic and experimental images demonstrate that the clustering robustly selects the desired local minimum and that primitive unit cells are estimated with sub-pixel accuracy, even in the presence of strong noise and ambiguities due to strong auto-correlation of the image along lattice vectors and inside the unit cells.

The proposed method offers the potential to turn powerful real-space processing methods for crystal images requiring prior knowledge about crystal symmetries into unsupervised methods. Lastly, let us point out that the proposed estimator for the fundamental frequency also suggests itself for pitch detection problems in sound analysis [9,22].

Acknowledgments. The authors would like to thank P.M. Voyles for providing experimental STEM images.

References

1. Akaike, H.: A new look at the statistical model identification. IEEE Trans. Autom. Control **19**(6), 716–723 (1974)
2. Boerdgen, M., Berkels, B., Rumpf, M., Cremers, D.: Convex relaxation for grain segmentation at atomic scale. In: Fellner, D. (ed.) Vision, Modeling and Visualization, pp. 179–186. Eurographics Association (2010)
3. Bragg, W.L.: The determination of parameters in crystal structures by means of fourier series. Proc. Roy. Soc. Lond. A Math. Phys. Eng. Sci. **123**, 537–559 (1929)
4. Browning, N., Chisholm, M., Pennycook, S.: Atomic-resolution chemical analysis using a scanning transmission electron microscope. Nature **366**(6451), 143–146 (1993)
5. Buades, A., Coll, B., Morel, J.M.: Image denoising methods: a new nonlocal principle. SIAM Rev. **52**(1), 113–147 (2010)
6. Burnham, K.P., Anderson, D.R.: Multimodel inference understanding AIC and BIC in model selection. Sociol. Methods Res. **33**(2), 261–304 (2004)
7. Cava, R., Ji, H., Fuccillo, M., Gibson, Q., Hor, Y.: Crystal structure and chemistry of topological insulators. J. Mater. Chem. C **1**(19), 3176–3189 (2013)
8. Dabov, K., Foi, A., Katkovnik, V., Egiazarian, K.: Image denoising by sparse 3-D transform-domain collaborative filtering. IEEE Trans. Image Process. **16**(8), 2080–2095 (2007)
9. De La Cuadra, P., Master, A., Sapp, C.: Efficient pitch detection techniques for interactive music. In: Proceedings of the 2001 International Computer Music Conference, pp. 403–406 (2001)
10. Elsey, M., Wirth, B.: Fast automated detection of crystal distortion and crystal defects in polycrystal images. Multiscale Model. Simul. **12**(1), 1–24 (2014)
11. Hamerly, G., Elkan, C.: Learning the k in k-means. In: Neural Information Processing Systems, p. 2003. MIT Press (2003)
12. Hanson, M.A., Roth, C.B., Jo, E., Griffith, M.T., Scott, F.L., Reinhart, G., Desale, H., Clemons, B., Cahalan, S.M., Schuerer, S.C., et al.: Crystal structure of a lipid g protein-coupled receptor. Science **335**(6070), 851–855 (2012)
13. Kimoto, K., Asaka, T., Yu, X., Nagai, T., Matsui, Y., Ishizuka, K.: Local crystal structure analysis with several picometer precision using scanning transmission electron microscopy. Ultramicroscopy **110**(7), 778–782 (2010)

14. Klug, A.: Image analysis and reconstruction in the electron microscopy of biological macromolecules. Chemica Scripta **14**, 245–256 (1978–1979)
15. Klug, H.P., Alexander, L.E., et al.: X-ray Diffraction Procedures, vol. 2. Wiley, New York (1954)
16. Mevenkamp, N., Binev, P., Dahmen, W., Voyles, P.M., Yankovich, A.B., Berkels, B.: Poisson noise removal from high-resolution stem images based on periodic block matching. Adv. Struct. Chem. Imag. **1**(1), 1–19 (2015)
17. Pelleg, D., Moore, A.W.: X-means: extending k-means with efficient estimation of the number of clusters. In: ICML, pp. 727–734 (2000)
18. Putnis, A.: An Introduction to Mineral Sciences. Cambridge University Press, Cambridge (1992)
19. Sang, X., LeBeau, J.M.: Revolving scanning transmission electron microscopy: correcting sample drift distortion without prior knowledge. Ultramicroscopy **138**, 28–35 (2014)
20. Wang, Z., Song, Y., Shi, H., Wang, Z., Chen, Z., Tian, H., Chen, G., Guo, J., Yang, H., Li, J.: Microstructure and ordering of iron vacancies in the superconductor system k y fe x se 2 as seen via transmission electron microscopy. Phys. Rev. B **83**(14), 140505 (2011)
21. Williams, D.B., Carter, C.B.: The Transmission Electron Microscope. Springer, New York (1996)
22. Zeng, Y.M., Wu, Z.Y., Liu, H.B., Zhou, L.: Modified amdf pitch detection algorithm. In: 2003 International Conference on Machine Learning and Cybernetics, vol. 1, pp. 470–473. IEEE (2003)

Copula Archetypal Analysis

Dinu Kaufmann[(⊠)], Sebastian Keller, and Volker Roth

Department of Mathematics and Computer Science,
University of Basel, Basel, Switzerland
{dinu.kaufmann,sebastianmathias.keller,volker.roth}@unibas.ch

Abstract. We present an extension of classical archetypal analysis (AA). It is motivated by the observation that classical AA is not invariant against strictly monotone increasing transformations. Establishing such an invariance is desirable since it makes AA independent of the chosen measure: representing a data set in meters or log(meters) should lead to approximately the same archetypes. The desired invariance is achieved by introducing a semi-parametric Gaussian copula. This ensures the desired invariance and makes AA more robust against outliers and missing values. Furthermore, our framework can deal with mixed discrete/continuous data, which certainly is the most widely encountered type of data in real world applications. Since the proposed extension is presented in form of a preprocessing step, updating existing classical AA models is especially effortless.

1 Introduction

Archetypal Analysis (AA), introduced by Cutler and Breiman in 1994 [5], approximates the convex hull of a set of multivariate observations with a small set of vertex points. These vertex points are called archetypes, because all observations can be approximated by a convex mixture of these vertex points plus a noise term.

An example from biology, presented in [18], makes this concept intuitively comprehensible: from a total of 108 species, Norberg and Rayner's study of bat wings [15] identified $K = 3$ archetypes which explain – to some degree – almost all different species. The archetypal bats were found as to outperform all other bats at a single given task, see Fig. 1.

The Problem with Classical Archetypal Analysis. Finding the archetypes is a geometric concept that crucially depends on the representation of the observations in $\mathbb{R}^p$. One major problem in classical AA, which we like to address, is its sensitivity to monotone transformations of the coordinate axes: it can make a huge difference if one measures a certain property for example in meters or log(meters). This problem is illustrated in Fig. 2: After a transformation of the original data by a strictly monotone increasing transformation, the lower left panel would suggest a total of four archetypes, one located at each corner. Whereas the lower right panel, reconstructed by a semi-parametric copula, identifies approximately the same three archetypes as in the original data.

© Springer International Publishing Switzerland 2015
J. Gall et al. (Eds.): GCPR 2015, LNCS 9358, pp. 117–128, 2015.
DOI: 10.1007/978-3-319-24947-6_10

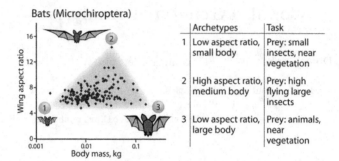

Fig. 1. Wing aspect ratio of bats versus their body mass [18]. Three archetypes were identified; their inferred tasks are listed in the above table. The convex hull is the border of the light blue area. Figure from [18].

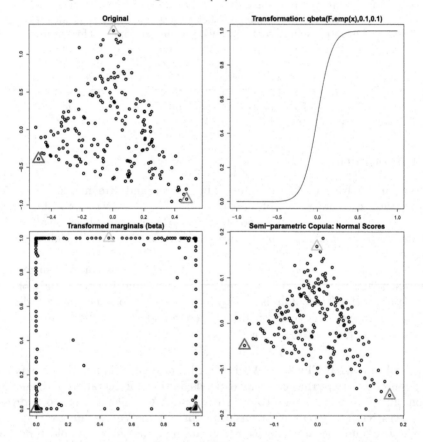

Fig. 2. Upper left panel: 200 points sampled as (noisy) convex mixtures of 3 archetypes (triangle symbols) in two dimensions. Upper right: Strictly monotone transformation applied to each dimension. Lower left: Transformed datapoints and location of the original archetypes after transformation. Lower right: Reconstruction of the transformed dataset by copula-PCA.

From a probabilistic viewpoint, classical AA can be seen as a linear latent variable model: The n observations are described as convex mixtures of K archetypes arranged as the rows of the matrix Z. The mixing components sum to one, i.e. $\sum_{i=1}^{K} \alpha_i = \mathbf{1}^t \boldsymbol{\alpha} = 1$. In a probabilistic archetype model we might assume that $\boldsymbol{a} \sim \mathrm{Dir}_K(\boldsymbol{\alpha})$, and the observations $\boldsymbol{x} \in \mathbb{R}^p$ scatter around the means $Z^t \boldsymbol{a}$ according to isotropic Gaussian noise with variance η, see also the model proposed in [17]:

$$\boldsymbol{x} | Z, \boldsymbol{a} \sim N(Z^t \boldsymbol{a}, \eta I_p). \tag{1}$$

As long as only Euclidean lengths are concerned, one might argue that the sensitivity to monotone transformations is a problem of somewhat artificial nature, but in high-dimensional real-world applications with features of different types and different domains, the above representation problem indeed defines an inherent limitation of classical AA.

Extending the Model. As a means for overcoming this representational problem we introduce a copula based preprocessing step thus making AA invariant against all (strictly) monotone increasing transformations: being inherently invariant against such strictly monotone increasing transformations, copula densities prove to be *exactly* the invariance class needed for this task.

Presumably the most elegant solution for the problem of inferring the archetypes would be to complement the model with priors over all (hyper-) parameters and analyse the posterior distribution of the archetypes in a fully Bayesian fashion. In general, we think this would be feasible but this is not the main focus of this work. Instead, we would like to maintain a probabilistic "flavour", but we still want to make use of existing highly efficient algorithms for identifying archetypes by minimising the negative log-likelihood

$$\sum_{i=1}^{n} (\boldsymbol{x}_i - Z^t \boldsymbol{a}_i)^2 = \| X - AZ \|_F^2 \tag{2}$$

under the additional constraint that the archetypes themselves are convex mixtures of the observations: $\boldsymbol{z} = X\boldsymbol{b}$, with $\mathbf{1}^t \boldsymbol{b} = 1$, or, in matrix form $Z = BX$. Formally, this defines a non-negative matrix factorisation problem, and efficient solution techniques have been proposed in the literature. The main computational idea in these models is to pre-select points on the convex hull by computing the convex hull in two-dimensional projections (e.g. pairwise PCA projections or random projections), see [1,3,11,23]. Models of this kind have been successfully applied to image collections [6,22], document collections [4], economic market studies [13], game strategies [19] etc. Extensions of archetypal analysis to nonlinear kernel models have been proposed in [2], probabilistic generalisations for exponential family models appeared in [17], and the use of sparse regression models that offer an elegant solution for the problem of automatically selecting the number of archetypes have been proposed in [16] (Fig. 2).

2 Copula Archetypal Analysis

In this section we show how to overcome the representational problem by embedding archetypal analysis in a copula framework [10,14]. The framework includes a strictly monotone increasing mapping h: $\boldsymbol{y} = h(\boldsymbol{x})$, $\mathbb{R}^p \mapsto \mathbb{R}^p$, thereby treating X as latent variables, which are estimated on the oberservations Y, as shown in the graphical model in Fig. 3. The formulation with latent variables allows to re-use existing algorithms for recovering the archetypes.

Sklar's theorem [20] allows the decomposition of every continuous multivariate cumulative distribution function (cdf) $F(Y_1, \ldots, Y_p)$ into it's univariate marginals $F_1(Y_1), \ldots, F_p(Y_p)$ and a copula C comprising the dependency pattern only. More precisely, the theorem states the existence and uniqueness of a copula C such that

$$F(Y_1, \ldots, Y_p) = C(U_1, \ldots, U_p), \tag{3}$$

where the uniformly distributed $U_j = F_j(Y_j)$ are generated with the probability integral transformation of the univariate marginal cdfs. In the following, we will look for a parametric copula C, which suitably represents the dependency structure in the space of U.

Motivation for Gaussian Copula. A parametric copula C is used in order to define a likelihood function $l(\theta; \{\boldsymbol{y}_i\}_{i=1}^n)$, which makes it possible to estimate the latent vectors $\boldsymbol{x}_i$. Subsequently these are used as input for classical archetype reconstruction. A particularly simple choice of a dependency structure is a Gaussian copula model C_Σ, which inherently implies a latent space by transforming $\tilde{X}_j = \Phi^{-1}(U_j)$ with the standard normal inverse cdf, i.e. the quantile function. The latent space $\tilde{X} \sim \mathcal{N}(0, \Sigma)$ is jointly normal distributed with zero mean and correlation Σ. A graphical model is given in Fig. 3, right panel. Clearly, the latent sample covariance

$$\tilde{X}^t \tilde{X} \sim \mathcal{W}_c(n, \Sigma) \tag{4}$$

is central Wishart. In general, Gaussian copulas are very restrictive examples of copulas, in particular if a certain application domain requires proper modeling of tail-dependencies. For the purpose of reconstructing archetypes, however, the Gaussian copula is highly suited, because in the generative archetype model

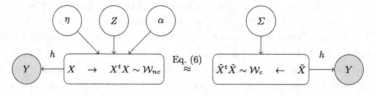

Fig. 3. Graphical models of Archetypal Analysis (left) and Gaussian Copula (right).

outlined in Eq. (1), the dependency structure is indeed approximately Gaussian. To see this, it is useful to rewrite Eq. (1) in matrix form:

$$X|Z, A \sim \mathcal{MN}(AZ_{K \times p}, I_n, \eta I_p), \tag{5}$$

where $X_{n \times p}$ contains the observations x_i as rows, $A_{n \times K}$ contains the mixing components α as rows and $\mathcal{MN}(M, \Omega, \Sigma)$ denotes the matrix normal distribution with mean matrix $M = AZ$, row covariance Ω and column covariance Σ. Since in Eq. (1), the individual components of x are independent given the means, we might say that the means M capture the full dependency structure of x. This interpretation can be formally expressed by analysing the covariance structure of the observations x_i. Since X is matrix normal with identity covariances, it follows that $X^t X$ is non-central Wishart with non-centrality matrix $M^t M$. The non-central Wishart distribution, on the other hand, can be approximated with a central Wishart, where the approximation is derived via moment matching, see [21]:

$$X^t X \sim \mathcal{W}_{nc}(n, \eta I, M^t M) \approx \mathcal{W}_c(n, \frac{1}{n} M^t M + \eta I_p). \tag{6}$$

Comparing Eq. (4) with Eq. (6) shows that under the generative archetype model in Eq. (1), the covariance structure of the observed vectors x is approximately Gaussian, which, in turn formally justifies the use of a Gaussian copula model for estimating the latent space.

Special Case: Continuous Observations Without Missing Values. If all observations Y are continuous and if there are no missing values, the simplest way of estimating each column $X_{\bullet,j}$, $j = 1, \ldots, p$ is to compute the *normal scores* based on the empirical marginal cdfs F_{emp} and the standard normal inverse cdf: $\hat{U}_{\bullet,j} = F_{emp}(Y_{\bullet,j}) = \text{ranks}(Y_{\bullet,j})/(n + 1)$ is a uniformly distributed random variable, and $X_{\bullet,j} = \Phi^{-1}(\hat{U}_{\bullet,j})$ further transforms the density (elementwise) to standard normal. Given the normal scores, the correlation matrix Σ which fully parametrises the Gaussian copula, is then just the expected covariance of the normal scores.

Using the empirical marginals F_{emp}, corresponds to the non-parametric part in the inference, since only the ranks are used in the transformation. This establishes invariance against arbitrary continuous cdfs F and also against their composition with an arbitrary strict monotone increasing transformation $(F \circ g)(y)$.

Data: Observations Y
Result: Archetypes Z
for *all dimensions* **do**
$\quad$ Compute normal scores $X_{\bullet,j} = \Phi^{-1}\left(\frac{\text{ranks}(Y_{\bullet,j})}{n+1}\right)$;
end
$Z \leftarrow \texttt{FindArchetypes(X)}$;

Algorithm 1. Copula Archetypal Analysis for continuous observations.

This makes inference invariant against different representations as well as insensitive against outliers. Note that we might have different cdfs and transformations in every component of y.

The algorithm, outlined in Algorithm (1), now proceeds by estimating the latent X based on the Gaussian copula model, and then calling an arbitrary function FindArchetypes(X) that minimises Eq. (2) and returns archetypes Z and mixing coefficients A. We assume that this function implements some classical archetype reconstruction algorithm, together with some mechanism for selecting the number of archetypes. In practice, we use the group-Lasso based algorithm proposed in [16] which uses the Bayesian Information Criterion (BIC)-score for automatically choosing an appropriate number of archetypes.

General Case: Mixed Data and Missing Values. In general, however, we allow the observations to be continuous and/or discrete (ordered factors), and we also allow missing values. For discrete observations, the ranks in the empirical cdf contain ties that might be broken in some arbitrary way. However, the resulting cdf-mapping will *not* make the marginal densities uniform, since transformations of discrete random variables do not change the distribution, but affect only the sampling space.

In order to deal with such situations, it has been proposed to use the extended rank likelihood [9]. The elementary observation is that for non-decreasing marginal cdfs, $y_{i,j} < y_{k,j}$ implies $x_{i,j} < z_{k,j}$. For the entire set of observations Y, this generalises such that X must lie in the set

$$\mathcal{D} = \left\{ X \in \mathbb{R}^{n \times p} : \max(x_{k,j} : y_{k,j} < y_{i,j}) < x_{i,j} < \min(x_{k,j} : y_{i,j} < y_{k,j}) \right\} \quad (7)$$

> **Data**: Observations Y
> **Result**: Archetypes Z
> initialise (X, Σ);
> **for** N *Gibbs sweeps* **do**
> > **for** *all observations* **do**
> > > **for** *all dimensions* **do**
> > > > conditioned on (Y, X), compute bounds $\{lo, up\}$;
> > > > conditioned on (Σ, X), compute
> > > > - conditional mean $\mu_{i,j}$ and conditional variance $\sigma_{i,j}^2$;
> > > > draw $x_{i,j} \sim N_{\text{trunc}}(\mu_{i,j}, \sigma_{i,j}^2, lo, up)$ from truncated normal;
> > > **end**
> > **end**
> > conditioned on X, draw Σ from inverse Wishart;
> > $A \leftarrow$ FindArchetypes(X);
> > update average archetypal scores in $\bar{A}_s(X)$
> **end**
> find clusters in set $\{x | \bar{A}_s(x) > 0\}$;
> return in every cluster the object with highest score $\bar{A}_s$;

Algorithm 2. Copula AA for mixed observations and missing values.

This enables us to see the marginal cdfs F_j as nuisance parameters in the likelihood and hence to estimate the correlation matrix Σ on $\mathcal{D}$.

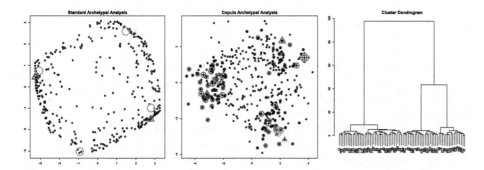

Fig. 4. Left: 400 datapoints sampled as (noisy) convex mixtures of 3 archetypes in 10 dimensions, monotonically transformed (beta marginal densities) and linearly quantised into 10 levels. Shown is the projection on the first two principal components, the reconstructed archetypes (red circles) and the original archetypes after transformation (triangles). Middle: reconstruction with Copula Archetypal Analysis. The size of the blue circles indicates the archetype score for each datapoint. Points with a non-zero archetype score are hierarchically clustered. The colored diamonds show the highest-scoring datapoint in every cluster found by cutting the dendrogram in the right panel (Color figure online).

Bayesian inference for Σ includes an inverse-Wishart prior distribution $p(\Sigma) \sim \mathcal{W}^{-1}(\nu_0, \nu_0 V_0)$, with degrees of freedom ν_0 and scale V_0. It can be achieved by constructing a Markov chain having its stationary distribution at Σ's posterior distribution $p(\Sigma | X \in \mathcal{D}) \propto p(\Sigma)p(X \in \mathcal{D}|\Sigma)$. Sampling is done in a Gibbs fashion, alternating between $X|\Sigma, Y$ and $\Sigma|X$, as outlined in Algorithm (2).

Resampling the latent variable $X|Y, \Sigma$ corresponds to sampling from a truncated normal

$$x_{i,j} \sim \mathcal{N}_{\text{trunc}} \left(\mu_{i,j}, \sigma_j^2, lo, up \right), \tag{8}$$

where the lower truncation $lo = \max(x_{i,j} : y_{i,j} < \text{unique}(y_{n,j}, \dots, y_{n,j})$ and the upper truncation $up = \min(x_{i,j} : y_{i,j} > \text{unique}(y_{n,j}, \dots, y_{n,j})$ are determined by the set $\mathcal{D}$ in Eq. (7). Thereby, the mean $\mu_{i,j} = X_{i,-j} \left(\Sigma_{j,-j} \Sigma_{-j,-j}^{-1} \right)^t$ and the variance $\sigma_{i,j}^2 = \Sigma_{j,j} - \Sigma_{j,-j} \Sigma_{-j,-j}^{-1} \Sigma_{-j,j}$ are conditioned on the remaining variables.

Resampling the correlation matrix $\Sigma|X$ means drawing from the inverse-Wishart, augmented with the data term $X^t X$

$$\Sigma \sim \mathcal{W}^{-1} \left(\nu_0 + n, \nu_o V_o + X^t X \right). \tag{9}$$

In order to accomodate for missing values $y_{i,j}$, the step in Eq. (8) is adjusted to use the unconstrained (i.e. untruncted) normal distribution.

Now, in every Gibbs iteration, we run an existing algorithm for drawing a set archetypes. For every object x, we update a score $\bar{A}_s(X)$, measuring the average proximity to the closest archetypes. Clustering of the score landscape and, within each cluster, selecting the objects with the highest score, finalises the algorithm. An example is given in Fig. 4.

3   Demo-Application in Computational Biology

We applied the Copula archetype model to analyze the genetic stress response induced by heat shock in *Saccharomyces cerevisiae* (yeast). Two different information sources are used: (i) time-resolved gene expression measurements of yeast genes under heat shock conditions, i.e. temporal changes in the process of synthesizing gene products under heat stress. (ii) Binding affinity scores for certain stress-related transcription factors. A transcription factor (TF) is a protein that binds to DNA sequences near genes and regulates gene expression. The first dataset has been published in [7] and can be downloaded from their web supplement, the second one refers to [8] and can be downloaded at http://fraenkel. mit.edu/Harbison/release_v24/ as *p*-values for TF binding events. Probe names in this dataset are matched to genes in order to combine the TF data with the gene expression data. The *p*-values are exponentially transformed to a binding affinity score on $[0, 1]$ such that the upper half of the unit interval is associated with highly significant bindings with $p < 5 \cdot 10^{-3}$. Combination of both datasets leads to a 10-dimensional description of 6105 yeast genes, expression values at 4 different timepoints and binding affinities to the 6 transcription factors ADR1, GAT1, HSF1, MSN2, SKN7, YAP1.

In the context of AA, we look for a few genes that show prominent expression/binding patterns that explain all observed patterns as convex mixtures in the latent copula space. Since roughly 13 % of the genes contain missing values in one or more dimensions, we use the Gibbs-sampling strategy in Alg. (2) for inferring archetypal genes. Figure 5 summarises the result of this analysis. Copula archetypal analysis identified 6 archetypal gene clusters that roughly correspond to the following patterns. **Stress response** (genes near the green diamond): these are known heat-stress response genes, they are highly overexpressed and have high binding affinity to the stress-related transcription factor SKN7, which is one of the two major transcriptional stress-response regulators in yeast. **Ribosomal RNA processing** (red): these genes play an essential role in protein synthesis. As expected, they are downregulated under heat stress, and this regulatory process is mediated by binding to YAP1, which is the second major regulator, cf. [12]. Two archetypes, depicted by the magenta and blue diamond, represent genes with mainly catalytic function that are regulated by exactly these two different stress response regulons, and two further archetypes (cyan and yellow diamond) have opposite binding affinity to the transcriptional activator ADR1. For further details see Fig. 5. Note that our findings nicely corroborate the results in [18], where essentially the same major groups of archetypal genes have been identified under environmental stress conditions

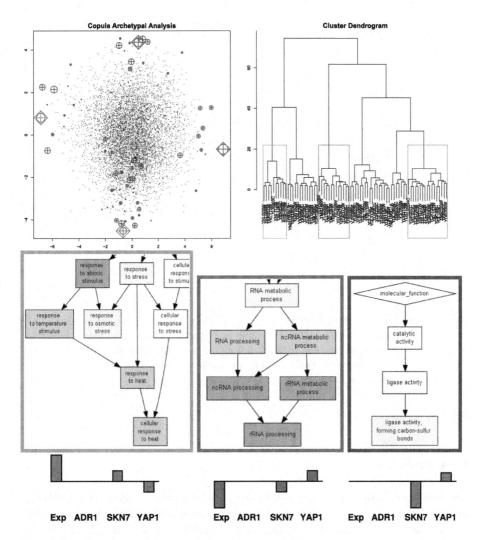

Fig. 5. Yeast genes under heat stress, characterised by gene expression values and binding affinity scores to stress-related transcription factors. Top left: PCA-plot of archetype reconstruction with our copula model. Colored diamonds show genes with highest archetype score in each of the clusters found by cutting the dendrogram in the top right panel (the boxes indicate clusters with significantly enriched gene functions represented by *Gene Ontology* (GO) terms). Middle row: enrichment analysis of genes in the cluster indicated by the green, red, and magenta boxes in the dendrogram, computed with the GOrilla software http://cbl-gorilla.cs.technion.ac.il/. Color encodes p-values of enriched GO-term: yellow $= 10^{-3}$ to 10^{-5}, orange $= 10^{-5}$ to 10^{-7}, dark-orange $= 10^{-7}$ to 10^{-9}. Bottom row: archetype-specific gene-expression and binding pattern (schematic) (Color figure online).

but in a different organism. Classical archetypal analysis has severe problems on this dataset: first, genes with missing values have to be removed, and second, several archetypes that have a clear biological interpretation (like the magenta one) could not be found by the classical algorithm, see Fig. 6.

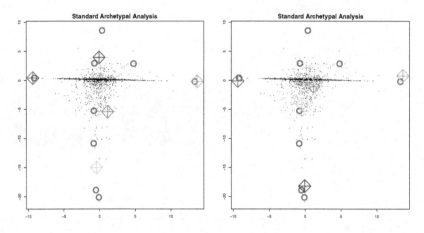

Fig. 6. Results of standard archetypal analysis. Left: 1st principal component (PC) vs 2nd one, Right: 1st PC vs 3rd PC. The red circles indicate the location of the archetypes. For comparison, the colored diamonds show the archetypal objects identified by Copula Archetypal Analysis. The projection in the right panel reveals that there is no archetype in close proximity of the magenta- and yellow-colored diamonds (Color figure online).

4   Conclusion

We introduced copula archetypal analysis, which wraps classical archetypal analysis into a copula framework. This ensures invariance of archetypal analysis against the class of strictly monotone increasing functions. We think, this is the largest invariance class since it only keeps the rank relation of the data, while the representation of the data can change. Furthermore, we devised the possibility to include mixed data and missing values. This is an important property, since in many real world datasets, mixed data and missing values are very common. Moreover, our algorithm is formulated as a preprocessing step, such that established algorithms can be re-used in order to efficiently recover the archetypes. Lastly, we have demonstrated that our model works well on both simulated data and in a real world application.

Acknowledgements. This work was partially supported by the Swiss National Science Foundation, project 200021_146178: Copula Distributions in Machine Learning.

References

1. Bauckhage, C.: A note on archetypal analysis and the approximation of convex hulls (2014). arXiv preprint arXiv:1410.0642
2. Bauckhage, C., Manshaei, K.: Kernel archetypal analysis for clustering web search frequency time series. In: 22nd International Conference on Pattern Recognition (ICPR), pp. 1544–1549. IEEE (2014)
3. Bauckhage, C., Thurau, C.: Making Archetypal analysis practical. In: Denzler, J., Notni, G., Süße, H. (eds.) Pattern Recognition. LNCS, vol. 5748, pp. 272–281. Springer, Heidelberg (2009)
4. Canhasi, E., Kononenko, I.: Weighted archetypal analysis of the multi-element graph for query-focused multi-document summarization. Expert Syst. Appl. **41**(2), 535–543 (2014)
5. Cutler, A., Breiman, L.: Archetypal analysis. Technometrics **36**(4), 338–347 (1994)
6. Ebert, S., Schiele, B.: Where next in object recognition and how much supervision do we need? In: Farinella, G.M., Battiato, S., Cipolla, R. (eds.) Advanced Topics in Computer Vision, pp. 35–64. Springer, London (2013)
7. Gasch, A.P., Spellman, P.T., Kao, C.M., Carmel-Harel, O., Eisen, M.B., Storz, G., Botstein, D., Brown, P.O.: Genomic expression programs in the response of yeast cells to environmental changes. Mol. Biol. cell **11**(12), 4241–4257 (2000)
8. Harbison, C.T., Gordon, D.B., Lee, T.I., Rinaldi, N.J., Macisaac, K.D., Danford, T.W., Hannett, N.M., Tagne, J.B., Reynolds, D.B., Yoo, J., et al.: Transcriptional regulatory code of a eukaryotic genome. Nat. **431**(7004), 99–104 (2004)
9. Hoff, P.D.: Extending the rank likelihood for semiparametric copula estimation. Ann. Appl. Stat. **1**(1), 265–283 (2007)
10. Joe, H.: Multivariate models and multivariate dependence concepts. CRC Press, Boca Raton (1997)
11. Kersting, K., Wahabzada, M., Thurau, C., Bauckhage, C.: Hierarchical convex nmf for clustering massive data. ACML **10**, 253–268 (2010)
12. Lee, J., Godon, C., Lagniel, G., Spector, D., Garin, J., Labarre, J., Toledano, M.B.: Yap1 and skn7 control two specialized oxidative stress response regulons in yeast. J. Biol. Chem. **274**(23), 16040–16046 (1999)
13. Li, S., Wang, P., Louviere, J., Carson, R.: Archetypal analysis: a new way to segment markets based on extreme individuals. In: Proceedings of the ANZMAC 2003 Conference, A Celebration of Ehrenberg and Bass: Marketing Knowledge, Discoveries and Contribution, pp. 1674–1679 (2003)
14. Nelsen, R.B.: An Introduction to Copulas. Science & Business Media. Springer, New York (1999)
15. Norberg, U.M., Rayner, J.M.: Ecological morphology and flight in bats (mammalia; chiroptera): wing adaptations, flight performance, foraging strategy and echolocation. Philos. Trans. R. Soc. B Biol. Sci. **316**(1179), 335–427 (1987)
16. Prabhakaran, S., Raman, S., Vogt, J.E., Roth, V.: Automatic model selection in Archetype analysis. In: Pinz, A., Pock, T., Bischof, H., Leberl, F. (eds.) DAGM and OAGM 2012. LNCS, vol. 7476, pp. 458–467. Springer, Heidelberg (2012)
17. Seth, S., Eugster, M.J.: Probabilistic archetypal analysis (2013). arXiv preprint arXiv:1312.7604
18. Shoval, O., Sheftel, H., Shinar, G., Hart, Y., Ramote, O., Mayo, A., Dekel, E., Kavanagh, K., Alon, U.: Evolutionary trade-offs, pareto optimality, and the geometry of phenotype space. Sci. **336**(6085), 1157–1160 (2012)

19. Sifa, R., Bauckhage, C.: Archetypical motion: Supervised game behavior learning with archetypal analysis. In: IEEE Conference on Computational Intelligence in Games (CIG), pp. 1–8. IEEE (2013)
20. Sklar, M.: Fonctions de répartition à n dimensions et leurs marges. Université Paris, vol. 8 (1959)
21. Steyn, H., Roux, J.: Approximations for the non-central wishart distribution. S. Afr. Stat. J. **6**, 165–173 (1972)
22. Thurau, C., Bauckhage, C.: Archetypal images in large photo collections. In: IEEE International Conference on Semantic Computing, ICSC 2009, pp. 129–136. IEEE (2009)
23. Thurau, C., Kersting, K., Bauckhage, C.: Convex non-negative matrix factorization in the wild. In: Ninth IEEE International Conference on Data Mining, ICDM 2009, pp. 523–532. IEEE (2009)

Interactive Image Retrieval for Biodiversity Research

Alexander Freytag[1,2](✉), Alena Schadt[1], and Joachim Denzler[1,2]

[1] Computer Vision Group, Friedrich Schiller University Jena, Jena, Germany
alexander.freytag@uni-jena.de
[2] Michael Stifel Center Jena, Jena, Germany

Abstract. On a daily basis, experts in biodiversity research are confronted with the challenging task of classifying individuals to build statistics over their distributions, their habitats, or the overall biodiversity. While the number of species is vast, experts with affordable time-budgets are rare. Image retrieval approaches could greatly assist experts: when new images are captured, a list of visually similar and previously collected individuals could be returned for further comparison. Following this observation, we start by transferring latest image retrieval techniques to biodiversity scenarios. We then propose to additionally incorporate an expert's knowledge into this process by allowing him to select must-have-regions. The obtained annotations are used to train exemplar-models for region detection. Detection scores efficiently computed with convolutions are finally fused with an initial ranking to reflect both sources of information, global and local aspects. The resulting approach received highly positive feedback from several application experts. On datasets for butterfly and bird identification, we quantitatively proof the benefit of including expert-feedback resulting in gains of accuracy up to 25 % and we extensively discuss current limitations and further research directions.

1 Introduction

In biodiversity research, experts are confronted with a growing amount of collected images which build the foundation for statistics over distributions of species, their habitats, or the overall biodiversity in ecosystems. Within this challenging process, classification of individuals is commonly done using field guides and by comparing the current object of investigation against known classes, thereby checking for the presence of unique characteristics (*e.g.*, a red dotted neck or a characteristically colored wing). Common image retrieval techniques, *e.g.*, [2,4,5,8,26,27,34,37], could greatly assist in this process by suggesting visually similar genera for further inspection to an expert. Simply applying these techniques to biodiversity scenarios, however, does not necessarily lead to satisfying results. One reason is that species, while visually similar on a global scale, often show significant differences in small and localized details which are easily missed. Furthermore, locations of discriminative details significantly differ between categories, which requires experts to investigate different sets of

© Springer International Publishing Switzerland 2015
J. Gall et al. (Eds.): GCPR 2015, LNCS 9358, pp. 129–141, 2015.
DOI: 10.1007/978-3-319-24947-6_11

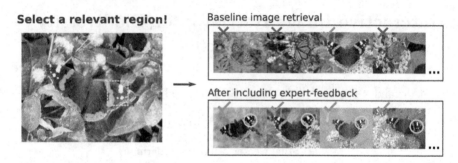

Fig. 1. Image retrieval techniques can assist biodiversity researchers by filtering collected datasets for individuals visually similar to an unseen object (*left and top row*). We present how an expert-in-the-loop can improve this baseline by selecting a must-have-region (*e.g., the dashed rectangle*). By training region-specific detection models, we can detect these regions in training images (*indicated as circles in bottom row*) to verify and update the initial ranking.

parts depending on the currently faced individual. In this paper, we therefore present an approach to improve existing image retrieval techniques by incorporating expert feedback about must-have-regions into the retrieval process. A visualization of the underlying idea is given in Fig. 1.

We will build on neural codes [4] as baseline, a recently introduced technique for image retrieval using activations of convolutional neural network architectures. Thereby, handing over a query image results in similarity scores for all previously collected training examples. Based on an image region specified by an expert, we then learn a detection model from only this single positive example following recent results for exemplar-models in patch discovery [12,19,30]. Efficient evaluations of the detection model on all training images result in a second score indicating the presence of the selected region. We finally update the ranking by fusing both results. In consequence, we obtain a list of visually similar individuals which additionally exhibit parts similar to the selected region. For the sake of quantitative results, we require ground truth labels of training images in the presented evaluations. However, our approach does *not* rely on class annotations at all and can thus be applied even in unsupervised tasks where no (machine-accessible) class information is available. Furthermore, the resulting approach runs within seconds on standard hardware and is thus also applicable for large image collections.

In the remainder of this paper, we first give a short review on state-of-the-art in image retrieval (Sect. 2) and then introduce our approach for interactive image retrieval in Sect. 3. Quantitative analyses of the resulting system are presented in Sect. 4 on computer vision datasets related to biodiversity applications. Depending on the tackled scenario, we report significant accuracy gains but also show and discuss limitations of the current approach and resulting future research directions. A short summary concludes the paper.

2   Image Retrieval in a Nutshell

Retrieving visually similar images given a newly captured query, *i.e.,* the task we motivated in the last section, is the central topic of an entire research area which is commonly referred to as *content-based image retrieval*. In more then 20 years of research, a variety of approaches has been developed, *e.g.,* [1,2,4,5,7,8,15, 26,27,31,37]. While differing in algorithmic details and required assumptions, the underlying pipeline mainly consists of three steps: (i) representing known images and organizing representations in a search structure, (ii) computing representations for a new query image, and (iii) matching of representations to build a ranked list from which top-ranked images are returned. A great amount of research and engineering art went into carefully designing and implementing all three steps. However, we noticed two crucial issues for image retrieval in biodiversity applications. First of all, latest findings from the image retrieval community are yet to be transferred to remaining areas of application. While this is partly successful, *e.g.,* in medical scenarios [38], we found in several discussions that this process works rather poorly in biodiversity research. Besides, we found that off-the-shelf retrieval algorithms are often not perfectly feasible for biodiversity applications. This observation mainly arises from the fact that a large fraction of retrieval algorithms aim at finding images of exactly the same object as the query   [2,4,5,8,26,27,31,37]. In this paper, we are instead interested in retrieving known individuals similar but not identical to a previously *unseen* sample. This task is by far not novel, and an entire sub-field known as *category retrieval* tackles this challenging problem by modeling or learning the occurring intra-category variances (*e.g.,* see [4,5,7] for latest impressive results as well as [22] for an application to plant species identification scenarios). While we received already promising feedback by simply applying image retrieval techniques in biodiversity scenarios, the resulting framework was often found to be too static. Instead, the possibility for selecting must-have-regions, *e.g.,* a unique wing pattern, was often desired. In terms of computer vision, we thus seek for distance metrics which are user- and exemplar-specific and interpretable.

A research area similar in spirit is local learning, where known images most similar to a test image are retrieved to then learn representations and models from those similar images only [7,12,13,17,32,39,40]. In the focus of this paper, we instead leave the decision process to the expert, but aim at providing him with a set of relevant images as helpful as possible and further allow him to interactively refine the query results.

The only related work we a aware of is [6] which allows to select outputs of an unsupervised segmentation for query refinement. We instead propose a more intuitive and precise technique for providing feedback as shown next.

3   Interactive Selection of Regions of Focus

Let us now introduce the aforementioned technique for interactive image retrieval. As a result of several discussions, we found that the selection of rectangles as must-have-regions for the current query is an intuitive, simple, and yet

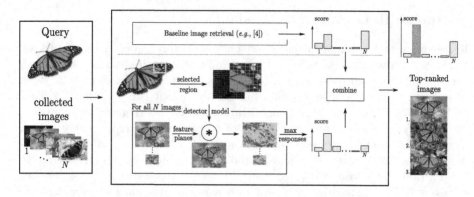

Fig. 2. Overview of our proposed approach for interactive image retrieval. Figure is best viewed in color and by zooming in. See text for details.

powerful way for receiving feedback from an application expert. To integrate this information into the retrieval process, we provide solutions for three questions:

i. how to train a detection model f from a single positive example,
ii. how to efficiently evaluate the model on all training images, and
iii. how to integrate detection responses into the process of image ranking.

An overview of the resulting approach is shown in Fig. 2.

Exemplar-models for Region Detection. Determining the existence or absence of a selected region in a collected training set can be done most easily by casting it as a part detection task. Thus, we aim at training a detection model from a single positive example and virtually everything else as negative data. While this task appears cumbersome on first glance, exemplar-models such as Exemplar-SVM [24] or Exemplar-LDA [16,19] provide an elegant solution and have been found useful for learning patch detectors from a single positive example [12,19,30]. Unfortunately, training of Exemplar-SVMs involves computationally expensive hard negative mining, In contrast, Exemplar-LDA models can be trained highly efficiently since the majority of computations is done only once in an offline stage. Since we are interested in fast responses after an expert selected a region, we thus follow [12,19] and apply LDA models as region detectors. In consequence, distributions of (the single) positive and all negative examples are assumed to be Gaussian with a shared covariance matrix Σ_0 and mean vectors μ_1 and μ_{-1}, respectively. Although this assumption might be far from being perfectly correct, it offers two advantages: (i) a discriminative linear separation of positive and negative data

$$w_{\mathrm{LDA}} = \Sigma_0^{-1} \left(\mu_1 - \mu_{-1} \right) \tag{1}$$

with (ii) fast training and model evaluations [16]. Furthermore, we can additionally view Eq. (1) as de-correlated nearest class mean [25] and it is known that reducing correlations in feature cells is beneficial for detection tasks [12,16]. We thus only need to compute $\boldsymbol{\Sigma}_0$ and $\boldsymbol{\mu}_{-1}$ from all possible locations, aspect ratios, and scales in all training samples once [16]. In practice, we add a scaled identity matrix $\boldsymbol{\Sigma}_0 + \sigma_n^2 \boldsymbol{I}$ to increase numerical stability. During the interaction process, it only remains to solve the linear equation system in Eq. (1) to obtain the desired detection model.

Efficient Convolutions for Region Detection. To reliably detect the selected region in training images, we need to densely evaluate the learned detector, *i.e.*, on all possible locations and scales. Let therefore $\boldsymbol{x}$ denote the feature vector extracted from a single position and scale. For a linear detector as in Eq. (1), the response on $\boldsymbol{x}$ is computed as additive combination of dimension-specific similarity scores (ignoring offsets for simplicity of notation):

$$f(\boldsymbol{x}) = \langle \boldsymbol{w}_{\mathrm{LDA}}, \boldsymbol{x} \rangle = \sum_{d=1}^{D} \boldsymbol{w}_{\mathrm{LDA}}(d) \cdot \boldsymbol{x}(d). \tag{2}$$

Evaluation of f on all possible locations can then be done in a sliding window manner by computing Eq. (2) for densely extracted features. In this case, we can also change the order of computations and can equivalently compute Eq. (2) by adding D convolutions of 1×1 filters with corresponding feature planes. As required later, this also holds if $\boldsymbol{x}$ follows a spatial tiling composed of $T \times T$ cells with D_C feature dimensions per cell (thus, $D = T \cdot T \cdot D_C$ in Eq. (2)). For prominent examples, *e.g.*, Spatial Pyramid Match Kernels [23] or HOG [11] for detection tasks, Eq. (2) translates to

$$f(\boldsymbol{x}) = \sum_{d_i, d_j = 1}^{T} \sum_{c=1}^{D_C} \boldsymbol{w}_{\mathrm{LDA}}\left((d_j T + d_i) D_C + c\right) \cdot \boldsymbol{x}\left((d_j T + d_i) D_C + c\right). \tag{3}$$

Again, we can exchange order of summations which leads to adding results of D_C convolutions of $T \times T$ filters with corresponding feature planes. By computing feature planes for all training images in an offline step, we can efficiently detect selected regions and reduce an expert's idle times to a minimum.

Fusion of Complementary Retrieval Scores. Given the previous steps, it now remains to combine detection results with the previously obtained ranking of the baseline retrieval system. As commonly done in object detection, we perform max-pooling over response maps from all scales and return the largest detection score for each image. Scores are linearly normalized into $[0, 1]$ to maintain their relative ordering and still allow for a well-defined range of outputs. Given results of baseline image retrieval and interactive selection, we now seek for examples with high scores reflected by both indicators. We therefore assume both sources of information to be complementary which justifies a simple product as combination rule [3,20]. Note that the assumption of complementary information is indeed justifiable, since a baseline retrieval is concerned with coarse distinctions regarding the entire image. Instead, interactive selection explicitly neglects the majority of this information and searches for the remaining parts

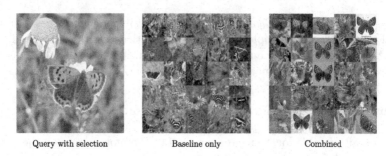

Query with selection   Baseline only   Combined

Fig. 3. Visualizing the influence of expert feedback. Figure is best viewed in color.

with arbitrarily different techniques. While we also experimented with other fusion techniques [20], we empirically found this strategy to be as simple as powerful. Combined scores are finally ordered and top-ranked results are returned. Putting all parts together, we obtain the framework as visualized in Fig. 2. The entire pipeline runs within seconds and allows experts to easily investigate results with different regions selected. A qualitative example is given in Fig. 3.

4   Experiments

By applying the previously introduced techniques to biodiversity tasks, we already obtained highly positive feedback from several experts which we took as a qualitative confirmation of our approach's usability. In this section, we additionally present quantitative results on two established computer vision datasets to analyze benefits, limitations, and future research directions.

4.1   Evaluation Criteria

To evaluate success of an image retrieval technique, a variety of different criteria have been put forward and the presumably most common measure is mean average precision (mAP) [2,4,5,8,26,27,37] based on precision and recall. When returning k top-ranked images, *precision* refers to the relative number of correctly retrieved images, *i.e.,* $\frac{\#\text{true positives}}{k}$, whereas *recall* denotes the number of correctly retrieved images relative to the absolute number of known positive examples, *i.e.,* $\frac{\#\text{true positives}}{\#\text{known positives}}$. Computing mAP is then done by plotting recall against accuracy individually for each possible category and averaging areas under the resulting curves. While mAP is excellent for evaluating an image retrieval system's performance over the entire range of possible working points, *i.e.,* different trade-offs between precision and recall, we observed that the majority of possible working points is not feasible in practice. Instead, application constraints often render high recall values as an irrelevant measure of quality. According to our experience, an application expert is in fact not interested in a supporting tool with perfect recall which returns almost all known images – only to not miss a single correct one. Instead, he is usually interested in inspecting

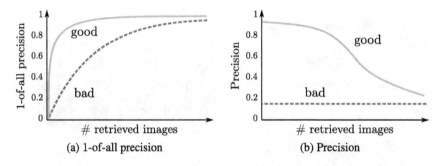

(a) 1-of-all precision

(b) Precision

Fig. 4. Illustrating different criteria for evaluating image retrieval accuracy.

just a small set of retrieved images, and this retrieved set should exhibit several properties. Interestingly, we also observed that these properties vary over task and expert, *e.g.,* experienced researchers are usually interested in inspecting visually similar examples to then make a final decision on their own. In this case, retrieving at least one example of the correct category is often sufficient which we refer to as 1-*of-all precision*. Less experienced researchers, though, often base their decision on relative frequencies of returned categories. In these cases, as many retrieved images as possible should be of the correct category, *i.e.,* a high precision matters. While several papers followed the second evaluation, *e.g.,* [7,37], we are not aware of any work applying the first principle, which however was found to be a useful criterion for application experts. We will see later that both criteria can cover orthogonal aspects of a system's performance and thus should be considered side by side. Both criteria are illustrated in Fig. 4 visualizing results for a strong and a poor retrieval system.

4.2   Datasets for Illustrating Biodiversity Applications

So far, we are not aware of any biodiversity dataset publicly available for computer vision researchers. To still allow for quantitative evaluations, we present experimental results on two datasets established in the computer vision community which cover areas of investigation relevant for biodiversity researchers. In the following, we give a short overview on both datasets.

Leeds – Identifying Butterflies. The Leeds Butterfly dataset [36] contains 832 images of butterflies captured in a natural environment. It covers ten distinct butterfly species with 55 to 100 images per category. Exemplary individuals of eight species are shown in Fig. 5a.

CUB2011 – Recognizing Birds. The Caltech-UCSD Birds-200-2011 (CUB200) [35] dataset covers 200 bird species native in North America. The provided dataset contains 11,788 individuals which are split in train and test set of approximately same size. We also conducted experiments on the frequently used subset (CUB14) by [10] which contains 14 categories of warblers and wood-

(a) Leeds Butterflies [36]

(b) Caltech-UCSD birds 200 [35]

(c) Acquisition of annotations

Fig. 5. *Left*: Examples of different species from datasets used in our evaluations showing butterflies [36] (*top*) and birds [35] (*bottom*). *Right*: GUI for acquisition of must-have-regions to allow for quantitative evaluations.

peckers with 817 images. Examples are shown in Fig. 5b. Noteworthy, category labels do not distinguish between male and female, nor between young and adult.

4.3   Experiments in a Butterfly Identification Scenario

We have already seen a qualitative example in Fig. 3. For a quantitative evaluation, we start with the previously introduced butterfly dataset Leeds [36].

Experimental Setup. As baseline retrieval technique, we apply neural codes by [4]. In detail, we use the AlexNet model [21] initially trained on ImageNet for general purpose feature extraction [14,18]. Features of several layers are extracted using the Caffe toolbox [18] and we empirically found conv3 to be well suited for our application. Since the dataset does not provide any part information, we asked six users to manually select a single region for each image which they rate as informative. Notably, the users' initial domain knowledge ranged from no knowledge at all to individual training for several weeks. For their guidance, we displayed individuals of each category as visualized in Fig. 5c. Following recent trends in fine-grained recognition [12], we represent selected regions using histograms of oriented gradients (HOG) [11] and histograms of ColorNames (CN) [33] to capture color, texture, and shape. Spatial information is kept by tiling the selected region using a regular grid and extracting features in each cell separately [11]. HOG and CN features are extracted using publicly available source-code of [16] and [33]. We train exemplar-specific LDA models using the code provided by [12]. For evaluation, we follow the leave-one-out principle and exclude each image once from the training set to serve as query image. Precision and 1-of-all precision curves are finally averaged over all images and shown in Fig. 6.

Evaluation. When averaging over all users (Fig. 6a), we notice a significant increase in both precision and 1-of-all precision. Noteworthy, the accuracy with respect to the first retrieved image is increased from 71 % to 90 %. From our

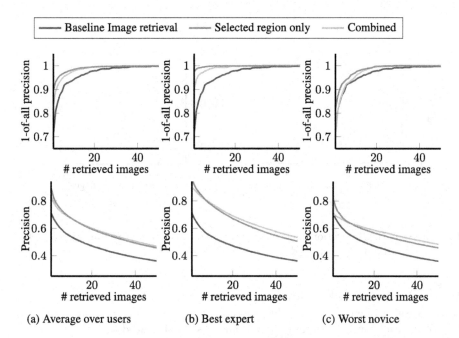

Fig. 6. Evaluating image retrieval with interactive feedback on the butterfly dataset Leeds [36]. Results are obtained from six annotators ranging from novices to experts.

experience, this result is indeed remarkable given the already sophisticated performance obtained with neural codes as baseline technique. Furthermore, we note that experienced annotators can easily lift the retrieval accuracy to ranges significantly over 95 % (Fig. 6b). However, even novices with little experience can add valuable information (Fig. 6c). We also observe that solely relying on outputs of detection models further boosts performance if k is extremely small but is inferior to combined results for larger retrieved sets. This behavior is plausible since images with extremely high detection scores are likely to contain the exact same pattern as the query. In contrast, medium scores likely result from examples of mixed-up categories which have a similar local pattern but are different at a global scale. Consequently, incorporating the baseline information can correct these cases. Interestingly, we also notice different trends when comparing precision and 1-of-all precision as a measure of accuracy. We therefore conclude that a decision for one evaluation strategy over the other should be based on the desired properties of the retrieved set of images.

4.4   Experiments in a Bird Recognition Task

In a second experiment, we evaluate limitations of our approach and further research directions using the previously introduced CUB200 bird dataset.

Experimental Setup. Following previous research [9,12,42], we crop images to the provided bounding box and apply the provided split in train and test images.

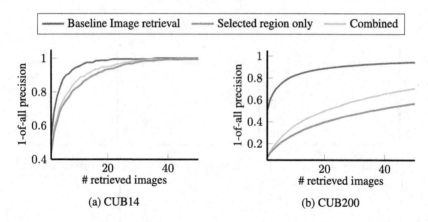

Fig. 7. Evaluating limitations and further research directions for the introduced interactive retrieval approach on bird recognition datasets by [35].

We simulate region selection using provided part annotations for anchoring a squared region of width and height proportional to $\frac{1}{10}$ of the box's main diagonal. For verification, we additionally asked our most experienced annotator to mark head regions on the small subset. The remaining setup is identical to the previous experiment except that neural codes are extracted from conv5. Due to the lack of space, we only present results in Fig. 7 obtained from head regions which are known to be most discriminative [42].

Evaluation. In contrast to the superior results on Leeds, we notice that selecting a single region is too restrictive for bird recognition tasks and can even hurt retrieval accuracy. Notably, even our most experienced expert was not able to improve the accuracy (Fig. 7a). On CUB200, the accuracy induced by detection scores finally drops significantly (Fig. 7b) and thus goes along with the combined results. We attribute this observation to three reasons. First of all, captured bird images are highly diverse, both with respect to pose (parts are often occluded, thus, no model can be trained) and appearance (male vs. female, young vs. adult, label errors). Besides, the number of species is significantly larger which renders the task significantly more difficult. Finally, single parts are often not visually discriminative with respect to different categories although their combination is. Since the usability of the current approach was confirmed in personal discussions, we can conclude several important directions for improvement. First of all, an extension to multiple selectable regions would be highly beneficial to specify parts which are only discriminative when appearing jointly. Besides, estimating the number of required annotations would be helpful for unexperienced researchers. Finally, providing relative positions of multiple parts and expressing their semantics would allow for more informative expert feedback.

5   Conclusions

In this paper, we introduced image retrieval techniques to assist in biodiversity research. Using neural codes as baseline, we then presented how to additionally incorporate expert feedback by interactively selecting must-have-regions. The provided information served for training of region-specific detection models which are efficiently evaluated on all training images with convolutions. Combining detection scores with baseline results finally allowed for verifying and updating the initial ranking. In a butterfly identification task, this intuitive way of providing feedback resulted in improved results for non-experts while more experienced users could even further boost the performance. The resulting approach is easy to use and already received highly positive feedback from several experts. In a last experiment, we evaluated limitations of our approach and discussed open research directions. As future work, we plan to incorporate relevance feedback [29, 41] which was suggested by medical experts. In addition, transferring our approach to different application areas, *e.g.,* retrieval of similar plants [22] or moths [28], could assists experts in other domains. Furthermore, replacing current region descriptions by efficiently computable CNN activations is likely beneficial. While their applicability is currently limited by hardware requirements, further progress in this field will allow for training even better region detection models.

References

1. Arandjelovic, R.: Advancing Large Scale Object Retrieval. Ph.D. thesis, University of Oxford (2013)
2. Arandjelovic, R., Zisserman, A.: Three things everyone should know to improve object retrieval. In: CVPR (2012)
3. Atrey, P.K., Hossain, M.A., El Saddik, A., Kankanhalli, M.S.: Multimodal fusion for multimedia analysis: a survey. Multimedia Syst. **16**(6), 345–379 (2010)
4. Babenko, A., Slesarev, A., Chigorin, A., Lempitsky, V.: Neural codes for image retrieval. In: CVPR (2014)
5. Cao, X., Zhang, H., Guo, X., Liu, S., Chen, X.: Image retrieval and ranking via consistently reconstructing multi-attribute queries. In: Fleet, D., Pajdla, T., Schiele, B., Tuytelaars, T. (eds.) ECCV 2014, Part I. LNCS, vol. 8689, pp. 569–583. Springer, Heidelberg (2014)
6. Carson, C., Belongie, S., Greenspan, H., Malik, J.: Blobworld: Image segmentation using expectation-maximization and its application to image querying. TPAMI **24**(8), 1026–1038 (2002)
7. Chatfield, K., Simonyan, K., Zisserman, A.: Efficient on-the-fly category retrieval using ConvNets and GPUs. In: Cremers, D., Reid, I., Saito, H., Yang, M.-H. (eds.) ACCV 2014. LNCS, vol. 9003, pp. 129–145. Springer, Heidelberg (2015)
8. Chum, O., Philbin, J., Sivic, J., Isard, M., Zisserman, A.: Total recall: Automatic query expansion with a generative feature model for object retrieval. In: ICCV (2007)
9. Donahue, J., Jia, Y., Vinyals, O., Hoffman, J., Zhang, N., Tzeng, E., Darrell, T.: Decaf: a deep convolutional activation feature for generic visual recognition. In: ICML (2014)

10. Farrell, R., Oza, O., Zhang, N., Morariu, V.I., Darrell, T., Davis, L.S.: Birdlets: Subordinate categorization using volumetric primitives and pose-normalized appearance. In: ICCV (2011)
11. Felzenszwalb, P.F., Girshick, R.B., McAllester, D., Ramanan, D.: Object detection with discriminatively trained part based models. TPAMI **32**(9), 1627–1645 (2010)
12. Freytag, A., Rodner, E., Darrell, T., Denzler, J.: Exemplar-specific patch features for fine-grained recognition. In: Jiang, X., Hornegger, J., Koch, R. (eds.) GCPR 2014. LNCS, vol. 8753, pp. 144–156. Springer, Heidelberg (2014)
13. Frome, A., Singer, Y., Sha, F., Malik, J.: Learning globally-consistent local distance functions for shape-based image retrieval and classification. In: ICCV, pp. 1–8 (2007)
14. Guadarrama, S., Rodner, E., Saenko, K., Zhang, N., Farrell, R., Donahue, J., Darrell, T.: Open-vocabulary object retrieval. In: Proceedings of Robotics: Science and Systems (2014). http://www.roboticsproceedings.org/rss10/p41.html
15. Gudivada, V.N., Raghavan, V.V.: Content based image retrieval systems. IEEE Comput. **28**(9), 18–22 (1995). (Special Issue on Content-Based Image Retrieval Systems)
16. Hariharan, B., Malik, J., Ramanan, D.: Discriminative decorrelation for clustering and classification. In: Fitzgibbon, A., Lazebnik, S., Perona, P., Sato, Y., Schmid, C. (eds.) ECCV 2012, Part IV. LNCS, vol. 7575, pp. 459–472. Springer, Heidelberg (2012)
17. Ionescu, R., Popescu, M., Grozea, C.: Local learning to improve bag of visual words model for facial expression recognition. In: ICML Workshop on Representation Learning (2013)
18. Jia, Y., Shelhamer, E., Donahue, J., Karayev, S., Long, J., Girshick, R., Guadarrama, S., Darrell, T.: Caffe: Convolutional architecture for fast feature embedding (2014). arXiv preprint arXiv:1408.5093
19. Juneja, M., Vedaldi, A., Jawahar, C., Zisserman, A.: Blocks that shout: Distinctive parts for scene classification. In: CVPR (2013)
20. Kittler, J., Hatef, M., Duin, R.P., Matas, J.: On combining classifiers. TPAMI **20**(3), 226–239 (1998)
21. Krizhevsky, A., Sutskever, I., Hinton, G.E.: Imagenet classification with deep convolutional neural networks. In: NIPS (2012)
22. Kumar, N., Belhumeur, P.N., Biswas, A., Jacobs, D.W., Kress, W.J., Lopez, I.C., Soares, J.V.B.: Leafsnap: a computer vision system for automatic plant species identification. In: Fitzgibbon, A., Lazebnik, S., Perona, P., Sato, Y., Schmid, C. (eds.) ECCV 2012, Part II. LNCS, vol. 7573, pp. 502–516. Springer, Heidelberg (2012)
23. Lazebnik, S., Schmid, C., Ponce, J.: Beyond bags of features: Spatial pyramid matching for recognizing natural scene categories. In: CVPR, pp. 2169–2178 (2006)
24. Malisiewicz, T., Gupta, A., Efros, A.: Ensemble of exemplar-svms for object detection and beyond. In: ICCV (2011)
25. Mensink, T., Verbeek, J., Perronnin, F., Csurka, G.: Distance-based image classification: Generalizing to new classes at near-zero cost. TPAMI **35**(11), 2624–2637 (2013)
26. Philbin, J., Chum, O., Isard, M., Sivic, J., Zisserman, A.: Object retrieval with large vocabularies and fast spatial matching. In: CVPR, pp. 1–8 (2007)
27. Philbin, J., Chum, O., Isard, M., Sivic, J., Zisserman, A.: Lost in quantization: Improving particular object retrieval in large scale image databases. In: CVPR, pp. 1–8 (2008)

28. Rodner, E., Simon, M., Brehm, G., Pietsch, S., Wgele, J.W., Denzler, J.: Fine-grained recognition datasets for biodiversity analysis. In: CVPR-WS (2015)
29. Rui, Y., Huang, T.S., Ortega, M., Mehrotra, S.: Relevance feedback: a power tool for interactive content-based image retrieval. IEEE Trans. Circuits Syst. Video Technol. **8**(5), 644–655 (1998)
30. Singh, S., Gupta, A., Efros, A.A.: Unsupervised discovery of mid-level discriminative patches. In: Fitzgibbon, A., Lazebnik, S., Perona, P., Sato, Y., Schmid, C. (eds.) ECCV 2012, Part II. LNCS, vol. 7573, pp. 73–86. Springer, Heidelberg (2012)
31. Sivic, J., Zisserman, A.: Video google: a text retrieval approach to object matching in videos. In: ICCV, pp. 1470–1477 (2003)
32. Urtasun, R., Darrell, T.: Sparse probabilistic regression for activity-independent human pose inference. In: CVPR (2008)
33. Van De Weijer, J., Schmid, C., Verbeek, J., Larlus, D.: Learning color names for real-world applications. IEEE Trans. Image Process. **18**(7), 1512–1523 (2009)
34. Vogel, J., Schiele, B.: Semantic modeling of natural scenes for content-based image retrieval. IJCV **72**(2), 133–157 (2007)
35. Wah, C., Branson, S., Welinder, P., Perona, P., Belongie, S.: The caltech-ucsd birds-200-2011 dataset. Technical report CNS-TR-2011-001, California Institute of Technology (2011)
36. Wang, J., Markert, K., Everingham, M.: Learning models for object recognition from natural language descriptions. In: BMVC (2009)
37. Wang, Q., Si, L., Zhang, D.: Learning to hash with partial tags: exploring correlation between tags and hashing bits for large scale image retrieval. In: Fleet, D., Pajdla, T., Schiele, B., Tuytelaars, T. (eds.) ECCV 2014, Part III. LNCS, vol. 8691, pp. 378–392. Springer, Heidelberg (2014)
38. Xu, X., Li, B.: Automatic classification and detection of clinically relevant images for diabetic retinopathy. Medical Imaging (2008)
39. Yu, A., Grauman, K.: Fine-grained visual comparisons with local learning. In: CVPR (2014)
40. Zhang, H., Berg, A.C., Maire, M., Malik, J.: Svm-knn: Discriminative nearest neighbor classification for visual category recognition. In: CVPR, pp. 2126–2136 (2006)
41. Zhang, L., Lin, F., Zhang, B.: Support vector machine learning for image retrieval. In: ICIP, pp. 721–724 (2001)
42. Zhang, N., Farrell, R., Iandola, F., Darrell, T.: Deformable part descriptors for fine-grained recognition and attribute prediction. In: ICCV (2013)

Temporal Acoustic Words for Online Acoustic Event Detection

Rene Grzeszick$^{(\boxtimes)}$, Axel Plinge, and Gernot A. Fink

Department of Computer Science, TU Dortmund, Dortmund, Germany
{rene.grzeszick,axel.plinge,gernot.fink}@tu-dortmund.de

Abstract. The Bag-of-Features principle proved successful in many pattern recognition tasks ranging from document analysis and image classification to gesture recognition and even forensic applications. Lately these methods emerged in the field of acoustic event detection and showed very promising results. The detection and classification of acoustic events is an important task for many practical applications like video understanding, surveillance or speech enhancement. In this paper a novel approach for online acoustic event detection is presented that builds on top of the Bag-of-Features principle. Features are calculated for all frames in a given window. Applying the concept of feature augmentation additional temporal information is encoded in each feature vector. These feature vectors are then softly quantized so that a Bag-of-Feature representation is computed. These representations are evaluated by a classifier in a sliding window approach. The experiments on a challenging indoor dataset of acoustic events will show that the proposed method yields state-of-the-art results compared to other online event detection methods. Furthermore, it will be shown that the temporal feature augmentation significantly improves the recognition rates.

1 Introduction

The detection and classification of acoustic events is an important task for many practical applications. In analysis of multimedia content, the classification of objects, visual actions or movements and sounds can be combined for the understanding high level semantic events in videos [9]. It is also possible to do this multimedia event classification based on acoustic features alone [13]. Live applications include the analysis of acoustic events in various environments. Surveillance in cluttered scenes can be improved by an acoustic analysis in order to detect unexpected scenarios that are not visually recognizable (e.g. screams or glass breaking) [2,5]. Another application is meeting analysis and multi-modal interaction [20]. A slightly different field are outdoor applications like mobile robots for security, urban planning [21,26] or wildlife observations where the goal is to determine the presence of certain animals by acoustic features [10,27]. The task is difficult because of the diversity of the acoustic events. A single event is usually comprised of a variety of individual sounds, e.g. chair movement can produce knocking and rubbing sounds, handling paper can include rustling and

© Springer International Publishing Switzerland 2015
J. Gall et al. (Eds.): GCPR 2015, LNCS 9358, pp. 142–153, 2015.
DOI: 10.1007/978-3-319-24947-6_12

knocking on the table and so on. Human laughter or speech are fundamentally different depending on the individual person. It is desirable for a classification method of acoustic events to handle these variabilities and generalize from single instances to the broad range of sounds within an event class.

In order to capture the temporal variability of different sounds, HMMs are widely used. However, the Viterbi decoding requires a full sequence in order to predict the past [4]. Consequentially, most HMM approaches work offline and assign event classes to time points for a past sequence of events. Thus they commonly only address the task of offline analysis.

There are several methods for online classification and detection of acoustic events. The basic method is to use a GMM to model each category, as is done in speaker identification. The mean and variance of the feature vector are modelled as Gaussians. This is also known as the *Bag-of-Frames* approach to acoustic classification [1,6]. Extensions of this approach include the use of a background model [24]. Lately, methods that build on the Bag-of-Features principle have emerged in the field of acoustic event detection [2,13,16]. Acoustic features such as MFCCs are extracted for each frame and clustered in order to build a set of representatives. The occurrences of these representatives in a short time window are then counted and the resulting histogram is used for classification. A very similar approach is the so called superframe, where a histogram over a pre-classification is used instead [14,15]. Given the task at hand, these representatives are often referred to as an audio or acoustic word. One advantage of the Bag-of-Features models is that due to their simplicity and fast computation it is easy to employ them for online analysis.

The basic Bag-of-Features approach employs unsupervised hard vector quantization in order to derive a codebook by which to quantize the input [13]. This strategy is not always optimal for acoustic classification. It is rather advantageous to follow the GMM approach of using soft quantization by assuming a Gaussian distribution of the feature vectors and perform the training in a supervised manner [16], which is termed *Bag-of-Super-Features*.

These approaches discard any temporal information within the analysis window by treating all frames with disregard of temporal order. One way to reintroduce temporal information is to use a pyramid scheme [11]. The short time windows that are used for classification are well suited for a subdivision as proposed by the pyramid scheme [16]. In contrast to the pyramid scheme there are approaches in computer vision that propose directly including this information at feature level [8,17]. This is sometimes referred to as feature augmentation.

In [17] features are augmented with continuous x, y coordinates that encode the position of a feature within an image. This directly builds on the encoding abilities of the Fisher Vector approach. Given a set of features, a GMM is estimated in order to compute a set of representatives, e.g. visual or, here, acoustic words. These represent the global distribution of the samples. For the encoding, each feature is assigned to the visual/acoustic words based on the GMM posteriors. Then, the differences of the local distribution with respect the global distribution of the acoustic words are encoded the mean and covariance deviation vectors of the feature vector and the visual/acoustic word. While this allows to append continuous coordinates and yields a very detailed encoding compared to a hard or soft quantization, it also requires enough samples in order to robustly estimate the local distributions. Given the low number of frames in a time window this is hardly possible in acoustic classification and event detection.

In [8] quantized x, y coordinates that roughly encode the position of a feature within an image are appended. This approach preserves a tiling structure similar to the pyramid scheme and does not estimate the local feature distributions. The augmentation of the features with quantized coordinates causes the clustering step in the Bag-of-Feature computation to form different codebooks for different regions of an image or a time window. It could be shown that these adaptive codebooks cover the information contained in each tile better than a global codebook and allow for reducing the dimensionality of the representation.

In this paper it will be shown that the detection and classification of acoustic events based on Bag-of-Super-Features representations of acoustic words can be improved by augmenting the features with a temporal component. The evaluation will show that a tiling with adaptive codebooks as proposed in [8] outperforms plain Bag-of-Features methods as well as pyramid schemes in recognition rates while at the same time having a lower dimensionality. Furthermore, the evaluation will show the influence of parameters such as window length and codebook size on the Bag-of-Super-Features approach and finally a comparison with recent methods will show that the proposed approach achieves state-of-the-art results.

2   Method

For the acoustic event detection and classification, a single microphone or beamformed signal is processed in short time windows of w seconds. An overview of the processing method is shown in Fig. 2. For a given window i, a set of feature vectors $Y_i = (\boldsymbol{y}_1 \dots \boldsymbol{y}_K)$ is calculated for all K frames in this window. All features in this set are augmented with additional temporal information with respect to t he window. These features are then softly quantized by a GMM that has been trained in a supervised manner so that a Bag-of-Features representation is computed. Finally, a multinomial maximum likelihood classifier is applied.[1]

2.1   Features

For sound and especially speech processing, the mel frequency cepstral coefficients (MFCCs) are one of the most widely used features. The input signal is filtered by a triangular mel frequency filter bank. In the computational modeling of the human hearing process [25], ERB-spaced gammatone filterbanks are

---

[1] A video of the proposed method applied in our lab can be found at: https://vimeo.com/134489154.

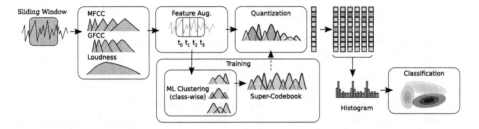

Fig. 1. Overview of the method: Given a window containing an acoustic signal, MFCCs, GFCCs and a loudness feature are computed. The resulting feature vector is augmented by a quantized time coordinate with respect to the window. A GMM is applied for clustering the features of each class in order to learn a supervised codebook. Finally, all features are quantized and the resulting histogram is classified by a multinomial maximum likelihood classifier.

used. From that the gammatone frequency cepstral coefficients (GFCCs) were derived [19]. The filterbank of the MFCCs is replaced by linear phase gamma-tone filters. The basic feature vector is comprised of regular MFCCs, GFCCs and the perceptual loudness derived from the A-weighted magnitude spectrum. A basic whitening step is performed by subtracting the mean and dividing by the standard deviation of the traning data.

2.2 Feature Augmentation

It has been shown that adding time information is able to improve the recognition rates of acoustic event detection and classification [16]. This idea is highly related to the encoding of spatial information in the vision domain [11]. In contrast to the popular pyramid approach, in the following, the time information is directly encoded at feature level [8].

Therefore, quantized time coordinates t are appended to the feature vector. Given a fixed window of w seconds in length, it is subdivided into N tiles of equal size so that the time is quantized into a value of $[1, .., N]$. Thus the augmented feature vector consists of 13 MFCCs m, 13 GFCCs g, loudness l and a temporal index t:

$$\boldsymbol{y}_k = (m_1, \ldots, m_{13}, g_1, \ldots, g_{13}, l, t)^T \qquad (1)$$

Note that when quantizing these features by a vector quantizer or a GMM in order to compute a Bag-of-Features representation this generates adaptive codebooks for each tile. This is a major difference to the spatial pyramid app-roach where the same codebook is used for each tile. Furthermore, the size of the codebook V determines the size of the overall feature representation whereas the size of the feature representation grows with each tile in the pyramid scheme [8,11]. In this approach only tiling is used and the upper levels of the pyramid are discarded as they usually do not carry much information (cf. [8]).

2.3   Bag-of-Super-Features

After augmenting the feature vectors with temporal information, a Bag-of-Features approach is applied. Hence, a codebook of *acoustic words* is estimated from the training set. Most Bag-of-Features approaches use clustering algorithms, e.g. k-means, on the complete training set to derive a codebook and later assign each feature to a centroid by hard quantization.

However, disregarding the labels in the clustering step can lead to mitigation of significant differences. A remedy for this effect is to build codebooks of size Z for all C classes Ω_c separately and then to concatenate them into a large super-codebook. This method is referred to as a *Bag-of-Super-Features* (cf. [16]) in analogy to the super-vector construct used in speaker identification [22].

Here, the expectation-maximization (EM) algorithm is applied to all feature vectors $\boldsymbol{y}_k$ for each class Ω_c in order to estimate Z means and deviations $\mu_{z,c}, \sigma_{z,c}$ for all C classes. All means and deviations are concatenated into a super-codebook $\boldsymbol{v}$ with $V = Z \cdot C$ elements

$$v_{j=(c \cdot Z+z)} = (\mu_{z,c}, \sigma_{z,c}) \tag{2}$$

where the index j is computed from the class index c and the Gaussian index z as $j = c \cdot Z + z$. Using this super-codebook, a soft quantization of a feature vector $\boldsymbol{y}_k$ can be computed as

$$q_{k,j}(\boldsymbol{y}_k, v_j) = \mathcal{N}(\boldsymbol{y}_k|v_j) \Big/ \sum_{j'} \mathcal{N}(\boldsymbol{y}_k|v_{j'}) . \tag{3}$$

Then, a histogram $\boldsymbol{b}$ can be computed over all K frames of an input window Y_i, where the occurrences of an acoustic word v_j in the window Y_i are estimated by

$$b_i(Y_i, v_j) = \frac{1}{K} \sum_k q_{k,j}(\boldsymbol{y}_k, v_j) . \tag{4}$$

These histograms can then be used as a feature representation of the window Y_i and as an input for a classifier.

2.4   Classification

The probability of an acoustic word v_j to occur in a given class Ω_c is estimated using a set of training windows $Y_i \in \Omega_c$ for each class c by Laplacian smoothing:

$$P(v_j|\Omega_c) = \frac{\alpha + \sum_{Y_i \in \Omega_c} b_i(Y_i, v_j)}{\alpha V + \sum_{u=1}^{V} \sum_{Y_m \in \Omega_c} b_m(Y_m, v_u)} , \tag{5}$$

where α is weighting factor for the smoothing (in practice $\alpha = 0.5$ showed good results). Hence, the probability is estimated by the fraction of the acoustic word v_j to occur in any window of class c with respect to all acoustic words occurring in any window class c. Rather than using a prior classification step to eliminate silence and background noise, as done in several systems (cf. [23]), the rejection class Ω_0 is trained with recordings where no event occurred.

Since all classes are assumed to be equally likely and have the same prior, maximum likelihood classification is used. The posterior is estimated using the relative frequency of all acoustic words

$$P(Y_i|\Omega_c) = \prod_{v_j \in v} P(v_j|\Omega_c)^{b_i(Y_i,v_j)} \ . \tag{6}$$

For the classification of a single window Y_i the maximum probability is chosen for deriving a label that is assigned to this window.

2.5   Detection

Due to the simplicity and rapid computation of this approach it can easily be adapted to event detection. Here, a sequence of acoustic events is given.

The classification window is applied as a sliding window that is moved forward for one frame k at a time. The recognition result is used for the frame that is centered in the window so that context information is available for a short time before and after the frame. As the window has a length of w sec, there is a processing delay of $w/2$ sec. As the implementation is running in real time, this delay is of high interest. In the experiments it will be shown that a delay of 300 ms is sufficient for practical purposes.

3   Evaluation

The proposed method has been evaluated on the very challenging office live task of the DCase (Detection and Classification of Acoustic Scenes and Events) challenge [6]. The temporal feature augmentation is compared with a Bag-of-Super-Features approach without feature augmentation and the pyramid scheme. Parameters with respect to temporal processing, like the windows size and tilings, as well as the influence of the codebook size are evaluated. The approach is then compared to the state of the art methods. In order to test for significant differences between classifiers and parameter configurations, a randomization test ($N = 1e5$) has been performed [7]. This method was chosen since it does avoid any distribution assumption.

3.1   D-Case Office Live Dataset

The dataset of this task is comprised of a variety of indoor sounds that could occur in an office or comparably a meeting room scenario. There are 16 sound classes *alert, clearthroat, cough, doorslam, drawer, keyboard, knock, laughter, mouse, pageturn, pendrop, phone, printer, speech, switch, keys* and additionally *silence* that have to be detected. The dataset provides a training set of segmented sequences for each of the 16 classes with a total length of 18 min and 49 s. Furthermore, there are three scripted test sequences which are publicly available with a total length of 5 min and 21 s. For each of these sequences two annotations are available. Since there is no training data for the silence/background class, the silence portions from the other two scripts were used to train the classifier for each script. The task is to detect the acoustic events in these sequences and classify them correctly. Hence, for different methods the precision and recall with respect to the number of frames that are correctly recognized are computed and the F-score is evaluated. All experiments were repeated 50 times using different codebooks each time over all sequences and annotations, yielding a total of 300 runs. Note that the differences in the scripts lead to a larger variance as the results for each script differ by about 3 %.

3.2 Temporal Processing

For the detection of acoustic events, two parameters are of interest with respect to the temporal processing. The first one is the length of the window w in seconds, the second one is the spatial setup within this window, i.e. the number of tiles. The F-scores of different window lengths and tilings for the temporal feature augmentation and the temporal pyramid scheme, as proposed in [16], are shown in Table 1. For the pyramids an additional max pooling step has been computed on top of the tilings. All parameter combinations have been evaluated using $Z = 30$, i.e. a super-codebook size of $V = 30 \cdot 17$.

It can be seen that for both methods, the best results are achieved by using a window length of 0.6 s. Furthermore, a baseline method with no spatial information has been evaluated with different window lengths as well. Again the best classification performance of $55.0 \pm 3.1\%$ has been achieved with a window length of 0.6 s. The results also show that the adaptive codebooks that are computed for each tile by the feature augmentation approach allow for a more fine grained analysis. The best results are achieved by using 6 or 8 tiles, while the pyramid scheme shows the best result with only two tiles.

Table 1. F-scores [%] and standard deviation for pyramids and temporal feature augmentation for different window lengths and tilings. The results are averaged over all three scripts, both annotations and 50 codebook generations using $Z = 30$.

		\multicolumn{6}{c}{tilings}					
	w	2	4	6	8	10	12
temporal	0.3	50.6±3.9	50.8±3.5	50.8±3.4	50.6±3.3	50.7±3.4	50.6±3.4
temporal	0.6	53.8±3.0	55.3±2.6	55.7±3.1	55.7±3.0	55.4±2.8	55.5±2.7
temporal	0.9	51.7±5.9	53.5±4.2	55.2±4.5	55.3±4.6	55.1±3.9	55.2±4.2
temporal	1.2	50.0±5.3	52.0±3.7	53.1±4.6	54.2±4.4	54.1±3.9	54.1±3.6
temporal	1.5	43.1±9.1	48.3±6.3	49.9±6.4	51.1±6.2	51.8±5.8	52.0±5.1
pyramid	0.3	50.3±3.6	50.1±3.5	50.0±3.5	49.7±3.5	49.5±3.4	49.6±3.4
pyramid	0.6	54.9±3.1	54.7±2.8	54.6±2.8	54.4±2.7	54.4±2.8	53.9±2.9
pyramid	0.9	54.6±3.9	54.2±3.8	54.0±3.9	53.8±4.0	53.6±4.1	53.5±4.2
pyramid	1.2	54.3±3.6	54.3±3.5	53.9±3.4	53.9±3.3	53.6±3.3	53.4±3.3
pyramid	1.5	50.7±5.4	50.6±5.1	50.2±5.0	50.1±5.0	49.7±5.0	49.4±5.0

Using the best configuration for each augmentation scheme, the permutation test has been performed. This revealed that the temporal augmentation significantly ($p < 0.01$) outperformed the pyramid and the unaugmented classification. It also showed that the pyramid did not outperform the unaugmented version.

3.3 Codebook Size

Different codebook sizes of $Z = 20, 30, 40, 60, 90, 120$ were evaluated for the pyramid approach, the temporal feature augmentation and a Bag-of-Super-Features approach without temporal information. For all methods the best performing temporal processing configurations are used. Hence, a window size of 0.6 s is used for all three approaches. For the pyramid two tiles and for the acoustic words with temporal feature augmentation six tiles are computed.

While for the augmented features the size of the overall feature representation is equal to the super-codebook size $V = C \cdot Z$, the concatenation in the pyramid scheme further increases the size of the final representation. Hence, a temporal pyramid with N tiles at the bottom and one top layer has a final feature representation of the size $(N + 1) \cdot V$.

In Table 2 the results are shown. It can be observed that small codebooks of 30 or 40 acoustic words per class yields good results and that the performance deteriorates with an increasing codebook size. The best performance is achieved using temporal feature augmentation and a codebook size that uses 40 centroids per class (i.e. a super-codebook size of $V = 680$).

3.4 Comparison with State-of-the-art

For comparison, some state-of-the-art methods were re-implemented and used in combination with the MFCC-GFCC features. Additionally, published results for the D-Case office live development set were used for comparing the performance.

Re-implemented methods. The Bag-of-Frames method [1], the Bag-of-Audio words method [13] and a Bag-of-Features approach using Fisher encoding and a linear SVM (cf. [3]) were evaluated. The Bag-of-Frames estimates one GMM per class. It achieves the best performance with a codebook size of $Z = 30$ per GMM. The Bag-of-Audio words uses hard vector quantization with $V = 1000$ as originally proposed and an SVM with a histogram intersection kernel. As Fisher

Table 2. F-scores [%] and standard deviation for pyramids and temporal feature augmentation for different codebook sizes. Best performing temporal configurations are used. Results are averaged over all three scripts, both annotations and 50 codebooks.

Classifier \ Z	20	30	40	60	90	120
feature augmentation	54.3±2.8	55.7±3.1	55.9±3.5	54.8±4.4	51.5±4.9	48.0±4.8
pyramid	54.3±3.2	54.9±3.1	55.1±3.2	54.5±4.0	52.2±4.6	48.9±4.7
w/o temp processing	54.4±2.7	55.0±3.1	54.8±3.3	54.1±4.1	51.6±5.0	48.0±4.9

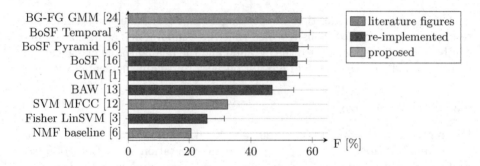

Fig. 2. Comparison of different classifiers and literature values on the D-Case office live development set with the proposed approach * as F-scores [%]. The re-implemented results are averaged over all three scripts, both annotations and 50 codebook generations. The best parameter configuration for each classifier was chosen (Color figure online).

encoding usually uses smaller codebooks, the best performance was achieved with a codebook size of $Z = 5$ and encoding the mean and covariance deviation vectors. Detailed results are shown in Fig. 2 in blue. The Bag-of-Audio words achieved an F-score of only 47 %, which is most likely due to the unsupervised codebook learning. Also the Fisher approach yields an F-score of only 26 %. This clearly demonstrates that short time windows do not cover enough frames in order to robustly estimate the local distributions around each centroid of the codebook. With an F-Score of 56 % the temporal augmentation outperformed the well known Bag-of-Audio-Words method. The difference was proven significant ($p < 0.01$) by the permutation test.

Results from the literature. When comparing these results with the ones published for the D-Case office live development set, shown in Fig. 2 in gray, it can be seen that the temporal augmentation outperforms most live detection methods. Note however, that it is difficult to accurately compare to these results as the protocol might deviate with respect to the number of runs or even more importantly scripts or annotations used in the evaluation. The offline HMM based results are not shown since the task of online detection is investigated. Typically, the best performing offline HMM approaches achieve a 20 % higher F-score (cf. [18]). The best performing online method is the GMM based approach using a separate background model [24]. With an F-score of 56.3 % it is well in the range of our proposed method. However, the authors state that it is not robust to noise.

3.5   Result Discussion

Figure 3 shows the class-wise F-Score over all sequences. The most difficult categories include switch and mouse, which usually last only a few ms and are therefore very difficult to detect in an online detection approach that relies on

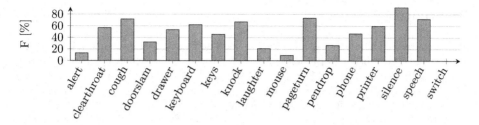

Fig. 3. Classwise F-Score on D-Case Develpment set sequences using the proposed method.

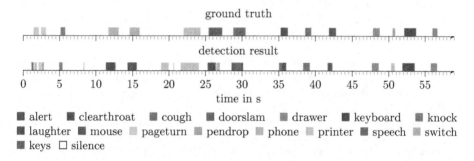

Fig. 4. Example detection results for the first 60 s of sequence 01 of the D-Case office live development set using the proposed method with temporal feature augmentation using six tiles over a window size of 0.6 s and a codebook size of $Z = 40$.

some context. In most cases those are mistaken for silence. Longer lasting (e.g. printing) or very distinctive acoustic events (e.g. knocks or coughs) are more easily recognized. An exemplary result on the first 60 s of a sequence is shown in Fig. 4.

4   Conclusion

In this paper a novel method for online acoustic event detection has been proposed. It builds on the Bag-of-Features principle and integrates feature augmentation with a temporal component and a supervised codebook learning step.

The experiments on a challenging indoor dataset of acoustic events show that the proposed method yields state-of-the-art results compared to other online event detection methods. Furthermore, it could be shown that the feature augmentation yields significant improvements over a basic Bag-of-Features approach and the well known pyramid scheme, while at the same time reducing the dimensionality of the representation. The results show that for practical purposes a processing delay of only 300 ms allows for the integration of enough context to robustly recognize acoustic events.

References

1. Aucouturier, J.J., Defreville, B., Pachet, F.: The Bag-of-Frames Approach to Audio Pattern Recognition: A Sufficient Model for Urban Soundscapes but Not for Polyphonic Music. J. Acoust. Soc. Am. **122**(2), 881–891 (2007)
2. Carletti, V., Foggia, P., Percannella, G., Saggese, A., Strisciuglio, N., Vento, M.: Audio Surveillance using a Bag of Aural Words Classifier. In: 2013 10th IEEE International Conference on Advanced Video and Signal Based Surveillance, pp. 81–86. IEEE (2013)
3. Chatfield, K., Lempitsky, V., Vedaldi, A., Zisserman, A.: The devil is in the details: an evaluation of recent feature encoding methods. In: Proceeding British Machine Vision Conference (BMVC) (2011)
4. Fink, G.A.: Markov Models for Pattern Recognition. From Theory to Applications. Advances in Computer Vision and Pattern Recognition, 2nd edn. Springer, London (2014)
5. Foggia, P., Saggese, A., Strisciuglio, N., Vento, M.: Cascade classifiers trained on Gammatonegrams for reliably detecting Audio Events. In: 11th IEEE International Conference on Advanced Video and Signal Based Surveillance (AVSS), pp. 50–55. IEEE (2014)
6. Giannoulis, D., Benetos, E., Stowell, D., Rossignol, M., Lagrange, M., Plumbley, M.D.: Detection and classification of acoustic scenes and events: an IEEE AASP challenge. In: IEEE Workshop on Applications of Signal Processing to Audio and Acoustics (WASPAA), pp. 1–4. IEEE (2013)
7. Good, P.: Permutation Tests - A Practical Guide to Resampling Methods for Testing Hypotheses. Springer Series in Statistics, 2nd edn. Springer, New York (2000)
8. Grzeszick, R., Rothacker, L., Fink, G.A.: Bag-of-Features Representations using Spatial Visual Vocabularies for Object Classification. In: Proceeding International Conference on Image Processing (ICIP) (2013)
9. Jiang, Y.G., Bhattacharya, S., Chang, S.F., Shah, M.: High-level event recognition in unconstrained videos. Int. J. Multimedia Inf. Retrieval **2**(2), 73–101 (2013)
10. Klinck, H., Stelzer, K., Jafarmadar, K., Mellinger, D.K.: AAS Endurance: An Autonomous Acoustic Sailboat for Marine Mammal Research. In: International Robotic Sailing Conference (2009)
11. Lazebnik, S., Schmid, C., Ponce, J.: Beyond bags of features: Spatial pyramid matching for recognizing natural scene categories. In: Proceeding IEEE Conference on Computer Vision and Pattern Recognition (CVPR), vol. 2, pp. 2169–2178 (2006)
12. Nogueira, W., Roma, G., Herrera, P.: Automatic Event Classification using Front End Single Channel Noise Reduction, MFCC Features and a Support Vector Machine Classifier. Technical report, IEEE AASP Challenge: Detection and Classification of Acoustic Scenes and Events (2013). http://c4dm.eecs.qmul.ac.uk/sceneseventschallenge/abstracts/OL/NR2.pdf
13. Pancoast, S., Akbacak, M.: Bag-of-audio-words approach for multimedia event classification. In: Interspeech, pp. 2105–2108 (2012)
14. Phan, H., Maasz, M., Mazur, R., Mertins, A.: Random regression forests for acoustic event detection and classification. IEEE/ACM Trans. Audio Speech Lang. Process. **23**(1), 20–31 (2014). http://ieeexplore.ieee.org/articleDetails.jsp?arnumber=6949625
15. Phan, H., Mertins, A.: Exploiting superframe cooccurence for acoustic event recognition. In: European Signal Processing Conference (2014)

16. Plinge, A., Grzeszick, R., Fink, G.A.: A bag-of-features approach to acoustic event detection. In: IEEE International Conference on Acoustics, Speech, and Signal Processing (2014)
17. Sánchez, J., Perronnin, F., De Campos, T.: Modeling the spatial layout of images beyond spatial pyramids. Pattern Recogn. Lett. **33**(16), 2216–2223 (2012)
18. Schröder, J., Cauchi, B., Schädler, M.R., Moritz, N., Adiloglu, K., Anemüller, J., Doclo, S., Kollmeier, B., Goetze, S.: Acoustic event detection using signal enhancement and spectro-temporal feature extraction. Technical report, IEEE AASP Challenge: Detection and Classification of Acoustic Scenes and Events (2013). http://c4dm.eecs.qmul.ac.uk/sceneseventschallenge/abstracts/OL/SCS.pdf
19. Shao, Y., Srinivasan, S., Wang, D.: Incorporating auditory feature uncertainties in robust speaker identification. In: IEEE International Conference on Acoustics, Speech, and Signal Processing, pp. 277–280 (2007)
20. Shivappa, S.T., Trivedi, M.M., Rao, B.D.: Audiovisual information fusion in human computer interfaces and intelligent environments: a survey. Proc. IEEE **98**(10), 1692–1715 (2010)
21. Steele, D., Krijnders, J.D., Guastavino, C.: The Sensor City Initiative: Cognitive Sensors for Soundscape Transformations. GIS Ostrava (2013)
22. Tang, H., Chu, S.M., Hasegawa-Johnson, M., Huang, T.S.: Partially supervised speaker clustering. IEEE Trans. Pattern Anal. Mach. Intell. **34**(5), 959–971 (2012)
23. Temko, A., Malkin, R.G., Zieger, C., Macho, D., Nadeu, C., Omologo, M.: CLEAR evaluation of acoustic event detection and classification systems. In: Stiefelhagen, R., Garofolo, J.S. (eds.) CLEAR 2006. LNCS, vol. 4122, pp. 311–322. Springer, Heidelberg (2007)
24. Vuegen, L., Broeck, B.V.D., Karsmakers, P., Gemmeke, J.F., Vanrumste, B., Hamme, H.V.: An MFCC-GMM approach for event detection and classification. Technical report, IEEE AASP Challenge: Detection and Classification of Acoustic Scenes and Events (2013). http://c4dm.eecs.qmul.ac.uk/sceneseventschallenge/abstracts/OL/VVK.pdf
25. Wang, D., Brown, G.J. (eds.): Computational Auditory Scene Analysis: Principles, Algorithms, and Applications. IEEE Press (2006)
26. Young, S.H., Scanlon, M.V.: Robotic vehicle uses acoustic array for detection and localization in Urban environments. in: SPIE Proceeding Mobile Robot Perception, vol. 4364, pp. 264–273 (2001)
27. Zeppelzauer, M., Stöger, A.S., Breiteneder, C.: Acoustic detection of elephant presence in noisy environments. In: Proceedings of the 2nd ACM international workshop on Multimedia analysis for ecological data, pp. 3–8. ACM (2013)

Human Pose Analysis

Biternion Nets: Continuous Head Pose Regression from Discrete Training Labels

Lucas Beyer[✉], Alexander Hermans, and Bastian Leibe

Visual Computing Institute, RWTH Aachen University, Aachen, Germany
beyer@vision.rwth-aachen.de

Abstract. While head pose estimation has been studied for some time, continuous head pose estimation is still an open problem. Most approaches either cannot deal with the periodicity of angular data or require very fine-grained regression labels. We introduce biternion nets, a CNN-based approach that can be trained on very coarse regression labels and still estimate fully continuous 360° head poses. We show state-of-the-art results on several publicly available datasets. Finally, we demonstrate how easy it is to record and annotate a new dataset with coarse orientation labels in order to obtain continuous head pose estimates using our biternion nets.

1 Introduction

The estimation of head poses is an important building block for higher-level computer vision systems such as social scene understanding, human-computer interfaces, driver monitoring, and security systems. For many of these tasks, a continuous head pose angle is arguably more useful than few discrete orientation classes as yielded by most current head pose systems [4,8,34].

While many face pose and gaze estimation methods have been covered in the literature, the task of regressing *head* pose is distinctly different in that it also handles people not facing the camera, resulting in poses spanning the full 360° spectrum. Thus, head pose estimators need to be able to cope with the periodicity of angular data, *i.e.* the fact that 361° corresponds to 1° and, for a head pose of 0°, a prediction of 359° is no worse than a prediction of 1°. Face pose and gaze estimators can conveniently sidestep this difficulty by constraining the prediction range to non-periodic intervals such as [−90°, 90°]. Another difficulty in learning a head pose regressor lies in obtaining enough training data with accurate regression labels [6,11]. All publicly available datasets, except [5], are either restricted to coarse orientation bins, or to the range of front-facing poses [2,6,9,10,14,15].

A multitude of approaches [25,32] has been proposed which solve only one of the two aforementioned problems: either they cannot cope with periodicity [24,26,34], or they need fine-grained regression data [16,33,35]. Since none

Electronic supplementary material The online version of this chapter (doi:10.1007/978-3-319-24947-6_13) contains supplementary material, which is available to authorized users.

J. Gall et al. (Eds.): GCPR 2015, LNCS 9358, pp. 157–168, 2015.
DOI: 10.1007/978-3-319-24947-6_13

of this is satisfactory, we propose a principled approach to solve both problems simultaneously.

Our approach is based on convolutional neural networks (CNNs), for which we propose a novel output layer embedding an angle into two dimensions, coupled with a fitting cost function. It is able to handle fully periodic, continuous regression while *only requiring coarse, discrete class-labels* as training data, which are easily obtainable from video recordings. We call our approach *biternion nets*. Before demonstrating the effectiveness of the biternion output layer, we validate our CNN architecture on several publicly available datasets and show that it yields state-of-the-art results.

In summary, our contributions are threefold: (1) We present a CNN architecture that outperforms state-of-the art results on several public head pose datasets. (2) We propose a novel combination of output layer and cost function to elegantly solve the problem of periodic orientation regression, which we call *biternion nets*. (3) We show that we can learn *continuous* head-pose regression from discrete training labels. To demonstrate this, we present continuous regression results obtained from a biternion net trained on data recorded and annotated in less than two and a half hours.

2   Related Work

Head pose estimation has been a very active research field for the past 20 years [25,32]. Over time, authors have developed many different methods to approach this problem. The probably most popular direction is the functional mapping of images to a feature space where classifiers or regressors can directly be applied. These mappings range from simple gradient-based features [7,21,24], over covariance features [34], to learned functional mappings [4,26,33]. These approaches often result in a manifold embedding of the images [26,34]. However, if training data is sparse, it is hard to ensure the quality of these manifolds [19]. Another approach is to find facial landmarks, such as eye and mouth locations, and use these to determine the pose of a face [9]. It is also possible to use tracking information to get a good prior for the head pose [7,10]. Here, interactions between the body pose and the head pose can be exploited [5,8]. Several of these techniques have also been used for objects such as cars or chairs [18,28,33].

While some of these approaches work on high resolution images [2,10,12,14], the majority of them is based on low resolution images [5,24,26,34]. With the recent availability of cheap RGB-D sensors, depth information has also been used to improve head pose estimation [12].

The high activity within this field has resulted in a large number of different datasets for head pose estimation [1,2,5,6,9,10,14,15,34], most of which are face pose rather than head pose datasets and often only contain sparse head poses and fairly coarse orientation labels. As we are interested in continuous head pose estimations, most of these datasets are not suitable for our experiments.

Based on the available datasets, most approaches focus on coarse face poses, while only few *head* pose estimation approaches and datasets exist [5,34,35].

Wu and Toyama [35] estimate gradient distributions from 1024 different viewpoints and match new views to the nearest viewpoint to determine the pose. Benfold and Reid [5] use the walking direction obtained from unsupervised people tracking in a video sequence to train a regression forest for the head pose. Tosato et al. [34] use covariance features to classify head poses into a small set of orientation bins.

CNNs have also been used for orientation estimation before. Qi [28] fine-tunes a large pre-trained CNN to classify the orientation of chairs using a large amount of rendered chairs with precise labels. However, using CNNs pre-trained on ImageNet for low-resolution head pose estimation makes no sense due to the significantly different filter resolution, type of data, and learning task. Most similar to our approach is the one by Osadchy et al. [26], which also uses a CNN for continuous head pose estimation. They learn a face manifold on (non-public) data with regression labels, which enables them to jointly detect and estimate the pose of faces. In contrast to us, they focus on using face pose data to improve face detection and do not address the periodicity problem.

Some approaches also aim at solving the periodicity problem [16,18,33]. However, their approaches are typically based on nearest-neighbor matching or kernel density estimation, meaning that they require dense orientation labels for training. All three of the above approaches use fine grained face datasets [1,14] and it is unclear how well they could perform for head pose estimation.

To the best of our knowledge, only Huang et al. [19] aim at learning continuous regressors from a discrete face pose dataset. They learn a mixture of local tangent subspaces that are robust to regression regions with bad coverage in the training set. Their representation is based on HOG features and they use high resolution images. It is questionable whether their approach can deal with head poses, as HOG features are not very expressive for the back of a head. Furthermore, they do not evaluate how continuous their regression really is.

In conclusion, based on existing approaches, the task of continuous periodic head pose estimation is still unsolved. Here our approach comes into play.

3   CNNs for Head Pose Estimation

Throughout this paper, we work in the framework of deep convolutional networks and stochastic, gradient-based optimization. In this section, we present the specific network architecture we use for all experiments, changing only the output layer and cost function to match the task at hand. We then apply it to multiple publicly available datasets, consistently outperforming current state-of-the-art methods on those datasets.

3.1   The Network Architecture

We use a moderately deep, batch-normalized [20], VGG-style network architecture [30] consisting of six convolutional layers with 24, 24, 48, 48, 64 and 64 feature channels, respectively, followed by a single hidden layer of 512 units, and train it for a fixed duration of 50 epochs in all our experiments. For all details about the network and the training procedure, please refer to the supplementary material. We implemented the network in Theano [3] using IPython notebook [27]. All numbers reported within this paper are averages over five runs. While we will show that this architecture already performs very well, it is likely possible to reduce the error even further by using deeper networks with more careful regularization and a bag of other well-known tricks [13,17,23,29,36]. We do not further go down that road, since the goal of this section is simply to demonstrate the suitability of CNNs in general, and our architecture in particular, for predicting head poses on low-resolution images.

3.2   Experimental Validation

We use the collection of datasets provided by Tosato *et al.* [34] to validate our approach. First, we show results on those datasets that treat pose estimation as a classification task in Table 1. These datasets contain very rough pose bins, such as Front, Back, Left and Right, with the addition of FrontLeft and FrontRight for HIIT and HOCoffee, and Background for the 5-class version of the QMUL dataset.

In this case, the network's output layer is a softmax-layer and the cost being optimized is the negative log-likelihood. While the accuracies obtained by state-of-the-art methods are already high, we show that our CNN architecture achieves a significant improvement as it reduces the error by about a third across all datasets.

Table 1. Class-average accuracies on the four classification datasets from [34]. The sample counts refer to the provided train/test splits. We obtain state-of-the-art results on all datasets.

	HIIT	HOCoffee	HOC	QMUL	
# Samples	12 000/12 007	9522/8595	6860/5021	7603/7618	9813/8725
# Classes	6	6	4	4	4 + 1
Tosato *et al.* [34]	96.5 %	81.0 %	78.69 %	94.25 %	91.18 %
Lallemand *et al.* [21]	-	-	79.9 %	-	-
Our CNN	**98.70 %**	**86.99 %**	**83.97 %**	**95.58 %**	**94.30 %**

We next turn to the datasets with continuous regression labels. Statistics about the datasets are shown in Table 2, together with our results. The IDIAP Head Pose dataset, which stems from a video recording of few people in a meeting room, has a very restricted range of angles; specifically, 94 % of the pan angles lie within the rather narrow, front-facing range of $[-60°, 60°]$. For this experiment, the output of our network is computed by a fully-connected layer with three outputs and the cost function is the mean absolute deviation. This simple approach to pan-tilt-roll regression outperforms the state-of-the art in all three dimensions. Please note that with a linear output layer and the MAD cost

Table 2. A comparison to two regression datasets from [34]. The first number is the mean absolute angular deviation, the second its standard deviation across test-samples. We obtain state-of-the-art results on all datasets.

# Samples	IDIAP Head Pose			CAVIAR-c	CAVIAR-o
	42 304/23 991			10 660/10 665	10 802/10 889
Pose range	pan	tilt	roll	pan	pan
	[-101,101]	[-73,23]	[-46,65]	[0, 360]	[0, 360]
Tosato *et al.* [34]	10.3°±10.6°	4.5°±5.3°	4.3°±3.8°	22.7°±18.4°	35.3°±24.6°
Ba & Odobez [2]	8.7°±9.1°	19.1°±15.4°	9.7°±7.1°	-	-
Our CNN	**5.9°±7.2°**	**2.8°±2.6°**	**3.5°±3.9°**	**19.2°±24.2°**	**25.2°±26.4°**

function, the network does not learn the pan, tilt and roll angles jointly; they merely share a common feature representation.[1]

The CAVIAR dataset comes in both a clean version containing only fully-visible heads, and an occluded version containing *only* partially-occluded heads. While they do come in the full range of angles, almost 40 % of the training samples lie within ±4° of the four canonical orientations. A major downside of this dataset is that most images have been upscaled to 50-by-50 pixels from their original size of, on average, 7-by-7 pixels. We still perform the comparison for the sake of completeness, and our network manages to beat the current state-of-the-art on such a difficult dataset.

These experiments show that the network architecture we use forms a solid basis by itself and we can now use it to further investigate continuous, periodic orientation regression.

4   Periodic Orientation Regression

None of the datasets in the previous section really uncover a crucial problem for full head-orientation regression: periodicity. We can demonstrate that this is a real problem by adding 360° to all negative pan values of the IDIAP dataset. With this semantically identical dataset, the exact same (naive) network used in the previous section becomes very unstable and only reaches errors of 12.9°, 4.5° and 5.3° for pan, tilt and roll, respectively.

For memory-based models such as k-NN and kernel-methods, periodicity only plays a role during the voting part of the algorithm, where it can easily be solved by a modulo operation. But this kind of model suffers from the inherent need of fine-grained training data, hence our focus on parametric models.

For parametric models such as CNNs, periodicity may cause problems in two different ways: (1) The cost function to be optimized is unaware of the fact that a prediction of 359° for a ground truth orientation of 0° should incur the same loss as 1°. Unfortunately, simply applying a `mod` operator to the output of the

---

[1] This becomes evident by computing the derivatives of the cost w.r.t. the parameters: the tilt and roll terms are absent from the derivative w.r.t. the pan and vice-versa.

network results in a discontinuous error function that can no longer be optimized robustly. (2) A regression output which results from a matrix-vector product, such as performed in most parametric models, is an inherently linear operation, while we ideally want a circular output.

Our biternion approach solves both of these problems in an elegant way.

4.1 Von Mises Cost Function

The first problem of discontinuity in the cost function can be addressed by turning to the von Mises distribution [22], which is a close approximation to the normal distribution on the unit circle:

$$p_{\text{VM}}(\varphi \mid \mu, \kappa) = \frac{e^{\kappa \cos(\varphi - \mu)}}{2\pi I_0(\kappa)} . \tag{1}$$

Equation (1) defines its probability density function, where φ is an angle, μ is the mean angle of the distribution, κ is inversely related to the variance of the approximated Gaussian, and $I_0(\kappa)$ is the modified Bessel function of order 0, which is a constant for fixed κ. Since it leverages the cosine function to avoid any discontinuity, it is well-suited for gradient-based optimization and we can derive the following cost function by inverting and scaling it accordingly:

$$C_{\text{VM}}(\varphi \mid t; \kappa) = 1 - e^{\kappa(\cos(\varphi - t) - 1)}. \tag{2}$$

In the cost formulation, we call t the target value and κ is a simple hyperparameter that controls the tails of the loss function.

4.2 Biternion Representation for Orientation Regression

While the von Mises cost presented above solves the first issue, the fundamental problem of predicting a periodic value using a linear operation persists. Also, $\|\mathbf{y}\| = 1$Inspired by the quaternion representation often found in computer graphics, we propose a natural alternative representation of an angle by the two-dimensional vector consisting of its sine and cosine $\mathbf{y} = (\cos\varphi, \sin\varphi)$, which we call the *biternion representation*. Surprisingly, the only use of a similar encoding we found in the related literature is that by Osadchy *et al.* [26], who also embed angles into a similar, albeit different, higher-dimensional space. Unfortunately, their approach does not solve the periodicity problem since it uses the discontinuous atan2 function.

The biternion representation immediately suggests the use of the continuous, cyclic cosine cost widely used in the NLP literature [31]:

$$C_{\cos}(\mathbf{y} \mid \mathbf{t}) = 1 - \frac{\mathbf{y} \cdot \mathbf{t}}{\|\mathbf{y}\| \, \|\mathbf{t}\|}. \tag{3}$$

Implementing a biternion output-layer in any framework for neural networks is relatively straightforward, since all that is needed is a fully-connected layer and a normalization layer. For clarity, Eq. 4 gives the operation performed by a biternion-layer during the forward pass, where $\mathbf{W} \in \mathbb{R}^{n \times 2}$ and $\mathbf{b} \in \mathbb{R}^2$ are the learnable parameters from the fully-connected layer:

$$f_{\mathrm{BT}}(\mathbf{x}; \mathbf{W}, \mathbf{b}) = \frac{\mathbf{Wx} + \mathbf{b}}{\|\mathbf{Wx} + \mathbf{b}\|} \qquad (4)$$

The derivative of the normalization, necessary for the backward pass, can then be stated as

$$\partial_{x_i} \frac{\mathbf{x}}{\|\mathbf{x}\|} = \partial_{x_i} \frac{\mathbf{x}}{\sqrt{\sum_j x_j^2}} = \frac{\sum_{j \neq i} x_j^2}{\left(\sum_j x_j^2\right)^{\frac{3}{2}}} = \frac{\sum_{j \neq i} x_j^2}{\|\mathbf{x}\|^3}. \qquad (5)$$

Notice how (1) the normalization in the biternion layer makes sure the output values are learned *jointly* and (2) the normalization terms in C_{cos} can subsequently be omitted.

Finally, the ensembling of multiple biternion predictions, as needed by some augmentation techniques, can simply be performed by averaging the vectors, since the average of unit vectors is again a unit vector, a fact also used by Hara *et al.* [16].

Biternions are Restricted Quaternions. We now show that biternions correspond to unit-quaternions restricted to a single reference axis of rotation. Let Q_φ be the quaternion $\left(a_x \sin(\frac{\varphi}{2}), a_y \sin(\frac{\varphi}{2}), a_z \sin(\frac{\varphi}{2}), \cos(\frac{\varphi}{2})\right)$ representing a rotation of φ around the axis $\mathbf{a}$ and Q_θ the quaternion representing a rotation of θ around the same axis. A quaternion representing the immediate rotation from Q_φ to Q_θ can be computed as $\frac{Q_\varphi}{Q_\theta}$, which corresponds to:

$$\begin{pmatrix} -\cos(\frac{\varphi}{2})a_x \sin(\frac{\theta}{2}) + a_x \sin(\frac{\varphi}{2})\cos(\frac{\theta}{2}) - a_y \sin(\frac{\varphi}{2})a_z \sin(\frac{\theta}{2}) + a_z \sin(\frac{\varphi}{2})a_y \sin(\frac{\theta}{2}) \\ -\cos(\frac{\varphi}{2})a_y \sin(\frac{\theta}{2}) + a_y \sin(\frac{\varphi}{2})\cos(\frac{\theta}{2}) - a_z \sin(\frac{\varphi}{2})a_x \sin(\frac{\theta}{2}) + a_x \sin(\frac{\varphi}{2})a_z \sin(\frac{\theta}{2}) \\ -\cos(\frac{\varphi}{2})a_z \sin(\frac{\theta}{2}) + a_z \sin(\frac{\varphi}{2})\cos(\frac{\theta}{2}) - a_x \sin(\frac{\varphi}{2})a_y \sin(\frac{\theta}{2}) + a_y \sin(\frac{\varphi}{2})a_x \sin(\frac{\theta}{2}) \\ \cos(\frac{\varphi}{2})\cos(\frac{\theta}{2}) + a_x \sin(\frac{\varphi}{2})a_x \sin(\frac{\theta}{2}) + a_y \sin(\frac{\varphi}{2})a_y \sin(\frac{\theta}{2}) + a_z \sin(\frac{\varphi}{2})a_z \sin(\frac{\theta}{2}) \end{pmatrix}$$

Using the fact that $\|\mathbf{a}\| = 1$, the last entry of the quaternion—which encodes the cosine of half the angle represented by the quaternion—simplifies to $\cos(\frac{\varphi}{2})\cos(\frac{\theta}{2}) + \sin(\frac{\varphi}{2})\sin(\frac{\theta}{2}) = \cos(\frac{\varphi - \theta}{2})$. The other entries can similarly be simplified, resulting in a quaternion representing a rotation of the angle from φ to θ around the same axis $\mathbf{a}$. This shows that biternions can be seen as quaternions around a fixed reference axis $\mathbf{a}$ and the cosine cost corresponds to the amplitude of the direct rotation between the predicted and the target biternions.

Relationship to the von Mises Cost. By comparing C_{VM} and C_{cos}, it is visible that they do *not* compute the same expression, *i.e.*, the biternion-layer coupled with the cosine cost does *not* optimize the von Mises cost. The von Mises cost for the biternion layer can be written as:

$$C_{\mathrm{VM,BT}}(\mathbf{y} \mid \mathbf{t}) = 1 - e^{\kappa(\mathbf{y} \cdot \mathbf{t} - 1)}. \qquad (6)$$

Notice the similarity to Eq. 3; the main difference is the presence of e, which "pushes down" the error around the target value, in effect penalizing small mistakes less strongly.

4.3   Experimental Results

In order to investigate the relative usefulness of the von Mises cost and the biternion representation for periodic regression, we now turn to the TownCentre dataset [5]. This dataset contains heads of tracked pedestrians in a shopping district, annotated with head pose regression labels. The prior distribution of the pose angle is shown in the middle of Fig. 1. For all experiments, we train on 7920 heads of 3960 persons and evaluate on 774 heads of 387 random but *different* persons. The results can be seen in Table 3.

As a first baseline, we train a shallow linear regressor on raw pixel values. We then train a deep CNN using a naive regression output and cost, as described in Sect. 3.2. While the depth of the architecture allows it to perform much better, it is still plagued by the two problems of cyclic regression. Using the von Mises cost solves the first problem in the cost function; this

Table 3. Quantitative regression results for the TownCentre dataset [5].

Method	MAE
Linear Regression	64.1°±45.0°
Naive Regression	38.9°±40.7°
Von Mises	29.4°±31.3°
Biternion	21.6°±25.2°
Biternion+Von Mises	**20.8°±24.7°**
Benfold&Reid [5]	25.6° / 64.9°

reduces the error by a significant amount, showing that the more appropriate cost function indeed does aid optimization. Following this, we evaluate the performance of a biternion net both with the cosine cost and the von Mises cost. As can be seen, the expressive power of the biternion layer solves both problems encountered in periodic regression and produces the best results.

It should be noted that we cannot fairly compare to most of the related work for various reasons: the results in [8] have been computed on only 15 persons, which is far from representative for this dataset. Chamveha *et al.* [7] use a tracker and scene-specific orientation priors. Even the numbers from Benfold and Reid [5] are not a fair comparison since they use walking direction as a prior. The first of their numbers in Table 3 is achieved by a regressor which has seen all persons and their walking direction during training[2], while the second of their numbers has not seen any of the persons since it has been trained on a different dataset.

5   Continuous Regression from Discrete Training Labels

We have shown that biternion nets are well-suited to fully-periodic head pose regression. We now turn to the third contribution of this paper, namely the ability to perform continuous head pose regression using only discrete pose labels for training. To simulate discrete pose labels, we discretize the continuous annotations of the TownCentre dataset. By varying the number of discrete bins, we generate multiple datasets on which we train various approaches using only *the centers of the bins* as training labels. We then evaluate the predictions made by these approaches by computing their mean angular deviation w.r.t. the full regression annotations of the test set. All results are reported in Table 4.

---

[2] Their setup is justified for their task, but makes a fair comparison impossible.

Table 4. Regression results from different approaches for different discretizations. Here infinity represents no discretization. Note that the Biternion layer handles the discrete labels very well, both with the cosine and the von Mises cost.

Class bins	Class center	Class interpolation	Naive regression	Von Mises	Biternion	Biternion + Von Mises
3	37.2°±32.8°	35.5°±30.4°	45.5°±39.7°	36.6°±34.5°	**32.1°±28.1°**	32.2°±28.8°
4	34.9°±30.5°	31.7°±29.3°	43.0°±40.6°	33.4°±32.2°	27.1°±27.3°	**26.9°±27.4°**
6	26.1°±28.4°	24.1°±27.6°	38.3°±38.5°	31.8°±33.1°	**22.1°±25.5°**	22.7°±26.7°
8	24.5°±28.6°	22.6°±28.0°	40.6°±39.7°	30.2°±32.3°	21.8°±24.9°	**21.3°±25.2°**
10	23.8°±27.5°	21.9°±26.9°	37.6°±38.3°	28.8°±30.8°	**21.4°±24.6°**	21.8°±25.5°
12	23.6°±29.4°	22.2°±28.8°	39.0°±38.2°	29.7°±31.5°	**21.4°±25.3°**	21.8°±25.3°
∞	-	-	38.9°±40.7°	29.4°±31.1°	21.6°±25.2°	**20.8°±24.7°**

We first apply two classification-based baselines, followed by all regression-based approaches introduced in Sect. 4.

In order to train a regressor using discrete pose labels, a first rather simplistic approach commonly found in the literature is to train a classifier which outputs the class center as prediction. For probabilistic classifiers, a natural extension of this approach is to output the argmax of a quadratic interpolation of the class with the highest posterior probability and its neighboring classes. On average, this improves the results by about 2°.

CNNs compute a continuous function of their input and, during training, each sample *pulls* the parameters of the CNN slightly into a direction leading to a better prediction of its pose. This intuition suggests that it should be possible for CNNs to learn a continuous mapping from images to pose angles even when only given very rough pose labels. This is shown in the last four columns of Table 4. As can be seen, this idea hardly works at all in the naive regression case and is only somewhat improved by the von Mises cost. Biternion nets, on the other hand, have no difficulty being trained this way and in fact outperform the class-based approaches with any number of realistically annotable classes, whether the cosine or the von Mises cost is used

Unfortunately, looking only at numbers representing an average error over a large amount of images does not reflect the real advantage of biternion nets over the classifier approach. For this reason, we plotted heatmaps of the predictions

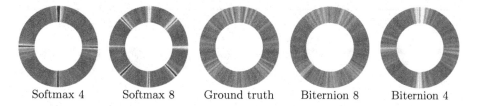

Softmax 4   Softmax 8   Ground truth   Biternion 8   Biternion 4

Fig. 1. Prediction distributions for softmax and biternion output layers trained on different discretizations. The classification results include the interpolation.

made by a CNN classifier with quadratic interpolation and the predictions made by a biternion net in Fig. 1. These heatmaps clearly show that, while the class-interpolation approach and biternion nets give similar scores, the predictions of the biternion nets are vastly superior because they are more continuous and similar to the distribution of the ground-truth angles.

5.1   Practicality

To show the potential of our approach, we recorded a small dataset using a common smartphone camera and annotated it with eight class labels. For this, we recorded 24 people in our lab and asked them to rotate on the spot. We then manually cropped a square region in the resulting videos containing their head and rescaled it to 50 × 50 pixels to make it compatible to our network architecture. In our scenario, the image sequence of a single person can easily be annotated based on temporal constraints. We split up the full annotation task into two annotation runs of four classes. First we annotate Front, Left, Back and Right, followed by the same annotation with boundaries shifted by 45°. We select temporal regions in the video through their start and end frames and mark any such region as one class. The resulting pair of annotations can then easily be merged into an eight-class annotation. The whole process, including the cropping of the head regions and the annotation itself, was done by a single person and took no longer than two and a half hours.

We train a biternion net on the resulting dataset except for one person, which we set aside for qualitative evaluation. We only train this network for five epochs since the number of people in this dataset is orders of magnitude smaller than in all previous datasets. We then let the biternion net predict the head pose of the left-out person *for each frame individually*. The result, which can be seen in Fig. 2, clearly shows that the network estimates a fairly smooth sinusoidal pose across the two turns the person made, despite having been trained on only eight discrete pose annotations.

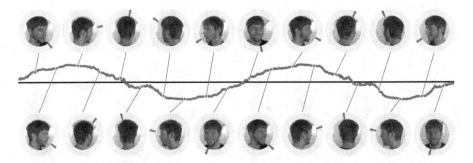

Fig. 2. Qualitative results. The purple line shows the sine of the predicted orientation angle across two full turns. For each head, the purple mark shows the orientation as seen from above. Results are equally spaced and not cherry-picked, more densely sampled results can be seen in the supplementary material.

6 Conclusion

In this paper, we have introduced biternion nets, a CNN based approach. We have validated our architecture on several public datasets and have shown that our biternion layer is essential for continuous periodic orientation regression. Our obtained results redefine the state of the art on all used datasets. We furthermore show that, using biternion nets, it becomes possible to collect data with discrete and coarse orientation labels, which can be annotated quickly and cheaply, in order to train a continuous and precise head pose regressor. This suggests that fine-grained regression annotations are no longer necessary for continuous orientation estimation. The work in this paper was funded by the EU projects STRANDS (ICT-2011-600623) and SPENCER (ICT-2011-600877). Code is available at http://github.com/lucasb-eyer/BiternionNet.

References

1. Aghajanian, J., Prince, S.: Face pose estimation in uncontrolled environments. In: BMVC (2009)
2. Ba, S.O., Odobez, J.M.: Evaluation of multiple cue head pose estimation algorithms in natural environments. In: ICME (2005)
3. Bastien, F., Lamblin, P., Pascanu, R., Bergstra, J., Goodfellow, I.J., Bergeron, A., Bouchard, N., Bengio, Y.: Theano: new features and speed improvements. In: Deep Learning and Unsupervised Feature Learning NIPS 2012 Workshop (2012)
4. Baxter, R.H., Leach, M.J., Mukherjee, S.S., Robertson, N.M.: An adaptive motion model for person tracking with instantaneous head-pose features. IEEE Signal Process. Lett. **22**(5), 578–582 (2015)
5. Benfold, B., Reid, I.: Unsupervised learning of a scene-specific coarse gaze estimator. In: ICCV (2011)
6. Black Jr., J.A., Gargesha, M., Kahol, K., Kuchi, P., Panchanathan, S.: A framework for performance evaluation of face recognition algorithms. In: Proceedings of the SPIE, vol. 4862, pp. 163–174 (2002)
7. Chamveha, I., Sugano, Y., Sugimura, D., Siriteerakul, T., Okabe, T., Sato, Y., Sugimoto, A.: Head direction estimation from low resolution images with scene adaptation. CVIU **117**(10), 1502–1511 (2013)
8. Chen, C., Odobez, J.M.: We are not contortionists: coupled adaptive learning for head and body orientation estimation in surveillance video. In: CVPR (2012)
9. Dantone, M., Gall, J., Fanelli, G., Van Gool, L.: Real-time facial feature detection using conditional regression forests. In: CVPR (2012)
10. Demirkus, M., Precup, D., Clark, J.J., Arbel, T.: Probabilistic temporal head pose estimation using a hierarchical graphical model. In: Fleet, D., Pajdla, T., Schiele, B., Tuytelaars, T. (eds.) ECCV 2014, Part I. LNCS, vol. 8689, pp. 328–344. Springer, Heidelberg (2014)
11. Dollár, P., Welinder, P., Perona, P.: Cascaded pose regression. In: CVPR (2010)
12. Fanelli, G., Dantone, M., Gall, J., Fossati, A., Van Gool, L.: Random forests for real time 3D face analysis. IJCV **101**(3), 437–458 (2013)
13. Goodfellow, I., Warde-Farley, D., Mirza, M., Courville, A., Bengio, Y.: Maxout networks. In: ICML (2013)

14. Gourier, N., Hall, D., Crowley, J.L.: Estimating Face orientation from robust detection of salient facial structures. In: ICPR 2004 FG Net Workshop (2004)
15. Gross, R., Matthews, I., Cohn, J., Kanade, T., Baker, S.: Multi-pie. Image Vis. Comput. **28**(5), 807–813 (2010)
16. Hara, K., Chellappa, R.: Growing regression forests by classification: applications to object pose estimation. In: Fleet, D., Pajdla, T., Schiele, B., Tuytelaars, T. (eds.) ECCV 2014, Part II. LNCS, vol. 8690, pp. 552–567. Springer, Heidelberg (2014)
17. He, K., Zhang, X., Ren, S., Sun, J.: Delving deep into rectifiers: surpassing human-level performance on imagenet classification (2015). arXiv preprint arXiv:1502.01852
18. He, K., Sigal, L., Sclaroff, S.: Parameterizing object detectors in the continuous pose space. In: Fleet, D., Pajdla, T., Schiele, B., Tuytelaars, T. (eds.) ECCV 2014, Part IV. LNCS, vol. 8692, pp. 450–465. Springer, Heidelberg (2014)
19. Huang, D., Storer, M., De la Torre, F., Bischof, H.: Supervised local subspace learning for continuous head pose estimation. In: CVPR (2011)
20. Ioffe, S., Szegedy, C.: Batch normalization: accelerating deep network training by reducing internal covariate shift (2015). arXiv preprint arXiv:1502.03167
21. Lallemand, J., Ronge, A., Szczot, M., Ilic, S.: Pedestrian orientation estimation. In: Jiang, X., Hornegger, J., Koch, R. (eds.) GCPR 2014. LNCS, vol. 8753, pp. 476–487. Springer, Heidelberg (2014)
22. Mardia, K.V., Jupp, P.E.: Directional Statistics, vol. 494. Wiley, New york (2009)
23. Montavon, G., Orr, G.B., Müller, K. (eds.): Neural Networks: Tricks of the Trade, 2nd edn. Springer, Berlin (2012)
24. Murphy-Chutorian, E., Doshi, A., Trivedi, M.M.: Head pose estimation for driver assistance systems: a robust algorithm and experimental evaluation. In: ITSC (2007)
25. Murphy-Chutorian, E., Trivedi, M.M.: Head pose estimation in computer vision: a survey. PAMI **31**(4), 607–626 (2009)
26. Osadchy, M., Cun, Y.L., Miller, M.L.: Synergistic face detection and pose estimation with energy-based models. JMLR **8**, 1197–1215 (2007)
27. Pérez, F., Granger, B.E.: IPython: a system for interactive scientific computing. Comput. Sci. Eng. **9**(3), 21–29 (2007). http://ipython.org
28. Qi, R.: Learning 3D Object Orientations From Synthetic Images (2015)
29. Saxe, A.M., McClelland, J.L., Ganguli, S.: Exact solutions to the nonlinear dynamics of learning in deep linear neural networks. In: ICLR (2014)
30. Simonyan, K., Zisserman, A.: Very deep convolutional networks for large-scale image recognition. In: ICLR (2015)
31. Singhal, A.: Modern information retrieval: a brief overview. IEEE Data Eng. Bull. **24**(4), 35–43 (2001)
32. Siriteerakul, T.: Advance in head pose estimation from low resolution images: a review. IJCSI 9(2) (2012)
33. Torki, M., Elgammal, A.: Regression from local features for viewpoint and pose estimation. In: ICCV (2011)
34. Tosato, D., Spera, M., Cristani, M., Murino, V.: Characterizing humans on riemannian manifolds. PAMI **35**(8), 1972–1984 (2013)
35. Wu, Y., Toyama, K.: Wide-range, person- and illumination-insensitive head orientation estimation. In: International Conference on Automatic Face and Gesture Recognition (2000)
36. Zeiler, M.D., Rob, F.: Stochastic pooling for regularization of deep convolutional neural networks. In: ICLR (2013)

A Physics-Based Statistical Model for Human Gait Analysis

Petrissa Zell[✉] and Bodo Rosenhahn

Institut Für Informationsverarbeitung (TNT), Leibniz Universität Hannover,
Hanover, Germany
{zell,rosenhahn}@tnt.uni-hannover.de

Abstract. Physics-based modeling is a powerful tool for human gait analysis and synthesis. Unfortunately, its application suffers from high computational cost regarding the solution of optimization problems and uncertainty in the choice of a suitable objective energy function and model parametrization. Our approach circumvents these problems by learning model parameters based on a training set of walking sequences. We propose a combined representation of motion parameters and physical parameters to infer missing data without the need for tedious optimization. Both a k-nearest-neighbour approach and asymmetrical principal component analysis are used to deduce ground reaction forces and joint torques directly from an input motion. We evaluate our methods by comparing with an iterative optimization-based method and demonstrate the robustness of our algorithm by reducing the input joint information. With decreasing input information the combined statistical model regression increasingly outperforms the iterative optimization-based method.

1 Introduction

The central endeavour in many biomechanical studies is to determine joint forces and torques, which act at and across a joint, respectively [6,9,11]. These forces summarize all active forces effecting a joint, e.g., exerted by tendons, ligaments and neighboring bone segments. The clinical standard to calculate joint torques is through inverse dynamics, based on the measurement of ground reaction forces (GRF) and joint positions by means of force plates and a motion capture (MoCap) system [18]. Despite being frequently used, the results of this approach have to be treated carefully, because various error sources exist which sometimes have non-negligable effects. Especially the length of estimated lever arms is highly sensitive to marker placement uncertainties and the chosen model for body segment parameters [10,16].

An alternative method for torque estimation is physical modeling of the human body and simulation of dynamical development via forward dynamics. There already exists a variety of physics-based models for human gait with differing complexity. A relatively simple approach is to model body parts by rigid segments that are linked by joints associated with spring torques. These mass-spring models qualify to describe the human walk adequately without the drawback of a

© Springer International Publishing Switzerland 2015
J. Gall et al. (Eds.): GCPR 2015, LNCS 9358, pp. 169–180, 2015.
DOI: 10.1007/978-3-319-24947-6_14

high dimensional parameter space. The simulation of movement can be achieved via forward dynamics, i.e. by integrating the equations of motion (EOM) and simultaneously optimizing model parameters to extremize an objective function (often defined as some form of energetic effort). This method has the advantage of directly accessible joint torques, implemented in the EOM, but provokes high computational cost due to the integration. The closer the model gets to reality, i.e. the higher the degree of freedom (DOF) becomes, the larger the computational cost. The iterative minimization of an objective function without prior knowledge of model parameters is referred to as optimization-based method in the following.

Our approach aims to adopt the benefits of physics-based motion analysis while simultaneously avoiding high computational cost by means of machine learning techniques. Methods like principal component analysis for pattern recognition have already been used to analyse and snythesize human motion by Troje et al. in 2002 [14]. We propose a statistical model that combines the physical parameters of a two dimensional mass-spring model based on [3] with corresponding gait characteristics following this approach.

The data driven learning of physical parameters allows us to include style dependent properties of walking into our framework. These properties comprise subject specific preferences to burden some joints more than others, which is an information usually lost when minimizing a general energy function. Simulations were executed on a training set of MoCap data from Troje et al. [14] to estimate a subspace from the physical and motion parameters. This combined representation, termed combined statistical model (CSM) in the following, enables us to directly infer force patterns from motion data without further optimization. Consequently, we achieve a massive reduction of computation time of force and torque estimation compared to optimization-based methods. The computation time of the regression with our CSM lies in the order of seconds. In contrast to that, the optimization-based method we applied for comparison requires computation times of up to several hours. Within the scope of our CSM we propose two different direct regression methods, namely a k-nearest-neighbours (k-NN) approach and asymmetrical principal component analysis (aPCA) [1]. We evaluate our methods by comparing GRFs and joint positions to ground truth data and knee torques to calculations via inverse dynamics.

To summarize, our **contributions** are as follows:

- We introduce a combined statistical model for human motion and corresponding physical parameters.
- The model allows us to estimate missing data in real-time.
- Finally, we analyze different regression methods for force and torque estimation.

2   Related Work

The incorporation of physics-based models into the analysis and synthesis of movement offers the benefit of physical validity. Typical errors like the sliding of feet on the ground or the simulation of unstable motions can be avoided. Techniques for motion generation and analysis divide into controller-based methods [13,15,21] and optimization-based methods [4,5,8,20].

In 1971 Chow and Jacobson introduced an optimization-based approach to simulate human gait [5]. Since then, optimization techniques have been widely used by researchers on the basis of increasingly complex skeletal and muscoskeletal models. Fleet et al. [4] used a 12-segment articulated body model to estimate joint torques and contact dynamics. Their results show consistently estimated torques for walking and running over a wide spread of subjects. The estimated ground reaction forces (GRF) are a good approximation of the ground truth data concerning the mean value, but differ regarding temporal development.

Xiang et al. [20] used a large-scale physical model in order to predict gait patterns. They applied a predictive dynamics approach to approximate joint angles and torques, minimizing the dynamic effort (sum of integrated squared joint torques). Furthermore, GRFs were calculated inversely. The predicted values are in overall similar to experimental data, though calculated GRFs display noticeable difference concerning shape from data available in the literature.

General issues of optimization-based generation of motion with a large degree of freedom (DOF) model are high computational cost and the need for numerous constraints on the model parameter space. Moreover, the minimization of an energy function to optimize walking parameters is a convenient tool for the synthesis of natural looking gaits in general, but often fails to predict subject specific walking styles. Liu et al. [8] adressed this problem by introducing Nonlinear Inverse Optimization to estimate physics-based style parameters from motion capture (MoCap) data. They used learned parameters for the synthesis of new motion in the respective style. Wei et al. [17] combined statistical motion priors with physical constraints in order to generate physically-valid human motion. These last two approaches aim at the generation of physically realistic motion but do not analyze the consistency of simulated force patterns with ground truth data.

In contrast to the existing works, we propose a framework, that encompasses geometrical properties, motion information and physical parameters in a combined statistical model. Relevant advantages of our method towards state-of-the-art methods are robustness in the case of incomplete input information and low computational cost. The combined parametrization enables us to deduce missing data, such as forces or joint trajectories, in real-time.

3   The Physics-Based Statistical Model

The generation of a statistical model that combines motion characteristics with a physical representation requires parameter learning on a training set S. For this purpose, MoCap data from Troje et al. [14] was used. The dataset contains walking sequences of 115 male and female subjects with varying weight (from 44.4 kg to 110 kg), height (from 1.52 m to 1.96 m) and age (from 13 years to 59 years).

3.1 Motion Model

Walking can be considered as a time series of postures p and is represented similiarly to [14] as a linear combination of principal component postures with sinusoidal variation of coefficients,

$$p(t) = p_0 + p_1 \sin(\omega t) + p_2 \sin(\omega t + \Phi_2) + p_3 \sin(2\omega t + \Phi_3) + p_4 \sin(2\omega t + \Phi_4). \quad (1)$$

p_0 is the mean posture and (p_1, p_2, p_3, p_4) are principal components, called eigenpostures in the following. ω is the fundamental frequency describing the gait and (Φ_2, Φ_3, Φ_4) are phase delays. In this framework, a posture consists of 15 three-dimensional joint positions, resulting in a 45-dimensional vector p. The complete motion parametrization is represented by

$$u = [p_0,\ p_1,\ p_2,\ p_3,\ p_4,\ \omega,\ \Phi_2,\ \Phi_3,\ \Phi_4]^T. \quad (2)$$

3.2 Physical Model

Our physical gait model is an extension of a two dimensional mass-spring-model of the lower extremeties and the torso by Brubaker et al. [3]. Our modifications are additional body segments (head and arms) with appropriate springs, a toe-off force, and nonlinear force characteristics for a spring that acts on the stance shank. The linear toe-off force F_{TO} is active during a finite timespan Δt_{TO} at the beginning of a gait step (half of a gait cycle) and accelerates the center of mass (COM) of the rear shank. The force is set to

$$F_{TO} = \iota (1 - \frac{t}{\Delta t_{TO}})[-\sin(\phi_{S2} + \alpha), \cos(\phi_{S2} + \alpha)]^T, \quad (3)$$

where ι indicates the initial magnitude and α defines the deviation of the force direction from the orientation of the rear shank segment, given by ϕ_{S2}.

Motivated by research on nonlinear spring design [12], we use a nonlinear spring torque that acts on the stance shank to improve the simulation of natural knee flexion and to cover a greater variety of gait patterns. More precisely we set the spring's resting angle $\phi^{(0)}$ to a fourth order polynomial over the x-position of the whole body's COM x_{CoM} resulting in the torque

$$\tau = -\kappa \left(\phi_{S1} - \phi^{(0)}(q, \sigma) \right) - d\dot{\phi}_{S1}, \quad (4)$$

$$\phi^{(0)}(q, \sigma) = \phi^{(0)} + \sum_{k=1}^{4} c_k x_{CoM}^k (q, \sigma). \quad (5)$$

The parameters κ and d are spring stiffness and attenuation constant, respectively and the angle ϕ_{S1} describes the orientation of the stance shank. The vector q defines the configuration of the model in the form of segment angles and σ describes the subject-dependent geometry, i.e. segment lengths. The temporal state of the physical model is given by the pair $(q(t), \dot{q}(t))$ and can be determined by integrating a set of equations of motion, resulting in the dynamic state function

$$(q(t), \dot{q}(t)) = D(t, q_0, \dot{q}_0, \theta, \sigma), \tag{6}$$

where $(q_0, \dot{q}_0)$ indicates the initial state and θ includes all modeled force parameters, i.e. spring and toe-off force parameters.

A detailed analysis of the effects, that these enhancements have on the simulated gait patterns exceeds the scope of this paper and remains for future work. The focus of this publication lies on the inclusion of statistic knowledge to estimate forces and joint torques.

3.3   Combined Representation

To combine the physical properties with the information about a subject's motion, single gait steps taken from the MoCap walking sequences are approximated using the physical model. The approximation process can be divided into two parts: First, subject-specific body parameters and angular dynamics are estimated from MoCap data. Afterwards, effective torques and forces are approximated via model simulation.

In the first step, the distance between two dimensional cartesian model and MoCap joint coordinates r_{model} and r_{MoCap}, respectively, is minimized by optimizing body segment lengths and angles over a timespan of several steps,

$$(q(t), \sigma) = \underset{q, \sigma}{\arg\min} \left\{ \sum_j \left| r_{\text{MoCap}, j}(t) - r_{\text{model}, j}(q(t), \sigma) \right|^2 \right\}. \tag{7}$$

We calculate angular velocities and accelerations by means of finite differences and define the consequent states $(q(t), \dot{q}(t))_{\text{targ}}$ as target for the following model simulation. These target states need to be temporally aligned. For this purpose, heel strike times have to be known and are assumed to take place at time points which exhibit a local maximum in step length.

In the second step of the approximation process we search for physical model parameters, that create a motion which has minimal distance to the target motion. In other words, we simulate a step of the model by evaluating function D from Eq. (6) for a set of key times $\{t_k\}_k$ and minimize the sum of squared approximation errors. The times t_k lie within the estimated timespan T_s for single support of the gait step because our physical model does not include a double support phase.

Since our main interest lies in generating realistic force patterns, we also constrain the model simulation to yield GRF values F_{sim} within the vicinity of ground truth data F_{true}. The values are normalized, i.e. divided by the total body mass M, for comparability. The optimization problem is formulated as follows,

$$(q_0, \dot{q}_0, \theta) = \underset{q_0, \dot{q}_0, \theta}{\arg\min} \left\{ \sum_k \left| D(t_k, q_0, \dot{q}_0, \theta, \sigma) - (q(t_k), \dot{q}(t_k))_{\text{targ}} \right|^2 \right\},$$

$$\text{s.t. } \left| F_{\text{sim}}(q(t_k), \dot{q}(t_k), \ddot{q}(t_k), \sigma) - \bar{F}_{\text{true}}(t_k) \right| \leq \eta_k, \tag{8}$$

with thresholds η_k. We calculate the effective normalized GRF via

$$F_{\text{sim}}(\boldsymbol{q}, \dot{\boldsymbol{q}}, \ddot{\boldsymbol{q}}, \boldsymbol{\sigma}) = \sum_i \frac{m_i}{M}(\boldsymbol{a}_i(\boldsymbol{q}, \dot{\boldsymbol{q}}, \ddot{\boldsymbol{q}}, \boldsymbol{\sigma}) - \boldsymbol{g}), \tag{9}$$

where $\boldsymbol{a}_i$ is the linear acceleration of segment i and $\boldsymbol{g}$ is the gravitational acceleration vector with magnitude $g = 9.81\,\text{m/s}^2$.

The optimization problems in Eqs. (7) and (8) are solved by the interior-point algorithm. The resulting physics-based model parameters are

$$\boldsymbol{v} = [\boldsymbol{q}_0, \dot{\boldsymbol{q}}_0, \boldsymbol{\theta}, M]^T, \tag{10}$$

with appended total body mass M which is known from the training set.

Based on the combined parametrization of $\boldsymbol{u}$ and $\boldsymbol{v}$, it is possible to infer joint torques from joint trajectories and vice versa. We do not perform the reverse regression, since joint torques are typically not available as ground truth data, but instead infer joint trajectories from the GRF. For this objective, we define a set of GRF features $\boldsymbol{f}$. The behaviour of $F_x(t)$ is approximately linear. Therefore, we use the slope of $F_x(t)$ as a feature. For $F_y(t)$ we choose the magnitudes at the two maximum points and the minimum point. This results in a four-dimensional feature vector. In the training set, no ground truth data on GRF vectors exists, which is why we learn the GRF parameters $\boldsymbol{f}$ by the use of our simulated values F_{sim}.

Along with the motion representation from Eq. (2) and the physical parameters from Eq. (10) this yields a combined description of walking in form of a 285-dimensional subject specific vector $\boldsymbol{w}_s = [\boldsymbol{u}_s^T, \boldsymbol{v}_s^T, \boldsymbol{f}_s^T]^T$. We obtain a parametrization for the whole training set by writing the vectors $\boldsymbol{w}_s$ into the columns of a matrix $\boldsymbol{W}$:

$$\boldsymbol{W} = \begin{bmatrix} \boldsymbol{u}_1 \cdots \boldsymbol{u}_{115} \\ \boldsymbol{v}_1 \cdots \boldsymbol{v}_{115} \\ \boldsymbol{f}_1 \cdots \boldsymbol{f}_{115} \end{bmatrix} \begin{matrix} \in \mathbb{R}^{229} & (\text{motion Eq. (2)}) \\ \in \mathbb{R}^{52} & (\text{physical model Eq. (10)}) \\ \in \mathbb{R}^4 & (\text{GRF features}) \end{matrix} \tag{11}$$

$$\underbrace{\phantom{\boldsymbol{u}_1 \cdots \boldsymbol{u}_{115}}}_{115 \text{ subjects}}$$

4 Missing Data Estimation

4.1 Direct Regression

The combined statistical model encompasses geometrical properties, dynamical behaviour and the physical basis of a walking subject. All of these features contribute to the characteristics of a gait pattern and their mutual dependency can be used to infer missing data from an incomplete parameter set. We apply two different regression methods: k-nearest-neighbour (k-NN) regression and an asymmetrical projection into the principal component space (aPCA), as introduced by [1] for the reconstruction of occluded facial images. Motivated by sparse representation methods [7, 19], our algorithm first performs a classification of the input data concerning predefined motion features, which divide the training set into five pairs of disjoint subclasses. The focus lies on lower body dynamic, e.g. the knee-flexion at different points of the gait cycle. We classify regarding object to class distances of the known part of the parameter set, as suggested by [2]. The intersection of the best matching classes is defined as sample space for the following regression. For the k-NN regression, we set k equal to the number of vectors $\boldsymbol{w}$ covered by this reduced subject set and iteratively reduce k, if the infered joint torque magnitudes surpass a fixed threshold.

4.2   Iterative Optimization

In order to emphasize the advantage of a combined statistical model, we compare the performance of our regression methods to an alternative iterative optimization-based approach, in which we optimize Eqs. (7) and (8) to approximate the motion and calculate suitable forces. In the case of incomplete motion input, i.e. incomplete joint trajectories, we augment Eq. (8) to include a penalty function $E(\boldsymbol{q}, \dot{\boldsymbol{q}}, \boldsymbol{\theta})$ in order to account for the missing joint position information. The energy function is based on dynamic effort,

$$E(\boldsymbol{q}, \dot{\boldsymbol{q}}, \boldsymbol{\theta}) = \frac{1}{T} \int_0^T \left(\alpha F_{TO}^2 + \sum_j \beta_j \tau_j^2 \right) dt. \tag{12}$$

We empirically set the weights to $\alpha = 0.1$, $\beta_j = 0.001$ for stance leg, spine and neck joints and $\beta_j = 0.0001$ for swing leg and arm joints. This way, a high penalty is placed on the toe-off force and on the stiff joint torques. We refer to this optimization-based method as OPT.

5   Experiments

We compare the performance of the methods for missing data estimation regarding the deviation of estimates from ground truth data. For this purpose, we measured joint trajectories and GRF vectors of three different test subjects. Recording motion and force data was synchronized and done by a Vicon T-series MoCap system and AMTI force plates, respectively. The laboratory setup is depicted in Fig. 2. The force plate system measures magnitude and direction of GRF vectors, which we compare to estimated two dimensional values, resulting from Eq. (9). Furthermore we determine knee extensor and flexor torques of the stance leg via inverse dynamics. The results are compared to simulated model torques τ_{K1}. We use symmetric mean absolute percentage error (SMAPE) as measure for the deviation of estimated magnitudes and first derivatives from ground truth values. The sum of the resulting SMAPE values is used as error measure ϵ. We include first derivatives in this measure in order to increase the weight of shape discrepancies.

5.1   GRF and Knee Torque Estimation

In the first part of the evaluation process our aim is to find the best approximation of the GRF and the stance knee torque given the full motion parametrization

u and with an incomplete set of motion parameters, respectively. Starting with missing left hand trajectory, we successively remove the trajectories of the left elbow, ankle and knee, so that at the final stage the entire motion information of limbs on the left-hand side is unknown. The number of missing input joint trajectories is denoted by N. The results for one example subject can be seen in Fig. 1. The depicted estimates are based on complete input information in (a) and missing joint information on the full left-hand side in (b). Associated SMAPE values ϵ_F and ϵ_τ of GRF and knee torque estimates, as well as computation times t_c, are listed in Table 1.

As expected the best approximation of ground truth data is achieved by the optimization-based method OPT with zero missing input trajectories. In this case the full joint information is used and no additional energy minimization affects the result. As the input information is reduced the CSM methods increasingly outperform OPT. Especially the k-NN approach shows consistently low SMAPE values. The error measure for the estimated knee torque even decreases with increasing N. Which can be explained by the low number of test subjects combined with the inaccuracy of the inverse dynamics calculation of joint torques, meaning that the corresponding errors coincidentally compensate the errors resulting from missing joint information. Consequently the comparison of GRFs has a higher value and should be the decisive measure for the evaluation of a method.

The computation times of the CSM methods are in the order of seconds for k-NN and deci-seconds for aPCA, respectively. In contrast to that, OPT requires computation times of several hours, highly depending on the initialization of the optimization parameters.

5.2   Joint Trajectory Estimation

We consider the reverse inference process in a second experiment. Now we want to estimate joint trajectories based on input GRF data. For this experiment we only apply our k-NN algorithm, since it outperformed the other methods in the previous experiment. Furthermore the optimization of joint positions to

Table 1. SMAPE values ϵ_F and ϵ_τ for GRF and knee torque estimates based on the regression methods described in Sect. 4 with related computation times t_c. N indicates the number of missing input joint trajectories.

	k-NN			aPCA			OPT		
N	ϵ_F	ϵ_τ	t_c [s]	ϵ_F	ϵ_τ	t_c [s]	ϵ_F	ϵ_τ	t_c [s]
0	1.504	1.624	2.994	1.726	2.019	**0.881**	**1.483**	**1.420**	8103
1	**1.504**	**1.586**	2.117	1.780	2.052	**0.934**	1.811	1.851	4358
2	**1.496**	**1.582**	2.112	2.005	2.083	**0.913**	1.890	1.793	3096
3	**1.524**	**1.562**	2.583	1.606	2.169	**0.619**	1.843	2.069	3229
4	**1.528**	**1.565**	2.538	1.594	2.072	**0.669**	1.911	2.188	2092

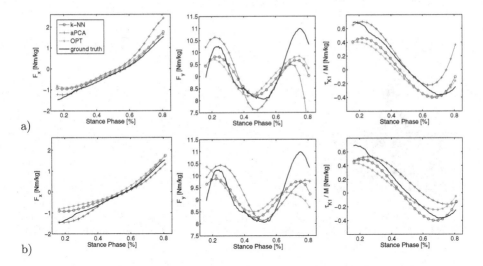

Fig. 1. Comparison between different regression and optimization methods concerning estimated GRF components F_y, F_x and knee torques τ_{K1}. Positive values correspond to flexor torques. The results are based on full joint trajectory information (in a)) and on partial information with $N = 4$ (in b)), respectively. In the case of GRF components, the black line illustrates ground truth data and in the case of joint torques, it represents torques calculated via inverse dynamics. The corresponding evaluation can be found in Table 1.

approximate a target GRF is a highly under-determined problem. Hence, approach OPT would need to be enhanced with multiple constraints on the motion and comparability could not be guaranteed. In addition to the motion feature classification, we reduce the subspace to walkers of matching height to ensure compliant y-positions of the estimated joints.

We deduce the motion vector $\boldsymbol{u}$ from GRF features $\boldsymbol{f}$ and the subjects mass M and height H via k-NN regression of the input vector $[M, H, \boldsymbol{f}]^T$. The results for one example subject are shown in Fig. 3 in form of two-dimensional joint trajectories of the head, the hip, the left knee and the left ankle. Black lines represent ground truth positions and colored lines the estimated values. The mean joint position discrepancy over the time equals 5.6 cm. It is worth mentioning, that the mean position error of the arm joints is 36 % higher than that of the remaining joints. By implication, we can assume that the arm movement has only a minor influence on the GRF. Figure 4 illustrates the estimated posture of the subject at several time points. Animations of the corresponding motion and the ground truth movement are provided as supplementary material.

6   Discussion

The experimental results demonstrate the benefit of a combined statistical representation. The method is robust to missing input information and the estimated results approximate the ground truth data as well as our extended physical

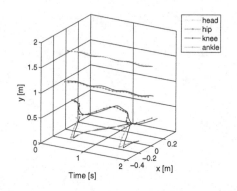

Fig. 2. A subject walking across the force plates in our laboratory setup

Fig. 3. Two-dimensional joint trajectories. Black lines illustrate ground truth positions and dotted colored lines the corresponding estimates via CSM (Color figure online).

Fig. 4. Frames of the estimated motion based on GRF features f. The blue arrow represents the GRF vector and the red discs represent knee joint torques (Color figure online).

model allows. The best results for the case of complete input joint information are achieved by means of the iterative optimization-based method OPT, but as soon as we reduce the available information, our k-NN approach outperforms the other methods. Considering the computational effort of the evaluated methods, the CSM causes a significant reduction of computation time from hours to the order of seconds, compared to the iterative optimization-based method. The fact that gradient-descent algorithms generally require a good initial guess of the parameters is not taken into consideration, since we provide our learned parameter space as a set of initial points for the optimization in OPT.

In addition to force estimation, the CSM also enables us to infer a motion from ground reaction force data and subject parameters based on a small set of four features.

References

1. Al-Naser, M., Söderström, U.: Reconstruction of occluded facial images using asymmetrical principal component analysis. Integr. Comput. Aided Eng. **19**(3), 273–283 (2012)
2. Boiman, O., Shechtman, E., Irani, M.: In defense of nearest-neighbor based image classification. In: CVPR. IEEE Computer Society (2008)
3. Brubaker, M.A., Fleet, D.J.: The kneed walker for human pose tracking. In: IEEE Conference on Computer Vision and Pattern Recognition (2008)
4. Brubaker, M.A., Sigal, L., Fleet, D.J.: Estimating contact dynamics. In: IEEE 12th International Conference on Computer Vision, ICCV 2009, September 27 - October 4 2009, Kyoto, Japan, pp. 2389–2396 (2009)
5. Chow, C.K., Jacobson, D.: Studies of human locomotion via optimal programming. Math. Biosci. **10**(3–4), 239–306 (1971)
6. Fregly, B.J., Reinbolt, J.A., Rooney, K.L., Mitchell, K.H., Chmielewski, T.L.: Design of patient-specific gait modifications for knee osteoarthritis rehabilitation. IEEE Trans. Biomed. Eng. **54**(9), 1687–1695 (2007)
7. Jiang, Z., Lin, Z., Davis, L.S.: Learning a discriminative dictionary for sparse coding via label consistent K-SVD. In: 2011 IEEE Conference on Computer Vision and Pattern Recognition (CVPR), pp. 1697–1704 (2011)
8. Liu, C.K., Hertzmann, A., Popović, Z.: Learning physics-based motion style with nonlinear inverse optimization. ACM Trans. Graph. **24**(3), 1071–1081 (2005)
9. Powers, C.M.: The influence of abnormal hip mechanics on knee injury: a biomechanical perspective. JOSPT **40**, 42–51 (2010)
10. Rao, G., Amarantini, D., Berton, E., Favier, D.: Influence of body segments' parameters estimation models on inverse dynamics solutions during gait. J. Biomech. **39**(8), 1531–1536 (2006)
11. Schmalz, T., Blumentritt, S., Jarasch, R.: Energy expenditure and biomechanical characteristics of lower limb amputee gait: the influence of prosthetic alignment and different prosthetic components. Gait Posture **16**(3), 255–263 (2002)
12. Schmidt, N., Okada, M.: Optimal design of nonlinear springs in robot mechanism: simultaneous design of trajectory and spring force profiles. Adv. Robot. **27**(1), 33–46 (2013)
13. Sok, K.W., Kim, M., Lee, J.: Simulating biped behaviours from human motion data. In: Proceedings of the ACM SIGGRAPH 2007, p. 107 (2007)
14. Troje, N.F.: Decomposing biological motion: a framework for analysis and synthesis of human gait patterns. J. Vis. **2**(5), 371–387 (2002)
15. Tsai, Y.Y., Lin, W.C., Cheng, K.B., Lee, J., Lee, T.Y.: Real-time physics-based 3d biped character animation using an inverted pendulum model. IEEE Trans. Vis. Comput. Graph. **16**(2), 325–337 (2010)
16. Vaughan, C.L.: Are joint torques the holy grail of human gait analysis? Hum. Mov. Sci. **15**(3), 423–443 (1996)
17. Wei, X., Min, J., Chai, J.: Physically valid statistical models for human motion generation. ACM Trans. Graph. **30**(3), 19:1–19:10 (2011)
18. Whittle, M.W.: Clinical gait analysis: a review. Hum. Mov. Sci. **15**(3), 369–387 (1996)
19. Wright, J., Yang, A.Y., Ganesh, A., Sastry, S.S., Ma, Y.: Robust face recognition via sparse representation. IEEE Trans. Pattern Anal. Mach. Intell. **31**(2), 210–227 (2009)

20. Xiang, Y., Arora, J.S., Abdel-Malek, K.: Optimization-based prediction of asymmetric human gait. J. Biomech. **44**(6), 683–693 (2011)
21. Yin, K., Loken, K., van de Panne, M.: Simbicon: simple biped locomotion control. ACM Trans. Graph. **26**(3) (2007)

Recognition and Scene Understanding

Joint 3D Object and Layout Inference from a Single RGB-D Image

Andreas Geiger[1][(✉)] and Chaohui Wang[2]

[1] Max Planck Institute for Intelligent Systems, Tübingen, Germany
andreas.geiger@tue.mpg.de
[2] Université Paris-Est, Marne-la-Vallée, Paris, France
Chaohui.wang@u-pem.fr

Abstract. Inferring 3D objects and the layout of indoor scenes from a single RGB-D image captured with a Kinect camera is a challenging task. Towards this goal, we propose a high-order graphical model and jointly reason about the layout, objects and superpixels in the image. In contrast to existing holistic approaches, our model leverages detailed 3D geometry using inverse graphics and explicitly enforces occlusion and visibility constraints for respecting scene properties and projective geometry. We cast the task as MAP inference in a factor graph and solve it efficiently using message passing. We evaluate our method with respect to several baselines on the challenging NYUv2 indoor dataset using 21 object categories. Our experiments demonstrate that the proposed method is able to infer scenes with a large degree of clutter and occlusions.

1 Introduction

Robotic systems (e.g., household robots) require robust visual perception in order to locate objects, avoid obstacles and reach their goals. While much progress has been made since the pioneering attempts in the early 60's [33], 3D scene understanding remains a fundamental challenge in computer vision. In this paper, we propose a novel model for holistic 3D understanding of indoor scenes (Fig. 1). While existing approaches to the 3D scene understanding problem typically infer only objects [16,17] or consider layout estimation as a pre-processing step [25], our method reasons jointly about 3D objects and the scene layout. We explicitly model visibility and occlusion constraints by exploiting the expressive power of high-order graphical models. This ensures a physically plausible interpretation of the scene and avoids undercounting and overcounting of image evidence.

Following [17,25,38], our approach also relies on a set of 3D object proposals and pursues model selection by discrete MAP inference. However, in contrast to previous works, we do not fit cuboids to 3D segments in a greedy fashion. Instead, we propose objects and layout elements by solving a set of "inverse graphics" problems directly based on the unary potentials in our model. This allows us to take advantage of the increasing availability of 3D CAD models and leads to more accurate geometric interpretations. We evaluate the proposed

© Springer International Publishing Switzerland 2015
J. Gall et al. (Eds.): GCPR 2015, LNCS 9358, pp. 183–195, 2015.
DOI: 10.1007/978-3-319-24947-6_15

Fig. 1. Illustration of our Results. Left-to-right: Inferred objects, superpixels (red=explained), reconstruction (blue=close to red=far) and semantics with color code (Color figure online).

method in terms of 3D object detection performance on the challenging NYUv2 dataset [38] and compare it to [25] as well as two simple baselines derived from our model. Our code and dataset are publicly available[1].

2   Related Work

3D indoor scene understanding is a fundamental problem in computer vison and has recently witnessed great progress enabled by the increasing performance of semantic segmentation and object detection algorithms [6,10] as well as the availability of RGB-D sensors. Important aspects of this problem include 3D layout estimation [15,36], object detection [35,39], as well as semantic segmentation [14,32]. A variety of geometric representations have been proposed, including cuboids [17,25,46], 3D volumetric primitives [8,47], as well as CAD models [1,24,35,39]. While the problem has traditionally been approached using RGB images [1,8,23,36,46] and videos [42], the availability of RGB-D sensors [30] and datasets [38] nourish the hope for more accurate models of the scene [12,16,18,47]. Towards this goal, a number of holistic models have been proposed which take into account the relationship between objects (often represented as cuboids) and/or layout elements in the scene [4,22,37,45]. While CRFs provide a principled way to encode such contextual interactions [43], modeling visibility/occlusion rigorously is a very challenging problem [37,41].

The approach that we present is particularly related to several recent works which model the 3D scene using geometric primitives (e.g., cuboids) [17,25]. Despite their promising performance, these works ignore some important aspects in their formulation. In [25], a pairwise graphical model is employed to incorporate contextual information, but visibility constraints are ignored, which leads to overcounting of image evidence. In [17], undercounting of image evidence is addressed by enforcing "explained" superpixels to be associated with at least one object. However, occlusions are not considered (e.g., an object which explains a superpixel might be occluded by another object at the same superpixel), which can lead to implausible scene configurations. Besides, semantic labels and related contextual information are ignored.

---

[1] http://www.cvlibs.net/projects/indoor_scenes/.

While 3D CAD models have been primarily used for object detection [24,35,39,48], holistic 3D scene understanding approaches typically rely on simpler cuboid models [17,25]. In this work, we leverage the precise geometry of CAD models for holistic 3D scene understanding. The advantages are two-fold: First, we can better explain the depth image evidence. Second, it allows for incorporating visibility and occlusion constraints in a principled fashion.

3   Joint 3D Object and Layout Inference

We represent indoor scenes by a set of layout elements (e.g., "wall", "floor", "ceiling") and objects (e.g., "chairs", "shelves", "cabinets"). Given an RGB-D image $\mathbf{I}$ partitioned into superpixels $\mathcal{S}$, our goal is to simultaneously infer all layout and object elements in the scene. In particular, we reason about the type, semantic class, 3D pose and 3D shape of each object and layout element. Towards this goal, we first generate a number of object and layout proposals given the observed image $\mathbf{I}$ (see Sect. 3.4), and then select a subset of layout elements and objects which best explain $\mathbf{I}$ and $\mathcal{S}$ via MAP inference in a CRF.

More formally, let $\mathcal{L}$ and $\mathcal{O}$ denote the set of layout and object proposals, respectively. Each proposal $\rho_i = (t_i, c_i, m_i, r_i, z_i)$ $(i \in \mathcal{L} \cup \mathcal{O})$ comprises the following attributes: the proposal type $t_i \in \{layout, object\}$, its semantic class $c_i \in \{mantel, \ldots, other\}$, a 3D object model indexed by $m_i \in \{1, \ldots, M\}$, the image region $r_i \subset \mathbf{I}$ which has generated the proposal, as well as a set of pose parameters z_i which characterize pose and scale in 3D space. For each proposal, the semantic class variable c_i takes a label from the set of classes corresponding to its type $t_i \in \{layout, object\}$. We pre-aligned the scene with the camera coordinate axis using the method of Silberman et al. [38] and assume that layout elements extend to infinity. Thus, for $t_i = layout$, m_i indexes a 3D plane model, and z_i comprises the normal direction and the signed distance from the camera center. For $t_i = object$, m_i indexes one of the 3D CAD models in our dataset or a 3D cuboid if no CAD model is available for an object category. Furthermore, z_i comprises the 3D pose (we only consider rotations around the up-vector). and scale parameters of the object, i.e., $z_i \in \mathbb{R}^3 \times [-\pi, +\pi) \times \mathbb{R}^3_+$.

We associate a binary random variable $X_i \in \{0, 1\}$ with each layout/object proposal ρ_i, taking 1 if scene element i is present and 0 otherwise. To impose visibility/occlusion constraints and avoid evidence undercounting, we also associate a binary random variable X_k $(k \in \mathcal{S})$ with each superpixel k to model if the superpixel is explained $(X_k = 1)$ or unexplained $(X_k = 0)$. A valid scene configuration should explain as many superpixels as possible while at the same time satisfying Occam's razor, i.e., simple explanations with a small number of layouts and objects should be preferred. We specify our CRF model on

$\mathbf{X} = \{X_i\}_{i \in \{\mathcal{L} \cup \mathcal{O} \cup \mathcal{S}\}}$ in terms of the following energy

$$E(\mathbf{x}|\mathbf{I}) = \sum_{i \in \mathcal{L}} \underbrace{\phi_i^{\mathcal{L}}(x_i|\mathbf{I})}_{\text{layout}} + \sum_{i \in \mathcal{O}} \underbrace{\phi_i^{\mathcal{O}}(x_i|\mathbf{I})}_{\text{object}} + \sum_{k \in \mathcal{S}} \underbrace{\phi_k^{\mathcal{S}}(x_k)}_{\text{superpixel}} + \sum_{i \in \mathcal{L} \cup \mathcal{O}, k \in \mathcal{S}} \underbrace{\psi_{ik}^{\mathcal{S}}(x_i, x_k|\mathbf{I})}_{\text{occlusion/visibility}}$$

$$+ \sum_{k \in \mathcal{S}} \underbrace{\kappa_k(\mathbf{x}_{c_k})}_{\text{occlusion/visibility}} + \sum_{i,j \in \mathcal{O}} \underbrace{\psi_{ij}^{\mathcal{O},\mathcal{O}}(x_i, x_j)}_{\text{object-object}} + \sum_{i \in \mathcal{L}, j \in \mathcal{O}} \underbrace{\psi_{ij}^{\mathcal{L},\mathcal{O}}(x_i, x_j)}_{\text{layout-object}} \qquad (1)$$

where $\mathbf{x}_{c_k} = (x_i)_{i \in c_k}$ denotes a joint configuration of all variables involved in clique c_k. The unary potentials $\phi_i^{\mathcal{L}}$ and $\phi_i^{\mathcal{O}}$ encode the agreement of proposal i with the image, and $\phi_k^{\mathcal{S}}$ adds a penalty to the energy function if superpixel k is not explained by any object or layout element. The pairwise potentials $\psi_{ik}^{\mathcal{S}}$ and the high-order potentials κ_c ensure consistency between the scene and superpixels while respecting visibility and occlusion constraints. Contextual information such as relative pose or scale is encoded in $\psi_{ij}^{\mathcal{O},\mathcal{O}}$ and $\psi_{ij}^{\mathcal{L},\mathcal{O}}$.

3.1 Unary Potentials

We assume that each proposal ρ_i originates from a candidate image region $r_i \subset \mathbf{I}$ which we use to define the layout and object unary potentials in the following. Details on how we obtain these proposal regions will be specified in Sect. 3.4.

Layout Unary Potentials: We model the layout unary terms as

$$\phi_i^{\mathcal{L}}(x_i|\mathbf{I}) = w^{\mathcal{L}} \left(h^{\mathcal{L}}(\rho_i) + b^{\mathcal{L}} \right) x_i \qquad (2)$$

where $w^{\mathcal{L}}$ and $b^{\mathcal{L}}$ are model parameters that adjust the importance and bias of this term and $h^{\mathcal{L}}(\rho_i)$ captures how well the layout proposal fits the RGB-D image. More specifically, we favour layout elements which agree with the depth image and occlude as little pixels as possible, i.e., we assume that the walls, floor and ceiling determine the boundaries of the scene. In particular, we define $h^{\mathcal{L}}(\rho_i)$ as the difference between the count of pixels occluded by proposal ρ_i and the number of depth inliers wrt. all pixels in region r_i.

Object Unary Potentials: Similarly, we define the object unary terms as

$$\phi_i^{\mathcal{O}}(x_i|\mathbf{I}) = w^{\mathcal{O}} \left(h^{\mathcal{O}}(\rho_i) + b^{\mathcal{O}} \right) x_i \qquad (3)$$

where $h^{\mathcal{O}}(\rho_i)$ captures how well the object fits the RGB-D image: We consider an object as likely if its scale (last 3 dimensions of z_i) agrees with the scale of the 3D object model s_i, its rendered depth map agrees with the RGB-D depth image and its re-projection yields a region that maximizes the overlap with the region r_i which has generated the proposal. We assume a log-normal prior for the scale s_i, which we learn from all instances of class c_i in the training data.

Superpixel Unary Potentials: For each superpixel k we define

$$\phi_k^{\mathcal{S}}(x_k) = w^{\mathcal{S}}(1 - x_k) \qquad (4)$$

where $w^S \geq 0$ is a penalty assigned to each superpixel k which is not explained. This term encourages the explanation of as many superpixels as possible. Note that without such a term, we would obtain the trivial solution where none of the proposals is selected. Due to the noise in the input data and the approximations in the geometry model we enforce this condition as a soft constraint, i.e., superpixels may remain unexplained at cost w^S, cf. Fig. 1.

3.2 Visibility and Occlusion Potentials

To ensure that the selected scene elements and superpixels satisfy visibility and occlusion constraints we introduce the potentials κ_k and ψ_{ik}^S.

High-Order Consistency Potentials: $\kappa_k(\mathbf{x}_{c_k})$ is defined as:

$$\kappa_k(\mathbf{x}_{c_k}) = \begin{cases} \infty & \text{if } x_k = 1 \wedge \sum_{i \in \mathcal{L} \cup \mathcal{O}} x_i = 0 \\ 0 & \text{otherwise} \end{cases} \tag{5}$$

Here, the clique $c_k \subseteq \{k\} \cup \mathcal{L} \cup \mathcal{O}$ comprises the superpixel k and all proposals $i \in \mathcal{L} \cup \mathcal{O}$ that are able to explain superpixel k. In practice, we consider a superpixel as explained by a proposal if its rendered depth map is within a threshold (in our case 0.2 m) of $\mathbf{I}$ for more than 50 % of the comprised pixels. Note that Eq. 5 ensures that only superpixels which are explained by at least one object can take label $x_k = 1$.

Occlusion Potentials: Considering $\kappa_k(\mathbf{x}_{c_k})$ alone will lead to configurations where a superpixel is explained by objects which are themselves occluded by other objects at the same superpixel, thus violating visibility. To prevent this situation, we introduce pairwise occlusion potentials ψ_{ik}^S between all scene elements $i \in \mathcal{L} \cup \mathcal{O}$ and superpixels $k \in \mathcal{S}$

$$\psi_{ik}^S(x_i, x_k | \mathbf{I}) = \begin{cases} \infty & \text{if } x_i = 1 \wedge x_k = 1 \wedge \text{ "}i \text{ occludes } k\text{"} \\ 0 & \text{otherwise} \end{cases} \tag{6}$$

where "i occludes k" is true if for more than 50 % of the pixels in superpixel k the depth of the rendered object i is at least 0.2 m smaller than the corresponding depth value in $\mathbf{I}$. In other words, we prohibit superpixels from being explained if one or more active scene elements occlude the view.

3.3 Context Potentials

We also investigate contextual cues in the form of pairwise relationships between object and layout elements as described in the following.

Object-Object Potentials: The pairwise potential between object i and j is modeled as the weighted sum

$$\psi_{ij}^{\mathcal{O},\mathcal{O}}(x_i, x_j) = \sum_{t \in \{p,s,ovlp\}} w^t \psi_{ij}^t(x_i, x_j) \tag{7}$$

where ψ_{ij}^{t} is a feature capturing the relative pose, scale or overlap between object i and object j. We encode the pose and scale correlation between objects conditioned on the pair of semantic classes. For the pose, let $\mathrm{dist}_{ij}(z_i, z_j)$ and $\mathrm{rot}_{ij}(z_i, z_j)$ denote the distance and the relative rotation (encoded as cosine similarity) between object i and j, respectively. For each pair (c, c') of semantic classes, we estimate the joint distribution $p_{c,c'}^{\mathrm{p}}(\mathrm{dist}_{ij}, \mathrm{rot}_{ij})$ from training data using kernel density estimation (KDE). The relative pose potentials between a pair of objects are then defined by the negative log-likelihood $\psi_{ij}^{\mathrm{p}}(x_i, x_j) = -x_i x_j \log p_{c_i,c_j}^{\mathrm{p}}(\mathrm{dist}_{ij}(z_i, z_j), \mathrm{rot}_{ij}(z_i, z_j))$. Similarly, we consider scale by the negative logarithm of the relative scale distribution between semantic classes c_i and c_j as $\psi_{ij}^{\mathrm{s}}(x_i, x_j) = -x_i x_j \log p_{c_i,c_j}^{\mathrm{s}}(\mathrm{s}_{ij})$. Here, the relative scale s_{ij} is defined as the difference of the logarithm in scale and $p_{c_i,c_j}^{\mathrm{s}}(\mathrm{s}_{ij})$ is learned from training data using KDE. To avoid objects intersecting each other, we further penalize the overlapping volume of two objects

$$\psi_{ij}^{\mathrm{ovlp}}(x_i, x_j) = x_i x_j \left(\frac{V(\rho_i) \cap V(\rho_j)}{V(\rho_i)} + \frac{V(\rho_i) \cap V(\rho_j)}{V(\rho_j)} \right)$$

where $V(\rho)$ denotes the space occupied by the 3D bounding box of proposal ρ.

Layout-Object Potentials: Regarding the pairwise potential between layout i and object j, we consider the relative pose and volume exclusion constraints in analogy to those for the object-object potentials specified above:

$$\psi_{ij}^{\mathcal{L},\mathcal{O}}(x_i, x_j) = w^{\mathrm{p}} \psi_{ij}^{\mathrm{p}}(x_i, x_j) + w^{\mathrm{ovlp}} \psi_{ij}^{\mathrm{ovlp}}(x_i, x_j) \tag{8}$$

Here, ψ_{ij}^{p} denotes the log-likelihood of the object-to-plane distance and $\psi_{ij}^{\mathrm{ovlp}}$ penalizes the truncation of an object volume by a scene layout element.

3.4   Layout and Object Proposals

As discussed in the previous sections, our discrete CRF takes as input a set of layout and object proposals $\{\rho_i\}$. We obtain these proposals by first generating a set of foreground candidate regions $\{r_i\}$ using [3,13] and then solving the "inverse graphics problem" by drawing samples from the unary distributions specified in Eqs. 2 and 3 for each candidate region r_i.

Foreground Candidate Regions: For generating foreground candidate regions, we leverage the CPMC framework [3] extended to RGB-D images [25]. Furthermore, we use the output of the semantic segmentation algorithm of [13] as additional candidate regions. While [3] only provides object regions, [13] additionally provides information about the background classes *wall*, *floor* and *ceiling*. In contrast to existing works on RGB-D scene understanding which often rely on simple 3D cuboid representations [17,25], we explicitly represent the shape of objects using 3D models. For indoor objects such data becomes increasingly available, e.g., searching for "chair", "sofa" or "cabinet" in Google's 3D Warehouse returns more than $10,000$ hits per keyword. In our case, we make use of a compact set of 66 models to represent object classes with non-cuboid shapes.

Proposals from Unary Distributions: Unlike [17,25], we do not fit the tightest 3D cuboid to each candidate region for estimating the proposal's pose parameters as this leads to an undesirable shrinking bias. Instead, we sample proposals directly from the unary distributions specified in Sect. 3.1 using Metropolis-Hastings [9,26], leveraging the power of our 3D models in a generative manner. More specifically, for each layout candidate region, we draw samples from $p_{\mathcal{L}}(z_i, m_i) \propto \exp\left(-\phi^{\mathcal{L}}(z_i, m_i|\mathbf{I})\right)$ and for each object candidate region we draw samples from $p_{\mathcal{O}}(z_i, m_i) \propto \exp\left(-\phi^{\mathcal{O}}(z_i, m_i|\mathbf{I})\right)$. Here, the potentials $\phi^{\mathcal{L}}$ and $\phi^{\mathcal{O}}$ are defined as the right hand sides of Eqs. 2 and 3, fixing $x_i = 1$. Note that for proposal generation $\phi^{\mathcal{L}}$ and $\phi^{\mathcal{O}}$ depend on the pose and model parameters while those arguments are fixed during subsequent CRF inference. By restricting z_i to rotations around the up-axis we obtain an 8-dimensional sampling space for objects. For layout elements the only unknowns are the normal direction and the signed distances from the camera coordinate origin.

We randomly choose between global and local moves. Our global moves sample new pose parameters directly from the respective prior distributions which we have learned from annotated objects in the NYUv2 training set [12]. Modes of the target distribution are explored by local Student's t distributed moves which slightly modify the pose, scale and shape parameters. For each candidate region r_i we draw $10,000$ samples using the OpenGL-based 3D rendering engine librender presented in [11] and select the 3 most dominant modes.

3.5 Inference

Despite the great promise of high-order discrete CRFs for solving computer vision problems [2,43], MAP inference in such models remains very challenging. Existing work either aims at accelerating message passing for special types of potentials [7,20,27,31,40] or exploits sparsity of the factors [19,21,34]. Here, we explore the sparsity in our high-order potential functions (cf., Eq. 5) and recursively split the state space into sets depending on whether they do or do not contain any special state as detailed in the supplementary material. The class of sparse high-order potentials which can be handled by our recursive space-partitioning is a generalization of the pattern-based potentials proposed in [21,34]. In contrast to [21,34], our algorithm does not make the common assumption that energy values corresponding to "pattern" states are lower than those assigned to all other states as this assumption is violated by the high-order potential in Eq. 5. For algorithmic details, we refer the reader to the supplementary material.

4 Experimental Results

We evaluate our method in terms of 3D object detection performance on the challenging NYUv2 RGB-D dataset [38] which comprises 795 training and 654 test images of indoor scenes including semantic annotations. For evaluation, we use the 25 object and layout (super-)categories illustrated in Fig. 1 and leverage

Table 1. 3D Detection Performance on 21 Object Classes of NYUv2. The first part of the table shows results for [25], our baselines and our full model (FullModel-CAD) when evaluating the full extent of all 3D objects (i.e., including the occluded parts) in terms of the weighted F1 score (%). The second part of the table shows F1 scores when evaluating only the visible parts. See text for details.

	mantel	counter	toilet	sink	bathtub	bed	headboard	table	shelf	cabinet	sofa	chair	chest	refrigerator	oven	microwave	blinds	curtain	board	monitor	printer	overall
#obj	10	126	30	36	25	169	23	455	242	534	228	703	137	42	29	40	111	91	50	81	25	3187
[25] - 8 Proposals	0	4	27	12	0	13	0	8	13	3	16	8	5	0	0	0	13	5	3	8	0	7.90
[25] - 15 Proposals	0	3	27	10	0	11	0	7	11	3	19	8	4	0	0	11	11	6	3	6	0	7.71
[25] - 30 Proposals	0	3	24	11	12	10	0	7	10	3	18	9	5	0	0	11	11	5	3	6	0	7.61
Base-Det-Cuboid	0	8	3	2	13	12	5	8	3	6	6	4	14	14	7	3	3	2	1	4	2	5.80
Base-NMS-Cuboid	0	3	16	0	0	51	6	11	8	14	12	7	24	10	6	0	10	7	2	7	4	11.93
NoOcclusion-Cuboid	0	5	8	3	22	51	7	15	9	17	17	10	21	17	0	0	6	6	2	1	5	13.68
NoContext-Cuboid	0	9	7	2	27	51	6	17	7	18	16	6	21	23	5	0	4	2	1	5	6	13.38
FullModel-Cuboid	0	6	8	3	23	51	7	15	8	18	17	7	24	21	0	0	6	6	2	6	5	13.45
Base-Det-CAD	0	8	13	2	11	10	5	10	4	6	8	9	14	14	7	4	5	3	4	4	1	7.66
Base-NMS-CAD	0	2	43	3	0	48	6	16	9	14	21	15	23	14	5	6	6	5	2	5	4	15.05
NoOcclusion-CAD	0	4	52	4	25	49	0	21	9	17	30	18	24	24	0	0	0	6	4	3	0	17.57
NoContext-CAD	0	8	47	4	28	45	7	23	8	20	28	20	25	22	0	4	2	4	5	4	0	18.61
FullModel-CAD	0	4	61	4	31	55	7	24	10	19	33	18	27	24	0	0	1	6	3	5	0	**19.22**
[25] - 8 Proposals	0	4	27	12	0	13	0	8	13	3	16	8	5	0	0	0	13	5	3	8	0	7.90
[25] - 15 Proposals (vis)	0	6	33	10	0	12	0	10	13	6	23	10	8	0	0	16	14	10	5	10	0	10.12
[25] - 30 Proposals (vis)	0	5	30	11	12	11	0	9	12	6	22	10	9	0	0	16	13	9	5	10	0	9.96
FullModel-CAD (vis)	0	7	61	8	31	56	7	25	13	21	31	18	26	16	0	0	2	11	5	6	0	**20.47**

the manually annotated 3D object ground truth of [12]. We extract 400 super-pixels from each RGB-D image using the StereoSLIC algorithm [44], adapted to RGB-D information and generate about 100 object proposals per scene. The parameters in our model ($w^{\mathcal{L}} = 1$, $b^{\mathcal{L}} = 0$, $w^{\mathcal{O}} = 1.45$, $b^{\mathcal{O}} = 1.3$, $w^{\mathcal{S}} = 1.3$, $w^{\mathrm{p}} = w^{\mathrm{s}} = 0.001$, and $w^{\mathrm{ovlp}} = 100$) are obtained by coordinate descent on the NYUv2 training set and kept fixed during all our experiments.

Evaluation Criterion: We evaluate 3D object detection performance by computing the F1 measure for each object class and taking the average over all classes, weighted by the number of instances. An object is counted as true positive if the intersection-over-union of its 3D bounding box with respect to the associated ground truth 3D bounding box is larger than 0.3. This threshold is chosen smaller than the 0.5 threshold typically chosen for evaluating 2D detection [5] as the 3D volume intersection-over-union criterion is much more sensitive compared to its 2D counterpart.

Ablation Study: In this section, we evaluate the importance of the individual components in our model. First, we compare our method when using *CAD* models vs. using only simple *Cuboid* models as object representation. As illustrated in Table 1, we obtain a relative improvement in F1 score of 42.2 % when using CAD object models in our full graphical model (*FullModel-CAD vs. FullModel-Cuboid*), highlighting the importance of accurate 3D geometry modeling for this task. Next, we compare our full model with versions which exclude the occlusion (*NoOcclusion*) or context (*NoContext*) terms in our model. From Table 1, it becomes evident that the occlusion term is more important than context, improving the F1 score by 9.1 %. Adding the contextual relationship improves

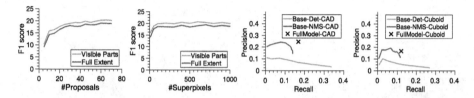

Fig. 2. 3D Object Detection. From left-to-right: Performance of full model wrt. number of proposals and wrt. number of superpixels. Precision-recall curves of the baselines wrt. the full model when using 3D CAD models and cuboid primitives (Color figure online).

performance by 3.2 %. Finally, Fig. 2 displays the 3D detection performance of our model with respect to the number of proposals (first subfigure) and super-pixels (second subfigure) evaluating objects to their full extent (blue) or only the visible part (red) by clipping all bounding boxes accordingly.

Baselines: In this section, we quantitatively compare our method against a recently published state-of-the-art algorithm [25] and two simpler baselines derived from our full model: For our first baseline (*Base-Det*), we simply threshold our unary detections at their maximal F1 score calculated over the training set. Our second baseline (*Base-NMS*) additionally performs greedy non-maximum-suppression, selecting only non-overlapping objects from the proposal set. As our results in Table 1 show, our method yields relative improvements in F1 score of 149.4 % and 27.2 % wrt. *Base-Det-CAD* and *Base-NMS-CAD*, respectively. Furthermore, the third and fourth plot of Fig. 2 show the perfor-mance of the baselines in terms of precision and recall when varying the detection threshold.

We further compare our method to [25] as their setup is most similar to ours and their code for training and evaluation is available. As [25] is only able to detect the visible part of objects and has been trained on a ground truth dataset biased towards cuboids, we re-train their method on the more recent and complete NYUv2 ground truth annotations by Guo et al. [12] clipped to the visible range and report results for different number of proposals (8, 15, 30). For a fair comparison, we evaluate only the visible parts of each object (*visible*, lower part of the table). On average, we double the F1 score wrt. [25]. The differences are especially pronounced for furniture categories such as *bathtub*, *bed*, *table*, *cabinet*, *sofa* and *chair*, showing the benefits of leveraging powerful 3D models during inference. Furthermore, we note that the performance of [25] drops with the number of proposals while the performance of our method keeps increasing (Fig. 2), which is a favorable property considering future work at larger scales. For completeness, we also show the performance of [25] on the unclipped bounding boxes (first rows of Table 1).

Qualitative Results: Figure 3 visualizes our inference results on a number of representative NYUv2 test images. Each panel displays (left-to-right) the inferred object wireframe models, virtual 3D renderings and the correspond-ing semantic segmentation. Note how our approach is able to recover even

Fig. 3. Inference Results. Each subfigure shows: Object wireframes, rendered depth map and induced semantic segmentation.

complex shapes (e.g., chair in row 1, right column) and detects heavily occluded 3D objects (e.g., bathtub and toilet in row 5, right column). The two lower rows show some failure cases of our method. In the top-left case, the sink is detected correctly, but intersects the volume of the containing cabinet which is removed from the solution. For most other cases, either the semantic class predictions which we take as input are corrupt, or the objects in the scene do not belong to the considered categories (such as *person*, *piano* or *billiard table*). However, note that even in those cases, the retrieved explanations are *functionally* plausible. Furthermore, flat objects are often missed due to the low probability of their volume intersecting the ground truth in 3D. Thus (and for completeness) we also provide an evaluation of the objects projected onto the 2D image (similar to the one carried out in [25]) in our supplementary material.

Runtime: On average, our implementation takes 119.2 s for generating proposals (∼6,000 samples/second via OpenGL), 7.9 s for factor graph construction and 0.7 s for inference on an i7 CPU running at 2.5 GHz.

5   Conclusion

In this paper, we have proposed a model for 3D indoor scene understanding from RGB-D images which jointly considers the layout, objects and superpixels. Our experiments show improvements with respect to two custom baselines as well as a state-of-the-art scene understanding approach which can be mainly attributed to two facts: First, we sample more accurate 3D CAD proposals directly from the unary distribution and second, the proposed model properly accounts for occlusions and satisfies visibility constraints. In the future, we plan to address more complete scene reconstructions, e.g., obtained via volumetric fusion in order to increase object visibility and thus inference reliability. Furthermore, we plan to extend our model to object based understanding of dynamic scenes from RGB/RGB-D video sequences by reasoning about 3D scene flow [28,29].

References

1. Aubry, M., Maturana, D., Efros, A., Russell, B., Sivic, J.: Seeing 3D chairs: exemplar part-based 2D–3D alignment using a large dataset of CAD models. In: CVPR (2014)
2. Blake, A., Kohli, P., Rother, C.: Markov Random Fields for Vision and Image Processing. MIT Press, Cambridge (2011)
3. Carreira, J., Sminchisescu, C.: CPMC: automatic object segmentation using constrained parametric min-cuts. PAMI 34(7), 1312–1328 (2012)
4. Choi, W., Chao, Y.W., Pantofaru, C., Savarese, S.: Understanding indoor scenes using 3D geometric phrases. In: CVPR (2013)
5. Everingham, M., Van Gool, L., Williams, C.K.I., Winn, J., Zisserman, A.: The pascal visual object classes (VOC) challenge. IJCV 88(2), 303–338 (2010)
6. Felzenszwalb, P.F., Girshick, R.B., McAllester, D.A.: Cascade object detection with deformable part models. In: CVPR (2010)
7. Felzenszwalb, P.F., Mcauley, J.J.: Fast inference with min-sum matrix product. PAMI 33(12), 2549–2554 (2011)
8. Fouhey, D.F., Gupta, A., Hebert, M.: Data-driven 3D primitives for single image understanding. In: ICCV (2013)
9. Gilks, W., Richardson, S.: Markov Chain Monte Carlo in Practice. Chapman & Hall, London (1995)
10. Girshick, R., Donahue, J., Darrell, T., Malik, J.: Rich feature hierarchies for accurate object detection and semantic segmentation. In: CVPR (2014)
11. Güney, F., Geiger, A.: Displets: resolving stereo ambiguities using object knowledge. In: CVPR (2015)
12. Guo, R., Hoiem, D.: Support surface prediction in indoor scenes. In: ICCV (2013)
13. Gupta, S., Arbelaez, P., Malik, J.: Perceptual organization and recognition of indoor scenes from RGB-D images. In: CVPR (2013)
14. Gupta, S., Girshick, R., Arbeláez, P., Malik, J.: Learning rich features from RGB-D images for object detection and segmentation. In: Fleet, D., Pajdla, T., Schiele, B., Tuytelaars, T. (eds.) ECCV 2014, Part VII. LNCS, vol. 8695, pp. 345–360. Springer, Heidelberg (2014)
15. Hedau, V., Hoiem, D., Forsyth, D.: Recovering the spatial layout of cluttered rooms. In: ICCV (2009)

16. Jia, Z., Gallagher, A., Saxena, A., Chen, T.: 3D-based reasoning with blocks, support, and stability. In: CVPR (2013)
17. Jiang, H., Xiao, J.: A linear approach to matching cuboids in RGB-D images. In: CVPR (2013)
18. Kim, B., Xu, S., Savarese, S.: Accurate localization of 3D objects from RGB-D data using segmentation hypotheses. In: CVPR (2013)
19. Kohli, P., Ladicky, L., Torr, P.H.S.: Robust higher order potentials for enforcing label consistency. IJCV **82**(3), 302–324 (2009)
20. Kohli, P., Kumar, M.P.: Energy minimization for linear envelope MRFs. In: CVPR (2010)
21. Komodakis, N., Paragios, N.: Beyond pairwise energies: efficient optimization for higher-order MRFs. In: CVPR (2009)
22. Lee, D., Gupta, A., Hebert, M., Kanade, T.: Estimating spatial layout of rooms using volumetric reasoning about objects and surfaces. In: NIPS (2010)
23. Lim, J.J., Khosla, A., Torralba, A.: FPM: fine pose parts-based model with 3D CAD models. In: Fleet, D., Pajdla, T., Schiele, B., Tuytelaars, T. (eds.) ECCV 2014, Part VI. LNCS, vol. 8694, pp. 478–493. Springer, Heidelberg (2014)
24. Lim, J.J., Pirsiavash, H., Torralba, A.: Parsing IKEA objects: fne pose estimation. In: ICCV (2013)
25. Lin, D., Fidler, S., Urtasun, R.: Holistic scene understanding for 3D object detection with RGB-D cameras. In: ICCV (2013)
26. Mansinghka, V., Kulkarni, T., Perov, Y., Tenenbaum, J.: Approximate bayesian image interpretation using generative probabilistic graphics programs. In: NIPS 2013 (2013)
27. Mcauley, J.J., Caetano, T.S.: Faster algorithms for max-product message-passing. JMLR **12**, 1349–1388 (2011)
28. Menze, M., Geiger, A.: Object scene flow for autonomous vehicles. In: CVPR (2015)
29. Menze, M., Heipke, C., Geiger, A.: Joint 3d estimation of vehicles and scene flow. In: ISA (2015)
30. Newcombe, R.A., Izadi, S., Hilliges, O., Molyneaux, D., Kim, D., Davison, A.J., Kohli, P., Shotton, J., Hodges, S., Fitzgibbon, A.: Kinectfusion: real-time dense surface mapping and tracking. In: ISMAR (2011)
31. Potetz, B., Lee, T.S.: Efficient belief propagation for higher-order cliques using linear constraint nodes. CVIU **112**(1), 39–54 (2008)
32. Ren, X., Bo, L., Fox, D.: RGB-(D) scene labeling: features and algorithms. In: CVPR (2012)
33. Roberts, L.G.: Machine perception of three-dimensional solids. Ph.D. thesis, Massachusetts Institute of Technology (1963)
34. Rother, C., Kohli, P., Feng, W., Jia, J.: Minimizing sparse higher order energy functions of discrete variables. In: CVPR (2009)
35. Satkin, S., Hebert, M.: 3DNN: viewpoint invariant 3D geometry matching for scene understanding. In: ICCV (2013)
36. Schwing, A.G., Urtasun, R.: Efficient exact inference for 3D indoor scene understanding. In: Fitzgibbon, A., Lazebnik, S., Perona, P., Sato, Y., Schmid, C. (eds.) ECCV 2012, Part VI. LNCS, vol. 7577, pp. 299–313. Springer, Heidelberg (2012)
37. Schwing, A.G., Fidler, S., Pollefeys, M., Urtasun, R.: Box in the box: joint 3D layout and object reasoning from single images. In: ICCV (2013)
38. Silberman, N., Hoiem, D., Kohli, P., Fergus, R.: Indoor segmentation and support inference from RGBD images. In: Fitzgibbon, A., Lazebnik, S., Perona, P., Sato, Y., Schmid, C. (eds.) ECCV 2012, Part V. LNCS, vol. 7576, pp. 746–760. Springer, Heidelberg (2012)

39. Song, S., Xiao, J.: Sliding shapes for 3D object detection in depth images. In: Fleet, D., Pajdla, T., Schiele, B., Tuytelaars, T. (eds.) ECCV 2014, Part VI. LNCS, vol. 8694, pp. 634–651. Springer, Heidelberg (2014)
40. Tarlow, D., Givoni, I.E., Zemel, R.S.: Hop-map: efficient message passing with high order potentials. In: AISTATS (2010)
41. Tighe, J., Niethammer, M., Lazebnik, S.: Scene parsing with object instances and occlusion ordering. In: CVPR (2014)
42. Tsai, G., Xu, C., Liu, J., Kuipers, B.: Real-time indoor scene understanding using Bayesian filtering with motion cues. In: ICCV (2011)
43. Wang, C., Komodakis, N., Paragios, N.: Markov random field modeling, inference & learning in computer vision & image understanding: a survey. CVIU **117**(11), 1610–1627 (2013)
44. Yamaguchi, K., McAllester, D., Urtasun, R.: Robust monocular epipolar flow estimation. In: CVPR (2013)
45. Zhang, H., Geiger, A., Urtasun, R.: Understanding high-level semantics by modeling traffic patterns. In: ICCV (2013)
46. Zhang, Y., Song, S., Tan, P., Xiao, J.: PanoContext: a whole-room 3D context model for panoramic scene understanding. In: Fleet, D., Pajdla, T., Schiele, B., Tuytelaars, T. (eds.) ECCV 2014, Part VI. LNCS, vol. 8694, pp. 668–686. Springer, Heidelberg (2014)
47. Zheng, B., Zhao, Y., Yu, J.C., Ikeuchi, K., Zhu, S.C.: Beyond point clouds: scene understanding by reasoning geometry and physics. In: CVPR (2013)
48. Zia, M., Stark, M., Schiele, B., Schindler, K.: Detailed 3D representations for object recognition and modeling. PAMI **35**(11), 2608–2623 (2013)

Object Proposals Estimation in Depth Image Using Compact 3D Shape Manifolds

Shuai Zheng[1]([✉]), Victor Adrian Prisacariu[1], Melinos Averkiou[2],
Ming-Ming Cheng[1,5], Niloy J. Mitra[2], Jamie Shotton[3], Philip H.S. Torr[1],
and Carsten Rother[4]

[1] University of Oxford, Oxford, UK
shuai.zheng@eng.ox.ac.uk
[2] University College London, London, UK
[3] Microsoft Research, Cambridge, UK
[4] TU Dresden, Dresden, Germany
[5] Nankai University, Tianjin, China

Abstract. Man-made objects, such as chairs, often have very large shape variations, making it challenging to detect them. In this work we investigate the task of finding particular object shapes from a single depth image. We tackle this task by exploiting the inherently low dimensionality in the object shape variations, which we discover and encode as a compact shape space. Starting from any collection of 3D models, we first train a low dimensional Gaussian Process Latent Variable Shape Space. We then sample this space, effectively producing infinite amounts of shape variations, which are used for training. Additionally, to support fast and accurate inference, we improve the standard 3D object category proposal generation pipeline by applying a shallow convolutional neural network-based filtering stage. This combination leads to considerable improvements for proposal generation, in both speed and accuracy. We compare our full system to previous state-of-the-art approaches, on four different shape classes, and show a clear improvement.

1 Introduction

Object detection has recently undergone significant advances, thanks to progress in GPU design [23], deep convolutional neural networks (ConvNets) [14,27,38], and big image recognition dataset [10] collected by e.g. Amazon Mechanical Turk. However, man-made objects, such as chairs, often have very large shape variations, making them still challenging to detect. On the other hand, there

S. Zheng, V.A. Prisacariu, M.-M. Cheng and P.H.S. Torr—This work has been supported by UK EPSRC EP/I001107/2 and EP/J014990 (VAP).

M. Averkiou and N.J. Mitra—This work has been supported by Starting Grant SmartGeometry (StG-2013-335373) and Melinos Averkiou is grateful for a scholarship from the Rabin Ezra Scholarship Trust.

M.-M. Cheng—This work has been partially supported by Youth Leader Program of Nankai University.

© Springer International Publishing Switzerland 2015
J. Gall et al. (Eds.): GCPR 2015, LNCS 9358, pp. 196–208, 2015.
DOI: 10.1007/978-3-319-24947-6_16

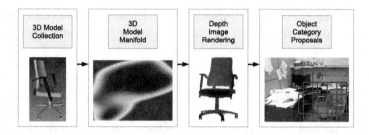

Fig. 1. System overview. Given a set of 3D shapes, we learn a low dimensional latent shape space using GP-LVM (3D Model Manifold). We then generate shapes from this space and render them from a number of random 3D poses. We use these to train a three layer proposal pipeline, based on SVM and ConvNets.

is a large number of CAD models available in 3D Warehouse. In this work we want to thoroughly analyse how to leverage this significantly large CAD model collections for the task of finding particular object shapes in a single depth image.

Most object detection approaches have focused on the 2D domain, with 3D being considered only recently, in works such as [3,16,34]. Gupta *et al.* [16] is an example of using a standard ConvNet pipeline. The authors use manually annotated RGB-D data from the NYU dataset to train a deep convolutional neural network for feature extraction and classification. At inference time, they classify only the proposed object locations returned from the accurate (but slow) proposal generator of [2]. An alternative approach is presented in [3,34], where the authors take a collection of 3D CAD models which they use to generate synthetic depth maps. Gupta *et al.* [15] used a convolutional neural network to predict the coarse pose of the object and then align the CAD models to the objects through a model fitting. In that work, however, object proposals are found using an exhaustive standard sliding window proposal generator.

A hallmark of current 3D object detection work is the focus on the classification/feature discovery phase. Finding object location proposals still uses standard 2D strategies, such as selective search or sliding window. In contrast, in this paper we explicitly tackle the problem of proposal generation, and exploit the inherently lower appearance variance of the 3D domain to provide a method that is both faster and more accurate than the current state of the art. Inspired by the work of Karpathy *et al.* [19], we show how to use a compact 3D shape space in detecting those objects with high shape variations.

In the 2D (RGB) domain, objects have often a large appearance variance, due to colour, texture and varying lighting conditions. These, however, do not manifest themselves in the 3D depth domain, which has enabled works like [31] to use primarily synthetic data for training. Inspired by such methods, we do not assume the existence of a large quantity of manually labelled training data, but instead interpolate between manually constructed 3D models, using a variance-preserving approach. We start from a collection of 3D models, obtained from the Trimble Google 3D warehouse. We use these to train a low dimensional latent space using the Gaussian Process Latent Variable Models (GL-LVM, [26]) method. Such spaces capture the intrinsic variance of the training data and have been used previously as shape priors for 3D tracking and reconstruction in [30] and semantic SLAM in [9]. Next we generate 3D shapes back from these spaces and finally render them into multiple 2.5D depth-only projections.

A second requirement for a proposal generator is fast and accurate inference. With this in mind, we train a cascaded object proposal method, comprising of *two* layers. The first is a traditional "objectness" proposal generator such as BING [7] or edgeBox [40], which are the fastest ones. We use this to generate a large number (over 1000) of low accuracy proposals, very quickly, at over 1000 fps. The last layer then is designed to filter out the noise and retain only a small number (about 100) of very accurate proposals. This is constructed using a shallow ConvNet and a linear SVM classifier.

As shown in Fig. 1, the output of this cascade is a set of proposals that can be classified by any downstream classifier, e.g. ConvNet [16,27]. This work therefore proposes a novel method for finding object location proposals, specific to the 3D depth domain. Using our test data, as outlined in the results section, the standard 2D selective search method result in an accuracy of 56.3 %, using 100 proposals, while ours has an accuracy of 82.9 %. Furthermore, whereas selective search required over 2.6 s per frame, our approach needs 0.88 s, giving a relative speed up of almost 3×. The improvement in accuracy and speed comes as a result of our two **main contributions**:

- We leverage the generative abilities of GP-LVM shape spaces, coupled with a random pose rendering stage, to generate effectively *infinite* amounts of shape variance-maintaining training data.
- We improve the standard 3D object category proposal pipeline, by integrating a proposal generator with a shallow ConvNet-based filtering stage. This leads to considerable improvements in both speed and accuracy of the proposal generation.

2   Related Work

We review related approaches for proposal generation, along with methods that use synthetic data for depth-based inference.

Object proposal methods have been developed to find a small number (e.g. 1,000) of category-independent bounding box candidates that are expected to cover all objects in an image [1,12]. Such pruning methods are extremely effective in object detection, as demonstrated in recent state-of-the-art approaches [14]. One category of object proposal methods [6,11] uses rough segmentations to generate the object candidates. While such methods successfully reduce the search space for category-based classifiers, they are computationally very expensive, requiring 2–7 min. to process a single image. Alexe *et al.* [1] developed an efficient method that integrates several objectness cues to predict the object candidates. Zhang *et al.* [39] proposed a cascaded ranking SVM approach with orientated gradient features to generate the object proposals. More recently, Uijlings et al. [38] proposed a selective search method that achieves higher recall prediction. The method, when integrated with an SVM classifier, has been demonstrated to achieve state-of-the-art performance in object detection. Recently, Cheng et al. [7], proposed a very fast cascaded SVM method that generates object proposals at over 300 fps. Zitnick et al. [40] use edge detection to generate reliable and relative fast proposals. Arbeláez et al. [2] develop a multiscale combinatorial grouping method which can provide very accurate segmentation proposals. Krähenbühl et al. [22] use a method to identify critical level sets in geodesic distance transforms computed for seeds placed in the image, based on which they generate a lot of reliable segmentation proposals.

Synthetic data has been used for object detection in two primary ways. One is to learn multi-view priors for object detectors from 3D models [21,29]. The other is to use transfer learning [8] to train a detector using the 3D model data in the 3D domain and use it in 2D images. Generating realistic RGB data from 3D models, however, is very difficult, as it requires realistic 3D shapes, textures, poses, and lighting. Related approaches have been used, for example, in model-based hand 3D tracking by [24,35,37]. Fortunately, in the context of depth images, rendering realistic synthetic depth is comparatively much easier, as it only requires realistic 3D models and pose. Such an approach was used successfully in detection based human pose estimation by [31].

Song et al. [34] and Aubry et al. [3] developed exemplar-based 3D object detectors trained on 3D CAD datasets. Our approach differs from theirs, as they explore 3D object detection with a sliding window whereas we propose a data-driven object category proposal generator. Our approach is complementary to Gupta et al. [16], who use the region-based convolutional neural network [14] framework to learn rich features for 3D object detection, and have achieved very high accuracy in 3D object detection. We leverage publicly available 3D CAD models to improve both the speed and quality of the object category proposal generators, which is the bottleneck of their system.

Another defining feature of our approach is the use of dimensionality reduction for variance-maintaining shape interpolation. This has been used before for e.g. 3D tracking and reconstruction, in e.g. [9,30], but, to our knowledge, has not yet employed in object proposal generation. Dimensionality reduction in detection has so far primarily targeted training data preconditioning, by removing unnecessary variance from local descriptors in e.g. [5,20,33], thereby leading to improved final results.

In this work we follow [31] and use synthetic depth generated from a collection of 3D models to train a detector. We learn low dimensional GP-LVM shape manifolds. We then sample the explicit shape manifolds to generate low variance 3D shapes, which we use to synthetically generate several depth images from multiple views. These are next used to train a fast SVM object category proposal generator method, similar to [7].

3   Algorithm

We propose an algorithm for generating category proposals for single view depth images, that is specialised in handling a particular shape family such as e.g. chairs, monitors, toilets, or sofas. The algorithm runs in three main stages: starting from a set of object models, we construct a corresponding shape manifold to model the in-category variations (Sect. 3.1); we then sample the extracted manifold to create representative shapes that are then used to synthetically produce depth images (Sect. 3.2); and finally we use the synthetic depth images to train a cascaded proposal generator (Sect. 3.3).

3.1   Constructing a 3D Shape Manifold

We learn Gaussian Process Latent Variable Models (GP-LVM, [25]) shape spaces [9,30], using the pipeline outlined in Fig. 2. In Sect. 4, we show how the access to

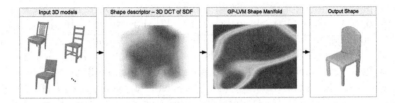

Fig. 2. 3D Parametrised Manifold: given an unorganised 3D chair model collection we build shape descriptors and learn low dimensional embeddings which we use to remove unnecessary shape and training dataset variance.

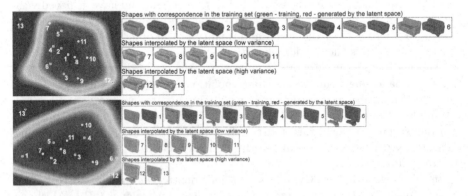

Fig. 3. Example Latent Shape Space: Each row shows a two dimensional latent space of 3D shapes (left) and samples from it (right). Warmer colours indicate higher variance, colder colours lower variance and the red dots point out the latent points corresponding to the training data. Red shapes are generated by the latent space and have the green shapes as ground truth. Blue shapes are interpolated by the latent space, with no correspondence in the training data (Color figure online).

parametrised shape manifolds improves the object category proposal generation, leading to a performance that is superior to several state-of-the-art alternatives.

We assume a given set of training 3D models from the Google Warehouse. These are then aligned (using ICP), voxelised to a volumetric representation, embedded inside 3D signed distance functions, and compressed using the 3D discrete cosine transform.

We next apply GP-LVM on the DCT-SDF descriptor to find a low dimensional shape embedding space. GP-LVM is a nonlinear and probabilistic dimensionality reduction technique. It is used to represent a set of N high dimensional observations $\mathbf{X} = [\mathbf{x}_1, \ldots, \mathbf{x}_N]$ with a set of corresponding low dimensional points $\mathbf{Y} = [\mathbf{y}_1, \ldots, \mathbf{y}_N]$, where the dimensionality of $\mathbf{Y}$ is (much) smaller than that of $\mathbf{X}$. In our case the observation variables are the DCT compressed SDF volumes, so we can write:

$$\mathbf{y}_i = \text{DCT}_{3D}(\text{SDF}(M_i)) \qquad M_i = H_e(\text{IDCT}_{3D}(\mathbf{y}_i)) \qquad (1)$$

where M_i is the volumetric representation of the i-th 3D shape, H_e is the smooth Heaviside function, SDF computes a signed distance function, and DCT/IDCT are the forward and reverse discrete cosine transforms. Figure 3 shows an example 2D latent space embedding 3D shapes of chairs. We use $256 \times 256 \times 256$ 3D volumes and $40 \times 40 \times 40$ 3D DCT harmonics, for a 64000D final shape descriptor.

Finding a GP-LVM embedding is done by maximising the probability of the observation data $\mathbf{Y}$ jointly given the latent variables $\mathbf{X}$ and the hyperparameters of a Gaussian Process (GP) [25] mapping $\mathbf{Y}$ into $\mathbf{X}$. This probability is formally written as:

$$P(\mathbf{Y}|\mathbf{X}) = \prod_{i=1}^{N} \mathcal{N}(\mathbf{y}_i|0, \mathbf{K}) \qquad (2)$$

where $\mathbf{K}$ is the covariance matrix of the GP with the following nonlinear kernel:

$$\mathbf{K}(\mathbf{x}_i, \mathbf{x}_j) = \kappa(\mathbf{x}_i, \mathbf{x}_j) = \theta_1 e^{-\frac{\theta_2}{2}||\mathbf{x}_i - \mathbf{x}_j||^2} + \theta_3 + \theta_4 \delta_{ij} \qquad (3)$$

with θ_{1-4} being the GP hyperparameters, δ_{ij} Kronecker's delta function and $\kappa(\cdot, \cdot)$ the GP covariance function. This model generates 3D shapes $\mathbf{y}_i$ from latent variables $\mathbf{x}_i$ as Gaussian distributions:

$$\mathbf{y}_i|\mathbf{X} \sim \mathcal{N}(\mu_i, \sigma_i^2) \qquad (4)$$

$$\mu_i = \kappa(\mathbf{x}_i, \mathbf{X})\mathbf{K}^{-1}\mathbf{Y} \qquad (5)$$

$$\sigma_i^2 = \kappa(\mathbf{x}_i, \mathbf{x}_i) - \kappa(\mathbf{x}_i, \mathbf{X})\mathbf{K}^{-1}\kappa(\mathbf{x}_i, \mathbf{X})^T. \qquad (6)$$

Identifying unusual shapes when using a GP-LVM shape space simply amounts to generating all training shapes back from the latent space and sorting them by variance, with the lowest variance corresponding to the most typical 3D models.

3.2   Depth Rendering and Data Synthesis

Real world objects have different shapes and can be placed in different poses, with different camera viewpoints. This leads to a very large possible appearance

Fig. 4. Shallow ConvNet model architecture. This figure presents our inference process during inference time. We adapted successful network configuration described in [28] for this task.

space, whose variability we need to deal with. Following Shotton *et al.* [31], we build a randomised depth image rendering pipeline based on the extracted 3D model manifold. Thus we generate a large number of depth images, from different viewpoints and with the object in different poses and displaying intrinsic shape variations. When rendering the depth images (the shapes M_i described above are converted to meshes), we randomly sample the set of 3D appearance parameters using a heuristic approximation of the variability we expected to observe in the real world. Also, in order to make our data more realistic, we use the intrinsic parameters used in NYU V2 data.

3.3 Cascaded Object Category Proposal Generator

Our depth-based object category proposal generator draws inspiration from recent object proposal generators, such as BING [7], EdgeBox [40], and ConvNet-based object detection approaches, such as [14]. We suggest a two-layer structure. The first layer follows the object proposal generator. At inference time, these produce a large number of detections very quickly (at over 1000 fps). Precision however can often be quite low. The second layer is then designed to remove some false positives and so reduce the number of proposals needed for an accurate detection from e.g. 1000 to e.g. 100, with little to no loss of recall. This layer is implemented using a shallow ConvNet.

Unlike in RGB images, the object contour information is very salient in depth images. One way to detect such contours is to use gradient convolution filters. This led us to adapt the 64D normalised gradients feature used for *2D RGB* object category proposal estimation in [7], to our depth-only scenario. In our proposed framework, we can also use a more accurate proposal generator approach, such as EdgeBox [40].

Refining the Object Category Pool. The first stage of our proposal generating cascade is very fast, but often leads to low quality proposals. In order to refine the proposal pool, we use a shallow 4-layer ConvNet and a following linear SVM, as shown in Fig. 4.

We trained the ConvNet first on the ImageNet dataset and next fine-tuned it on the NYU V2 depth training data and the synthetic data generated from the GP-LVM low dimensional latent space. Using both real and artificial examples prevents the network from overfitting. Compared to the standard deep networks [18] used in the ImageNet object detection task, our network is shallower than the deep networks [18,36], while having lower accuracy, is faster at runtime, making it better suited for the task at hand.

4 Experiments

We evaluate our method on the NYU V2 [32] dataset using four categories of objects (chairs, sofas, toilets and TV). The remainder of this section is split into four parts: (i) Sect. 4.1 describes our experimental setup; (ii) Sect. 4.2 shows that using our variance-preserving synthetic data and random view rendering improves accuracy; (iii) Sect. 4.3 shows that the extra ConvNet filtering further improves accuracy.

4.1 Experimental Setup

Dataset. The NYU V2 dataset [32] contains 1449 RGB and depth images with pixel-level segmentation annotations. We split data set according to the standard NYU V2 train/test split to obtain 495 training and validation images, and 404 testing images.

To train our latent space and classifiers we also use 3D models downloaded from the Google 3D Warehouse. We select 374 chairs, 42 TV, 36 sofas, and 24 toilets 3D CAD models. After passing through the latent space filtering, we use them to render the depth images, 37400 for the chair class, 25200 for TV, 21600 for sofa, and 14400 for toilet. Here we considered 600 different random pose and viewpoint configurations, which excluded the top and bottom viewpoints, as these are rarely seen in indoor scenes.

Evaluation Criteria. We use standard DR-#WIN accuracy measure [1], which quantifies detection rate (DR) given #WIN proposals. A proposal covers an object if the strict VOC [13] criterion is satisfied, i.e. if INT-UNION> 0.5.

Implementation. Our approach is implemented based on the Caffe [17] library. We fine-tune the network-in-network model [28] on the NYU V2 dataset and the synthetic data. The learning step size is 5000, the momentum is 0.9, and the weight decay is 0.0005. Using a NVIDIA Titan Black GPU, the per frame inference processing is 0.88 s per frame, with a pool of 1000 category proposal candidates from BING[1].

4.2 Synthetic Data

We first investigate the effect of the *number of rendered depth images* on the classification result. As shown in the Fig. 5, we observe the clear trend that adding

---

[1] https://github.com/bittnt/Objectness.

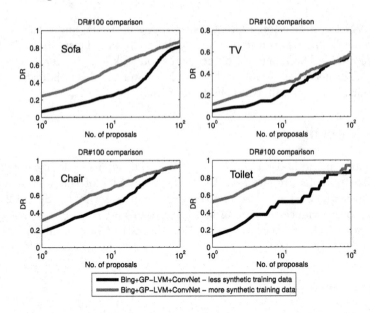

Fig. 5. Logarithmic plot measuring the DR#100 (50 % Intersection-over-union) accuracy when we double the amount of synthetic data (i.e. sofa: 43200 (red), 21600 (black); TV: 50400 (red), 25200 (black); chair: 74800 (red), 37400 (black); tiolet: 28800 (red), 14400 (black).). The extra data leads to much higher accuracy when using fewer proposals. As the number of proposals increases the extra training points do not help much, as the BING discrimination ability saturates (Color figure online).

more synthetic renderings into the training set helps boost the performance of the approach.

We next investigate the effect of the *data preconditioning* (i.e. the number of GP-LVM dimensions and variance of the 3D shapes) on the classification result. Not all object 3D models are realistic and not all 3D shape details are important in the classification. The GP-LVM shape manifold allows us to remove both unusual shapes and unnecessary intra-shape variance from the training data. To showcase this feature we used 374 3D chair shapes to train 3, 4, 5, 6 and 7 dimensional GP-LVM shape spaces. The results are shown in Tables 1 (left and right) and 2. In Table 1 (left) we show the results obtained from the original training set (i.e. not compressed with GP-LVM) and when learning a 5D GP-LVM latent space and training with (i) the top 100, 150 and 200 shapes with the lowest variance, and (ii) the full training set. Initially, as the number of training shapes increases (between 100 and 150 models) accuracy improves. At some point between 150 and 200 though unusual shapes start being added to the training set, which decreases the accuracy. In Table 1 (right) we vary the number of dimensions used for the trained GP-LVM spaces from 3 to 7. The same trend as in Table 1 (left) can be observed. Initially (when using between 3 and 5 dimensions) we add useful shape variance to the training set which improves the final accuracy. When more than 5 dimensions are used (and that includes the full uncompressed training set) we add unnecessary variance to the training set thus decreasing accuracy. Finally, in Table 2[2], we use the chair class and 1000 BING proposals to evaluate our method of shape generation (BING + GPLVM) against (i) BING + the alternative shape generation method of ShapeSynth [4] and (ii) other methods for proposal generations that do not use synthetic data: BING [7], OBN [1], CSVM [39], SEL [38], and random guessing. OBN, CSVM and BING are trained on the NYU V2 training set whereas SEL does not require any data. BING + ShapeSynth and BING + GPLVM are trained on the NYU V2 training data and the sampled ShapeSynth or GPLVM synthetic shapes. Our method outperforms all the other proposal generators. Of particular note is that BING + GP-LVM outperforms BING + ShapeSynth, in spite of ShapeSynth usually generating much more realistic looking shapes. This result complements the experiment from Table 1 and shows that sampling only low variance shapes from the manifold is beneficial.

Table 1. Effect of data preconditioning. Left - accuracy results obtained when training on the chair category with the original dataset not compressed with GP-LVM and when using a 5D low dimensional GP-LVM space and training with (i) the top 100, 150 and 200 shapes with the lowest variance (ii) the full training set. Right - accuracy obtained when generating data from 3–7D low dimensional spaces and selecting the top 150 shapes with the lowest variance. #DIM indicates the number of latent space dimensions and #SAM the number of samples from each latent space.

BING-GPLVM		BING-GPLVM	
#DIM(#SAM)	DR-#1000W	#DIM(#SAM)	DR-#1000W
5–100	88.7	3–150	88.0
5–150	**89.7**	4–150	89.6
5–200	89.2	**5–150**	**89.7**
5–374	88.4	6–150	89.3
Original-374	87.8	7–150	89.2

4.3   ConvNet Filtering Layer

In Fig. 6 we compare selective search, BING + GP-LVM and BING + GP-LVM + ConvNet, when using *only 100* proposals, and all four object classes. The best results are obtained when using our full approach (BING + GP-LVM + ConvNet), with BING + GP-LVM following with 59.2 % respectively, and selective search being the last with 56.3 %. Of course both selective search would reach higher accuracy with more proposals, as shown before. However, no method other than BING + GP-LVM + ConvNet is able to reach this level of accuracy with *just 100 proposals*. We also note that per-frame processing with our full approach was 0.88 s, whereas for selective search it was 2.6 s.

---

[2] Experiments are carried out on a machine with a Intel Xeon E5-2687w(32 Cores).

Table 2. Quantitative results on different proposal estimation approaches.
We compared different approaches on the chair category using the NYU V2 depth image dataset. We follow the standard evaluation criteria, which is the detection rate over 1000 object proposals [1]. The best result are obtained when using BING + GP-LVM.

Method	Random Guess	OBN [1]	CSVM [39]	SEL [38]	BING [7]	BING-ShapeSynth [4]	BING-GPLVM our approach
DR-#1000W	42.0	83.0	84.5	85.9	85.6	88.5	**89.7**
Time (s)	N/A	2.10	1.20	2.6	**0.0009**	**0.0009**	**0.0009**

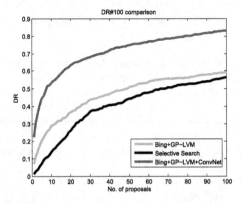

Fig. 6. DR#100 Comparison. We compare three methods, selective search (which we consider to be the state of the art), BING + GP-LVM, and BING + GP-LVM + ConvNet, when using *only 100* proposals, and all four object classes. Our full approach is the most accurate, with an accuracy of 82.9 % whereas selective search produces 56.3 %.

5   Conclusions

We presented an algorithm for generating depth-based proposals for high-variation specific object categories. Our main message is that (i) the use of synthetic data, sampled from variance-maintaining compact shape manifolds, boosts the accuracy of object category proposal estimation, as it enables the classifier to focus on the intrinsic 'classness' variance and ignore unusual shape details; and (ii) a final shallow ConvNet layer further dramatically improve the overall accuracy. As future work, we intend to investigate the use of this proposal generator in various applications, such as depth fusion or 3D reconstruction.

References

1. Alexe, B., Deselaers, T., Ferrari, V.: Measuring objectness of image windows. IEEE Trans. Pattern Anal. Mach. Intell. **34**(11), 2189–2202 (2012)

2. Arbeláez, P., Pont-Tuset, J., Barron, J., Marques, F., Malik, J.: Multiscale combinatorial grouping. In: CVPR, pp. 328–335 (2014)
3. Aubry, M., Maturana, D., Efros, A.A., Russel, B., Sivic, J.: Seeing 3D chairs: exemplar part-based 2D-3D alignment using a large dataset of CAD models. In: CVPR, pp. 3762–3769 (2014)
4. Averkiou, M., Kim, V., Zheng, Y., Mitra, N.J.: Shapesynth: parameterizing model collections for coupled shape exploration and synthesis. Comput. Graph. Forum **33**(2), 125–134 (2014)
5. Brown, M., Hua, G., Winder, S.: Discriminative learning of local image descriptors. IEEE Trans. Pattern Anal. Mach. Intell. **33**(1), 43–57 (2011)
6. Carreira, J., Sminchisescu, C.: CPMC: automatic object segmentation using constrained parametric min-cuts. IEEE Trans. Pattern Anal. Mach. Intell. **34**(7), 1312–1328 (2012)
7. Cheng, M.M., Zhang, Z., Lin, W.Y., Torr, P.: BING: Binarized normed gradients for objectness estimation at 300 fps. In: CVPR, pp. 3286–3293 (2014)
8. Chiu, H.P., Kaelbling, L.P., Lozano-Perez, T.: Virtual training for multi-view object class recognition. In: CVPR, pp. 1–8 (2007)
9. Dame, A., Prisacariu, V.A., Ren, C.Y., Reid, I.: Dense reconstruction using 3d object shape priors. In: CVPR, pp. 1288–1295 (2013)
10. Deng, J., Dong, W., Socher, R., Li, L.J., Li, K., Fei-Fei, L.: ImageNet: a large-scale hierarchical image database. In: CVPR, pp. 248–255 (2009)
11. Endres, I., Hoiem, D.: Category independent object proposals. In: Daniilidis, K., Maragos, P., Paragios, N. (eds.) ECCV 2010, Part V. LNCS, vol. 6315, pp. 575–588. Springer, Heidelberg (2010)
12. Endres, I., Hoiem, D.: Category-independent object proposals with diverse ranking. IEEE Trans. PAMI **36**(2), 222–234 (2014)
13. Everingham, M., Van Gool, L., Williams, C.K.I., Winn, J., Zisserman, A.: The pascal visual object classes (VOC) challenge. Int. J. Comput. Vision **88**(2), 303–338 (2010)
14. Girshick, R., Donahue, J., Darrell, T., Malik, J.: Rich feature hierarchies for accurate object detection and semantic segmentation. In: CVPR, pp. 580–587 (2014)
15. Gupta, S., Arbeláez, P.A., Girshick, R.B., Malik, J.: Aligning 3D models to RGB-D images of cluttered scenes. In: CVPR, pp. 4731–4740 (2015)
16. Gupta, S., Girshick, R., Arbeláez, P., Malik, J.: Learning rich features from RGB-D images for object detection and segmentation. In: Fleet, D., Pajdla, T., Schiele, B., Tuytelaars, T. (eds.) ECCV 2014, Part VII. LNCS, vol. 8695, pp. 345–360. Springer, Heidelberg (2014)
17. Jia, Y.: Caffe: An open source convolutional architecture for fast feature embedding (2013). http://caffe.berkeleyvision.org/
18. Simonyan, K., Zisserman, A.: Very deep convolutional networks for large-scale image recognition (2014). arXiv:1409.1556v2
19. Karpathy, A., Miller, S., Li, F.F.: Object discovery in 3d scenes via shape analysis. In: ICRA, pp. 2088–2095 (2013)
20. Ke, Y., Sukthankar, R.: PCA-SIFT: a more distinctive representation for local image descriptors. In: CVPR, pp. 506–513 (2004)
21. Kim, Y.M., Mitra, N.J., Huang, Q., Guibas, L.: Guided real-time scanning of indoor objects. Comput. Graph. Forum (Proc. Pacific Graph.) **32**, 177–186 (2013)
22. Krähenbühl, P., Koltun, V.: Geodesic object proposals. In: Fleet, D., Pajdla, T., Schiele, B., Tuytelaars, T. (eds.) ECCV 2014, Part V. LNCS, vol. 8693, pp. 725–739. Springer, Heidelberg (2014)

23. Krizhevsky, A., Sutskever, I., Hinton, G.E.: ImageNet classification with deep convolutional neural networks. In: NIPS, pp. 1106–1114 (2012)
24. de La Gorce, M., Paragios, N., Fleet, D.: Model-based hand tracking with texture, shading and self-occlusions. In: CVPR, pp. 1–8 (2008)
25. Lawrence, N.: Probabilistic non-linear principal component analysis with Gaussian process latent variable models. JMLR **6**, 1783–1816 (2005)
26. Lawrence, N.D.: Gaussian process latent variable models for visualisation of high dimensional data. In: NIPS, pp. 329–336 (2003)
27. LeCun, Y., Bottou, L., Bengio, Y., Haffner, P.: Gradient-based learning applied to document recognition. In: Proceedings of the IEEE, pp. 2278–2324 (1998)
28. Lin, M., Chen, Q., Yan, S.: Network in network. In: ICLR (2013)
29. Pepik, B., Stark, M., Gehler, P., Schiele, B.: Multi-view priors for learning detectors from sparse viewpoint data (2014). arXiv:1312.6095
30. Prisacariu, V.A., Segal, A.V., Reid, I.: Simultaneous monocular 2D segmentation, 3D Pose recovery and 3D reconstruction. In: Lee, K.M., Matsushita, Y., Rehg, J.M., Hu, Z. (eds.) ACCV 2012, Part I. LNCS, vol. 7724, pp. 593–606. Springer, Heidelberg (2013)
31. Shotton, J., Fitzgibbon, A.W., Cook, M., Sharp, T., Finocchio, M., Moore, R., Kipman, A., Blake, A.: Real-time human pose recognition in parts from single depth images. In: CVPR, pp. 1297–1304 (2011)
32. Silberman, N., Hoiem, D., Kohli, P., Fergus, R.: Indoor segmentation and support inference from RGBD images. In: Fitzgibbon, A., Lazebnik, S., Perona, P., Sato, Y., Schmid, C. (eds.) ECCV 2012, Part V. LNCS, vol. 7576, pp. 746–760. Springer, Heidelberg (2012)
33. Simonyan, K., Vedaldi, A., Zisserman, A.: Learning local feature descriptors using convex optimisation. IEEE Trans. Pattern Anal. Mach. Intell. **36**(8), 1573–1585 (2014)
34. Song, S., Xiao, J.: Sliding shapes for 3D object detection in depth images. In: Fleet, D., Pajdla, T., Schiele, B., Tuytelaars, T. (eds.) ECCV 2014, Part VI. LNCS, vol. 8694, pp. 634–651. Springer, Heidelberg (2014)
35. Stenger, B., Thayananthan, A., Torr, P.H.S., Cipolla, R.: Model-based hand tracking using a hierarchical bayesian filter. IEEE Trans. Pattern Anal. Mach. Intell. **28**(9), 1372–1384 (2006)
36. Szegedy, C., Liu, W., Jia, Y., Sermanet, P., Reed, S., Anguelov, D., Erhan, D., Vanhoucke, V., Rabinovich, A.: Going deeper with convolutions (2014). arXiv:1409.4842
37. Tang, D., Yu, T.H., Kim, T.K.: Real-time articulated hand Pose estimation using semi-supervised transductive regression forests. In: ICCV, pp. 3224–3231 (2013)
38. Uijlings, J.R.R., van de Sande, K.E.A., Gevers, T., Smeulders, A.W.M.: Selective search for object recognition. IJCV **104**(2), 154–171 (2013)
39. Zhang, Z., Warrell, J., Torr, P.H.: Proposal generation for object detection using cascaded ranking SVMS. In: CVPR, pp. 1497–1504 (2011)
40. Zitnick, C.L., Dollár, P.: Edge boxes: locating object proposals from edges. In: Fleet, D., Pajdla, T., Schiele, B., Tuytelaars, T. (eds.) ECCV 2014, Part V. LNCS, vol. 8693, pp. 391–405. Springer, Heidelberg (2014)

The Long-Short Story of Movie Description

Anna Rohrbach[1]([✉]), Marcus Rohrbach[2], and Bernt Schiele[1]

[1] Max Planck Institute for Informatics, Saarbrücken, Germany
arohrbach@mpi-inf.mpg.de
[2] UC Berkeley EECS and ICSI, Berkeley, CA, USA

Abstract. Generating descriptions for videos has many applications including assisting blind people and human-robot interaction. The recent advances in image captioning as well as the release of large-scale movie description datasets such as MPII-MD [28] and M-VAD [31] allow to study this task in more depth. Many of the proposed methods for image captioning rely on pre-trained object classifier CNNs and Long Short-Term Memory recurrent networks (LSTMs) for generating descriptions. While image description focuses on objects, we argue that it is important to distinguish verbs, objects, and places in the setting of movie description. In this work we show how to learn robust visual classifiers from the weak annotations of the sentence descriptions. Based on these classifiers we generate a description using an LSTM. We explore different design choices to build and train the LSTM and achieve the best performance to date on the challenging MPII-MD and M-VAD datasets. We compare and analyze our approach and prior work along various dimensions to better understand the key challenges of the movie description task.

1 Introduction

Automatic description of visual content has lately received a lot of interest in our community. Multiple works have successfully addressed the image captioning problem [6,16,17,35]. Many of the proposed methods rely on Long Short-Term Memory networks (LSTMs) [13]. In the meanwhile, two large-scale movie description datasets have been proposed, namely MPII Movie Description (MPII-MD) [28] and Montreal Video Annotation Dataset (M-VAD) [31]. Both are based on movies with associated textual descriptions and allow studying the problem how to generate movie description for visually disabled people. Works addressing these datasets [28,33,38] show that they are indeed challenging in terms of visual recognition and automatic description. This results in a significantly lower performance then on simpler video datasets (e.g. MSVD [2]), but a detailed analysis of the difficulties is missing. In this work we address this by taking a closer look at the performance of existing methods on the movie description task.

This work contributes (a) an approach to build robust visual classifiers which distinguish verbs, objects, and places extracted from weak sentence annotations; (b) based on the visual classifiers we evaluate different design choices to train an LSTM for generating descriptions. This outperforms related work on the

J. Gall et al. (Eds.): GCPR 2015, LNCS 9358, pp. 209–221, 2015.
DOI: 10.1007/978-3-319-24947-6_17

MPII-MD and M-VAD datasets, using automatic and human evaluation (only on MPII-MD); (c) we perform a detailed analysis of prior work and our approach to understand the challenges of the movie description task.

2   Related Work

Image captioning. Automatic image description has been studied in the past [9,19,20,23], gaining increased attention just recently [6,8,16,17,22,35]. Many of the proposed works rely on Recurrent Neural Networks (RNNs) and in particular on Long Short-Term Memory networks (LSTMs). New datasets have been released, Flickr30k [39] and MS COCO Captions [3], where [3] also presents a standardized protocol for image captioning evaluation. There are attempts to analyze the performance of recent methods, e.g. [5] compares them with respect to the novelty of generated descriptions and additionally proposes a nearest neighbor baseline that improves over recent methods.

Video description. In the past video description has been addressed in controlled settings [1,18], on a small scale [4,11,30] or in single domains like cooking [26,29]. Donahue *et al.* [6] first proposed to describe videos using an LSTM, relying on precomputed CRF scores from [26]. Later [34] extended this work to extract CNN features from frames which are max-pooled over time. Pan *et al.* [24] propose a framework with a visual-semantic embedding to ensure better coherence between video and text. Xu *et al.* [37] jointly address the language generation and video/language retrieval tasks by learning a joint embedding for a deep video model and compositional semantic language model.

Movie description. Recently two large-scale movie description datasets have been proposed, MPII Movie Description [28] and Montreal Video Annotation Dataset [31]. Compared to previous video description datasets, they have broader domain and are more varied and challenging with respect to the visual content and the associated descriptions. They also do not have any additional annotations, as e.g. TACoS Multi-Level [26], thus one has to rely on the weak sentence annotations. To handle this challenging scenario [38] proposes an attention based model which selects the most relevant temporal segments in a video, incorporates 3-D CNN and generates a sentence using an LSTM. Venugopalan *et al.* [33] propose an encoder-decoder framework, where a single LSTM encodes the input video frame by frame and decodes it into a sentence, outperforming [38]. Our approach for sentence generation is most similar to [6] and we rely on their LSTM implementation based on Caffe [15].

3   Approach

In this section we present our two-step approach. The first step performs visual recognition using the visual classifiers which we train according to labels' semantics and "visuality". The second step generates textual descriptions using an LSTM. We explore various design choices for building and training the LSTM.

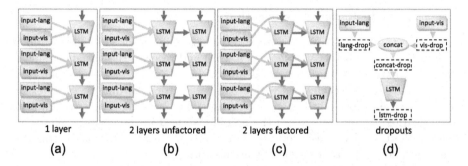

Fig. 1. (a–c) LSTM architectures. (d) Variants of placing the dropout layer.

3.1 Visual Labels for Robust Visual Classifiers

For training we rely on a parallel corpus of videos and weak sentence annotations. As in [28] we parse the sentences to obtain a set of labels (single words or short phrases, e.g. *look up*) to train visual classifiers. However, in contrast to [28], we do not want to keep all of these initial labels as they are noisy, but select only visual ones which actually can be robustly recognized.

Avoiding parser failure. Not all sentences can be parsed successfully, as e.g. some sentences are incomplete or grammatically incorrect. To avoid loosing the potential labels in these sentences, we match our set of initial labels to the sentences which the parser failed to process.

Semantic groups. Our labels correspond to different semantic groups. In this work we consider three most important groups: verbs, objects and places. We propose to treat each label group independently. First, we rely on a different representation for each semantic group, which is targeted to the specific group. Namely we use the activity recognition features Improved Dense Trajectories (DT) [36] for verbs, large scale object detector responses (LSDA) [14] for objects and scene classification scores (PLACES) [40] for places. Second, we train one-vs-all SVM classifiers for each group separately. The intuition behind this is to avoid "wrong negatives" (e.g. using *object* "bed" as negative for *place* "bedroom").

Visual labels. Now, how do we select *visual* labels for our semantic groups? In order to find the verbs among the labels we rely on the semantic parser of [28]. Next, we look up the list of "places" used in [40] and search for corresponding words among our labels. We look up the object classes used in [14] and search for these "objects", as well as their base forms (e.g. "domestic cat" and "cat"). We discard all the labels that do not belong to any of our three groups of interest as we assume that they are likely not visual and thus are difficult to recognize. Finally, we discard labels which the classifiers could not learn, as these are likely noisy or not visual. For this we require the classifiers to have certain minimum area under the ROC-curve (Receiver Operating Characteristic).

3.2   LSTM for Sentence Generation

We rely on the basic LSTM architecture proposed in [6] for video description. At each time step an LSTM generates a word and receives the visual classifiers (*input-vis*) as well as the previous generated word (*input-lang*) as input (see Fig. 1(a)). We encode each word with a one-hot-vector according to its index in a dictionary and project it in a lower dimensional embedding. The embedding is jointly learned during training of the LSTM. We feed in the classifier scores as input to the LSTM which is equivalent to the best variant proposed in [6]. We analyze the following aspects for this architecture:

Layer structure. We compare a 1-layer architecture with a 2-layer architecture. In the 2-layer architecture, the output of the first layer is used as input for the second layer (Fig. 1b) and was used by [6] for video description. Additionally we also compare to a 2-layer factored architecture of [6], where the first layer only gets the language as input and the second layer gets the output of the first as well as the visual input.

Dropout placement. To learn a more robust network which is less likely to overfit we rely on a dropout [12], i.e. a ratio r of randomly selected units is set to 0 during training (while all others are multiplied with $1/r$). We explore different ways to place dropout in the network, i.e. either for language input (*lang-drop*) or visual (*vis-drop*) input only, for both inputs (*concat-drop*) or for the LSTM output (*lstm-drop*), see Fig. 1(d). While the default dropout ratio is $r = 0.5$, we evaluate the effect of other ratios.

Learning strategy. By default we use a step-based learning strategy, where a learning rate is halved after a certain number of steps. We find the best learning rate and step size on the validation set. Additionally we compare this to a polynomial learning strategy, where the learning rate is continuously decreased. This learning strategy has been shown to give good results faster without tweaking the step size for GoogleNet implemented by Sergio Guadarrama in Caffe [15].

4   Evaluation

In this section we first analyze our approach on the MPII-MD [28] dataset and explore different design choices. Then, we compare our best system to prior work.

4.1   Analysis of Our Approach

Experimental setup. We build on the labels discovered by the semantic parser of [28]. To be able to learn classifiers we select the labels that appear at least 30 times, resulting in 1,263 labels. The parser additionally tells us whether the label is a verb. We use the visual features (DT, LSDA, PLACES) provided with the MPII-MD dataset [28]. The LSTM output/hidden unit as well as memory cell have each 500 dimensions. We train our method on the training set (56,861 clips) and evaluate on the validation set (4,930 clips) using the METEOR [21] score.

According to [7,32], METEOR supersedes previously used measures such as BLEU [25] in terms of agreement with human judgments. METEOR also outperforms CIDEr [32] when the number of references is small and in the case of MPII-MD we have only a single reference.

Table 1. Comparison of different choices of labels and visual classifiers. All results reported on the validation set of MPII-MD.

Approach	Labels	Classifiers Retrieved	Classifiers Trained
Baseline: all labels treated the same way			
(1) DT	1263	-	6.73
(2) LSDA	1263	-	7.07
(3) PLACES	1263	-	7.10
(4) DT+LSDA+PLACES	1263	-	7.24
Visual labels			
(5) Verbs(DT), Others(LSDA)	1328	7.08	7.27
(6) Verbs(DT), Places(PLACES), Others(LSDA)	1328	7.09	7.39
(7) Verbs(DT), Places(PLACES), Objects(LSDA)	913	7.10	7.48
(8) + restriction to labels with $ROC \geq 0.7$	263	7.41	**7.54**
Baseline: all labels treated the same way, labels from (8)			
(9) DT+LSDA+PLACES	263	7.16	7.20

Robust visual classifiers. In a first set of experiments we analyze our proposal to consider groups of labels to learn different classifiers and also to use different visual representations for these groups (see Sect. 3.1). In Table 1 we evaluate our generated sentences using different input features to the LSTM. In our baseline, in the top part of Table 1, we treat all labels equally, i.e. we use the same visual descriptors for all labels. The PLACES feature is best with 7.10 METEOR. Combination by stacking all features (DT + LSDA + PLACES) improves further to 7.24 METEOR.

The second part of the table demonstrates the effect of introducing different semantic label groups. We first split the labels into "Verbs" and all remaining. Given that some labels appear in both roles, the total number of labels increases to 1328 (line 5). We analyze two settings of training the classifiers. In the case of "Retrieved" we retrieve the classifier scores from the general classifiers trained in the previous step. "Trained" corresponds to training the SVMs specifically for each label type (e.g. for "Verbs"). Next, we further divide the non-"Verb" labels into "Places" and "Others" (line 6), and finally into "Places" and "Objects" (line 7). We discard the unused labels and end up with 913 labels. Out of these labels, we select the labels where the classifier obtains a ROC higher or equal to 0.7 (threshold selected on the validation set). After this we obtain 263 labels and the best performance in the "Trained" setting (line 8). To support our intuition about the importance of the label discrimination (i.e. using different features for different semantic groups of labels), we propose another baseline (line 9). Here we use the same set of 263 labels but provide the same feature for all of them, namely the best performing combination DT + LSDA + PLACES. As we see, this results in an inferior performance.

Table 2. LSTM architectures, MPII-MD val set. Labels, classifiers as Table 1(8).

Architecture	METEOR
1 layer	**7.54**
2 layers unfact.	**7.54**
2 layers fact.	7.41

(a) LSTM architectures (lstm-dropout 0.5).

Dropout	METEOR
no dropout	7.19
lang-drop	7.13
vis-drop	7.34
concat-drop	7.29
lstm-drop	**7.54**

(b) Dropout strategies (1-layer, dropout 0.5).

Dropout ratio	METEOR
r=0.1	7.22
r=0.25	7.42
r=0.5	**7.54**
r=0.75	7.46

(c) Dropout ratios (1-layer, lstm-dropout).

We make several observations from Table 1 which lead to robust visual classifiers from the weak sentence annotations. (a) It is beneficial to select features based on the label semantics. (b) Training one-vs-all SVMs for specific label groups consistently improves the performance as it avoids "wrong" negatives. (c) Focusing on more "visual" labels helps: we reduce the LSTM input dimensionality to 263 while improving the performance.

LSTM architectures. Now, as described in Sect. 3.2, we look at different LSTM architectures and training configurations. In the following we use the best performing "Visual Labels" approach, Table 1, line (8).

We start with examining the architecture, where we explore different configurations of LSTM and dropout layers. Table 2a shows the performance of three different networks: "1 layer", "2 layers unfactored" and "2 layers factored" introduced in Sect. 3.2. As we see, the "1 layer" and "2 layers unfactored" perform equally well, while "2 layers factored" is inferior to them. In the following experiments we use the simpler "1 layer" network. We then compare different dropout placements as illustrated in (Fig. 2b). We obtain the best result when applying dropout after the LSTM layer ("lstm-drop"), while having no dropout or applying it only to language leads to stronger over-fitting to the visual features. Putting dropout after the LSTM (and prior to a final prediction layer) makes the entire system more robust. As for the best dropout ratio, we find that 0.5 works best with lstm-dropout (Table 2c).

Next we look at different learning rates and strategies[1]. We find that the best learning rate in the step-based learning is 0.01, while step size 4000 slightly improves over step size 2000 (which we used in Table 1). We explore an alternative learning strategy, namely decreasing learning rate according to a polynomial decay. We experiment with different exponents (0.5 and 0.7) and numbers of iterations (25 K and 10 K), using the base-learning rate 0.01. Our results show that the step-based learning is superior to the polynomial learning.

In most of the experiments we trained our networks for 25,000 iterations. After looking at the METEOR performance for intermediate iterations we found that for the step size 4000 at iteration 15,000 we achieve best performance overall. Additionally we train multiple LSTMs with different random orderings of the training data. In our experiments we combine three in an ensemble, averaging

---

[1] More details can be found in our corresponding arXiv version [27].

Table 3. Comparison to prior work. Human eval ranked 1 to 3, lower is better.

Approach	*METEOR* in %	Human evaluation: rank Correct. Grammar Relev.		
Best of [28]	5.59	2.11	2.39	2.08
S2VT [33]	6.27	2.02	**1.67**	2.06
Visual-Labels (our)	**7.03**	**1.87**	1.94	**1.86**
NN-upperbound	19.43	-	-	-

Approach	*METEOR* in %
[38]	4.33
S2VT [33]	5.62
Visual-Labels (our)	**6.36**

(a) Test Set of MPII-MD.   (b) Test Set of M-VAD.

the resulting word predictions. In most cases the ensemble improves over the single networks in terms of METEOR score (see Footnote 1).

To summarize, the most important aspects that decrease over-fitting and lead to a better sentence generation are: (a) a correct learning rate and step size, (b) dropout after the LSTM layer, (c) choosing the training iteration based on METEOR score as opposed to only looking at the LSTM accuracy/loss which can be misleading, and (d) building ensembles of multiple networks with different random initializations. In the following section we compare our best ensemble (selected on the validation set) to related work on the test sets of MPII-MD and M-VAD.

4.2   Comparison to Related Work

Experimental setup. First we compare the best method of [28], the recently proposed method S2VT [33] and our proposed "Visual Labels"-LSTM on the test set of the MPII-MD dataset (6,578 clips). In addition to METEOR [21], we perform a human evaluation, by randomly selecting 1300 video snippets and asking AMT turkers to rank three systems with respect to correctness, grammar and relevance, similar to [28]. Next we evaluate our method on the test set of the M-VAD dataset [31] (4,951 clips) and compare it to [33] and [38]. We train our method on M-VAD and use the same LSTM architecture and parameters as for MPII-MD, but select the number of iterations on the M-VAD validation set.

Results on MPII-MD. Table 3a summarizes the results on the test set of MPII-MD (see Footnote 1). While we rely on identical features and similar labels as [28], we significantly improve the performance, specifically by 1.44 METEOR points. Moreover, we improve over the recent approach of [33], which also uses LSTM to generate video descriptions. Exploring different strategies to label selection and classifier training, as well as various LSTM configurations allows to obtain best result to date on the MPII-MD dataset. Human evaluation mainly agrees with the automatic measure. We outperform both prior works in terms of Correctness and Relevance, however we lose to S2VT in terms of Grammar. This is due to the fact that S2VT produces overall shorter (7.4 versus 8.7 words per sentence) and simpler sentences, while our system generates longer sentences and therefore has higher chances to make mistakes. We also propose a retrieval upperbound. For every test sentence we retrieve the closest training sentence according to the METEOR score. The rather low METEOR score of 19.43 reflects the difficulty of the dataset.

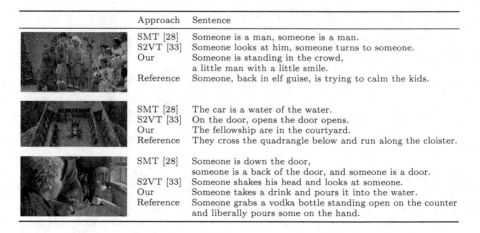

Approach	Sentence
SMT [28]	Someone is a man, someone is a man.
S2VT [33]	Someone looks at him, someone turns to someone.
Our	Someone is standing in the crowd, a little man with a little smile.
Reference	Someone, back in elf guise, is trying to calm the kids.
SMT [28]	The car is a water of the water.
S2VT [33]	On the door, opens the door opens.
Our	The fellowship are in the courtyard.
Reference	They cross the quadrangle below and run along the cloister.
SMT [28]	Someone is down the door, someone is a back of the door, and someone is a door.
S2VT [33]	Someone shakes his head and looks at someone.
Our	Someone takes a drink and pours it into the water.
Reference	Someone grabs a vodka bottle standing open on the counter and liberally pours some on the hand.

Fig. 2. Qualitative comparison of prior work and our proposed method. Examples from the test set of MPII-MD. Our approach identifies activities, objects, and places better than related work.

An interesting characteristic of the compared methods is the size of the output vocabulary, which is *94* for [28], *86* for [33] and *605* for our method, while it is *6,422* for the reference test sentences. This clearly shows a higher diversity of our output. Unlike other methods ours can generate e.g. verbs as *grab, drive, sip, climb, follow*, objects as *suit, chair, cigarette, mirror, bottle* and places as *kitchen, corridor, restaurant*. We show some qualitative results in Fig. 2. Here, the verb *pour*, object *drink* and place *courtyard* only appear in our output. We attribute this, on one hand, to our diverse and robust visual classifiers. On the other hand, the architecture and parameter choices of our LSTM allow us to learn better correspondence between the words and the visual classifiers' scores.

Results on M-VAD. Table 3b shows the results on the test set of M-VAD dataset. Our method outperforms the other two in METEOR score. As we see, the results overall agree with Table 3a, but are consistently lower suggesting that M-VAD is more challenging than MPII-MD. We attribute this to more precise manual alignments of the MPII-MD dataset.

5   Analysis

Despite the recent advances in the video description task, the performance on the movie description datasets (MPII-MD and M-VAD) remains rather low. In this section we want to look closer at three methods, SMT of [28], S2VT [33] and ours, in order to understand where these methods succeed and where they fail. In the following we evaluate all three methods on the MPII-MD test set.

5.1   Difficulty Versus Performance

As the first study we suggest to sort the test reference sentences by difficulty, where difficulty is defined in multiple ways.

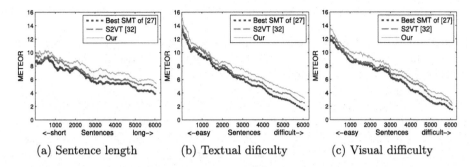

Fig. 3. Y-axis: METEOR score per sentence. X-axis: test sentences 1 to 6,578 sorted by (a) length (increasing); (b) textual difficulty (increasing); (c) visual difficulty (increasing). Shown values are smoothed with a mean filter of size 500.

Sentence length and Word frequency. Some of the intuitive sentence difficulty measures are its length and average frequency of its words. When sorting the data by difficulty (increasing sentence length or decreasing average word frequency), we find that all three methods have the same tendency to obtain lower METEOR score as the difficulty increases. Figure 3a shows the performance of compared methods w.r.t. the sentence length. For the word frequency the correlation is even stronger (see Footnote 1). Our method consistently outperforms the other two, most notable as the difficulty increases.

Textual and Visual difficulty. Next, for each test reference sentence we search for the closest training sentence (in terms of the METEOR score). We use the obtained best scores to sort the reference sentences by *textual difficulty*, i.e. the "easy" sentences are more likely to be retrieved. If we consider all training sentences, we obtain a textual Nearest Neighbor. We plot the performance of three methods w.r.t. the textual difficulty in Fig. 3b. All methods "agree" and ours is best throughout the difficulty range, in particular in the most challenging part of the plot (right). We can also use visual features to find the k visual Nearest Neighbors in the Training set, select the best one (in terms of the METEOR score) and use this score to sort the reference sentences. We call this a *visual difficulty*. The intuition behind it is to consider a video clip as visually "easy" if the most similar training clips also have similar descriptions (the "difficult" clip might have no close visual neighbours). We rely on our best visual representation (8) from Table 1 and *cos* similarity measure to define the visual difficulty and sort the reference sentences according to it, using $k = 10$ (Fig. 3c). Again, we see a clear correlation between the visual difficulty and the performance of all methods (Fig. 3c).

Summary. (a) All methods perform better on shorter, common sentences and our method notably wins on longer sentences. (b) Our method also wins on sentences that are more difficult to retrieve. (c) Visual difficulty, defined by *cos* similarity and representation (8) from Table 1, strongly correlates with the performance of all methods.

5.2 Semantic Analysis

WordNet Verb Topics. Next we analyze the test reference sentences w.r.t. verb semantics. We rely on WordNet Topics (high level entries in the WordNet ontology), e.g. "motion", "perception", defined for most synsets in WordNet [10]. Sense information comes from the semantic parser of [28], thus it might be noisy. We select sentences with a single verb, group them according to the verb's Topic and compute an average METEOR score for each group (see Footnote 1). We find that our method is best for all Topics except "communication", where [28] wins. The most frequent verbs there are "look up" and "nod", which are also frequent in the dataset and in the sentences produced by [28]. The best performing Topic, "cognition", is highly biased to "look at" verb. The most frequent Topics, "motion" and "contact", which are also visual (e.g. "turn", "walk", "open"), are nevertheless quite challenging, which we attribute to their high diversity. Topics with more abstract verbs (e.g. "be", "have", "start") get lower scores.

Top 100 best and worst sentences. We look at 100 test reference sentences, where our method obtains highest and lowest METEOR scores. Out of 100 best sentences 44 contain the verb "look" (including phrases such as "look at"). The other frequent verbs are "walk", "turn", "smile", "nod", "shake", i.e. mainly visual verbs. Overall the sentences are simple. Among the worst 100 sentences we observe more diversity: 12 contain no verb, 10 mention unusual words (specific to the movie), 24 have no subject, 29 have a non-human subject. This leads to a lower performance, in particular, as most training sentences contain "Someone" as subject and generated sentences are biased towards it.

Summary. (a) The test reference sentences that mention verbs like "look" get higher scores due to their high frequency in the dataset. (b) The sentences with more "visual" verbs tend to get higher scores. (c) The sentences without verbs (e.g. describing a scene), without subjects or with non-human subjects get lower scores, which can be explained by dataset biases.

6 Conclusion

We propose an approach to automatic movie description which trains visual classifiers and uses their scores as input to LSTM. To handle the weak sentence annotations we rely on three ingredients. (1) We distinguish three semantic groups of labels (verbs, objects and places). (2) We train them separately, removing the noisy negatives. (3) We select only the most reliable classifiers. For sentence generation we show the benefits of exploring different LSTM architectures and learning configurations. As the result we obtain the highest performance on the MPII-MD and M-VAD datasets as shown by automatic and human evaluation.

We analyze the challenges in the movie description task using our and two prior works. We find that the factors which contribute to higher performance include: presence of frequent words, sentence length and simplicity as well as presence of "visual" verbs (e.g. "nod", "walk", "sit", "smile"). We observe a high bias in the data towards humans as subjects and verbs similar to "look".

Future work has to focus on dealing with less frequent words and handle less visual descriptions. This potentially requires to consider external text corpora, modalities other than video, such as audio and dialog, and to look across multiple sentences. This would allow exploiting long- and short-range context and thus understanding and describing the story of the movie.

Acknowledgements. Marcus Rohrbach was supported by a fellowship within the FIT weltweit-Program of the German Academic Exchange Service (DAAD). The authors thank Niket Tandon for help with the WordNet Topics analysis.

References

1. Barbu, A., Bridge, A., Burchill, Z., Coroian, D., Dickinson, S., Fidler, S., Michaux, A., Mussman, S., Narayanaswamy, S., Salvi, D., Schmidt, L., Shangguan, J., Siskind, J.M., Waggoner, J., Wang, S., Wei, J., Yin, Y., Zhang, Z.: Video in sentences out. In: UAI (2012)
2. Chen, D., Dolan, W.: Collecting highly parallel data for paraphrase evaluation. In: ACL (2011)
3. Chen, X., Fang, H., Lin, T., Vedantam, R., Gupta, S., Dollr, P., Zitnick, C.L.: Microsoft coco captions: data collection and evaluation server (2015). arXiv:1504.00325
4. Das, P., Xu, C., Doell, R., Corso, J.: Thousand frames in just a few words: lingual description of videos through latent topics and sparse object stitching. In: CVPR (2013)
5. Devlin, J., Cheng, H., Fang, H., Gupta, S., Deng, L., He, X., Zweig, G., Mitchell, M.: Language models for image captioning: the quirks and what works (2015). arXiv:1505.01809
6. Donahue, J., Hendricks, L.A., Guadarrama, S., Rohrbach, M., Venugopalan, S., Saenko, K., Darrell, T.: Long-term recurrent convolutional networks for visual recognition and description. In: CVPR (2015)
7. Elliott, D., Keller, F.: Image description using visual dependency representations. In: EMNLP, pp. 1292–1302 (2013)
8. Fang, H., Gupta, S., Iandola, F.N., Srivastava, R., Deng, L., Dollár, P., Gao, J., He, X., Mitchell, M., Platt, J.C., Zitnick, C.L., Zweig, G.: From captions to visual concepts and back. In: CVPR (2015)
9. Farhadi, A., Hejrati, M., Sadeghi, M.A., Young, P., Rashtchian, C., Hockenmaier, J., Forsyth, D.: Every picture tells a story: generating sentences from images. In: Daniilidis, K., Maragos, P., Paragios, N. (eds.) ECCV 2010, Part IV. LNCS, vol. 6314, pp. 15–29. Springer, Heidelberg (2010)
10. Fellbaum, C.: WordNet: An Electronic Lexical Database. The MIT Press, Cambridge (1998)
11. Guadarrama, S., Krishnamoorthy, N., Malkarnenkar, G., Venugopalan, S., Mooney, R., Darrell, T., Saenko, K.: Youtube2text: Recognizing and describing arbitrary activities using semantic hierarchies and zero-shoot recognition. In: ICCV (2013)
12. Hinton, G.E., Srivastava, N., Krizhevsky, A., Sutskever, I., Salakhutdinov, R.R.: Improving neural networks by preventing co-adaptation of feature detectors (2012). arXiv:1207.0580
13. Hochreiter, S., Schmidhuber, J.: Long short-term memory. Neural Comput. **9**(8), 1735–1780 (1997)

14. Hoffman, J., Guadarrama, S., Tzeng, E., Donahue, J., Girshick, R., Darrell, T., Saenko, K.: LSDA: large scale detection through adaptation. In: NIPS (2014)
15. Jia, Y., Shelhamer, E., Donahue, J., Karayev, S., Long, J., Girshick, R., Guadarrama, S., Darrell, T.: Caffe: Convolutional architecture for fast feature embedding (2014). arXiv:1408.5093
16. Karpathy, A., Fei-Fei, L.: Deep visual-semantic alignments for generating image descriptions. In: CVPR (2015)
17. Kiros, R., Salakhutdinov, R., Zemel, R.S.: Unifying visual-semantic embeddings with multimodal neural language models. TACL (2015)
18. Kojima, A., Tamura, T., Fukunaga, K.: Natural language description of human activities from video images based on concept hierarchy of actions. IJCV **50**(2), 171–184 (2002)
19. Kulkarni, G., Premraj, V., Dhar, S., Li, S., Choi, Y., Berg, A.C., Berg, T.L.: Baby talk: understanding and generating simple image descriptions. In: CVPR (2011)
20. Kuznetsova, P., Ordonez, V., Berg, T.L., Hill, U.C., Choi, Y.: Treetalk: composition and compression of trees for image descriptions. In: TACL (2014)
21. Lavie, M.D.A.: Meteor universal: language specific translation evaluation for any target language. In: ACL 2014, p. 376 (2014)
22. Mao, J., Xu, W., Yang, Y., Wang, J., Huang, Z., Yuille, A.: Deep captioning with multimodal recurrent neural networks (m-RNN). In: ICLR (2015)
23. Mitchell, M., Dodge, J., Goyal, A., Yamaguchi, K., Stratos, K., Han, X., Mensch, A., Berg, A.C., Berg, T.L., Daume III, H.: Midge: generating image descriptions from computer vision detections. In: EACL (2012)
24. Pan, Y., Mei, T., Yao, T., Li, H., Rui, Y.: Jointly modeling embedding and translation to bridge video and language (2015). arXiv:1505.01861
25. Papineni, K., Roukos, S., Ward, T., Zhu, W.J.: BLEU: a method for automatic evaluation of machine translation. In: ACL (2002)
26. Rohrbach, A., Rohrbach, M., Qiu, W., Friedrich, A., Pinkal, M., Schiele, B.: Coherent multi-sentence video description with variable level of detail. In: Jiang, X., Hornegger, J., Koch, R. (eds.) GCPR 2014. LNCS, vol. 8753, pp. 184–195. Springer, Heidelberg (2014)
27. Rohrbach, A., Rohrbach, M., Schiele, B.: The long-short story of movie description (2015). arXiv:1506.01698
28. Rohrbach, A., Rohrbach, M., Tandon, N., Schiele, B.: A dataset for movie description. In: CVPR (2015)
29. Rohrbach, M., Qiu, W., Titov, I., Thater, S., Pinkal, M., Schiele, B.: Translating video content to natural language descriptions. In: ICCV (2013)
30. Thomason, J., Venugopalan, S., Guadarrama, S., Saenko, K., Mooney, R.J.: Integrating language and vision to generate natural language descriptions of videos in the wild. In: COLING (2014)
31. Torabi, A., Pal, C., Larochelle, H., Courville, A.: Using descriptive video services to create a large data source for video annotation research (2015). arXiv:1503.01070v1
32. Vedantam, R., Zitnick, C.L., Parikh, D.: Cider: Consensus-based image description evaluation. In: CVPR (2015)
33. Venugopalan, S., Rohrbach, M., Donahue, J., Mooney, R., Darrell, T., Saenko, K.: Sequence to sequence - video to text (2015). arXiv:1505.00487
34. Venugopalan, S., Xu, H., Donahue, J., Rohrbach, M., Mooney, R., Saenko, K.: Translating videos to natural language using deep recurrent neural networks. In: NAACL (2015)
35. Vinyals, O., Toshev, A., Bengio, S., Erhan, D.: Show and tell: A neural image caption generator. In: CVPR (2015)

36. Wang, H., Schmid, C.: Action recognition with improved trajectories. In: ICCV (2013)
37. Xu, R., Xiong, C., Chen, W., Corso, J.J.: Jointly modeling deep video and compositional text to bridge vision and language in a unified framework. In: AAAI (2015)
38. Yao, L., Torabi, A., Cho, K., Ballas, N., Pal, C., Larochelle, H., Courville, A.: Describing videos by exploiting temporal structure (2015). arXiv:1502.08029v4
39. Young, P., Lai, A., Hodosh, M., Hockenmaier, J.: From image descriptions to visual denotations: New similarity metrics for semantic inference over event descriptions. TACL **2**, 67–78 (2014)
40. Zhou, B., Lapedriza, A., Xiao, J., Torralba, A., Oliva, A.: Learning Deep Features for Scene Recognition using Places Database. In: NIPS (2014)

Graph-Based Deformable 3D Object Matching

Bertram Drost[1]([⊠]) and Slobodan Ilic[2]

[1] MVTec Software GmbH, Munich, Germany
drost@mvtec.com
[2] Siemens AG, Munich, Germany

Abstract. We present a method for efficient detection of deformed 3D objects in 3D point clouds that can handle large amounts of clutter, noise, and occlusion. The method generalizes well to different object classes and does not require an explicit deformation model. Instead, deformations are learned based on a few registered deformed object instances. The approach builds upon graph matching to find correspondences between scene and model points. The robustness is increased through a parametrization where each graph vertex represents a full rigid transformation. We speed up the matching through greedy multi-step graph pruning and a constant-time feature matching. Quantitative and qualitative experiments demonstrate that our method is robust, efficient, able to detect rigid and non-rigid objects and exceeds state of the art.

1 Introduction

The accurate and robust detection and localization of 3D objects in cluttered and noisy real-world data is crucial for many robotic and industrial applications. We present a method that is able to efficiently localize deformed 3D object instances in 3D point clouds. For this, we solve the assignment problem through graph matching and return a consistent set of scene-model-correspondences.

Recently, features that describe pairs of oriented 3D points were used successfully in 3D object recognition, rigid 3D object detection and as 3D feature point descriptors [1–3]. Such point pairs are invariant against rigid transformations, robust, fast to compute, and – due to their low dimension – fast to match. We show that the set of possible point pair features that describe the deformations of a model can be learned based on only a few training examples.

Drost *et al.* [3] use point pair features in a local voting scheme to find the best matching rigid transformation between a reference model and a 3D scene. We train their method using the point pairs of the deformed models to obtain an initial set of potentially inconsistent scene-model-correspondences. Based on this, we use a graph matching model similar to the one proposed by Leordeanu and Hebert [4] to assign relaxed weights to the assignment candidates based on their overall consistency. We augment the model by using an extended correspondence parametrization that takes 3D motion into account. Finally, a greedy dense subgraph extraction is performed to convert the relaxed assignment weights into a set of consistent correspondences. In essence, the graph matching globally

© Springer International Publishing Switzerland 2015
J. Gall et al. (Eds.): GCPR 2015, LNCS 9358, pp. 222–233, 2015.
DOI: 10.1007/978-3-319-24947-6_18

optimizes the correspondences by finding the largest subset of consistent scene-model-correspondences.

The proposed method generalizes well over different object classes and requires no explicit deformation model. Most parameters can remain constant over a large range of objects, making the method general and easy to use. In terms of performance, we obtain runtimes of around one second for an unoptimized implementation on large scenes. The method requires no feature detector and instead uniformly samples scene and model point clouds.

Note that this work concentrates on the recovery of approximate, but consistent scene-model-correspondences. Additional model and deformation dependent refinement steps, such as deformable ICP [5] or model fitting, are not performed. We evaluate the approach quantitatively and qualitatively on synthetic and real-world datasets, showing its generality, performance and robustness.

2   Related Work

Chui and Rangarajan [6] approach the point correspondence problem in 2D using their TPS-RPM framework that can deal with outliers and uses thin-plate-splines as deformation model. However, their approach was demonstrated on artificial 2D data only. It does not scale well to 3D data with large amounts of clutter due to the worst-case performance of $O(N^3)$. Anguelov et al. [7] solve the correspondence problem in 3D using a joint probabilistic model that preserves local geometry. Their method shows very good results when registering meshes of humans using a deformation model that preserves geodesic distance. While the two preceding methods are able to register deformed variants of point clouds, they are unable to deal with larger amounts of outliers, clutter, noise, or occlusion. They are also limited to a single or few deformation models. Those restrictions make the approaches unsuitable as generic 3D deformable object detectors.

Ruiz-Correa et al. [8] propose a deformable shape detector that uses a symbolic representation of shape components to represent and detect deformable objects. Their method can deal with occlusion and noise, and generalizes well over different deformation models in a "learn by example" way similar to our proposed approach. However, they report runtimes of over 12 min, making their method impractical for real-world robotic applications.

The usage of graph matching algorithms in Computer Vision has a long tradition. An extensive overview is given by Conte et al. [9]. Graph matching allows a robust localization of deformed objects and is a promising method for such a challenge. While it has been shown extensively to work in 2D applications, its applications in 3D are mostly limited and restricted to artificial perfect-data scenarios (see, for example, Duchenne et al. [10]). Berg et al. [11] model the assignment problem as an Integer Quadratic Programming (IQP) problem and use a thin-plane spline for post-processing and outlier removal. Leordeanu and Hebert [4] proposed a relaxation of the binary assignment problem, showing that it's orders of magnitudes faster and more robust than IQP. The graph structure in our proposed method is based on their graph, where vertices represent point-to-point assignments, while edges connect geometrically consistent assignments. They also show the connection between the energy optimization and the eigenvector problem of the adjacency matrix. However, no evaluation on deformable 3D matching was performed.

Recently, hypergraphs were used for efficient image and point cloud registration. Zass and Shashua [12] proposed to use hypergraphs to model more complex relations between two feature sets. Chertok and Keller [13] build upon that work and show efficient hypergraph matching for 2D images. Duchenne *et al.* [10] use higher-order relations for the graph creation, showing good results in both 2D and 3D. However, they evaluate only on perfect 3D meshes and show no quantitative results in 3D. Also, their creation of the adjacency matrix is expensive and makes their method impractical for real-world applications. Leordeanu *et al.* [14] propose a new hypergraph matching algorithm, which they use to efficiently register images that contain deformations. Lee *et al.* [15] extend a random walk strategy to hyper-graphs and can include similarity measures of arbitrary orders. They outperform other methods on 2D when matching feature points on 2D images.

Several of the mentioned methods require feature point detectors and were shown on 2D image data only. While robust feature point detectors in 2D are available, 3D data often exhibits too little distinctive geometry for robust salient point or feature point extraction. The method proposed in this paper thus uses a all-to-all matching that does not require feature point extraction.

Several approaches deal with shape retrival, *i.e.*, the identification of 3D point clouds or meshes. Passalis *et al.* [16] use a wavelet representation of objects for efficient shape retrieval in large databases. Mahmoudi and Sapiro [17] identify point clouds based on the distribution of several intrinsic measurements on that cloud, such as geodesic distances. While those approaches generalize well to rigid and non-rigid object classes, they require the objects to be segmented, making the approaches unsuitable to scenes with large amounts of clutter.

Drost *et al.* [3] detects rigid 3D objects in 3D point clouds using point-pair features and a voting scheme with local parametrization. Hinterstoisser *et al.* [18] demonstrate rigid 3D object detection using a high-performance template matching approach in RGB-D data. While both methods show robust results, they do not immediately generalize to non-rigid objects.

3   Method

Both model and scene are subsampled uniformly, to avoid any bias from different point densities throughout the point clouds. In practice, we use sampling distances between 3% and 5% of the model's diameter. We denote $\mathbf{m}_i \in M$ for points on the sampled model and $\mathbf{s}_j \in S$ for points on the sampled scene surface. Both point clouds are oriented, i.e., each point has a normal $\mathbf{n}$ associated with it. The objective is to find a deformed instance of the model in the scene by giving consistent correspondences between scene and model points. Due to occlusion, clutter, and noise, not every scene point has a corresponding model point and vice versa.

Overview. In order to find those correspondences, we build a graph $G = (V, E)$, where each vertex $v \in V$ represents a possible correspondence between a scene point and a model point. An edge $e = (v_1, v_2) \in E$ indicates that some non-rigid transformation exists such that both correspondences v_1 and v_2 are aligned simultaneously. In other words, vertices that represent consistent correspondences are connected. This graph model is based on [4]. If an instance of the model is present in the scene, the graph's vertices that connect the visible model points to their ground-truth scene points will be connected and form a dense subgraph of G. We will extract this subgraph using standard techniques, and thus recover the model-scene-correspondences. We will also show how the graph can be constructed sparsely (aiding performance) and how to extend the vertices by adding another parameter to the correspondence (aiding robustness).

3.1   Model Generation

Feature and Database. We use oriented pairs of 3D points as features for the matching, similar to [1–3]. Each pair $(\mathbf{m}_1, \mathbf{m}_2)$ with normals $\mathbf{n}_1$ and $\mathbf{n}_2$ is described by

$$\mathbf{F}(\mathbf{m}_1, \mathbf{m}_2) = (|\mathbf{d}|, \angle(\mathbf{n}_1, \mathbf{d}), \angle(\mathbf{n}_2, \mathbf{d}), \angle(\mathbf{n}_1, \mathbf{n}_2)) . \tag{1}$$

where $\mathbf{d} = \mathbf{m}_2 - \mathbf{m}_1$. $\mathbf{F}$ is fast to compute, asymmetric and invariant against rigid motions.

In the online phase, given a scene point pair, we will need to identify all model point pairs that might be similar to the scene point pair under any trained deformation. For this, similar to [3], we discretize $\mathbf{F}$ by uniformly sampling its components and use a hash table H to store a mapping between sampled features and lists of corresponding point pairs. This allows constant-time lookup for similar point pairs.

Deformation Model. Real-world object classes exhibit a large variety of different deformations. In order to be independent from any particular deformation model, we learn the range of possible deformations based only on registered examples $M_1, M_2, \ldots, M_n$ given by the user. We write $\mathbf{m}_i^k \in M_k$ as position of model point $\mathbf{m}_i$ in the deformed example M_k. For each pair $(\mathbf{m}_i, \mathbf{m}_j) \in M^2$, we first collect all its deformations

$$D(\mathbf{m}_i, \mathbf{m}_j) = \{(\mathbf{m}_i^k, \mathbf{m}_j^k) : k = 1, \ldots n\} \tag{2}$$

from the provided examples. We then add all features of the point pairs within the convex hull of D to the database. Note that additionally, the discretization of the feature vectors adds a small range of possible deformations, since variations that do not change the discretized value do not affect the value retrieved from the hash table.

3.2 Vertex Parametrization

Our graph models correspondences between model and scene points. In 2D, a single point-to-point correspondence completely captures a rigid motion, assuming that normal vectors or gradients are available. In 3D, however, a single correspondence misses one degree of freedom: After aligning a scene and a model point as well as their normal vectors, one can still rotate around the normal vector. Using correspondences only is thus an underparametrization of an underlying rigid motion. For graph matching, this has the effect of aggregating vertices and thus probably introducing undesired cliques, making it more difficult to extract the correct correspondences.

To counter this, we explicitly include the rotation around the normal in the vertex parametrization. Each vertex in the graph then represents not only two corresponding points $\mathbf{s}$, $\mathbf{m}$, but also a rotation angle α around the normal vector. $(\mathbf{m}, \alpha)$ are also called the *local parameters* w.r.t. $\mathbf{s}$. Together with the normals, those parameters completely parametrize a rigid transformation T. Formally, we follow [3] and define T as

$$T(\mathbf{s}, \mathbf{m}, \alpha) = L(\mathbf{s})^{-1} R_x(\alpha) L(\mathbf{m}) \tag{3}$$

where $L(\mathbf{x}) \in SE(3)$ is a transformation with $L(\mathbf{x}) = 0$ and $L(\mathbf{n}(\mathbf{x})) = (1, 0, 0)^T$, and $R_x(\alpha)$ is a rotation around the x-axis with angle α. The rotation angle α is sampled in d intervals, such that each vertex can be parametrized as $S \times (M \times [0; 2\pi]_d)$. The number of vertices in the full graph is then $|S||M|d$.

3.3 Graph Creation and Local Voting Scheme

Handling a graph with $|S||M|d$ vertices can become computationally expensive for larger scenes. In order to improve the matching speed, we prune the graph based on the results of the local voting scheme of [3], thus effectively removing parts which we deem unlikely to be relevant. Figure 1 outlines the graph creation.

At its core, the local voting scheme is a Hough Transform that recovers the best local parameters $(\mathbf{m}, \alpha)$ given some fixed scene reference point $\mathbf{s}_1 \in S$, *i.e.*, the parameters for which the most scene points are aligned with the model. For this, the parameter space $M \times [0; 2\pi]$ is discretized using $[0; 2\pi]_d$ as described above. The method then iterates over all other scene points $\mathbf{s}_2 \in S$, computes $\mathbf{F}(\mathbf{s}_1, \mathbf{s}_2)$ and matches $\mathbf{F}$ against the hash table H. This returns a list of model point pairs $(\mathbf{m}_1, \mathbf{m}_2)$ for which a deformation exists such that the two point pairs are similar. For each such matching point pair, α_1 is computed by solving (3), and a vote is cast for $(\mathbf{m}_1, \alpha_1)$.

Contrary to [3], we perform the voting for all reference points simultaneously. For each model point pair that matches a scene point pair, we obtain the symmetric parameter α_2 and cast a vote for reference point $\mathbf{s}_2$ at $(\mathbf{m}_2, \alpha_2)$. The two corresponding nodes of the graph, $(\mathbf{s}_1, \mathbf{m}_1, \alpha_1)$ and $(\mathbf{s}_2, \mathbf{m}_2, \alpha_2)$, are connected with an edge, since they can both be fulfilled simultaneously. We create a sparse graph by adding only those vertices that have a high voting score. This removes

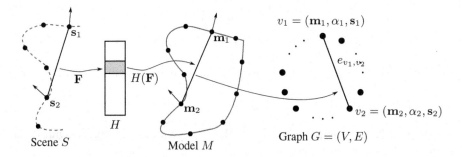

Fig. 1. Graph Construction. *From left to right*: For each scene point pair $(\mathbf{s}_1, \mathbf{s}_2)$, **F** is computed. The hash table returns a list $H(\mathbf{F})$ of all model point pairs that can be deformed to match $(\mathbf{s}_1, \mathbf{s}_2)$. *Right*: Each vertex v in the graph represents a possible correspondence between a scene and a model point. Edges are created between vertices that are consistent, *i.e.*, a deformable transformation between scene and model exists that fulfills both correspondences: For each match $(\mathbf{m}_1, \mathbf{m}_2) \in H(\mathbf{F})$, an edge is created.

vertices and edges that are unlikely to be a part of the object. In practice, for each scene reference point, we use the references with the highest 3 % of voting scores.

The left images in Fig. 6 show an example of the pruned graph creation. For a full graph, each model vertex would be connected to each scene point. For our pruned graph, only a small subset of those connections remains. As outlined in Fig. 2, the pruning step improves the runtime of the graph matching by several orders of magnitude.

3.4   Graph Matching

In the following, we follow the notation of [10]. The problem is to find an assignment vector $X \in \{0, 1\}^V$, where X_v is 1 if the scene and model point represented by v correspond and 0 otherwise. This problem is relaxed, such that $X_v \in R^+$, and modeled as an energy optimization problem

$$X^* = \underset{|X|=1}{\text{argmax}} \sum_{e=(v_i,v_j) \in E} X_{v_i} X_{v_j}. \tag{4}$$

In terms of the graph's adjacency matrix $A = (w)_{i,j}$, this becomes

$$X^* = \underset{|X|=1}{\text{argmax}} \sum_{i,j \in V} w_{i,j} X_{v_i} X_{v_j}. \tag{5}$$

Note that for the normalization $|X| = 1$, any norm can be used, since we will use the relative values of X only. The problem is then a scaled Rayleight quotient problem [4, 10], and X^* is an eigenvector associated to the largest eigenvalue of A.

We solve the optimization problem through gradient descend. X^0 is initialized to all ones, the update step is

$$X^{k+1} = \frac{AX^k}{|AX^k|} \tag{6}$$

	$|S|$	$|M|$	Vertices $|V|$	Edges $|E|$	Runtime
Dense	13106	300	135.566	98.886.050	1163.6 s
Sparse	13106	300	34.095	42.832	1.1 s

Fig. 2. Effect of matching with a sparse graph using the local voting scheme for the scene shown in Fig. 6

This is equivalent to the power iteration that has proven convergence against an eigenvector of the largest eigenvalue of A.

Voting Scheme Interpretation. The iteration (6) can also be seen as a repeated, re-weighted voting scheme: In the first step, each vertex votes for all connected vertices with a weight of 1, such that X_v^1 is the degree of v, *i.e.*, the number of connected edges. In subsequent steps, each vertex v votes again for all connected vertices, but this time with the number of votes it received in the last round, instead of 1. Through this feedback cycle, vertices of a strongly connected subgraph amplify each other, while the values of weakly connected vertices fall due to normalization. With this interpretation, the graph pruning is equivalent to performing the first iteration of (6) on the full graph and then removing vertices with low scores.

3.5 Dominant Consistent Subgraph Extraction

The power iteration gives us a weighted set of vertices or scene-model-correspondences. However, even though the correct correspondences obtain high scores, the set is not necessarily consistent. It might contain outliers as well as non-unique correspondences, i.e., two or more connections to a model or scene point. In [4], a greedy approach for extracting the most dominant, consistent dense subgraph was proposed. Their approach, however, is computationally expensive and requires a strong deformation model. [10] modeled the optimization based on the l_1-norm, giving an almost binary correspondence vector, which is easier to threshold. However, we found that this approach has a slower convergence and tends to drop correct nodes. We instead use a simple greedy subgraph extraction. Though this is somewhat of an ad-hoc solution, we found it performs well with little computational costs.

The vertex $v^* = \mathrm{argmax}_{v \in V} X^*(v)$ with the largest score is used as seeding point, and the set of all vertices reachable over no more than two edges ("two hops") is extracted. We found that a single hop is not enough, since the desired subgraph is not a clique, while three hops has too much a chance of introducing incorrect correspondences. To avoid double-correspondences of scene or model points, if a scene of model point is part of two or more extracted correspondences, we only keep the correspondence with the highest value in X^*. Such double-correspondences mostly connect two neighboring points of one set to a single point in the other set, a result of the allowed deformation.

4   Results

We evaluated the proposed approach with several quantitative and qualitative experiments. Synthetic and real data with available ground truth was used for the quantitative evaluation, while the qualitative experiments were performed on a real dataset only.

Note that all parameters were kept constant over all experiments, showing that the method's robustness w.r.t. its parameters. Model and scene were sub-sampled with distance 3 % of the model's diameter. For the hash table, the distance of feature **F** was also quantized in steps of 5 % of the model's diameter, while angles were quantized in steps of 12°. Figure 5 (left) motivates the choice for the distance sampling parameter, which is a tradeoff between matching accuracy and matching speed. For each scene, 10 iterations of Eq. 6 were performed.

The method was implemented in C and tested on a Core i5, 3.33 GHz. The off-line learning phase, i.e., creation of the Hash Table H, took less than 1 min for all objects. Feature matching required 0.05 to 2 seconds, the power iterations 0.1 to 2.5 secs, depending on the complexity of the scene and the amount of clutter. Timings for the remaining steps, such as scene sampling and greedy dense subgraph extraction, were neglectable. We believe that an improved implementation and a better control over the number of iterations would significantly improve the runtime.

4.1   Quantitative

Synthetic Data. A first set of experiments was performed on synthetic data, where ground truth is available. We selected three different objects with different surface characteristics, a clamp, a pipe joint and the Stanford Bunny [19] (Fig. 4, left). For each object, 100 scenes were rendered with different amounts of clutter, occlusion, and deformation (Fig. 4, right). The objects were deformed using free-form deformation [20]. For training, 10 deformed instances of each object, which were not part of any of the evaluation scenes, were used.

Model	Precision	Recall	Rel. Error
Clamp	0.93	0.57	3.6%
Pipe joint	0.99	0.69	2.2%
Bunny	0.96	0.51	4.1%

Fig. 3. Average precision, recall, and relative error of the returned correspondences for the synthetic scenes

We measure the performance of the method in terms of precision, recall, and error of the recovered correspondences. A recovered correspondence is a true positive if its scene point is on the object and its model point is at most 10 %

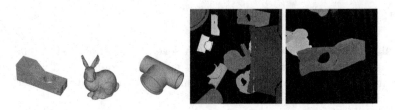

Fig. 4. *Left*: Objects used for the synthetic tests (clamp, bunny, pipe joint). *Right*: Example scenes of the synthetic dataset, showing clutter and deformation.

away from its ground truth position. The relative error measures for each true positive correspondence the distance of the corresponding model point to the ground truth model point, divided by the diameter of the object.

Figure 3 shows the average results for the three objects. The recovered correspondences show a very high precision, indicating that most of the recovered correspondences were correct. The average recall is larger than 0.5, meaning that on average more than half of the correct correspondences were recovered.

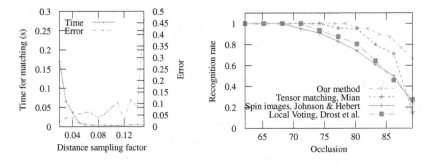

Fig. 5. *Left*: Effect of changing the distance sampling parameter of the feature database for an exemplary synthetic scene. Matching accuracy and robustness drops significantly when sampling with more than 0.1, while matching time raises significantly when sampling with less than 0.05. In practice, we use 0.05 over all our experiments. **Right**: Detection results on the dataset of Mian *et al.* [21]. Our approach exceeds the rigid baseline method of Drost *et al.* [3] and successfully detects 96.3 % (181 of 188) of all objects, and 98.8 % (168 of 170) of objects with less than 84 % occlusion. Our method also outperforms spin images of Johnson and Hebert [22] and the tensor voting of Mian *et al.* [23].

Real Data. We evaluated our approach on the dataset of Mian *et al.* [23, 24]. The dataset contains 50 scenes of 5 rigid objects, obtained with a high-precision laser scanner and with available ground truth. Figure 5 (right) shows the detection rates w.r.t. the occlusion of the objects

Note that even though the objects are rigid, detection still benefits from using our graph approach. This is evident from the fact that we exceed the baseline method of Drost *et al.*, which we use to initialize our graph. We also outperform several other state of the art methods.

4.2 Qualitative

We evaluated the proposed method on a set of real-world scenarios. Over 50 scenes containing pretzels, bananas, cappys and stressballs were acquired using both an industrial stereo sensor and a Primesense RGB-D sensor and matched against the corresponding model. Note that since the stereo sensor does not return an RGB-image, its scenes are visualized in 3D only.

For training, several deformed instances of each object were acquired, manually segmented and registered using deformable ICP [5]. We used only 5 to 15 examples for each class for the training, showing that the method is able to generalize from only few examples.

Figure 7 show several example scenes. Figure 6 shows on two examples how the graph creation leads to a sparse graph (1) and how the graph matching extracts a consistent set of correspondences from that graph (2). The effect on the computational costs are shown in Fig. 2. Additional examples are available in the supplementary material.

Overall, we found that the method performs very well even in cases of severe clutter, occlusion, and noise.

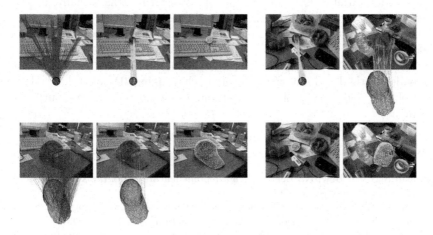

Fig. 6. Graph matching examples. **Left three images**: (1) Initial correspondences, created by thresholding the results of the local voting scheme. Each correspondence is a vertex in our graph. (2) Correspondences extracted after graph matching by the greedy subgraph extraction. Note that only a consistent set of correspondences from the original set of correspondences remains. (3) The correspondences were transformed into a rigid transformation. **Right two images**: Additional examples. The matching was performed on the depth image only, while the RGB image was used for visualization only. Images best viewed in color (Color figure online).

Fig. 7. Qualitatives results on scenes acquired with a stereo sensor. Challenges include clutter, occlusion, multiple instances and strong deformations. The rightmost scene shows the model (bottom) and fitted result (top).

4.3 Conclusion

We presented a deformable 3D object detection scheme that generalizes well over different object classes and requires few parameters. We showed how the combination of all possible deformations can be learned based on only a few deformed training samples. The graph matching scheme of [4] was extended by augmenting the correspondences with another parameter, making them more expressive in 3D. We prune the graph by using the method of [3] to create only a sparse set of correspondences that are likely to be correct. Using 3D point pairs makes the method invariant against any rigid 3D transformations. Finally, a greedy dense subgraph extraction is used to find a consistent set of correspondences, which can be used to obtain an approximate rigid transformation or to initialize a deformable ICP.

Our experiments show that the proposed method is able to robustly and quickly detect rigid and non-rigid objects in challenging 3D point clouds despite heavy clutter and partial object occlusion. For rigid objects, we outperform prior art.

References

1. Rusu, R.B., Blodow, N., Beetz, M.: Fast point feature histograms (FPFH) for 3D registration. In: ICRA (2009)
2. Wahl, E., Hillenbrand, G., Hirzinger, G.: Surflet-pair-relation histograms: a statistical 3d-shape representation for rapid classification. In: 3DIM (2003)
3. Drost, B., Ulrich, M., Navab, N., Ilic, S.: Model globally, match locally: efficient and robust 3D object recognition. In: CVPR (2010)
4. Leordeanu, M., Hebert, M.: A spectral technique for correspondence problems using pairwise constraints. In: ICCV (2005)
5. Myronenko, A., Song, X.: Point set registration: coherent point drift. PAMI **32**(12), 2262–2275 (2010)
6. Chui, H., Rangarajan, A.: A new point matching algorithm for non-rigid registration. CVIU **89**(2), 114–141 (2003)
7. Anguelov, D., Srinivasan, P., Pang, H.C., Koller, D., Thrun, S., Davis, J.: The correlated correspondence algorithm for unsupervised registration of nonrigid surfaces. NIPS. **17**, 33–40 (2004)

8. Ruiz-Correa, S., Shapiro, L.G., Meila, M.: A new paradigm for recognizing 3-d object shapes from range data. In: ICCV, pp. 1126–1133. Citeseer (2003)
9. Conte, D., Foggia, P., Sansone, C., Vento, M.: Thirty years of graph matching in pattern recognition. IJPRAI **18**(03), 265–298 (2004)
10. Duchenne, O., Bach, F., Kweon, I.S., Ponce, J.: A tensor-based algorithm for high-order graph matching. PAMI **33**(12), 2383–2395 (2011)
11. Berg, A.C., Berg, T.L., Malik, J.: Shape matching and object recognition using low distortion correspondences. In: CVPR (2005)
12. Zass, R., Shashua, A.: Probabilistic graph and hypergraph matching. In: CVPR (2008)
13. Chertok, M., Keller, Y.: Efficient high order matching. PAMI **32**(12), 2205–2215 (2010)
14. Leordeanu, M., Zanfir, A., Sminchisescu, C.: Semi-supervised learning and optimization for hypergraph matching. In: ICCV, pp. 2274–2281. IEEE (2011)
15. Lee, J., Cho, M., Lee, K.M.: Hyper-graph matching via reweighted random walks. In: CVPR, pp. 1633–1640. IEEE (2011)
16. Passalis, G., Kakadiaris, I.A., Theoharis, T.: Intraclass retrieval of nonrigid 3D objects: application to face recognition. PAMI **29**(2), 218–229 (2007)
17. Mahmoudi, M., Sapiro, G.: Three-dimensional point cloud recognition via distributions of geometric distances. Graph. Models **71**(1), 22–31 (2009)
18. Hinterstoisser, S., Cagniart, C., Ilic, S., Sturm, P., Navab, N., Fua, P., Lepetit, V.: Gradient response maps for real-time detection of textureless objects. PAMI **34**(5), 876–888 (2012)
19. Turk, G., Levoy, M.: Zippered polygon meshes from range images. In: Proceedings 21st Annual Conference on Computer Graphics and Interactive Techniques, p. 318. ACM (1994)
20. Sederberg, T.W., Parry, S.R.: Free-form deformation of solid geometric models. In: ACM Siggraph Computer Graphics, vol. 20, pp. 151–160. ACM (1986)
21. Mian, A.S., Bennamoun, M., Owens, R.A.: Automatic correspondence for 3D modeling: an extensive review. Int. J. Shape Model. **11**(2), 253 (2005)
22. Johnson, A.E., Hebert, M.: Using spin images for efficient object recognition in cluttered 3d scenes. PAMI **21**(5), 433–449 (1999)
23. Mian, A.S., Bennamoun, M., Owens, R.: Three-dimensional model-based object recognition and segmentation in cluttered scenes. PAMI **28**(10), 1584–1601 (2006)
24. Mian, A., Bennamoun, M., Owens, R.: On the repeatability and quality of keypoints for local feature-based 3D object retrieval from cluttered scenes. Int. J. Comput. Vision **89**(2–3), 348–361 (2010)

Posters

Line3D: Efficient 3D Scene Abstraction for the Built Environment

Manuel Hofer$^{(\boxtimes)}$, Michael Maurer, and Horst Bischof

Institute for Computer Graphics and Vision, Graz University of Technology,
Graz, Austria
hofer@icg.tugraz.at
http://www.icg.tugraz.at

Abstract. Extracting 3D information from a moving camera is traditionally based on interest point detection and matching. This is especially challenging in the built environment, where the number of distinctive interest points is naturally limited. While common Structure-from-Motion (SfM) approaches usually manage to obtain the correct camera poses, the number of accurate 3D points is very small due to the low number of matchable features. Subsequent Multi-view Stereo approaches may help to overcome this problem, but suffer from a high computational complexity. We propose a novel approach for the task of 3D scene abstraction, which uses straight line segments as underlying features. We use purely geometric constraints to match 2D line segments from different images, and formulate the reconstruction procedure as a graph-clustering problem. We show that our method generates accurate 3D models, with a low computational overhead compared to SfM alone.

1 Introduction

Recovering 3D information from an image sequence used to be a very challenging and time consuming task. Today, thanks to freely available software such as Bundler [24] or VisualSfM [26], even non-expert users are able to generate accurate 3D models from arbitrary scenes within hours. Since these so-called Structure-from-Motion (SfM) approaches operate on a sparse set of distinctive feature points (e.g. SIFT [18] features), the resulting 3D point cloud is usually quite sparse as well. The more important part of the SfM result are the obtained camera poses for each input image, which enable subsequent Multi-View Stereo (MVS) pipelines (e.g. PMVS [8] or SURE [21]) to create a (semi-) dense point cloud.

While the first part of this two-step procedure (pose estimation via SfM) can be computed very efficiently even for large crowd-sourced datasets [7,10], the second part (dense reconstruction via MVS) is still computationally expensive and can take up to several days even on modern desktop computers. Moreover, the resulting 3D point cloud might easily consist of millions of points and just viewing it in a point-cloud viewer quickly becomes a very tedious task. The same holds for any kind of automatic data analysis or post processing (e.g. meshing [17]). This is due

© Springer International Publishing Switzerland 2015
J. Gall et al. (Eds.): GCPR 2015, LNCS 9358, pp. 237–248, 2015.
DOI: 10.1007/978-3-319-24947-6_19

  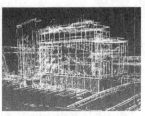

SfM [15]	PMVS [8]	Line3D (proposed)
46, 572 points	12, 156, 664 points	13, 489 lines
(a) runtime: 2.25 hours	(b) runtime: > 11 hours	(c) runtime: **375.63 sec**

Fig. 1. Three different 3D representations of the *BUILDING* sequence (344 images). (a) Sparse 3D model [15]. (b) Semi-dense point-cloud (PMVS [8]). (c) 3D line model using *Line3D*. As we can see, it is hardly possible to recognize the building in the sparse 3D model, while it is clearly recognizable in both the semi-dense- and the line-based 3D model. Compared to PMVS, our method has much lower runtime- and memory requirements.

to the nature of using point clouds as a representation of a 3D model. On the one hand, shapes of arbitrary complexity can be described by a set of 3D points, but on the other hand, the number of points needed to do so can quickly exceed the capabilities of your system.

What would be desirable is an efficient way of abstracting the 3D model, so that as much 3D information as possible can be encoded with only as much data as really necessary. A natural choice would be to use more complex geometric primitives as data representation, such as planes (e.g. [20]) or lines (e.g. [12]). While this might not be sufficient for natural scenes (e.g. forests, etc.), it is especially useful for the built environment, where most of the structures are piece-wise planar/linear.

We propose a novel approach for the task of 3D scene abstraction, denoted as *Line3D*, which makes use of straight line segments as data representation. Our method works as an efficient SfM post-processing tool and positions itself in between sparse and dense 3D reconstruction. We build on recent methods [11–14], which use epipolar-guided line segment matching and formulate the 3D reconstruction as a clustering problem. Our main contributions are the reformulation of the scoring procedure of matched 2D segments in a less restrictive way, the replacement of the simple graph-clustering procedure in [11,12] with a more recent matrix-diffusion based method [4], as well as the computation of affinities between potentially matching segments using a linear function of their estimated depth and user specified regularization parameters in the pixel space. These modifications ultimately result in more complete 3D models without negatively influencing the runtime.

Figure 1 shows a comparison between a sparse-, dense-, and a line-based 3D model for an urban scene. As we can see, our reconstruction provides a high amount of 3D information, despite its sparsity compared to the dense model. Moreover, running our method is only a low computational overhead, even for this relatively large-scale dataset. The source code of our method is publicly available and can be downloaded from http://aerial.icg.tugraz.at.

2   Related Work

While line segments have been used for tasks such as image registration or 3D reconstruction for a long time (e.g. [2]), in recent years image-based 3D reconstruction has been dominated by the use of image feature-points and their invariant descriptors (e.g. SIFT [18]). Only quite recently, the principles of feature-point descriptors have been successfully ported to the task of line segment matching (e.g. [28–30]), but line-based 3D reconstruction for real-world scenarios is still rarely used. While earlier methods have severe limitations (e.g. Manhattan-world assumption [23]), more recent approaches [11–14,16] have successfully been deployed on challenging datasets. They all require known camera poses (e.g. by running a conventional SfM pipeline beforehand), since pose estimation using line segments can only be done in special scenarios (e.g. by using triplets of two parallel and one orthogonal lines [5]), with given 3D lines [27], or when explicit endpoint correspondences can be established [19].

Jain et al. [16] proposed a method that does not require explicit correspondences between line segments from different images, which enables 3D reconstruction under difficult lighting conditions or around highly non-planar objects (such as power pylons), where patch-based line descriptors would fail. They formulate the reconstruction procedure as an optimization problem, where the unknown depth of the endpoints of 2D line segments in the images is modelled as a random variable. They compute the most probable 3D locations for the segment endpoints by minimizing the reprojection error among several neighboring views, and compute a final 3D model by merging individual 3D hypotheses that are sufficiently close together. While their approach generates visually pleasant results, the continuous optimization of the endpoint depths, in a potentially large range, renders the method inefficient for large-scale datasets.

To overcome these issues, Hofer et al. [13,14] replaced the continuous depth estimation with epipolar guided line segment matching, to limit the number of possible 3D locations to a discrete set. They further replaced the greedy line-merging from [16] with a scale invariant graph clustering formulation [12], which can also be evaluated on-the-fly for incremental SfM applications [11].

We build up on the core principles presented in [11–14], which are appearance-less line segment matching and global graph-clustering of corresponding segments across images. We demonstrate how the resulting 3D reconstructions can be improved by making several adaptions to their original formulation, without sacrificing runtime performance.

3   3D Reconstruction Using Line Segments

Given an (unordered) image sequence $I = \{I_1, \ldots, I_N\}$, we first run an arbitrary SfM pipeline to obtain the corresponding camera poses as well as a sparse set of

3D points $X = \{X_1, \ldots, X_K\}$, which is needed solely to define which images are visual neighbors. We further define $X(i) \subset X$ to be the set of 3D points which are visible in image I_i. We require a set of 2D line segments $L_i = \{l_1^i, \ldots, l_{m_i}^i\}$ for each image, where each segment l_m^i simply consists of two endpoints $p_m^i, q_m^i \in \mathbb{R}^2$. The line segments can be obtained by any line segment detector, such as LSD [9] or EDL [1].

Similar to [11, 12], our method consists of several steps: (1) establishing potential correspondences between line segments from different images, (2) evaluating these correspondences based on their support in neighboring views, (3) selecting the most plausible correspondence for each 2D segment as its 3D position hypothesis, and (4) clustering 2D segments based on their spatial proximity in 3D to obtain the final correspondence set and 3D model.

3.1 Establishing Line Segment Correspondences

To generate a line-based 3D model we need to establish correspondences between 2D line segments from different images. Theoretically, this could be done by one of the numerous line-matching approaches presented in the past (e.g. [28–30]). However, most of these approaches are patch-based and are therefore only suitable for line segments located on planar surfaces. Most of the line segments in natural images correspond to depth discontinuities, which results in line descriptors describing the potentially far away background. To overcome this drawback, recent methods have demonstrated how correspondences can be established and verified using purely geometric principles, without any kind of appearance [12–14], or with color histogram-based line descriptors [3] as weak support [11].

We follow [11–14] and use epipolar matching constraints to establish a set of potential correspondences for each line segment l_m^i individually. Since it would be infeasible (and unnecessary) to match all images with each other, we first compute a set of visual neighbors $V_i \subset \{1, \ldots, N\} \backslash \{i\}$ for each image I_i, by finding its M nearest neighbors in terms of Dice's similarity coefficient

$$S_I(i, j) = \frac{2 \cdot |X(i) \cap X(j)|}{|X(i)| + |X(j)|}, \tag{1}$$

which sets the number of common worldpoints in relation to the total number of worldpoints for each image (the higher the more similar).

We then match all segments in L_i to all segments in L_j (if $j \in V_i$). For a specific segment pair, $l_m^i \in L_i$ and $l_{\bar{m}}^j \in L_j$, we compute the epipolar lines of their endpoints in the opposite image. We then simply intersect the infinite lines passing through the segments l_m^i and $l_{\bar{m}}^j$ with the epipolar lines, and compute the overlap of the region between the intersection points with the original segments. If both relative overlaps (normalized by the length of the respective segment l_m^i or $l_{\bar{m}}^j$) are above a fixed threshold τ, we consider l_m^i and $l_{\bar{m}}^j$ to be potentially matching ($\tau = 0.25$ in all our experiments).

As shown in [11–14], we can transform each 2D correspondence into a 3D line $H_{m,\bar{m}}^{i,j}$ by intersecting the two planes passing through the respective camera centers $C_i, C_j \in \mathbb{R}^3$, and the 2D segments. We compute two 3D line segment hypotheses ($h_{m,\bar{m}}^{i,j}$ and $h_{\bar{m},m}^{j,i}$) for each correspondence, which are defined as 3D line segments on $H_{m,\bar{m}}^{i,j}$, whose projected endpoints coincide with the endpoints of the 2D line segments l_m^i and $l_{\bar{m}}^j$ respectively. Similar to the 2D case, a 3D line segment consists of two 3D points ($h_{m,\bar{m}}^{i,j} = \{P_{m,\bar{m}}^{i,j}, Q_{m,\bar{m}}^{i,j}\}$). Note that $H_{m,\bar{m}}^{i,j} = H_{\bar{m},m}^{j,i}$, while in general $h_{m,\bar{m}}^{i,j} \neq h_{\bar{m},m}^{j,i}$ (due to occlusions and imprecise 2D segment detections).

3.2   Evaluating Line Segment Correspondences

The matching procedure enables us to establish a potentially large set of correspondences, most of which are of course incorrect. Since we only use weak epipolar constraints, it is not possible to distinguish correct from incorrect matches during matching. However, we can assign confidence values for correspondences after L_i has been matched with all visual neighbors. This can either be done using gradient-based backprojection and scoring of the 3D hypotheses over multiple images [14, 16] (which is time consuming), or by directly analysing their 3D similarity to each other [11–13] (which requires some scale information). Both methods are based on the observation that correct hypotheses of a 2D segment always support each other (e.g. they are close together in 3D space and project to similar locations in the images), while this does not hold for incorrect ones.

To be scale invariant and fast, we use a novel similarity measure based on positional- and angular reprojection errors between a 3D hypothesis and 2D segments. We assign a confidence

$$c(h_{m,\bar{m}}^{i,j}) = \sum_{x \in V_i \setminus \{j\}} \max_{y \in \{1,\ldots,m_x\}} \left\{ A_{2D}(\Gamma_x(h_{m,\bar{m}}^{i,j}), l_y^x) \right\}, \qquad (2)$$

to a correspondence $h_{m,\bar{m}}^{i,j}$, where Γ_x projects a 3D line segment into an image I_x, and A_{2D} computes a truncated affinity between two 2D segments. This affinity is defined as

$$A_{2D}(l_1, l_2) = \begin{cases} S_{2D}^a(l_1, l_2) \cdot S_{2D}^p(l_1, l_2) & \text{if } S_{2D}^a(l_1, l_2) \cdot S_{2D}^p(l_1, l_2) > 0.5 \\ 0 & \text{otherwise} \end{cases}, \quad (3)$$

with S_{2D}^a being an *angular* similarity, and S_{2D}^p being a *position* similarity defined as

$$S_{2D}^a(l_1, l_2) = \exp\left(-\frac{\angle(l_1, l_2)^2}{2\sigma_a^2}\right) \qquad S_{2D}^p(l_1, l_2) = \exp\left(-\frac{d_{\max}(l_1, l_2)^2}{2\sigma_p^2}\right), \quad (4)$$

where $\angle(l_1, l_2)$ denotes the angle between the two line segments (in degrees), and $d_{\max}(l_1, l_2)$ is the maximum normal distance between the endpoints of l_1 to the infinite line passing through l_2, and vice versa. σ_a and σ_p are user specified regularization parameters.

With this formulation we are able to determine whether a matching hypothesis makes sense or not. We only keep hypotheses for further processing for which

$c(h_{m,\bar{m}}^{i,j}) > 1$, which means that at least two segments from two additional images (apart from I_i and I_j) have to support $h_{m,\bar{m}}^{i,j}$. We end up with a much sparser set of correspondences, with a significantly lower number of outliers, while correct hypotheses are only seldom removed.

3.3   Assigning 3D Locations to 2D Segments

As in [11–13], given all hypotheses $h_{m,\bar{m}}^{i,j}$ for a 2D segment l_m^i, we want to estimate its most probable 3D position, since each 2D segment can only be a projection of one specific 3D structure. We then use this 3D information for the following clustering procedure, as first shown in [11,12]. For each 2D segment l_m^i we define its 3D location as

$$\hat{h}_m^i = \operatorname*{argmax}_{h_{m,\bar{m}}^{i,j}} \left\{ c(h_{m,\bar{m}}^{i,j}) \right\}, \tag{5}$$

which is simply its 3D hypothesis with the highest confidence. We additionally normalize the associated confidence $c(\hat{h}_m^i) = \min\{1, c(\hat{h}_m^i)/2\}$, such that $c(\hat{h}_m^i) = 1$ means a hypothesis is supported by ≥ 4 images (see Sect. 3.2). In contrast to [11,12], where confidences are always normalized linearly by the locally highest confidence value (per image), we normalize by a fixed value. We have seen that 3D segment hypotheses verified by 4 or more images are almost never incorrect, which can also be observed for SfM point-clouds on the 3D point level. This enables correct matches which are only found in a low number of visual neighbor images (due to occlusions, etc.) to obtain a high confidence, despite the potential occurrence of other correspondences from the same image which might be occluded less often. Since this procedure is purely local, it can be easily done even for large-scale datasets.

3.4   Clustering 2D Segments Across Images

To perform the segment clustering we need an affinity matrix W, which holds the pairwise similarities between all potentially matching 2D segments. Since we only need to consider segment pairs which have been matched before, this matrix is usually very sparse. The question is how these similarities should be computed. We could use the same metric as for the hypothesis confidence above, by projecting 3D segments into images and evaluating the projective score (see Eq. 3). The problem with this procedure is that the reprojection error is not necessarily an appropriate indicator for a good correspondence, since it might be small despite a large spatial displacement. Hence, it is desirable to compute similarities directly in the 3D space.

To achieve this, we need some scale information. Since it is not possible to obtain a metric 3D reconstruction from a conventional SfM pipeline (unless further knowledge about the scene is provided, e.g. ground control points [22]), we have to find a way to derive a scale estimate from the reconstruction. Motivated by [11–13], we use user defined uncertainty thresholds in the pixel space, which are then brought into the local 3D space of the reconstruction. Unlike in these approaches, where an estimate about spatial uncertainty thresholds is made using all potential 3D line segment hypotheses (correct as well as incorrect ones), we formulate the uncertainty estimation as a linear function of the scene depth with respect to the underlying camera geometry, which is more robust to outlier hypotheses.

We aim at converting an uncertainty threshold t from the pixel space into the 3D space, for each image I_i individually. Therefore, we define z_i to be the center point of I_i, and $\tilde{z}_i$ to be z_i shifted by t (in any direction). We unproject z_i from the image at a distance of 1, and obtain a 3D point Z_i. We then shoot a 3D ray through $\tilde{z}_i$ and compute the normal distance k_t^i between Z_i and this ray. We use this distance as the slope of our linear uncertainty function

$$u_i(X, t) = k_t^i \cdot \|C_i - X\|_2, \qquad (6)$$

where $\|C_i - X\|_2$ is the Euclidean distance between a 3D point X and the camera center C_i of I_i (i.e. its scene depth along the viewing ray). In other words, $u_i(X, t)$ assigns a spatial uncertainty to a 3D point X, with respect to a maximally allowed reprojection error t, in the image I_i.

To avoid the possibility that the allowed spatial uncertainty grows too large for points far away from the camera center, we analyse the configuration of the final 3D hypotheses of all segments in L_i, to obtain a depth range in which this estimation makes sense. We therefore compute the median scene depth D_i over all final 3D hypotheses $\hat{h}_m^i$, by using both segment endpoints, and truncate our uncertainty function at the median. We obtain a modified uncertainty estimator

$$\hat{u}_i(X, t, D_i) = \begin{cases} u_i(X, t) & \text{if } \|C_i - X\|_2 < D_i \\ k_t^i \cdot D_i & \text{otherwise} \end{cases}, \qquad (7)$$

which can then be finally used to estimate similarities between clusterable 2D segments.

To compute the pairwise segment affinities, we use two separate uncertainty thresholds t_l (lower bound) and t_u (upper bound), with $t_l < t_u$. Since we always have small inaccuracies throughout the reconstruction procedure (e.g. in the SfM or the line segment detection), we cannot assume we will have perfect 3D hypotheses with zero distance to each other. We therefore do not punish deviations below t_l, and fit a Gaussian model between t_l and the cutoff value t_u. For two potentially matching 2D segments l_m^i and $l_{\tilde{m}}^j$, their similarity is computed as

$$W(l_m^i, l_{\tilde{m}}^j) = \frac{1}{2}\left(c(\hat{h}_m^i) + c(\hat{h}_{\tilde{m}}^j)\right) \cdot A_{3D}(\hat{h}_m^i, \hat{h}_{\tilde{m}}^j). \qquad (8)$$

The similarity function A_{3D} is defined in a similar way as for the 2D case (Eq. 3):

$$A_{3D}(\hat{h}_m^i, \hat{h}_{\tilde{m}}^j) = S_{3D}^a(\hat{h}_m^i, \hat{h}_{\tilde{m}}^j) \cdot \min\left\{S_{3D}^p(\hat{h}_m^i, \hat{h}_{\tilde{m}}^j), S_{3D}^p(\hat{h}_{\tilde{m}}^j, \hat{h}_m^i)\right\}, \qquad (9)$$

where the angular similarity S_{3D}^a is equivalent to its 2D counterpart S_{2D}^a (Eq. 4), and the position similarity S_{3D}^p is defined as

$$S_{3D}^p(\hat{h}_m^i, \hat{h}_{\tilde{m}}^j) = \min\left\{E(\hat{P}_m^i, \hat{h}_{\tilde{m}}^j), E(\hat{Q}_m^i, \hat{h}_{\tilde{m}}^j)\right\}, \qquad (10)$$

with the point-to-line affinity E being computed as

$$E(X, h) = \begin{cases} 1 & \text{if } dist(X, h) < \hat{u}_i(X, t_l, D_i) \\ \exp\left(-\frac{(dist(X,h) - \hat{u}_i(X, t_l, D_i))^2}{2\sigma_{i,X}^2}\right) & \text{otherwise} \end{cases},$$

(11)

where $dist(X, h)$ is the Euclidean distance between a point X and a line h. The distance regularisation parameter $\sigma_{i,X}$ is derived from t_l and t_u, such that the affinity E drops to 0.01 if the maximum allowed distance $\hat{u}_i(X, t_u, D_i)$ is reached.

The resulting affinity matrix could now be directly fed to an arbitrary graph clustering algorithm, which takes a simple pairwise affinity matrix as an input. Related methods [11,12] used [6] as a clustering algorithm, which delivers visually pleasant results for the general case. To further improve the clustering result, we deploy a more recent clustering strategy [4], which is based on diffusing the given affinity matrix W, by implicitly considering the underlying data manifold. Compared to [6], there is virtually no computational overhead, since the diffusion procedure can be efficiently computed in parallel on the GPU.

The clustering result from [4] is post-processed by removing all clusters which do not contain 2D segments from at least four different images. We estimate the final 3D line for each remaining cluster from the 3D segments of the contained 2D residuals, as first shown in [16]. The line direction can be computed by a Singular Value Decomposition of the scatter matrix containing all endpoints of clustered 3D segment hypotheses, and a point on the line can easily be obtained by computing the center of gravity among all these endpoints. We finally project all individual segments onto the averaged 3D line, and compute a set of 3D line segments on this line, such that each of these segments is fully covered by at least three of the projected hypotheses. Figure 2 visualises the different steps of the reconstruction procedure for the *BUILDING* sequence.

4   Experimental Results

We demonstrate the capabilities of our algorithm on two challenging real-world datasets, and quantitatively compare our results to the state-of-the-art [12] on

(a) Selected 3D Hypotheses   (b) Final Clusters

Fig. 2. Visualisation of the reconstruction procedure. (a) Individual 3D hypotheses $\hat{h}_m^i$ for all segments l_m^i. (b) Result of the graph-clustering [4] using random colors (one per cluster).

Ground truth	Hofer et al. [12]	Line3D (proposed)
(laser scan)	RMSE: 0.0598	RMSE: 0.0568
	6.61 seconds	3.64 seconds

Fig. 3. Quantitative evaluation on the *Herz-Jesu-P8* [25] dataset (Color figure online).

a publicly available dataset with ground truth. We further set our line-based reconstructions in relation to conventional dense point-clouds, obtained from PMVS [8], to give an idea of the pros and cons of both methods in terms of runtime vs. level of abstraction.

The parameters are kept fixed for all datasets. We set the 2D confidence regularisation parameters to $\sigma_p = 2px$ and $\sigma_a = 5°$, and the uncertainty thresholds to $t_l = 2px$ and $t_u = 6px$. As a line segment detector we use LSD [9], and as an SfM pipeline we use [15]. Our algorithm is implemented in C++ and CUDA, making use of parallel computing whenever possible.

Figure 3 shows a quantitative comparison between our method and the method by Hofer et al. [12] on the *Herz-Jesu-P8* [25] dataset. The lines are colored by their root-mean-square error (RMSE) to the ground truth surface. As we can see, both approaches have a comparably high accuracy while our method manages to reconstruct more 3D segments. Please note that not all valid 3D lines are actually contained in the ground truth. This is especially notable on the railings at the main entrance (colored in dark red).

Figure 4 shows qualitative results for two real-world test sequences. Please note that the runtime for PMVS is measured in hours, while for [12] and *Line3D* it is in seconds. As can be seen, both line-based approaches generate virtually outlier-free results very efficiently, but our method in general manages to reconstruct more 3D segments. This is mainly due to the different uncertainty- and confidence estimation procedures, as well as the modified clustering process, which enable 3D segments that are not visible in many images to be reconstructed more likely. The comparison to the dense point-clouds underlines once more how a lot of 3D information can be extracted in a very short time when only straight line segments are used as features. Our 3D line models give the viewer a very good impression of what is going on in the scene, but in a compact way and requires a very short amount of computational time.

5   Conclusion

We proposed a new method to generate abstract 3D models for built environments. We have shown how a significant amount of 3D information about a

390, 762 points   1, 689 lines   2, 697 lines
0.83 hours   50.67 seconds   55.85 seconds

PYLON, 66 images, 4320 × 3240px

12, 156, 664 points   12, 565 lines   13, 489 lines
11.34 hours   368.28 seconds   375.63 seconds

BUILDING, 344 images, 4912 × 3264px

Fig. 4. Qualitative reconstruction results. Left column: PMVS [8], Middle column: Hofer et al. [12], Right column: *Line3D* (proposed method).

scene can be encoded very efficiently, by using line segments in contrast to a large point-cloud. However, our goal was not to replace dense 3D reconstruction, but rather to provide an alternative for all scenarios in which 3D edge information is preferred over a point-cloud.

At the moment, our method can be seen as an SfM post-processing tool, which takes camera poses and images as an input, and returns a 3D model. In our future work, we intend to use the obtained 3D line segments (and their 2D residuals) to refine the camera poses from the SfM. We believe that using a combination of points and lines has the potential to improve SfM for indoor- and urban environments, where distinctive feature-points are rare.

Acknowledgements. This work has been supported by the Austrian Research Promotion Agency (FFG) project FreeLine (Bridge1/843450) and OMICRON electronics GmbH.

References

1. Akinlar, C., Topal, C.: EDLines: real-time line segment detection by edge drawing. In: International Conference on Image Processing (ICIP) (2011)
2. Ayache, N., Faverjon, B.: Efficient registration of stereo images by matching graph descriptions of edge segments. Int. J. Comput. Vis. (IJCV) **1**(2), 107–113 (1987)

3. Bay, H., Ferrari, V., van Gool, L.: Wide-baseline stereo matching with line segments. In: International Conference on Computer Vision and Pattern Recognition (CVPR) (2005)

4. Donoser, M.: Replicator graph clustering. In: British Machine Vision Conference (BMVC) (2013)

5. Elqursh, A., Elgammal, A.: Line-based relative pose estimation. In: International Conference on Computer Vision and Pattern Recognition (CVPR) (2011)

6. Felzenszwalb, P., Huttenlocher, F.: Efficient graph-based image segmentation. Int. J. Comput. Vis. (IJCV) **59**(2), 167–181 (2004)

7. Frahm, J.-M., Fite-Georgel, P., Gallup, D., Johnson, T., Raguram, R., Wu, C., Jen, Y.-H., Dunn, E., Clipp, B., Lazebnik, S., Pollefeys, M.: Building Rome on a cloudless day. In: Daniilidis, K., Maragos, P., Paragios, N. (eds.) ECCV 2010, Part IV. LNCS, vol. 6314, pp. 368–381. Springer, Heidelberg (2010)

8. Furukawa, Y., Ponce, J.: Towards internet-scale multi-view stereo. In: International Conference on Computer Vision and Pattern Recognition (CVPR) (2010)

9. von Gioi, R., Jakubowicz, J., Morel, J.M., Randall, G.: LSD: a fast fine segment detector with a false detection control. Trans. Pattern Anal. Mach. Intell. (PAMI) **32**(4), 722–732 (2010)

10. Havlena, M., Schindler, K.: VocMatch: efficient multiview correspondence for structure from motion. In: Fleet, D., Pajdla, T., Schiele, B., Tuytelaars, T. (eds.) ECCV 2014, Part III. LNCS, vol. 8691, pp. 46–60. Springer, Heidelberg (2014)

11. Hofer, M., Donoser, M., Bischof, H.: Semi-global 3D line modeling for incremental structure-from-motion. In: British Machine Vision Conference (BMVC) (2014)

12. Hofer, M., Maurer, M., Bischof, H.: Improving sparse 3D models for man-made environments using line-based 3D reconstruction. In: International Conference on 3D Vision (3DV) (2014)

13. Hofer, M., Wendel, A., Bischof, H.: Incremental line-based 3D reconstruction using geometric constraints. In: British Machine Vision Conference (BMVC) (2013)

14. Hofer, M., Wendel, A., Bischof, H.: Line-based 3D reconstruction of wiry objects. In: Computer Vision Winter Workshop (CVWW) (2013)

15. Irschara, A., Zach, C., Bischof, H.: Towards wiki-based dense city modeling. In: International Conference on Computer Vision (ICCV) (2007)

16. Jain, A., Kurz, C., Thormaehlen, T., Seidel, H.: Exploiting global connectivity constraints for reconstruction of 3D line segments from images. In: International Conference on Computer Vision and Pattern Recognition (CVPR) (2010)

17. Labatut, P., Pons, J., Keriven, R.: Efficient multi-miew reconstruction of large-scale scenes using interest points, delaunay triangulation and graph cuts. In: International Conference on Computer Vision (ICCV) (2007)

18. Lowe, D.: Distinctive image features from scale-invariant keypoints. Int. J. Comput. Vis. (IJCV) **60**(2), 91–110 (2004)

19. Micusik, B., Wildenauer, H.: Structure from motion with line segments under relaxed endpoint constraints. In: International Conference on 3D Vision (3DV) (2014)

20. Raposo, C., Antunes, M., Barreto, J.P.: Piecewise-planar StereoScan:structure and motion from plane primitives. In: Fleet, D., Pajdla, T., Schiele, B., Tuytelaars, T. (eds.) ECCV 2014, Part II. LNCS, vol. 8690, pp. 48–63. Springer, Heidelberg (2014)

21. Rothermel, M., Wenzel, K., Fritsch, D., Haala, N.: SURE: photogrammetric surface reconstruction from imagery. In: LCD Workshop (2012)

22. Rumpler, M., Daftry, S., Tscharf, A., Prettenthaler, R., Hoppe, C., Mayer, G., Bischof, H.: Automated end-to-end workflow for precise and Geo-accurate reconstructions using fiducial markers. In: Annals of Photogrammetry, Remote Sensing and Spatial Information Sciences (ISPRS) (2014)
23. Schindler, G., Krishnamurthy, P., Dellaert, F.: Line-based structure from motion for urban environments. In: International Symposium on 3D Data Processing, Visualization, and Transmission (3DPVT) (2006)
24. Snavely, N., Seitz, S., Szeliski, R.: Photo tourism: exploring image collections in 3D. ACM Trans. Graph. (SIGGRAPH) **25**, 835–846 (2006)
25. Strecha, C., von Hansen, W., Van Gool, L., Fua, P., Thoennessen, U.: On benchmarking camera calibration and multi-view stereo for high resolution imagery. In: International Conference on Computer Vision and Pattern Recognition (CVPR) (2008)
26. Wu, C.: Towards linear-time incremental structure-from-motion. In: International Conference on 3D Vision (3DV) (2013)
27. Zhang, L., Koch, R.: Line matching using appearance similarities and geometric constraints. In: Pinz, A., Pock, T., Bischof, H., Leberl, F. (eds.) DAGM and OAGM 2012. LNCS, vol. 7476, pp. 236–245. Springer, Heidelberg (2012)
28. Zhang, L., Xu, C., Lee, K.-M., Koch, R.: Robust and efficient pose estimation from line correspondences. In: Lee, K.M., Matsushita, Y., Rehg, J.M., Hu, Z. (eds.) ACCV 2012, Part III. LNCS, vol. 7726, pp. 217–230. Springer, Heidelberg (2013)
29. Zhang, Y., Yang, H., Liu, X.: A line matching method based on local and global appearance. In: International Congress on Image and Signal Processing (ICISP) (2011)
30. Zhiheng, W., Fuchao, W., Zhanyi, H.: MSLD: a robust descriptor for line matching. Pattern Recogn. **39**, 889–896 (2009)

An Efficient Linearisation Approach for Variational Perspective Shape from Shading

Daniel Maurer[1]([✉]), Yong Chul Ju[1], Michael Breuß[2], and Andrés Bruhn[1]

[1] Institute for Visualization and Interactive Systems,
University of Stuttgart, Stuttgart, Germany
{maurer,ju,bruhn}@vis.uni-stuttgart.de
[2] Applied Mathematics and Computer Vision Group,
Brandenburg University of Technology Cottbus-Senftenberg, Cottbus, Germany
breuss@b-tu.de

Abstract. Recently, variational methods have become increasingly more popular for perspective shape from shading due to their robustness under noise and missing information. So far, however, due to the strong nonlinearity of the data term, existing numerical schemes for minimising the corresponding energy functionals were restricted to simple explicit schemes that require thousands or even millions of iterations to provide accurate results. In this paper we tackle the problem by proposing an efficient linearisation approach for the recent variational model of Ju *et al.* [14]. By embedding such a linearisation in a coarse-to-fine Gauß-Newton scheme, we show that we can reduce the runtime by more than three orders of magnitude without degrading the quality of results. Hence, it is not only possible to apply variational methods for perspective SfS to significantly larger image sizes. Our approach also allows a practical choice of the regularisation parameter so that noise can be suppressed efficiently at the same time.

1 Introduction

The recovery of the 3-D shape of an object from a single image given only information on the illumination direction and the surface reflectance – so called *Shape from Shading (SfS)* – is one of the classical tasks in computer vision. In particular in scenarios, in which huge baselines or space constraints do not allow the use of a stereo setup with two or more cameras, monocular SfS can be a highly appealing alternative to traditional stereo. Moreover SfS, in contrast to other 3-D shape reconstruction methods, does not rely on the presence of texture. Hence, it is not surprising that SfS has a wide field of applications, covering large scale reconstruction problems such as astronomy [24] and terrain reconstruction [4] as well as small scale tasks such as dentistry [1] and endoscopy [31]. Further important applications are the reconstruction of archaeological findings [9] and the visual inspection of manufactured parts [17].

Most of the classical methods for SfS have been developed in the context of astronomy and are hence based on a simple orthographic projection [11,12].

© Springer International Publishing Switzerland 2015
J. Gall et al. (Eds.): GCPR 2015, LNCS 9358, pp. 249–261, 2015.
DOI: 10.1007/978-3-319-24947-6_20

However, in recent applications in endoscopy or macro photography, camera and light source are relatively close to the photographed scene, so that the consideration of a *perspective* camera [8, 18, 22] is required. The corresponding camera model not only improves the results in such applications, it also offers a decisive theoretical advantage compared to the orthographic model: When considering a *point light source at the optical centre* and combining the resulting model with a physically motivated light attenuation term based on a *quadratic intensity fall-off*, the resulting SfS model is *well-posed* in the viscosity sense [23], such that concave-convex ambiguities inherent to orthographic models [29] are dissolved to some extent [5]. This makes explicit that the use of a perspective camera model is very beneficial from both a practical and a theoretical viewpoint.

Taking a closer look at the underlying modelling framework, most approaches for perspective SfS are based on the solution of a hyperbolic partial differential equation (PDE) of Hamilton-Jacobi type; see e.g. [23, 27]. While such approaches allow the application of efficient numerical solvers such as fast marching schemes [15, 26, 30], they are prone to noise and missing data. In particular, they have no mechanisms to handle such cases, since they rely completely on the correctness of the input data.

In this context, *variational methods* have proven to be very useful [13, 14]. Since such methods are based on the minimisation of an energy functional that complements a data fidelity term with a smoothness term, they do not strictly enforce the consistency with the input data, as they also regularise by adaptively averaging the information. However, when it comes to numerical schemes for the minimisation, the literature on perspective SfS is restricted so far to the application of simple explicit schemes [2, 13, 14, 31, 32]. Explicit schemes have the advantage that they are easy to code, but the computation of the minimiser as steady state of an artificial time evolution typically requires thousands or even millions of iterations to provide useful results. This slow convergence does not only pose a problem for large image sizes. It also turns out to be problematic in the presence of noise and missing data, since a larger amount of regularisation typically requires a significant decrease of the time step size. As a consequence, the number of iterations has to be increased even further which makes the application of explicit schemes inefficient if not infeasible even for small image sizes. Summarising: While variational methods for perspective SfS offer a high degree of robustness under noise and missing data, their long runtimes make them hardly applicable in practice.

Our Contributions. Using the recent model of Ju *et al.* [14] that extends previous work of the authors [13] by a depth parametrisation along the optical axis, our paper contributes to the design of efficient solvers for variational perspective SfS in three ways: (i) On the one hand, we propose an efficient numerical scheme that embeds a linearisation approach based on a lagged upwind discretisation into a Gauß-Newton like coarse-to-fine solver. Compared with the alternating explicit scheme in [14] that already relies on a coarse-to-fine estimation with the same discretisation, this solver allows to speed up the computation by more than three orders of magnitude. (ii) On the other hand, when linearising the reflectance model in the data term, we propose to compute its derivatives numerically. As a consequence, the proposed approach can be extended in a straightforward way to more advanced reflection models such as the Oren-Nayar model for rough surfaces [19] or the Phong model for specular reflections [21]. (iii) Finally, we demonstrate that the proposed numerical scheme is highly useful in those cases where large parts of the input information is missing or when a large amount of regularisation is needed, e.g. due to noise. Also significant larger image sizes can be handled than with the alternating explicit scheme from [14].

Related Work. Since the field of variational perspective SfS is rather new, there exist only a few works that address the problem of the efficient computation. On the one hand, Ju *et al.* [14] propose to embed an alternating simplified explicit scheme into a coarse-to-fine estimation. However, the overall convergence is still rather slow and the algorithm needs hundreds of thousands of iterations to provide accurate results. On the other hand, Abdelrahim *et al.* [2] propose to speed up the computation by initialising the explicit scheme with the result of a PDE-based approach. This, however, contradicts the idea of using variational methods to render the estimation more robust, since PDE-based approaches have no mechanisms to handle noise or missing information.

First approaches to linearise the reflectance model go back to the early works of Pentland [20] and Tsai and Shah [28] in the context of local methods for orthographic SfS. Recently, also Barron and Malik [3] suggested to perform such a linearisation within a joint variational approach for estimating shape, illumination, and reflectance. However, also in this case, the camera model was assumed to be orthographic. The only linearisation approach for SfS in the context of a perspective camera so far was proposed by Lee *et al.* [16]. Their method, however, was specifically designed for a triangular element surface model and did not consider any explicit form of regularisation. Finally, none of the aforementioned approaches considered any form of upwind schemes for discretising occurring derivatives. While such schemes are not often used in computer vision, they are highly important for obtaining a stable numerical method.

Organisation. In Sect. 2 we review the recent model of Ju *et al.* [14] as a representative for variational perspective SfS. In Sect. 3 we then show how this model can be discretised appropriately and minimised efficiently using a linearised coarse-to-fine approach. A qualitative and quantitative evaluation of the model and the minimisation framework is conducted in Sect. 4. Finally, Sect. 5 concludes with a summary.

2   Variational Perspective SfS

In this section, we review the variational method of Ju *et al.* [14] that serves as a prototype for the development of our efficient linearisation scheme in Sect. 3. To this end, we first derive the surface parametrisation as well as the underlying model assumptions and then discuss their embedding into a variational framework.

Surface Parametrisation and Model Assumptions. Let us start by discussing the parametrisation of the surface. Assuming a *perspective* camera the unknown surface $S : \Omega_{\mathbf{x}} \to \mathbb{R}^3$ can be parametrised as $S(\mathbf{x}, z(\mathbf{x})) = [z\,x/\mathtt{f}, z\,y/\mathtt{f}, -z]^\top$, where $\mathbf{x} = (x, y)^\top \in \Omega_{\mathbf{x}}$ is the pixel position in the image plane $\Omega_{\mathbf{x}} \subset \mathbb{R}^2$, $\mathtt{f}$ denotes the focal length of the camera and $z(\mathbf{x})$ the depth orthogonal to the image plane.

Furthermore, assuming a *Lambertian* reflectance model and a *light attenuation term* that follows the inverse square law, the resulting brightness equation reads [23]:

$$I = \frac{1}{r^2}\left(\mathbf{N} \cdot \mathbf{L}\right), \tag{1}$$

where $I = I(\mathbf{x})$ is the recorded image, $\mathbf{N}$ is the surface normal, $\mathbf{L} = \mathbf{L}(\mathbf{x})$ is the direction of incoming light and $r = r(\mathbf{x})$ denotes the distance from the light source to the surface. For a *point light source* located in the *camera centre* at the origin, this distance r as well as the direction of the incoming light $\mathbf{L}$ read

$$r(\mathbf{x}) = \frac{z}{Q}, \qquad \mathbf{L}(\mathbf{x}) = \frac{1}{\sqrt{|\mathbf{x}|^2 + \mathtt{f}^2}}\begin{bmatrix} -x \\ -y \\ \mathtt{f} \end{bmatrix} = \frac{Q}{\mathtt{f}}\begin{bmatrix} -x \\ -y \\ \mathtt{f} \end{bmatrix}, \tag{2}$$

with $Q(\mathbf{x}) = \mathtt{f}/\sqrt{|\mathbf{x}|^2 + \mathtt{f}^2}$ being the conversion factor between the radial depth r and the Cartesian depth z. Note that light rays and optical rays have opposite direction.

Moreover, the surface normal can be computed by taking the normalised cross-product of the partial derivatives S_x, S_y of the parametrised surface in x- and y-direction:

$$\mathbf{N}(\mathbf{x}, z, \nabla z) = \frac{S_x \times S_y}{|S_x \times S_y|} = \frac{1}{W}\begin{bmatrix} \mathtt{f} z_x \\ \mathtt{f} z_y \\ (\nabla z \cdot \mathbf{x}) + z \end{bmatrix}, \tag{3}$$

$$W(\mathbf{x}, z, \nabla z) = \sqrt{\mathtt{f}^2\,|\nabla z(\mathbf{x})|^2 + [(\nabla z \cdot \mathbf{x}) + z(\mathbf{x})]^2}. \tag{4}$$

Finally, plugging the surface normal (3) and the light direction (2) into the brightness Eq. (1), we obtain the following constraint for perspective SfS [14]:

$$I(\mathbf{x}) - \frac{Q(\mathbf{x})^3}{zW(\mathbf{x}, z, \nabla z)} = 0. \tag{5}$$

Variational Model. Following [14], we embed the previous constraint as quadratic data term into a variational framework and complement it with a discontinuity-preserving second order smoothness term. Please note that from a theoretical viewpoint first order data terms are not advisable for SfS, since the data term already contains first order derivatives. Consequently, we use a second order smoothness term based on the Hessian and compute the unknown depth z as minimiser of the following energy

$$E\left(z(\mathbf{x})\right) = \int_{\Omega_{\mathbf{x}}} c(\mathbf{x}) \underbrace{D(\mathbf{x}, z(\mathbf{x}), \nabla z(\mathbf{x}))^2}_{\text{Data term}} + \alpha \underbrace{\Psi\left(S(\text{Hess}(z)(\mathbf{x}))^2\right)}_{\text{Smoothness term}} d\mathbf{x}, \quad (6)$$

where D of the data term and S of the smoothness term are given by

$$D(\mathbf{x}, z, \nabla z) = \left(I(\mathbf{x}) - \frac{Q(\mathbf{x})^3}{z\,W(\mathbf{x}, z, \nabla z))}\right), \quad (7)$$

$$S\left(\text{Hess}(z)(\mathbf{x})\right) = \sqrt{z_{xx}(\mathbf{x})^2 + 2z_{xy}(\mathbf{x})^2 + z_{yy}(\mathbf{x})^2}, \quad (8)$$

respectively. Here, the penaliser $\Psi(s^2) = 2\lambda^2\sqrt{1 + s^2/\lambda^2}$ is the Charbonnier function [7] with the contrast parameter λ, the weight α is the regularisation parameter that steers the amount of smoothness of the surface, and $c : \mathbf{x} \in \Omega_{\mathbf{x}} \subset \mathbb{R}^2 \rightarrow \{0,1\}$ is a confidence function that allows to exclude unreliable image regions from the data term.

3 An Efficient Linearisation Approach

Let us now discuss how the minimiser of the previous energy functional in Eq. (6) can be computed efficiently. To this end, we first approximate the spatial derivatives in the data term using a similar scheme as the one proposed by [28] in the context of non-variational orthographic SfS. In a second step, we then linearise the corresponding constraint in the data term and deduce a numerical scheme motivated by [6] that make use of two nested fixed point iterations and a coarse-to-fine strategy.

Approximation. In order to minimise the proposed energy functional, we first introduce approximations for z_x and z_y using the upwind scheme from [25]. Please note that standard finite differences schemes (e.g. central differences) are not appropriate, due to the hyperbolic nature of the SfS data term. Employing grid spacings h_x, h_y in x- and y-direction, respectively, the approximation for z_x reads

$$\tilde{z}_x = \max\left(\mathcal{D}^- z, -\mathcal{D}^+ z, 0\right), \quad (9)$$

$$\mathcal{D}^- z = \frac{z(x, y) - z(x - h_x, y)}{h_x}, \quad \mathcal{D}^+ z = \frac{z(x + h_x, y) - z(x, y)}{h_x}, \quad (10)$$

where, for the simplicity of our presentation, $z(\cdot, \cdot)$ is identified with the corresponding grid values. Since the forward difference $\mathcal{D}^+ z$ enters Eq. (9) with a negative sign, one has to restore the correct sign afterwards via [5,14]

$$z_x \approx \begin{cases} -\tilde{z}_x & \text{if } \tilde{z}_x = -\mathcal{D}^+ z, \\ \tilde{z}_x & \text{else.} \end{cases} \quad (11)$$

After approximating z_y accordingly and replacing all derivatives in the data term with the corresponding approximations, we obtain the following expression for

D that only depends on z (at the expense of including values at neighbouring locations):

$$D(\mathbf{x}, z, \nabla z) \approx D(x, y, z(x, y), z(x - h_x, y), z(x + h_x, y), z(x, y - h_y), z(x, y + h_y)).$$
(12)

Minimisation. According to the calculus of variations [10] any stationary point (and in particular the minimiser) of the approximated energy functional must fulfil the associated Euler-Lagrange equation [10]. In order to write down this equation compactly, let us introduce the following abbreviations

$$
\begin{aligned}
D^{xy} &= D\big(x, y, z(x, y), z(x - h_x, y), z(x + h_x, y), z(x, y - h_y), z(x, y + h_y)\big), \\
D^{x^- y} &= D\big(x - h_x, y, z(x - h_x, y), z(x - 2h_x, y), z(x, y), \\
&\qquad z(x - h_x, y - h_y), z(x - h_x, y + h_y)\big), \\
D^{x^+ y} &= D\big(x + h_x, y, z(x + h_x, y), z(x, y), z(x + 2h_x, y), \\
&\qquad z(x + h_x, y - h_y), z(x + h_x, y + h_y)\big),
\end{aligned}
$$
(13)

with D^{xy^-} and D^{xy^+} being defined analogously. Here, the superscripts denote the central point of the approximation. Moreover, we use the same style of notation for the abbreviations of the confidence function c and the smoothness term S. Then, the Euler-Lagrange equation of our approximated energy is given by

$$
\begin{aligned}
0 = {}& c^{xy} D^{xy} \left[D^{xy}\right]_z + c^{x^- y} D^{x^- y} \left[D^{x^- y}\right]_z + c^{x^+ y} D^{x^+ y} \left[D^{x^+ y}\right]_z \\
&+ c^{xy^-} D^{xy^-} \left[D^{xy^-}\right]_z + c^{xy^+} D^{xy^+} \left[D^{xy^+}\right]_z \\
&+ \alpha \left(\left[\Psi'\left((S^{xy})^2\right) z_{xx}\right]_{xx} + 2\left[\Psi'\left((S^{xy})^2\right) z_{xy}\right]_{yx} + \left[\Psi'\left((S^{xy})^2\right) z_{yy}\right]_{yy} \right),
\end{aligned}
$$
(14)

where $[\cdot]_*$ denotes partial derivatives of the enclosed expressions. Moreover, the derivative of the penaliser function $\Psi(s^2)$ reads $\Psi'(s^2) = 1/\sqrt{1 + s^2/\lambda^2}$. Due to the approximation of ∇z, the data term contributions $\frac{\partial}{\partial x}[D]_{z_x}$ and $\frac{\partial}{\partial y}[D]_{z_y}$ stated in [14] do not arise. Instead they are replaced by four terms considering additional points in the neighbourhood. With the purpose of obtaining a linear system of equations, we now introduce a first fixed point iteration on z, with the iteration index k, using a semi-implicit scheme in the terms related to the data term and an implicit scheme in the terms related to the smoothness term. Then z^{k+1} can be obtained as the solution of

$$
\begin{aligned}
0 = {}& c^{xy} D^{xyk+1} \left[D^{xyk}\right]_{z^k} + c^{x^- y} D^{x^- yk+1} \left[D^{x^- yk}\right]_{z^k} + c^{x^+ y} D^{x^+ yk+1} \left[D^{x^+ yk}\right]_{z^k} \\
&+ c^{xy^-} D^{xy^- k+1} \left[D^{xy^- k}\right]_{z^k} + c^{xy^+} D^{xy^+ k+1} \left[D^{xy^+ k}\right]_{z^k} \\
&+ \alpha \Big(\left[\Psi'\left((S^{xyk+1})^2\right) z_{xx}^{k+1}\right]_{xx} + 2\left[\Psi'\left((S^{xyk+1})^2\right) z_{xy}^{k+1}\right]_{yx} \\
&+ \left[\Psi'\left((S^{xyk+1})^2\right) z_{yy}^{k+1}\right]_{yy} \Big).
\end{aligned}
$$
(15)

In the first iteration, z^0 is initialised as suggested in [14]. In order to remove the nonlinearity of the terms related to the data term we furthermore linearise D^{xyk+1} around D^{xyk} using a first order Taylor expansion:

$$D^{xyk+1} = D^{xyk} + \left[D^{xyk}\right]_{z^{xyk}} dz^{xyk} + \left[D^{xyk}\right]_{z^{x-yk}} dz^{x-yk}$$
$$+ \left[D^{xyk}\right]_{z^{x+yk}} dz^{x+yk} + \left[D^{xyk}\right]_{z^{xy-k}} dz^{xy-k} + \left[D^{xyk}\right]_{z^{xy+k}} dz^{xy+k}.$$

Here, dz denotes the unknown depth increment $dz^k = z^{k+1} - z^k$ and the superscripts are used analogously to those of the previous terms. Accordingly, we linearise D^{x-yk+1}, D^{x+yk+1}, D^{xy-k+1} and D^{x-yk+1}. Thus we introduce an incremental computation as in [6] and only compute the increment dz in each iteration. Please note that our data term is *substantially different* from linearised data terms in optical flow estimation and stereo reconstruction, since it includes *neighbouring locations*. To remove the last remaining nonlinearity in Ψ' we introduce a second fixed point iteration on dz with the iteration index l, which we initialise with $dz^{k,0} = 0$. For the argument of the Ψ'-function $dz^{k,l}$ is employed and for the other terms $dz^{k,l+1}$. After plugging the linearised expressions in Eq. (15), we finally obtain a linear system of equations with respect to $dz^{k,l+1}$.

Coarse-to-Fine Scheme. As in [6,14] we embed the first fixed point iteration in a coarse-to-fine scheme to overcome local minima and thus better approximate the global minimizer. To this end, we introduce the parameter $\eta \in (0,1)$ that specifies the downsampling factor between two consecutive resolution levels and the parameter κ that specifies after how many iterations k the resolution level is adopted.

Computation. Finally, we compute the derivatives of D with respect to z numerically. To this end, we vary the current z estimate by $\pm h_z$ and re-evaluate the D terms. This proceeding allows to compute the derivatives of D with a standard central difference scheme. In addition the contributions of the smoothness term are discretised using standard central differences. In order to solve the sparse linear system of equations in $dz^{k,l+1}$ efficiently we apply the successive over-relaxation method (SOR). After sufficient solver iterations as well as sufficient fix point iterations l we crop the computed increments $dz^{k,l_{\max}}$ such that $|dz^{k,l_{\max}}| \leq dz_{\text{limit}}$ and then update the depth via $z^{k+1} = z^k + dz^{k,l_{\max}}$. This avoids that erroneous increments misdirect the computation in case the linearisation provides a poor approximation in **x**. Let us note that controlling the size of updates is a standard procedure in many numerical algorithms.

4   Experimental Evaluation

To investigate the performance of our algorithm, we made use of the synthetic test images shown in Fig. 1 that have already been used in Ju *et al.* [14]. For a suitable comparison we also employ the same error measures as in their original paper: the *relative surface error* (RSE) which determines how well the reconstructed surface matches the ground truth and the *relative image error* (RIE)

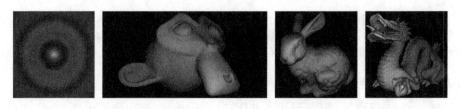

Fig. 1. Synthetic images. **From left to right:** *Sombrero, Suzanne, Stanford Bunny* and *Dragon*.

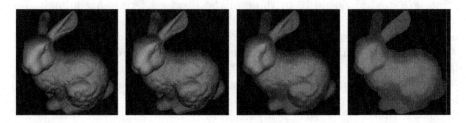

Fig. 2. Impact of the smoothness term under increasing α using the *Stanford Bunny* test image. **From left to right:** Input image, reprojected image with $\alpha = 1$, $\alpha = 20$ and $\alpha = 100$.

that indicates how well the reprojected image fits the input image. For the purpose of using a minimum number of parameters and of demonstrating that the proposed algorithm does not need a time-consuming fine tuning we choose a set of parameters which will be used throughout the following experiments, namely a downsampling factor of $\eta = 0.9$, $\kappa = 5$, $l_{\max} = 9$, 10 SOR iterations, $dz_{\text{limit}} = 0.01$, $h_z = 10^{-12}$ and a contrast parameter of $\lambda = 10^{-3}$. Further, the confidence function c is set to 0 at the background pixels and otherwise set to 1.

Impact of the Smoothness Term. In our first experiment we investigate the impact of the smoothness term under increasing values of the regularisation parameter α. In Fig. 2 the original input image is shown as well the reprojected images of computations with increasing α. As one can see, increasing α leads to an estimation of a smoothed surface while details are gradually eliminated. This is not only a very important property in the presence of noise, it also allows to specify the level of detail of the reconstruction.

Comparison with Other Methods. In the second experiment we compare our method with the PDE-based approach of Vogel *et al.* [30] with Lambertian reflectance model (= baseline model of Prados *et al.* [23]) and the variational approach of Ju *et al.* [14]. In order to demonstrate the advantages and shortcomings of these approaches we consider the original input images as well as noisy versions (Gaussian noise with $\sigma = 20$). The computed error measures are listed in Table 1. It can be seen that for the original input images our new linearised approach yields slightly higher error values, especially in the case of the *Dragon*. However, except for the *Dragon*, the errors are below one percent. Moreover,

Table 1. Comparison between the PDE-based method of Vogel *et al.* [30], the variational method of Ju *et al.* [14] and our approach in terms of error measures (RSE, RIE) for the four test images without and with noise ($\sigma = 20$). The parameters of our approach are: *Sombrero* ($\alpha = 0.003$), *Stanford Bunny* ($\alpha = 0.08$), *Dragon* ($\alpha = 0.2$), *Suzanne* ($\alpha = 0.04$), *Noisy Sombrero* ($\alpha = 0.02$), *Noisy Stanford Bunny* ($\alpha = 3$), *Noisy Dragon* ($\alpha = 1$), *Noisy Suzanne* ($\alpha = 2$). For the other two approaches the same parameters have been used as in the original papers.

	Vogel *et al.* [30]		Ju *et al.* [14]		Our method	
	RSE	RIE	RSE	RIE	RSE	RIE
Sombrero	0.00301	0.00495	0.00318	0.00209	0.00768	0.00925
Stanford Bunny	0.00266	0.00154	0.00439	0.00007	0.00928	0.00327
Dragon	0.00422	0.00255	0.01376	0.00028	0.02904	0.02333
Suzanne	0.00253	0.00082	0.00251	0.00002	0.00696	0.00224
Noisy Sombrero	0.19530	0.27254	0.05118	0.13239	0.01542	0.03851
Noisy Stanford B.	0.10973	0.17347	0.03235	0.15279	0.01359	0.12285
Noisy Dragon	0.12240	0.19409	0.05395	0.18767	0.03391	0.17732
Noisy Suzanne	0.12134	0.16783	0.01256	0.14302	0.00826	0.12038

the results for the noisy test images show the advantage of variational methods that include a regularisation mechanism contrary to PDE-based SfS approaches. While the PDE-based approach produces strongly deteriorated results due to its crucial dependence on the initialisation at singular points, both variational approaches achieve much lower surface errors. Furthermore, our novel scheme does not suffer from the problem that the regularisation parameter α has to be chosen sufficiently small to allow convergence within a reasonable number of iterations - as in the case of the alternating explicit scheme of Ju *et al.* [14]. This explains why our optimal parameters do not necessarily have to coincide with the optimal parameters of Ju *et al.* [14] that have been tuned for a fixed number of 10^6 iterations (to keep runtimes within a day).

We repeated the noise experiment with an additional pre- and post-processing step, respectively. While for the pre-processing a variational image denoising method with TV-regularisation was used, we employed a similar method with second order smoothness term corresponding to our regulariser in (6) for the post-processing. The outcome of this experiment is shown in Table 2. Although the approach of Vogel *et al.* [30] benefits significantly from both steps (in particular from denoising the input image) our variational model still yields better results (even without the corresponding steps). This clearly demonstrates the usefulness of the built-in regularisation of variational methods.

Reconstruction with Inpainting. Our third experiment considers the inpainting capabilities of the smoothness term given via Eqs. (6) and (8). A similar experiment has been carried out in [13,14]. However, the inpainted domains were rather small in those works. The explicit schemes used there would have

Table 2. Comparison of the method of Vogel *et al.* [30] and our approach under noise when using an additional pre-processing step (image denoising) or post-processing step (depth smoothing).

	Vogel *et al.* [30]			Our method		
	orig. RSE	pre-p	post-p	orig. RSE	pre-p	post-p
Noisy Sombrero	0.19530	0.02008	0.19197	0.01542	0.01741	0.01538
Noisy Stanford B.	0.10973	0.01434	0.06164	0.01359	0.01470	0.01357
Noisy Dragon	0.12240	0.04623	0.08226	0.03391	0.03322	0.03390
Noisy Suzanne	0.12134	0.01245	0.06169	0.00826	0.00917	0.00824

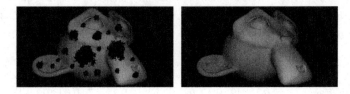

Fig. 3. Inpainting of the *Suzanne* image: Deteriorated input image, reprojected image ($\alpha = 0.5$).

needed more iterations to fill in larger regions resulting in tremendous computation time. In contrast, our new approach may inpaint larger regions without significant increase in runtime. To demonstrate this, we defined a degraded domain for inpainting considerably larger than those in [13, 14] and set the confidence function to 0 in the degraded domain. As shown in Fig. 3 our reprojected image of the reconstruction looks quite reasonable in spite of the huge amount of missing information. In case of rather flat regions no differences to the original image are noticeable, whereas missing regions with varying surface orientations, as e.g. at the ear, seem to be smoothed. However, an RSE of 0.00793 shows that the quality of the reconstruction is comparable to the RSE achieved by computing the reconstruction based on the original input image without missing regions (RSE = 0.00696).

Table 3. Runtime comparison between Vogel *et al.* [30], Ju *et al.* [14] and our approach.

	Vogel *et al.* [30]	Ju *et al.* [14]	Our method
Sombrero (256×256)	1 s	29113 s	17 s
Stanford Bunny (256×256)	1 s	23969 s	11 s
Dragon (256×256)	1 s	25350 s	12 s
Suzanne (512×256)	2 s	48395 s	21 s
Blunderbuss Pete (1080×1920)	33 s	Infeasible computation time	340 s

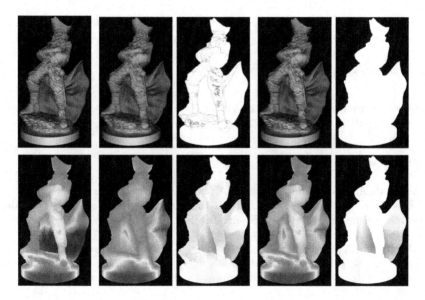

Fig. 4. From top to bottom: Reprojected image and colour-coded depth of the *Blunderbuss Pete* test image (3-D model by *BenDasie*). **From left to right:** Ground truth, our approach + difference plots, method of Vogel *et al.* [30] + difference plots (Color figure online).

High-Resolution Image. Since variational SfS approaches mainly use simple explicit schemes, they usually require thousands or even millions of iterations to converge. Hence, the runtime becomes a critical issue. As can be noticed in Table 3, our approach achieves a speed up of approximately 2000 for small images compared to the explicit approach in [14]. In particular, it allows a reasonable computation time for high resolution images such as *Blunderbuss Pete* depicted in Fig. 4, where runtimes with explicit schemes become infeasible. Moreover, the quality is still highly competitive. As shown in Fig. 4, the reprojected image of our approach is close to the ground truth (RIE = 0.03414), whereas the difference plots reveal some difficulties at the cloak (RSE = 0.02930). In contrast, the approach of Vogel *et al.* [30] achieves an almost perfect reprojected image (RIE = 0.00067). With respect to the surface it shows similar errors at the cloak, while the reconstruction at the knee and torso is better (RSE = 0.01593).

5   Conclusion

In this paper we have introduced an efficient numerical scheme for variational perspective SfS based on a linearisation of the reflectance model. The proposed scheme not only yields speed ups of more than three orders of magnitude compared to standard explicit schemes without significantly compromising the quality of the reconstruction. It also allows to select sufficiently large values for the regularisation parameter without compromising the runtime, which enables us to deal adequately and efficiently with noise and missing information. Finally, the proposed numerical strategy is rather general such that it can be carried over to other variational models form the SfS literature that are based on standard explicit schemes so far.

Acknowledgements. This work has been partly funded by the Deutsche Forschungs-gemeinschaft (BR 2245/3-1, BR 4372/1-1).

References

1. Abdelrahim, A.S., Abdelrahman, M.A., Abdelmunim, H., Farag, A., Miller, M.: Novel image-based 3D reconstruction of the human jaw using shape from shading and feature descriptors. In: Proceedings of the British Machine Vision Conference, pp. 1–11 (2011)
2. Abdelrahim, A.S., Abdelmunim, H., Graham, J., Farag, A.: Novel variational approach for the perspective shape from shading problem using calibrated images. In: Proceedings of the IEEE International Conference on Image Processing, pp. 2563–2566 (2013)
3. Barron, J.T., Malik, J.: Shape, illumination, and reflectance from shading. IEEE Trans. Pattern Anal. Mach. Intell. **37**(8), 1670–1687 (2015)
4. Bors, A.G., Hancock, E.R., Wilson, R.C.: Terrain analysis using radar shape-from-shading. IEEE Trans. Pattern Anal. Mach. Intell. **25**, 974–992 (2003)
5. Breuß, M., Cristiani, E., Durou, J.-D., Falcone, M., Vogel, O.: Perspective shape from shading: ambiguity analysis and numerical approximations. SIAM J. Imaging Sci. **5**(1), 311–342 (2012)
6. Brox, T., Bruhn, A., Papenberg, N., Weickert, J.: High accuracy optical flow estimation based on a theory for warping. In: Pajdla, T., Matas, J.G. (eds.) ECCV 2004. LNCS, vol. 3024, pp. 25–36. Springer, Heidelberg (2004)
7. Charbonnier, P., Blanc-Féraud, L., Aubert, G., Barlaud, M.: Deterministic edge-preserving regularization in computed imaging. IEEE Trans. Image Process. **6**(2), 298–311 (1997)
8. Courteille, F., Crouzil, A., Durou, J.-D., Gurdjos, P.: Towards shape from shading under realistic photographic conditions. In: Proceedings of the IEEE International Conference on Pattern Recognition, pp. 277–280 (2004)
9. Fassold, H., Danzl, R., Schindler, K., Bischof, H.: Reconstruction of archaeological finds using shape from stereo and shape from shading. In: Proceedings of the Computer Vision Winter Workshop, pp. 21–30 (2004)
10. Gelfand, I.M., Fomin, S.V.: Calculus of Variations. Dover, New York (2000)
11. Horn, B.K.P.: Shape from shading: a method for obtaining the shape of a smooth opaque object from one view. Ph.D. thesis, Department of Electrical Engineering, MIT, Cambridge, Massachusetts, USA (1970)
12. Ikeuchi, K., Horn, B.K.P.: Numerical shape from shading and occluding boundaries. Artif. Intell. **17**(1–3), 141–184 (1981)
13. Ju, Y.C., Bruhn, A., Breuß, M.: Variational perspective shape from shading. In: Aujol, J.-F., Nikolova, M., Papadakis, N. (eds.) SSVM 2015. LNCS, vol. 9087, pp. 538–550. Springer, Heidelberg (2015)
14. Ju, Y.C., Maurer, D., Breuß, M., Bruhn, A.: Direct variational perspective shape from shading with Cartesian depth parametrisation. In: Perspectives in Shape Analysis, Mathematics and Visualization. Springer (2015, to appear)

15. Kimmel, R., Sethian, J.A.: Optimal algorithm for shape from shading and path planning. J. Math. Imaging Vis. **14**(3), 237–244 (2001)
16. Lee, K.M., Kuo, C.-C.J.: Shape from shading with a generalized reflectance map model. Comput. Vis. Image Underst. **67**, 143–160 (1997)
17. Nayar, S.K.: Shape recovery methods for visual inspection. In: Proceedings of the IEEE Workshop on Applications in Computer Vision, pp. 136–145 (1992)
18. Okatani, T., Deguchi, K.: Shape reconstruction from an endoscope image by shape from shading technique for a point light source at the projection center. Comput. Vis. Image Underst. **66**, 119–131 (1997)
19. Oren, M., Nayar, S.: Generalization of the Lambertian model and implications for machine vision. Int. J. Comput. Vis. **14**(3), 227–251 (1995)
20. Pentland, A.: Shape information from shading: a theory about human perception. In: Proceedings of the IEEE International Conference on Computer Vision, pp. 404–413 (1988)
21. Phong, B.T.: Illumination for computer-generated pictures. Commun. ACM **18**(6), 311–317 (1975)
22. Prados, E., Faugeras, O.: "Perspective shape from shading" and viscosity solutions. In: Proceedings of the IEEE International Conference Computer Vision, pp. 826–831 (2003)
23. Prados, E., Faugeras, O.: Shape from shading: a well-posed problem? In: Proceedings of the IEEE Conference on Computer Vision and Pattern Recognition, pp. 870–877 (2005)
24. Rindfleisch, T.: Photometric method for lunar topography. Photogram. Eng. **32**(2), 262–277 (1966)
25. Rouy, E., Tourin, A.: A viscosity solution approach to shape-from-shading. SIAM J. Numer. Anal. **29**(3), 867–884 (1992)
26. Sethian, J.: Level Set Methods and Fast Marching Methods. Cambridge University Press, Cambridge (1999)
27. Tankus, A., Sochen, N., Yeshurun, Y.: Shape-from-shading under perspective projection. Int. J. Comput. Vis. **63**(1), 21–43 (2005)
28. Tsai, P.-S., Shah, M.: Shape from shading using linear approximation. Image Vis. Comput. **12**(8), 487–498 (1994)
29. Vogel, O., Bruhn, A., Weickert, J., Didas, S.: Direct shape-from-shading with adaptive higher order regularisation. In: Sgallari, F., Murli, A., Paragios, N. (eds.) SSVM 2007. LNCS, vol. 4485, pp. 871–882. Springer, Heidelberg (2007)
30. Vogel, O., Breuß, M., Leichtweis, T., Weickert, J.: Fast shape from shading for Phong-type surfaces. In: Tai, X.-C., Mørken, K., Lysaker, M., Lie, K.-A. (eds.) SSVM 2009. LNCS, vol. 5567, pp. 733–744. Springer, Heidelberg (2009)
31. Wu, C., Narasimhan, S., Jaramaz, B.: A multi-image shape-from-shading framework for near-lighting perspective endoscopes. Int. J. Comput. Vis. **86**, 211–228 (2010)
32. Zhang, L., Yip, A.M., Tan, C.T.: Shape from shading based on Lax-Friedrichs fast sweeping and regularization techniques with applications to document image restoration. In: Proceedings of the IEEE Conference on Computer Vision and Pattern Recognition, pp. 1–8 (2007)

TomoGC: Binary Tomography by Constrained GraphCuts

Jörg Hendrik Kappes[(✉)], Stefania Petra, Christoph Schnörr,
and Matthias Zisler

Heidelberg University, Heidelberg, Germany
kappes@math.uni-heidelberg.de

Abstract. We present an iterative reconstruction algorithm for binary
tomography, called TomoGC, that solves the reconstruction problem
based on a constrained graphical model by a sequence of graphcuts.
TomoGC reconstructs objects even if a low number of measurements are
only given, which enables shorter observation periods and lower radiation doses in industrial and medical applications. We additionally suggest
some modifications of established methods that improve state-of-the-art
methods. A comprehensive numerical evaluation demonstrates that the
proposed method can reconstruct objects from a small number of projections more accurate and also faster than competitive methods.

1 Introduction

Limited-data tomography deals with the problem of reconstructing 3D-volumes
or 2D-images denoted by $x \in \mathbb{R}^N$, from a small number of (noisy) projections
given by $b = Ax + \nu \in \mathbb{R}^M$. The range of applications for tomography includes
industrial [21] and medical [29] applications. In many situations it is desirable to
reduce the number of required measurements M that are represented by the rows
of the matrix $A \in \mathbb{R}^{M \times N}$. If M is much smaller than N, then the reconstruction
problem is ill-posed and regularization is required.

The tomography reconstruction problem can be formulated as a regularized
least squares (1) or a constrained minimization of the regularizer (2).

$$x^* \in \underset{x \in \mathbb{R}^N}{\arg\min}\, R(x) + \|Ax - b\|_2^2 \tag{1}$$

$$x^* \in \underset{x \in \mathbb{R}^N}{\arg\min}\, R(x), \qquad \text{s.t.} \quad \underline{b} \le Ax \le \overline{b} \tag{2}$$

While problem (1) is searching for a solution that has a low score of the regularizer and good data-fidelity, problem (2) is searching in the feasible set (given by
the data-constraints) for the solution with the lowest score of the regularizer.

Early approaches such as filtered back projection (FBP) [7], deal with the
tomography problem by analytical reconstruction methods, which provides reasonably accurate reconstructions in very short times, but usually require many
projection angles. The algebraic reconstruction methods (ARMs) such as ART,

© Springer International Publishing Switzerland 2015
J. Gall et al. (Eds.): GCPR 2015, LNCS 9358, pp. 262–273, 2015.
DOI: 10.1007/978-3-319-24947-6_21

SIRT or SART solve problem (1) without any regularization term $R(x)$. They fall into the category of row-action methods [10,11] also known as iterated projection methods for systems of linear (in)equalities. ARMs give better results than FBP, but due to the lack of regularization usually the number of required projections is still large.

For a further reduction of required observations, several regularization techniques have been proposed depending on the prior knowledge at hand. Convex sparsity promoting priors like ℓ_1- or total variation minimization [17], smoothness priors [36] or box constraints conserve the convexity of the overall problem. Such non-smooth, constrained, distributed and large-scale optimisation problems can be addressed by proximal algorithms in an unified fixed point theoretical framework [9,14] as finding solutions to monotone inclusion problems or more specifically by projections on convex sets [5,8]. In this context the alternating direction method of multipliers [28] and in particular the Chambolle Pock Algorithm [12], which is a decomposable method for minimizing the sum of two convex functions subject to linear constraints, can be considered for tomographic inversion [31]. Interestingly, the ADMM framework can be adopted also when considering a non-convex regularization term like the ℓ_0-prior as done in [32]. However several questions concerning convergence remain open. For a sufficient uniqueness condition for the ℓ_0-regularized tomographic reconstruction problem in terms of the image gradient sparsity and the number of tomographic measurements, we refer to [15].

A further reduction of required measurements can be obtained if the range of x is a finite set. The tomography problems (1) and (2) with the additional constraint that $x \in \{v_1, \ldots, v_K\}^N$ is known as *discrete tomography* problem, the subject of the present paper. A special case of this problem is *binary tomography* where the set is restricted to two possible values ($K = 2$) for each x_i, which in practice occurs e.g. when air pockets in work pieces need to be detected without destroying the object.

We underline that several heuristics have been designed to intervene between consecutive steps of a non-binary iterative image reconstruction algorithm in order to gradually steer the iterates towards a binary solution. Batenburg *et al.* suggested a (Soft) Discrete Algebraic Reconstruction Technique known as (S)DART [4,6], which is a very fast heuristic that starts from a continuous reconstruction, applies a segmentation step to restrict the reconstruction to the allowed values, and then restarts the continuous reconstruction on boundary regions of the segmentation, iteratively. While this leads to good results quite fast, it does not optimize an objective function. In another line of research Batenburg and Sijbers [2,3] presented an algorithm for the binary tomography problem that is based on a sequence of minimum cost flow problems. For two projection directions (with non-overlapping rays for each direction) this method is exact. In the general case, it is a greedy approximation.

An alternative ansatz is to reformulate problem (1) into a discrete graphical model. For the binary tomography problem (1) this leads to a fully connected second-order binary model [30]. The multi-label case can be reduced to a sequence of such binary problems in a α-expansion framework [30]. As this is in general not sub-modular, Raj *et al.* [30] have suggested to use QPBO [25] to solve a relaxation of the problem which give additional persistence certificates. The main limitation of this approach is that the number of pairwise terms grows quadratically with the number of pixels and the complexity of QPBO roughly grows cubically with the number of pairwise terms in the worst case, which caused e.g. [30] to consider only restricted projection matrices A. To overcome this problem, Tuysuzoglu *et al.* [34] consider local approximations of the non-sub-modular terms around a working point which is iteratively improved. Similar methods have been also studied for more general graphical models [16,33].

Weber *et al.* [35,36] suggested to solve problem (1) by a quadratic program. The binary constraints are enforced by iteratively increasing a non-convex balloon-term that pushes the labels to zeros and ones. The subproblems are solved by the difference-of-convex-function programming technique that iteratively and locally approximates the non-convex part of the objective by an affine upper bound. While there is no guarantee that this method finds the global optimum, it generally returns good results.

Gouillart *et al.* [18] have proposed a belief propagation algorithm for the discrete tomography problem (1). In order to handle the higher order interactions induced by the projection constraints, they include Lagrangian multipliers that enforce that these constraints are fulfilled on average. However, this algorithm only estimates the marginal distributions, which then are rounded to obtain a discrete reconstruction.

Outside the application area of tomography, Lagrangian relaxation has been used amongst others for multicommodity max flow [37], graphical models [26], and graphical models with a few constraints [27]. While in [26], contrary to our work, variable duplication is used to relax the problem, [27,37] use the same mathematical idea as we do in the present context of discrete tomography.

Contributions. We present a novel method for solving the binary tomography problem, which solves the dual of a relaxation of problem (2) by a sequence of graphcut problems. The size of these problems scales linearly with the number of primal variables and, besides the graphcut computation, only a few simple matrix-vector operations are required. Consequently, the proposed method is very efficient and scales up well to large data. On the other side, it is mathematically sound and is the only currently available method that provides a lower bound on the optimal objective value. Furthermore, we provide a comprehensive experimental comparison of state-of-the-art methods, which was lacking so far in the literature. We also suggest some modifications of standard methods which improve their performance or are even necessary to make these methods applicable in all considered scenarios.

2   Constrained GraphCuts for Binary Tomography

We consider problem (2) for $K = 2$. To ease the presentation, we temporarily consider the noise-free case where $\underline{b} = \overline{b} = b$ and generalize it later on. Without loss of generality, we assume that $v_1 = 0$ and $v_2 = 1$. We define a grid graph

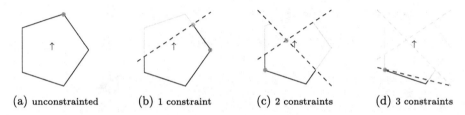

(a) unconstrainted   (b) 1 constraint   (c) 2 constraints   (d) 3 constraints

Fig. 1. Polyhedral illustration of the constrained linear program. In the unconstrained case **(a)**, the optimal solution is integral. With one additional constrained **(b)**, the LP-solution (•) and optimal integer solution in the constrained set (•) are not identical. When adding another constrained **(c)**, the LP-solution moves in the interior of the original polytope. By adding more constraints **(d)**, the feasible set gets smaller and finally the LP solution gets integral.

$G = (V, E)$, with V corresponding to image pixels and $E \subset V \times V$ defining the neighborhood system. As regularization term, we use $R(x) := \sum_{uv \in E} \beta \cdot |x_u - x_v|$, so the problem at hand is given by

$$x^* \in \underset{x \in \{0,1\}^{|V|}}{\arg\min} \sum_{uv \in E} \beta \cdot |x_u - x_v|, \qquad \text{s.t.} \quad Ax = b. \tag{3}$$

Without the additional constraints $Ax = b$ and $\beta \geq 0$, this problem can be solved as a linear program by relaxing the $\{0, 1\}$ constraints to $[0, 1]$ constraints and by representing $|x_u - x_v|$ linearly by means of additional auxiliary variables. This would be even the case if additional unary terms are added [13, 23]. However, in the presence of projection constraints as part of the problem, this is no longer true, as illustrated in Fig. 1. The relaxed linear program can then have non-binary solutions.

In order to find efficiently a solution of the relaxed problem (3), we consider its Lagrangian dual

$$\max_{\lambda} \min_{x \in [0,1]^{|V|}} \sum_{uv \in E} \beta \cdot |x_u - x_v| + \langle \lambda, Ax - b \rangle \tag{4}$$

$$= \max_{\lambda} \underbrace{\min_{x \in [0,1]^{|V|}} \sum_{uv \in E} \beta \cdot |x_u - x_v| + \langle \lambda, Ax \rangle - \langle \lambda, b \rangle}_{=:g(\lambda)}. \tag{5}$$

By weak duality, we know that for every feasible primal x and feasible dual value λ, the inequality (6) holds.

$$\sum_{uv \in E} \beta \cdot |x_u - x_v| \geq g(\lambda) \tag{6}$$

If the optima x^* and λ^* exist, equality in (6) holds (strong duality). If a feasible finite primal solution exists, then also the dual has a feasible finite solution. In the case that no feasible primal value exists, the dual problem is unbounded.

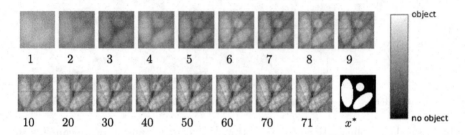

Fig. 2. Shows the evolution of the unary data-term $A^\top \lambda$ during the iterations. After 71 iterations, the data term leads to a duality gap of zero. This illustrates that after a few iterations, the data term does not change so much any more.

As a consequence, if a feasible primal solution exists, then we may solve the dual problem instead of the primal, followed by recovering a primal solution from the dual solution.

The most simple algorithm to optimize the dual problem (5) is iterative subgradient ascent with a proper stepsize sequence γ_i. For any λ and

$$x^\lambda \in \arg\min_{x \in [0,1]^{|V|}} \sum_{uv \in E} \beta \cdot |x_u - x_v| + \langle \lambda, Ax \rangle,$$

a lower bound on the optimal value is given by $\sum_{uv \in E} \beta \cdot |x_u^\lambda - x_v^\lambda| + \langle \lambda, Ax^\lambda - b \rangle$. For the dual objective $g(\lambda)$ and its subdifferential $\partial g(\lambda)$, we compute a subgradient by

$$\partial g(\lambda) \ni Ax^\lambda - b, \quad x^\lambda \in \arg\min_{x \in [0,1]^{|V|}} \sum_{uv \in E} \beta \cdot |x_u - x_v| + \langle \lambda, Ax \rangle. \tag{7}$$

The calculation of x^λ can be further simplified by making use of the relation to graphcuts [13,23], which guarantees that a binary solution exists, that is globally optimal. This can be efficiently calculated by a graphcut (max-flow) algorithm. As long as $\beta > 0$, the optimal solution x^* does not depend on the value of β. Only the optimal dual variable λ^* will scale according to β.

An interesting observation is that by optimizing the dual objective, we iteratively build up a unary data term $A^\top \lambda$, as illustrated in Fig. 2. Due to regularization, the unary terms do not have to be perfect. While a reasonable data term is found after a few iterations, most of the iterations are required to close the primal-dual-gap without changing the dual variables much.

The construction of a feasible primal solution is non-trivial. While general primal construction rules exists [20], these produce an optimal and feasible solution only in the limit. More advanced methods for solving the dual, for example bundle methods [22], have a faster convergence and also provide primal estimates. However, a study of those methods is beyond the present work.

As we are interested in binary solutions anyway, we have come up with the following framework to generate primal solutions. Each subgradient yields a primal solution x^λ. If this solution is feasible and strong duality holds, *i.e.*

Algorithm 1. TomoGC (noise free case)

Require: $A \in \mathbb{R}^{M \times N}$, $b \in \mathbb{R}^{M \times 1}$, $\beta > 0$, $E \subset [N]^2$
Ensure: $v \leq \min_{x \in [0,1]^N,\, Ax=b} \sum_{uv \in E} \beta \cdot |x_u - x_v|$ if feasible
1: **initialize:** $i = 0$, $\quad \lambda = [0]^{1 \times M}$, $\quad \bar{x} = [0]^{N \times 1}$
2: $x^\lambda \in \arg\min_{x \in \{0,1\}^{|V|}} \sum_{uv \in E} \beta \cdot |x_u - x_v| + \langle \lambda, Ax \rangle$
3: **while** $(\|Ax^\lambda - b\| > 0$ and $\langle \lambda, Ax^\lambda - b \rangle \neq 0)$ and $i < i_{\max}$ **do**
4: $\quad \lambda = \lambda + \gamma_i(x^\lambda) \cdot [Ax^\lambda - b]$
5: $\quad x^\lambda \in \arg\min_{x \in \{0,1\}^{|V|}} \sum_{uv \in E} \beta \cdot |x_u - x_v| + \langle \lambda, Ax \rangle$
6: $\quad$ **if** $\|A\bar{x} - b\| > \|Ax^\lambda - b\|$ **then**
7: $\quad\quad \bar{x} = x$
8: $\quad$ **end if**
9: $\quad i = i + 1$
10: **end while**
11: $x = \bar{x}$
12: $v = \sum_{uv \in E} \beta \cdot |x_u - x_v| + \langle \lambda, Ax - b \rangle$

$\langle \lambda, Ax^\lambda - b \rangle = 0$, this is an optimal primal solution. If the optimal primal solution is non-binary, the sub-gradients will oscillate around the non-binary solution. But if the solution is binary and unique, the dual objective will have the optimal primal solution as subgradient at the optimal dual point.

The pseudocode of our method is given in Algorithm 1. In each iteration, we update the dual variable in the direction of the subgradient. The non-summable diminishing step length that ensures convergence, is defined by $\gamma_i(x) = \frac{20}{(0.1 \cdot i + 1) \cdot \|Ax - b\|_2}$, $i \in \mathbb{N}$.

Noisy Data Case. In the case where we have to deal with noise and $\underline{b} < \bar{b}$, we have to replace $Ax - b$ in Eq. 4 and Algorithm 1 by $\max\{0, Ax - \underline{b}\} + \min\{Ax - \bar{b}, 0\}$. The values $\underline{b}$ and $\bar{b}$ have to be selected with respect to the noisy measurements b and the assumed noise level such that a feasible solution exists.

3 Experiments

For our experimental evaluation, we used the binary test-datasets of Weber et al. [35] and Batenburg and Sijbers [4]. We generated the projection matrices with the ASTRA-toolbox [1] and simulated parallel projections within the range of 0 and 180 degrees. The width of the sensor-array is 1.5 times the image size and each sensor has the same size as a pixel. The entries of the projection matrix A are given by the length of the intersection of the pixels and the rays. We restricted our evaluation to algorithms that can deal with arbitrary projection matrices and excluded methods that make additional assumptions such as $A \in \{0,1\}^{M \times N}$. Table 1 lists all methods that we evaluated.

As a baseline for continuous methods we considered Filtered Back Projection (**FBP**) [7], Simultaneous Iterative Reconstruction Technique (**SIRT**) [19], and a total variation regularized reconstruction with hard projection constraints

Table 1. Compared Methods. Methods marked with * are either novel methods or extensions of existing methods proposed in the present work.

Shortcut	Reference	Label	Regularization	Implementation	Objective
FBP	[7]	cont	no	ASTRA-toolbox	-
SIRT	[19]	cont	no	ASTRA-toolbox	Eq. (1)
tomoTV	[15]	cont	TV	Denitiu et al.	Eq. (2)
tomoDC	[36]	binary	Potts	ours	Eq. (1)
tomoFTR*	[16,34]	binary	Potts	ours	Eq. (1)
tomoPB*	[33,34]	binary	Potts	ours	Eq. (1)
tomoGC*	Sect. 2	binary	Potts	ours	Eq. (2)
DART	[4]	discrete	-	ASTRA-toolbox	-
DART-S*	[4]	discrete	Potts	ASTRA-toolbox + TRWS	-

(**tomoTV**) [15]. For the former two, we used the implementation available in the ASTRA-toolbox, the latter was kindly provided by Denitiu et al..

We furthermore compared to the Discrete Algebraic Reconstruction Technique (**DART**) [4]. We used the publicly available implementation of the ASTRA-toolbox. For the continuous iterative reconstructions we used SIRT. We set the smoothing intensity and percentage of random points to 0.1, which are the suggested default values, and run DART for 20 iterations. Additionally, we suggest a variation of the DART method by replacing the elementary nearest neighbor segmentation of the DART-method by a structured segmentation that also includes a smoothness-term. In order to be able to deal with multi-label problems, we used TRWS [24] to solve the segmentation problems. To the best of our knowledge, this combination of DART and structured segmentation (**DART-S**) has not been considered before.

For the binary case, we implemented the difference-of-convex-functions approach (**tomoDC**) from Weber et al. [36] which is known to give good results even with a low number of projections. We used the same parameter setting as described in [35] and the implementation of the spectral projected gradient (SPG) method of Mark Schmidt[1] for solving the subproblems. When running tomoDC on the large instances from [4], we observed that the method got stucked in non-binary equilibriums due to numerical reasons. Because adding some additional noise as suggested by Weber et al. did not solve the problem, we initialized tomoDC with the solution of FBP. This resolved all numerical problems for all our problem instances.

In recent work Tuysuzoglu et al. [34] solve binary tomography problems by a set of surrogate problems that approximate the original function around the current solution. The surrogate problems are designed to be solvable by graph-cut (max-flow) methods. If the best solution of all surrogate problems improves the original energy, then the current solution is updated accordingly and the

---

[1] http://www.cs.ubc.ca/~schmidtm/Software/minConf.html.

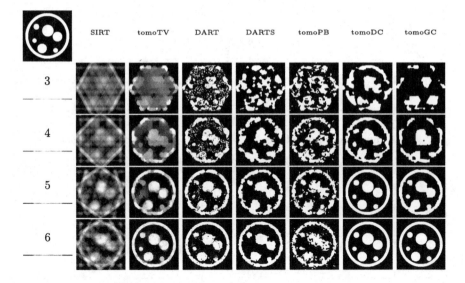

Fig. 3. *Phantom 3* from Weber [35] with no noise

procedure continues, otherwise it stops. The downside of this approach is that the selection of the surrogate problems in [34] is rather greedy and inefficient. Inspired by this work, we recognize some relations to recent works in the area of discrete optimization [16,33] which better indicate how to choose these surrogate problems. Tang *et al.* [33] consider all possible surrogate problems (pseudo bounds) with respect to the free parameter, and find all possible solutions by parametric max-flow. By using parametric max-flow a greedy selection is only required if the number of possible solutions is too large - this can be the case if the current solution is bad. In such a case, we simply greedy-like suppress nearby solutions. Typically, after a few iterations, the solution is good enough such that the number of possible solutions is small. We call this method tomography with pseudo bounds (**tomoPB**). A similar approach was suggested by Gorelick *et al.* [16] - originally also not applied to tomography problems. They use also a first-order Taylor expansion as an upper bound of the original function around the working point. An additional trust region term, based on the Euclidean distance, enforces solutions in the local region where the objective function is approximated well. We call this method tomography with fast trust region (**tomoFTR**).

A full evaluation of all test-instances is reported in the supplementary material. Due to lack of space, we can only show here two examples and some reconstructions. Figures 3 and 5 show in the first row the original data and the sinograms (*b*) which are measured with *k* projection angles. Figure 4 shows the ratio of wrongly reconstructed pixels and runtime for a different number of projection angles for two examples. In the noise free case tomoDC and tomoGC give the best results, but tomoGC is typically one magnitude faster. As shown in Figs. 3

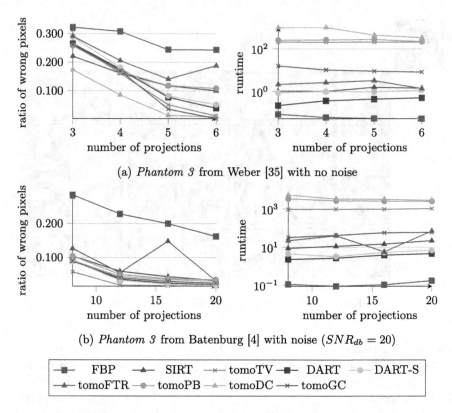

(a) *Phantom 3* from Weber [35] with no noise

(b) *Phantom 3* from Batenburg [4] with noise ($SNR_{db} = 20$)

Fig. 4. Exemplary plots for the runtime and pixel accuracy in the noise free and noisy case for small number of projections. In the noise free case, tomoDC, tomoTV and tomoGC give the best results, but tomoGC is typically one magnitude faster. In the presence of noise tomoTV, DART and DART-S give the best results, since their greediness/rounding make them robust against noise.

and 4a, those are able to obtain nearly optimal reconstructions with only 5 projections. DART-S gives a reasonable result with 5 projections, which is much better than the original DART method with only slightly increased runtime. FBP, SIRT, tomoFTR and tomoPB have problems with this small number of projections and require more projections for reasonable reconstructions.

We also simulated noisy observations by adding Poisson noise to the sinograms (*b*). The reconstruction results shown in Figs. 4b and 5 are obtained with a signal to noise ratio (SNR) of 20 db. None of the problem formulations are designed to deal with Poisson noise, which is the most realistic approximation of noise in tomography. DART, DART-S and tomoTV include a rounding procedure, which removes noise in a greedy way. This seemed to work better than more sophisticated approaches, like tomoDC or tomoGC, which use a "wrong" noise model and added some artefacts to fulfill the projection constraints. The best results are obtained by tomoTV after rounding and DART-S, which again

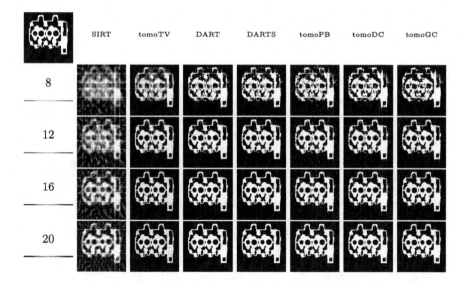

Fig. 5. *Phantom 3* from Batenburg [4] with noise ($SNR_{db} = 20$)

gives better results compared to the original DART method. In the presence of noise, tomoFTR got sometimes stuck in local fixed points, and tomoPB performs better than tomoDC, but worse than tomoGC.

4   Conclusion and Future Work

We presented a new method for efficient binary reconstruction problems. In each iteration, our method only has to perform simple matrix vector operations and a graphcut problem of the size of the image/volume. For large-scale problems, solving the graphcut problem becomes the limiting factor, but efficient parallel implementations for this problem have been suggested in the recent literature. Even without this specialized implementations, our method is by more than one magnitude faster than competitive methods and provides additional theoretical guarantees, which makes it appealing to be used as a sub-solver within a α-expansion like algorithm, as suggested in [34].

For the generalization to multi-label tomography, we obtained some first promising results by replacing graph cuts with graphical models, which is equivalent in the binary case. However, in the multi-label case two additional problems have to be considered. Firstly, the discrete inference problem is no longer tractable in polynomial time and secondly, the allowed values span a simplex and no longer live on an one-dimensional space.

In future work, we also plan to replace naive subgradient ascent by the more advanced bundle method with automatic stepsize choice [22]. This should give a further speedup and non-binary primal estimates which can be used to suppress noise similar to tomoTV.

Acknowledgements. Financial support of our research work by the DFG, grant GRK 1653. is gratefully acknowledged.

References

1. van Aarle, W., Palenstijn, W.J., Beenhouwer, J.D., Altantzis, T., Bals, S., Batenburg, K.J., Sijbers, J.: The ASTRA-toolbox: a platform for advanced algorithm development in electron tomography. Ultramicroscopy (2015)
2. Batenburg, K.J.: A network flow algorithm for reconstructing binary images from continuous x-rays. J. Math. Imaging Vis. **30**(3), 231–248 (2008)
3. Batenburg, K.J., Sijbers, J.: Generic iterative subset algorithms for discrete tomography. Discrete Appl. Math. **157**(3), 438–451 (2009)
4. Batenburg, K.J., Sijbers, J.: DART: a practical reconstruction algorithm for discrete tomography. IEEE Trans. Image Process. **20**(9), 2542–2553 (2011)
5. Bauschke, H.H., Borwein, J.M.: On projection algorithms for solving convex feasibility problems. SIAM Rev. **38**(3), 367–426 (1996)
6. Bleichrodt, F., Tabak, F., Batenburg, K.J.: SDART: an algorithm for discrete tomography from noisy projections. Comput. Vis. Image Underst. **129**, 63–74 (2014)
7. Bracewell, R.N., Riddle, A.C.: Inversion of fan-beam scans in radio astronomy. Astron. J. **150**(2), 427–434 (1967)
8. Capricelli, T., Combettes, P.: A convex programming algorithm for noisy discrete tomography. In: Advances in Discrete Tomography and its Applications. Birkhäuser, Boston (2007)
9. Cegielski, A.: Iterative Methods for Fixed Point Problems in Hilbert Spaces. Lecture Notes in Mathematics, vol. 2057. Springer, Heidelberg (2013)
10. Censor, Y.: Row-action methods for huge and sparse systems and their applications. SIAM Rev. **23**(4), 444–466 (1981)
11. Censor, Y., Zenios, S.: Parallel Optimization: Theory, Algorithms, and Applications. Oxford University Press, New York (1997)
12. Chambolle, A., Pock, T.: A first-order primal-dual algorithm for convex problems with applications to imaging. J. Math. Imaging Vis. **40**(1), 120–145 (2011)
13. Chambolle, A.: Total variation minimization and a class of binary MRF models. In: Rangarajan, A., Vemuri, B.C., Yuille, A.L. (eds.) EMMCVPR 2005. LNCS, vol. 3757, pp. 136–152. Springer, Heidelberg (2005)
14. Combettes, P.: Solving monotone inclusions via compositions of nonexpansive averaged operators. Optimization **53**(5–6), 475–504 (2004)
15. Denitiu, A., Petra, S., Schnörr, C., Schnörr, C.: Phase transitions and cosparse tomographic recovery of compound solid bodies from few projections. Fundamenta Informaticae **135**, 73–102 (2014)
16. Gorelick, L., Schmidt, F.R., Boykov, Y.: Fast trust region for segmentation. In: 2013 IEEE Conference on Computer Vision and Pattern Recognition, Portland, OR, USA, 23–28 June, 2013, pp. 1714–1721 (2013)
17. Goris, B., Van den Broek, W., Batenburg, K., Mezerji, H., Bals, S.: Electron tomography based on a total variation minimization reconstruction techniques. Ultramicroscopy **113**, 120–130 (2012)
18. Gouillart, E., Krzakala, F., Mezard, M., Zdeborova, L.: Belief-propagation reconstruction for discrete tomography. Inverse Prob. **29**(3), 035003 (2013)
19. Gregor, J., Benson, T.: Computational analysis and improvement of SIRT. IEEE Trans. Med. Imaging **27**(7), 918–924 (2008)

20. Gustavsson, E., Patriksson, M., Strömberg, A.B.: Primal convergence from dual subgradient methods for convex optimization. Math. Program. **150**(2), 365–390 (2015)
21. Hanke, R., Fuchs, T., Uhlmann, N.: X-ray based methods for non-destructive testing and material characterization. Nucl. Instrum. Meth. Phys. Res. Sect. A: Accelerators, Spectrometers, Detectors Associated Equipment **591**(1), 14–18 (2008). Radiation Imaging Detectors 2007 Proceedings of the 9th International Workshop on Radiation Imaging Detectors
22. Kiwiel, K.C.: Proximity control in bundle methods for convex nondifferentiable minimization. Math. Program. **46**, 105–122 (1990)
23. Kolmogorov, V., Zabin, R.: What energy functions can be minimized via graph cuts? IEEE Trans. Pattern Anal. Mach. Intell. **26**(2), 147–159 (2004)
24. Kolmogorov, V.: Convergent tree-reweighted message passing for energy minimization. IEEE Trans. Pattern Anal. Mach. Intell. **28**(10), 1568–1583 (2006)
25. Kolmogorov, V., Rother, C.: Minimizing nonsubmodular functions with graph cuts-a review. IEEE Trans. Pattern Anal. Mach. Intell. **29**(7), 1274–1279 (2007)
26. Komodakis, N., Paragios, N., Tziritas, G.: MRF energy minimization and beyond via dual decomposition. IEEE Trans. Pattern Anal. Mach. Intell. **33**(3), 531–552 (2011)
27. Lim, Y., Jung, K., Kohli, P.: Efficient energy minimization for enforcing label statistics. IEEE Trans. Pattern Anal. Mach. Intell. **36**(9), 1893–1899 (2014)
28. Parikh, N., Boyd, S.: Proximal algorithms. Found. Trends Optim. **1**(3), 1–108 (2013)
29. Smith-Bindman, R., Lipson, J., Marcus, R., et al.: Radiation dose associated with common computed tomography examinations and the associated lifetime attributable risk of cancer. Arch. Intern. Med. **169**(22), 2078–2086 (2009)
30. Raj, A., Singh, G., Zabih, R.: MRF's for MRI's: Bayesian reconstruction of MR images via graph cuts. In: 2006 IEEE Computer Society Conference on Computer Vision and Pattern Recognition (CVPR 2006), New York, NY, USA, 17–22 June 2006, pp. 1061–1068 (2006)
31. Sidky, E.Y., Jakob, H., Jörgensen, J.H., Pan, X.: Convex optimization problem prototyping for image reconstruction in computed tomography with the Chambolle-Pock algorithm. Phys. Med. Biol. **57**(10), 3065 (2012)
32. Storath, M., Weinmann, A., Frikel, J., Unser, M.: Joint image reconstruction and segmentation using the Potts model. Inverse Prob. **31**(2), 025003 (2015)
33. Tang, M., Ben Ayed, I., Boykov, Y.: Pseudo-bound optimization for binary energies. In: Fleet, D., Pajdla, T., Schiele, B., Tuytelaars, T. (eds.) ECCV 2014, Part V. LNCS, vol. 8693, pp. 691–707. Springer, Heidelberg (2014)
34. Tuysuzoglu, A., Karl, W., Stojanovic, I., Castanon, D., Unlu, M.: Graph-cut based discrete-valued image reconstruction. IEEE Trans. Image Process. **24**(5), 1614–1627 (2015)
35. Weber, S., Nagy, A., Schüle, T., Schnörr, C., Kuba, A.: A benchmark evaluation of large-scale optimization approaches to binary tomography. In: Kuba, A., Nyúl, L.G., Palágyi, K. (eds.) DGCI 2006. LNCS, vol. 4245, pp. 146–156. Springer, Heidelberg (2006)
36. Weber, S., Schnörr, C., Hornegger, J.: A linear programming relaxation for binary tomography with smoothness priors. Electron. Notes Discrete Math. **12**, 243–254 (2003)
37. Xiao, L., Johansson, M., Boyd, S.: Simultaneous routing and resource allocation via dual decomposition. IEEE Trans. Commun. **52**(7), 1136–1144 (2004)

An Improved Eikonal Method for Surface Normal Integration

Martin Bähr and Michael Breuß[(✉)]

Applied Mathematics Group, BTU Cottbus-Senftenberg,
Platz der Deutschen Einheit 1, 03046 Cottbus, Germany
{martin.baehr,breuss}@b-tu.de

Abstract. The integration of surface normals is a classic problem in computer vision. Recently, an approach to integration based on an equation of eikonal type has been proposed. A crucial component of this model is the data term in which the given data is complemented by a convex function describing a squared Euclidean distance. The resulting equation has been solved by a classic fast marching (FM) scheme. However, while that method is computationally efficient, the reconstruction error is considerable, especially in diagonal grid directions. In this paper, we present two improvements in order to deal with this problem. On the modeling side, we present a novel robust formulation of the data term. Moreover, we propose to use a semi-Lagrangian discretisation which improves the rotational invariance while it allows to keep the FM strategy. Our experiments confirm that our novel method gives a superior quality compared to the previous methods.

1 Introduction

The integration of surface normals is a fundamental task in computer vision. As an important classic example for the application of this technique let us mention the photometric stereo process introduced by Woodham [17]. There the normal field of the surface of a static object observed from one and the same camera position under different lighting conditions is retrieved. Then the computed normal field has to be integrated to obtain the unknown shape in terms of the depth map. To handle the crucial integration step, many different approaches and methods have been developed during the last decades. As examples for classic methods let us mention here the scheme of Frankot and Chellappa relying on the fast Fourier transform [5], the approach of Horn and Brooks based on a variational formulation [10] which has been explored in terms of its necessary optimality condition by Simchony et al. [15], and the more direct line-integration method of Wu and Li [18]. As examples for modern extensions of the variational method of Horn and Brooks let us mention here the methods of Durou and his co-workers [2,3] and the scheme of Harker and O'Leary [7].

However, while many methods have been proposed there is still a need for approaches that combine *accuracy*, *numerical robustness* and *efficiency*. In order to explore the potential of the highly efficient fast marching (FM) algorithm

© Springer International Publishing Switzerland 2015
J. Gall et al. (Eds.): GCPR 2015, LNCS 9358, pp. 274–284, 2015.
DOI: 10.1007/978-3-319-24947-6_22

for the purpose of surface normal integration, Ho *et al.* [9] formulated a suitable model in the format of an eikonal-type partial differential equation (PDE). Making use of the equivalent formulation of surface normals in terms of corresponding gradients of an unknown surface, a crucial part of this model complements the input gradient field by the gradient field of a convex function. We denote this part of the model of Ho *et al.* as the *data term* and the mentioned convex function as f.

However, while some promising results for synthetic, very smooth surfaces were presented in [9], also severe problems were reported that made the method difficult to apply. In the paper of Galliani *et al.* [6] some of the fundamental problems of the original scheme of Ho *et al.* were solved by introducing a well-engineered discrete formulation of the function f. This takes into account the hyperbolic nature of the underlying eikonal-type PDE. To summarise, the method of Galliani *et al.* is a computationally *efficient* FM scheme for the intended purpose. However, this scheme is still based on the original model of Ho *et al.* and relies on a conventional formulation of the FM scheme. The question arises if the complete approach could be improved with respect to *accuracy* and *numerical robustness* without compromising the efficiency of the approach.

Our Contributions. We improve upon the method of Galliani *et al.* in two ways. On the *modeling side* we propose to substitute the squared Euclidean distance chosen as the function f in [6,9] by the more robust absolute value function. The intuition behind our choice is to avoid numbers in different orders of magnitude that contribute in the data term when using the squared Euclidean distance, and we conjecture that in this way we may reduce numerical errors. In terms of the *numerical method* we propose to use a more sophisticated semi-Lagrangian FM discretisation [1,4] that is conceptually to a high degree rotationally invariant. By employing dedicated experiments we discuss the benefits of our novel method, especially we show that our method yields superior quality compared to the method of Galliani *et al.*

Paper Organisation. Section 2 gives a brief overview of previous FM based methods. In Sect. 3 we show in detail the impact of our improvements in model and numerics. A complementary experimental evaluation is given in Sect. 4. The paper ends with a conclusion.

2   The Previous Models

The problem of reconstruction is to recover a surface from a given normal field $n:=n(x,y)$. To this regard the surface can be represented as a depth map $v(x,y)$ over $(x,y) \in \Omega$ where Ω is the computational domain. A normal field n of a function v for every $(x,y) \in \Omega$ is given through

$$n(x,y) = \frac{(v_x, v_y, -1)^\top}{\sqrt{\|\nabla v\|^2 + 1}} \qquad \text{where} \qquad v_x = \frac{\partial v}{\partial x}, \; v_y = \frac{\partial v}{\partial y}. \tag{1}$$

Given the components n_x, n_y, n_z of a normal vector n, this can be made equivalent to the partial derivatives of v via

$$\begin{pmatrix} v_x \\ v_y \end{pmatrix} = \begin{pmatrix} -\frac{n_x}{n_z} \\ -\frac{n_y}{n_z} \end{pmatrix} =: \begin{pmatrix} p \\ q \end{pmatrix}. \qquad (2)$$

Setting $g(x,y) := (p(x,y), q(x,y))$, we obtain from (1) and (2) the equation

$$-\nabla v(x,y) = g(x,y) \qquad (3)$$

and taking the Euclidean norm of ∇v, Eq. (3) leads directly to the following eikonal-type equation:

$$\|\nabla v\| = \sqrt{p^2 + q^2} =: 1/F. \qquad (4)$$

The latter equation is a hyperbolic PDE. For PDEs of eikonal type, a solution can be computed efficiently by the FM scheme [8,13,14,16].

Let us briefly describe the FM strategy. In order to apply this method we need an initial point $v(x_0, y_0) = 0$. Starting from this the computed values of $v(x,y)$ describe the arrival time of a wavefront from the initial point to every point (x,y) in the computational domain. The known function $F(x,y)$ corresponds to the speed function of the expanding wavefront. The solution of FM describes the propagation of the wave in the order from the minimum of v to its maximum on the domain of interest. In our application, we will consider the centre point in our image domains as the starting point for the FM process.

The Method of Ho et al. In their work Ho *et al.* [9] suggest to solve the eikonal equation for a function w of the form

$$w := v + \lambda f \qquad (5)$$

with a parameter $\lambda > 0$ and a user-defined function f, so that the new function w has a known minimum in (x_0, y_0). To obtain v one has to solve the eikonal equation for w, where we note that ∇v and ∇f are known, and recover v from the computed w by subtracting the known function f.

Let us give some more details. In [9] it is proposed to use the squared Euclidean distance function

$$f := (x - x_0)^2 + (y - y_0)^2 \qquad (6)$$

around the point (x_0, y_0). To ease notation, let us locate the minimum of f at the centre of the domain $(x_0, y_0) = (0,0)$ and write

$$f = x^2 + y^2. \qquad (7)$$

Keeping in mind the analytic derivative of f, the gradient of (5) with respect to $n = (p,q)$ leads to

$$\nabla w = \begin{pmatrix} p + \lambda 2x \\ q + \lambda 2y \end{pmatrix}. \qquad (8)$$

With the help of the Euclidean norm we get the eikonal equation

$$\|\nabla w\| = \sqrt{(p + \lambda 2x)^2 + (q + \lambda 2y)^2} \qquad (9)$$

with the boundary condition $w(0,0) = 0$. After the computation of w we obtain the sought depth map via

$$v = w - \lambda f. \tag{10}$$

Let us emphasize that the proceeding of Ho *et al.* as above yields a highly unstable scheme, cf. the detailed discussion and evaluation in [6]. Therefore we refrain from showing numerical results of the corresponding method in this paper.

Improvements of Galliani et al. As elaborated in [6], the disadvantage of the previous method is its lack of stability caused by a too simple formulation of ∇f, leading to a high sensitivity with respect to the choice of λ. The problem is, that the analytic derivative used by Ho *et al.* for ∇f is identical to the central difference

$$f_x := \frac{f_{i+1,j} - f_{i-1,j}}{2\Delta x} \quad \text{(analogous for } f_y\text{)} \tag{11}$$

and for this the numerical scheme is not monotone. If one takes an upwind discretisation as proposed in [12] of f as

$$\nabla f = \begin{pmatrix} \left[\max\left(\frac{f_{i,j} - f_{i-1,j}}{\Delta x}, \frac{f_{i,j} - f_{i+1,j}}{\Delta x}, 0 \right) \right]^2 \\ \left[\max\left(\frac{f_{i,j} - f_{i,j-1}}{\Delta y}, \frac{f_{i,j} - f_{i,j+1}}{\Delta y}, 0 \right) \right]^2 \end{pmatrix} \tag{12}$$

instead of the analytic expression for ∇f, then the problem can be resolved.

Let us note that the upwind discretisation as employed in (12) makes use of the values aligned with the grid directions only. This type of discretisation is in the work of Galliani *et al.* also employed for resolving the solution v. This implies that one can expect a poor approximation of important solution features in case these are not aligned with the grid.

3   Our Improvements

The main design drawbacks one may infer from the described construction are twofold. First, as already commented, there may be a problem with resolving structures not aligned with the grid. Secondly, the use of the squared Euclidean distance for f implies that numerical inaccuracies of small size in numbers will be put together with rapidly increasing contributions by f. Therefore, the second objective of us will be to propose a better choice for the function f.

3.1   The Absolute Value Function

The approach of Ho *et al.* has two degrees of freedom, *(i)* the parameter λ and *(ii)* the choice of the function f. By the reformulation in [6], the choice of λ is not a true degree of freedom anymore since the resulting method is robust vs. the variation of λ. Therefore, we study the second degree of freedom and consider a possible function f so that w has only one minimum. We propose to change the previous model by employing instead of the Euclidean distance function

$$f := \| \cdot \|_1, \tag{13}$$

Fig. 1. The obstacle experiment: reconstruction of a white image with a black square for $\lambda = 100000$. **Left.** Original image, image size is 256×256. **Centre.** Second quadrant of computational domain, reconstruction by the method of Galliani *et al.* using the squared Euclidean distance function. **Right.** Reconstruction using the absolute value function instead.

i.e. in $2D$ for example $f = |x| + |y|$ is used. This choice is similar in style as the total variation norm often employed in image processing applications.

The Obstacle Experiment. In Fig. 1 we illustrate by a toy example the effect of our new model. The aim is to reconstruct a white image with a single black square located in diagonal direction from the centre. The left image in Fig. 1 shows the ground truth from which we computed an initial gradient field. The other two images in Fig. 1 shows the lower right quadrant of this domain together with the solutions obtained by the method of Galliani *et al.* and via our first improvement, respectively.

This toy experiment addresses a difficult problem for many surface normal integrators, namely the presence of a strong discontinuity as discussed in [2]. For the discussed methods, an important area is the region exactly behind the obstacle. Here the squared Euclidean distance function shows its biggest weakness, in contrast to the proposed L_1 data function. The benefit of the latter is quantified in Table 1, where the values of MSE and L_∞ are clearly lower.

The Sombrero Experiment. Our second experiment here is concerned the problem of rotational invariance, for which we consider the sombrero hat function as depicted in Fig. 2 over a grid of size 201×201. Let us note, that complementary to the previous experiment, the solution is here smooth.

In order to compare the error of computed solutions as depicted in Fig. 2 we employed in the figure the same error scaling for both error visualisations, so that one can see here the significant decrease in the error caused by our choice. Note also that we observe after our first improvement still a relatively high numerical inaccuracy along the grid diagonals. The impact of our model improvement is also confirmed quantitatively via Table 1.

3.2   Semi-Lagrangian Discretisation

We now tackle the inaccuracy by using the traditional FM discretisation along diagonal directions. To this end we propose to employ the semi-Lagrangian FM

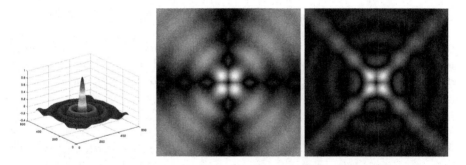

Fig. 2. The sombrero experiment: reconstruction of a rotationally invariant function for $\lambda = 1$. **Left.** Sombrero function, i.e. the ground truth. **Centre.** Visualisation of the absolute error of the scheme proposed in [6]. White represents a high error. **Right.** Visualisation of the error after our first improvement using the L_1 norm for f.

method (SL method) as described in [1,4]. While the SL method is a standard technique in numerics, it is probably not widely used in computer vision. Thus we now give a brief account of its principles.

The main idea behind the SL method relies on the relation between an eikonal-type equation and the minimum time problem of control theory, see e.g. [4] for a detailed exposition. The eikonal-type equation

$$F(\mathbf{x})\|\nabla w(\mathbf{x})\| = 1 \quad \mathbf{x} \in \mathbb{R}^2 \setminus \Omega_0 \tag{14}$$

$$w(\mathbf{x}) = 0 \quad \mathbf{x} \in \partial\Omega_0 \tag{15}$$

with $F(\mathbf{x}) > 0$, can be transformed by the *Kruzkov function*

$$k(\mathbf{x}) := 1 - e^{-w(\mathbf{x})} \tag{16}$$

to the following special Hamilton-Jacobi-Bellman equation of a minimum time problem

$$k(\mathbf{x}) + \max_{a \in B(0,1)} \{-F(\mathbf{x})a \cdot \nabla k(\mathbf{x})\} = 1 \quad \mathbf{x} \in \mathbb{R}^2 \setminus \Omega_0 \tag{17}$$

$$k(\mathbf{x}) = 0 \quad \mathbf{x} \in \partial\Omega_0. \tag{18}$$

Table 1. Comparison of MSE and L_∞ for (left) the reconstruction in our *obstacle experiment* with $\lambda = 100000$, and (right) for the *sombrero experiment* with $\lambda = 1$. L_∞ is defined as the maximum absolute error between the ground truth and the reconstruction.

f	$\|\cdot\|_2^2$	$\|\cdot\|_1$
MSE	205.80	18.28
L_∞	259.904	244.754

f	$\|\cdot\|_2^2$	$\|\cdot\|_1$
MSE	0.109	0.023
L_∞	0.707	0.689

Thereby, $a \in \mathbb{R}^2$ is the optimal control and it is determined in the closed unit ball $B(0,1)$ in $\mathbb{R}^2$. In order to vividly describe this we can say: we search the time t to reach the target $T = \Omega_0$ from a point $\mathbf{x}$ in the domain $\mathbb{R}^2 \setminus \Omega_0$. Furthermore the SL scheme for Hamilton-Jacobi equations on a grid G stems from a discrete version of the Dynamic Programming Principle. The corresponding formulation reads as

$$k(\mathbf{x}_i) = \min_{a \in B(0,1)} \{\beta_i k(\mathbf{x}_i - \tilde{h}a)\} + 1 - \beta_i \qquad \mathbf{x}_i \in G \setminus \Omega_0 \qquad (19)$$

$$k(\mathbf{x}_i) = 0 \qquad \mathbf{x}_i \in G \cap \partial\Omega_0, \qquad (20)$$

with $\beta_i = e^{-h_i}$, $h_i = \tilde{h}/F_i$ and $F(\mathbf{x}_i) = F_i$. To approximate the value of $k(\mathbf{x}_i - \tilde{h}a)$, we use linear interpolation. However, we search the minimum just on $\partial B(0,1)$ and therefore the optimisation problem is written in $2D$ in parametric form with

$$k((x_i, y_i) - \tilde{h}a) \qquad (21)$$

where $a = (\cos\theta, \sin\theta)$ and $\theta \in [0, \pi)$. This minimisation problem has low dimensional costs since we compute the values $k(\mathbf{x}_i - \tilde{h}a)$ through a linear interpolation by using just the three nearest grid nodes.

Employing then the idea behind the SL method is rather simple. One has to follow all steps of the classical FM except the computed values at the node $\mathbf{x}_i$. Here we use the SL scheme and this leads to the main difference. The interpolation of $k(\mathbf{x}_i - \tilde{h}a)$ needs eight nodes around $\mathbf{x}_i$ instead four nodes in the case of the traditional FM scheme. This corresponds to a larger stencil using values from all grid directions, which implies that the narrow band used in the FM technique must include the diagonal neighbors of $\mathbf{x}_i$.

Let us now discuss the resulting improvements at hand of the obstacle experiment and the sombrero experiment discussed in the previous paragraph. In Fig. 3 we display in an analogous fashion as in previous experiments the SL solutions. We may observe especially a much lower error behind the obstacle and a good resolution along any direction on the grid with no observable alignment as intended. These observations are confirmed again quantitatively, see Table 2.

Finally we combine both of our advantageous improvements into one method, the results of which we depict in Fig. 4 for our toy problems. In case of the obstacle problem the error is largely reduced when comparing with all the previous methods. However, we see that it is still located behind the obstacle from the perspective of the starting point of the integration. In the sombrero problem we observe now again a slight error of similar shape as present in Fig. 2, but it is reduced. Visually the plot of the error of our final method shows an state inbetween the behaviour of the schemes introduced in our two individual improvement steps. In Table 2 we also see that our novel scheme shows a significantly reduced error rate compared with the method of Galliani et al., cf. Table 1.

4   Further Experiments

Complementary to our toy model problems we now study the performance of our novel method for the reconstruction of surfaces of more complex synthetic data as well as for data from a real-world application.

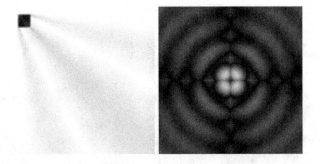

Fig. 3. Toy experiments with the SL method with Euclidean distance function. **Left.** Result for the obstacle experiment with SL method. **Right.** Visualisation of the error for the sombrero experiment.

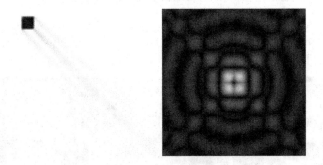

Fig. 4. Toy experiments with our novel method. **Left.** Obstacle experiment. **Right.** Visualisation of the error for the sombrero experiment.

The Visual Experiment. Our first experiment intends to show a visual comparison of the scheme of Galliani *et al.* and our new method. To this end we compute the derivatives in x- and y-direction of the well-known Lena test image (not shown here) using the Sobel operator; we employ the latter because of the higher order accuracy (compared to our methods) and good rotational invariance properties. The results of the reconstruction are presented in Fig. 5 and they confirm the qualitative results from our toy problems as we can observe in general a better quality in the reconstruction with our novel scheme. Let us

Table 2. Comparison of MSE and L_∞ for the reconstructions in the *obstacle experiment* and the *sombrero experiment* (left) with the SL method, and (right) for our final, novel scheme combining SL and L_1 data function.

	obstacle	sombrero		obstacle	sombrero
MSE	85.058	0.024	MSE	14.019	0.0131
L_∞	232.792	0.613	L_∞	223,724	0.611

Fig. 5. Artificial but difficult integration experiment. **Left.** Reconstruction of Lena with the method of Galliani *et al.*. **Right.** Result using our novel combing $L1$-norm for f and SL discretisation.

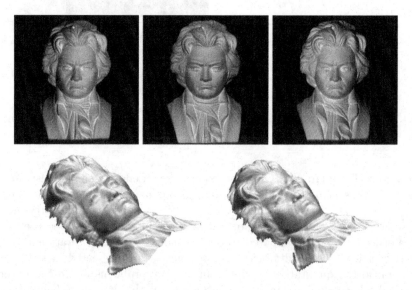

Fig. 6. Reconstruction of "Beethoven". **Top row: (a)–(c).** The three input images of Beethoven with different illumination conditions. Size of the input images is 256×256. **Bottom left: (d).** Reconstruction using the method of Galliani *et al.*. **Bottom right: (e).** Reconstruction by our novel method with $L1$-norm for f and SL discretisation.

note in this context of our construction criteria, that the Lena test image shows a mixture of smooth regions and discontinuous structures in all grid directions.

Application: Photometric Stereo with Real-World Test Images. Finally we present a computer vision application of our proposed method, namely the

Fig. 7. Reconstruction of "Beethoven" from a frontal perspective, ordered from left to right by (a)–(d). Reconstruction by the method from **(a)** [6] and **(b)** by our scheme, with the centre point as starting point for surface normal integration. **(c), (d).** Analogously, this time using a point at the forehead as initial point for integration.

photometric stereo (PS) reconstruction of the real-world data set *Beethoven* shown in Fig. 6 (*a*)–(*c*). In order to compute the normal field of the surface we employ the recent uncalibrated PS method of Queau *et al.* [11]. Again we compare here our method with the method from [6]. The solutions computed by both methods are visualised in Fig. 6(*d*), (*e*). One can observe that the reconstruction obtained via our method is smoother. The method of Galliani *et al.* introduces artefacts extending from strong features of the shape as e.g. noticeable at the alar wing of the nose.

Via a different, frontal perspective as depicted in Fig. 7(a), (b) we can confirm the latter result. However, let us note that even with our improved method there are still some artifacts left. Choosing a different starting point for integration of surface normals, see Fig. 7(c), (d), we especially note the high error introduced by the method of Galliani *et al.* at the nose of the Beethoven bust, as predicted by our obstacle experiment.

5   Conclusion

We have presented a significant improvement of the FM integrator for surface normals over previous work. We conjecture that our method can be used e.g. for computing initial states for more accurate iterative solvers. An interesting point in our model is that it yields better results than the method relying on the rotational invariant L_2 data function. This may be not completely intuitive. In a future work we plan to give a detailed evaluation of this issue.

References

1. Cristiani, E., Falcone, M.: Fast semi-Lagrangian schemes for the eikonal equation and applications. SIAM J. Numer. Anal. **45**(5), 1979–2011 (2007)
2. Durou, J.D., Aujol, J.F., Courteille, F.: Integrating the normal field of a surface in the presence of discontinuities. Energy Minimization Methods Comput. Vis. Pattern Recogn. **5681**, 261–273 (2009)

3. Durou, J.D., Courteille, F.: Integration of a normal field without boundary condition. In: Proceedings of the First International Workshop on Photometric Analysis for Computer Vision (2007)
4. Falcone, M., Ferretti, R.: Semi-Lagrangian Approximation Schemes for Linear and Hamilton–Jacobi Equations. Society for Industrial and Applied Mathematics (2011)
5. Frankot, R.T., Chellappa, R.: A method for enforcing integrability in shape from shading algorithms. IEEE Trans. Pattern Anal. Mach. Intell. **10**(4), 439–451 (1988)
6. Galliani, S., Breuß, M., Ju, Y.C.: Fast and robust surface normal integration by a discrete eikonal equation. In: Proceedings of British Machine Vision Conference, pp. 1–11 (2012)
7. Harker, M., O' Leary, P.: Least squares surface reconstruction from measured gradient fields. In: Proceedings of the IEEE Conference on Computer Vision and Pattern Recognition (2008)
8. Helmsen, J.J., Puckett, E.G., Colella, P., Dorr, M.: Two new methods for simulating photolithography development in 3d. Opt. Microlithography IX **2726**, 253–261 (1996)
9. Ho, J., Lim, J., Yang, M.H., Kriegman, D.: Integrating surface normal vectors using fast marching method. Proc. Eur. Conf. Comput. Vis. **3953**, 239–250 (2006)
10. Horn, B.K.P., Brooks, M.J.: The variational approach to shape from shading. Comput. Vis. Graphics Image Process. **33**(2), 174–208 (1986)
11. Queau, Y., Lauze, F., Durou, J.D.: Solving uncalibrated photometric stereo using total variation. J. Math. Imaging Vis. **52**(1), 87–107 (2015)
12. Rouy, E., Tourin, A.: A viscosity solutions approach to shape-from-shading. SIAM J. Numer. Anal. **29**(3), 867–884 (1992)
13. Sethian, J.A.: A fast marching level set method for monotonically advancing fronts. Proc. Natl. Acad. U.S.A. PNAS **93**(4), 1591–1595 (1996)
14. Sethian, J.A.: Level Set Methods and Fast Marching Methods, 2nd edn. Cambridge Press, Cambridge (1996)
15. Simchony, T., Chellappa, R., Shao, M.: Direct analytical methods for solving poisson equations in computer vision problem. IEEE Trans. Pattern Anal. Mach. Intell. **12**(5), 435–446 (1990)
16. Tsitsiklis, J.N.: Efficient algorithms for globally optimal trajectories. IEEE Trans. Autom. Control **40**(9), 1528–1538 (1995)
17. Woodham, R.J.: Photometric method for determining surface orientation from multiple images. Opt. Eng. **19**(1), 139–144 (1980)
18. Wu, Z., Li, L.: A line-integration based method for depth recovery from surface normals. Comput. Vis. Graphics Image Process. **43**(1), 53–66 (1988)

GraphFlow – 6D Large Displacement Scene Flow via Graph Matching

Hassan Abu Alhaija[1,2]($\boxtimes$), Anita Sellent[1,3], Daniel Kondermann[2],
and Carsten Rother[1]

[1] TU Dresden, Dresden, Germany
hassan.abu_alhaija@tu-dresden.de
[2] Heidelberg University, Heidelberg, Germany
[3] TU Darmstadt, Darmstadt, Germany

Abstract. We present an approach for computing dense scene flow from
two large displacement RGB-D images. When dealing with large displacements the crucial step is to estimate the overall motion correctly.
While state-of-the-art approaches focus on RGB information to establish guiding correspondences, we explore the power of depth edges. To
achieve this, we present a new graph matching technique that brings
sparse depth edges into correspondence. An additional contribution is
the formulation of a continuous-label energy which is used to densify the
sparse graph matching output. We present results on challenging Kinect
images, for which we outperform state-of-the-art techniques.

1 Introduction

In this work, we tackle a fundamental problem in computer vision – that is
to estimate a dense correspondence field between a pair of images. While for
some scenarios, e.g., small motion in a highly textured scene, this task is considered to be solved, there are still a number of outstanding challenges in the
general case. The particular challenge we are addressing in this work is when the
scene and/or the camera are subject to large movements. This occurs frequently
when objects move at high speed or humans perform articulated actions, such
as gesturing, walking or doing sport. Also, large displacements occur in time
lapse photography, e.g., when a camera surveils a building site or observes the
growth of a plant. Another scenario is when intermediate frames in a video
sequence have to be deleted and the task is to find a smooth transition between
the remaining frames. Unfortunately, large displacements violate the assumptions of most state-of-the-art scene flow estimation techniques, i.e. variational
approaches [14,17]. They achieve very high accuracy when the overall motion
is small. However, for large displacements the main problem is to estimate the
general motion of all objects correctly. The task of this work is to show how
this general motion can be recovered reliably. We here ask the specific question of computing dense 6D scene flow between a pair of RGB-D images with
independently moving and deforming objects. This means that for each pixel
we aim at recovering the 3D translation and 3D rotation, that matches a pixel

© Springer International Publishing Switzerland 2015
J. Gall et al. (Eds.): GCPR 2015, LNCS 9358, pp. 285–296, 2015.
DOI: 10.1007/978-3-319-24947-6_23

(and its local neighborhood) to the corresponding point in the other image. To compute dense flow for large displacements, many works have proposed to first find some sparse matches between the two frames and then, subsequently, utilize this information to estimate a dense flow field, e.g. [6,15,29]. Distinctive points can be matched using, e.g., SURF [3] or SIFT [19]. However, this assumes that the scene contains sufficiently textured surfaces and non-repetitive patterns. While man-made environments often violate those assumptions, they are highly suitable for using active depth cameras, e.g., active stereo or time-of-flight sensors [11]. These devices provide depth maps even for untextured surfaces. In our two stage scene flow approach, instead of using sparse texture matches only, we utilize depth edges extracted from the RGB-D images that describe object boundaries well. However, in the presence of large motion, they are actually not trivially described and matched. While exact edge description suffers from occlusion and distortion effects, more robust edge descriptors often lead to ambiguous matches. To disambiguate edge matches with robust descriptors, we use a structured matching approach in the form of graph matching that profits from non-local information to assign edge matches. The structure-preserving properties of an underlying loopy graph allows the strong and unique matches to guide the weak and ambiguous ones. While building the structure graph for a moving camera in a static scene is a relatively straight forward task, in this work we show how the depth information can be used to construct 3D graphs that respect independently moving objects in addition to camera motion. In the second stage, we show how dense scene flow can be obtained from graph matching by extending the recent SphereFlow method of Hornacek et al. [15]. For this we propose a new energy function that incorporates a left-right consistency check as well as standard smoothness and data terms. The energy is optimized with alpha expansion, and we demonstrate an improvement in performance with respect to SphereFlow. To summarize, the main contributions are

- A state-of-the-art method for large displacement scene flow from RGB-D image pairs.
- A new graph matching technique that exploits depth information.
- A new continuous-label energy for scene flow that jointly models a left-right consistency check, as well as spatial smoothness and local appearance.

2 Related Work

Since the introduction of scene flow by Vedula et al. [26] numerous approaches to scene flow estimation have been proposed. Many of them use multi-view video frames as input and employ the input images to compute depth structure and 3D motion, e.g. [16,21,28]. However, with recent depth cameras, RGB-D images have become readily available. Variational approaches to scene flow estimation from RGB-D images, e.g. [14,17], combine pixel-wise brightness and gradient constancy with depth velocity constraints, and additional regularization of the 3D motion, to obtain a global solution. Since they rely on iterative linearization or second order approximation, e.g. [9], variational approaches without appropriate initialization are restricted to small or moderately large motion even when iterative warping and coarse-to-fine schemes are used. In contrast, discrete scene flow approaches demonstrate good performance also for large motion. Hadfield and Bowden [12] estimate scene flow with a particle based formulation, and can deal also with large 3D motion. However, they assume constant velocity in a multi-frame image sequence. Hornacek et al. [15] and Wang et al. [29] use a PatchMatch based algorithm [2] with a local data term to generate 6D motion proposals between two frames. For large displacement motion, these approaches define currently the state-of-the-art. But they still fail in the absence of sufficiently textured surfaces, as we will show. In our approach we extend the model of [15] by a term for the left-right consistency check, which has been done before for, e.g., variational optical flow [1].

The information of landmark matching is currently exploited in a few scene flow approaches. Hornacek et al. [15] use sparse SURF feature matches in addition to random initialization; Quiroga et al. [20] match SURF features on each level of the image pyramid and encourage dense scene flow to behave accordingly. Similar approaches are known from the optical flow literature. For example, Brox and Malik [6] or Weinzaepfel et al. [30] use the strength of feature matches to support large displacement estimation while still using an image pyramid. Leordeanu et al. [18] and Revaud et al. [22] use semi-dense matches to replace the image pyramid. However, single feature matches are often too unreliable to be directly included into dense motion estimation. Sellent et al. [23] use additional images to improve feature matches, while Xu et al. [31] decide on each pyramid level anew, if and what feature matches are utilized. In our approach we use a graph matching strategy to improve the reliability of feature matches. Graph matching has a very wide field of applications in pattern recognition and machine vision, see [8,10]. It provides non-local information on landmarks by embedding them in a graph structure. In our approach we formulate the graph structure on depth edge features. In contrast to edge or line matching in RGB images [4,27] we can extract these features robustly. Additionally, we can use the depth channel to build the structure of the graph by avoiding to connect features across depth discontinuities. This is an advantage over, e.g., Zhang et al. [33] which cannot profit from depth information for graph construction.

3 Method

Our graph matching scene flow approach proceeds in two steps. In the first step, we determine depth edges in the two input RGB-D frames, construct the associated graphs, and then match them. In the second step, we use the sparse motion information obtained from the graph matching to assign dense, smooth and consistent 6D rigid body motion to each observed pixel in both frames.

3.1 Graph Matching

For $\Omega, \Omega' \subset \mathbb{R}^2$ let $I : \Omega \to \mathbb{R}^4$, $I' : \Omega' \to \mathbb{R}^4$ be two RGB-D images with depth and color channel I_d, I_c and 3D-to-2D mapping $\pi : \mathbb{R}^3 \to \Omega$. We pre-process the

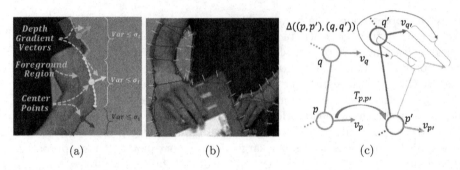

Fig. 1. Details of graph matching. (a) Our edge description segments are represented by their center point, average appearance descriptor that describe the foreground region and normalized depth gradient vector. In order to compute a description segment we accumulate neighboring edge pixels whose descriptor variance is lower than a threshold σ_t and whose count is between $r_{min} = 20$ and $r_{max} = 30$ pixels. (b) For graph matching, the description segments centers are connected to form a graph. In particular, each description segment center is connected to its $N = 3$ nearest neighbors with respect to the geodesic distance of the depth map to avoid connections across large depth changes. (c) Illustration of the geometry term $\Delta((p, p'), (q, q'))$ for graph matching, see Eq. (3) and text.

depth channel to fill-in the unknown depths via morphological operations and apply a median filter to suppress noise. We extract edges in the depth map with the Canny edge detector [7]. For each edge pixel we use the orientation of the depth gradient to determine the foreground region around this point. We use the SIFT descriptor with three different sizes $(8, 16, 32)$ [19] on the foreground region to describe the appearance of the edge point. As edges might change length and appearance between frames we do not use this pixel-wise description directly, but instead group edge pixels with similar appearance into *description segments*, see derivation in Fig. 1(a). Each description segment is represented by its center point which is the median of all its points, its normalized depth gradient vector and the mean of all its pixels' descriptors.

Based on these description segments we construct the graph structure. Let R and R' be the set of all descriptor segments centers in image I and I' respectively. For each element in R we create graph edges to its $N = 3$ nearest description segments, considering the geodesic distance of the depth map, see Fig. 1(b). Using the geodesic distance for graph edge construction we ensure that segments are not connected over depth discontinuities, which often coincide with object boundaries, hence motion boundaries. The set of all graph edges between description segments centers are represented by the graph edge sets E, E'. This gives the two graphs $G = (R, E)$ and $G' = (R', E')$ defined on image I and I' respectively. We denote by $A \subseteq R \times R'$ the set of all potential assignments between the two sets of description segment centers. A matching configuration between the two graphs is represented by the binary vector $\mathbf{x} \in \{0, 1\}^{|A|}$ where for each $a = (p, p') \in A$ the entry $x_a = 1$ means that p matches p'. Thereby each matching configuration must satisfy a uniqueness constraint where each description segment has at most one match. Our matching objective function is

$$E(x) = \lambda^{app} E^{app}(x) + \lambda^{geom} E^{geom}(x) + \lambda^{occ} E^{occ}(x) . \tag{1}$$

The energy consists of three terms, each weighted individually (here we use $\lambda^{app} = 300, \lambda^{geom} = 0.1, \lambda^{occ} = 50$).

The **appearance term** E^{app} is a unary term that measures similarity in appearance of matched descriptor segments. We use the Euclidean distance between the concatenated SIFT feature vectors and set

$$E^{app}(x) = \sum_{a=(p,p')\in A} ||desc(p) - desc(p')||_2 \, x_a \tag{2}$$

where $desc(p)$ is the average descriptor of the description segment of center p.

The **geometry term** E^{geom} is a pairwise term that defines the relationship between pairs of neighboring assignments, see Fig. 1(c). The tuples $a = (p, p')$ and $b = (q, q')$ are in a neighbor set N when either the edge $\vec{pq} \in E$ or $\vec{p'q'} \in E'$ exist. Let $T_{p,p'}$ be the 2D translation and rotation that maps $\vec{pv_p}$ to $\vec{p'v_{p'}}$, where $v_p = p + d_p$, $v_{p'} = p' + d_{p'}$ and $d_p, d_{p'}$ are the normalized depth gradient vectors at p, p' respectively. A geometry preserving matching should then map neighboring description segments to description segments that satisfy a similar transformation, i.e. $\Delta((p, p'), (q, q')) = ||T_{p,p'}(q) - q'||_2 + ||T_{p,p'}(v_q) - v_{q'}||_2$ should be small. Thus our geometry term

$$E_{geom}(x) = \sum_{(a,b)\in N} (\Delta(a, b) + \Delta(b, a)) \, x_a \, x_b \tag{3}$$

penalizes differences in length between the vectors $\vec{pq}$ and $\vec{p'q'}$ and inconsistency in their rotations. Meanwhile, arbitrary consistent rotations are allowed. Note that in [25] the pairwise term penalizes all rotations regardless of their consistency with neighbors, which had in our experiments a negative effect.

The **occlusion term** E^{occ} penalizes unmatched description segments by adding a negative value to the energy for each active assignment. In contrast to [25], which uses a constant value, we utilize a variable value that models the confidence of occlusion at an image location. Thereby a strong decrease in depth at an image location $I_d(p) \gg I'_d(p)$ is an indicator of occlusion with a closer object. Using the weights $w_I(p) = I_d(p) - \min(I_d(p), I'_d(p))$ and $w_{I'}(p) = I'_d(p) - \min(I_d(p), I'_d(p))$ normalized over the full image to the range $[0, 1]$, we set

$$E^{occ}(x) = \sum_{a=(p,p')\in A} - (1 - \frac{w_I(p) + w_{I'}(p')}{2}) \, x_a . \tag{4}$$

In general, finding the global minimum of the energy function Eq. (1) is an NP-hard problem. However, the *Dual Decomposition Graph Matching* developed by Torresani et al. [25] finds a good approximative solution that is in practice often close to the global optimum, see Sect. 4.

3.2   Scene Flow

The result of the graph matching step is a set of sparse matches of descriptor segments. We use this result to get a dense 6D flow field by optimizing a discrete-domain energy. Extending the work from [15], we want the 6D scene flow g: $\mathbb{R}^3 \to \mathbb{R}^3$ from I to I' and g' from I' to I to minimize the energy

$$E(g, g') = \sum_{p \in \Omega \cup \Omega'} D(g_p^*) + \sum_{(p,q) \in N_4} V(g_p^*, g_q^*) + \sum_{p \in \Omega, p' \in \Omega'} C(g_p, g_{p'}') \qquad (5)$$

where $g_p^* \in \{g_p, g_p'\}$. The data term is from [15]:

$$D(g_p) = \sum_{H \in S_p} w(p, \pi(H))(\|\nabla I_c(\pi(H)) - \nabla I_c'(\pi'(g_p(H)))\|_2^2$$
$$+ \alpha \|g_p(H) - NN_{I'}(g_p(H))\|_2^2), \qquad (6)$$

which measures RGB gradient constancy and geometric consistency of the scene flow g, for all 3D points H in a sphere S_p around the 3D back-projection of pixel p. Here ∇I_c is the image gradient, $\pi(H)$ is the projection of H onto image plane I, $NN_I(H)$ is the nearest neighbor of H in 3D back-projection of I, $\alpha > 0$ is a weighting constant and $w(p, p') = exp(-\|I(p) - I(p')\|_2/\gamma)$ is an adaptive support weighting [32]. The pairwise smoothness term

$$V(g_p, g_q) = \beta \|g_p(\bar{P}) - g_q(\bar{P})\|_2^2 \qquad (7)$$

is also similar to [15]. Weighted with $\beta > 0$, it enforces smoothness by applying the motion of pixels p and q in the 4-connected neighborhood N_4 to the middle point $\bar{P} = \frac{1}{2}(P+Q)$ of their 3D back-projections P, Q. Additionally, we introduce the term $C(g_p, g_{p'}')$ which enforces consistency between forward and backward scene flow by penalizing the deviation from the "starting point"

$$C(g_p, g_{p'}') = \begin{cases} \|p - \pi(g_{p'}'(g_p(P)))\|_2 & \text{if } p' = \pi'(g_p(P)) \\ 0 & \text{otherwise} \end{cases} . \qquad (8)$$

We minimize this energy in *three phases*. In the first phase, we obtain 6D rigid body motions for all sparse matches by mapping the corresponding 3D points and their surface normals into one-another such that the rotation is minimal [15]. Afterwards, pixels without an associated sparse match are assigned the 6D motion of their geodesically closest matched point with respect to the depth map. In the second phase, we use the PatchMatch variant of Hornacek et al. [15] to minimize the data term D only. The smoothness term V and consistency term C are in this phase only optimized implicitly by considering proposals from spatial neighbors and potential matches of the forward/backward scene flow, respectively. For the third phase, we cluster the 6D motions of the second phase that satisfy $C(g_p, g_{p'}') < \tau$ with $\tau = 1$ into $K = 50$ clusters using the K-means clustering of the corresponding Rodriguez representations. The clustered 6D motions from this step serve as scene flow proposals for a global minimization of the energy in Eq. (5) via alpha expansion [5]. Here each expansion

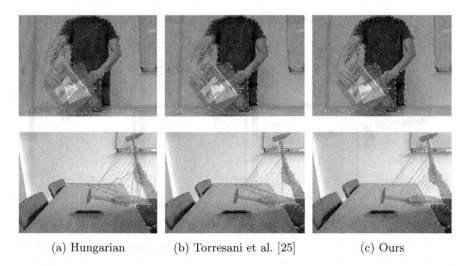

(a) Hungarian   (b) Torresani et al. [25]   (c) Ours

Fig. 2. Visual comparison of graph matching results. For illustration purpose both RGB images are super-imposed. Green means a correct match (or occlusion), blue is an almost correct match (definition in text) and red is a wrong match. Our result is clearly superior to the other techniques (Color figure online).

move runs QPBO [13], since the move-energy can be non-submodular. The alpha expansion is initialized with the motions from the second phase. Note, in contrast to [15] we optimize one global energy which includes consistency, smoothness, and appearance. This leads to considerably improved results, see Sect. 4.

4   Experiments

We recorded a dataset of seven RGB-D image pairs with the MS Kinect V1 camera.[1] Each image pair captures objects that undergo very large motion – see examples in Fig. 2. We present both quantitative results for graph matching, as well as qualitative evaluation of the final dense scene flow. In order to quantify the graph matching results, we use our algorithm to build description segments on image pairs. Then we generate ground truth matching by manually labeling each description segment in one image with its best corresponding description segment in the other image, or marking it as occlusion. Note that by construction, description segments centers in two images may not correspond exactly to the same physical 3D points. Therefore, we define *almost correct* matches to be those which are within the radius $r_{max} = 30$ of the correct description segments centers, see Fig. 1. Given ground truth matches, we can assign three class labels to each description segment matched by the graph matching algorithm: (a) correct match; (b) almost correct match and (c) wrong match. Exemplary results are shown in Fig. 2. A full quantitative evaluation is given in Table 1.

---

[1] Available on our web page
http://cvlab-dresden.de/research/image-matching/graphflow/.

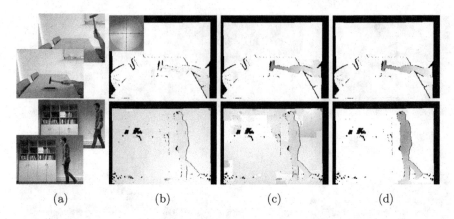

(a)   (b)   (c)   (d)

Fig. 3. Comparison to SphereFlow [15] for the sequence *Hammer* and *Walking*. Only the flow field of the left image is shown. (a) Original image pair. (b) Result of SphereFlow, where black pixels are unobserved depth values. For visualization, the magnitude of flow vectors is multiplied by 100. For these two sequences the result is an almost constant small motion everywhere. (c) Result of SphereFlow with graph matching points added to the pipeline of [15], before PatchMatch is applied. Only for the *Hammer* sequence gives better results, where the "pink-colored motion" on the hammer points towards the "up-right" direction (see flow color encoding). The *Walking* sequence is still degenerate (d) Our result. In both cases the motion estimation looks visually pleasing.

The percentages of correct matches are shown first, whereas the almost correct matches are denoted in brackets. We compare our graph matching with conventional nearest neighbor (SIFT) matching and Hungarian matching of the description segments that admits at most one-to-one matching [24]. Both methods do not exploit any graph structure and have a considerably lower performance. We also compare ours to the graph matching approach of Torresani et al. [25]. Both approaches use the same appearance term and optimization method, but different geometry and occlusion terms. In all but two cases our method outperforms the results of Torresani et al. [25] and a gain of up to 24.4 % can be observed in the *Tea* scene. Finally, we evaluated the impact of our weighted occlusion term by fixing it to a constant value, denoted by "Const. Occ.". For nearly all scenes variable occlusion weights result in better performance.

As our final aim is the computation of scene flow, we are not only interested whether matches are correct or wrong, but also in the Euclidean distance between wrong matches and correct ones. These distances are shown in Table 2. Our approach has the smallest average error distance of all methods.

To better understand the optimization process, we finally analyze the energy of the dual decomposition framework with respect to the computed lower bounds for each scene, see Table 2 right. In four cases we reach global optimality while in the other three cases the lower bound is relatively tight. Given those results on our dataset, we conclude that our model seems to be a close approximation to an optimal energy formulation.

Table 1. Quantitative evaluation of the graph matching results. The percentages of correct matches and almost correct matches (in brackets). Our algorithm consistently outperforms a naive approach as well as a comparable approach [25] by up to 24.4 % for the *Tea* sequence. Here "Const. Occ." means our full energy with a constant occlusion term. Best results are marked in bold.

Sequence	SIFT	Hungarian [24]	Torresani [25]	Const. Occ	Our
Board	63.3 (80.0)	70.0 (91.7)	70.0 (93.3)	**85.0 (95.0)**	**85.0 (95.0)**
Books	38.9 (64.3)	46.0 (71.4)	**59.5** (80.2)	55.6 **(83.3)**	**59.5 (83.3)**
Dinner	80.0 (89.5)	86.7 (93.3)	**88.6 (97.1)**	87.6 **(97.1)**	87.6 (96.2)
Hammer	34.6 (42.0)	51.9 (65.4)	59.3 (76.5)	65.4 (76.5)	**67.9 (81.5)**
Party	64.6 (86.5)	57.3 (81.3)	63.5 (88.5)	66.7 (90.6)	**67.7 (92.7)**
Tea	54.4 (90.0)	73.3 (85.6)	55.6 (88.9)	78.9 (91.1)	**80.0 (93.3)**
Walking	54.2 (72.9)	66.7 (81.3)	79.2 **(85.4)**	**83.3** (83.3)	**83.3** (83.3)

Table 2. Quantitative evaluation of the graph matching results and associated optimization problem. (Left) Average Euclidean distances of wrong matches as compared to ground truth. Overall, our matching results have equal or smaller error compared to all other methods. (Right) Lower and upper bound of the graph matching energy, where we reach in four out of seven cases global optimality.

Sequence	SIFT	Hungarian [24]	Torresani [25]	Const. Occ	Our	Lower	Upper
Board	17.32	11.00	7.32	**3.78**	**3.78**	−2262.7	−2262.7
Books	47.90	36.75	15.03	7.50	**6.93**	−4170.6	−4103.8
Dinner	16.52	9.72	3.71	2.26	**2.24**	−3602.5	−3602.5
Hammer	56.77	33.62	29.75	23.11	**21.81**	−2101.4	−2097.8
Party	12.33	20.39	9.49	6.92	**6.41**	−3631.0	−3629.9
Tea	11.79	9.56	9.05	4.12	**3.69**	−3126.9	−3126.9
Walking	21.01	15.89	8.15	**7.66**	**7.66**	−1625.8	−1625.8

Dense 6D Scene Flow. We evaluate our method for obtaining dense scene flow, from the graph matches, on the same RGB-D scenes as they contain large displacements and untextured regions. Datasets with similar challenging data and ground truth scene flow are not available. Therefore, we restrict ourselves to qualitative evaluation. Our dataset is publicly available for future comparisons. We compare to SphereFlow [15], which is the state-of-the-art for large displacement scene flow estimation, as shown in their work. While for our scenes the result of SphereFlow is often decent, we observed that it sometimes returns a degenerate result where all motions are close to zero[2] – see examples in Fig. 3. The reason for such degenerate results is two-fold: First, SphereFlow [15] relies on SURF matches that are only available in textured areas. While our graph matching provides good matches even in the absence of texture. Second, [15]

---

[2] Adjusting the weighting parameters of [15] did not improve the results.

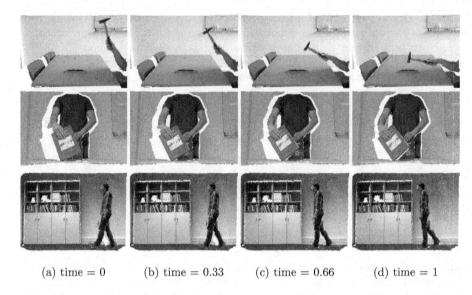

(a) time = 0   (b) time = 0.33   (c) time = 0.66   (d) time = 1

Fig. 4. Visualizing our results as a 3D point cloud from a slightly different viewpoint. (a–d) We warp the point clouds of the left and right images to generate intermediate images for different time points. Note that white pixels are due to missing depth measurements. We refer to our web page for a video.

does not optimize one energy but rather does a sequence of consistency checks before optimizing an energy with a smoothness term and a simplified data term. In contrast, we optimize an energy that includes a consistency term, which results in better and more stable solutions, see Fig. 3(d). Additional results can be found on our web page.

To further evaluate the accuracy of our method, we interpolate between the image pairs using the estimated scene flow and render intermediate frames from a slightly different viewpoint, see Fig. 4. The resulting interpolated videos are realistic and show smooth transition.

5   Conclusion and Future Work

We propose to use graph matching of depth edges to estimate sparse, large displacement motions between two RGB-D images. Combining this with a new continuous-label energy for dense 6D scene flow, we are able to achieve state-of-the-art results. In a next step we will add additional fine-tuning, e.g. gradient descent, on top of the discrete optimization. In a broader context, this work may inspire new directions for optical flow estimation from RGB images, since depth edges are the locations in the image which are most challenging for correspondence search, and at the same time often the most important locations when creating new visual effects.

References

1. Alvarez, L., Deriche, R., Papadopoulo, T., Sánchez, J.: Symmetrical dense optical flow estimation with occlusions detection. In: Heyden, A., Sparr, G., Nielsen, M., Johansen, P. (eds.) ECCV 2002, Part I. LNCS, vol. 2350, pp. 721–735. Springer, Heidelberg (2002)
2. Barnes, C., Shechtman, E., Finkelstein, A., Goldman, D.: PatchMatch: a randomized correspondence algorithm for structural image editing. TOG **28**(3), 24 (2009)
3. Bay, H., Tuytelaars, T., Van Gool, L.: SURF: speeded up robust features. In: Leonardis, A., Bischof, H., Pinz, A. (eds.) ECCV 2006, Part I. LNCS, vol. 3951, pp. 404–417. Springer, Heidelberg (2006)
4. Belongie, S., Malik, J., Puzicha, J.: Shape matching and object recognition using shape contexts. TPAMI **24**(4), 509–522 (2002)
5. Boykov, Y., Veksler, O., Zabih, R.: Fast approximate energy minimization via graph cuts. TPAMI **23**(11), 1222–1239 (2001)
6. Brox, T., Malik, J.: Large displacement optical flow: descriptor matching in variational motion estimation. TPAMI **33**(3), 500–513 (2011)
7. Canny, J.: A computational approach to edge detection. TPAMI **8**(6), 679–698 (1986)
8. Conte, D., Foggia, P., Sansone, C., Vento, M.: Thirty years of graph matching in pattern recognition. IJPRAI **18**(03), 265–298 (2004)
9. Ferstl, D., Riegler, G., Ruether, M., Bischof, H.: CP-Census: a novel model for dense variational scene flow from RGB-D data. In: Proceedings of BMVC (2014)
10. Foggia, P., Percannella, G., Vento, M.: Graph matching and learning in pattern recognition in the last 10 years. IJPRAI 28(01) (2014)
11. Grzegorzek, M., Theobalt, C., Koch, R., Kolb, A. (eds.): Time-of-Flight and Depth Imaging. LNCS, vol. 8200. Springer, Heidelberg (2013)
12. Hadfield, S., Bowden, R.: Scene particles: unregularized particle-based scene flow estimation. TPAMI **36**(3), 564–576 (2014)
13. Hammer, P., Hansen, P., Simeone, B.: Roof duality, complementation and persistency in quadratic 0–1 optimization. Math. Program. **28**(2), 121–155 (1984)
14. Herbst, E., Ren, X., Fox, D.: RGB-D flow: Dense 3-d motion estimation using color and depth. In: Proceedings of ICRA, pp. 2276–2282. IEEE (2013)
15. Hornácek, M., Fitzgibbon, A., Rother, C.: Sphereflow: 6 DoF scene flow from RGB-D pairs. In: Proceedings of CVPR. IEEE (2014)
16. Huguet, F., Devernay, F.: A variational method for scene flow estimation from stereo sequences. In: Proceedings of ICCV. IEEE (2007)
17. Jaimez, M., Souiai, M., Gonzalez-Jimenez, J., Cremers, D.: A primal-dual framework for real-time dense RGB-D scene flow. In: Proceedings of ICRA. IEEE (2015)
18. Leordeanu, M., Zanfir, A., Sminchisescu, C.: Locally affine sparse-to-dense matching for motion and occlusion estimation. In: Proceedings of ICCV. IEEE (2013)
19. Lowe, D.: Distinctive image features from scale-invariant keypoints. IJCV **60**(2), 91–100 (2004)
20. Quiroga, J., Devernay, F., Crowley, J.: Local/global scene flow estimation. In: Proceedings of ICIP. IEEE (2013)
21. Rabe, C., Müller, T., Wedel, A., Franke, U.: Dense, robust, and accurate motion field estimation from stereo image sequences in real-time. In: Daniilidis, K., Maragos, P., Paragios, N. (eds.) ECCV 2010, Part IV. LNCS, vol. 6314, pp. 582–595. Springer, Heidelberg (2010)

22. Revaud, J., Weinzaepfel, P., Harchaoui, Z., Schmid, C.: Epicflow: edge-preserving interpolation of correspondences for optical flow (2015). arXiv:1501.02565
23. Sellent, A., Ruhl, K., Magnor, M.: A loop-consistency measure for dense correspondences in multi-view video. Image Vis. Comput. **30**(9), 641–654 (2012)
24. Smith, D.K.: Network flows: theory, algorithms, and applications. J. Oper. Res. Soc. **45**(11), 1340–1340 (1994)
25. Torresani, L., Kolmogorov, V., Rother, C.: A dual decomposition approach to feature correspondence. TPAMI **35**(2), 259–271 (2013)
26. Vedula, S., Baker, S., Rander, P., Collins, R., Kanade, T.: Three-dimensional scene flow. In: Proceedings of ICCV, vol. 2, pp. 722–729. IEEE (1999)
27. Verhagen, B., Timofte, R., Van Gool, L.: Scale-invariant line descriptors for wide baseline matching. In: Proceedings of WACV. IEEE (2014)
28. Vogel, C., Schindler, K., Roth, S.: Piecewise rigid scene flow. In: Proceedings of ICCV. IEEE (2013)
29. Wang, Y., Zhang, J., Liu, Z., Wu, Q., Chou, P., Zhang, Z., Jia, Y.: Completed dense scene flow in RGB-D space. In: Jawahar, C.V., Shan, S. (eds.) ACCV 2014 Workshops. LNCS, vol. 9008, pp. 191–205. Springer, Heidelberg (2015)
30. Weinzaepfel, P., Revaud, J., Harchaoui, Z., Schmid, C.: Deepflow: large displacement optical flow with deep matching. In: Proceedings of ICCV. IEEE (2013)
31. Xu, L., Jia, J., Matsushita, Y.: Motion detail preserving optical flow estimation. TPAMI **34**(9), 1744–1757 (2012)
32. Yoon, K.J., Kweon, I.S.: Locally adaptive support-weight approach for visual correspondence search. In: IEEE Computer Society Conference on Computer Vision and Pattern Recognition. CVPR 2005, vol. 2, pp. 924–931. IEEE (2005)
33. Zhang, L., Koch, R.: An efficient and robust line segment matching approach based on LBD descriptor and pairwise geometric consistency. J. Vis. Commun. Image Represent. **24**(7), 794–805 (2013)

Fast Techniques for Monocular Visual Odometry

M. Hossein Mirabdollah[(✉)] and Bärbel Mertsching

GET Lab, University of Paderborn, Pohlwegstr 47-49, 33098 Paderborn, Germany
mirabdollah@get.upb.de

Abstract. In this paper, fast techniques are proposed to achieve real time and robust monocular visual odometry. We apply an iterative 5-point method to estimate instantaneous camera motion parameters in the context of a RANSAC algorithm to cope with outliers efficiently. In our method, landmarks are localized in space using a probabilistic triangulation method utilized to enhance the estimation of the last camera pose. The enhancement is performed by multiple observations of landmarks and minimization of a cost function consisting of epipolar geometry constraints for far landmarks and projective constraints for close landmarks. The performance of the proposed method is demonstrated through application to the challenging KITTI visual odometry dataset.

1 Introduction

Monocular visual odometry is known as a demanding problem in robotic and computer vision communities. The main challenge of a monocular odometry system is that feature depths are not measurable but rather they should be estimated. Unknown depths of features are mainly handled in literature based on two approaches. In the first approach, camera and feature positions are concurrently estimated in the context of extended Kalman filters. The methods belonging to this approach are mostly known as EKF-Monocular-SLAM methods (e.g. [3,9,16]). The main focus of this approach is how to parametrize large uncertainties of landmark positions in Gaussian forms in order to handle the problem in EKF filters. A good survey and comparison of these methods can be found in [15]. Among the EKF-based methods, the inverse depth parameterization (IDP) method [3] is known to be well established and has shown the best performance. However, it usually diverges if cameras move in depth. The reason is that this method localizes landmarks observed at low parallax angles very often behind cameras (negative depth problem). Additionally, complexity of the EKF based methods increases exponentially with respect to the number of landmarks, which makes them inappropriate for large scale robust visual odometry purposes. The second approach is based on bundle adjustment, in which a cost function between observed and predicted measurements (feature positions on the retina of a camera) at different camera poses is defined. Then the camera poses and feature positions are estimated by the minimization of the cost function. These methods require good initial guesses of camera poses. The initial guesses can be obtained from the epipolar geometry or based on the assumption

© Springer International Publishing Switzerland 2015
J. Gall et al. (Eds.): GCPR 2015, LNCS 9358, pp. 297–307, 2015.
DOI: 10.1007/978-3-319-24947-6_24

that the motion parameters of the camera do not change abruptly. Based on the epipolar geometry, a 3×3 matrix known as the essential matrix (for calibrated cameras) is estimated, which encodes camera motion. Essential matrices can be estimated using the 8-point [6], the 7-point [7] and the 5-point [13] methods.

In [19], the authors used bundle adjustment to minimize a cost function in which feature positions parametrized using IDP. This method is not real-time and may diverge if the camera moves in depth (due to the negative depth problem of the IDP). In [20], the 8-point method and a delayed parameterization technique known as the parallax angle parameterization are utilized to avoid the negative depth problem. This method essentially relies on the landmarks observed at high parallax angles. In [12], the authors used the perspective n point method (PnP) to estimate camera motion iteratively. The PnP method is mainly applicable if the positions of features in space are known (for instance from a stereo system). In case of a monocular system, it is assumed that the motion parameters do not change noticeably in consecutive frames; therefore, features can roughly be localized in space. Obviously, this method can only utilize features observed at high parallax angles and highly depends on the previous estimation of landmark positions. Hence, if the landmarks are not localized well in the previous steps, for instance due to measurement noise or small errors in the estimation of motion parameters, the method diverges. One common problem among the last three mentioned methods is that they cannot detect translation scale appropriately without using loop closure techniques. The reason is that visual features are hardly observed at high parallax angles in multiple frames. Consequently, the features cannot be used to detect scale drifts efficiently. Hence in the recent years, the scale detection problem has been approached in a different way. In case that a camera is installed on a wheeled vehicle and the height of the camera over the ground plane is known, absolute scale of camera motion can be determined. Geiger et al. in [5] used the 8-point method and the height of the camera over the ground plane to come up with the method known as libviso. Due to the usage of the 8-point method, libviso has a poor performance, especially in the estimation of rotation matrices. Additionally, in this method, they did not use any constraint to distinguish between the ground plane features from other features, resulting in large drifts in scale estimation. In [17,18], Song et al. developed multicore real time methods in which PnP is used to estimate motion parameters. Due to the usage of PnP, the methods produce large errors in case of bad localization of landmarks in previous steps. In another recent work proposed in [11], the 7-point method is modified to regularize roll and pitch angles of rotation matrices to enhance rotation estimations. This method is relatively time consuming and the rotation estimation is not as good as the PnP based methods.

In this paper, we propose a new visual odometry method which can handle far and close landmarks robustly. Our contribution to the monocular visual odometry is fourfold. First, using an iterative 5-point method to estimate initial guesses of motion parameters. Second, proposing a probabilistic triangulation method to obtain uncertainties of landmark positions. Third, robust tracking of low quality features on ground planes to estimate scale of camera motion. Fourth, enhancing the last camera pose by minimization of a cost function containing epipolar and projective constraints to handle far and close landmarks intuitively. In our method, only camera poses are iteratively estimated and landmark positions are estimated based on the probabilistic triangulation method. This technique allows us to leverage hundreds of features in the optimization process in real time.

The paper is organized as follows: in Sect. 2, the iterative 5-point method is discussed. The probabilistic triangulation method is presented in Sect. 3. In Sect. 4, our method to detect scale of camera motion is proposed. Leverage of multiple observations of features is discussed in Sect. 5. The proposed algorithm is evaluated in Sect. 6. Section 7 concludes this paper.

2   Inter Frame Camera Motion Estimation

A typical approach to estimate camera motion parameters between two frames is using epipolar geometry. For a calibrated camera, given a set of matched points $\{(x, y), (x', y')\}$, the following equation holds:

$$[x'\, y'\, 1]E[x\, y\, 1]^T = 0 \tag{1}$$

where E is known as the essential matrix. Assuming that a coordinate frame is attached to each camera pose, each point in space in the first camera frame such as $\mathbf{p} = [p_x,\ p_y,\ p_z]^T$ will have the coordinate of $\mathbf{p}' = [p'_x,\ p'_y,\ p'_z]^T$ in the second frame obtained as follows:

$$\mathbf{p}' = R(\mathbf{p} - \mathbf{t}) \tag{2}$$

where R is a rotation matrix encoding the rotation from the second frame to the first frame and $\mathbf{t} = [t_x,\ t_y,\ t_z]^T$ is the translation of the second frame with respect to the first frame. It can be shown that the essential matrix is related to R and $\mathbf{t}$ as follows:

$$E = \begin{bmatrix} e_1\ e_2\ e_3 \\ e_4\ e_5\ e_6 \\ e_7\ e_8\ e_9 \end{bmatrix} = RT \tag{3}$$

where $T = [\mathbf{t}]_\times$ is an antisymmetric matrix.

As Nister discussed in [13], the 5-point method is the best algebraic method to estimate essential matrices. The good performance of the 5-point method stems from two facts: first, it deals with degenerate cases efficiently; second, it uses the minimal number of points to estimate essential matrices, which makes the 5-point method more robust against outliers in the context of a RANSAC algorithm [4]. Unfortunately, the 5-point method is complex and demanding to apply it for real time purposes. In [8], an iterative 5-point method is proposed, which runs in real time. Nevertheless, in this method, the possibility of more solutions is not considered and it delivers only one solution. Additionally, in this work, translation vectors are parametrized using two independent angles. This parametrization produces more degree of nonlinearity and consequently more local minima in which the optimization process may get stuck. Here, we form a nonlinear equation system based on the Sampson distance [7] and two more constraints over the rotation and translation parameters. If we parametrize the rotation matrix with a quaternion $\mathbf{q} = [q_0, q_1, q_2, q_3]^T$, given five matched points such as $\{(x_i, y_i), (x'_i, y'_i)\}$, $i = 1 \ldots 5$, the equation system will be:

$$\frac{\mathbf{e}^T \mathbf{f}_1}{\sqrt{a_1^2 + b_1^2 + a_1'^2 + b_1'^2}} = 0$$

$$\vdots$$

$$\frac{\mathbf{e}^T \mathbf{f}_n}{\sqrt{a_5^2 + b_5^2 + a_5'^2 + b_5'^2}} = 0$$

$$q_0^2 + q_1^2 + q_2^2 + q_3^2 = 1$$

$$t_x^2 + t_y^2 + t_z^2 = 1 \tag{4}$$

where, $\mathbf{e} = [e_1, \ldots, e_9]^T$, $\mathbf{f}_i = [x'_i x_i, x'_i y_i, x'_i, y'_i x_i, y'_i y_i, y'_i, x_i, y_i, 1]^T$, $[a_i, b_i, c_i]^T = E[x_i, y_i, 1]^T$ and $[a'_i, b'_i, c'_i] = E^T[x'_i, y'_i, 1]^T$ (c and c' are not used in Eq. 4). The last two equations in Eq. 4 are due to the property of quaternions and the fact that the translation vector can only be estimated up to a scale factor. The above system of equations can be solved using the Gauss-Newton method. In iterative methods, initial guesses of parameters determine the converged solution. Thus, given five matched points, we obtain maximally up to 3 solutions based on the following initial guesses: $\mathbf{q} = [1, 0, 0, 0]^T$, $\mathbf{t} \in \{[1, 0, 0]^T, [0, 1, 0]^T, [0, 0, 1]^T\}$. Using the 5-point method in [13], we may obtain more solutions. However, in practical cases where rotations are not large, the other solutions are not either feasible or they are close to the solutions from the iterative method. Hence, the solutions are good enough to be used in the optimization process based on the multiple observations of landmarks.

3   Probabilistic Triangulation

We denote a camera pose at time t with respect to a global frame as $P_t = \{R_t, \mathbf{c}_t\}$, where R_t is a rotation matrix encoding the orientation of the camera and $\mathbf{c}_t$ shows the position of the camera in the global frame. If a landmark with the coordinate $\mathbf{p} = [p_x, p_y, p_z]^T$ is observed at two camera poses $P_k = \{R_k, \mathbf{c}_k\}$ and $P_t = \{R_t \ \mathbf{c}_t\}$ ($k < t$), at the points (x_k, y_k) and (x_t, y_t) on the retina of the camera, the landmark can be localized in space using triangulation. Our triangulation method is based on the fact that the point should lie on the lines drawn from the center of each camera pose in the directions of the observations. As a result, the following equations hold:

$$\mathbf{p} = \mathbf{c}_k + d_k \mathbf{v}_k \tag{5}$$

$$\mathbf{p} = \mathbf{c}_t + d_t \mathbf{v}_t \tag{6}$$

where $\mathbf{v}_k = R_k[x_k, y_k, 1]^T$ and $\mathbf{v}_t = R_t[x_t, y_t, 1]^T$. d_k and d_t are the depths of the landmark in the camera frames attached to each camera pose. Using the two equations, the following linear equation system is obtained:

$$[\mathbf{v}_k| - \mathbf{v}_t]\begin{bmatrix} d_k \\ d_t \end{bmatrix} = \mathbf{c}_t - \mathbf{c}_k = \mathbf{c}_{t,k} \tag{7}$$

By solving the above equation system, the depth of the landmark in the kth camera frame will be:

$$d_k = \frac{\nu}{\rho} = \frac{(\mathbf{v}_t^T\mathbf{v}_t\mathbf{v}_k^T - \mathbf{v}_k^T\mathbf{v}_t\mathbf{v}_t^T)\mathbf{c}_{t,k}}{\mathbf{v}_t^T\mathbf{v}_t\mathbf{v}_k^T\mathbf{v}_k - (\mathbf{v}_k^T\mathbf{v}_t)^2} \tag{8}$$

It can be shown that if there are measurement noise or errors in the estimation of rotation and translation parameters, ρ and ν will be joint Gaussian random variables: $[\rho, \nu]^T \sim \mathcal{N}([\bar{\rho}, \bar{\nu}]^T, \Sigma)$. As a result, d_k has the distribution of the ratio of two dependent Gaussian random variables. It can be shown that:

$$p(d_k|\rho) = \frac{1}{\sqrt{2\pi}\sigma_\nu} \frac{|\rho|}{d_k^2} \exp\left(-\frac{(\rho - \bar{\nu}d_k)^2}{2\sigma_\nu^2 d_k^2}\right) \tag{9}$$

where σ_ν^2 is the variance of ν obtained from the marginalization of ρ from the joint distribution of ρ and ν. The goal of probabilistic triangulation is to find a confidence range for d_k such as $[d_k^{min}, d_k^{max}]$ at each new observation of the landmark. To this end, we use Eq. 9 for $\rho = \bar{\rho} - 2\sigma_\rho$ and $\rho = \bar{\rho} + 2\sigma_\rho$ and find two positive d_k at which the probability of $p(d_k|\rho)$ is equal to a small ratio of the maximum pick of the distribution. In Fig. 1, the two distributions for $\rho = 1$, $\sigma_\rho = 0.1$, $\nu = 0.1$ and $\sigma_\nu = 0.1$ are depicted.

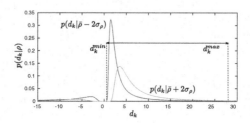

Fig. 1. Distribution of the depth parameter based on the probabilistic triangulation method.

It can be verified that the depth distribution tends to a Gaussian distribution in high parallax angles. In Eq. 8, the parallax angle is the angle between $\mathbf{v}_t$ and $\mathbf{v}_k$ ($\alpha = acos(\frac{\mathbf{v}_t^T\mathbf{v}_k}{|\mathbf{v}_t||\mathbf{v}_k|})$). We trim the range $[d_k^{min}, d_k^{max}]$ based on the new observations of the landmark such that $|d_k^{max} - d_k^{min}|$ reduces or stays the same. In another word, the uncertainty of a landmark position does not increase (in analogy to Bayesian filters) as the landmarks are assumed stationary.

4   Scale Detection

In case that a camera is installed on a wheeled vehicle parallelly to the ground plane, scale of translations can be obtained by using the height of the camera over the ground plane as a known parameter. Given R and $\mathbf{t}$ ($\|\mathbf{t}\| = 1$) for two consecutive frames and the matched points $\{(x, y), (x', y')\}$, we use triangulation to localize the corresponding 3D point in the first camera frame as follows:

$$\mathbf{p} = d_1 \mathbf{v}_1 \tag{10}$$

where d_1 is the depth of the point in the first camera frame and $\mathbf{v}_1 = [x, y, 1]^T$. It can be shown that d_1 is linearly proportional to the scale factor: $d_1 = \eta s$. Thus, given the known height of the camera h, we have: $s = \frac{h}{y\eta}$.

To utilize the above mentioned method, it is required to track features on typically highly homogeneous ground planes. In this regard, we extract features at different resolutions from a rectangular region of interest in the half bottom of both images. Then for each feature in the first frame, we find two matches in the second frame based on the feature descriptor used in libviso [5]. An important criterion by which many of wrong matches can be filtered is the distances of the matched features to their corresponding epipolar lines. Using all of the matches, different scale factors are calculated and then by applying a median filter, the most probable scale factor is found. This method is fast and much more accurate than the the method used in libviso.

5   Multiple Observations of Landmarks

To deal with degenerate cases and also uncertainties of scale factors, multiple observations of landmarks should be leveraged. Hence, we optimize the current camera pose P_t based on the multiple observations of landmarks. To this end, we use two types of constraints: the epipolar constraint for landmarks observed at low parallax angles as their uncertainties are far from Gaussian distributions and the projective constraint for landmarks observed at high parallax angles. For a landmark observed for the first time at the camera pose $P_k = \{R_k, \mathbf{c}_k\}$ with the coordinate (x_k, y_k), the Sampson distance is defined as follows:

$$S_e = \frac{\mathbf{e}_{t,k}^T \mathbf{f}_{t,k}}{\sqrt{a^2 + b^2 + a'^2 + b'^2}} = 0 \tag{11}$$

where $\mathbf{e}_{t,k} = vect(R_{t,k}T_{t,k})$, $R_{t,k} = R_t^T R_k$, $T_{t,k} = [\mathbf{c}_t - \mathbf{c}_k]_\times$, $[a, b, c]^T = R_{t,k}T_{t,k}[x_k, y_k, 1]^T$, $[a', b', c']^T = T_{t,k}^T R_{t,k}^T [x_t, y_t, 1]^T$ and $\mathbf{f}_{t,k} = [x_t x_k, x_t y_k, x_t, y_t x_k, y_t y_k, y_t, x_k, y_k, 1]^T$.

In case of close landmarks, we can use the projective constraint:

$$(\mathbf{x}_t - \hat{\mathbf{x}}_t)^T M^{-1} (\mathbf{x}_t - \hat{\mathbf{x}}_t) = 0 \tag{12}$$

where $\mathbf{x}_t = [x_t, y_t]^T$ is the vector of the real measurement, $\hat{\mathbf{x}}_t = [\hat{x}_t, \hat{y}_t]^T$ is the vector of predicted measurement and M is a covariance matrix encoding the uncertainty of the measurement. $\hat{x}_t$ and $\hat{y}_t$ are calculated as follows:

$$\hat{x}_t = \frac{\{R_t^T(\mathbf{c}_k + d_k R_k[x_k, y_k, 1]^T)\}_1}{\{R_t^T(\mathbf{c}_k + d_k R_k[x_k, y_k, 1]^T)\}_3}$$

$$\hat{y}_t = \frac{\{R_t^T(\mathbf{c}_k + d_k R_k[x_k, y_k, 1]^T)\}_2}{\{R_t^T(\mathbf{c}_k + d_k R_k[x_k, y_k, 1]^T)\}_3} \qquad (13)$$

where $\{\}_i$ is the ith element of a vector. In Eq. 12, M is calculated at each frame based on the uncertainty of the depth of the landmark. Hence to calculate M, we insert three samples: d_k, d_k^{min} and d_k^{max} in Eq. 13 and obtain three samples for the predicted measurement. Finally, based on the three samples, M is calculated. Now we can form a cost function which contains Sampson distances, projective constraints and a regularization constraint as follows:

$$C = \sum_{i=1}^{n_1} S_{e,i}^2 + \sum_{i=1}^{n_2} (\hat{\mathbf{x}}_{i,t} - \mathbf{x}_{i,t})^T M_i^{-1}(\hat{\mathbf{x}}_{i,t} - \mathbf{x}_{i,t}) + (\mathbf{y}_t - \hat{\mathbf{y}}_t)^T N^{-1}(\mathbf{y}_t - \hat{\mathbf{y}}_t)$$

$$(14)$$

where, n_1 and n_2 are the number of landmarks observed at low and high parallax angles respectively. $\mathbf{y}_t = [c_{x,t}, c_{y,t}, c_{z,t}, q_{0,t}, q_{1,t}, q_{2,t}, q_{3,t}]^T$ is a vector containing the parameters of the last camera pose. $\hat{\mathbf{y}}_t$ is the initial guess of the camera pose which is calculated based on the following motion model:

$$\mathbf{c}_t = \mathbf{c}_{t-1} + R_{t-1}(\mathbf{q}_{t-1})st$$

$$R_t(\mathbf{q}_t) = R_{t-1}(\mathbf{q}_{t-1})R^T \qquad (15)$$

where R and $\mathbf{t}$ are obtained from the inter frame camera motion estimation and s comes from the scale detection module. In Eq. 14, N is a covariance matrix obtained by the linearization of the motion model and error propagation through the linear model. In this regard, we consider some uncertainties for the instantaneous motion parameters. Experimentally, we found that the variance 0.0001 for the quaternion and translation elements works well. Additionally, the standard deviation of s is calculated dynamically based on the difference of two consecutive scale factors. The last term in the cost function is essential as the cost function could have several minima and the term regularizes the optimization process to converge to a state near to the initial guess (in the sense of Mahalanobis distances). The covariance matrix is also fed to the triangulation part, based on which the probabilistic triangulation is conducted. It should be mentioned that at each step the uncertainty of the previous camera pose is set to zero as we only use N as a regularization term in a smoothing scheme not a filtering scheme. In another word, we establish an intuitive relation between the unknown parameters and predefine the ranges of changes for each parameter in the optimization process. The overall method can be summarized as follows:

1. Given the last two images, calculate inter frame motion: R and $\mathbf{t}$.
2. Estimate scale of translation: s.
3. Predict the last camera pose and the covariance matrix N.
4. Minimize the cost function in Eq. 14. Use the Sampson distance for a land-mark if $d_k^{max} - d_k^{min} > \Delta d_{threshold}$, otherwise use the projective constraint.
5. Run probabilistic triangulation.

6   Experimental Results

We implemented the proposed method in C++ and used the KITTI visual odom-etry dataset for the evaluation. Concerning feature tracking, Shi-Thomasi cor-ner features [14] with the minimum quality of 0.01 were extracted and tracked using the Lucas-Kanade optical flow method (LK) [10]. Both of the algorithms are implemented in OpenCV [2]. The minimum distance between features was 30 pixels and the maximum number of features was 300. For the estimation of motion parameters between two frames, the iterative 5-point method discussed in Sect. 2 was used. The parameters were updated in fixed number of 5 iterations. The features were tracked maximally within 10 frames and $\Delta d_{threshold} = 15$. Based on multiple observations of features, the cost function in Eq. 14 was opti-mized with 5 iterations. With this setup, we achieved a real time performance (10 Hz) on a PC with an Intel Xeon E31270 @ 3.40GHz CPU without using any parallelism technique. For the evaluation, two measures are used: translation and rotation errors. Given the real position of a camera at time t as $\mathbf{c}_t$ and the estimated camera position as $\hat{\mathbf{c}}_t$, the average translation error is calculated as follows:

$$\epsilon_{\mathbf{c}} = \frac{1}{N_f} \sum_{t=0}^{N_f-1} \|\mathbf{c}_t - \hat{\mathbf{c}}_t\| \tag{16}$$

where N_f is the number of frames. The average rotation error is defined as:

$$\epsilon_R = \frac{180}{\pi N_f} \sum_{t=0}^{N_f-1} \left| acos \left(\frac{trace(R_t^e) - 1}{2} \right) \right| \tag{17}$$

where $R_t^e = R_t^T \hat{R}_t$. We compared our method based on the multiple observa-tions (MO) and only two view optimization using our iterative 5-point method (TVO) with libviso (LV) [5], the iterative method in [8] (I5p) and a visual odom-etry method based on the normalized 8-point method [6] and the LK tracker (8pLK). In Table 1, the translation and rotation errors for some of the chal-lenging training sequences of the KITTI dataset and also the average errors for all 11 sequences are presented. Interestingly, we see that only applying our iterative 5-point method (TVO) yields dramatically better estimations in com-parison to the other two view based methods. In average, I5p has the poorest performance as it neglects possibility of multiple solutions and also gets stuck in local minima due to the way it parametrizes the essential matrix. Especially, it performs poorly for sequences where the car often drives through sharp bends (due to the occurrence of degenerate cases). Interestingly, 8pLK performs better than libviso, which signifies superiority of LK tracker over the feature matching technique used in libviso as LK provides sub-pixel accuracies resulting in less measurement noise. As expected, the multiple view observation technique enhances the results from TVO, especially for the sequences where the ratio of outliers is high or the number of observed features at high parallax angles is low (for instance sequence 1). In Fig. 2, the estimated paths for the sequence 1 using MO, TVO and LV are visualized. In this sequence, the car drives in an autobahn and the number of landmarks observed at high parallax angles is low. As can be seen, TVO has a poor performance when estimating the elevation of the camera (originated from the error in the estimation of roll and pitch angles); whereas MO is able to estimate the path well.

Table 1. Average of translation and rotation errors using different methods for the training sequences of KITTI dataset.

Seq.	N_f	Method	MO	TVO	8pLK	LV	I5p	MO	TVO	8pLK	LV	I5p
		Length [m]	ϵ_c [m]					ϵ_R [deg]				
0	4541	3723.6	**10.4**	29.6	65.5	283.2	129.2	**1.4**	2.1	32.4	43.2	37.7
1	1101	2453.1	**97.9**	171.7	495.7	867.0	312.7	**4.7**	7.1	49.1	50.15	13.3
2	4661	5067.0	**32.3**	39.9	63.9	229.5	491.9	**1.2**	1.5	5.8	17.6	39.1
7	1101	694.7	**25.7**	89.6	123.3	115.1	99.3	**2.6**	3.7	4.3	40.9	22.1
Avg.	2109.2	2016.1	**21.3**	38.6	83.2	224.0	233.1	**1.9**	2.8	8.7	22.9	31.8

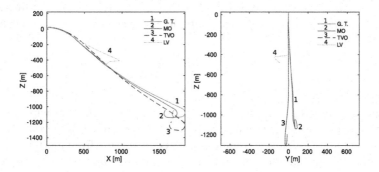

Fig. 2. Ground truth (G. T.) and estimated paths using different methods for the sequence 1 of the KITTI dataset.

We also submitted our results for the test sequences to the KITTI website under the name of FTMVO [1]. In the KITTI website, the methods are evaluated based on the percentage of errors until 800 meters with the step of 100 meters. In Table 2, the average of translation and rotation errors for our method and two recent methods of state-of-the-art are presented. As can be seen, our method outperforms the two methods MLM-SFM [17] and RCMPE+GP [11]. In [1], it can be seen that our method also outperforms many of the stereo vision based

Table 2. Average of translation and rotation errors for the test sequences of KITTI dataset: our method (FTMVO), MLM-SFM (M. 1) and RCMPE+GP (M. 2).

Method	FTMVO	M. 1	M. 2	Method	FTMVO	M. 1	M. 2
Tr. error [%]	2.24	2.54	2.55	Rot. error [deg/m]	0.049	0.057	0.087

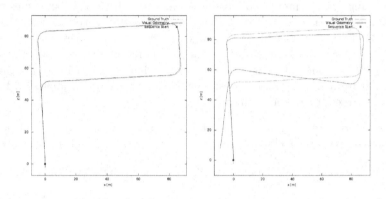

Fig. 3. Estimated (blue) and ground truth (red) paths for test sequence 14 based on our method (left) and MLM-SFM (right) (Colour figure online).

methods. From the test sequences, the $X - Z$ path of the first five sequences are visualized in the KITTI website. In Fig. 3, the estimated paths using our method and MLM-SFM for the sequence 14 are shown. The poor performance of MLM-SFM for this sequence lies in using the PnP method which degrades the estimations if the landmarks are badly localized in the previous frames. This situation occurs often if the camera experiences relatively large rotations and small translations.

7   Conclusion

An intuitive monocular visual odometry method is proposed, in which far and close landmarks are robustly handled. Through the proposed probabilistic triangulation technique, unlike the common SLAM or structure from motion methods, we can run the optimization process only on the last camera pose and exclude the localization of landmarks from the optimization process. Such an approach results in speeding up the algorithm to a great extent and also robustness of the algorithm against outliers. The performance of the method is demonstrated based on the large and demanding KITTI dataset for visual odometry.

References

1. Kitti visual odometry data set. http://www.cvlibs.net/datasets/kitti/eval_odometry.php
2. Bradski, G.: OpenCv library. Dr. Dobb's J. Softw. Tools **25**(11), 120–126 (2000)

3. Civera, J., Davison, A., Montiel, J.: Inverse depth parametrization for monocular SLAM. IEEE Trans. Robot. **24**(5), 932–945 (2008)
4. Fischler, M., Bolles, R.: Random sample consensus: a paradigm for model fitting with applications to image analysis and automated cartography. Commun. ACM **24**(6), 381–395 (1981)
5. Geiger, A., Ziegler, J., Stiller, C.: StereoScan: Dense 3d reconstruction in real-time. In: Proceeding of Intelligent Vehicles Symposium (2011)
6. Hartley, R.: In defense of the eight-point algorithm. IEEE Trans. Pattern Anal. Mach. Intell. **19**(6), 580–593 (1997)
7. Hartley, R., Zisserman, A.: Multiple View Geometry in Computer Vision, 2nd edn. Cambridge University Press, Cambridge (2004). (ISBN: 0521540518)
8. Hedborg, B., Felsberg, M.: Fast iterative five point relative pose estimation. In: Proceeding of IEEE Workshop on Robot Vision, pp. 60–67 (2013)
9. Kwok, N.M., Dissanayake, G., Ha, Q.: Bearing-only slam using a SPRT based Gaussian sum filter. In: Proceedings of IEEE International Conference on Robotics and Automation, pp. 1109–1114 (2006)
10. Lucas, B., Kanade, T.: An iterative image registration technique with an application to stereo vision. In: Proceedings of International Joint Conference on Artificial Intelligence, pp. 674–679 (1981)
11. Mirabdollah, M.H., Mertsching, B.: On the second order statistics of essential matrix elements. In: Jiang, X., Hornegger, J., Koch, R. (eds.) GCPR 2014. LNCS, vol. 8753, pp. 547–557. Springer, Heidelberg (2014)
12. Mur-Artal, R., Tardos, J.: ORB-SLAM: tracking and mapping recognizable features. In: Proceeding of Robotics: Science and Systems (RSS) Workshop on Multi View Geometry in Robotics (2014)
13. Nistér, D.: An Efficient solution to the five-point relative pose problem. IEEE Trans. Pattern Anal. Mach. Intell. **26**(6), 756–777 (2004)
14. Shi, J., Tomasi, C.: Good features to track. Technical report (1993)
15. Solà, J., Vidal-Calleja, T., Civera, J., Montiel, L.M.: Impact of landmark parametrization on monocular EKF-SLAM with points and lines. Int. J. Comput. Vis. **97**(3), 339–368 (2012)
16. Sola, J., Monin, A., Devy, M., Lemaire, T.: Undelayed initialization in bearing-only SLAM. In: Proceedings IEEE International Conference on Intelligent Robots and Systems, pp. 2499–2504 (2005)
17. Song, S., Chandraker, M.: Robust scale estimation in real-time monocular SFM for autonomous driving. In: Proceeding of Computer Vision and Pattern Recognition (2014)
18. Song, S., Chandraker, M., Guest, C.: Parallel, real-time monocular visual odometry. In: Proceeding of IEEE International Conference on Robotics and Automation, pp. 4698–4705 (2013)
19. Strasdat, H., Montiel, J.M.M., Davison, A.: Scale drift-aware large scale monocular SLAM. In: Proceedings of Robotics: Science and Systems (2010)
20. Zhao, L., Huang, S., Yan, L., Dissanayake, G.: Parallax angle parametrization for monocular SLAM. In: Proceeding of IEEE International Conference on Robotics and Automation, pp. 3117–3124 (2011)

Iterative Automated Foreground Segmentation in Video Sequences Using Graph Cuts

Tomislav Hrkać[✉] and Karla Brkić

Faculty of Electrical Engineering and Computing, University of Zagreb,
Unska 3, HR-10000 Zagreb, Croatia
tomislav.hrkac@fer.hr

Abstract. In this paper we propose a method for foreground object segmentation in videos using an improved version of the GrabCut algorithm. Motivated by applications in de-identification, we consider a static camera scenario and take into account common problems with the original algorithm that can result in poor segmentation. Our improvements are as follows: (i) using background subtraction, we build GMM-based segmentation priors; (ii) in building foreground and background GMMs, the contributions of pixels are weighted depending on their distance from the boundary of the object prior; (iii) probabilities of pixels belonging to foreground or background are modified by taking into account the prior pixel classification as well as its estimated confidence; and (iv) the smoothness term of GrabCut is modified by discouraging boundaries further away from the object prior. We perform experiments on CDnet 2014 Pedestrian Dataset and show considerable improvements over a reference implementation of GrabCut.

1 Introduction

Video surveillance has become common in public spaces such as airports, subway stations, banks, shopping centres etc. Although valuable in terms of crime prevention, video surveillance raises privacy concerns when the person being filmed is not involved in any sort of illegal activity. We consider the problem of object detection and segmentation in videos, constrained with the target application of pedestrian de-identification in video surveillance data, i.e. reversibly obfuscating the identity of the person in the video to make the person unrecognizable to human observers. Finely segmenting the pedestrians instead of just considering pedestrian bounding boxes is necessary to preserve the naturalness of the scene and enable building de-identified representations such as e.g. stick figures or rendered 3D models of humans.

Given the target application, our goals and assumptions are as follows: (i) we are considering a static camera, (ii) the motion in the scene is mainly due

This work has been supported by the Croatian Science Foundation, within the project "De-identification Methods for Soft and Non-Biometric Identifiers" (DeMSI, UIP-11-2013-1544), and by the COST Action IC1206 "De-Identification for Privacy Protection in Multimedia Content". This support is gratefully acknowledged.

© Springer International Publishing Switzerland 2015
J. Gall et al. (Eds.): GCPR 2015, LNCS 9358, pp. 308–319, 2015.
DOI: 10.1007/978-3-319-24947-6_25

to pedestrians, and (iii) we wish to achieve as precise per-pixel segmentation of humans as possible. Due to the introduced constraints, we assume that background subtraction can be used to obtain a prior on pedestrian locations. We propose a method based on graph cuts that builds on GrabCut [19], addressing common problems with the original algorithm that can result in poor segmentation in certain cases, e.g. when parts of the object share characteristics with parts of the background, when high contrast color changes are present in the background near the object, or when the objects are concave. We build object priors using a GMM-based background subtraction algorithm [27] and use them as input for an improved version of GrabCut. We start with an assumption that foreground/background priors can be reliably obtained using background subtraction. In building the GrabCut Gaussian mixture model, we introduce weighting each pixel depending on its distance from the boundary of the object prior. When determining whether a pixel belongs to foreground or background, we take into account the prior pixel classification along with its estimated confidence. Finally, we modify the smoothness term of GrabCut to discourage boundaries further away from the object prior.

2   Related Work

A number of methods for pedestrian detection have been proposed in recent years. Examples include the well-known HOG detector [7] (histograms of oriented gradients), extensions [24] of the boosted cascade of Haar-like features of Viola and Jones [23], deformable part models [10], multi-cue iterative algorithms [15], integral channel features [8] and their extensions [2], approaches based on convolutional neural networks [16,17,20], etc.

In spite of the progress in recent years, several review papers point out that pedestrian detection is a hard problem [2,8,9]. As our target application area is de-identification of pedestrians in videos, and the primary focus of this paper is correct pedestrian segmentation, we simplify the pedestrian detection problem by assuming a surveillance scenario with a static camera and employing background subtraction to determine possible pedestrian locations. In the future, we plan to factor in a dedicated detector that would be combined with the output of background subtraction, as in e.g. the work of Harville [11].

The basic idea of background subtraction is simple: a background model is built using frames of the video, and to determine foreground pixels in a frame the background model is subtracted from that frame [5,6,13]. Given that experimental evidence [13] supports the notion that Gaussian mixture-based algorithms [21,26,27] are among the top-performing background subtraction techniques, we employ the improved adaptive Gaussian mixture model of Zivkovic [27] to detect possible pedestrian locations to be processed by our segmentation algorithm.

Our segmentation algorithm is based on GrabCut, proposed by Rother et al. [19] for segmenting objects in static images. The GrabCut algorithm is semi-automatic in the sense that the user is required to draw a rectangle around an object, specifying the area outside the rectangle as sure background and the area inside the rectangle as the approximation of the foreground. GrabCut formulates the segmentation task as energy minimization problem and solves it by an iterative graph cut optimization technique, as proposed by Boykov and Jolly [3]. A number of extensions of GrabCut have been proposed, e.g. [1,12,14,18].

While background subtraction often gives imprecise results and is sensitive to lighting conditions, it can be straightforwardly combined with GrabCut, making the process of segmentation fully automatic and eliminating the need of human intervention. Several methods of combining motion-based foreground segmentation with GrabCut have been proposed in the literature. Sun et al. [22] note that straightforward use of the result of background subtraction as a mask for GrabCut often gives unsatisfactory results if the static background contains high-contrast elements. In order to fix this shortcoming, they propose an adaptive background contrast attenuation method. This method starts from the fact that the background is known from background subtraction and attenuates the contrast in the background, preserving simultaneously the contrast at the foreground/background boundary.

Hernandez-Vela et al. [12] present a fully automatic spatio-temporal GrabCut human segmentation methodology that combines tracking and segmentation. GrabCut initialization is performed by HOG-based subject detection, face detection and skin color model. In order to improve the segmentation results in concave regions (typical in images of humans), the authors refine the background mask by adding to it the pixels that have greater probability of belonging to the background, based on foreground and background color models. Temporal component is also included, by favoring segmentations that are close to the results obtained in the previous frame.

Poullot and Satoh [18] propose a method called VabCut for video foreground object segmentation in moving camera applications. VabCut works on an extension of the RGB color domain to the RGBM, where M is the motion layer. The motion layer is calculated after the RANSAC based frame alignment. Bounding box and a larger super bounding box around the moving object are calculated and only the area between these two bounding boxes is used for background modeling, in order to avoid visual similarities between foreground and background in case of large backgrounds. Additionally, the numbers of Gaussians in the GMMs for foreground and background models are independently optimized.

In contrast to the considered works, our method is designed to explicitly take into account situations when high contrast changes inside the object occur, or when background subtraction produces irregular and imprecise boundaries. In the following section, we review the basic GrabCut algorithm, followed by a description of our method.

3   Basic GrabCut Segmentation

In this section, we describe the original GrabCut algorithm [19] in some detail, as it is a foundation on which our method is built.

The color image I is represented as an array $z = (z_1, ..., z_n, ..., z_N)$ of N pixels in RGB space, where $z_i = (R_i, G_i, B_i)$. The segmentation of the image is defined as an array $\alpha = (\alpha_1, ..., \alpha_N)$, $\alpha_i \in \{0, 1\}$, assigning a label to each pixel of the image, indicating if it belongs to background ($\alpha_i = 0$) or foreground ($\alpha_i = 1$). The algorithm is semi-automatic, requiring the user to define an initial trimap T over the image. The trimap consists of three regions: T_B, T_F and T_U, specifying pixels belonging to sure background, sure foreground, and uncertain pixels, respectively. Most commonly, the user draws the rectangle that completely surrounds the object, specifying thereby the area outside the rectangle as T_B and the area inside the rectangle as T_U, while T_F is initially set to $\emptyset$. Initially, α_i is set to 0 for pixels in T_B and to 1 for pixels in $T_F \cup T_U$.

Then, both foreground and background are modeled by two separate full covariance Gaussian mixture models (GMM) of K components, parametrized as

$$\theta = \{\pi(\alpha, k), \mu(\alpha, k), \Sigma(\alpha, k), \alpha \in \{0, 1\}, k = 1, ..., K\}, \tag{1}$$

where π are the weights of the components, μ the means and Σ the covariance matrices of the model. Additionally, the array $k = \{k_1, ..., k_n, ..., k_N\}$ is introduced, where $k_i \in \{1, ..., K\}$ indicates the component of the background or foreground GMM (according to α_i) the pixel z_i belongs to.

The algorithm then formulates the segmentation task as an energy minimization problem w.r.t. the parameter α. The energy function consists of two terms, one enforcing consistency with the observed foreground and background color models, and another enforcing the solidity of the object:

$$E(\alpha, k, \theta, z) = U(\alpha, k, \theta, z) + V(\alpha, z), \tag{2}$$

where U is the "data term" that evaluates the fit of the segmentation to the background and foreground GMMs, while V is the "smoothness term" that evaluates the coherence of the segmentation in terms of color similarity. The data term is defined as:

$$U(\alpha, k, \theta, z) = \sum_i (-\log(\pi(\alpha_i, k_i) p(z_i | \alpha_i, k_i, \theta))). \tag{3}$$

The above expression will take on small values when most or all pixels have large probabilities of belonging to the models of foreground and background according to the current segmentation, while it will take on large values when this is not the case.

The smoothness term is defined as:

$$V(\alpha, z) = \gamma \sum_{\{m,n\} \in C} [\alpha_n \neq \alpha_m] \exp(-\beta ||z_m - z_n||^2), \tag{4}$$

where C is the set of pairs of neighbouring pixels according to 8-way connectivity, $[\alpha_n \neq \alpha_m]$ denotes the indicator function taking values 0 or 1 if the specified condition is false or true, and β is a robust parameter that weights the color contrast. The authors suggest setting $\beta = (2\langle ||z_m - z_n||2\rangle)^{-1}$, where $\langle \cdot \rangle$ is the expectation operator. The expression $\exp(-\beta ||z_m - z_n||^2)$ corresponds to the contrast between the neighbouring pixels and is low if the contrast is high and vice versa. Note that the factor $[\alpha_n \neq \alpha_m]$ allows this term to capture the contrast information only along the segmentation boundary. In this way, the smoothness term penalizes the segmentations where adjacent pixels of similar colors are labeled differently.

The minimization of the energy is performed by an iterated graph cut algorithm proposed by Boykov and Jolly [3]. In each iteration a refined segmentation is obtained, allowing more precise modeling of GMMs in the next iterations. The iterations are repeated either until convergence or some fixed number of times.

4   Our Method

Although the original GrabCut algorithm gives very good results in many situations, it has some deficiencies. The first and obvious one is the semi-automatic character of the algorithm, requiring certain (although minimal) user input. This drawback can be avoided in videos in a straightforward way, by using the result of background subtraction instead of manual initialization by the user. For example, a bounding box can be found around the foreground areas of sufficient size or, more appropriately, the raw results of background subtraction can be used as an initialization seed, marking certain pixels as sure foreground or background.

However, there are sometimes other problems with the original algorithm, resulting in imperfect and sometimes even significantly deficient segmentation. This becomes noticable especially in more challenging scenes, where parts of the object share characteristics with parts of the background, while other parts of the object stand out more clearly (see e.g. Figure. 2), forcing the algorithm to segment the object only partially and incorrectly. Another problematic scenario is when there are high contrast color changes in the unlabeled pixels T_U, leading the algorithm wrongly to regard such high contrast transitions as the object boundary. Furthermore, there is frequently the problem with the segmentation of concave objects. Because every bordering pixel contributes to the energy via the smoothness term V, the algorithm prefers shorter (i.e. convex) object boundaries.

We propose the modification of the original algorithm, taking into account the preliminary detection of the moving objects and resulting in a significantly improved segmentation.

We start by applying background subtraction [27] to each video frame. We call this step a preliminary step. In more difficult video sequences, the results of background subtraction are often noisy and disconnected. We apply morphological opening to remove noise, followed by morphological closing in order to connect disconnected components of the single foreground object. This results in a foreground/background mask that roughly corresponds to the desired segmentation but is too imprecise to be used as a final result. This mask represents the input into the modified GrabCut algorithm. The algorithm should find the more precise object boundary, relatively close to the boundary found by preliminary step, but not completely equal with it.

We propose a threefold modification of the GrabCut algorithm: (i) instead of evenly taking into account all pixels in building foreground and background GMMs, the contribution of each pixel is weighted depending on its distance from the boundary of the object found in the preliminary step; (ii) probabilities of a pixel belonging to foreground or background, needed to compute the data term U, are modified by taking into account the classification of the pixel in the preliminary step, as well as by taking into account the reliability of this classification based on the pixel's distance from the preliminary object's boundary; and (iii) the smoothness term V is modified by discouraging boundaries further away from the object's boundary found in the preliminary step. We describe each of these modifications in more detail in the following subsections.

4.1   Weighted Modeling of Foreground and Background GMMs

In order to estimate each pixel's probability of belonging to foreground or background based on its color, GrabCut models both foreground and background by a separate GMM, based on initial marking of pixels. In the original algorithm, GMM models of foreground and background are fitted to the image data by equally taking into account all the pixels initially classified as foreground or background. However, this can be misleading in cases when there are parts of the background relatively distant from the object but having similar appearance to the object. Intuitively, the contribution of a pixel to the background GMM should be lower the further the pixel is from the object boundary. The appearance of such far removed parts of the background is irrelevant to the segmentation, i.e. to finding the border between the object and its immediate surrounding. On the other hand, the object boundary found in the preliminary step is imprecise, so it is possible that the pixels classified as background that are very close to the object boundary do in fact belong to the foreground. Due to this imprecision and potential misclassification, the contribution of pixels very close to the object boundary to the background GMM should also be downweighted. The most weight should be given to the pixels at some (relatively small) distance from the object boundary, but not too close to it.

Similar reasoning can be applied to the modeling of the foreground GMM, however, because the objects are generally of a smaller size compared to the background, there is usually no need to downweight the contribution of the pixels inside the object further removed from the boundary (i.e. pixels in the center of the object are still relevant for the foreground GMM, unlike the distant background pixels). But the pixels near the boundary are still unreliable and should hence be downweighted.

We therefore propose a modification in the building of the GMM models of foreground and background where each pixel contributes to its respective model by a factor $w_i(\alpha_i, z_i)z_i$, where w_i is the weight determined by:

$$w_i(\alpha_i, z_i) = \begin{cases} \kappa_F d_{\min}(i) & \text{for } \alpha(i) = 1 \\ \kappa_G d_{\min}(i) \exp(-\tau d_{\min}(i)) & \text{for } \alpha(i) = 0 \end{cases} \tag{5}$$

In the above equation, $d_{\min}(i)$ is the distance of the i-th pixel to the nearest preliminary boundary point (determined by applying distance transform to the binary image obtained in the preliminary step), τ is a constant influencing at what distance the weight associated with background pixels will reach the maximum and how soon will it begin to decrease (i.e. at which distances the pixels are most relevant to the background GMM model), and κ_F and κ_B are normalizing constants ensuring that all the weights are in the interval $[0,1]$.

4.2 Modifications to the Data Term

The modification described in Subsect. 4.1 helps in building better and more relevant GMM models of foreground and background and thus indirectly influences the data term of the GrabCut energy calculated based on these models. However, we propose an additional, direct modification of the data term according to the following equation:

$$U(\alpha, k, \theta, z) = \sum_i - \log(P_i(\alpha_i, z_i) \pi(\alpha_i, k_i) p(z_i | \alpha_i, k_i, \theta)), \qquad (6)$$

where $P_i(\alpha_i, zi)$ represents the prior probability of each pixel belonging to foreground or background (according to α_i), based on the mask found in the preliminary step. Note that Eq. 6 can be obtained by multiplying each term of Eq. 3 with P_i. Since the preliminary step often results in imprecise object localization, we calculate $P(\alpha_i, zi)$ as:

$$P_i(\alpha_i, z_i) = \begin{cases} 1 \text{ for } d_{\min}(i) > D(\alpha_i) \\ 0 \text{ for } d_{\min}(i) < D(1 - \alpha_i) \\ 1 - d_{\min}(i)/D_{\max}(1 - \alpha_i) \text{ otherwise} \end{cases} \qquad (7)$$

The factor $D(\alpha_i)$ is the so-called distance threshold. The distance threshold regulates how far should the pixel be away from the preliminary object boundary inside the foreground or background in order to consider its preliminary classification as accurate (it is determined empirically depending on the expected error of the preliminary step). The distance $D_{\max}(\alpha_i)$ is the maximum distance of all foreground or background pixels from the preliminary object boundary. In other words, if the pixel is classified as foreground or background in the preliminary step and it is sufficiently far away from the preliminary object boundary, we set P_i of its belonging to the opposite category to 0, thus strongly favoring the classification of the pixel according to the preliminary step. For the pixels close to preliminary object boundary, however, to allow the posibility of their initial misclassification, we multiply the original GrabCut color-based probability of belonging to the opposite category by a value that decreases with the distance of the pixel from the preliminary object boundary (last branch in Eq. 7).

4.3 Modifications to the Smoothness Term

In the original algorithm, the smoothness term V discourages placing the boundary at positions where the color values of the neighbouring pixels are similar, by increasing the energy for each boundary point by the amount that depends on the contrast between neighbouring pixels at that point (Eq. 4). As already explained, this can lead to two kinds of problems. When there is an emphasized discontinuity of color values inside the object (e.g. a pedestrian wearing a shirt and trousers of significantly different colors) and some of the colors are much more different from the background than others, the algorithm will wrongly "cut through" the object and place the boundary at this discontinuity. Aditionally, if the real object boundary is long and concave, the contribution of all its points to the energy will be significant. This is even more the case if the contrast between the object and background is relatively low, e.g. a pedestrian wearing gray trousers on gray background. The algorithm will prefer shorter paths, either through the object or by enclosing parts of the background inside the concavities.

In order to fix these kinds of problems, we propose a modification of the smoothness term in a way that will additionally discourage both (i) placing the border deeply inside the approximation of the object obtained in the preliminary step ("cutting through the object"), as well as (ii) placing the border through the background in the concave areas, further from the approximate preliminary boundary. The proposed modified smoothness term can be expressed as:

$$V(\alpha, z) = \gamma \sum_{\{m,n\} \in C} [\alpha_n \neq \alpha_m] \exp(-\beta(||z_m - z_n||^2 + \lambda(d_{\min}(i) - \delta_0))). \quad (8)$$

Equation 8 can be obtained by multiplying the original smoothnes term (Eq. 4) by another exponential, $\exp(\beta\lambda(d_{\min}(i) - \delta_0))$, where λ and δ_0 are empirically determined constants. δ_0 ensures that the penalization is not high for pixels near the preliminary object boundary, while λ serves as a normalizing factor and makes the influence of the additional exponential comensurate with the influence of the original smoothness term.

5   Experiments

Our method was experimentally validated on the CDnet 2014 Pedestrian Detection dataset [25] and compared to a reference implementation of GrabCut [4].

5.1   The CDnet 2014 Pedestrian Dataset

The CDnet 2014 Pedestrian Dataset is a subset of the CDnet 2014 dataset [25], intended for change detection in dynamic sequences. The CDnet 2014 Pedestrian Dataset consists of ten videos of pedestrians with a total of 26248 frames. Several sequences were filmed in challenging conditions that include intermittent object motion, shadows and bad weather. As the dataset is a compilation of sequences from a number of sources, the image resolution varies with each sequence, with the maximum image size of 720 × 576. Example images from each of the ten sequences are shown in Fig. 1.

Fig. 1. Example frames from the CDnet 2014 Pedestrian Dataset sequences.

Table 1. Average precisions, recalls and F1 measures for each of the ten sequences in the CDnet 2014 Pedestrian Dataset.

Sequence	GrabCut			Ours		
	AP	AR	F1	AP	AR	F1
Backdoor	0.9938	0.3784	0.5481	0.9298	0.9175	0.9236
Bus station	0.9770	0.1186	0.2115	0.8569	0.5039	0.6346
Cubicle	0.9901	0.3642	0.5325	0.7339	0.7924	0.7620
Copy machine	0.9900	0.2266	0.3687	0.5847	0.3988	0.4741
Office	0.9943	0.1184	0.2116	0.7625	0.2400	0.3650
Pedestrians	1.0000	0.5917	0.7434	1.0000	0.9383	0.9681
PETS 2006	1.0000	0.4171	0.5886	1.0000	0.7169	0.8351
People in shade	0.8890	0.5364	0.6690	0.7555	0.7233	0.7390
Skate	1.0000	0.5102	0.6756	1.0000	0.6788	0.8086
Sofa	0.9659	0.1651	0.2819	0.6841	0.5449	0.6066

5.2 Experimental Results

We evaluated our method on the CDnet 2014 Pedestrian Dataset [25], comparing it to a reference implementation of the GrabCut algorithm [19] from the OpenCV library [4]. The run time performance of our algorithm was comparable to the reference implementation of GrabCut. Both algorithms were initialized using the same mask obtained by background subtraction [27] and morphologically pre-processed. The evaluation was done on a per-pixel basis in accordance with the guidelines for testing on the CDnet 2014 dataset [25]. We used the following values of the proposed algorithm parameters: opening of 5 pixels, closing of 9 pixels, $\tau = 10$. $D(\alpha_i) = 0.2 \cdot D_{max}(\alpha_i)$, $\lambda = 20000$, $\delta_0 = 8$, which were determined experimentally. For best performance we recommend optimizing the parameters using cross-validation.

The average precisions, recalls and F1 measures calculated over all frames for each of the ten sequences in the CDnet 2014 Pedestrian Dataset are shown in Table 1. In terms of F1 measure (the harmonic mean of precision and recall),

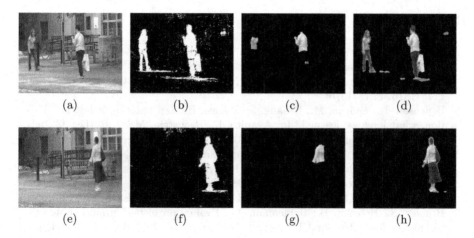

Fig. 2. Output comparisons for two frames from the sequence "backdoor": (a, e) original frames, (b, f) background ubtraction, (c, g) GrabCut, (d, h) our method.

our method outperforms the reference GrabCut implementation in all the considered sequences. The increase in the F1 measure is due to drastically improved recall as more pixels of the object are correctly segmented. The downside is that there are some false positives resulting in a relatively small drop of precision. Example output for two frames of the sequence "backdoor" is shown in Fig. 2. We see that in spite of good initialization with the background subtraction mask, GrabCut performs poorly due to a significant color difference in the clothing of the observed pedestrians. In contrast, our method succesfully segments all pedestrians. We attribute the success of our method to all the three improvements that we outlined in Sect. 4, resulting in the background subtraction outline being smoothed and pixel contributions that depend on the position of the pixels relative to the object prior.

6   Conclusion

We proposed a fully automatic method for segmenting pedestrians in video sequences based on modification of the GrabCut algorithm initialized with the mask obtained by background subtraction. In the modified version of the algorithm, the more relevant GMM models of foreground and background are built by weighting pixel contributions depending on their distance from the boundary of the object prior, and the data and smoothness terms of the energy equation are modified in a way that discourages placing boundaries far from the object prior boundary. We evaluated the proposed algorithm on the CDnet 2014 Pedestrian Dataset and showed that our proposed algorithm significantly outperforms the baseline implementation in all the sequences. In general, our algorithm offers much better F1 measure rates and enables segmenting full objects regardless of their local contrast and color changes.

References

1. Bai, X., Wang, J., Simons, D., Sapiro, G.: Video snapcut: robust video object cutout using localized classifiers. In: ACM SIGGRAPH 2009 Papers. SIGGRAPH 2009, pp. 70:1–70:11. ACM, New York (2009). http://doi.acm.org/10. 1145/1576246.1531376
2. Benenson, R., Omran, M., Hosang, J., Schiele, B.: Ten years of pedestrian detection, what have we learned? In: Agapito, L., Bronstein, M.M., Rother, C. (eds.) ECCV 2014 Workshops. LNCS, vol. 8926, pp. 613–627. Springer, Heidelberg (2015)
3. Boykov, Y., Jolly, M.P.: Interactive graph cuts for optimal boundary and region segmentation of objects in n-d images. In: Proceedings of the Eighth IEEE International Conference on Computer Vision. ICCV 2001, vol. 1, pp. 105–112 (2001)
4. Bradski, G.: The OpenCV library. Dr. Dobb's J. Softw. Tools **25**, 120–126 (2000)
5. Brutzer, S., Hoferlin, B., Heidemann, G.: Evaluation of background subtraction techniques for video surveillance. In: Proceedings of the 2011 IEEE Conference on Computer Vision and Pattern Recognition. CVPR 2011, pp. 1937–1944. IEEE Computer Society, Washington, DC (2011)
6. Cheung, S.C.S., Kamath, C.: Robust techniques for background subtraction in urban traffic video. In: Visual Communications and Image Processing, vol. 5308(1), pp. 881–892 (2004)
7. Dalal, N., Triggs, B.: Histograms of oriented gradients for human detection. In: Proceedings of CVPR, pp. 886–893 (2005)
8. Dollar, P., Tu, Z., Perona, P., Belongie, S.: Integral channel features. In: Proceedings of the British Machine Vision Conference. BMVA Press (2009). doi:10.5244/ C.23.91
9. Dollar, P., Wojek, C., Schiele, B., Perona, P.: Pedestrian detection: an evaluation of the state of the art. IEEE Trans. Pattern Anal. Mach. Intell. **34**(4), 743–761 (2012). doi:10.1109/TPAMI.2011.155
10. Felzenszwalb, P.F., Girshick, R.B., McAllester, D., Ramanan, D.: Object detection with discriminatively trained part-based models. IEEE Trans. Pattern Anal. Mach. Intell. **32**(9), 1627–1645 (2010). doi:10.1109/TPAMI.2009.167
11. Harville, M.: A framework for high-level feedback to adaptive, per-pixel, mixture-of-gaussian background models. In: Heyden, A., Sparr, G., Nielsen, M., Johansen, P. (eds.) ECCV 2002, Part III. LNCS, vol. 2352, pp. 543–560. Springer, Heidelberg (2002)
12. Hernandez-Vela, A., Reyes, M., Ponce, V., Escalera, S.: Grabcut-based human segmentation in video sequences. Sensors **12**, 15376–15393 (2012). doi:10.3390/ s121115376
13. Herrero, S., Bescós, J.: Background subtraction techniques: systematic evaluation and comparative analysis. In: Blanc-Talon, J., Philips, W., Popescu, D., Scheunders, P. (eds.) ACIVS 2009. LNCS, vol. 5807, pp. 33–42. Springer, Heidelberg (2009)
14. Kroeger, T., Kappes, J.H., Beier, T., Koethe, U., Hamprecht, F.A.: Asymmetric cuts: joint image labeling and partitioning. In: Jiang, X., Hornegger, J., Koch, R. (eds.) GCPR 2014. LNCS, vol. 8753, pp. 199–211. Springer, Heidelberg (2014)
15. Leibe, B., Seemann, E., Schiele, B.: Pedestrian detection in crowded scenes. In: Proceedings of the 2005 IEEE Computer Society Conference on Computer Vision and Pattern Recognition (CVPR 2005), vol. 1, pp. 878–885. IEEE Computer Society, Washington (2005). http://dx.doi.org/10.1109/CVPR.2005.272

16. Ouyang, W., Wang, X.: A discriminative deep model for pedestrian detection with occlusion handling. In: 2012 IEEE Conference on Computer Vision and Pattern Recognition (CVPR), pp. 3258–3265, June 2012
17. Ouyang, W., Zeng, X., Wang, X.: Modeling mutual visibility relationship in pedestrian detection. In: 2013 IEEE Conference on Computer Vision and Pattern Recognition (CVPR), pp. 3222–3229, June 2013
18. Poullot, S., Satoh, S.: Vabcut: a video extension of grabcut for unsupervised video foreground object segmentation. In: Proceedings of VISAPP (2014)
19. Rother, C., Vladimir, K., Blake, A.: "GrabCut" - interactive foreground extraction using iterated graph cuts. In: Proceedings of SIGGRAPH (2004)
20. Sermanet, P., Kavukcuoglu, K., Chintala, S., LeCun, Y.: Pedestrian detection with unsupervised multi-stage feature learning. In: Proceedings of CVPR, pp. 3626–3633 (2013)
21. Stauffer, C., Grimson, W.E.L.: Adaptive background mixture models for real-time tracking. In: CVPR, pp. 2246–2252 (1999)
22. Sun, J., Zhang, W., Tang, X., Shum, H.-Y.: Background cut. In: Leonardis, A., Bischof, H., Pinz, A. (eds.) ECCV 2006. LNCS, vol. 3952, pp. 628–641. Springer, Heidelberg (2006)
23. Viola, P., Jones, M.: Robust real-time object detection. Int. J. Comput. Vis. **57**, 137–154 (2001)
24. Viola, P., Jones, M.J., Snow, D.: Detecting pedestrians using patterns of motion and appearance. Int. J. Comput. Vis. **63**(2), 153–161 (2005). doi:10.1007/s11263-005-6644-8
25. Wang, Y., Jodoin, P.M., Porikli, F., Konrad, J., Benezeth, Y., Ishwar, P.: CDnet 2014: an expanded change detection benchmark dataset. In: Proceedings of IEEE Workshop on Change Detection (CDW 2014) at CVPR 2014, pp. 387–394 (2014)
26. Wren, C.R., Azarbayejani, A., Darrell, T., Pentland, A.P.: Pfinder: real-time tracking of the human body. IEEE Trans. Pattern Anal. Mach. Intell. **19**(7), 780–785 (1997)
27. Zivkovic, Z.: Improved adaptive gaussian mixture model for background subtraction. In: ICPR (2), pp. 28–31 (2004)

A Novel Tree Block-Coordinate Method for MAP Inference

Christopher Zach$^{(\boxtimes)}$

Toshiba Research Europe, Cambridge, UK
`christopher.zach@crl.toshiba.co.uk`

Abstract. Block-coordinate methods inspired by belief propagation are among the most successful methods for approximate MAP inference in graphical models. The set of unknowns optimally updated in such block-coordinate methods is typically very small and spans only single edges or shallow trees. We derive a method that optimally updates sets of unknowns spanned by an arbitrary tree that is different from one reported in the literature. It provides some insight why "tree block-coordinate" methods are not as useful as expected, and enables a simple technique to makes these tree updates more effective.

1 Introduction

Determining the maximum a-posteriori (MAP) assignment in graphical models or in random fields defined over an image domain is one of the most important tasks in computer vision and related fields. Since exact MAP inference is intractable in general, much research has focused on effective approximate MAP inference algorithms. In computer vision two complementary classes for approximate MAP inference are well-established: (a) move making algorithms aiming to improve a current label assignment such as the graph cut method [1] or fusion moves [8], and (b) message passing algorithms indirectly seeking the MAP assignment by optimizing a dual objective (e.g. [4,7,14]). In this work we focus on message passing algorithms, since they have a wide applicability, and they also have strong connections with the celebrated (min-sum) belief propagation (BP) method [9] (see also [5,13,15]).

A class of message passing algorithms is based on a block-coordinate approach and is known to monotonically improve the (dual) objective. Since the underlying objective is not strictly convex (or concave), in such methods convergence to the a true optimum is not guaranteed, and only a suboptimal limit point may be reached. One way to escape "local minima" is by updating larger sets of unknowns in the block-coordinate method, e.g. by updating all unknowns that are attached to a subtree of the graph. Another argument for larger updates is

Electronic supplementary material The online version of this chapter (doi:10. 1007/978-3-319-24947-6_26) contains supplementary material, which is available to authorized users.

that information about the value of states is propagated non-locally through the graph, hence one can expect faster improvements in the objective.

In this work we derive a novel tree block-coordinate method for MAP inference via message passing. It will reveal why block-coordinate methods do in practice not perform very well, and how to remedy that shortcoming. Finally, in our experiments we observe that problems defined over a random field require two passes over the image domain to reach an "almost converged" objective.

Background. This section presents some material on MAP inference, the underlying linear programming relaxation, and dual coordinate ascent methods for fast approximate inference. A labeling or MAP inference problem is determining the optimal label $x_s \in \mathcal{L}_s$ assigned at each node $s \in \mathcal{V}$, where the objective is over unary and pairwise terms,

$$\mathbf{x}^* \stackrel{\text{def}}{=} \arg\min_{\mathbf{x}} \sum_{s \in \mathcal{V}} \theta_s(x_s) + \sum_{(s,t) \in \mathcal{E}} \theta_{st}(x_s, x_t), \tag{1}$$

where $\mathbf{x} = (x_s)_{s \in \mathcal{V}} \in \bigotimes_{s \in \mathcal{V}} \mathcal{L}_s$. For simplicity we restrict ourselves to at most pairwise cliques, but all results can be generalized to higher order cliques. θ are the *potentials* or costs for assigning particular states to nodes or edges. This label assignment problem is generally intractable to solve, and one highly successful approach to approximately solve this problem is to employ the corresponding linear programming (LP) relaxation (see e.g. [16]),

$$E_{\text{MAP}}(\mathbf{b}) \stackrel{\text{def}}{=} \sum_{s,x_s} \theta_s(x_s) b_s(x_s) + \sum_{(s,t)} \sum_{x_s,x_t} \theta_{st}(x_s, x_t) b_{st}(x_s, x_t)$$

$$\text{s.t. } b_s(x_s) = \sum_{x_t} b_{st}(x_s, x_t) \qquad \sum_{x_s} b_s(x_s) = 1 \qquad b_{st}(x_s, x_t) \geq 0. \tag{2}$$

The unknowns $\{b_s\}_{s \in \mathcal{V}}$ and $\{b_{st}\}_{st}$ are "one-hot" encodings of the assigned labels, e.g. if $\mathbf{b}^*$ is the optimal solution of E_{MAP} and the relaxation is tight, then $b_s(x_s)$ is ideally 1 iff state x_s is the optimal label at node s, and 0 otherwise. The first set of constraints are usually called *marginalization constraints*, and the unit sum constraint is typically referred as *normalization constraint*. The primal program Eq. 2 is not optimized directly, since it turns out that the dual program can be solved more efficiently. Note that the linear program in Eq. 2 is not unique, and redundant non-negativity and normalization constraints can be added to E_{MAP} without affecting the optimal solution or value. Consequently, different duals are solved in the literature. The particular LP dual of E_{MAP}, which we will use in the remainder, is given by[1]

$$E^*_{\text{MAP}}(\lambda) = \sum_s \rho_s \qquad \text{s.t. } \forall x_s : \rho_s = \theta_s(x_s) + \sum_{t \in N(s)} \lambda_{t \to s}(x_s) \tag{3}$$

$$\forall x_s, x_t : \lambda_{t \to s}(x_s) + \lambda_{s \to t}(x_t) \leq \theta_{st}(x_s, x_t).$$

---

[1] Since the unknowns $(\rho_s)_{s \in \mathcal{V}}$ play only the role of auxiliary variables, we drop them as argument to E^*_{MAP} to simplify the notation.

Our convention is that the dual program is *maximized*. We will refer to the first set of constraints as the *balance constraint* and the second set of constraints is termed *capacity constraints*. W.l.o.g. we require $\theta \geq 0$ (pointwise) such that $\lambda \equiv 0$ is dual feasible.

A different dual often employed in the literature (e.g. [5,11,12]) is the following unconstrained dual program,

$$J_{\text{MAP}}(\lambda) = \sum_s \min_{x_s} \left\{ \theta_s(x_s) + \sum_{t \in N(s)} \lambda_{t \to s}(x_s) \right\}$$

$$+ \sum_{(s,t) \in \mathcal{E}} \min_{x_s, x_t} \left\{ \theta_{st}(x_s, x_t) - \lambda_{t \to s}(x_s) - \lambda_{s \to t}(x_t) \right\}. \quad (4)$$

The reparametrized unary potentials in Eq. 3, $\theta_s(x_s) + \sum_{t \in N(s)} \lambda_{t \to s}(x_s)$, are uninformative about the value of a state x_s (all reparametrized unaries are the same), and the effective value of a state is entirely attached to the edges. More precisely, complementary slackness tells us nothing about $b_s(x_s)$ in the primal program Eq. 2, but $\lambda_{t \to s}^*(x_s) + \lambda_{s \to t}^*(x_t) < \theta_{st}(x_s, x_t)$ for a dual optimal solution λ^* implies $b_{st}(x_s, x_t) = 0$. This is in contrast to the program in Eq. 4, where reparametrized unary *and* pairwise potentials encode the value of a state, and algorithms to optimize J_{MAP} search for agreement between these values. This property has pros and cons which will be mentioned briefly in Sect. 3.

Even if Eq. 3 (and Eq. 4) is a concave maximization problem (a linear program), optimizing E_{MAP}^* is not straightforward. Generic LP codes do not exploit the very particular structure of the problem, and first order methods exhibit slow convergence in practice due to the non-smooth objective. A successful class of algorithms to solve E_{MAP}^* approximately is based on block-coordinate ascent (e.g. [4,5,11,12,16,17]), which performs repeated optimization over a small but varying subsets of unknowns. Different algorithms are obtained by different choices of dual energies and subsets of optimized unknowns. One important aspect for the success of these algorithms, that the subproblems can be solved efficiently, typically in closed form. These algorithms usually resemble the classical belief propagation algorithm (which has few guarantees if run on cyclic graphs) and fall under the umbrella term *convex belief propagation*. These algorithms have in common, that the dual objective improves monotonically in each iteration, which renders them convergent.

Dual Coordinate Ascent. We review a convex belief propagation algorithm that is very simple to derive [17] and forms the basis for the tree block-coordinate method in Sect. 2. This method optimizes over all variables $\lambda_{t \to s}$ for all edges (s, t) in each step (i.e. all messages incoming at node s).

If we consider a particular node s and fix all unknowns other than ρ_s and $\{\lambda_{t \to s}\}_{(s,t)}$, the subproblem induced by Eq. 3 reads as

$$\max_{\rho_s, \{\lambda_{t \to s}\}} \rho_s \quad \text{s.t.} \quad \rho_s = \theta_s(x_s) + \sum_{t \in N(s)} \lambda_{t \to s}(x_s) \quad (5)$$

$$\lambda_{t \to s}(x_s) \leq \min_{x_t} \left\{ \theta_{st}(x_s, x_t) - \lambda_{s \to t}(x_t) \right\}.$$

We define the r.h.s. of the inequality constraints as $\mu_{t \to s}(x_s)$,

$$\mu_{t \to s}(x_s) \overset{\text{def}}{=} \min_{x_t} \left\{ \theta_{st}(x_s, x_t) - \lambda_{s \to t}(x_t) \right\}. \tag{6}$$

We introduce non-negative weights $w_{t \to s}$ such that $\sum_{t \in N(s)} w_{t \to s} = 1$ (but otherwise chosen arbitrarily) and use the ansatz $\lambda_{t \to s}(x_s) = \mu_{t \to s}(x_s) - w_{t \to s}\delta_s(x_s)$ for some $\delta_s(x_s) \geq 0$ to obtain the equivalent problem to Eq. 5,

$$\max_{\rho_s, \delta_s \geq 0} \rho_s \quad \text{s.t.} \quad \rho_s = \theta_s(x_s) + \sum_{t \in N(s)} \mu_{t \to s}(x_s) - \delta_s(x_s). \tag{7}$$

The weights $w_{t \to s}$ will play an important role in Sect. 2. Since $\delta_s(x_s) \geq 0$, the largest allowed value for ρ_s is given by

$$\rho_s \leftarrow \min_{x_s} \left\{ \theta_s(x_s) + \sum_{t \in N(s)} \mu_{t \to s}(x_s) \right\} = \min_{x_s} \nu_s(x_s), \tag{8}$$

where we define $\nu_s(x_s) \overset{\text{def}}{=} \theta_s(x_s) + \sum_{t \in N(s)} \mu_{t \to s}(x_s)$. $\delta_s(x_s)$ and $\lambda_{t \to s}$ are consequently given by

$$\delta_s(x_s) \leftarrow \theta_s(x_s) + \sum_{t \in N(s)} \mu_{t \to s}(x_s) - \rho_s = \nu_s(x_s) - \rho_s(x_s)$$

$$\lambda_{t \to s} \leftarrow \mu_{t \to s}(x_s) - w_{t \to s}\delta_s(x_s).$$

Via complementary slackness it is easy to see that if λ is dual optimal, then $\nu_s(x_s) > \rho_s$ implies $b_s(x_s) = 0$ in the primal solution of E_{MAP}. Algorithm 1 summarizes this convex BP method. We will see in Sect. 2 that this algorithm is equivalent to performing dual coordinate ascent with respect to both incoming messages $\lambda_{t \to s}$ and reverse messages $\lambda_{s \to t}$, $t \in N(s)$.

2   Tree Block-Coordinate Message Passing

In this section we derive a tree block-coordinate method to optimize the dual objective E^*_{MAP} (Eq. 3). The quantities $\mu_{t \to s}$ and ν_s in Algorithm 1 are analogous to the messages and the min-marginals, respectively, obtained by standard (min-sum) belief propagation on a tree graph. Thus, the ansatz for a more general tree block-coordinate update of messages will be to identify messages $m_{s \to t}$ returned by min-sum BP with $\mu_{s \to t}$ (up to an additive constant). Let $\mathcal{T}$ be a collection of trees, where each tree $T \in \mathcal{T}$ has a node set $V_T \subseteq V$ and edges $\mathcal{E}_T \subseteq \mathcal{E}$. For $s \in V_T$ let $N_T(s)$ be the adjacent nodes of s with respect to the tree edges.

By running belief propagation (or dynamic programming) on T we obtain messages $m_{s \to t}$ and $m_{t \to s}$ for all edges (s,t) belonging to T, and the min-marginals are given by $\nu_s(x_s) = \theta_s(x_s) + \sum_t m_{t \to s}(x_s)$. For an optimal assignment $\mathbf{x}^* = (x_s)_s$ we have the following relations connecting the BP and the dual

---

Algorithm 1. Node-based message passing

Require: Arbitrary feasible λ and ρ, weights $w_{t \to s}$
1: **while** not converged **do**
2:    **loop** over $s \in \mathcal{V}$ and assign for all $t \in N(s)$
3:      *Node update:*

$$\mu_{t \to s}(x_s) \leftarrow \min_{x_t} \left\{ \theta_{st}(x_s, x_t) - \sum_{t \in N(s)} \lambda_{s \to t}(x_t) \right\}$$

$$\rho_s \leftarrow \min_{x_s} \left\{ \theta_s(x_s) + \sum_{t \in N(s)} \mu_{t \to s}(x_s) \right\}$$

$$\delta_s(x_s) \leftarrow \theta_s(x_s) + \sum_{t \in N(s)} \mu_{t \to s}(x_s) - \rho_s$$

$$\lambda_{t \to s} \leftarrow \mu_{t \to s}(x_s) - w_{t \to s} \delta_s(x_s) \tag{9}$$

4:    **end loop**
5: **end while**

---

unknowns in Eq. 3:

$$\nu^* = \theta_s(x_s^*) + \sum_t m_{t \to s}(x_s^*) \qquad \lambda_{t \to s}(x_s^*) = \mu_{t \to s}(x_s^*)$$

$$\rho_s = \theta_s(x_s^*) + \sum_t \lambda_{t \to s}(x_s^*) = \theta_s(x_s^*) + \sum_t \mu_{t \to s}(x_s^*). \tag{10}$$

Therefore, by using an ansatz $\sum_t m_{t \to s}(x_s^*) = \sum_t \mu_{t \to s}(x_s^*) + \Delta_s$ (with $\Delta_s \geq 0$) we obtain

$$\nu^* - \theta_s(x_s^*) = \rho_s - \theta_s(x_s^*) + \Delta_s,$$

which provides $\Delta_s = \nu^* - \rho_s$, and consequently $\sum_t \mu_{t \to s}(x_s^*) = \sum_t m_{t \to s}(x_s^*) + \rho_s - \nu^*$. We distribute the "slack" Δ_s to the edges adjacent to s by setting $\mu_{t \to s}(x_s) = m_{t \to s}(x_s) + w'_{t \to s}(\rho_s - \nu^*)$. The non-negative weights $(w'_{t \to s})_{t \in N_T(s)}$ reside in the probability simplex satisfying $\sum_{t \in N_T(s)} w'_{t \to s} = 1$.

Further constraints on w': With our assumed relation between $m_{t \to s}$ and $\mu_{t \to s}$ the capacity constraint for optimal states reads as

$$\lambda_{t \to s}(x_s^*) + \lambda_{s \to t}(x_t^*) = \mu_{t \to s}(x_s^*) + \mu_{s \to t}(x_t^*)$$
$$= m_{t \to s}(x_s^*) + m_{s \to t}(x_t^*) + w'_{t \to s}(\rho_s - \nu^*) + w'_{s \to t}(\rho_t - \nu^*)$$
$$= \nu^* + \theta_{st}(x_s^*, x_t^*) + w'_{t \to s}(\rho_s - \nu^*) + w'_{s \to t}(\rho_t - \nu^*),$$

since $m_{t \to s}(x_s^*) + m_{s \to t}(x_t^*) = \nu^* + \theta_{st}(x_s^*, x_t^*)$. In general we have $m_{t \to s}(x_s) + m_{s \to t}(x_t) \leq \nu_s(x_s) + \theta_{st}(x_s, x_t)$, which follows from

$$m_{t \to s}(x_s) + m_{s \to t}(x_t) = m_{t \to s}(x_s) + \min_{x_s'} \left\{ \theta_{st}(x_s', x_t) + \theta_s(x_s') + \sum_{v \neq t} m_{v \to s}(x_s') \right\}$$

$$\leq m_{t \to s}(x_s) + \theta_{st}(x_s, x_t) + \theta_s(x_s) + \sum_{v \neq t} m_{v \to s}(x_s)$$

$$= \theta_{st}(x_s, x_t) + \nu_s(x_s). \tag{11}$$

A symmetric reasoning reveals $m_{t \to s}(x_s) + m_{s \to t}(x_t) \leq \nu_t(x_t) + \theta_{st}(x_s, x_t)$, which combines to

$$m_{t \to s}(x_s) + m_{s \to t}(x_t) \leq \min\{\nu_s(x_s), \nu_t(x_t)\} + \theta_{st}(x_s, x_t). \tag{12}$$

Since we require that $\lambda_{t \to s}(x_s^*) + \lambda_{s \to t}(x_t^*) = \theta_{st}(x_s^*, x_t^*)$ we obtain the following constraint on allowed weights, $\nu^* = w'_{t \to s}(\nu^* - \rho_s) + w'_{s \to t}(\nu^* - \rho_t)$, or

$$(w'_{t \to s} + w'_{s \to t} - 1)\nu^* = w'_{t \to s}\rho_s + w'_{s \to t}\rho_t. \tag{13}$$

Note that the r.h.s. are the terms ρ_s and ρ_t reparametrized to the edge (s, t), hence $\sum_{(s,t) \in T} (w'_{t \to s}\rho_s + w'_{s \to t}\rho_t) = \sum_s \rho_s = \nu^*$. Similar, for the l.h.s. we have $\sum_{(s,t) \in T} (w'_{t \to s} + w'_{s \to t} - 1)\nu^* = (2 - 1)\nu^* = \nu^*$, since $\sum_{t \in N_T(s)} w'_{t \to s} = 1$ by construction. Thus, one equation is linearly dependent. In Eq. 13 we have the choice of fixing the weights w' or the node contributions ρ_s. For numerical reasons it turns out to be beneficial to fix ρ_s and determine w' subject to the constraints. If $N = |\mathcal{V}_T|$ is the number of nodes in T, then we have $2(N - 1)$ unknowns and $N - 1$ constraints from Eq. 13 (of which one is linear dependent) and N normalization constraints. Hence, given ρ_s we obtain a unique assignment for w'. Let w_s be non-negative weights such that $\sum_s w_s = 1$ and set $\rho_s = w_s \nu^*$. Hence, we obtain $(w'_{t \to s} + w'_{s \to t} - 1)\nu^* = w'_{t \to s}\rho_s + w'_{s \to t}\rho_t = (w'_{t \to s}w_s + w'_{s \to t}w_t)\nu^*$, or

$$w'_{t \to s}(1 - w_s) + w'_{s \to t}(1 - w_t) = 1. \tag{14}$$

If s is a leaf node we have $w'_{t \to s}$ fixed to 1 (via the normalization constraint) and therefore $w'_{s \to t} = \frac{1 + w'_{t \to s}(w_s - 1)}{1 - w_t} = w_s/(1 - w_t)$. Thus, all weights for incoming edges are fixed at level 1, and the incoming weight from the parent node is determined via the normalization constraint. Overall, the weights w' are assigned via bottom-up traversal from the leaves to the root: for s not equal the root set

$$w'_{t \to s} \leftarrow 1 - \sum_{v \in ch(s)} w'_{v \to s} \qquad w'_{s \to t} \leftarrow \frac{1 + w'_{t \to s}(w_s - 1)}{1 - w_t}. \tag{15}$$

Message updates: We extend the relation between BP messages m and the values μ, $\sum_t \mu_{t \to s}(x_s^*) = \sum_t m_{t \to s}(x_s^*) + \rho_s - \nu^*$, to all states, i.e. $\sum_t \mu_{t \to s}(x_s) = \sum_t m_{t \to s}(x_s) + \rho_s - \nu^*$ for all x_s. Consequently, we obtain

$$\theta_s(x_s) + \sum_t \mu_{t \to s}(x_s) = \theta_s(x_s) + \sum_t m_{t \to s}(x_s) + \rho_s - \nu^* = \rho_s + \nu_s(x_s) - \nu^*.$$

As in the node-based message passing algorithm we use the following ansatz (introducing non-negative weights $w_{t \to s}$ with $\sum_{t \in N_T(s)} w_{t \to s} = 1$)

$$\lambda_{t \to s}(x_s) = \mu_{t \to s}(x_s) - w_{t \to s}\delta_s(x_s) = \mu_{t \to s}(x_s) - w_{t \to s}(\nu_s(x_s) - \nu^*)$$
$$= m_{t \to s}(x_s) + w'_{t \to s}(\rho_s - \nu^*) - w_{t \to s}(\nu_s(x_s) - \nu^*). \tag{16}$$

Since λ assigned this way has to satisfy the capacity constraints, $\lambda_{t \to s}(x_s) + \lambda_{s \to t}(x_t) \leq \theta_{st}(x_s, x_t)$, we obtain constraints on $w_{t \to s}$ and $w_{s \to t}$ as follows (for brevity we omit the state arguments to BP messages and λ):

$$
\begin{aligned}
\lambda_{t\to s} + \lambda_{s\to t} &= m_{t\to s} + m_{t\to s} + w'_{t\to s}(\rho_s - \nu^*) \\
&\quad + w'_{s\to t}(\rho_t - \nu^*) - w_{t\to s}(\nu_s - \nu^*) - w_{s\to t}(\nu_t - \nu^*) \\
&= m_{t\to s} + m_{t\to s} + \nu^* \underbrace{(w'_{t\to s}(w_s - 1) + w'_{s\to t}(w_t - 1))}_{=-1} \\
&\quad - w_{t\to s}(\nu_s - \nu^*) - w_{s\to t}(\nu_t - \nu^*) \\
&= m_{t\to s} + m_{t\to s} - \nu^* - w_{t\to s}(\nu_s - \nu^*) - w_{s\to t}(\nu_t - \nu^*) \\
&\leq \theta_{st} + \min\{\nu_s, \nu_t\} - \nu^* - w_{t\to s}(\nu_s - \nu^*) - w_{s\to t}(\nu_t - \nu^*) \overset{!}{\leq} \theta_{st},
\end{aligned}
$$

or $\min\{\nu_s, \nu_t\} - w_{t\to s}(\nu_s - \nu^*) - w_{s\to t}(\nu_t - \nu^*) \overset{!}{\leq} \nu^*$. A sufficient condition for this inequality to hold is $w_{t\to s} + w_{s\to t} \geq 1$. Note that we can choose $w = w'$, since the constraint $w'_{t\to s}(1 - w_s) + w'_{s\to t}(1 - w_t) = 1$ together with $1 - w_s \in [0, 1]$ and $1 - w_t \in [0, 1]$ already implies $w'_{t\to s} + w'_{s\to t} \geq 1$. In this setting the update for $\lambda_{t\to s}$ simplifies to

$$
\begin{aligned}
\lambda_{t\to s}(x_s) &= m_{t\to s}(x_s) + w_{t\to s}(\rho_s - \nu^*) - w_{t\to s}(\nu_s(x_s) - \nu^*) \\
&= m_{t\to s}(x_s) + w_{t\to s}(\rho_s - \nu_s(x_s)). \tag{17}
\end{aligned}
$$

In the following (and in our implementation) we will always choose $w = w'$. The full tree block-coordinate method for MAP inference is presented in Algorithm 2. The statement in line 3 ("preprocess messages", in bold) is discussed in Sect. 3.

Not Updating Messages to Leaves. If s is a leaf node in the tree T, then by setting $w = w'$ and $w_s = 0$ the new values for $\lambda_{t\to s}$ are essentially unchanged after a tree block-coordinate update. Note that $w_{s\to t} = 1$, since s is a leaf (recall Eq. 15). The reparametrized unary potentials at the leaf s are as follows,

$$
\hat{\theta}_s(x_s) = \theta_s(x_s) + \sum_{v\neq t}\lambda^{\mathrm{old}}_{v\to s}(x_s) = \rho^{\mathrm{old}}_s - \lambda^{\mathrm{old}}_{t\to s}(x_s), \tag{18}
$$

For the new values $\lambda^{\mathrm{new}}_{t\to s}(x_s)$ after the update we obtain

$$
\begin{aligned}
\lambda^{\mathrm{new}}_{t\to s}(x_s) &\leftarrow m_{t\to s}(x_s) + w_{t\to s}(\rho_s - \nu_s(x_s)) = m_{t\to s}(x_s) - \nu_s(x_s) \\
&= m_{t\to s}(x_s) - \hat{\theta}_s(x_s) - m_{t\to s}(x_s) = \lambda^{\mathrm{old}}_{t\to s}(x_s) - \rho^{\mathrm{old}}_s,
\end{aligned}
$$

where we used the facts that $\rho_s = w_s\nu^* = 0$ and $\nu_s(x_s) = \hat{\theta}_s(x_s) + m_{t\to s}(x_s)$ for a leaf s. We are free to add or subtract constants from the used reparametrized potentials, and if we subtract ρ^{old}_s from $\hat{\theta}_s(x_s)$, then $\lambda^{\mathrm{new}}_{t\to s} = \lambda^{\mathrm{old}}_{t\to s}$ for a leaf s. In particular, this observation shows that the loop body in Algorithm 2 (which updates only messages incoming at the root) is equivalent to jointly optimizes over incoming and outgoing messages.

Algorithm 2. Tree-based message passing

Require: Arbitrary feasible λ and ρ
1: **while** not converged **do**
2:     **loop**over trees $T \in \mathcal{T}$
3:         **Preprocess messages for** T **(Alg. 3)**
4:         Choose weights $w_s \geq 0$, $s \in \mathcal{V}_T$ s.t. $\sum_{s \in \mathcal{V}_T} w_s = 1$
5:         Determine weights $w_{t \to s}/w_{s \to t}$ (Eq. 15)
6:         For each $s \in T$ define reparamtrized unary potentials:

$$\hat{\theta}_s(x_s) \leftarrow \theta_s(x_s) + \sum_{v \notin N_T(s)} \lambda_{v \to s}(x_s)$$

7:         Run min-sum BP on T using reparametrized unary potentials $\hat{\theta}_s$
8:         Obtain min-marginals $\nu_s(x_s)$ and messages $m_{t \to s}$, $m_{s \to t}$
9:         Set $\nu^* \leftarrow \min_{x_s} \nu_s(x_s)$ (using any node s)
10:         *Tree update:* update $\lambda_{t \to s}$ and $\lambda_{s \to t}$ for all edges (s, t) in T (Eq. 17)

$$\lambda_{t \to s}(x_s) \leftarrow m_{t \to s}(x_s) + w_{t \to s}(w_s \nu^* - \nu_s(x_s))$$
$$\lambda_{s \to t}(x_t) \leftarrow m_{s \to t}(x_t) + w_{s \to t}(w_t \nu^* - \nu_t(x_t))$$

11:     **end loop**
12: **end while**

Monotone TRW Algorithm. As described in [12] one can use the tree updates of messages as a subroutine to tree-reweighted messages passing (TRW [7,14]) to obtain a monotone TRW algorithm. Message updates are performed *in parallel* for each tree $T \in \mathcal{T}$, and the final messages are averaged (potentially using a weighted average, i.e. convex combination). Since the constraints in E^*_{MAP} (Eq. 3) are convex, the convex combination of obtained messages remains feasible. Further, due to the objective being linear, the resulting dual objective is also the (weighted) average of the objectives induced by the individual tree. As already observed in [12], sequential application of tree updates is superior to TRW-like parallel updates in practice.

3   Improving Tree Updates

We show that in some sense a tree block-coordinate update of messsages resembles a node update for a node with very high degree: let $\breve{T}$ denote the set of internal nodes in T, then for the total weight outgoing from leaves we have

$$\sum_{(v,s):v \text{ is leaf}} w_{v \to s} = \sum_{(v,s):v \text{ is leaf}} \frac{w_v}{1 - w_s} \leq \frac{1}{\min_{s \in \breve{T}}\{1 - w_s\}} \sum_{v \text{ is leaf}} w_v$$

$$= \frac{1}{\min_{s \in \breve{T}}\{\sum_{s' \neq s} w_{s'}\}} \sum_{v \text{ is leaf}} w_v \leq \frac{1}{\sum_{s' \text{ is leaf}} w_{s'}} \sum_{v \text{ is leaf}} w_v = 1.$$

This implies that total weight coming from leaves is bounded by 1. In terms of information propagated to the leaves the tree-BCD method is comparable to a node update for a node with the number of leaves as its degree.

Thus, we have the following observations: (i) tree updates potentially improve the dual objective faster and pass information non-locally, but (ii) tree updates propagate no information to external (non-tree) edges, and very little information to leaf edges. Hence, the expected behavior of Algorithm 2 *without line 3* is a fast increase of the dual objective that levels off quickly. If the trees are "orthogonal" in the sense that they have no edge in common (e.g. chains corresponding to rows and columns in the image), then Algorithm 2 will converge to a (likely non-optimal) objective value in a finite number of tree updates (since reparametrized unary potentials at nodes are uninformative). Our approach to solve this dilemma is given in line 3 of the algorithm: messages are reparametrized such that tree edges are as informative as possible. This is achieved by invoking node updates (Eq. 9) with suitably chosen weights (see Algorithm 3): weights are close to 0 for non-tree edges, and large for tree edges (such that the normalization constraint is satisfied).

Such a preprocessing step of messages in not required for agreement seeking approaches to optimize J_{MAP} (Eq. 4), since both reparametrized unary and pairwise potentials carry the effective value of a state (see e.g. [11]). On the other hand, this property limits how effective information can be spread through the graph, and consequently the tree block-coordinate method proposed in [12] shows rather slow convergence as we will demonstrate in the next section.

Algorithm 3. Message preprocessing

Require: Arbitrary feasible λ, tree T, $0 < \varepsilon \ll 1$
  1: **loop** over $s \in \mathcal{V}_T$
  2:    Choose weights $w_{t \to s}$, $t \in N(s)$: $w_{t \to s} = \begin{cases} \varepsilon & \text{if } (s,t) \notin \mathcal{E}_T \\ \varepsilon + \frac{1-\varepsilon}{\deg_T(s)} \deg(s) & \text{otherwise.} \end{cases}$
  3:    Update $\lambda_{t \to s}$ (Eq. 9) using $\{w_{t \to s}\}$
  4: **end loop**

---

4   Results

In Fig. 1 we show the evolution of dual energies for dense stereo correspondence problems (the standard 450×375 and high resolution 900×750 "Cones" and "Teddy" stereo image pair [10]). The unary potentials (data term) are a Hamming distance of 9×7 census-transformed patches, and the pairwise potentials are given by the (gradient-adapted) P_1-P_2 penalizer [6] (with $P_1 = P_2/2$). We show the increase of the energy with respect to CPU time for 4 methods: (i) "Sontag-Jaakkola" is the method propsed in [12] using two spanning trees (one with horizontal chains connected by a vertical one, and another tree consisting of vertical chains linked by a horizontal one), "naive tree BCD" running Algorithm 2 *without*

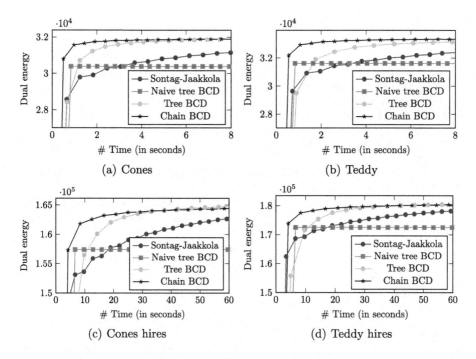

Fig. 1. Evolution of (dual) objective versus CPU time for dense stereo estimation.

message preprocessing (line 3) on the same trees, "tree BCD" refers to running Algorithm 2 *including message preprocessing*, and "chain BCD" corresponds to Algorithm 2 (with message preprocessing) run on "generalized" horizontal chains (i.e. chains defined by image rows extended by edges to pixels in neighboring rows). These chains are alternately traversed in top-to-bottom and bottom-to-top order. As expected for trees (almost) not having any edge in common, "naive tree BCD" converges to a suboptimal solution after two iterations, whereas all other method continue to improve their objectives. "Chain BCD" shows the fastest convergence and reaches a close to its final objective in only two passes over the images (i.e. one downward and one upward pass with generalized chains). Hence, it is an interesting candidate for "truncated" MAP inference that is allowed only a small number of message updates (see e.g. [2], and the popular semi-global matching approach [6] can be seen as instance of a one-step truncated TRW method [3]). More details on the setup and further numerical results and visualization can be found in the supplementary material.

5   Conclusion

In this work we present a novel tree block-coordinate method for MAP inference via message passing. As a byproduct it allows us to have a better understanding why tree updates of messages are less effective than expected, and how to overcome its poor performance. Future work includes utilizing our inference method in the context of parameter learning for structured prediction.

References

1. Boykov, Y., Veksler, O., Zabih, R.: Fast approximate energy minimization via graph cuts. IEEE Trans. Pattern Anal. Mach. Intell. **23**(11), 1222–1239 (2001)
2. Domke, J.: Parameter learning with truncated message-passing. In: Proceedings of the CVPR, pp. 2937–2943 (2011)
3. Drory, A., Haubold, C., Avidan, S., Hamprecht, F.A.: Semi-global matching: a principled derivation in terms of message passing. In: Jiang, X., Hornegger, J., Koch, R. (eds.) GCPR 2014. LNCS, vol. 8753, pp. 43–53. Springer, Heidelberg (2014)
4. Globerson, A., Jaakkola, T.: Fixing max-product: convergent message passing algorithms for MAP LP-relaxations. In: NIPS (2007)
5. Hazan, T., Shashua, A.: Norm-prodcut belief propagtion: primal-dual message-passing for LP-relaxation and approximate-inference. IEEE Trans. Inf. Theory **56**(12), 6294–6316 (2010)
6. Hirschmüller, H.: Accurate and efficient stereo processing by semi-global matching and mutual information. In: Proceedings CVPR, pp. 807–814 (2005)
7. Kolmogorov, V.: Convergent tree-reweighted message passing for energy minimization. IEEE Trans. Pattern Anal. Mach. Intell. **28**(10), 1568–1583 (2006)
8. Lempitsky, V., Rother, C., Roth, S., Blake, A.: Fusion moves for Markov random field optimization. IEEE Trans. Pattern Anal. Mach. Intell. **32**(8), 1392–1405 (2010)
9. Pearl, J.: Probabilistic Reasoning in Intelligent Systems. Morgan Kaufmann, Mountain view (1988)
10. Scharstein, D., Szeliski, R.: High-accuracy stereo depth maps using structured light. In: Proceedings of the CVPR, pp. 195–202 (2003)
11. Sontag, D., Globerson, A., Jaakkola, T.: Optimization for machine learning. In: Introduction to Dual Decomposition for Inference. MIT Press (2011)
12. Sontag, D., Jaakkola, T.: Tree block coordinate descent for MAP in graphical models. J. Mach. Learn. Res. **5**, 544–551 (2009)
13. Wainwright, M.J., Jordan, M.I.: Graphical models, exponential families, and variational inference. Found. Trends Mach. Learn. **1**, 1–305 (2008)
14. Wainwright, M.J., Jaakkola, T.S., Willsky, A.S.: MAP estimation via agreement on trees: message-passing and linear programming. IEEE Trans. Inf. Theory **51**(11), 3697–3717 (2005)
15. Weiss, Y., Yanover, C., Meltzer, T.: MAP estimation, linear programming and belief propagation with convex free energies. In: UAI (2007)
16. Werner, T.: A linear programming approach to max-sum problem: a review. IEEE Trans. Pattern Anal. Mach. Intell. **29**(7), 1165–1179 (2007)
17. Zach, C.: A principled approach for coarse-to-fine MAP inference. In: Proceedings of the CVPR, pp. 1330–1337 (2014)

A Parametric Spectral Model for Texture-Based Salience

Kasim Terzić[(✉)], Sai Krishna, and J.M.H. du Buf

Vision Laboratory/LARSys, University of the Algarve, Faro, Portuga
{kterzic,dubuf}@ualg.pt

Abstract. We present a novel saliency mechanism based on texture. Local texture at each pixel is characterised by the 2D spectrum obtained from oriented Gabor filters. We then apply a parametric model and describe the texture at each pixel by a combination of two 1D Gaussian approximations. This results in a simple model which consists of only four parameters. These four parameters are then used as feature channels and standard Difference-of-Gaussian blob detection is applied in order to detect salient areas in the image, similar to the Itti and Koch model. Finally, a diffusion process is used to sharpen the resulting regions. Evaluation on a large saliency dataset shows a significant improvement of our method over the baseline Itti and Koch model.

1 Introduction

Texture is known to be a powerful cue in early vision [20,32] and has consequently received much attention from the Computer Vision and Neuroscience communities. The seminal work on saliency maps by Itti and Koch included an orientation component, calculated by a bank of Gabor filters [16], and there has been much work on texture segmentation. However, texture remains one of the hardest feature channels to model, and most recent work on saliency focuses on colour, contrast and local region descriptors.

In this paper, we return to the problem of texture in saliency models by extending the Itti and Koch model. By interpreting oriented Gabor filter responses as a local power spectrum of the image, we define a simple parametric model in order to characterise local texture in terms of orientation, anisotropy, scale and complexity. The model parameters are then used as features and processed by a set of centre-surround cells, as in [16] and followed by a simple diffusion process to obtain preliminary results. Evaluation on a standard saliency dataset shows that our texture-based saliency model outperforms other texture-based models. It is competitive with the original Itti and Koch model, despite only using texture. A combination of texture and colour outperforms the baseline Itti and Koch model and achieves promising results.

Our texture model is built on top of responses of complex cells in V1 which can be efficiently computed [30]. Consequently, it not only adds a powerful feature to saliency estimation methods, but could also serve as a plausible texture model for early vision.

© Springer International Publishing Switzerland 2015
J. Gall et al. (Eds.): GCPR 2015, LNCS 9358, pp. 331–342, 2015.
DOI: 10.1007/978-3-319-24947-6_27

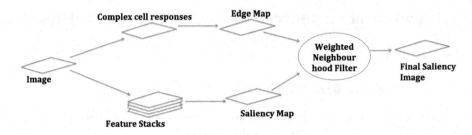

Fig. 1. Overview of our texture-based saliency method. First, the input image is processed using a bank of Gabor filters. The responses are used to obtain complex cell responses and the edge map (top), and to obtain a stack of texture features which are processed by a set of centre-surround cells to obtain a saliency map (bottom). The saliency map is combined with the edge map in a diffusion filtering step to provide the final texture-based saliency map.

2   Related Work

Much work on visual saliency is motivated by the early processing in the visual cortex. One of the first biological models was created by Itti, Koch and Niebur [16,18], where intensity, colour and orientation maps are processed by a bank of centre-surround filters. This influential model shaped much of later work on saliency and attention. Related work includes weighting of different feature maps after identifying useful features [15] and exploring the role of saliency in overt attention [25]. It has been noted that the original Itti and Koch model, designed for eye movement simulation, is not well-suited for object-based salience, and an extended model was shown to reach state-of-the-art results [8]. Similarly, eye fixation maps were combined with traditional segmentation methods in [22].

In recent years, there has been a shift towards detecting complete salient objects in scenes, with a large region covering most of an object. Often, an image is segmented, and regions are labelled according to colour and luminance [1], region-based contrast [5,6] or dissimilarity between image patches [7]. One approach attempts to learn a correct foreground object segmentation from training images [23]. Object-based saliency is important for interfacing with scene-understanding systems from AI [24,28] or for cognitive robotics [29], where sequential scene processing is common.

Other approaches from Computer Vision include image regions which represent the scene in terms of visual perception [10], graph-based visual saliency [13], and object-based saliency features [12]. There have also been attempts to model saliency as a discriminant process [9], a regression problem [19], or using a Bayesian surprise criterion [17]. It has been shown that hierarchical, multi-scale processing can improve saliency on small-scale, high-contrast patterns [33].

Very few saliency methods explicitly use spatial frequency or texture. In addition to the approaches related to the Itti and Koch model, which use orientation as one of the feature channels, there have been several approaches using the frequency spectrum. Achanta et al. [2] used bandpass filtering to obtain uniform regions with sharp boundaries, but their features were still based on colour. Two approaches extracted saliency from the frequency spectrum of the image. Hou and Zhang introduced a method based on the global Fourier transform [14]. By subtracting the average log-spectrum of many images from the log-spectrum of the individual image, they obtain a spectral residual which, when transformed back into the spatial domain, indicates salient regions which potentially correspond to objects. Guo et al. [11] built on this concept, but argued that the phase, not amplitude, of the spectrum is key to finding salient regions. They extended this concept to the Quaternion Fourier Transform which can represent intensity, colour and motion of each pixel. Neither of these methods is biologically plausible, or based on texture. We are not aware of any recent work on saliency which attempts to explicitly model and compare texture.

In the rest of this paper we present a new and more biological interpretation of the local Gabor filter responses. We describe the local texture using a parametric model. The parameters of this model represent new features, which are then processed using centre-surround filters.

3 Method

Our method attempts to find consistent regions which are different from their surroundings, using centre-surround blob detection. To this end, we characterise local texture at each pixel using a parametric model, where the four parameters correspond to orientation selectivity (isotropic-anisotropic), dominant orientation, scale selectivity, and dominant scale (from coarse to fine). Figure 1 shows an overview of our method. We calculate the edge map based on the responses of complex cells. In parallel we extract four feature maps based on texture and calculate a salience map by performing blob detection. The salience map is combined with the edge map in a weighted-filtering step.

3.1 V1 Model

Our method begins by extracting responses of oriented Gabor filters at multiple orientations and scales. Gabor filters are commonly used as a model of so-called simple cells in the early visual cortex. In our implementation, we rely on the fast V1 model from [31], applying default parameters: 8 orientations and 7 logarithmically spaced scales. Complex Gabor filters are modelled by

$$G_{\lambda,\sigma,\theta}(x,y) = \exp\left(-\frac{\tilde{x}^2 + \gamma\tilde{y}^2}{2\sigma^2}\right) \exp\left(i\frac{2\pi\tilde{x}}{\lambda}\right), \tag{1}$$

where

$$\tilde{x} = x\cos\theta + y\sin\theta \tag{2}$$

$$\tilde{y} = y\cos\theta - x\sin\theta, \tag{3}$$

λ is the wavelength in pixels, and σ the receptive field size in pixels. We apply default parameters from [31]: $\sigma/\lambda = 0.56$, $\gamma = 0.5$ and θ assumes 8 values, equally spaced on $[0, \pi)$.

Responses of simple cells are obtained by convolving the image with the complex Gabor filters:

$$S_{\lambda,\theta} = I * G_{\lambda,\theta}. \tag{4}$$

The moduli of simple cell responses are used to model complex cortical cells:

$$C_{\lambda,\theta}(x,y) = |S_{\lambda,\theta}(x,y)|. \tag{5}$$

3.2 Local Texture Model

Since Gabor filters are bandpass filters, it is evident that the responses of all complex cells computed at a particular position represent the frequency spectrum of the local region. Each filter response represents a sample in this power spectrum. Although Gabor filtering is typically expensive, it is the first step of any biological model, and there are optimised and GPU-accelerated solutions [31].

Like the corresponding Gabor filters, the spectrum has two dimensions: orientation (corresponding to filter orientation) and frequency (corresponding to filter wavelength), which effectively yields a 2D matrix. This matrix is cyclic in the orientation, i.e., a cylinder. In our model, we assume that the power spectrum can be approximated by a 2D-separable Gaussian function. This is obviously a very rough approximation, but we are not interested in reconstructing the texture, only in measuring whether there is a noticeable difference between the textures at neighbouring positions. In practice, we found that approximating the marginals by two 1D Gaussians is simpler and also produces good results.

The processing of each 2D matrix is very simple and fast. First, the noisy spectrum is smoothed by applying a 3×3 lowpass block filter. Then, the 2D array is projected (summed) into two 1D arrays: the scale array S_i and the (cyclic) orientation array O_i. In both arrays, the local maximum is detected, yielding the "means" μ_s and μ_o, after which the standard deviations σ_s and σ_o are computed, taking into account the periodicity of O_i. Experimental results revealed no significant differences between using the maxima as means and using the real means as computed by moments. Figure 2 illustrates this process.

As described above, the local power spectrum is modelled by four parameters: the means and standard deviations in the orientation and frequency dimensions. The mean orientation of the Gaussian μ_o thus encodes the dominant orientation of the texture, and the standard deviation σ_o is a measure of isotropy: small values of σ_o indicate a strong preference for a particular direction, while large values mean that many different orientations are present. In terms of frequency, μ_s encodes the characteristic scale of the texture, coarse vs. fine, while σ_s tells us whether there is one characteristic scale or a mixture of coarse and fine scales. Figure 3 shows the four texture features extracted from a real image.

This model is obviously not very discriminative: it does not deal with multimodal and non-Gaussian spectra. However, it is considerably more powerful than just using the dominant local orientation, and the additional complexity is minimal – Gabor filtering is far more expensive than curve fitting. The four

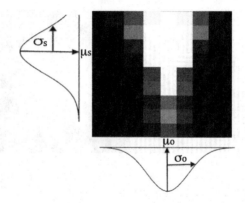

Fig. 2. Our texture model. A local power spectrum is a 2D matrix where the dimensions represent orientation (horizontal axis) and frequency (vertical). The spectrum resembles a 2D Gaussian function. We can fit two 1D Gaussians to the 1D marginals of the spectrum to obtain the means and standard deviations of orientation and frequency, which we use as features.

Fig. 3. Our texture features extracted from a real image. Blob detection on these feature maps is used to produce a saliency map.

parameters described above are then used with blob-detection kernels to extract salient textured regions. Then blob extraction is applied as shown in Fig. 4.

3.3 Blob Detection

The blob detection step is the same as in [16]. The four parameters $\mu_o, \sigma_o, \mu_s, \sigma_s$ are calculated for each pixel of the image and stored in four maps with the same dimensions as the image: M_μ^o, M_μ^s, M_σ^o and M_σ^s. The algorithm works on full-sized images, but subsampling is possible for improving the speed of the filtering operations.

The four maps are then processed by a bank of centre-surround Difference-of-Gaussian filters with different sizes, as is common. In our implementation, we use three sizes and the filters are typical "mexican hat" kernels which combine a positive Gaussian and a negative one with a larger standard deviation. For the three different filter sizes, the standard deviations of the positive Gaussians are 45, 90 and 180 pixels, and those of the negative Gaussians are 90, 180 and 360,

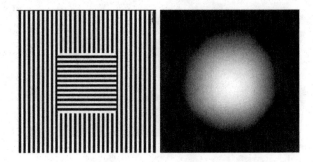

Fig. 4. An example of texture saliency. The image on the left has a salient region identified only by texture (average intensity and colour are the same). Blob detection based on colour fails in this case, but blob detection based on texture features as described in this paper detects a salient blob (right image).

respectively. The filters need to be large in order to capture large salient objects, but this presents a problem with smaller images. We therefore apply extensive border-replicating padding of the feature images to avoid this problem. The resulting 12 saliency maps are summed and normalised to 0-255 to obtain the pre-final saliency map.

3.4 Region Sharpening

Blob detection is good at identifying the centres of salient regions, but blob boundaries are poorly defined. It may be useful for overt attention models, but less useful for localising and segmenting salient objects. In order to sharpen region boundaries and to create more homogeneous regions which better correspond to complete objects, we apply a non-linear diffusion step. Although the idea of diffusion in early vision is not without controversy, it has been suggested that colouring and surface interpolation mechanisms take place in V1 [21], especially as a result of feedback from higher areas V2 and V4 [27].

We begin by taking the sum of all complex cell responses extracted at the finest scale:

$$C_{\text{edge}}(x, y) = \sum_{\theta} C_{\lambda,\theta}(x, y), \tag{6}$$

where λ corresponds to the finest scale applied in the previous step. The combined map C_{edge} resembles an edge map, where large values correspond to narrow bars or sharp transitions between different intensity values. This map is normalised to the range 0–1.

We then apply a weighted neighbourhood filter to each point in the saliency map S, based on the values of its neighbours:

$$s(x, y) = \frac{1}{8} \sum_{i \in 1}^{8} w_i S_i, \tag{7}$$

w1	w2	w3
w8		w4
w7	w6	w5

Fig. 5. Weights used in the diffusion filtering step. We simulate the diffusion process by repeated weighted average filtering.

where s_i are the 8 neighbours of the central pixel $s(x, y)$: $S_1 = s(x - 1, y - 1)$, $S_2 = s(x, y - 1)$, etc. (see Fig. 5 for an illustration). The weights w_i depend on the strength of the edge map C_{edge} at that pixel:

$$w_i = (1 - C_i), \tag{8}$$

where C_i is the value of the edge map C_{edge} at relative position i.

The result of this filtering is a strong influence of neighbouring pixels not lying on an edge, and no influence of pixels located on edges. This can be seen as a dynamical diffusion process in the early visual cortex, where neighbouring cells (representing saliency) excite each other, but the connections are inhibited by complex cells. In our model, we repeat the filtering process a set number of times to approximate the equilibrium solution. A further improvement can be obtained by extracting closed contours from the image before filtering.

The filtering process ensures that closed regions become more uniformly salient, while outside regions become less salient. Figure 6 shows an example of this process on a real image. It can be seen that the shape of the blob is acceptable although it is too big because of the sizes of the Difference-of-Gaussian filters. It is also stronger close to the edges, and some parts of the object have low salience. The diffusion filtering on the basis of responses of complex cells at the finest scale is able to correct the size and, because responses outside the blob are suppressed, thresholding can be applied to obtain a binary mask. Below, the threshold value will be used as a free parameter in quantitative evaluation.

4   Evaluation

We evaluated the texture-based saliency method on the standard saliency dataset developed by Achanta et al. [2] The dataset consists of 1000 images, each containing a single salient object, plus hand-annotated ground-truth masks.

Figure 7 shows the results of our algorithm on some of the images from the dataset. It can be seen that our algorithm consistently highlights the salient regions in the images. The diffusion step results in well-defined region boundaries which correspond to entire objects.

Figure 8 (left) shows a comparison of our texture-only algorithm against similar algorithms: the Itti and Koch baseline model on this dataset and two

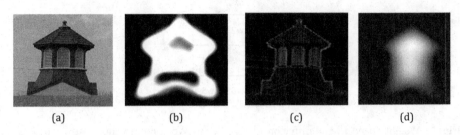

(a)   (b)   (c)   (d)

Fig. 6. Left to right: input image, the result of blob detection, edges obtained from the responses of complex cells, and saliency corrected by diffusion filtering. Texture saliency responds strongly to areas where texture is different from its surrounding, but it does not uniformly cover the entire object and, due to large blob detection kernels, it also responds outside object boundaries. Combining saliency with image edges during the diffusion filtering step results in smoother, object-based saliency.

approaches based on texture or frequency. We plot the precision-recall curves obtained by varying the threshold used to binarise the saliency images. Precision and recall are computed by comparing each pixel in the saliency map with the hand-annotated ground truth map, counting all true and false positives and negatives in all 1000 images. Our algorithm outperforms the other methods, significantly improving the state of the art in terms of texture-based saliency. It can be seen that our texture saliency alone can slightly outperform the classic Itti and Koch model. This is most likely due to the selection of kernel sizes for blob detection, since their model was designed before this dataset became popular, and was optimised for modelling sequential saccadic eye movements. Figure 8 (right) shows a comparison with two state-of-the-art methods. We added three colour features to our model and averaged the salience maps for this experiment.

5   Discussion

The texture parameters applied in the salience model are based on a more complex model [3], but extremely simplified in order to be applicable in real-time applications. Nevertheless, the very good results in terms of salience suggest that further refinements may not be required if texture is going to be combined with colour, motion and stereo disparity. More advanced texture models exist, for example based on models of cortical grating cells on top of which the texture symmetry order could be detected (linear, rectangular, hexagonal, etc.) [4], but this information may not be very accurate in real-world applications where almost no textures show perfect symmetries.

There are several recent methods which obtain better results than our method on this dataset. We stress that our work was aimed at creating novel texture-based features and that results presented here are preliminary. Integration of our features with state-of-the-art methods and a wider selection of features is expected to make our model more competitive. In this paper, we concentrated on the improvement in texture-based saliency, which is a much overlooked part of saliency models.

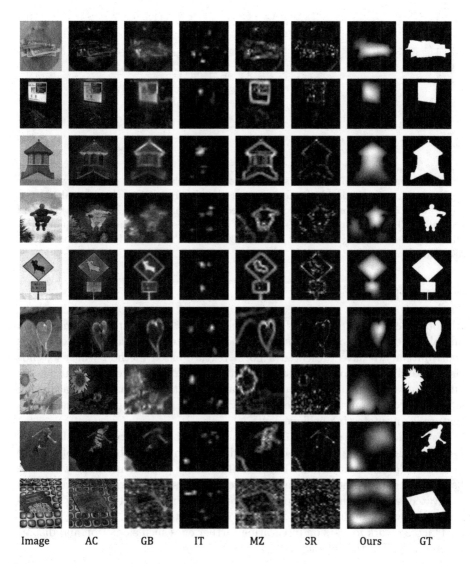

Fig. 7. Visual comparison of results on the saliency dataset. The input images are shown in the left column. The ground truth annotations are shown in the right column. The remaining columns, from left to right, show the results of AC [2], GB [13], IT [16], MZ [11], SR [14], and our algorithm, before thresholding. The bottom three rows show some difficult examples. Our algorithm responds strongly to the alternating textures of the leaves and the wall in the bottom left corner of the sunflower image (third from below), and fails completely with the passport image (bottom row). In the second row from below, we also detect the rock, which is salient but not annotated.

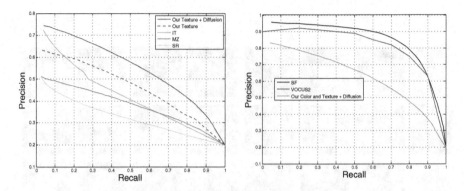

Fig. 8. Comparison against some state-of-the-art models. The left graph shows a comparison against methods which incorporate texture or frequency: the original Itti and Koch model (IT) [16], and the spectrum-based models of Hou and Zhang (SR) [14] and Guo et al. [11]. The right graph shows our model extended with colour against two state-of-the-art models: Perazzi et al. (SF) [26] and the improved Itti and Koch model VOCUS2 [8].

6   Conclusion

Although texture is considered an important cue for attention, segmentation and object detection, only few saliency models currently exploit texture. In this contribution, we have presented a novel texture-based method which extends the Itti and Koch model and shows that texture can be a very useful cue for advancing saliency models. We are not aware of any texture-based work achieving significant results on standardised saliency datasets, so showing results using only texture is an interesting achievement.

Evaluation on the standard dataset shows that our saliency model alone outperforms the baseline Itti and Koch model, and that a combination of texture and colour adds an additional boost. Unlike many popular methods which are based on region segmentation and local descriptors, our method is biologically motivated and could help to explain the role of texture in early saliency processing, and how it can drive saccadic eye movements to objects.

Ongoing work focuses on integrating further cues such as motion and disparity, and applying the saliency model on a real-time robot.

Acknowledgements. This work was supported by the EU under the FP-7 grant ICT-2009.2.1-270247 *NeuralDynamics* and by the FCT under the grants LarSYS UID/EEA/50009/2013 and SparseCoding EXPL/EEI-SII/1982/2013.

References

1. Achanta, R., Estrada, F.J., Wils, P., Süsstrunk, S.: Salient region detection and segmentation. In: Gasteratos, A., Vincze, M., Tsotsos, J.K. (eds.) ICVS 2008. LNCS, vol. 5008, pp. 66–75. Springer, Heidelberg (2008)

2. Achanta, R., Hemami, S.S., Estrada, F.J., Süsstrunk, S.: Frequency-tuned salient region detection. In: CVPR, pp. 1597–1604 (2009)
3. du Buf, J.: Abstract processes in texture discrimination. Spat. Vis. **6**, 221–242 (1992)
4. du Buf, J.: Improved grating and bar cell models in cortical area V1 and texture coding. Image Vis. Comput. **25**, 873–882 (2007)
5. Cheng, M.M., Mitra, N.J., Huang, X., Torr, P.H.S., Hu, S.M.: Global contrast based salient region detection. IEEE T-PAMI **37**(3), 569–582 (2015)
6. Cheng, M., Zhang, G., Mitra, N.J., Huang, X., Hu, S.: Global contrast based salient region detection. In: CVPR, pp. 409–416 (2011)
7. Duan, L., Wu, C., Miao, J., Qing, L., Fu, Y.: Visual saliency detection by spatially weighted dissimilarity. In: CVPR, pp. 473–480 (2011)
8. Frintrop, S., Werner, T., Martin-Garcia, G.: Traditional saliency reloaded: a good old model in new shape. In: CVPR (2015)
9. Gao, D., Vasconcelos, N.: Bottom-up saliency is a discriminant process. In: ICCV, pp. 1–6 (2007)
10. Goferman, S., Zelnik-Manor, L., Tal, A.: Context-aware saliency detection. In: CVPR, pp. 2376–2383 (2010)
11. Guo, C., Ma, Q., Zhang, L.: Spatio-temporal saliency detection using phase spectrum of quaternion fourier transform. In: CVPR (2008)
12. Han, J., Ngan, K.N., Li, M., Zhang, H.: Unsupervised extraction of visual attention objects in color images. IEEE Trans. Circuits Syst. Video Techn. **16**(1), 141–145 (2006)
13. Harel, J., Koch, C., Perona, P.: Graph-based visual saliency. In: NIPS, pp. 545–552 (2006)
14. Hou, X., Zhang, L.: Saliency detection: a spectral residual approach. In: CVPR (2007)
15. Hu, Y., Xie, X., Ma, W.-Y., Chia, L.-T., Rajan, D.: Salient region detection using weighted feature maps based on the human visual attention model. In: Aizawa, K., Nakamura, Y., Satoh, S. (eds.) PCM 2004. LNCS, vol. 3332, pp. 993–1000. Springer, Heidelberg (2004)
16. Itti, L., Koch, C.: A saliency-based search mechanism for overt and covert shifts of visual attention. Vision Res. **40**(10–12), 1489–1506 (2000)
17. Itti, L., Baldi, P.: Bayesian surprise attracts human attention. In: NIPS, pp. 547–554 (2005)
18. Itti, L., Koch, C., Niebur, E.: A model of saliency-based visual attention for rapid scene analysis. IEEE Trans. Pattern Anal. Mach. Intell. **20**(11), 1254–1259 (1998)
19. Jiang, H., Wang, J., Yuan, Z., Wu, Y., Zheng, N.: Salient object detection: a discriminative regional feature integration approach. In: CVPR (2013)
20. Julesz, B.: Textons, the elements of texture perception, and their interactions. Nature **290**(5802), 91–97 (1981)
21. Lee, T.S., Mumford, D., Romero, R., Lamme, V.F.: The role of the primary visual cortex in higher level vision. Vision Res. **38**, 2429–2454 (1998)
22. Li, Y., Hou, X., Koch, C., Rehg, J.M., Yuille, A.L.: The secrets of salient object segmentation. In: CVPR, pp. 280–287 (2014)
23. Liu, T., Sun, J., Zheng, N., Tang, X., Shum, H.: Learning to detect a salient object. In: CVPR (2007)
24. Neumann, B., Terzić, K.: Context-based probabilistic scene interpretation. In: IFIP AI, pp. 155–164, September 2010
25. Parkhurst, D., Law, K., Niebur, E.: Modeling the role of salience in the allocation of overt visual attention. Vision Res. **42**(1), 107–123 (2002)

26. Perazzi, F., Krähenbühl, P., Pritch, Y., Hornung, A.: Saliency filters: Contrast based filtering for salient region detection. In: IEEE CVPR, pp. 733–740 (2012)
27. Self, M.W., van Kerkoerle, T., Super, H., Roelfsema, P.R.: Distinct roles of the cortical layers of area V1 in figure-ground segregation. Curr. Biol. **23**, 2121–2129 (2013)
28. Terzić, K., Hotz, L., Šochman, J.: Interpreting structures in man-made scenes: combining low-level and high-level structure sources. In: International Conference on Agents and Artificial Intelligence. Valencia, Spain, January 2010
29. Terzić, K., Lobato, D., Saleiro, M., Martins, J., Farrajota, M., Rodrigues, J.M.F., du Buf, J.M.H.: Biological models for active vision: towards a unified architecture. In: Chen, M., Leibe, B., Neumann, B. (eds.) ICVS 2013. LNCS, vol. 7963, pp. 113–122. Springer, Heidelberg (2013)
30. Terzić, K., Rodrigues, J., du Buf, J.: Fast cortical keypoints for real-time object recognition. In: ICIP, pp. 3372–3376. Melbourne, September 2013
31. Terzić, K., Rodrigues, J., du Buf, J.: BIMP: a real-time biological model of multi-scale keypoint detection in V1. Neurocomputing **150**, 227–237 (2015)
32. Wolfe, J.M., Horowitz, T.S.: What attributes guide the deployment of visual attention and how do they do it? Nat. Rev. Neurosci. **5**, 495–501 (2004)
33. Yan, Q., Xu, L., Shi, J., Jia, J.: Hierarchical saliency detection. In: CVPR (2013)

High Speed Lossless Image Compression

Hendrik Siedelmann[1,2(✉)], Alexander Wender[1], and Martin Fuchs[1]

[1] University of Stuttgart, Stuttgart, Germany
hendrik.siedelmann@googlemail.com
[2] Heidelberg University, Heidelberg, Germany

Abstract. We introduce a simple approach to lossless image compression, which makes use of SIMD vectorization at every processing step to provide very high speed on modern CPUs. This is achieved by basing the compression on delta coding for prediction and bit packing for the actual compression, allowing a tuneable tradeoff between efficiency and speed, via the block size used for bit packing. The maximum achievable speed surpasses main memory bandwidth on the tested CPU, as well as the speed of all previous methods that achieve at least the same coding efficiency.

1 Introduction

For applications which need to process large amounts of image data such as high speed video or high resolution light fields, the I/O subsystem can easily become the bottleneck, even when using a RAID0 or SSDs for storage. This makes compression an attractive tool to widen this bottleneck, increasing overall performance. As lossy compression incurs signal degradation and may interfere with further processing, we will only consider lossless compression in the following. While dictionary based compression methods like `lzo` [18] can reach a high bandwidth, the compression ratio of such generic compression methods is quite low compared to dedicated image compression methods. However, research in lossless image compression has mainly been concerned with the maximization of the compression ratio, and even relatively fast image compression schemes like `jpeg-ls` are not able to keep up with the transfer rates of fast I/O configurations.

In this article, we present a simple lossless image compression scheme, which makes use of the SIMD instructions of modern CPUs to achieve extremely high performance. Our implementation allows a configurable tradeoff between speed and compression and exceeds the memory transfer speeds of modern CPUs in its fastest configuration, allowing incorporation of lossless compression into many areas where compression was not feasible before. Our specific use case, which motivated this work, is an example of such an application: recording a very large and dense light field data set (several terabytes in size), requiring a continuous compression bandwidth of 360 MiB/s, a rate which the used I/O configuration was not able to guarantee on its own.

© Springer International Publishing Switzerland 2015
J. Gall et al. (Eds.): GCPR 2015, LNCS 9358, pp. 343–355, 2015.
DOI: 10.1007/978-3-319-24947-6_28

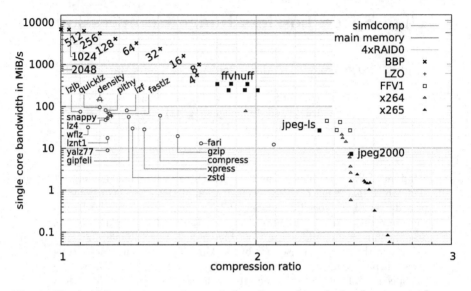

Fig. 1. Bandwidth vs. compression ratio for all tested methods, showing single core results on an Intel® Core™ i7-2600 CPU on the "blue sky" test sequence from the SVT data set [12]. "BBP" denotes our method for several block sizes from 2048 to 4 bytes. An example 4xRAID0 configuration and main memory bandwidth are included for comparison. The `simdcomp` method is the C implementation of [14] and can, in general, not compress image data, but is shown for bandwidth comparison. For `lzo`, and `ffvhuff` all configurations are shown, as well as all available presets for `x264` and `x265`.

1.1   Applications of Lossless Image Compression

Compression is always a tradeoff of processing resources against bandwidth and storage. While lossy compression provides high compression ratios, its application is limited to areas where the distortion of the signal due to lossy compression does not pose a problem. But in some cases losses are not acceptable. Examples for this include reference data sets for image processing or sophisticated image processing, like superresolution. In this case, lossless compression may still provide an overall performance increase due to bandwidth savings as well as reduced storage requirements. However lossless compression provides less compression, which reduces the gain obtained from using it. In many capture scenarios, the required bandwidth for on the fly compression, before initial storage, imposes a hard constraint. This is addressed by the proposed scheme, as compression bandwidth can be adjusted to speeds that surpass memory transfer speeds, a hard limit for any hardware configuration.

2   Related Work

In the following, we briefly discuss lossless compression methods that focus on high speed, see Fig. 1 for an overview of evaluated methods. The methods are ordered by the dimensionality of the compression scheme, starting with generic 1D compression algorithms. Any compression method with lower dimensionality may be used to compress data with a higher dimensionality at reduced efficiency, as correlation in the missing dimensions cannot be exploited. On the other hand, lower dimensionality can lead to lower algorithmic complexity and therefore higher speed. While the method discussed in this paper is a pure image compression method, we will regard and evaluate compression from the basis of compressing a video stream, which allows the inclusion of advanced lossless video compression methods like AVC and HEVC which allow higher compression ratios by exploiting the 3D correlation. Also applications for high bandwidth image processing like light field, or high speed video capture, may allow the use of video compression methods, making an evaluation based on video data adequate.

2.1 Dictionary and 1D Compression

General purpose compression methods like deflate (zlib/gzip) [10] or bzip2 [23] achieve good compression ratios for most types of inputs, but are quite slow, with a maximum bandwidth of around 30 MiB/s on an off-the-shelf Intel Core i7-2600 CPU. Faster methods, including lzo, lz4 and gipfeli [9,15,18] are more directly based on the original LZ77 compression scheme [28] and provide a bandwidth of up to 152 MiB/s for our configuration, see Fig. 1. This performance has led to the utilization for lossless 4 K image transmission [11], but compared to image based methods the compression ratio is rather poor, as dictionary based methods are not well suited to the task of image coding. Specialized methods adapted for specific tasks, like integer or floating point compression, provide a much higher speed of several gigabytes per second, by using a simple bit packing approach [8,14] and exploiting the SIMD instructions provided by modern CPU architectures [14]. However, those methods operate on 32 bit integers or 64 bit floating point values and are thus not directly applicable to the compression of 8 bit image data. We have developed an algorithm which uses SIMD bit packing for the actual compression, combining it with a prediction scheme and small block sizes, allowing efficient compression of image data. See Sect. 3 for details.

2.2 Image Compression

Dedicated lossless image compression methods like jpeg-ls [27] peak at around 25MiB/s, with modifications reaching 75MiB/s on an Intel® Core™ i7-920 processor at 2.67 GHz [26]. The jpeg-ls codec was standardized in 1999 and is still widely used as the baseline for the evaluation of lossless image compression methods. To our knowledge there are no significantly faster methods available, even though the gap to the fastest 1D compression method [14] amounts to more than two orders of magnitude. Later works mainly concentrate on increasing compression efficiency at reduced speed, which is not the focus of this work.

2.3 Video Compression

State of the art video standards like HEVC, as well as its predecessor AVC, include lossless profiles which provide high compression ratios. The ffvhuff coder from the `ffmpeg` library [3] based on `HuffYUV` [24], which uses the `jpeg-ls` predictor together with simple Huffmann coding, obtains a speed of 343 MiB/s, the highest speed for any video codec we evaluated, see Fig. 1. Another interesting compressor is the `ffv1` coder [17] at 44 MiB/s, also from `ffmpeg`, which combines a `jpeg-ls` style predictor with a context adaptive entropy coder, based on similiar principles as the one from `AVC`, with context adaption over several frames. The `ffv1` coder achieves a compression ratio and speed competitive to `AVC`, see Fig. 1.

2.4 GPU Aided Compression

There have been various efforts to improve the performance of different compression techniques by using the massively parallel computation capabilities of modern GPUs. For 1D compression a text based method has been ported to the GPU by Ozsoy et al. [21] demonstrating a speedup of up to 2.21x for the GPU solution. Floating point compression based on bit packing has also been shown to reach a speedup of 5x [20], but at the cost of a reduced compression efficiency and in comparison to a CPU version which does not make use of SIMD for bit packing, like implemented in [14].

An approach for GPU based predictive lossless image coding has been presented by Kau and Chen, showing a speedup of up to 5x with a combined system utilizing GPU and CPU [13], however absolute performance is quite low at less than 1 MiB/s. The `cuj2k` library, implementing `jpeg2000` on the GPU provides similar performance to a parallel `jpeg2000` implementation for the CPU [2]. The work presented by Treib et al. [25], implementing a simple wavelet based compressor, provides results with slightly worse compression than `jpeg2000` but with a compression speed of up to 700 MiB/s, which is significantly higher than previous approaches.

The difficulties in porting standard image compression methods to the GPU are analyzed by Richter and Simon [22], specifically for `jpeg` and `jpeg2000`. They conclude that especially the entropy coding part proves difficult for modern GPUs, together with the codestream build-up. Their observations include also the case where a highly optimized CPU implementation outperforms a GPU based approach. These considerations have led us to the conclusion that a carefully implemented CPU image compression algorithm that takes advantage of modern SIMD instruction sets may already provide a significant boost in lossless compression speed. Another advantage of the CPU only implementation is that the GPU remains free for image based processing tasks, for which it is better suited. However, there still is the opportunity for further research to investigate the potential of a GPU based implementation, but a CPU implementation is needed for a thorough comparison.

3 Compression Scheme

From the above methods, we found the SIMD based integer compression method to be the most promising approach for a fast compression scheme, due to the

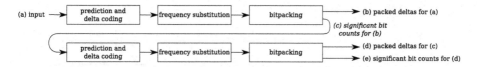

Fig. 2. Flow chart illustrating the compression procedure. An input stream (a) is processed with delta coding, frequency substitution and bit packing, see Sects. 3.2 to 3.5, producing a packed output stream (b), as well as the number of significant bits per block (c). The number of significant bits can change slowly from block to block, therefore (c) is fed through the same compression procedure to produce the final output streams (d) and (e) which, together with (b), compose the compressed output.

demonstrated high performance. However, bit packing is not directly possible with image data. A prediction scheme enables decorrelation of neighboring pixels and allows bit packing of the residuals, see Sect. 3.2, but the scheme still has to overcome several hurdles compared to the bit packing method using 32 bit integers from [14]:

Less Latitude: For image data, the bit depth is normally 8 bit compared to at least 32 bit in database indices, so each additional bit needed for the encoding has four times the impact on the overall compression performance.

Large Block Size: While SIMD on x86 has a width of 16 bytes, the implementation in [14] uses block sizes of 128 integers, respectively 512 bytes. Image data has a much higher variance compared to database indices, especially considering the smaller range for 8 bit data. Therefore, a smaller block size is required for efficient image compression, resulting in an increased overhead for signaling significant bit counts, which is especially problematic considering the greater impact of this overhead. Also, constant per block computations like signaling and branching depending on significant bit counts, have a higher impact on processing times with smaller block sizes.

Missing SIMD Instructions: On x86 many instructions that are available for processing 32 bit integers, as for example shifts, are not available in byte variants and have to be replaced by a more expensive combination of 32 bit shift and mask operations.

Size Increase Due to Delta Coding: In contrast to database indices, pixels in an image are not sorted by value and deltas between consecutive pixels therefore require one extra sign bit, increasing the compressed size by 12.5 % for naive delta coding.

3.1 Overview

Our approach, see Fig. 2, revolves around the concept of bit packing, which is the compression of integers by storing only the significant bits for each input value. To facilitate vectorization and to avoid excessive overhead due to the coding of significant bit counts, we apply bit packing to whole blocks of bytes, with larger

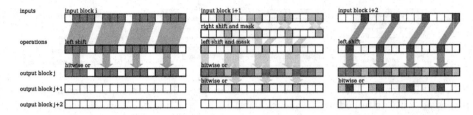

Fig. 3. Illustration of the interleaved bit packing scheme. For clarity the depicted blocks have a size of four samples with four bits each, instead of 8 bits as in the actual implementation. Bits are represented by boxes, significant bits are colored, white blocks have a value of zero. The packing routine distinguishes two cases: either there is enough space to store the significant bits, as is the case with block i and i+2, or the block has to be split between the current and next output block, as with block i+1 in the illustration. The colored arrows denote executed operations. Please note that the operations are always performed with the whole SIMD width and not per element.

block sizes resulting in higher performance at reduced compression efficiency. We use a very simple prediction scheme, trading coding efficiency for higher speed: We refer to this whole scheme as block-wise bit packing (BBP). Compared to Huffmann or arithmetic coding, bit packing cannot adapt to the distribution of symbols. Therefore, we employ *frequency substitution* in order to encode more frequent values, i.e. values with a higher probability of occurrence, with less significant bits, see Sect. 3.4. As bit packing results in a variable length code which is not prefix free, and correct decoding thus requires that the number of significant bits is known to the decoder via external means, the significant bit lengths have to be signaled separately. The need to store the number of significant bits is another reason, apart from vectorization, for the division into blocks. As the block size approaches one byte, the overhead of signaling the number of significant bits outweighs the increase in coding efficiency. To reduce the efficiency loss at all block sizes, which occurs due to the overhead for signaling significant bit lengths, the whole scheme is also applied to the data stream which signals those bit lengths, exploiting the correlation between successive blocks.

3.2 Prediction in 1 Dimension

Delta coding can be regarded as the most simple form of prediction based compression: each sample is predicted to have the same value as the last one, so calculation of the residual simplifies to the calculation of the difference between the two samples. A problem with such prediction schemes is the necessity to calculate a prefix sum when decoding. While parallel calculation of the prefix sum is possible, performance is still reduced. The integer coding by Lemire et al. [14] avoids the problem by using a fixed offset of 16 Bytes, which the authors report to increase the average delta by a factor of four.

In contrast to the database indexes they address, image data is correlated in two dimensions. Normally, this is exploited to improve compression efficiency by using a 2D predictor, such as the median edge predictor in `jpeg-ls`. We exploit the two-dimensional correlation to accelerate performance by coding the delta between vertical pixel neighbors, followed by the packing of horizontal blocks using SIMD. The correlation in the vertical direction provides residuals that are smaller than the actual sample values, while horizontal correlation means that a horizontal block tends to group samples with similar significant bit lengths, reducing efficiency loss due to block-wise handling.

Additionally, this gives a large flexibility for the layout of the input data. Because of the in-memory layout as continuous chunks of memory, the vertical prediction can be implemented with simple pointer arithmetic. The address of the previous line is calculated using the address of the current line minus a fixed offset, which is normally the width of the image. If the input data consists of interleaved samples, e.g. RGB images or raw Bayer patterns, then the offset may be adjusted, so that prediction is always executed from the same sample type, avoiding costly preprocessing steps for format conversion.

3.3   Modulo Delta Coding

As the difference between predicted and observed value may be anywhere between -255 and 255, it cannot be coded naively inside an 8 bit range. To avoid the necessity of expanding the coding range to 9 bit, which would halve the effective SIMD width and waste one bit of space, we utilize modular arithmetic over $\mathbb{Z}/256\mathbb{Z}$.

3.4   Frequency Substitution

The prediction residuals from delta coding tend to follow a two sided geometric distribution [16, 19], where small differences are very common. While small values are well suited for bit packing, the use of non-saturated wrapping arithmetics maps small differences, like -1, to potentially large values (255 in this case), which requires all 8 bits for encoding. To compensate for this effect, we apply a substitution, ordered by the minimal absolute difference: 0 stays 0, $-1 \equiv 255$ maps to 1, $-255 \equiv 1$ maps to 2, $-2 \equiv 254$ maps to 3, etc. This mapping is identical to the scheme often used when mapping signed to unsigned integers in the context of universal codes, as used by `jpeg-ls` and `AVC` when using Golomb codes for the entropy stage, just applied with respect to the implied modulo operation.

This mapping describes a triangle function with a slope of 2, where the first slope maps to even values and the second slope to odd values. This function is suitable for SIMD implementation, leading to high performance.

3.5   Block-Wise Interleaved Bit Packing

The packing uses a vertical layout, where a block of n bytes is interleaved into a block of the same size, with unused bits remaining at the same position in every byte. Consecutive blocks are interleaved into the unused bits for each byte in a block, until no unused bit remains, which leads to the write out of the current block and allocation of the next one, see Fig. 3 for a visualisation of the procedure. Compared to a computed jump to one of the different bit packing routines, depending on unused and required bits, as implemented in [14], we only branch over the block full condition and process any bit combination using the same code, with computed shifts and masks. This single branch is the only one within the compression loop, leading to low misprediction rates. This approach results in a lower performance penalty for small block sizes, which are necessary for efficient image compression.

4 Evaluation

The following sections will outline the conditions of the evaluation, which was performed on an Intel® Core™ i7-2600 Processor running at 3.4 GHz.

4.1 Implementations

Our implementation for the introduced method is executed in C, making extensive use of compiler intrinsics for SIMD operations as well as constant propagation and link time optimizations to realize portable, modular and easily extended code. As SSE3 instructions, released in 2006, have become quite ubiquitous on the x86 platform, we have targeted it in the evaluations presented in this article (AVX, which became available in 2011, focused on floating point operations and was therefore not considered). To allow a more detailed insight into the actual implementation, our code – including non-vectorized C fallback and an unoptimized implementation for the ARM NEON SIMD extension – will be released online under an open source license.

The implementations for the image and video compression methods were taken from the `ffmpeg` library [3], except the `AVC` (libx264 [6]), `HEVC` (libx265 [1]) and `jpeg2000` encoders (libopenjpeg [4]), which are provided by external libraries, but are still integrated within `ffmpeg`. The implementation of Lemire et al. [14] was also evaluated to show the performance possible when executing pure bit packing, although no compression could be achieved on the used data set. To test the dictionary methods the open source squash library [5] was used, which incorporates a broad range of generic compression methods, using the respective reference implementations.

4.2 Method

To minimize the effect of memory transfers for the fastest methods, the compression was executed on chunks of 64 KiB, which allows the whole compression to take place within the 256 KiB L2 cache of the Intel® Core™ i7-2600, for which we measured a bandwidth of 25 GiB/s. Timings were obtained for each coder, by reading the file in chunks, measuring 16 repeated runs of the coder in one go, to avoid the influence of the execution time of the timing syscall on the measured bandwidth. Measuring only a single iteration resulted in a bandwidth up to 30 % lower for the fastest coders. Note that the results of the video compression methods were obtained by running ffmpeg in benchmark mode, thus including memory transfer and management overhead. However extra measurement of the pure decoding performance of ffmpeg indicate an overhead of less than 3 % for the fastest measured video compression method.

4.3 Data Set

The results shown in Fig. 1 were obtained by executing the benchmark described in Sect. 4.1 on the uncompressed "blue sky" test sequence from the SVT data set [12]. The specific sequence was selected because it is easy enough as a compression challenge that all methods achieved at least minimal compression, while still being a recording of a natural scene, containing noise and other artifacts, which make compression more challenging than computer generated imagery. The scene was converted to grayscale as this was the only format compatible with all tested implementations. More complex scenes caused some coders, specifically lzo, to fall back into a non-compressing mode with a much higher bandwidth of nearly 1.7 GiB/s, see Table 1. While such a mode is a useful fallback if compression is not possible, such a behavior does not provide useful data for this evaluation. Please refer to the supplemental materials for a more extensive list of benchmark results for several different sources.

4.4 Results

A comparison of the performances of all evaluated compression algorithms can be found in Fig. 1. Positions in the plot show the relative performance of methods against each other, with faster methods towards the top and better compressing methods to the right. The evaluation of the performance of the different compression methods can be summarized as follows:

- Even the fastest generic compression methods are dominated by the dedicated image and video compression methods, as they achieve relatively low compression ratios without higher speed.
- Most of the methods optimized for image or video compression can provide better compression ratios, but at a significantly lower bandwidth.
- Our implementation can provide a very high bandwidth of over 6 GiB/s, much faster than previous methods, while it is also able to provide a compression ratio approaching that of the previously fastest dedicated image compression methods.

Regarding encoding speed, the closest contender to our method is ffvhuff, which is several times slower, but achieves slightly higher compression of up to 1:2.0. The two video coders x264 and x265 produce the highest compression at up to 1:2.48 and 1:2.68 respectively, but at a noticeable penalty in encoding speed. The `jpeg-ls` coder can not keep up with this performance but is still notable as the relatively high compression ratio of 1:2.32 is achieved by a pure image coder, which is unable to exploit the temporal correlation.

4.5   Minor Findings

The performance of the different compression methods depends to a varying degree on the specific data set, please see Table 1 for benchmark results of a few coders on different sources, more are available in the supplemental materials. While a detailed analysis of the speed variability was out of scope for this work, the basic pattern seems to be that the more complex a method the higher the dependency of the performance on the input characteristics. Specifically the relatively simple method implemented in this work, as well as the method in [14] and `ffvhuff` show a moderate dependency on the input characteristics, while most video compression methods and the dictionary based methods show a more complex behavior. The most variability was observed by the `lzo` coder for which performance varied by a factor of ten depending on the input.

Table 1. As this extract from our tests (see the supplemental material for all results) shows, compression ratio and speed vary a lot with the content, with some correlation between high throughput and better compression rates. The results for `lzo` indicate a special mode for non-compressible input. The best results for bandwidth and compression ratio are marked in bold for each file, the fastest and slowest result for each coder in italic. For our method block sizes of 8 and 128 bytes were selected as representative tradeoffs, please refer to Fig. 1 for an overview of all possible block sizes and their respective performance.

	Bandwidth in MiB/s					Compression Ratio				
Coder	File 1	File 2	File 3	File 4	File 5	File 1	File 2	File 3	File 4	File 5
BBP-8	975	992	*947*	*1307*	1022	1.31	1.71	1.38	5.16	1.51
BBP-128	**3993**	**4236**	***3957***	*4835*	**4199**	1.16	1.28	1.14	3.42	1.31
ffvhuff	329	343	*308*	*479*	339	1.45	**1.96**	1.39	3.47	1.59
x264-ultrafast	101	76	*72*	*206*	109	**1.49**	1.95	**1.47**	**9.17**	**1.84**
density	245	*150*	*311*	198	227	1.02	1.20	0.99	1.66	1.04
lzo1x	633	*141*	*1668*	334	427	1.02	1.21	1	3.69	1.04

5   Discussion and Future Work

As shown in Sect. 4.4, the performance achieved by our method is significantly higher than any previous method. In the fastest configuration the achievable performance surpasses the memory bandwidth, although at a considerable loss in compression efficiency, while the simple bitpacking method of Lemire et al.

[14] roughly doubles this performance, without achieving any compression for the evaluated content.

While one could expect the performance of an implementation to scale well with the SIMD width, which is effectively the level of parallism, preliminary results for the new AVX2 extensions, operating with a SIMD width of 256 bits, indicate a speedup of less than 40 % compared to the 128 bit wide SSSE3 implementation, suggesting that a large portion of the execution time is not spent on pure arithmetics, but on cache misses and branch misprediction. The expected AVX-512/AVX3 instructions will warrant further examination of this property.

In the introduced method, compression is based solely on 2D correlation. A candidate for an efficient disparity compensation based solution could be based on PatchMatch [7], which could be used to evaluate only few candidates per pixel over several iterations, propagating good solutions over the frame.

Also, the high performance of the method has implications for applications limited by main memory size or bandwidth. The compression scheme supports in-memory compression to increase available memory as well as to increase memory bandwidth, provided access patterns permit the decompression and processing to execute from within the CPU caches.

6   Conclusion

This work shows how to overcome the bandwidth limitations of previous lossless generic and image specific compression methods, while providing a reasonable compression performance. This does not only enable lossless image compression for applications which could not previously make use of it, but also provides interesting possibilities for image processing tasks, regarding memory bandwidth and utilization optimizations.

Acknowledgements. This research was financially supported by the Juniorprofessorenprogramm Baden-Württemberg.

References

1. x265 HEVC high efficiency video coding H.265 encoder (last accessed on 17 December 2014). http://x265.org/
2. JPEG 2000 on CUDA (last accessed on 27 May 2015). http://cuj2k.sourceforge.net/
3. A complete, cross-platform solution to record, convert and stream audio and video. (last accessed on 27 May 2015). https://www.ffmpeg.org
4. OpenJPEG library : an open source JPEG 2000 codec (last accessed on 27 May 2015). http://www.openjpeg.org/
5. Squash - compression abstraction library (last accessed on 27 May 2015). http://quixdb.github.io/squash

6. VideoLAN - x264, the best H.264/AVC encoder (last accessed on 27 May 2015). http://www.videolan.org/developers/x264.html

7. Barnes, C., Shechtman, E., Finkelstein, A., Goldman, D.B.: PatchMatch: A randomized correspondence algorithm for structural image editing. In: Proceeding of SIGGRAPH ACM Transactions on Graphics vol. 28, no. 3, August 2009

8. Burtscher, M., Ratanaworabhan, P.: FPC: a high-speed compressor for double-precision floating-point data. IEEE Trans. Comput. **58**(1), 18–31 (2009)

9. Collet, Y.: LZ4 explained, May 2011. http://fastcompression.blogspot.co.at/2011/05/lz4-explained.html

10. Deutsch, P.: Deflate compressed data format specification version 1.3. RFC 1951, May 1996. https://tools.ietf.org/html/rfc1951

11. Gomes, R.D., Costa, Y.G.G.d., Aquino Júnior, L.L., Silva Neto, M.G.d., Duarte, A.N., Souza Filho, G.L.d.: A solution for transmitting and displaying UHD 3d raw videos using lossless compression. In: Proceedings of the 19th Brazilian Symposium on Multimedia and the Web, pp. 173–176, WebMedia 2013. ACM, New York (2013). http://doi.acm.org/10.1145/2526188.2526228

12. Haglund, L.: The SVT high definition multi format test set. Swedish Television Stockholm (2006). https://media.xiph.org/video/derf/

13. Kau, L.J., Chen, C.S.: Speeding up the runtime performance for lossless image coding on GPUs with CUDA. In: IEEE International Symposium on Circuits and Systems (ISCAS), 2013, pp. 2868–2871, May 2013

14. Lemire, D., Boytsov, L.: Decoding billions of integers per second through vectorization. CoRR abs/1209.2137 (2012). http://arxiv.org/abs/1209.2137

15. Lenhardt, R., Alakuijala, J.: Gipfeli-high speed compression algorithm. In: Data Compression Conference (DCC), 2012, pp. 109–118. IEEE (2012)

16. Netravali, A., Limb, J.O.: Picture coding: a review. Proc. IEEE **68**(3), 366–406 (1980)

17. Niedermayer, M.: FFV1 video codec specification, August 2013. http://www1.mplayerhq.hu/michael/ffv1.html

18. Oberhumer, M.F.: oberhumer.com: LZO real-time data compression library (last accessed on 27 May 2015). http://www.oberhumer.com/opensource/lzo/

19. O'Neal, J.: Predictive quantizing systems (differential pulse code modulation) for the transmission of television signals. Bell Syst. Tech. J. **45**(5), 689–721 (1966)

20. O'Neil, M.A., Burtscher, M.: Floating-point data compression at 75 Gb/s on a GPU. In: Proceedings of the Fourth Workshop on General Purpose Processing on Graphics Processing Units, pp. 7:1–7:7, GPGPU-4. ACM, New York (2011). http://doi.acm.org/10.1145/1964179.1964189

21. Ozsoy, A., Swany, M., Chauhan, A.: Pipelined parallel lzss for streaming data compression on GPGPUs. In: IEEE 18th International Conference on Parallel and Distributed Systems (ICPADS), 2012, pp. 37–44, December 2012

22. Richter, T., Simon, S.: Coding strategies and performance analysis of GPU accelerated image compression. Picture Coding Symp. (PCS) **2013**, 125–128 (2013)

23. Seward, J.: bzip2 and libbzip2 (1996). http://www.bzip.org

24. Togni, R.: Description of the HuffYUV (HFYU) codec, March 2003. http://multimedia.cx/huffyuv.txt

25. Treib, M., Reichl, F., Auer, S., Westermann, R.: Interactive editing of gigasample terrain fields. In: Proceeding Eurographics Computer Graphics Forum, vol. 31, no. 2, pp. 383–392 (2012). http://diglib.eg.org/EG/CGF/volume31/issue2/v31i2pp383-392.pdf

26. Wang, Z., Klaiber, M., Gera, Y., Simon, S., Richter, T.: Fast lossless image compression with 2d golomb parameter adaptation based on JPEG-LS. In: Proceedings of the 20th European Signal Processing Conference, EUSIPCO 2012, Bucharest, Romania, August 27–31, 2012, pp. 1920–1924 (2012). http://ieeexplore.ieee.org/xpl/freeabs_all.jsp?arnumber=6334076

27. Weinberger, M., Seroussi, G., Sapiro, G.: The LOCO-I lossless image compression algorithm: principles and standardization into JPEG-LS. IEEE Trans. Image Process. **9**(8), 1309–1324 (2000)

28. Ziv, J., Lempel, A.: A universal algorithm for sequential data compression. IEEE Trans. Inf. Theor. **23**(3), 337–343 (1977)

Learning Reaction-Diffusion Models
for Image Inpainting

Wei Yu[1]([⊠]), Stefan Heber[1], and Thomas Pock[1,2]

[1] Institute for Computer Graphics and Vision,
Graz University of Technology, Graz, Austria
wei.yu@icg.tugraz.at
[2] Safety & Security Department,
AIT Austrian Institute of Technology, Graz, Austria

Abstract. In this paper we present a trained diffusion model for image inpainting based on the structural similarity measure. The proposed diffusion model uses several parametrized linear filters and influence functions. Those parameters are learned in a loss based approach, where we first perform a greedy training before conducting a joint training to further improve the inpainting performance. We provide a detailed comparison to state-of-the-art inpainting algorithms based on the TUM-image inpainting database. The experimental results show that the proposed diffusion model is efficient and achieves superior performance. Moreover, we also demonstrate that the proposed method has a texture preserving property, that makes it stand out from previous PDE based methods.

1 Introduction

Image inpainting is a fundamental problem in Computer Vision (CV) with great practical importance. Given an image with lost, deteriorated or simply unknown regions, the task of image inpainting is to convincingly fill-up those unknown image regions. Hence, the main goal is to produce natural-looking and visually pleasant images. Inpainting applications can be roughly divided into two classes. First, there are inpainting applications where one considers the task of reconstructing a set of small connected image regions. Example applications include the restoration of old photos, damaged videos [21], or artwork [30], and the removal of logos, superimposed text, or other unwanted objects in images, to name but a few. The second class of inpainting applications considers the task of restoring large regions of scattered pixels. Inpainting methods belonging to this class are closely related to image compression methods [8,15,26]. Galić et al. [15] for instance proposed a method for image compression based on edge-enhancing diffusion. Liu et al. [26] proposed a framework for image compression, where the main idea is to extract edge-based assistant information in the encoding step and use this information to guide the inpainting in the decoding step.

This research was supported by the FWF-START project *Bilevel optimization for Computer Vision*, No. Y729 and the Vision+ project *Integrating visual information with independent knowledge*, No. 836630.

© Springer International Publishing Switzerland 2015
J. Gall et al. (Eds.): GCPR 2015, LNCS 9358, pp. 356–367, 2015.
DOI: 10.1007/978-3-319-24947-6_29

Proposed inpainting methods in the literature tend to fall into one of the following categories. First, there are exemplar-based or patch-based methods [5,11,40], that try to fill the inpainting regions by propagating information from the remaining parts of the image at the patch-level. Thus those methods reconstruct the corrupted regions by sampling and copying uncorrupted patches taken from the same image (or from a certain dictionary). Those methods are usually based on the self-similarity principle, i.e. one assumes that images include a lot of repetitions of local information. It is not surprising, that the main idea of patch-based methods can be traced back to texture synthesis techniques [12]. Due to their non-local property, patch-based methods are well suited to inpaint large connected image regions with texture, but most of those methods are unable to handle densely scattered inpainting domains. One exception is the non-local inpainting method by Facciolo et al. [14], that allows inpainting from sparse data. The second category of inpainting methods involves either variational principles or is Partial Differential Equation (PDE) based, noticeable examples include [2,6,7,13,28]. Those methods have been successfully used to smoothly inpaint small image regions. A common drawback of PDE based methods is their inability to properly reconstruct image texture, which is clearly visible when trying to reconstruct large inpainting domains. However, PDE based methods remain applicable in compression-like applications, i.e. inpainting task based on sparse data. Masnou and Morel [28] for example proposed an inpainting model based on variational principles, where they interpolated the inpainting regions by extending the isophotes, which are lines of constant intensities. Bertalmio et al. [2] proposed a PDE based inpainting method, that is inspired by the methodology of art conservators, where a transport process is interlinked with an anisotropic diffusion process. The overall idea is to fill the inpainting region such that the isophote lines are completed. In [6] authors extended the Rudin Osher Fatemi (ROF) image denoising model [35] to image inpainting, i.e. their variational model is based on the Total Variation (TV) and produces inpainting result with smallest possible isophotes. In a subsequent paper [7] a curvature driven diffusion equation was introduced to realize the connectivity principle. Esedoglu and Shen [13] proposed the so-called Mumford Shah Euler model. This model combines the celebrated Mumford Shah segmentation model [29] with Euler's elastica curve model. Besides the aforementioned two categories of inpainting methods, authors also proposed methods that attempt to combine the advantages of PDE based and patch-based methods [1,3,4,11,17,22,31]. Bugeau et al. [3] for instance proposed a framework that combines patch-based methods with PDE based methods by enforce coherence among neighboring pixels. Cao et al. [4] proposed to extract level lines from a simplified version of the image to guide the patch-based inpainting. Peter and Weickert [31] proposed a method, where patch-based and PDE based approaches are used block wise. In [24,33,34,41] authors investigated image statistics from natural images. Roth and Black [33] for example proposed a framework to learn generic, expressive image priors that capture the statistics of natural scenes. The so-called Fields of Experts (FoE) [33] uses continuous heavy-tailed potential functions and learns the parameters of experts by contrastive divergence learning in high-order Markov Random Field (MRF) models. In [36], Schmidt et al. modified the FoE model by using Gaussian scale mixtures as potential functions. In [10], Chen et al. simplified the diffusion coefficients and then generalized the conventional nonlinear reaction diffusion model by using learned filters and influence functions. They showed that the resulting energy functional of the proposed diffusion model is a generalization of the FoE model [33]. They trained models for Gaussian denoising and JPEG deblocking. Both models achieved a superior performance compared to the state-of-the-art and are highly efficient as well.

Contribution. In this paper we will modify the diffusion model proposed in [10] for the task of image inpainting. Contrary to [10], where a Peak Signal to Noise Ratio (PSNR) based training is used, we propose a training based on the Structural Similarity Image Measure (SSIM) [39], which seems to be more suitable for the task of image inpainting. In the experimental section we will present generic models, that are trained based on a complete dataset, and specific models, that are trained on the uncorrupted image regions of the image to be inpainted. We will provide a detailed evaluation on the TUM-image inpainting database [37,38], which will show that the proposed method is able to achieve superior performance compared to state-of-the-art inpainting methods, and is highly efficient at the same time. Further we will show that although our method falls into the category of PDE based methods it is also capable to perform texture inpainting to a certain extent.

2   Diffusion Model

In this section, we first present a brief overview of the trained reaction diffusion model proposed in [10] before extending it to the task of image inpainting.

Trained reaction-diffusion model. Let $\Omega \subset \mathbb{R}^2$ be the image domain and consider an image as a mapping $u : \Omega \times [0, \infty) \to \mathbb{R}$, $u = u(x, t)$, where $t \geqslant 0$ denotes the stage or the time. Then a general anisotropic diffusion model is given as

$$\partial_t u = \operatorname{div}(\Gamma(u)\nabla u), \tag{1}$$

with the original image $f : \Omega \to \mathbb{R}$ as the initial state, i.e. $u(x, 0) = f(x)$, and with reflecting boundary conditions, i.e. $\partial_n u = 0$ on the image boundary $\partial\Omega$, where n denotes the normal to $\partial\Omega$. Note that in Eq. (1) ∇ is taken w.r.t. the spatial variables x and $\Gamma(u)$ denotes the diffusion tensor, which is a positive definite symmetric matrix. In the case of isotropic diffusion $\Gamma(u)$ can be replaced by a positive scalar-valued diffusion coefficient also called diffusivity.

In [10] the authors modified Eq. (1) in the following way: (i) they generalized the ∇ operator to a set of filters represented by $\mathbf{K}_i^t$, (ii) they equipped each filter with its own diffusion coefficient represented by so-called influence functions $\phi_i^t : \mathbb{R}^N \to \mathbb{R}^N$, and (iii) they added a reaction term $\psi : \mathbb{R}^N \times \mathbb{R}^N \to \mathbb{R}^N$, which basically yields a non homogenous diffusion equation. Finally, they proposed the following diffusion model in the discrete setting

$$\mathbf{u}_t = \mathbf{u}_{t-1} - \sum_{i=1}^{N_k} \mathbf{K}_i^{t\top} \phi_i^t(\mathbf{K}_i^t \mathbf{u}_{t-1}) - \psi(\mathbf{u}_{t-1}, \mathbf{f}), \tag{2}$$

where $\mathbf{u}_t \in \mathbb{R}^N$ denotes the vectorized representation of an image at stage t, N_k denotes the number of filters, $\mathbf{f} \in \mathbb{R}^N$ is the vectorized corrupted input image, and $\mathbf{K}_i^t \in \mathbb{R}^{N \times N}$ is a sparse matrix representing a convolution operation with the kernel $\mathbf{k}_i^t$ (i.e. $\mathbf{K}_i^t \mathbf{u} = \mathbf{k}_i^t * \mathbf{u}$). Note that the influence functions ϕ_i^t and filters $\mathbf{K}_i^t$ vary for different stages t. Chen et al. [10] proposed to train the parameters of the diffusion model in Eq. (2). They showed that the reaction term changes for different applications, like Gaussian denoising, or JPEG deblocking. They also illustrated that the model is related to the FoE [33] and to convolutional networks [20], which are popular models in the field of computer vision and pattern recognition.

Diffusion model for image inpainting. For the inpainting task tackled in this paper, the given gray-valued images $\mathbf{u}$ are assumed to be noisefree. Hence the proposed method only updates the gray-values inside the unknown or missing image regions $\mathcal{A} \subset \Omega$. Unlike Gaussian denoising or JPEG deblocking discussed in [10], a challenge of image inpainting is that it has no available reaction term within the inpainting domain. Hence the proposed model relies on the information at the boundary of the inpainting domain $\partial \mathcal{A}$ and on the learned information from uncorrupted parts of the image (i.e. $\mathcal{A}^c$), or from a given set of images. Thus the main idea of the proposed model is to propagate the known information from outside the inpainting region in a meaningful way in order to reconstruct the values inside the unknown image regions. For this purpose we define the following diffusion model

$$\mathbf{u}_t = \mathbf{u}_{t-1} - \mathbf{m} \cdot \sum_{i=1}^{N_k} \mathbf{K}_i^{t\top} \phi_i^t(\mathbf{K}_i^t \mathbf{u}_{t-1}), \tag{3}$$

where $\cdot$ denotes the Hadamard product (i.e. pointwise multiplication), and $\mathbf{m} \in \mathbb{R}^N$ is a vectorized mask indicating the inpainting domain $\mathcal{A}$, i.e.

$$\mathbf{m}[j] = \begin{cases} 1 & j \in \mathcal{A}, \\ 0 & \text{otherwise}, \end{cases} \tag{4}$$

where $\mathbf{m}[j]$ denotes the value at the jth position of the vector $\mathbf{m}$. In order to reduce the computational complexity the influence functions ϕ_i^t are set to be continuous piecewise linear functions [18].

The iterative process in Eq. (3) can be summarized as follows: (i) filter the current image $\mathbf{u}_{t-1}$ with the kernel $\mathbf{k}_i^t$ for $1 \leqslant i \leqslant N_k$, (ii) calculate the output of the influence function ϕ_i^t and filter the result with the kernel $\overline{\mathbf{k}}_i^{t\,1}$ for $1 \leqslant i \leqslant N_k$, where $\overline{\mathbf{k}}_i^t$ is obtained by rotating $\mathbf{k}_i^t$ by 180 degrees, (iii) sum up the N_k results and calculate the Hadamard product with the mask $\mathbf{m}$, and (iv) update $\mathbf{u}_{t-1}$ with the obtained result.

---

[1] $\mathbf{K}_i^{t\top} \phi_i^t(\mathbf{K}_i^t \mathbf{u}_{t-1})$ can be rewritten as $\overline{\mathbf{k}}_i^t * \phi_i^t(\mathbf{K}_i^t \mathbf{u}_{t-1})$.

3   Learning

In this section we briefly outline the learning approach. We propose a SSIM based learning approach to estimate the parameters $\Theta_t = \{\mathbf{k}_i^t, \phi_i^t\}$ on the right-hand side of Eq. (3) for all stages $1 \leqslant t \leqslant T$. We start with a greedy training, where we optimize the parameters at the stage t and then use the optimal parameters to calculate the inpainted image $\mathbf{u}_t$. After that we optimize the parameters of the next stage, till we reach the maximum number of stages T. The result of the greedy training is used as an initialization for the following joint training, where we train all stages simultaneously. Let $\{\mathbf{f}^j, \mathbf{g}^j, \mathbf{m}^j\}_{j=1}^{K}$ denote the K training samples, where $\mathbf{f}^j$ is the jth corrupted image with unknown values at the inpainting regions indicated by the mask $\mathbf{m}^j$, and $\mathbf{g}^j$ is the jth ground truth image. Then the greedy training minimizes

$$\mathcal{L}(\Theta_t) = \sum_{j=1}^{K} \ell(\mathbf{u}_t^j, \mathbf{g}^j), \qquad (5)$$

for each stage $1 \leqslant t \leqslant T$. The loss function $\ell(\mathbf{u}_t^j, \mathbf{g}^j)$ is defined based on the SSIM [39], which has already been used for image denoising [23,32], where it has shown its superiority over PSNR [39]. SSIM assesses the luminance, the contrast, and the structure of two images $\mathbf{I}_1 : \Omega \to \mathbb{R}^2$ and $\mathbf{I}_2 : \Omega \to \mathbb{R}^2$ on the patch level. In this context the SSIM index of two image patches $\mathbf{p}_1$ and $\mathbf{p}_2$ is calculated as follows

$$\text{SSIM}(\mathbf{p}_1, \mathbf{p}_2) = \frac{(2\mu_1\mu_2 + c_1)(2\sigma_{12} + c_2)}{(\mu_1^2 + \mu_2^2 + c_1)(\sigma_1^2 + \sigma_2^2 + c_2)}, \qquad (6)$$

where c_j is a predefined constant, μ_j and σ_j^2 denote the average and the variance of the image patch $\mathbf{p}_j$, $j \in \{1, 2\}$, and σ_{12} is the covariance of the two patches. The final image measure, denoted as $\mathcal{S}(\mathbf{I}_1, \mathbf{I}_2)$, is obtained as the mean SSIM index of all image patches. Note that $\mathcal{S}(\mathbf{I}_1, \mathbf{I}_2)$ attains its maximum of 1 only if $\mathbf{I}_1 = \mathbf{I}_2$. Thus we define the loss function in Eq. (5) as

$$\ell(\mathbf{u}_t^j, \mathbf{g}^j) = 1 - \mathcal{S}(\mathbf{u}_t^j, \mathbf{g}^j), \qquad (7)$$

and minimize the resulting energy. For optimization we use the L-BFGS algorithm [27], which is a batch-based optimization algorithm. Using L-BFGS we need to specify the loss function (cf. (5)) and the according gradient. The gradient of Eq. (5) is obtained by applying the chain rule, i.e.

$$\frac{\partial \mathcal{L}(\Theta_t)}{\partial \Theta_t} = \sum_{j=1}^{K} \frac{\partial \ell(\mathbf{u}_t^j, \mathbf{g}^j)}{\partial \Theta_t} = \sum_{j=1}^{K} \frac{\partial \mathbf{u}_t^j}{\partial \Theta_t} \frac{\partial \ell(\mathbf{u}_t^j, \mathbf{g}^j)}{\partial \mathbf{u}_t^j}, \qquad (8)$$

where $\mathbf{u}_t^j$ is defined in Eq. (3). After the greedy training we continue with the joint training, where we learn the parameters of all stages simultaneously. We seek to minimize the loss of the last stage. Thus the energy functional for the joint training can be formulated as

Table 1. Quantitative inpainting results for 80 % and 90 % random missing pixels.

		Laplacian	EED [15]	Chen [9]	Schmidt MRF [36]	Schmidt FoE [36]	TD (PSNR)	TD (SSIM)
80%	PSNR	21.5998	21.6823	22.5123	21.4210	21.8630	22.7306	22.6301
	SSIM	0.7864	0.7896	0.8185	0.7781	0.8028	0.8243	0.8267
	GSIM	0.7417	0.7454	0.7947	0.7451	0.7844	0.7910	0.8048
90%	PSNR	20.0751	20.1172	20.4899	19.7449	20.1043	20.7618	20.6663
	SSIM	0.6689	0.6721	0.7094	0.6519	0.6905	0.7128	0.7287
	GSIM	0.6636	0.6660	0.7119	0.6562	0.7106	0.7072	0.7409

$$\mathcal{L}(\Theta_1, \ldots, \Theta_T) = \sum_{j=1}^{K} \ell(\mathbf{u}_T^j, \mathbf{g}^j), \tag{9}$$

where, similar as in (8), we use the chain rule to obtain the gradient for the jth training sample as

$$\frac{\partial \ell(\mathbf{u}_T^j, \mathbf{g}^j)}{\partial \Theta_t} = \frac{\partial \mathbf{u}_t^j}{\partial \Theta_t} \frac{\partial \mathbf{u}_{t+1}^j}{\partial \mathbf{u}_t^j} \cdots \frac{\partial \ell(\mathbf{u}_T^j, \mathbf{g}^j)}{\partial \mathbf{u}_T^j} \quad \text{for} \quad 1 \leqslant t \leqslant T. \tag{10}$$

Further details on calculating the gradient can be found in the supplementary material.

4 Experiments

When trying to evaluate inpainting algorithms one recognizes that there exists no well-defined ground truth. This is apparent when considering inpainting problems involving large image regions, where multiple natural-looking solutions might exist. However, in order to provide a quantitative evaluation for inpainting methods authors mainly use predefined ground truth images and compare their methods based on the PSNR or similar measures. Within this paper we follow this type of evaluation, and we will present a comprehensive comparison to state-of-the-art inpainting methods based on the TUM-image inpainting database [37,38] using the following three measures: PSNR, SSIM [39], and GSIM [25].

We will consider two types of trained diffusion models. First, we present generic models, that are learned on an entire dataset. The generic models are used to restore large regions of scattered pixels (e.g. 80 % and 90 % random missing pixels), and to inpaint small connected image regions. The second type of models are specifically learned for inpainting a certain image, i.e. those models are trained based on the uncorrupted parts of the given image. We will show that those specific models are able to learn the texture of a given image. Thus they are applicable for the task of texture inpainting.

Fig. 1. Qualitative inpainting result for 80 % and 90 % random missing pixels. The closeup views clearly show the advantage of the proposed trained diffusion (TD) model.

To optimize the involved parameters in Eq. (3) we use L-BFGS[2] [27], which minimizes the energy by iteratively approximating the inverse Hessian matrix. For all experiments we first conduct a greedy training, where L-BFGS runs for 200 iterations in each stage. Afterwards we jointly train the parameters of all stages. The filters $\mathbf{k}_i^t$ are initialized with the Discrete Cosine Transform (DCT) bases, and the influence functions are initialized as $\phi_i^t(x) = 0.01x$. The joint training is then initialized with the result of the greedy training. In the following we will use the short notation TD(SSIM) to denote the obtained trained diffusion model with SSIM learning. For comparison, we also apply TD(PSNR) which is a trained diffusion model with PSNR learning.

For the generic models, the training dataset includes 400 images of size 180×180 as in [10]. The test dataset is the TUM-image inpainting database [38], which includes 17 images of size 640×480. In [38], the authors suggested four state-of-the-art inpainting algorithms for comparison [3,16,19,40]. Algorithms [3,19,40] cannot be used for compression type inpainting tasks. Therefore, we will compare in this case to Laplacian, and edge enhancing diffusion-based inpainting (EED) [15], to the learned MRF prior proposed by Chen et al. [9], to the learned

---

[2] Used solver: http://www.cs.toronto.edu/~liam/software.shtml.

Table 2. Quantitative results for inpainting a small connected image region.

	Lap.	EED [15]	Chen [9]	Schmidt MRF [36]	Schmidt FoE [36]	Bugeau [3]	Herling [19]	Xu [40]	TD (PSNR)	TD (SSIM)
PSNR	35.1529	35.1700	35.5031	34.7119	35.1434	33.5746	33.1427	35.3308	35.8205	35.9084
SSIM	0.9902	0.9902	0.9907	0.9897	0.9905	0.9880	0.9864	0.9900	0.9913	0.9915
GSIM	0.9910	0.9910	0.9910	0.9909	0.9920	0.9917	0.9915	0.9919	0.9920	0.9925

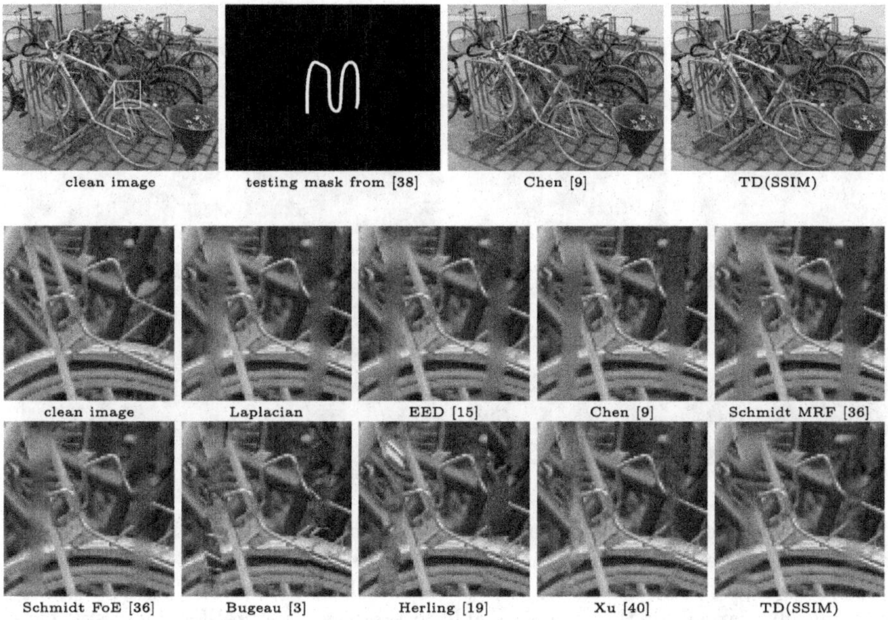

Fig. 2. Qualitative results for inpainting a small connected image region.

pairwise MRF model, and to the FoE model with Gaussian scale mixtures as experts, both proposed by Schmidt et al. [36]. For the remaining experiments we will compare to all algorithms mentioned above if a ground truth is available.

Inpainting of 80 % and 90 % random missing pixels. For this experiment we train two generic diffusion models, where we use 30 stages with 48 filters. In the case of 80 % missing pixels we use a kernel size of 7×7. Inpainting of 90 % random missing pixels is a more challenging problem, thus we allow the model to explore more available information by increasing the kernel size to 11×11. The parameters of the trained diffusion models are optimized in the joint training using 100 iterations of L-BFGS. We evaluate the results based on the TUM-image inpainting database [38]. Table 1 provides quantitative results in terms of the mean PSNR, SSIM, and GSIM. We observe that the proposed TD(SSIM) model achieves the best SSIM and GSIM results, and it is on par with the TD(PSNR) model based on the PSNR evaluation. Figure 1 provides corresponding qualitative results, where we also observe clearly visible qualitative improvements.

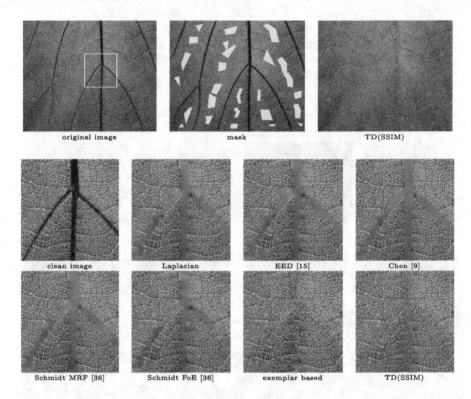

Fig. 3. Qualitative results for texture inpainting. Besides the original image of a leaf and the mask, that indicates the inpainting regions (blue) and the training regions (green), the figure provides closeup views that clearly show that the TD model, that is specifically learned for this image, is able to produce a natural-looking result close to the result obtained with an exemplar based method (Color figure online).

Inpainting of small regions. In this experiment, we train a 30-stage generic diffusion model with 24 filters of size 5×5. For the training, we randomly generate several small regions, where each region occupies about 300 connected pixels. Quantitative result for this experiment are provided in Table 2, where the proposed model achieves superior results compared to state-of-the-art methods. The table shows the mean PSNR, SSIM, and GSIM values for inpainting the images of the TUM-image inpainting database [38], where the inpainting region is defined by the mask shown in Fig. 2. We observe that the TD(SSIM) model is able to outperform all other models, even the TD(PSNR) model based on the PSNR evaluation. Closeup views are presented in Fig. 2, where we observe that the proposed method better preserves the image edges than the other PDE based image inpainting methods. The methods by Bugeau et al. [3] and Herling and Broll [19] introduce visual artifacts, e.g. at the tire of the bike (bottom left in the closeup views). The result of the method by Xu and Sun [40] has less visual artifacts, but it also introduces some noise. The proposed TD model on the other hand provides a convincing result with less artifacts.

Inpainting of a specific texture. Now we present an experiment for texture inpainting, where we learn the specific texture within a single given image **I**. The task is to inpaint a predefined image region within the same image (e.g. the blue regions indicated in Fig. 3). In order to train a specific diffusion model we generate $K = 200$ training images $\mathbf{f}^j$, where pixels within a mask **m** (Fig. 3 indicates the training mask in green) are set to random gray values. If we initialize with the results of linear diffusion, then we can get similar inpainted images by using only 5 training images, cf. supplementary material. Hence we obtain the training set $\{\mathbf{f}^j, \mathbf{g}^j, \mathbf{m}^j\}_{j=1}^K$ (cf. Sect. 3), where $\mathbf{g}^j = \mathbf{I}$ and $\mathbf{m}^j = \mathbf{m}$ for $1 \leqslant j \leqslant K$. Based on this training set we learn a 7 stage diffusion model with 24 filters of size 13×13. Figure 3 provides some qualitative inpainting results, where only the TD model is trained on the given image. Because of the smoothness assumption and the local property of PDE based image inpainting methods, those type of methods are in general not well suited for the task of texture inpainting. Exemplar based image inpainting methods on the other hand are non-local and have achieved good performance for texture inpainting [3,19,40]. Anyhow, our experiments show that the proposed TD model is also able to perform texture inpainting. The TD inpainting result and the exemplar based result shown in Fig. 3 are like two of a kind.

5   Conclusion

In this paper we proposed a trained diffusion model for image inpainting. We used a combination of a greedy training with a joint training to optimized the parameters of the diffusion model. In the experimental section we showed that by learning the parameters of a simple diffusion model one obtains an inpainting method, which is competitive to sophisticated and highly complex state-of-the-art inpainting methods. The diffusion model and the learning method lay the foundation of pleasant inpainted results. In principle, PDE based inpainting methods are known to be inapplicable for texture inpainting. However our experimental evaluation revealed the somehow surprising result, that the proposed trained diffusion model can be used for texture reconstruction. We hope that this work raises awareness for the potential of learned PDE based methods for image inpainting. In future work, we are interested in inpainting larger image regions, in compression applications with lower point densities (e.g. 5 %), and in training a unified diffusion model for different image inpainting tasks.

References

1. Bertalmio, M., Vese, L., Sapiro, G., Osher, S.: Simultaneous structure and texture image inpainting. In: proceedings of CVPR, vol. 2, pp. II-707-12 (2003)
2. Bertalmio, M., Sapiro, G., Caselles, V., Ballester, C.: Image inpainting. In: Conference on Computer graphics and interactive techniques, pp. 417–424. ACM Press/Addison-Wesley Publishing Co. (2000)
3. Bugeau, A., Bertalmio, M., Caselles, V., Sapiro, G.: A comprehensive framework for image inpainting. Image Process. **19**(10), 2634–2645 (2010)

4. Cao, F., Gousseau, Y., Masnou, S., Pérez, P.: Geometrically guided exemplar-based inpainting. SIAM J. Img. Sci. **4**(4), 1143–1179 (2011)
5. Caselles, V.: Exemplar-based image inpainting and applications. SIAM News **44**(10), 1–3 (2011)
6. Chan, T.F., Shen, J.: Local inpainting models and TV inpainting. SIAM J. Appl. Math. **62**(3), 1019–1043 (2001)
7. Chan, T.F., Shen, J.: Nontexture inpainting by curvature-driven diffusions. J. Vis. Commun. Image Represent. **12**(4), 436–449 (2001)
8. Chen, Y., Ranftl, R., Pock, T.: A bi-level view of inpainting-based image compression (2014). arXiv preprint arXiv:1401.4112
9. Chen, Y., Ranftl, R., Pock, T.: Insights into analysis operator learning: from patch-based sparse models to higher order MRFs. Image Process. **23**(3), 1060–1072 (2014)
10. Chen, Y., Yu, W., Pock, T.: On learning optimized reaction diffusion processes for effective image restoration. In: Proceeding of CVPR (2015)
11. Criminisi, A., Pérez, P., Toyama, K.: Region filling and object removal by exemplar-based image inpainting. Trans. Img. Proc. **13**(9), 1200–1212 (2004)
12. Efros, A., Leung, T.: Texture synthesis by non-parametric sampling. In: proceeding of ICCV, vol. 2, pp. 1033–1038 (1999)
13. Esedoglu, S., Shen, J.: Digital inpainting based on the Mumford-Shah-Euler image model. Eur. J. Appl. Math. **13**(04), 353–370 (2002)
14. Facciolo, G., Arias, P., Caselles, V., Sapiro, G.: Exemplar-based interpolation of sparsely sampled images. In: Cremers, D., Boykov, Y., Blake, A., Schmidt, F.R. (eds.) EMMCVPR 2009. LNCS, vol. 5681, pp. 331–344. Springer, Heidelberg (2009)
15. Galić, I., Weickert, J., Welk, M., Bruhn, A., Belyaev, A., Seidel, H.P.: Image compression with anisotropic diffusion. JMIV **31**(2–3), 255–269 (2008)
16. Getreuer, P.: Total variation inpainting using split bregman. Image Process. On Line **2**, 147–157 (2012)
17. Grossauer, H.: A combined PDE and texture synthesis approach to inpainting. In: Pajdla, T., Matas, J.G. (eds.) ECCV 2004. LNCS, vol. 3022, pp. 214–224. Springer, Heidelberg (2004)
18. Hel-Or, Y., Shaked, D.: A discriminative approach for wavelet denoising. IEEE Trans. Image Process. **17**(4), 443–457 (2008)
19. Herling, J., Broll, W.: Pixmix: A real-time approach to high-quality diminished reality. In: International Symposium on Mixed and Augmented Reality (ISMAR), pp. 141–150. IEEE (2012)
20. Jain, V., Seung, S.: Natural image denoising with convolutional networks. In: Advances in Neural Information Processing Systems, pp. 769–776 (2009)
21. Kokaram, A.C., Morris, R.D., Fitzgerald, W.J., Rayner, P.J.: Interpolation of missing data in image sequences. Image Process. **4**(11), 1509–1519 (1995)
22. Komodakis, N., Tziritas, G.: Image completion using efficient belief propagation via priority scheduling and dynamic pruning. Trans. Img. Proc. **16**(11), 2649–2661 (2007)
23. Kong, X., Li, K., Yang, Q., Wenyin, L., Yang, M.H.: A new image quality metric for image auto-denoising. In: Proceeding of ICCV, pp. 2888–2895. IEEE (2013)
24. Levin, A., Zomet, A., Weiss, Y.: Learning how to inpaint from global image statistics. In: poceeding of ICCV, pp. 305–312 (2003)
25. Liu, A., Lin, W., Narwaria, M.: Image quality assessment based on gradient similarity. Image Process. **21**(4), 1500–1512 (2012)
26. Liu, D., Sun, X., Wu, F., Li, S., Zhang, Y.Q.: Image compression with edge-based inpainting. Circuits Syst. Video Technol. **17**(10), 1273–1287 (2007)

27. Liu, D.C., Nocedal, J.: On the limited memory BFGS method for large scale optimization. Math. Program. **45**(1–3), 503–528 (1989)
28. Masnou, S., Morel, J.M.: Level lines based disocclusion. In: Proceeding of ICIP, vol. 3, pp. 259–263 (1998)
29. Mumford, D., Shah, J.: Optimal approximations by piecewise smooth functions and associated variational problems. Comm. Pure Appl. Math. **42**(5), 577–685 (1989)
30. Nikolaidis, N., Pitas, I.: Digital image processing in painting restoration and archiving. In: proceeding of ICCV, vol. 1, pp. 586–589. IEEE (2001)
31. Peter, P., Weickert, J.: Compressing images with diffusion- and exemplar-based inpainting. In: Aujol, J.-F., Nikolova, M., Papadakis, N. (eds.) SSVM 2015. LNCS, vol. 9087, pp. 154–165. Springer, Heidelberg (2015)
32. Rehman, A., Wang, Z.: Ssim-based non-local means image denoising. In: proceeding of ICIP, pp. 217–220. IEEE (2011)
33. Roth, S., Black, M.: Fields of experts: a framework for learning image priors. In: proceeding of CVPR, vol. 2, pp. 860–867 (2005)
34. Roth, S., Black, M.: Steerable random fields. In: proceeding of ICCV, pp. 1–8 (2007)
35. Rudin, L.I., Osher, S., Fatemi, E.: Nonlinear total variation based noise removal algorithms. Physica D: Nonlinear Phenomena **60**(1–4), 259–268 (1992)
36. Schmidt, U., Gao, Q., Roth, S.: A generative perspective on MRFs in low-level vision. In: proceeding of CVPR, pp. 1751–1758. IEEE (2010)
37. Tiefenbacher, P., Bogischef, V., Merget, D., Rigoll, G.: Subjective and objective evaluation of image inpainting quality. In: proceeding of ICIP. IEEE (2015)
38. TUM-image inpainting database. http://www.mmk.ei.tum.de/tumiid/
39. Wang, Z., Bovik, A.C., Sheikh, H.R., Simoncelli, E.P.: Image quality assessment: from error visibility to structural similarity. Image Process. **13**(4), 600–612 (2004)
40. Xu, Z., Sun, J.: Image inpainting by patch propagation using patch sparsity. Image Process. **19**(5), 1153–1165 (2010)
41. Zhu, S.C., Mumford, D.: Prior learning and gibbs reaction-diffusion. Pattern Anal. Mach. Intell. **19**(11), 1236–1250 (1997)

Image Orientation Estimation
with Convolutional Networks

Philipp Fischer[✉], Alexey Dosovitskiy, and Thomas Brox

Department of Computer Science, University of Freiburg,
Freiburg im Breisgau, Germany
{fischer,dosovits,brox}@cs.uni-freiburg.de

Abstract. Rectifying the orientation of scanned documents has been
an important problem that was solved long ago. In this paper, we focus
on the harder case of estimating and correcting the exact orientation of
general images, for instance, of holiday snapshots. Especially when the
horizon or other horizontal and vertical lines in the image are missing, it
is hard to find features that yield the canonical orientation of the image.
We demonstrate that a convolutional network can learn subtle features
to predict the canonical orientation of images. In contrast to prior works
that just distinguish between portrait and landscape orientation, the
network regresses the exact orientation angle. The approach runs in real-
time and, thus, can be applied also to live video streams.

1   Introduction

Sometimes, taking a picture can take time. Everybody in front of the lens is
smiling happily, but while the amateur photographer tries to get all lines perfectly horizontal struggling with the lens distortion, the subjects of interest start
to become a little uneasy. Would it not be nice, if one could just press the button
and the orientation of the picture would be corrected automatically?

The inertial sensors, which are already built into modern cameras to correct
the orientation of pictures in 90° steps, could potentially do the job, but this
function is usually not implemented. In this paper, we present a way to automatically correct the image orientation based just on the visual data. It can be
applied as a post-processing step to pictures taken with any camera, including
older models without inertial sensors.

Orientation correction is a long standing task in document analysis [2,3,9,
13,16,21]. However, all these methods exploit the special structure of document
images, such as text layout in lines and precise shapes of letters. In the general
setting, the task is harder, since important features, such as text or picture
boundaries are not available and even image features, such as the horizon or
other dominant horizontal or vertical lines in the scene can be missing. Figure 1
shows an example, where traditional line-based approaches will most likely fail.

In such cases, the result depends on very subtle features that require some
understanding of the image content. In the last three years, deep convolutional

P. Fischer—Supported by a scholarship of the Deutsche Telekom Stiftung.

J. Gall et al. (Eds.): GCPR 2015, LNCS 9358, pp. 368–378, 2015.
DOI: 10.1007/978-3-319-24947-6_30

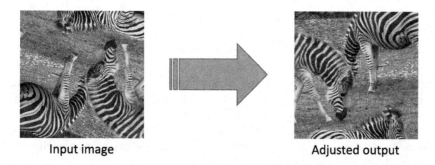

Input image   **Adjusted output**

Fig. 1. Automatic orientation adjustment. The rotation angle of the input image is estimated by a convolutional network. With this information the image can be adjusted to its canonical orientation. In this example, there are hardly any useable horizontal or vertical lines. The existing lines are in fact confusing.

networks have been shown to be very good at learning such features. The initial success was on classification tasks [8], but also other problems that require the use of initially unspecified features, such as depth map prediction from single images, have been approached successfully with convolutional networks [4].

In this paper, we train a convolutional network to predict the orientation of an image. We consider the problem at three difficulty levels. In the easiest setting, we assume that the rotation is at most $\pm 30°$. The task becomes more difficult if the rotation can be between $-45°$ and $+45°$, as this can lead to confusion between horizontal and vertical lines and, consequently, to an ambiguity between the landscape and portrait orientation. The most difficult setting is orientation estimation without any prior knowledge about the coarse orientation, i.e., all angles (0–360°) are equally likely.

Training powerful, deep convolutional networks used to require a large amount of annotated training data. Often this is a strong restriction as the collection of such data can be very tedious. For the present task, however, training data can be generated very easily in almost arbitrary amounts, since any unlabeled set of images can serve as training set. Training samples can be generated by just rotating these images by random angles.

We demonstrate that the proposed networks successfully learn to predict the orientation with an average accuracy of $3°$ in the setting with $\pm 30°$. It outperforms baselines built upon Hough transform or Fourier transform by a large margin. The network runs in real time on a GPU. Hence, it can also be used to stabilize a live video stream. Experiments with a webcam show that the network generalizes and has not learned to make use of potential artifacts that result from the synthesized training and test set.

2   Related Work

We are not aware of work on precise estimation of the orientation of general natural images. Existing methods either reduce the domain of application or they do not predict the precise angle but only classify between a restricted set of standard orientations.

Some methods explicitly use fine structure of the image to estimate the rotation. Wei et al. [20] make use of interpolation artifacts introduced by applying rotation to digital images. However, this method would not work for images which were not taken upright. Solanki et al. [15] estimate the rotation of printed images by analyzing the pattern of printer dots. Clearly, this method does not apply to images taken with a digital camera.

Horizon detection [5,10] is a special case of image orientation estimation. However, the horizon is not visible in most photos.

In other works the continuous-valued prediction task has been reduced to classification by restricting the rotations to multiples of 90°. This problem can be solved fairly efficiently [17,19].

While we are not aware of applications of neural networks to estimating orientation of general images, there has been work on pose estimation with neural networks, in particular head and face orientation estimation [12,14,18]. Interestingly, the following networks trained to estimate orientation of arbitrary images also work well for face images.

3   Experimental Setup

3.1   Data

Ideally, for training a network to predict orientation, one requires a dataset of natural images annotated with how much their rotation angle deviates from the upright orientation. In theory it would be possible to collect such a dataset using a camera with a sensitive tilt sensor like an accelerometer. However, such a procedure would be time-consuming and expensive, while being susceptible to accelerated motions of the camera.

Hence, we rather use the publicly available Microsoft COCO dataset [1] as training set and apply rotations artificially. This makes data collection trivial, but the resulting data is noisy: Microsoft COCO includes tilted images and images with undefined orientations. For the test set we discarded those images (see examples in Fig. 2). While this procedure is infeasible for the large training set, our results show that a network trained on these noisy data still performs very well.

Augmentation. To prevent overfitting, we perform image augmentation, i.e., we apply random transformations to input samples during network training on the fly. We use translations (up to 5 % of the image width), brightness adjustment in the range $[-0.2, 0.2]$, gamma adjustment with $\gamma \in [-0.5, 0.1]$ and Gaussian pixel noise with a standard deviation in the range $[0, 0.02]$.

Manually verified test set. Images in the COCO dataset are not always perfectly straight. In order to precisely evaluate the performance of our method and compare it to the baselines, we manually selected a subset of 1030 images from the

Fig. 2. Examples of images that were dismissed for the test set. We discarded slanted images, framed images and images which do not have a well-defined orientation.

COCO validation set. For these images we ensured that they are correctly oriented. Moreover, we labeled test images as "easy" if they contained significant vertical or horizontal lines, for example, buildings, horizon, walls or doors. Other images we labeled as "difficult". In total there are 618 "easy" images and 412 "difficult" ones. Figures 3, 5 and 6 show several example test images, both "easy" and "difficult".

3.2 Tasks and Networks

We consider orientation estimation at three difficulty levels: $\pm30°$, $\pm45°$, and the full 360°. We call the corresponding networks trained for these tasks Net-30, Net-45, and Net-360. For all three tasks we built upon the AlexNet architecture from Krizhevsky et al. [8] implemented in Caffe [6] and pretrained on ImageNet. This architecture consists of 5 convolutional layers, followed by 3 fully connected layers. After each fully connected layer, a rectified linear unit is used as nonlinearity. Additionally normalization and dropout are applied. For more details see [8].

Using ImageNet pretraining worked better than training the network from scratch despite the good availability of training data for our tasks. It seems that the class labels from ImageNet help learn semantic features that are useful for the task but too difficult for the network to learn from the orientation objective. After pretraining, all fully connected layers were initialized with Gaussian noise. Moreover, the last prediction layer of the AlexNet was replaced by one with two output units. We chose two output units to distinguish clockwise and counterclockwise rotations. The first output is to be active for positive rotations, while the second one is active for negative rotations. Given an angle α, the desired output vector is $[\max(0, \alpha), \max(0, -\alpha)]$. We trained the network with L1 loss.

We also set up a network with 4 class outputs corresponding to 0, 90, 180, and 270°. It is trained with a 4-way softmax output and cross-correlation loss. This network can be used for the conventional task of distinguishing landscape from portrait and upside-down images. We used this network to make a coarse prediction in the 360° task before estimating the exact angle with the regression architecture described above.

All of the networks were trained using the Adam optimization method [7]. The momentum parameters we fixed as recommended in [7] to $\beta_1 = 0.9$ and $\beta_2 = 0.999$. As the main learning rate we set $\lambda = 1e{-}4$ and then decrease it in steps until we reach $\lambda = 2e{-}7$. Additionally we use a slow start, i.e. starting with a low learning rate $\lambda = 1e{-}6$ and increasing it until the main learning rate is reached.

3.3   Baseline Methods

We did not find prior work on precisely estimating the orientation of natural images. Hence, for comparison we evaluated three simple baselines that are built upon the "Straighten image" function in Matlab Central [11] and use two traditional computer vision techniques: Hough transform and Fourier transform. All methods are based on dominant gradient or line orientations to straighten the image.

In the first method, which we refer to as *Hough-var*, edges are detected with a Prewitt filter. We then perform a Hough transform and compute the variance of each column in the Hough space, that is, for each angle we compute the variance of all values corresponding to this angle. The Hough space is folded to a range of $90°$ such that angles with the same value modulus 90 contribute to the same bin. For the Hough space we chose a bin size of $0.5°$. The angle estimate is computed as the angle with maximum variance.

Also the second method, *Hough-pow*, uses the Hough transform. We use the Canny edge detector and then apply the Hough transform. We raise all the values to a power α (we found $\alpha = 6$ to work well in the experiments) and sum each column. Again, after folding the space to a range of $90°$, the estimated angle is the one for which this sum takes the largest value.

Fig. 3. Orientation adjustment with Net-30 and Hough-pow. Although dominant horizontal and vertical lines are missing in most of these examples, the network predicts the correct angle.

The third method makes use of the fast Fourier transform (FFT), we hence refer to it as *Fourier*. After performing FFT, we again fold the space such that rotations with a difference of 90° match. For each angle, we then sum all magnitudes corresponding to this angle to obtain its score. The angle with the maximum score determines the estimated image orientation.

4   Results

We evaluated the networks on the three subtasks and compared them quantitatively to the above mentioned baselines. Additionally we show some qualitative results, demonstrating strengths as well as limitations of the approach. As an example application, we use an orientation-estimating network for real-time video stabilization.

4.1   Fine Orientation Adjustment

We first evaluated the scenario in which the rough image orientation is known, and only fine adjustment, in the range of $[-30; 30]$ degrees or $[-45; 45]$ degrees, is needed. Table 1 shows the average error in degrees for the test set. The average error of the network is much lower than that of the three baselines. The histograms in Fig. 4 reveal that the better performance is mainly because the network fails far less often in hard cases when traditional line features are absent. For Net-30, the average error for the ±30° range reaches the accuracy level of the training data set. Allowing for up to ±45° makes the task harder, since horizontal and vertical lines can now be confused. Figure 4b reveals that the accuracy is the same for good cases, but there are more failure cases at the far end of the histogram due to portrait vs. landscape confusion (please use zoom in the

Table 1. Average absolute errors of the estimated angles. The networks clearly outperform the baseline methods and achieve very good accuracies on the fine orientation adjustment tasks. The full orientation estimation task is significantly harder. Here it helps to first classify the coarse orientation succeeded by a fine adjustment.

Task	Net-30	Net-45	Net-360	Net-rough+45	Hough-var	Hough-pow	Fourier
±30°-all	**3.00**	4.00	19.74	19.64	11.41	10.62	10.66
±30°-easy	**2.17**	2.83	19.48	17.90	8.44	7.04	8.64
±30°-hard	**4.26**	5.75	20.12	22.24	15.88	15.99	13.69
±45°-all	-	**4.63**	20.64	19.24	16.92	13.06	16.51
±45°-easy	-	**3.24**	21.26	19.29	14.08	9.01	13.32
±45°-hard	-	**6.71**	19.70	19.15	21.16	19.13	21.28
±180°-all	-	-	20.97	**18.68**	-	-	-
±180°-easy	-	-	20.29	**18.70**	-	-	-
±180°-hard	-	-	21.98	**18.65**	-	-	-

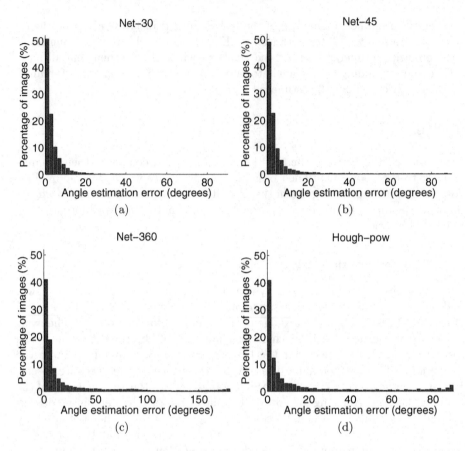

Fig. 4. Error histograms for the three networks on the ±30°, the ±45°, and the full orientation estimation task, as well as for the Hough-pow baseline on the ±45° task. The networks fail less often than the baseline. Note that Net-30, Net-45 and Net-360 are run on progressively harder tasks.

electronic version of the paper). Figure 3 shows some examples for the orientation adjustment. Visually, the results look very good. In Fig. 5 we show cases that caused the largest errors. The optimal rotation for most of these examples is also hard to decide for humans.

4.2   Orientation Estimation with Full Rotations

We also evaluated the case where the given image is rotated arbitrarily between 0 and 360°. We tested two different approaches to solve this problem. First, we applied a network similar to those from Sect. 4.1 with two output units. Since a direct prediction of the angle as a scalar would break continuity at one point of the cycle, the network predicts the cosine and sine of the angle and the actual angle is then obtained by the arc tangent. In a second approach, we predict

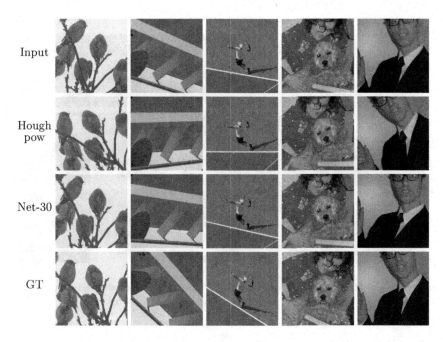

Input

Hough
pow

Net-30

GT

Fig. 5. Failure cases with Net-30 (samples with particularly large errors between 14 and 38°). For comparison we also show the Hough-pow results. Even for humans it is hard to decide on the optimal orientation.

a 90° rough orientation followed by a fine orientation adjustment in the range $[-45, 45]$ degrees.

Table 1 reveals that the second approach performed better. In general, the full rotation task comes with significantly larger average errors than the fine adjustment. The histograms in Fig. 4 reveal that this is mostly due to failure cases with very large errors. The left part of the histogram of Net-360 is still comparable to those of the other two networks. Figure 6 shows some examples for Net-360 including one larger failure case and one slight inaccuracy. It is worth noting that, in order to make use of semantic information such as faces, the network has to recognize faces although they can be upside-down in the input image.

4.3 Video Stabilization

A single forward pass of our networks takes 45 ms at an input resolution of 280×280 pixels on an NVIDIA GTX Titan GPU, which enables us to use it in real-time applications like video stabilization. Our video stabilization implementation can be used with any webcam and shows the original as well as the rectified image live on the screen. We used Net-45 in this experiment.

Fig. 6. Results with Net-360. **Top row:** input image. **Middle row:** adjusted output. **Bottom row:** ground truth. Despite large rotations, the network can often estimate the correct angle.

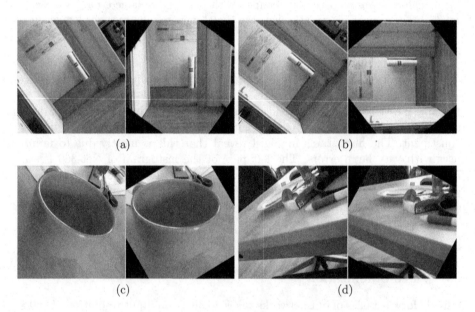

Fig. 7. Results of real-time video stabilization with Net-45. Images come in pairs: input on the left and the straightened image on the right. (a) and (b) demonstrate how the angle estimation flips at 45°, because the network expects angles between ±45°. In (c) and (d) the network predicts the correct orientation, even though the images do not contain useful vertical or horizontal gradients.

The network successfully generalizes to images captured with the webcam. Some examples are shown in Fig. 7, and the reader is referred to the supplementary video for more examples. The fact that the network works with raw webcam images proves that it does not make use of interpolation artifacts which appear when artificially applying rotations. The network was trained to estimate rotations not larger than 45°, hence when presented with larger rotations, it jumps to the 90°-rotated image (Fig. 7(a) and (b)). Interestingly, the network works well even in the absence of strong vertical and horizontal edges, successfully retrieving upright images; see Fig. 7(c) and (d).

5   Conclusions

We have presented an approach based on convolutional networks that can predict the orientation of an arbitrary natural photograph. This orientation prediction can be used to adjust the image to its canonical orientation. The use of convolutional networks is advantageous for this task, since large numbers of training samples can be generated synthetically and the network is able to learn subtle contextual features that allow it to estimate the correct orientation even when straightforward features, such as vertical or horizontal lines are not present in the image. The network runs in realtime, which allows us to apply it to live video streams. In future work the network architecture will be optimized to run in realtime on smaller graphic chips (such as the NVIDIA Tegra), which would make the approach also applicable to orientation estimation in quadcopters, providing acceleration-independent measurements besides IMUs.

References

1. Microsoft COCO dataset. http://mscoco.org
2. Ávila, B.T., Lins, R.D.: A fast orientation and skew detection algorithm for monochromatic document images. In: Proceedings of the 2005 ACM Symposium on Document Engineering, pp. 118–126 (2005)
3. Chen, S.S., Haralick, R.M.: An automatic algorithm for text skew estimation in document images using recursive morphological transforms. In: ICIP, pp. 139–143 (1994)
4. Eigen, D., Puhrsch, C., Fergus, R.: Depth map prediction from a single image using a multi-scale deep network. In: NIPS (2014)
5. Fefilatyev, S., Smarodzinava, V., Hall, L.O., Goldgof, D.B.: Horizon detection using machine learning techniques. In: ICMLA, pp. 17–21 (2006)
6. Jia, Y., Shelhamer, E., Donahue, J., Karayev, S., Long, J., Girshick, R., Guadarrama, S., Darrell, T.: Caffe: Convolutional architecture for fast feature embedding. arXiv preprint (2014). arXiv:1408.5093
7. Kingma, D.P., Ba, J.: Adam: A method for stochastic optimization. In: ICLR (2015). http://arxiv.org/abs/1412.6980
8. Krizhevsky, A., Sutskever, I., Hinton, G.E.: Imagenet classification with deep convolutional neural networks. In: NIPS, pp. 1106–1114 (2012)
9. Kwag, H.K., Kim, S.H., Jeong, S.H., Lee, G.S.: Efficient skew estimation and correction algorithm for document images. Image Vis. Comput. 20(1), 25–35 (2002)

10. Lipschutz, I., Gershikov, E., Milgrom, B.: New methods for horizon line detection in infrared and visible sea images. Int. J. Comput. Eng. Res. **3**(3) (2013). ijceronline.com
11. Motl, J.: Straighten image function in Matlab Central. http://www.mathworks.com/matlabcentral/fileexchange/40239-straighten-image
12. Osadchy, M., LeCun, Y., Miller, M.L.: Synergistic face detection and pose estimation with energy-based models. J. Mach. Learn. Res. **8**, 1197–1215 (2007)
13. Peake, G.S., Tan, T.N.: A general algorithm for document skew angle estimation. In: ICIP, vol. 2, pp. 230–233 (1997)
14. Pingali, G.S., Zhao, L., Carlbom, I.: Real-time head orientation estimation using neural networks. In: ICIP, pp. 297–300 (2002)
15. Solanki, K., Madhow, U., Manjunath, B.S., Chandrasekaran, S.: Estimating and undoing rotation for print-scan resilient data hiding. In: ICIP, pp. 39–42 (2004)
16. Sun, C., Si, D.: Skew and slant correction for document images using gradient direction. In: 4th International Conference Document Analysis and Recognition (ICDAR 1997), pp. 142–146 (1997)
17. Vailaya, A., Zhang, H., Member, S., Yang, C., Liu, F.I., Jain, A.K.: Automatic image orientation detection. IEEE Trans. Image Process. **11**(7), 600–604 (2002)
18. Voit, M., Nickel, K., Stiefelhagen, R.: Neural network-based head pose estimation and multi-view fusion. In: Stiefelhagen, R., Garofolo, J.S. (eds.) CLEAR 2006. LNCS, vol. 4122, pp. 291–298. Springer, Heidelberg (2007)
19. Wang, Y.M., Zhang, H.: Detecting image orientation based on low-level visual content. Comput. Vis. Image Underst. **93**(3), 328–346 (2004)
20. Wei, W., Wang, S., Zhang, X., Tang, Z.: Estimation of image rotation angle using interpolation-related spectral signatures with application to blind detection of image forgery. Trans. Info. For. Sec. **5**(3), 507–517 (2010)
21. Yan, H.: Skew correction of document images using interline cross-correlation. CVGIP: Graph. Model Image Process. **55**(6), 538–543 (1993)

Semi-Automatic Basket Catheter Reconstruction from Two X-Ray Views

Xia Zhong[1], Matthias Hoffmann[1(✉)], Norbert Strobel[2],
and Andreas Maier[1,3]

[1] Pattern Recognition Lab, Friedrich-Alexander-Universität Erlangen-Nürnberg,
Erlangen, Germany
`matthias.hoffmann@cs.fau.de`
[2] Siemens Healthcare GmbH, Forchheim, Germany
[3] Erlangen Graduate School in Advanced Optical Technologies (SAOT),
Erlangen, Germany

Abstract. Ablation guided by focal impulse and rotor mapping (FIRM) is a novel treatment option for atrial fibrillation, a frequent heart arrhythmia. This procedure is performed minimally invasively and at least partially under fluoroscopic guidance. It involves a basket catheter comprising 64 electrodes. The 3-D position of these electrodes is important during treatment. We propose a novel model-based method for 3-D reconstruction of this catheter using two X-ray images taken from different views. Our approach requires only little user interaction. An evaluation of the method found that the electrodes of the basket catheter can be reconstructed with a median error of 1.5 mm for phantom data and 3.4 mm for clinical data.

1 Introduction

Atrial (Afib) fibrillation is one of the most common heart arrhythmia. In particular, for persistent Afib, ablation guided by focal impulse and rotor mapping (FIRM) has been proposed as an alternative to traditional treatment options [11]. To perform a FIRM-based ablation procedure, a multielectrode basket catheter is placed first in the right atrium and then into left atrium during the case. The basket catheter's shape resembles an ellipsoid when imaged under X-ray (see Fig. 1). It has eight splines, each spline comprising eight electrodes. One marker electrode can be identified by its larger size. The catheter is used to record the electrical signals in the atria. Using the Topera RhythmView 3-D electrophysiological mapping system (Topera Inc., Palo Alto, CA, USA), the position of electrical anomalies, so-called rotors can be found. This position is determined relative to the splines and the electrode positions of the basket catheter and indicates endocardial substrate maintaining the arrhythmia, that may be ablated. A method is required to remap the rotor position from its basket catheter-based coordinate system to the anatomical positions in the left and right atrium.

© Springer International Publishing Switzerland 2015
J. Gall et al. (Eds.): GCPR 2015, LNCS 9358, pp. 379–389, 2015.
DOI: 10.1007/978-3-319-24947-6_31

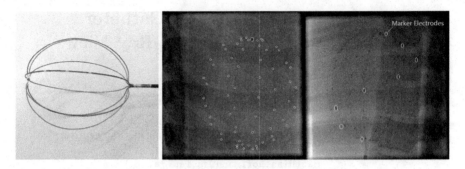

Fig. 1. Basket catheter, displayed left, as seen in two X-ray views taken from different directions. The basket catheter comprises eight splines carrying eight electrodes. Each spline has a marker electrode highlighted with ellipses (right).

As of now, remapping and associated catheter navigation is performed using the EnSite Velocity mapping system (St. Jude Medical, St. Paul, MN, USA). However, the use of the EnSite system is problematic for at least two reasons. First, current healthcare economics leave very little financial room to use a second mapping system during an Afib ablation procedure. Second, it is known that an impedance-based localization system such as Ensite Velocity may suffer from electrical field distortions [6]. As an alternative to the mapping system, we propose a method based on two X-ray images taken from different directions to detect and reconstruct the basket catheter in 3-D. This is a challenging task as the catheter is usually deformed by the atria. This results in a complex structure compared with other electrophysiological catheters such as the coronary sinus catheter and the circumferential mapping catheter [9].

1.1   Related Work

Image based 3-D catheter detection or reconstruction methods require usually the detection of features, e.g., the center line or electrodes of the catheter. The 3-D catheter can then either be generated bottom up from these features, or, in a top-down manner, i.e., an initialization of 3-D curve can be approximated towards the features. Hoffman et al. [9] proposed to use a bottom up strategy which detects the center line of a catheter in two different views first. Then it uses epipolar geometry to reconstruct an 3-D point cloud. They also proposed a method to find the correct order of a subset of points in the point cloud to reconstruct the catheter. Using 3-D curve segments as the feature rather than a 3-D point cloud, Delmas et al. [5] proposed a method to estimated the optimal ordered subset of 3-D curve segments and applied constraints to reconstruct the catheter. Using top-down strategy, Mauri [3] proposed a method using B-snakes to formulate the catheter detection and reconstruction as an energy minimization problem. Unfortunately, none of these approaches can be applied to our problem as the basket catheter has a complex structure. Furthermore, it is not always possible to extract the basket catheter splines as the contrast can be very low.

We present a top-down approach to reconstruct the shape of a basket catheter in 3-D using two 2-D X-ray images acquired from different directions. For reconstruction of the rather complex structure of the basket catheter, we propose to use a statistical shape model. The model is adapted to the electrodes and wires extracted in two 2-D images. Our method has been designed for the basket catheter, but can inspire reconstruction methods for other complex catheters.

2 Method

The method to detect the basket catheter comprises three steps. In the first step, we train the shape model of the basket catheter based on annotated ground truth data. In the second step, we detect the electrodes and splines of the basket catheter in the X-ray images taken from two different viewing directions. Using these 2-D points, we reconstruct all possible 3-D electrode candidates using triangulation. In this step, the user is also asked to specify the start and the end of the basket catheter at least one of the marker electrodes. The marker electrodes determine the order of the catheter splines. In the last step, the initialization of the model will be performed and the model will be matched to the extracted features in the 2-D images. A different, possibly more intuitive approach, may have been to assign electrodes to splines followed by 3-D reconstruction. However, it might be difficult to compute this assignment, especially if splines connecting the electrodes are not well visible, and an exhaustive search would possibly take too long to execute in a clinical environment.

2.1   Basket Catheter Spline Model

We describe each single spline of the basket catheter using a statistic shape model [4]. The choice to use a shape model was motivated by the desire to constrain the basket catheter reconstruction problem as much as possible yet being able to use prior knowledge about the expected deformation. The model is trained using the 3-D electrode positions of M splines which origin from several, differently deformed catheters. We combine the basket catheter's start point $\boldsymbol{p}_{i1} \in \mathbb{R}^3$, eight electrodes $\boldsymbol{p}_{i2}, \ldots, \boldsymbol{p}_{i9}$ and the basket's end point $\boldsymbol{p}_{i10}$ of the ith spline in a vector $\boldsymbol{x}'_i$

$$\boldsymbol{x}'_i = \left(\boldsymbol{p}_{i1}^T, \ldots, \boldsymbol{p}_{ik}^T, \ldots, \boldsymbol{p}_{i10}^T\right)^T \tag{1}$$

Such a description is established for each of the M basket catheter splines. To build the statistical shape model, the data needs to be normalized first. The normalization involves a rotation and translation in 3-D, scaling is not necessary, as the size of the catheter is standardized. We normalized the data $\boldsymbol{x}'_i$ so that the start point $\boldsymbol{p}_{i1}$ and the end point $\boldsymbol{p}_{i10}$ lie both on the y-axis. The middle point between these two points is defined as origin. Furthermore, during alignment we make sure that the eight electrodes $\boldsymbol{p}_{i2}, \ldots, \boldsymbol{p}_{i9}$ have minimum distance to the $X - Y$ plane and that their x-coordinates are positive. So, the alignment for point $\boldsymbol{p}_{ik}$ in i^{th} catheter spline can be formulated as

$$\boldsymbol{x}_{ik} = \mathbf{R}_i^Y \mathbf{R}_i (\boldsymbol{p}_{ik} + \boldsymbol{t}_i) \tag{2}$$

where $x_i = \left(x_{i1}^T, \ldots, x_{i10}^T\right)^T \in \mathbb{R}^{30}$ denotes the normalized and aligned points, t_i and $\mathbf{R}_i$ denote the translation and rotation for normalization, and $\mathbf{R}_i^Y$ denotes the rotation along the Y axis for alignment. Then we follow the steps from Cootes et al. [4], calculate the mean shape $\bar{x}$, the deviation dx_i from the mean and the covariance matrix Σ as

$$\bar{x} = \frac{1}{M}\sum_{i=1}^{M} x_i \qquad dx_i = x_i - \bar{x} \qquad \Sigma = \frac{1}{M}\sum_{i=1}^{M} dx_i dx_i^T \qquad (3)$$

By calculating an eigenvalue and eigenvector decomposition of the covariance matrix Σ, we get unit eigenvectors v_k ($k = 1, \ldots, 30$) with corresponding eigenvalues λ_k in descending order. Using the first N_m modes of variation $\mathbf{V} = (v_1, \ldots, v_{N_m})$ and the corresponding weight factors $b' = (b_1, \ldots, b_{N_m})$, we can generate new shapes x' of the model as

$$x' = \bar{x} + \mathbf{V}b' \qquad (4)$$

In the remainder of the paper, we use $N_m = 3$ modes of variations.

2.2   Electrode and Spline Detection

We detect the electrodes in the image $\mathbf{I}(x, y)$ using the determinant of the Hessian matrix $\mathbf{H}$ [10] of a scale space representation

$$\mathbf{L}(x, y; \sigma^2) = \mathbf{I}(x, y) * \mathbf{G}(x, y; \sigma^2) \qquad (5)$$

obtained by a convolution with a Gaussian kernel $\mathbf{G}(x, y; \sigma^2)$ of size σ. To detect blobs of different sizes, different values of σ should be chosen. Steger [12] stated that the center point of a bar-shaped profile with a width of $2w$ can be extracted when $\sigma \geq w/\sqrt{3}$. With prior knowledge of electrodes' dimensions w_p and the projection geometry information of the C-arm, we can estimate a minimal scale σ_{min}. Let m be the perspective magnification factor of the X-ray system and s_p be pixel spacing. Based on the length w_{im} of the electrode as it appears in the X-ray image (in pixels), we select the scale as

$$\sigma_{min} = \frac{w_{im}}{2\sqrt{3}} \qquad \text{with} \quad w_{im} = \frac{w_p \cdot m}{s_p} \qquad (6)$$

We use two different scales, σ_{min} and $2\sigma_{min}$, to calculate the determinant of the Hessian matrix for each pixel. Then we apply a threshold on the determinant of the Hessian to obtain an electrode mask image. The threshold level is selected such that a certain percentage of image pixels is extracted as the number of image pixels covered by electrodes is roughly known in advance. We then select the possible positions of the electrodes denoted as e_i^A and e_i^B in image A and B. Therefore, the local maximum of the determinant of the Hessian in each connected component of the mask image is selected as electrode center. Finally, the user is required to mark the start point $\tilde{p}_1^A$, $\tilde{p}_1^B$ and the end point $\tilde{p}_{10}^A$, $\tilde{p}_{10}^B$

of the basket catheter by clicking on them in the 2-D images of plane A and B, respectively. Additionally, either one or eight spline marker points are marked in both views. The 3-D position of the start point $\tilde{p}_1$, end point $\tilde{p}_{10}$ and the marker electrode(s) are obtained using triangulation.

2.3   Point Cloud Generation

We use epipolar geometry to search for correspondences between electrodes in associated two-view images. When searching for correspondences, we introduce some margin for acceptance. This acceptance range depends on the X-ray system used. For a bi-plane system, the acceptance range will be only a few pixels to compensate the blob detection error due to limited precision or residual camera calibration error. For mono-plane systems, patient motion might occur between the two acquisitions from different views. Therefore, we accept a higher margin and apply additionally a motion compensation using the marked 2-D catheter start points $\tilde{p}_1^A$, $\tilde{p}_1^B$ and the marked 2-D endpoints $\tilde{p}_{10}^A$, $\tilde{p}_{10}^B$ of image plane A and B, respectively. This motion compensation is applied to the projection matrix $\mathbf{P}^A$ associated with plane A by multiplying it with a 3-D translation matrix $\mathbf{T} = \left(1 \mid (t_x, t_y, t_z)^T\right)$. The $\mathbf{T}$ are selected such that the distance between the projection rays from $\tilde{p}_1^A$ and $\tilde{p}_1^B$ and the distance between the projection rays of $\tilde{p}_{10}^A$ and $\tilde{p}_{10}^B$ is minimal. For each possible point correspondence, a 3-D point is triangulated [8].

Finally, the catheter splines are extracted using a vesselness filter [2,7]. After applying a threshold, distance maps $\mathbf{I}_{ds}^A$ and $\mathbf{I}_{ds}^B$ to the splines in image A and B, respectively, are computed.

2.4   Model Initialization and Adaption

Length Adaption. Using the 3-D start point $\tilde{p}_1$ and the end point $\tilde{p}_{10}$ marked by the user, we perform an initialization of all single splines of the basket catheter model. Let $\hat{p}_{k1}(b')$ and $\hat{p}_{k10}(b')$ be the start point and end point of kth spline when using b' as parameters. We select the parameter vector $b_k = (b_{k1}, b_{k2}, b_{k3})^T$ of the kth spline such that $\|\tilde{p}_1 - \tilde{p}_{10}\| = \|\hat{p}_1(b') - \hat{p}_{10}(b')\|$. As this is an under-termined problem, we propose two different ways of adding constraints. One is called most probable model which is estimated by optimizing following equation

$$b_k = \underset{b'}{\operatorname{argmin}} \|\tilde{p}_1 - \tilde{p}_{10}\| - \|\hat{p}_1(b') - \hat{p}_{10}(b')\| - a_0 \cdot \mathcal{N}(b'; 0, \Sigma) \qquad (7)$$

For the second approach, we manually define a set of different ratios between b_{k1}, b_{k2} and b_{k3}. With these extra constraints, the problem becomes determined and can be solved. We use these parameters for all eight splines and distribute them with equal angle spacing around the axis defined by the start point $\tilde{p}_1$ and the end point $\tilde{p}_{10}$ to get a model of the whole basket catheter. As shown in Fig. 5, the shape of the model can be very different subject to the same start and end point.

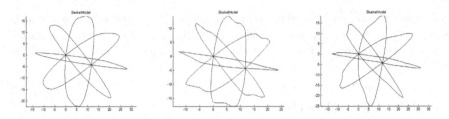

Fig. 2. Different possible shapes with same start point $\tilde{p}_1$ and end point $\tilde{p}_{10}$

Rotation Initialization. Starting with this initial model, we also need to estimate the rotation $\boldsymbol{\alpha} = (\alpha_1, \ldots, \alpha_8)$ of each single spline. In case we have eight marker electrodes as input, the rotation for all single splines is computed such that their distance to their respective marker electrode is minimal. With one marker electrode input, the whole basket catheter is rotated such that the distance of the marker electrode to its respective spline is minimal. Based on the result, we estimate further the rotation of the other remaining splines. We define therefore an energy-term $\mathcal{D}$ to describe the difference between the projected model and the extracted features in both images as

$$
\mathcal{D}(\mathbf{b}, \boldsymbol{\alpha}) = a_1 \cdot \underbrace{\left(\sum_i \min_k d\left(e_i^{\mathrm{A}}, \mathbf{S}_k^{\mathrm{A}}(\boldsymbol{b}_k, \alpha_k) \right) + \sum_i \min_k d\left(e_i^{\mathrm{B}}, \mathbf{S}_k^{\mathrm{B}}(\boldsymbol{b}_k, \alpha_k) \right) \right)}_{\text{Distance of each detected electrode to projected splines of the model}}
$$

$$
a_2 \cdot \underbrace{\left(\sum_i \min_{j,k} d\left(e_i^{\mathrm{A}}, \boldsymbol{p}_{k,j}^{\mathrm{A}}(\boldsymbol{b}_k, \alpha_k) \right) + \sum_i \min_{j,k} d\left(e_i^{\mathrm{B}}, \boldsymbol{p}_{k,j}^{\mathrm{B}}(\boldsymbol{b}_k, \alpha_k) \right) \right)}_{\text{Distance of each detected electrode to projected electrodes of the model}}
$$

$$
a_3 \cdot \underbrace{\left(\sum_{k,j} \min_i d\left(e_i^{\mathrm{A}}, \boldsymbol{p}_{k,j}^{\mathrm{A}}(\boldsymbol{b}_k, \alpha_k) \right) + \sum_{k,j} \min_i d\left(e_i^{\mathrm{B}}, \boldsymbol{p}_{k,j}^{\mathrm{B}}(\boldsymbol{b}_k, \alpha_k) \right) \right)}_{\text{Distance of each projected electrode of the model to detected electrodes}}
$$

$$(8)$$

where $\boldsymbol{p}_{kj}^{\mathrm{A}} \in \mathbb{R}^2$ denotes the projection of the jth electrode on the kth spline in the image A. The projection of the complete k^{th} 3-D spline in image A is denoted as $\mathbf{S}_k^{\mathrm{A}}$. Their projections in image B are denoted by $\boldsymbol{p}_{k,j}^{\mathrm{B}}$ and $\mathbf{S}_k^{\mathrm{A}}$, respectively. The rotation is estimated by minimizing the energy $\mathcal{D}$

$$
\boldsymbol{\alpha} = \underset{\alpha_1, \ldots, \alpha_8}{\operatorname{argmin}} \mathcal{D}(\mathbf{b}, \alpha_1, \ldots, \alpha_8) \tag{9}
$$

Outlier Reduction. The initialization described at the beginning of this section assumes that the basket catheter is symmetrical, i.e. the parameter vector $\boldsymbol{b}_k$ is the same for each spline. To cover also asymmetrical cases, we will

---

Algorithm 1. Iterative Outlier Reduction and Model Estimation

---

1: Compute for all electrodes e_i^A detected in image plane A the set $\mathcal{C}(e_i^A)$ of corresponding electrodes in image B
2: **for** each iteration step $t = 1 : N$ **do**
3:     **for** each e_i^A **do**
4:         find the two splines $\mathbf{S}_t^1$, $\mathbf{S}_t^2$ for which their projection $\mathbf{S}_t^{1A}$, $\mathbf{S}_t^{2A}$ in image A is closest to e_i^A
5:         compute their projections $\mathbf{S}_t^{1B}$, $\mathbf{S}_t^{2B}$ in image B
6:         delete from $\mathcal{C}(e_i^A)$ the point $\mathbf{c}_k$ which maximizes $\min(d(\mathbf{c}_k, \mathbf{S}_t^{1B}), d(\mathbf{c}_k, \mathbf{S}_t^{2B}))$
7:     **end for**
8:     reconstruct a new 3-D point cloud using the remaining correspondences
9:     estimate the model $\mathbf{M}_t$ with respect to the new point cloud
10:    estimate the rotation α_t
11: **end for**

---

use the 3-D electrode point cloud to adapt the initialization. As we have potentially many outliers in the 3-D point cloud, we will perform an iterative outlier reduction and model estimation algorithm. This Algorithm, which is described in Algorithm 1, assigns 2-D electrodes to 3-D splines to detect and eliminate spurious correspondences.

Image-Based Model Adaption. Finally, we adapt the model such that it fits to both images by altering the weighting $b = (b_1^T, \ldots, b_k^T)$ and rotation $\alpha = (\alpha_1, \ldots, \alpha_8)$. We introduce therefore an additional energy term

$$\mathcal{R}(b, \alpha) = a_4 \cdot \underbrace{\sum_k \mathcal{N}(b_k; 0, \Sigma)}_{\text{Model likelyhood}} + a_5 \cdot \underbrace{\sum_k \mathbf{I}_{ds}^A(\mathbf{S}_k^A(b_k, \alpha_k)) + \mathbf{I}_{ds}^B(\mathbf{S}_k^B(b_k, \alpha_k))}_{\text{Distance of projected splines to detected 2-D splines}}$$
$$(10)$$

for the final optimization of b and the rotation α

$$b, \alpha = \underset{b, \alpha}{\operatorname{argmin}} \mathcal{D}(b, \alpha) + \mathcal{R}(b, \alpha) \qquad (11)$$

3 Evaluation and Results

For evaluation, we used three different setups. In the first case, the basket catheter was deformed by tape and put into a bottle. A total of 18 different experiments were performed by inserting the basket catheter such that it assumed a different shape each time. Then, a C-arm CT was acquired. As a result, 18 3-D volumes were generated, each containing a differently deformed basket catheter. Also, a series of associated X-ray images taken from different angles was acquired for each volume. In each of the 18 volumes, the positions of the 3-D electrodes were annotated and served as ground truth. For evaluation, two X-ray images, taken from perpendicular view directions, were selected for each of the 18 basket catheter placements. They were taken as the input for our algorithm.

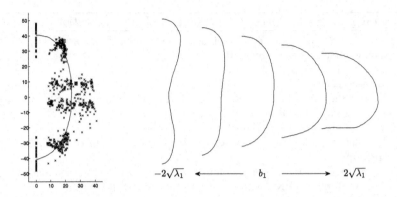

Fig. 3. The coordinates of a subset of the annotated electrodes, normalized and aligned with mean shape of the basket catheter spline model (shown left) and the first mode of variation (displayed right). As most of the variation spreads in the X-Y plane, we projected the mean shape and the variation of the basket into the X-Y plane.

For the second setup, the catheter was placed into a thorax phantom. Then we took four bi-plane image pairs with perpendicular viewing angles at different dose settings. Unlike in the previous experiment, in this case the basket catheter was identically deformed. We used this set to evaluate the performance of our approach with respect to different noise levels.

We also included one clinical data set in the evaluation taken from a mono-plane system. Here, the basket was placed in the right atrium along with other electrophysiological catheters. The ground truth positions of the electrodes of the basket catheter were obtained, both for the bi-plane setup and the clinical data, by triangulation of annotated electrodes in both views.

3.1   Result of the Spline Model Training

For training of the basket catheter model, we used the 3-D electrode coordinates annotated from the C-arm CT data sets. For evaluation using the C-arm CT data set, a leave-one-out crossvalidation was performed. The resulting model and the first mode of variation is shown in Fig. 3.

3.2   Basket Catheter Reconstruction Results

C-arm CT Data Set. The results of the evaluation using the C-arm CT data sets are shown in Fig. 4. We also investigated how marking all instead of a single spline marker electrode and outlier reduction changed our outcomes. We found that the median error was between 1.7 mm and 1.5 mm. The maximum errors are 24.2 mm and 32.2 mm for single marker annotation without and with outlier reduction, respectively. The respective maximum errors when all markers are annotated are 15.3 mm 24.1 mm. However, we did also encounter outliers of up to 32.2 mm depending on the kind of information provided by the user.

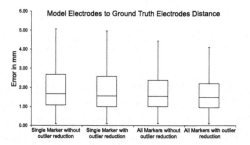

Fig. 4. Evaluation result of C-arm CT data with different electrode selection strategies. The median errors are 1.7 mm and 1.6 mm for single marker annotation without and with outlier reduction, respectively. The respective median errors when all markers are annotated are 1.6 mm 1.5 mm. Results with an error of a 1.5 inter-quartile range above the median error are not shown in the figure.

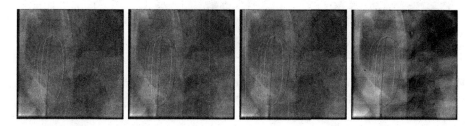

Fig. 5. Images of basket catheter in phantom and overlay of the reconstructed basket catheter. The X-ray dose and image quality improved from left to right.

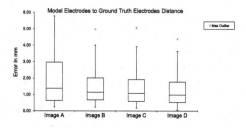

Fig. 6. Evaluation result with biplane X-ray data acquired at different dose levels. Image A has the poorest SNR, image D has the best SNR.

Comparing different user interactions, we see that the result improved somewhat when the positions of the eight marker electrodes were provided. Unfortunately, the improvements were limited, both for knowing all marker electrodes and also when applying outlier reduction methods.

Bi-Plane Views with Different X-Ray Dose. Figure 2 shows qualitative results using images from the bi-plane data set, quantitative results are presented in Fig. 6. The result shown in Fig. 6 indicate that our method performed better as the signal to noise ratio improved, i.e., as the X-ray dose was increased. This experiment shows that our method can also perform well at a low SNR.

Clinical Data. In Fig. 7, we show the clinical data with the basket catheter in the right atrium. In this case, we used single marker selection without outlier reduction. The result is also shown in this figure. With our method, we reached a median error of 3.4 mm and a maximum error of 12.5 mm, respectively.

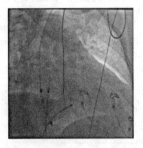 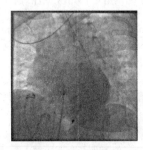 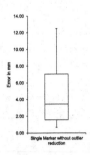

Fig. 7. Left anterior oblique (LAO) 45° view and right anterior oblique (RAO) 30° view of the basket catheter in the right atrium.

4   Discussion and Conclusion

When comparing a 3-D representation of a basket catheter computed by our method from two views to its counterpart generated using C-arm CT, we found a median error below the clinical important threshold of 3 mm [1]. Unfortunately, we also encountered large maximum errors. They were caused by heavily deformed and twisted basket catheters in the data set, these cases are not very clinically relevant as the basket catheters would need to be repositioned in such a situation to obtain a signal reading that can then be reliably processed further. The performance of outlier reduction is also restricted as in some case, some of the electrodes are positioned where multiple splines cross. In such a case, it is also hard for the algorithm to decide which spline the electrode should be assigned to. This problem could be approached by using a consensus based method in the future. In the clinical data set, however, the result was less satisfactory with a median error of 3.4 mm. This error is the consequence of very low-dose data acquisition resulting in X-ray images with a low SNR. In such a situation our electrode detection algorithm identifies many potential electrode positions which do not belong to the basket catheter. Any overlap of the basket catheter with other catheters is also problematic. In such a case, some electrodes of the basket catheter might not be visible and additional electrodes may be introduced that are not associated with the basket catheter. More work on robust basket electrode detection is needed to improve the result. Furthermore, the outlier reduction algorithm should be extended to assign e.g. probabilities to point correspondences. This which might also improve the result.

Acknowledgments. We gratefully acknowledge the feedback by the Klinikum Coburg, Germany, and would also like to thank them for the test images. This work was supported by Siemens Healthcare. The concepts and information presented in this paper are based on research, and are not commercially available.

References

1. Bourier, F., Fahrig, R., Wang, P., Santangeli, P., Kurzidim, K., Strobel, N., Moore, T., Hinkel, C., Amin, A.A.: Accuracy assessment of catheter guidance technology in electrophysiology procedures. J. Cardiovasc. Electrophysiol. **25**(1), 74–83 (2014)
2. Budai, A., Bock, R., Maier, A., Hornegger, J., Michelson, G.: Robust vessel segmentation in fundus images. Int. J. Biomed. Imaging 2013, 11 pages (2013)
3. Canero, C., Radeva, P., Toledo, R., Villanueva, J., Mauri, J.: 3d curve reconstruction by biplane snakes. In: Proceedings of the 15th International Conference on Pattern Recognition, vol. 4, pp. 563–566 (2000)
4. Cootes, T.F., Taylor, C.J., Cooper, D.H., Graham, J.: Active shape models - their training and application. Comput. Vis. Image Underst. **61**(1), 38–59 (1995)
5. Delmas, C., Berger, M.O., Kerrien, E., Riddell, C., Trousset, Y., Anxionnat, R., Bracard, S.: Three-dimensional curvilinear device reconstruction from two fluoroscopic views (2015)
6. Eitel, C., Hindricks, G., Dagres, N., Sommer, P., Piorkowski, C.: Ensite velocity cardiac mapping system: a new platform for 3d mapping of cardiac arrhythmias. Expert Rev. Med. Devices **7**(2), 185–192 (2010). http://www.tandfonline.com/doi/abs/10.1586/erd.10.1
7. Frangi, A.F., Niessen, W.J., Vincken, K.L., Viergever, M.A.: Multiscale vessel enhancement filtering. In: Wells, W.M., Colchester, A.C.F., Delp, S.L. (eds.) MICCAI 1998. LNCS, vol. 1496, pp. 130–137. Springer, Heidelberg (1998)
8. Hartley, R.I., Sturm, P.: Triangulation. Comput. Vis. Image Underst. **68**(2), 146–157 (1997)
9. Hoffmann, M., Brost, A., Jakob, C., Bourier, F., Koch, M., Kurzidim, K., Hornegger, J., Strobel, N.: Semi-automatic catheter reconstruction from two views. In: Ayache, N., Delingette, H., Golland, P., Mori, K. (eds.) MICCAI 2012, Part II. LNCS, vol. 7511, pp. 584–591. Springer, Heidelberg (2012)
10. Lindeberg, T.: Feature detection with automatic scale selection. Int. J. Comput. Vision **30**(2), 79–116 (1998)
11. Narayan, S.M., Krummen, D.E., Shivkumar, K., Clopton, P., Rappel, W.J., Miller, J.M.: Treatment of atrial fibrillation by the ablation of localized sourcesconfirm (conventional ablation for atrial fibrillation with or without focal impulse and rotor modulation) trial. J. Am. Coll. Cardiol. **60**(7), 628–636 (2012)
12. Steger, C.: An unbiased detector of curvilinear structures. IEEE Trans. Pattern Anal. Mach. Intell. **20**(2), 113–125 (1998)

Fast Brain MRI Registration with Automatic Landmark Detection Using a Single Template Image

Olga V. Senyukova[✉] and Denis S. Zobnin

Faculty of Computational Mathematics and Cybernetics,
Lomonosov Moscow State University, GSP-1, Leninskie Gory,
Moscow 119991, Russian Federation
osenyukova@graphics.cs.msu.ru

Abstract. Automatic registration of brain MR images is still a challenging problem. We have chosen an approach based on landmarks matching. However, manual landmarking of the images is cumbersome. Existing algorithms for automatic identification of pre-defined set of landmarks usually require manually landmarked training bases. We propose the registration algorithm that involves automatic detection of landmarks with the use of only one manually landmarked template image. Landmarks are detected using Canny edge detector and point descriptors. Evaluation of four types of descriptors showed that SURF provides the best trade-off between speed and accuracy. Thin plate spline transformation is used for landmark-based registration. The proposed algorithm was compared with the best existing registration algorithm without the use of local features. Our algorithm showed significant speed-up and better accuracy in matching of anatomical structures surrounded by the landmarks. All the experiments were performed on the IBSR database.

1   Introduction

Registration of magnetic resonance images (MRI) of human brain is a problem from the field of image matching. Usually this problem is formulated in terms of finding such a transformation of one image that makes it the most similar to the other image. Brain MRI registration has numerous applications in practice. For example, comparison of brain MR images of different subjects or one subject at different moments allows observing anatomical changes caused by some pathological process. Matching an input brain MR image with an atlas, i.e. an image along with its manual anatomical labelling, implies finding such a transformation of the atlas image that makes it the most similar to the input image, so that it is possible to transfer the labelling from the atlas to the input image. Currently, it is the most promising approach to brain MRI segmentation into anatomical structures [6].

The algorithms for brain MRI registration can be classified by different criteria. Firstly, registration can be linear or nonlinear. Linear registration algorithms use linear transformations, affine or rigid, and allow compensating for general

© Springer International Publishing Switzerland 2015
J. Gall et al. (Eds.): GCPR 2015, LNCS 9358, pp. 390–399, 2015.
DOI: 10.1007/978-3-319-24947-6_32

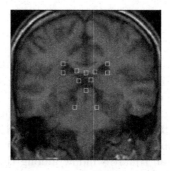

Fig. 1. Example of a manually landmarked brain MR slice

differences in scale, position, etc. These algorithms are fast, but they are not able to match anatomical structures locally. Thus, they are usually used as the first step of the registration process. One of the most widely used algorithms of this group is implemented as FSL FLIRT tool [21]. Another group of registration algorithms involves nonlinear transformations of the images that can locally refine image matching result after coarse linear registration. Numerous existing algorithms varying by the type of transformation used, image similarity metric and regularization method are outlined and compared in the review [14]. According to [14], Symmetric Normalization algorithm (SyN) [4] that uses nonlinear image transformations called *diffeomorphisms*, is the most accurate. Comparison of MRI registration methods [10] confirms that the method is state-of-the-art. However, SyN is one of the most computationally expensive methods, requiring a lot of time and memory.

The second criterion for classification of registration algorithms splits them into two groups: intensity-based algorithms and feature-based algorithms.

The algorithms of the first group try to find the image transformation that optimizes some intensity-based image similarity metric. Different types of metrics are used for that purpose, such as cross-correlation in [4,8], mutual information in [17], sum of squared differences (SSD) in [3,22]. These registration algorithms do not require any additional information but in some cases the result is hard to predict. If the anatomical differences are more than average, the most critical anatomical structures can be poorly matched.

Feature-based algorithms are less susceptible to this problem. First of all, they try to match specific features in the images, that correspond to well-distinguishable points with unique local neighbourhood. These features are called *landmarks* or *key points*. In early works, the landmarks were specified manually by an expert [11] or semi-automatically [18]. An example is shown in Fig. 1.

Manual landmarking is a tedious and time-consuming process, especially in 3D. Because of that, recent efforts in this direction concentrate on automatic detection of these points. Some algorithms involve automatic selection of key points from the whole set of local features [20,23], while others are searching for pre-defined landmark locations [12,13].

In this work we propose an algorithm for registration of two input brain MR images that is based on matching of the set of automatically detected landmarks in these images. The set of landmarks to be detected is given in a manually marked image, a template. Therefore, the algorithm does not require training bases, like the algorithms in [12,13]. Although the algorithm was implemented for 2D images, it can be further adapted for the 3D case. Before starting the process of automatic detection of landmarks in the input image, the template image, along with its landmarks, is linearly registered to the input image. For each landmark in the template image, its corresponding landmark in the input image is searched in a small square window among the non-zero points of the Canny edge map by comparing point descriptors. Image registration of the two input images by the set of key points is performed using thin plate splines transformation [9].

The proposed registration algorithm was evaluated on 18 2D slices extracted from each of the 18 brain MR images from IBSR database [2]. We evaluated and compared the accuracy and run time of landmarks detection using patch comparison by normalized cross-correlation (NCC) and three types of descriptors: local self-similarity descriptor (LSSD) [19], SIFT [15] and SURF [5]. The proposed algorithm was also compared with SyN [4], state-of-the-art algorithm without the use of key points.

2 Method

2.1 Template

As it was mentioned above, the proposed algorithm requires only one manually landmarked image. This image along with its landmarks will serve as the template for landmarks detection in each of the two input images.

We can define a template MR image, $T(\mathbf{x})$, as

$$T : \mathbf{x} \in \mathbb{R}^2 \to T(\mathbf{x}) \in \mathbb{R}, \tag{1}$$

where $\mathbf{x} = (x, y)$ specifies a point location, and $T(\mathbf{x})$ is intensity value in this point. A set of n manually specified landmarks in the template image can be defined as $P^T = \{\mathbf{p}_1^T, ..., \mathbf{p}_n^T\}$, where $\mathbf{p}_i^T = (x, y), i = 1, ..., n$ specifies the i's landmark location.

2.2 Preparation of the Images to the Detection of Landmarks

Two input images to be registered, $I(\mathbf{x})$ and $J(\mathbf{x})$, are defined similarly to (1):

$$I : \mathbf{x} \in \mathbb{R}^2 \to I(\mathbf{x}) \in \mathbb{R}, \tag{2}$$

$$J : \mathbf{x} \in \mathbb{R}^2 \to J(\mathbf{x}) \in \mathbb{R}, \tag{3}$$

where $\mathbf{x} = (x, y)$ specifies a point's location, and $I(\mathbf{x})$ (respectively, $J(\mathbf{x})$) is intensity value in this point.

Before starting the landmarks detection process, both images, $I(\mathbf{x})$ and $J(\mathbf{x})$, are preprocessed by anisotropic diffusion filter [16] that removes noise, while preserving edges. This saves meaningful anatomical information. Template image $T(\mathbf{x})$ can be preprocessed *once*, after it has been defined.

For each landmark $\mathbf{p}_i^T$ in the template image its corresponding landmark $\mathbf{p}_i^I$ ($\mathbf{p}_i^J$) in the input image will be searched in a square window of the size $2r + 1 \times 2r + 1$ around the point with the same coordinates as $\mathbf{p}_i^T$. So the template image $T(\mathbf{x})$ should be globally matched with the input image $I(\mathbf{x})$ ($J(\mathbf{x})$). Linear registration algorithm can achieve this goal. Let's assume that we have two copies of the template image $T(\mathbf{x})$ along with its landmark set P^T. The first copy of $T(\mathbf{x})$ is linearly transformed in order to match the input image $I(\mathbf{x})$. The landmarks positions P^T are changed accordingly. The second copy of $T(\mathbf{x})$ is linearly transformed in order to match the input image $J(\mathbf{x})$. The landmarks positions P^T are changed accordingly.

2.3   Detection of Landmarks

Anatomical landmarks, if specified properly, usually lie on the edges of anatomical structures, not in uniform regions. This allows making the algorithm faster and, at the same time, more robust by constraining the search area with the points having non-zero values on the edge map. Landmarks detection procedure is described below for the input image $I(\mathbf{x})$. The procedure will be the same for the input image $J(\mathbf{x})$.

Edge map is generated for the image $I(\mathbf{x})$ by Canny algorithm [7], one of the best existing edge detectors. Thus, the search area for the landmark $\mathbf{p}_i^I$ will be the following:

$$X_s = \{\mathbf{x}^I = (x^I, y^I) : x^I \in [x^T - r, x^T + r] \wedge y^I \in [y^T - r, y^T + r] \wedge C(\mathbf{x}^I) = 1\}, \quad (4)$$

where $C(\mathbf{x}^I)$ corresponds to the value of the Canny edge map in the point $\mathbf{x}$.

In order to characterize each landmark by its local context, we use a *descriptor*, i.e. a vector of values, computed for a point's neighbourhood. Let $D(\mathbf{x})$ be the descriptor of a point $\mathbf{x}$. So, for a landmark $\mathbf{p}_i^T$ in the template image $T(\mathbf{x})$ its corresponding point $\mathbf{p}_i^I$ in the input image $I(\mathbf{x})$ can be found as following:

$$\mathbf{p}_i^I = argmin_{\mathbf{x}^I \in X_s} ||D(\mathbf{p}_i^T) - D(\mathbf{x}^I)||. \quad (5)$$

In this work, we use three different types of descriptors in order to compare them in application to the posed problem and choose the best one.

Local Self-Similarity Descriptor (LSSD) [19] is based on computation of the similarity metric for the considered point and every other point in the window around it. This similarity space is represented in polar coordinates and the 80-bin histogram is built.

Scale Invariant Feature Transform (SIFT) descriptor [15] is built for the square patch around the point which is co-directional with the main gradient orientation in the local neighbourhood. The patch is split into 16 equal parts, for each of which a 8-bin histogram of gradient magnitude and orientations is built.

This results in a vector of 128 values. The descriptor is invariant to uniform scaling, rotation and slight intensity variations.

Speeded-up Robust Features (SURF) [5] is based on the ideas, similar to SIFT but is faster to compute. It uses integral images and Haar wavelets. The vector consists only of 64 values which makes it faster to match.

Besides comparison of descriptors, we also try one of the simplest methods to compare points by their local neighbourhood that is based on computation of normalized cross-correlation (NCC) metric for small square image patches around these points:

$$NCC(A, B) = \frac{\sum_{i=1}^{M}(A_i B_i)}{\sqrt{\sum_{i=1}^{M} A_i^2 \sum_{i=1}^{M} B_i^2}}, \tag{6}$$

where A_i is the intensity value in the ith point of the patch in the image A, B_i is the intensity value in the ith point of the patch in the image B, and M is the number of points in each of the patches.

Anatomical landmarks usually belong to internal structures. However, this is not enough for correct registration of the whole brain. In order to resolve this issue, we introduce *quasi-landmarks* that belong to the bounding box of the brain. The algorithm for their identification can be outlined as follows. On the Canny edge map we find four points with non-zero values, i.e. lying on the edges, with a minimum value of x (leftmost point), maximum value of x (rightmost point), minimum value of y (bottommost point) and maximum value of y (topmost point). These four points define the bounding box. Four points lying in the middle of each of the edges of the bounding box are considered to be quasi-landmarks. They are included into the landmark sets P^T, P^I and P^J.

2.4   Image Registration

During the registration process, one of the images is transformed in order to match the other image. The image, that is transformed, is called *moving image*. The other image is called *fixed image*. Let $I(\mathbf{x})$ be a moving image, and $J(\mathbf{x})$ be a fixed image.

According to the review of existing registration methods, state-of-the-art algorithms start from fast coarse linear registration. So, first of all, the image $I(\mathbf{x})$ is linearly registered to the image $J(\mathbf{x})$ along with its landmarks detected in the previous step of the proposed algorithm.

After that, the images can be registered non-linearly by matching of the set of landmarks. We have to find such a transformation $t(I(\mathbf{x}))$ that minimizes the distances between the corresponding landmarks:

$$t(I(\mathbf{x})) = argmin_t \sum_{i=1}^{n} ||\mathbf{p}_i^I - \mathbf{p}_i^J||, \tag{7}$$

In this work we use thin plate spline transformation [9] that was already used previously for landmark-based registration of brain MR images [18,23].

3 Experiments and Results

3.1 Dataset

The algorithm was evaluated on the set of real T1-weighted MR images of 18 subjects provided by the Center of Morphometric Analysis at the Massachusetts General Hospital and available on the Internet Brain Segmentation Repository (IBSR) [2]. Each MRI scan has $256 \times 256 \times 128$ image resolution. Spatial resolution is varying from scan to scan ($0.84 \times 0.84 \times 1.55\, mm^3$, $0.94 \times 0.94 \times 1.5\, mm^3$, $1.0 \times 1.0 \times 1.5\, mm^3$). Manual segmentation into 43 anatomical structures is provided for each MRI scan.

The experiments were performed on 18 2D slices each of which was extracted from the middle of the corresponding brain volume (slice number varies from 49 to 53 in the coronal plane). These slices contain large number of anatomical structures.

12 ground truth landmarks in each of the 18 slices were specified manually by the authors of the present work for validation purpose.

3.2 Comparison of Descriptors

The proposed algorithm for landmarks detection was implemented in Matlab and evaluated using cross-validation. 18 series of tests were performed. In the ith series the ith slice was considered as a template, and the landmarks were automatically detected in each of the rest 17 slices. 18×17 tests in total were performed. For each detected landmark the error in pixels was computed as the

Table 1. Comparison of detection accuracy for each of 12 anatomical landmarks using four different methods. Values in the Table are errors in pixels.

L.no	Mean				Std. dev			
	NCC	LSSD	SIFT	SURF	NCC	LSSD	SIFT	SURF
1	2.32	2.69	**1.57**	1.72	2.72	3.16	2.38	2.42
2	2.05	4.49	**1.74**	1.78	3.04	4.50	2.63	2.61
3	5.01	5.61	**3.72**	3.91	5.62	5.25	4.21	4.63
4	4.21	5.14	**2.61**	2.73	4.50	4.55	2.97	2.66
5	1.54	3.98	**1.25**	1.33	2.76	4.57	2.53	2.54
6	2.58	4.77	**2.21**	2.25	2.48	4.05	2.19	2.20
7	3.30	4.14	3.09	**2.85**	3.14	3.40	2.84	2.45
8	3.07	4.88	2.35	**2.18**	4.32	5.32	3.35	3.15
9	2.50	3.47	2.25	**1.72**	3.03	3.67	3.19	2.41
10	3.21	3.54	1.89	**1.86**	4.00	3.47	1.45	1.36
11	3.07	5.13	**2.68**	2.82	3.09	4.66	3.11	3.31
12	2.71	4.52	**2.59**	2.60	2.71	4.25	3.24	3.03

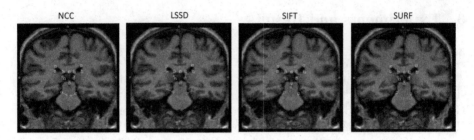

Fig. 2. Results example: boxes denote ground truth landmarks, asterisks denote automatically detected landmarks

distance to the ground truth landmark. Search window for each landmark was 21×21 ($r = 10$). The results are presented in Table 1. An example is shown in Fig. 2.

Another type of comparison was based on evaluation of the time consumed for landmarks detection on PC with Intel Core i5-2410M (2.3 GHz), 4 GB RAM. The results are shown in Fig. 3.

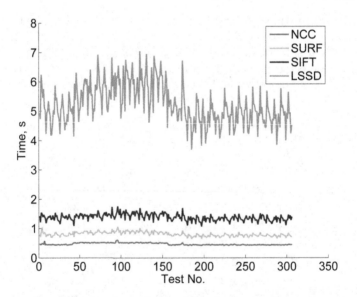

Fig. 3. Comparison of the algorithms by runtime

According to the experimental results SIFT and SURF descriptors provide the best accuracy. SIFT slightly over-performs SURF in 2/3 cases (no more than 0.2 pixels), but SURF is ≈ 2 times faster. The fastest algorithm is comparison of patches by NCC, however, it is not invariant to rotation and scaling, and it is more sensitive to intensity variations. Thus, SURF descriptor can be considered

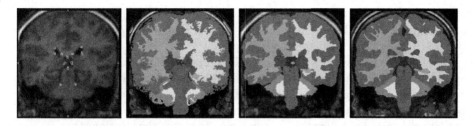

Fig. 4. Registration result. From left to right: landmarks on the moving image; SyN; proposed algorithm; ground truth labelling of the fixed image

the best one for this purpose. In most cases, landmark detection errors are within the limits of inter-expert variability.

3.3 Evaluation of Registration

Linear registration and non-linear registration by thin plate spline transformation were performed using Insight Segmentation and Registration Toolkit (ITK) [1]. Linear registration was performed using 2D affine transformation with NCC as similarity metrics and gradient descent as optimization algorithm. Parameters are the following: Iterations = 500; MinStep = 0.001; MaxStep = 0.3. Parameters for Symmetric Normalization (SyN) algorithm, which our method was compared with, are the following: Iterations = 100; Standard deviation (gaussian kernel) = 1.0; other parameters were set to default.

In order to evaluate the quality of matching of anatomical structures, we also used expert labelling of the images from IBSR database. The quality of registration is characterized by the similarity of the moving image labelling, transformed with the moving image, and the fixed image labelling. The result example is shown in Fig. 4.

From Fig. 4, it can be seen that SyN matches the gyrus better, but internal anatomical structures, if surrounded by landmarks, are much better matched by the proposed algorithm.

As for runtime comparison for the same PC as above, both algorithms require linear registration as the first step. It takes $\approx 0.6\,s$. SyN takes $\approx 5\,s$. The proposed algorithm consists of two steps: landmarks detection takes $\approx 0.5\,s$ and image registration by landmarks matching with thin plate spline transformation takes $\approx 0.04\,s$. In total, SyN takes $\approx 5.6\,s$ and the proposed algorithm takes only $\approx 1.1\,s$ which is about 5 times faster.

4   Conclusion and Discussion

In this work, we have proposed an algorithm for brain MR image registration by matching of automatically detected landmarks. We have demonstrated that one manually landmarked template image is enough for automatic detection of a set of well-distinguished landmarks in other images. Comparison of different types of descriptors for landmark identification showed that SURF descriptor provides the best trade-off between speed and accuracy.

Evaluation of image registration by the proposed algorithm showed that the approach based on matching of the pre-defined landmark set allows matching critical anatomical locations with good speed and accuracy. On the one hand, the result becomes more predictable for the specified locations, and on the other hand, the algorithm does not spend extra time on trying to match the locations that are not critical for the considered problem or cannot be matched at all. All three steps of the algorithm, linear registration, landmarks detection and registration by thin plate spline transformation, are so fast that the expert can get the results for 2D images in real-time and add landmarks into the template if necessary.

One of the future work directions can be introducing of varying search window size for handling the situations when the landmark is outside the search window. This situations may happen in the case of significant anatomical differences or damaged brain.

The algorithm can be further extended into 3D case. However, manual specification of landmarks is non-trivial for the 3D case. Therefore, the landmarks for the whole brain can be specified in consequent 2D slices of the template image. For each template slice with the landmarks, the most similar slice in the input brain volume can be found automatically. For example, this can be done by comparing normalized cross-correlation metrics, and the key points can be detected in it.

Acknowledgments. The authors would like to thank Alexey V. Petraikin, M.D. from Pirogov Russian National Research Medical University (RNRMU) for valuable discussion.

References

1. Insight segmentation and registration toolkit (ITK). http://www.itk.org
2. Internet brain segmentation repository. http://www.nitrc.org/projects/ibsr
3. Andersson, J., Smith, S., Jenkinson, M.: FNIRT – FMRIB's non-linear image registration tool. Human Brain Mapping. Poster 496 (2008)
4. Avants, B.B., Epstein, C.L., Grossman, M., Gee, J.C.: Symmetric diffeomorphic image registration with cross-correlation: evaluating automated labeling of elderly and neurodegenerative brain. Med. Image Anal. 12(1), 26–41 (2008)
5. Bay, H., Ess, A., Tuytelaars, T., Van Gool, L.: Speeded-up robust features (SURF). Comput. Vis. Image Underst. 110(3), 346–359 (2008)
6. Cabezas, M., Oliver, A., Llad, X., et al.: A review of atlas-based segmentation for magnetic resonance brain images. Comput. Methods Programs Biomed. 104(3), e158–e177 (2011)
7. Canny, J.: A computational approach to edge detection. IEEE Trans. Pattern Anal. Mach. Intell. 8(6), 679–698 (1986)
8. Collins, D.L., Evans, A.C.: ANIMAL: validation and applications of nonlinear registration-based segmentation. Int. J. Pattern Recognit Artif Intell. 11(8), 1271–1294 (1997)

9. Davis, M.H., Khotanzad, A., Flamig, D.P., Harms, S.E.: A physics-based coordinate transformation for 3-D image matching. IEEE Trans. Med. Imaging **16**(3), 317–328 (1997)
10. Diez, Y., Gubern-Mérida, A., Wang, L., Diekmann, S., Martí, J., Platel, B., Kramme, J., Martí, R.: Comparison of methods for current-to-prior registration of breast DCE-MRI. In: Fujita, H., Hara, T., Muramatsu, C. (eds.) IWDM 2014. LNCS, vol. 8539, pp. 689–695. Springer, Heidelberg (2014)
11. Evans, A.C., Dai, W., Collins, L., et al.: Warping of a computerized 3-D atlas to match brain image volumes for quantitative neuroanatomical and functional analysis. In: Proceedings SPIE, pp. 236–246. SPIE Press, Bellingham (1991)
12. Guerrero, R., Pizarro, L., Wolz, R., Rueckert, D.: Landmark localization in brain mr images using feature point descriptors based on 3D local self-similarities. In: 2012 9th IEEE International Symposium on Biomedical Imaging (ISBI), pp. 1535–1538. IEEE Press, New York (2012)
13. Han, D., Gao, Y., Wu, G., Yap, P.-T., Shen, D.: Robust anatomical landmark detection for MR brain image registration. In: Golland, P., Hata, N., Barillot, C., Hornegger, J., Howe, R. (eds.) MICCAI 2014, Part I. LNCS, vol. 8673, pp. 186–193. Springer, Heidelberg (2014)
14. Klein, A., Andersson, J., Ardekani, A.B., et al.: Evaluation of 14 nonlinear deformation algorithms applied to human brain MRI registration. NeuroImage **46**(3), 786–802 (2009)
15. Lowe, D.G.: Distinctive image features from scale-invariant keypoints. Int. J. Comput. Vision **60**(2), 91–110 (2004)
16. Perona, P., Malik, J.: Scale-space and edge detection using anisotropic diffusion. IEEE Trans. Pattern Anal. Mach. Intell. **12**(7), 629–639 (1990)
17. Pluim, J.P.W., Maintz, J.B.A., Viergever, M.A.: Mutual-information-based registration of medical images: a survey. IEEE Trans. Med. Imaging **22**(8), 986–1004 (2003)
18. Rohr, K., Stiehl, H.S., Sprengel, R., et al.: Landmark-based elastic registration using approximating thin-plate splines. IEEE Trans. Med. Imaging **20**(6), 526–534 (2001)
19. Shechtman, E., Irani, M.: Matching local self-similarities across images and videos. In: IEEE Conference on Computer Vision and Pattern Recognition, CVPR 2007, pp. 1–8. IEEE Press, New York (2007)
20. Shen, D.: Fast image registration by hierarchical soft correspondence detection. Pattern Recogn. **42**(5), 954–961 (2009)
21. Smith, S.M., Jenkinson, M., Woolrich, M.W., et al.: Advances in functional and structural MR image analysis and implementation as FSL. Neuroimage **23**(1), 208–219 (2004)
22. Vercauteren, T., Pennec, X., Perchant, A., Ayache, N.: Non-parametric diffeomorphic image registration with the demons algorithm. In: Ayache, N., Ourselin, S., Maeder, A. (eds.) MICCAI 2007, Part II. LNCS, vol. 4792, pp. 319–326. Springer, Heidelberg (2007)
23. Wu, G., Kim, M., Wang, Q., Shen, D.: S-HAMMER: hierarchical attribute-guided, symmetric diffeomorphic registration for MR brain images. Hum. Brain Mapp. **35**(3), 1044–1060 (2014)

Photorealistic Face Transfer in 2D and 3D Video

Daniel Merget[⊠], Philipp Tiefenbacher, Mohammadreza Babaee,
Nikola Mitov, and Gerhard Rigoll

Institute for Human-Machine Communication, TUM, Munich, Germany
daniel.merget@tum.de

Abstract. 3D face transfer has been employed in a wide field of settings such as videoconferencing, gaming, or Hollywood movie production. State-of-the-art algorithms often suffer from a high sensitivity to
tracking errors, require manual post-processing, or are overly complex in
terms of computation time. Addressing these issues, we propose a lightweight system which is capable to transfer facial features in both 2D and
3D. This is accomplished by finding a dense correspondence between a
source and target face, and then performing Poisson cloning. We solve
the correspondence problem efficiently by a sparse initial registration and
a subsequent warping, which is refined in a surface matching step using
topological projections. Additional processing power is saved by converting extrapolation problems to simple interpolation problems without loss
of precision. The final results are photorealistic face transfers in either
2D or 3D between arbitrary facial video streams.

1   Introduction

Given the high availability of consumer 3D capturing devices, there is a rising
demand for 3D video content processing. The film and gaming industry have
shown particular interest in human face transfer. The applications range from
photorealistic lip (re-)synchronization [7] over face manipulation for movies [2,4]
to videoconferencing [12], puppeteering [10,17] or virtual avatar control [5,9].

In general, the approaches can be divided into photorealistic and virtual
(avatar) approaches. However, the latter group of approaches could just as well
be adapted for photorealistic face transfer. Since the correspondences can always
be found by registering each individual face to a template or avatar, an adequate
algorithm to blend the registered result back into the target scene is basically
the only difference. Hence, we will treat both types of approaches as de-facto
equivalent.

Bouaziz and Weise et al. use a PCA face model that is subsequently refined
in order to account for personal details [5,22]. Vlasic et al. instead use a multilinear model to learn missing data from a sparse set of recordings [21]. Dale
et al. use FaceGen [18] and a matching algorithm of Vlasic et al. [21] in order
to find the correspondences [7]. Afterwards, they re-time the video sequences for
better lip synchronization and apply Poisson cloning, using graph cuts in order
to find an appropriate mask.

© Springer International Publishing Switzerland 2015
J. Gall et al. (Eds.): GCPR 2015, LNCS 9358, pp. 400–411, 2015.
DOI: 10.1007/978-3-319-24947-6_33

Our approach mostly differs in the way we achieve dense correspondence between the two faces. Using only sparse correspondences between the two individuals, we warp the source to the target face and refine the result in a single non-iterative step. The type of feature transfer is flexible in that it depends on the type of interpolation used in the warping step (e.g., shape, texture, viseme). Finally, we apply a variant of Poisson image cloning in order to blend the warped face back into the video sequence in a photorealistic fashion, waiving the costly graph cuts from [7].

2 Overview

In order to guide the reader trough the following sections, we provide a brief overview of the system. Before a source face can be transferred to a target scene, the two faces have to be in correspondence. Once a set of sparse correspondences is given, a dense correspondence has to be found. Usually, this problem is solved via a registration process. Non-rigid point registration, however, is computationally very costly since state-of-the-art algorithms typically require a number of iterations to converge to a satisfactory solution.

Instead, if no additional information is used, this step is generally known as *warping*. In general, the key purpose of warping is to find transformations for every point in the source to the target, only by inter- and extrapolating from known correspondences. Popular warping algorithms for three-dimensional shapes include weighted nearest neighbor search and tetrahedralized inter- and extrapolation [6]. Any warping technique can be used as long as the resulting transformations are continuous, i.e., close points should be affected by similar transformations. For this reason, we choose to employ tetrahedralized warping.

In order to achieve the best performance, we apply a topological projection after the initial warping. A topological projection is particularly easy to compute for human faces because their surface can be assumed to be nearly star-shaped. After applying this type of projection, the projected shape is identical for both source and target. This permits a second tetrahedralized warping step to be implemented in terms of interpolation only, instead of both inter- and extrapolation. This is advantageous, given that extrapolation is much less accurate and also more costly than interpolation. The whole registration pipeline for the three-dimensional case is illustrated in Fig. 1.

Finally, the refined result is merged with the target by means of Poisson image cloning, which is a mathematically elegant way to seamlessly paste the warped face into the target scene.

3 Finding Correspondences

First of all, we require a set of corresponding points between the source Φ and target Θ, so-called landmarks, denoted Λ^{Φ} and Λ^{Θ}, respectively. There are a number of approaches dealing with automatic landmark detection. For example, Face++ [25] uses a deep convolutional neural network in order to find such

Fig. 1. Pipeline of the registration process. First, a sparse correspondence between two faces is established (Sect. 3). Next, the source is warped onto the target using these correspondences (Sect. 4). Finally, the surfaces are refined via topologial projection (Sect. 5).

landmarks in human faces. Other approaches learn facial landmarks via structured output SVM [20] or employ exemplar-based graph matching [26]. We use the landmarks provided by the Microsoft Kinect 2.0 face model which is based on a fusion of an active appearance model and a 3D tracker, providing 1347 distinct landmarks per face. In general, any method being capable of finding landmarks in a reliable way is suitable for the purpose of this paper. One advantage of the Microsoft Kinect face model is that the correspondences are fairly spread out, hence there is no need to extrapolate later on in the warping step. Figure 2 provides a quick analysis about the required number and accuracy of the landmarks.

4   Rigid Alignment and Warping

Because the tetrahedralized warping is not invariant to rotation, an initial rigid alignment using the correspondences is required. Although a full rigid registration would be feasible, it is sufficient to find a least-squares approximation of a rotation matrix $\boldsymbol{R}$ which rotates the source landmarks $\boldsymbol{\Lambda}^{\boldsymbol{\Phi}} = \{\boldsymbol{\lambda}_i^{\boldsymbol{\Phi}}\}$ to be aligned with the target landmarks $\boldsymbol{\Lambda}^{\boldsymbol{\Theta}} = \{\boldsymbol{\lambda}_i^{\boldsymbol{\Theta}}\}$. Assuming that $\boldsymbol{\Lambda}^{\boldsymbol{\Phi}}$ and $\boldsymbol{\Lambda}^{\boldsymbol{\Theta}}$ are normalized to have zero mean (i.e., their centroids are in the origin), the objective to be minimized is the following:

$$\min_{\boldsymbol{R}} \sum_i^N ||\boldsymbol{R}\boldsymbol{\lambda}_i^{\boldsymbol{\Phi}} - \boldsymbol{\lambda}_i^{\boldsymbol{\Theta}}||^2 \tag{1}$$

An efficient method to compute $\boldsymbol{R}$ is via Singular Value Decomposition (SVD) of the sum of outer products between the corresponding landmarks [19]:

$$[\boldsymbol{U}, \boldsymbol{\Sigma}, \boldsymbol{V}] = \text{SVD}\left(\sum_i^N \boldsymbol{\lambda}_i^{\boldsymbol{\Phi}}(\boldsymbol{\lambda}_i^{\boldsymbol{\Theta}})^T\right) \tag{2}$$

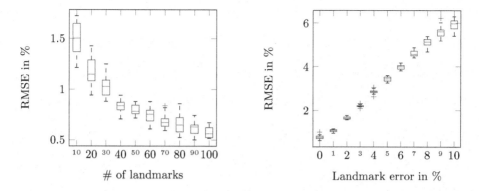

Fig. 2. Registration error for different number of landmarks and landmark accuracies. The results were obtained using randomly selected landmarks from 8 different faces of the Basel face model [14], warping each to the seven ground truth correspondences provided by the model (see Sect. 4 for details). So for each iteration, a total of 56 trials were evaluated. All of those trials were again averaged over 10 runs in order to compensate for outliers.

$$R = V U^T \tag{3}$$

In the following, it will be assumed that the source $\boldsymbol{\Phi}$ is prealigned to the target $\boldsymbol{\Theta}$ by means of this rotation matrix $\boldsymbol{R}$.

In order to do the warping, we proceed with a Delaunay tetrahedralization $\boldsymbol{\Delta}^{\Theta}$ on the target landmarks $\boldsymbol{\Lambda}^{\Theta}$ and adopt the edges for the source landmarks $\boldsymbol{\Lambda}^{\Phi}$ to receive the topoligically identical $\boldsymbol{\Delta}^{\Phi}$. Barycentric coordinates $\boldsymbol{b}_i^{\Phi}$ within the respective encompassing tetrahedron $\boldsymbol{D}_i^{\Phi}$ are assigned to all source points ϕ_i within $\boldsymbol{\Delta}^{\Phi}$. These coordinates are then used as a weight in order to interpolate between the landmarks and receive the warped result $\boldsymbol{\Omega} = \{\omega_i\}$. More specifically:

$$\omega_i = \boldsymbol{D}_i^{\Phi} \boldsymbol{b}_i^{\Phi} \tag{4}$$

Points which lie outside of the convex hull of $\boldsymbol{\Delta}^{\Phi}$ have to be extrapolated. This can be achieved by projecting the outer points smoothly onto the convex hull and then again perform barycentric interpolation using Eq. 4 [6]. If the landmarks are picked adequately, the extrapolation can also be avoided completely.

5   Surface Matching via Topological Projection

After the initial warping, the source $\boldsymbol{\Phi}$ and target $\boldsymbol{\Theta}$ are non-rigidly aligned, where the surfaces are interpolated from the sparse correspondence set. Using a topological projection, this intermediate result can be refined, so that the interpolated surfaces are again aligned to each other. Physically, this can be interpreted as a pressing a source surface patch into a mould of the target surface [13]. The accurate physical model from [13], however, is computationally expensive. Other approaches implement this type surface matching via Thin-Plate Splines [23] or

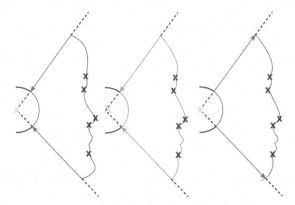

Fig. 3. Illustration of surface matching via topological projection. The first two images represent the prealigned source and target, respectively. Both are projected onto the unit sphere and put into correspondence. The interpolated source coordinates are then projected back onto the target, yielding the refined surface. The method can handle overlap as well as missing or non-isotropic data

using game theory [1], but the approaches are not very robust to noisy real-world data. Instead, we employ a mathematically simple approach which is inspired by Kent et al. [11]. The basic idea can be summarized as this: The source and target points are projected onto a common topology (e.g., sphere) before the projected source is merged and finally projected back onto the target. The process is illustrated in Fig. 3.

Any topology shared between the source and target is a suitable candidate, for example, the surface mesh which covers the known correspondences. Since human faces are typically (nearly) star-shaped objects, the projection onto a sphere provides the same amount of detail, while computations are kept to a minimum. The center c of the sphere can easily be found by intersecting all surface normal half-spaces. The center point can be precomputed relative to the landmarks and therefore does not contribute to the complexity of the system. Given an adequate center point c, computing the projection ρ of a point p is straightforward:

$$\rho = \frac{p - c}{||p - c||} \tag{5}$$

In the projected domain, the source and target are now in correspondence. In order to propagate this correspondence back to the original shape, yet another warping step is required. The projected points will lie on the surface of a unit sphere around the center point c. In other words, the projected source points are not within the convex hull of the target points (and vice versa). Consequently, warping would be based on extrapolation only. By introducing additional, virtual correspondences in the eight corners of the surrounding unit cube, a tetrahedralized warping step can be implemented solely in terms of interpolation, thereby reducing the computational effort considerably.

6   Poisson Cloning and Rendering

When blending the warped result Ω into the scene in a photorealistic fashion, lighting conditions and texture mismatch have to be compensated. Recent advances in image processing propose several variants of Poisson image cloning in order to tackle this problem [8,15,24]. Indeed, Poisson cloning is a powerful tool in providing a smooth boundary between source and target regions, where the cloning takes place in two dimensions. In order to apply Poisson cloning in three dimensions without adding considerable overhead, we solve the Poisson equation for the interpolated 2D projection of the warped 3D point set Ω. Afterwards, the result can be projected back to 3D.

In the original target scene, a perspective projection with respect to the camera origin guarantees that there are no ambiguous surfaces mapped to the same space. This is not generally the case for the warped source Ω, however, since the original source Φ may be oriented differently than the target Θ. We resolve possible ambiguities by a simple z-buffering approach, i.e., only those surfaces which are closest to the camera plane are rendered. After a bilinear interpolation in the 2D plane, the warped source Ω is ready to be rendered back into the target scene Θ using Poisson image cloning.

Alternatively, one can choose an area-preserving map projection from the sphere used in the refinement step to a 2D image. In this way, surface matching and Poisson cloning are combined in a single step. This approach is especially useful in 3D scenarios with multiple cameras, since a perspective projection covering the whole area of interest may not exist in that case.

The Poisson equation to be solved is

$$\min_{\Theta} \iint_{\Gamma} \left| \nabla\Theta - \nabla\Omega \right|^2 \partial\Gamma, \tag{6}$$

using the Dirichlet boundary condition

$$\Omega|_{\partial\Gamma} = \Theta|_{\partial\Gamma} \tag{7}$$

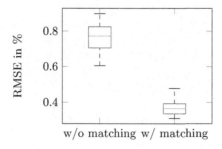

Fig. 4. Registration error with and without surface matching. The results were obtained using 50 randomly selected landmarks from 8 different faces of the Basel face model [14], in the same way as for Fig. 2.

and satisfying the Euler-Lagrange equation

$$\Delta\Omega = \Delta\Theta, \tag{8}$$

where Γ is the region to be cloned [15]. Simply choosing the convex hull of the warped source Ω as the boundary $\partial\Gamma$ may result in inaccuracies due to the possibly sparse outer regions. Hence, we predefine Γ relative to the landmark positions Λ^Θ, conserving important features (i.e., eyes, mouth and nose), thereby truncating sparse regions near the theoretical boundary. A more elaborate but computationally far more demanding approach by Dale et al. uses graph cuts to find an appropriate region Γ which minimizes the gradients on $\partial\Gamma$ [7].

7 Results and Discussion

Using the Basel Face Model [14], we demonstrate that the surface matching step from Sect. 5 reduces the Root Mean Square Error (RMSE) of the warped result by approximately 50 %, irrespective of the number of correspondences used. The results for 50 correspondences are depicted in Fig. 4.

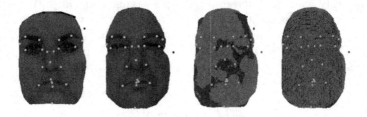

Fig. 5. 3D surface matching using 22 landmarks of the Bosphorus database [16]. From left to right: Source, target, warped (without matching), and using the proposed surface matching. There is clearly more overlap in the matched result, indicating a good correspondence.

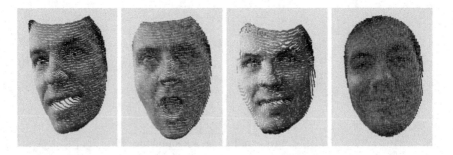

Fig. 6. Warping the geometry in a 3D video sequence. The results stem from three different pairings of 3D video captures. No further processing was applied.

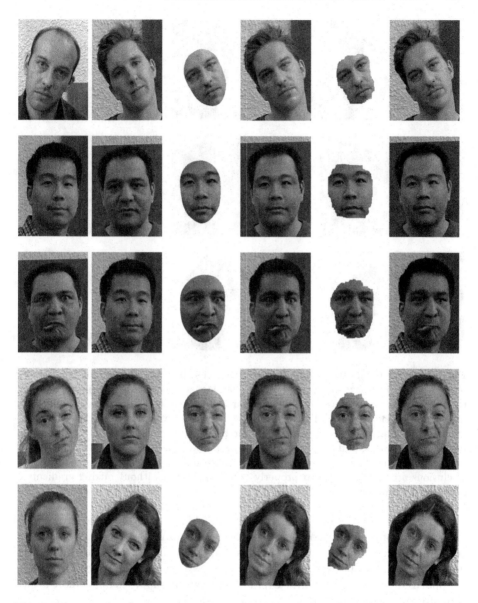

Fig. 7. Warping the geometry using Poisson cloning for 2D images. 1st to 4th column: Source, target, warped and the cloned result. 5th and 6th column: Our approach combined with the graph cuts from [7]. The approach is robust to varying head poses, lighting conditions and can also handle facial expression. All images are taken from video sequences that were captured from a distance of approximately 1 m in an uncontrolled office environment. The depicted results are fully auto-generated without manual corrections. Clearly, the graph cuts outperform the simple approach, e.g., bottom row. In many cases, however, the differences are barely noticeable.

Fig. 8. Typical failure cases. The first two columns show the source and target face, respectively. First row: Combining male and female faces yields unrealistic results even in the absence of obvious errors. In this particular case, the Kinect correspondences aggravate this effect, being slightly off. Second row: The warping from closed to open mouth cannot be handled properly in 2D (no z-buffering). Furthermore, a slight offset in the found correspondences results in an unproperly aligned mask which leads to artifacts (e.g., eyebrows, hair), which can be mitigated by graph cuts. Third row: Occlusions are not yet handled properly (Poisson cloning without mixing gradients), even in the graph cut case.

We also apply the approach to the Bosphorus database [16]. Since the dense correspondences are unknown in this case, the matching quality has to be evaluated by visual inspection. Figure 5 depicts two matched 3D faces from the Bosphorus database. Clearly, the overlap between the shapes is much more accurate after the refinement via topological projection.

Finally, Fig. 6 depicts different surface-matched warping results on 3D video sequences captured with Microsoft Kinect 2.0.

In order to illustrate the synergy of Poisson cloning with warping, we apply the combined approach to a set of 2D images, interpolating only the shape. In the same way, one could also interpolate texture or other visual features in order to obtain different results. Figure 7 shows the results of Poisson cloning applied with an intermediate warping step. Clearly, the approach is robust to varying lighting conditions and head poses. The warping achieves a much more realistic result compared to unwarped cloning, the cloning boundary $\partial\Gamma$ being much less prominent.

Our implementation of the whole processing chain runs at approximately $1 - 2\,\text{fps}$ on a notebook with an i7-4500U CPU and 8GB of RAM, where Poisson cloning is by far the most time-consuming step (typically $> 70\,\%$). On top of that, using the graph cut technique of [7] increases the computational effort by another factor of 3 to 4. Using an optimized and parallelized version, we are confident that a realtime-capable implementation of our baseline is feasible, i.e., providing the native Kinect 2.0 time resolution of 30 fps.

The most obvious limitation of the presented appoach is the missing occlusion handling as shown in Fig. 8. However, it is possible to extend the system by first detecting the occluded area(s) and then using mixing gradients for the Poisson cloning step [15]. Other problems occur when combining male and female faces. Especially when facial features such as beards are transferred, the results may look unnatural and artificial. This is probably due to the task itself being ill-posed rather than the employed algorithms being inadequate. After all, this limitation is not present for the transfer of facial expressions, for example.

8   Conclusion

We proposed a lightweight system to transfer facial features between different 2D/3D video scenes. The approach is applicable in real-world scenarios as it is robust to head pose and irregular illumination such directed light or shadows and does not rely on expensive hardware. The processing chain is very general and flexible, i.e., the different steps can be easily exchanged or extended. For example, the framework can be adapted in order to control virtual avatars instead of photorealistic individuals, omitting the Poisson cloning step completely. Alternatively, one could imagine other types of objects being transferred, given that the approach is not restricted to faces.

For future work, one could address small occlusions such as glasses by means of mixing gradients in the Poisson equation. Furthermore, it will be interesting to evaluate whether large occluded areas can be reconstructed, e.g., by fitting a model [3] or by exploiting symmetries. Finding a way to flexibly determine the boundary for the cloning which is computationally more efficient than the approach of Dale et al. [7] is another topic that should be investigated further, given that the results are very promising.

References

1. Albarelli, A., Rodolà, E., Torsello, A.: Fast and accurate surface alignment through an isometry-enforcing game. Pattern Recogn. **48**(7), 2209–2226 (2015)
2. Alexander, O., Rogers, M., Lambeth, W., Chiang, M., Debevec, P.: The digital emily project: photoreal facial modeling and animation. In: SIGGRAPH 2009 Courses, pp. 12:1–12:15. ACM (2009)
3. Blanz, V., Scherbaum, K., Seidel, H.P.: Fitting a morphable model to 3D scans of faces. In: International Conference on Computer Vision and Pattern Recognition (CVPR), pp. 1–8 (2007)

4. Borshukov, G., Piponi, D., Larsen, O., Lewis, J.P., Tempelaar-Lietz, C.: Universal capture - image-based facial animation for "The Matrix Reloaded". In: SIGGRAPH 2005 Courses. ACM (2005)

5. Bouaziz, S., Wang, Y., Pauly, M.: Online modeling for realtime facial animation. Trans. Graph. (SIGGRAPH) **32**(4), 40:1–40:10 (2013)

6. Cupisz, R.: Light probe interpolation using tetrahedral tessellations. In: Game Developers Conference (GDC) (2012). http://gdcvault.com/play/1015312/Light-Probe-Interpolation-Using-Tetrahedral

7. Dale, K., Sunkavalli, K., Johnson, M.K., Vlasic, D., Matusik, W., Pfister, H.: Video face replacement. Trans. Graphics (SIGGRAPH) 30 (2011)

8. Farbman, Z., Hoffer, G., Lipman, Y., Cohen-Or, D., Lischinski, D.: Coordinates for instant image cloning. Trans. Graph. (SIGGRAPH) **28**(3), 67:1–67:9 (2009)

9. Indiegogo: Facerig (2013). http://www.facerig.com

10. Kemelmacher-Shlizerman, I., Sankar, A., Shechtman, E., Seitz, S.M.: Being John Malkovich. In: Daniilidis, K., Maragos, P., Paragios, N. (eds.) ECCV 2010, Part I. LNCS, vol. 6311, pp. 341–353. Springer, Heidelberg (2010)

11. Kent, J.R., Carlson, W.E., Parent, R.E.: Shape transformation for polyhedral objects. Trans. Graph. (SIGGRAPH) **26**(2), 47–54 (1992)

12. Kuster, C., Popa, T., Bazin, J.C., Gotsman, C., Gross, M.: Gaze correction for home video conferencing. Trans. Graph. (SIGGRAPH) **31**(6), 1–6 (2012)

13. Litke, N., Droske, M., Rumpf, M., Schröder, P.: An image processing approach to surface matching. In: Proceedings of the Eurographics Symposium on Geometry Processing. Eurographics Association (2005)

14. Paysan, P., Knothe, R., Amberg, B., Romdhani, S., Vetter, T.: A 3D face model for pose and illumination invariant face recognition. In: Proceedings of the Advanced Video and Signal-based Surveillance (AVSS). IEEE (2009)

15. Prez, P., Gangnet, M., Blake, A.: Poisson image editing. Trans. Graph. (SIGGRAPH) **22**(3), 313–318 (2003)

16. Savran, A., Alyüz, N., Dibeklioğlu, H., Çeliktutan, O., Gökberk, B., Sankur, B., Akarun, L.: Bosphorus database for 3D face analysis. In: Schouten, B., Juul, N.C., Drygajlo, A., Tistarelli, M. (eds.) BIOID 2008. LNCS, vol. 5372, pp. 47–56. Springer, Heidelberg (2008)

17. Shiratori, T., Mahler, M., Trezevant, W., Hodgins, J.K.: Symposium on 3D User Interfaces (3DUI), pp. 59–66 (2013)

18. Singular Inversions Inc: Facegen modeller manual (2011). http://www.facegen.com

19. Umeyama, S.: Least-squares estimation of transformation parameters between two point patterns. Trans. Pattern Anal. Mach. Intell. (PAMI) **13**(4), 376–380 (1991)

20. Uřičář, M., Franc, V., Thomas, D., Akihiro, S., Hlaváč, V.: Real-time multi-view facial landmark detector learned by the structured output SVM. In: BWILD 2015: Proceedings of the Automatic Face and Gesture Recognition Conference and Workshops. IEEE (2015)

21. Vlasic, D., Brand, M., Pfister, H., Popović, J.: Face transfer with multilinear models. Trans. Graph. (SIGGRAPH) **24**(3), 426–433 (2005)

22. Weise, T., Bouaziz, S., Li, H., Pauly, M.: Realtime performance-based facial animation. Trans. Graph. (SIGGRAPH) **30**(4), 77:1–77:10 (2011)

23. Wu, Y., Ijiri, Y., Yang, M.H.: Multiple non-rigid surface detection and registration. In: International Conference on Computer Vision (ICCV), pp. 1992–1999 (2013)

24. Yoshizawa, S., Yokota, H.: Poisson image analogy: texture-aware seamless cloning. In: Eurographics - Posters. Eurographics Association (2013)

25. Zhou, E., Fan, H., Cao, Z., Jiang, Y., Yin, Q.: Extensive facial landmark localization with coarse-to-fine convolutional neural network. In: ICCV Workshop on 300 Faces in-the-Wild Challenge (2013)
26. Zhou, F., Brandt, J., Lin, Z.: Exemplar-based graph matching for robust facial landmark localization. In: International Conference on Computer Vision (ICCV) (2013)

FlowCap: 2D Human Pose from Optical Flow

Javier Romero$^{(\boxtimes)}$, Matthew Loper, and Michael J. Black

Max Planck Institute for Intelligent Systems, Tübingen, Germany
{jromero,mloper,black}@tuebingen.mpg.de

Abstract. We estimate 2D human pose from video using *only optical flow*. The key insight is that dense optical flow can provide information about 2D body pose. Like range data, flow is largely invariant to appearance but unlike depth it can be directly computed from monocular video. We demonstrate that body parts can be detected from dense flow using the same random forest approach used by the Microsoft Kinect. Unlike range data, however, when people stop moving, there is no optical flow and they effectively disappear. To address this, our *FlowCap* method uses a Kalman filter to propagate body part positions and velocities over time and a regression method to predict 2D body pose from part centers. No range sensor is required and FlowCap estimates 2D human pose from monocular video sources containing human motion. Such sources include hand-held phone cameras and archival television video. We demonstrate 2D body pose estimation in a range of scenarios and show that the method works with real-time optical flow. The results suggest that optical flow shares invariances with range data that, when complemented with tracking, make it valuable for pose estimation.

1 Introduction

Human pose estimation from monocular video has been extensively studied but currently there are no widely available, general, efficient, and reliable solutions. The problem is challenging due to the dimensionality of articulated human pose, the complexity of human motion, and the variability of human appearance in images due to clothing, lighting, camera view, and self occlusion. There has been extensive work on 2D human pose estimation using part-based models [8,11, 12,19,27,29], but existing solutions are still brittle. Systems like the Microsoft Kinect [21] address the above issues by using a specialized depth sensor that simplifies the problem by exploiting additional information. Depth data enables direct estimation of 3D pose while providing invariance to appearance.

What is missing is a robust solution like Kinect for the general 2D human pose estimation problem from video; that is, one that applies to archival video sources and can be used with devices such as cell phones and laptops that are currently equipped only with a monocular video camera. We propose optical flow as a key ingredient for such a solution, and demonstrate its potential with a system called *FlowCap* that estimates 2D pose using only optical flow.

Our method is made possible by the following observation: *Optical flow contains much of the same information as range data.* An optical flow field is much

© Springer International Publishing Switzerland 2015
J. Gall et al. (Eds.): GCPR 2015, LNCS 9358, pp. 412–423, 2015.
DOI: 10.1007/978-3-319-24947-6_34

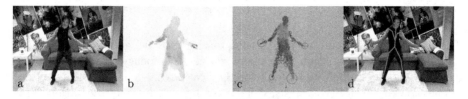

Fig. 1. FlowCap overview. a. Example frame from a video sequence shot with a phone camera. **b.** Optical flow computed with GPU flow [1]. **c.** Per-pixel part assignments based on flow with overlaid uncertainty ellipses (red). **d.** Predicted 2D part centroids connected in a tree (Colour figure online).

like a depth map in that the effects of appearance are essentially removed (see **Supp. Mat.**). Flow captures information about the overall shape and pose of the body and the boundary between the body and the background (Fig. 1b). Moreover, flow has an advantage beyond range data: 2D flow also captures the *motion* of body parts and we use this to good effect.

The first component of our approach follows that of Shotton et al. [21] except we replace range data with optical flow. We train a regression forest using flow and body part segmentations of realistic synthetic bodies in motion. As in [21] we predict per-pixel body part assignments and identify the part centroids (Fig. 1c).

Optical flow has one key disadvantage relative to range data: When a person is stationary, flow does not tell us where they are. It does however tell us something important – that the person is not moving. To take advantage of this, the second component of our method adds a temporal prediction process on top of the body part detections. We use a Kalman filter to estimate the locations and velocities of all body parts in 2D. By estimating velocities, we are able to incorporate information from the optical flow into the Kalman observation model. This improves part estimation when the person is moving as well as when they are still. When a person stops moving, the flow is near zero and the Kalman filter predicts the body is not moving, resulting in a stable pose estimate.

Using the HumanEva benchmark [23] we compare FlowCap with a state-of-the-art single-frame method [27] and find that, when people are moving, Flow-Cap is more stable. We demonstrate that the accuracy of real time optical flow estimation (GPU4Vision [26]) is sufficient for our task. We also test FlowCap on video sequences captured outdoors, with a moving hand-held cell-phone camera, and with archival video from television.

We do not propose FlowCap as a complete, stand-alone, system. Our approach, using only flow, cannot compete with Kinect's use of range data for accuracy or for 3D estimation. Rather our goal is to show that optical flow has a role in human pose estimation and that it shares properties with depth data. Clearly a full solution will include color data but here we demonstrate how far one can get with flow alone. To facilitate further work, we will make our training set of flow data available for research purposes[1].

---

[1] http://ps.is.tuebingen.mpg.de/project/FlowCap.

2 Prior Work

There is a huge literature on pose estimation in static images, video sequences, and using depth information from many sources. We focus on 2D human pose, which is widely studied and useful for applications such as person detection, human tracking, activity analysis, video indexing, and gesture recognition. Here we focus on the two areas most closely related to our method: Microsoft's Kinect and articulated pose estimation from optical flow.

Kinect: Kinect performs human motion capture from an inexpensive device in a person's home with sufficient accuracy for entertainment purposes. While popular, range sensing devices like Kinect are still not widely deployed when compared with traditional video cameras. Since the Kinect works only on range data it cannot be used for human pose estimation with archival data from television and films. Additionally, the Kinect's IR illumination can be swamped by natural light, rendering it useless outside.

One key to the success of Kinect is the use of regression forests [21]. Unfortunately, it is not feasible to apply this method directly to regular video images due to the huge variability in human appearance. Range data is important for the success of Kinect for two reasons. First it provides direct observations of scene depth, removing the ambiguities inherent in the 2D projection of people onto the image plane of a monocular camera. Second, and just as important, is that the range data simplifies the signal processing problem by removing the irrelevant effects of appearance and lighting while maintaining the important information about body structure. Our observation is that optical flow provides similar benefits, in particular with respect to this second point.

The first step of our method uses the regression forest of [21] but replaces depth training data with optical flow. After this we deviate from [21] because, unlike range, when the person stops moving the flow is zero. Consequently to know where the person is, our method requires a temporal model to integrate information; [21] does not use a temporal model but rather, finds the person again in every frame.

Pose from flow: There are many 2D and 3D model-based methods for estimating human pose from video that exploit optical flow (e.g. [6,17,22,24]). These methods relate the 2D image motion to the parameters of an articulated figure. Motion History Images [5] have also been used for pose classification.

Fablet and Black [10] use a synthetic character and motion capture data to generate training flow fields from different views. They use PCA to construct a low-dimensional representation of the flow and represent simple activities as trajectories in that low-dimensional space. They use a multi-view representation to cope with changing 3D viewpoint but do not estimate articulated pose.

Efros et al. [7] use optical flow patterns to estimate pose. They focus on low resolution people in video, which makes the flow information limited and noisy. Consequently they treat it as a spatio-temporal pattern, which becomes a motion descriptor, used to query a database for the nearest neighbor with a similar pattern and known 2D and 3D pose. They require similar sequences of full body poses in the database.

Bissacco et al. [3] train a boosted regression method to recognize pose from image and motion features. They do not use optical flow directly, but rather work on image differences. Schwarz et al. [20] use flow between time of flight range images to help differentiate body parts that occlude each other but do not estimate body pose from flow.

Recently, several methods augment traditional 2D pose estimation with optical flow information. In [13] they use flow to help segment body parts while jointly reasoning about pose, segmentation, and motion. In [29] they use flow to propagate putative 2D body models to neighboring frames. This enables an image likelihood function that incorporates information from multiple frames. In [16] the authors train a deep convolutional neural network (CNN) to use images and flow to estimate upper body pose. These approaches rely primarily on non-flow image cues, with flow as an extra cue. Here we explore the question of how far we can go with flow alone.

3 Data

Like [21] we generate training data using a realistic 3D human body model. However, generating a good flow training set, differs from their approach. First, the same body pose at time t can move to many different poses at $t+1$ resulting in different flow fields. Consequently, the training data must cover a range of both poses and changes in pose. Second, camera motions change the observed flow. While we robustly estimate and remove camera motion we assume there will be some residual camera motion and consequently build this into our training set to improve robustness. Third, optical flow computed on real images is not perfect and can be affected by lighting, shadows, and image texture (or lack thereof); we need to realistically model this noise. To do so, we synthesize pairs of frames with varied foreground and background texture, and various types of noise, and then run a flow algorithm to compute the training flow. The training dataset contains realistic human bodies in varying home environments performing a variety of movements. Example training data is shown in Fig. 2a.

Body shape variation. We use a 3D body model [15] that allows us to generate 3D human bodies with realistic shapes in arbitrary poses. We use separate body shape models for men and women and generate a wide variety of body shapes. The model represents people in tight clothing, but future work could add synthetic clothing and hair.

As in [21], the body model is segmented into parts, which are color coded for visualization (Fig. 2a bottom). The training data includes the 2D projection of these part segments and the 2D centroids of each part. Note that we use 19 parts, fewer and larger than in [21]; these provide more reliable part detection.

Body pose variation. To capture a wide range of human poses and motions we generate training pairs of poses representing plausible human movements between two frames. We do this in two ways. For experiments with the HumanEva dataset, we take the motion capture data from the training set and animate bodies using these motions. While appropriate for the HumanEva evaluation, the set of motions is somewhat limited. Consequently for our other experiments, we create a *generic* motion dataset. We create a distribution of natural poses from a dataset of 3D registrations like [4]. Then we sample pairs of poses and generate paths between them in pose space. Finally, we sample points along these paths, biased towards one of the originals, to define the pose change between frames.

Appearance variation. The performance of optical flow methods is affected by image texture and contrast. For example, when the background is homogeneous the estimated optical flow field may be overly smooth, blurring the foreground motion with the background motion; this can be clearly seen in Fig. 2a. We posit that these effects should be present in our dataset to be able to successfully estimate human pose from real flow.

We created high resolution texture maps from 3D scans of over 30 subjects. For each body shape, we randomly select a texture map and render the body in a basic 3D environment with a wall, floor, some simple objects, and some independently moving objects to simulate clutter and background motion. While not photo-realistic, the scenes have relatively realistic lighting, blur, and noise.

Flow computation. Flow algorithms make different trade-offs between accuracy and speed. To evaluate whether the real-time estimation of 2D body pose is feasible, we compare two methods using [1]: one non-real-time (3 seconds/frame) and the other real-time but noisier. For the former we use the Huber-L1 method from [26]. For the latter we use FAST_HL1 in [1].

Scale variation. As is common in the 2D human pose literature, we train two separate models at different scales (Fig. 2a left and right). The appropriate model is manually picked depending on the test sequence. The first captures upper body movement common in archival video like TV sitcoms. The second captures the full body and is aimed at game applications like in [21]. Within each category we generate training samples with a range of scales to provide some scale invariance. This scale invariance is demonstrated in our experiments with HumanEva, in which the size of the person varies substantially.

Training data summary. The HumanEva training set is composed of approximate 7,000 training examples of the full body. We generate two generic datasets: The upper body dataset is composed of approximately 7,000 training examples, while the full body dataset has approximately 14,000.

4   Method

The goal is to sequentially estimate the 2D pose of a human body from a series of images. As in [21], we consider two subproblems: A classification problem of assigning a body part identifier to each pixel, and a regression problem of inferring the position of the body joints. We add an additional tracking component that is essential when using flow.

Fig. 2. a) Training data. Top row: example synthetic frames from pairs of training frames. Middle: Estimated optical flow for each frame. Bottom: Ground truth body part segmentations. **b) Visual summary of the method.** Left to right: image capture with Kinect RGB camera, optical flow (color coded as in [2]), per pixel part labels, part centers with uncertainty (red circles) and motion vectors (10× actual magnitude), estimated kinematic structure of the part centers, predicted Kinect kinematic structure using linear regression (Colour figure online).

Problem definition: Our input consists of a sequence of $k + 1$ images, Y_i, of dimensions $m \times n$. For each image Y_i, we estimate the optical flow field, V_i, between Y_i and Y_{i+1} as described in Sect. 3. To reduce the effect of camera motion we also robustly estimate a dominant global homography for the image pair using RANSAC. Let the flow field at every pixel, given by the homography, be H_i. Then we define the residual flow field to be $\hat{V}_i = V_i - H_i$.

For every residual flow field, $\hat{V}_i$, our goal is to estimate the 2D locations of j joints, X_i, of size $j \times 2$; like [21], we use body part assignments to p parts as an intermediary between observables and joint locations. This is achieved in three steps. First, we estimate per-pixel body part assignments with a matrix, P_i, of size $m \times n \times (p + 1)$; labels correspond to either one of p body parts or the background. A label matrix, L_i, of size $m \times n$ is simply computed as $L_i(\mathbf{x}) = \arg\max_l P_i(\mathbf{x}, l)$, where $\mathbf{x} = (x, y)$ is an image pixel location. Second, we compute a matrix, M_i, of size $p \times 2$ containing the 2D centroids of the body parts in the image. Finally, the matrix, X_i, of 2D joint locations is predicted from M_i using linear regression.

Flow difference features: Following [21], each pixel is described by a t dimensional feature vector $F_i(\mathbf{x})$. Here we take $F_i(\mathbf{x})$ to include the flow magnitude $\|\hat{V}_i(\mathbf{x})\|$ at the pixel and a set of $t - 1$ flow differences, $\|\hat{V}_i(\mathbf{x}) - \hat{V}_i(x + \delta_x, y + \delta_y)\|$, computed with random surrounding pixels. The maximum displacements, δ_x, δ_y are set to 160 pixels for the full body training set and 400 pixels for the upper body set. A full body typically occupies around 100×300 pixels. Inspired by [21], we chose $t = 200$ and draw the samples δ_x, δ_y from a Gaussian distribution.

Body part classification: FlowCap classifies each feature vector, $F_i(\mathbf{x})$, at each pixel into one of $p+1$ classes representing the p body parts and the background. Randomized decision forests (implementation from [18]) are used to classify flow difference features. For each training image, we randomly sample 2000 pixel locations uniformly per part and use the associated feature vectors to train the classifier. Six trees are trained with maximum depth so that leaves contain a minimum of four samples. Given a flow field as input, the output of the decision forest is a matrix P_i from which we compute the label matrix L_i.

In the absence of motion, the classification, L_i, is ambiguous (row 2 in Fig. 2b). A static pixel surrounded by static pixels is classified as background. However, the lack of motion is a strong, complementary, feature that we can exploit in a tracking scheme. In this way, optical flow is used in two ways: first, as a static, appearance-invariant, feature for per-frame pose estimation, and second, as an observation of the pixel velocities for effective part tracking.

Part centroid tracking: The per-pixel part classifications are now used to track the part positions. For simplicity, we track a single hypothesis $\hat{M}_i(l)$ of the centroid of each part l. Considering multiple modes is promising and left for future work. While the most straightforward estimation of the 2D centroids would be a weighted average according to probabilities P_i, we seek a more robust estimation based on the following approximation of the mode

$$\hat{M}_i(l) = \sum_{\mathbf{x}} P_i(\mathbf{x}, l)^\alpha \mathbf{x} / \sum_{\mathbf{x}} P_i(\mathbf{x}, l)^\alpha \tag{1}$$

where $\alpha = 6$ in our experiments. Alternatively, this could be done by retraining the regression tree leaves to infer pixel offsets to the joint centroids, $\hat{M}_i - \mathbf{x}$ [21].

The modes can be very inaccurate in the absence of movement. To address this we perform temporal tracking of the centroids (independently per part) using a linear Kalman filter [25]. The state of the filter contains the estimation of the position and velocity of each part centroid, $M_i(l), M_i'(l)$. The measurements are the centroid estimates, $\hat{M}_i(l)$, and the velocities, $\hat{M}_i'(l)$, which we compute from the optical flow in a region around the current estimate. Since we are directly observing estimations of our state, the observation model is the identity. The states are initialized with their corresponding measurement $M_0(l) = \hat{M}_0(l)$, $M_0'(l) = \hat{M}_0'(l)$. The state-transition model assumes constant velocity:

$$M_i(l) = M_{i-1}(l) + M_{i-1}'(l) \tag{2}$$
$$M_i'(l) = M_{i-1}'(l). \tag{3}$$

The definition of the process and measurement noise is not so straight-forward. All noise models are considered uncorrelated. We empirically set the transition noise standard deviations to values between 2 and 20 pixels depending on the body part. The velocity component of the measurement noise, related to the flow accuracy, is empirically set to standard deviations of 5 pixels. The position component of the measurement noise Q_i^M depends on the accuracy of the decision forest estimation, through its estimations of the per-part probability matrices P_i

$$Q_i^M(l) = k_i^2 / \Big(\sum_{\mathbf{x}} P_i(\mathbf{x}, l) \Big)^2 \tag{4}$$

where k_i is a part-dependent constant, with empirical values between 40 and 100 pixels, reflecting the accuracy differences of the random forest across body parts.

Predicting joints: Tracking results in estimations of the body part centroids, M_i; Fig. 2b, fifth column, shows estimated part centers connected by purple lines. For many applications, however, we want the locations of the joints in an articulated model. One could directly learn these using the regression forest but it is more straightforward to estimate part centers and then estimate joint locations from these.

The relation between part centroids and joint locations is learned from the training dataset described in Sect. 3. Joint positions are predicted linearly from centroids, both represented in 2D. On HumanEva training data, we regress from detected part centroids to the ground truth 2D marker locations with an L1 loss. For the other experiments we use the generic training data and train the regression function from 'the ground truth part centroids to the ground truth model joints using elastic net [28]. Figure 2b, sixth column, shows the kinematic tree corresponding to predicted joints in turquoise.

5   Experiments

We summarize the experiments here; see supplemental video for more.

1. HumanEva. We compare FlowCap's performance on monocular 2D human pose estimation with [27]. This single-frame method estimates human pose based on the image gradients. In contrast, FlowCap completely disregards the visual appearance of a single frame, exploiting solely optical flow. The comparison is performed on the validation set of HumanEva I [23], which contains sequences of multiple subjects performing a variety of actions. We evaluate the methods on video from the single color camera, C1, for sequences containing movement for every body part, namely "Walking" and "Jog". The motions involve significant changes in scale and a full 360 degree change in orientation of the body.

Figure 3a shows 2D marker error, and confirms that FlowCap outperforms [27] on this subset of HumanEva I. The method of [27] has large errors in some frames due to misdetections on the background or large errors of the arm joints. This is reflected in larger standard deviations. While not a comprehensive comparison, this suggests flow can be a useful cue for 2D human pose.

2. Outdoors. While Kinect works well indoors, we captured a game-like sequence outside using the Kinect camera (Fig. 2). The natural lighting causes Kinect pose estimation to fail on almost every frame of the sequence. In contrast, FlowCap recovers qualitatively good 2D pose.

3. Cellphone camera. A truly portable system for human pose estimation would open up many applications. Figure 4a shows FlowCap run on video from

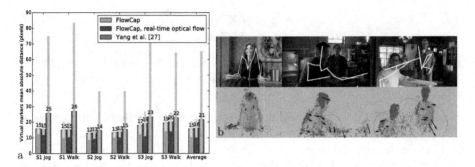

Fig. 3. a) Ground truth evaluation. Average (and std) absolute marker distance (as in [23]) for Walking and Jog validation sequences in HumanEva for FlowCap, FlowCap with real-time flow and [27]. **b) Failure cases.** Lack of representative data (e.g. long hair), back person's view, and multiple people.

a hand-held Samsung Nexus S mobile phone. Despite the camera-motion removal step (Sect. 4), residual background flow is observable in the sequence. Nonetheless, the estimated 2D poses are qualitatively good. This is a proof of concept since our software is not designed to run on a phone and all processing is done off-line.

4. Television. We do not claim to have a complete solution for human pose estimation from archival data but Fig. 4b shows a few results on the TV series "Buffy the Vampire Slayer" and "Friends." Results on videos with mostly-frontal views of a single moving person are promising. Here we envision FlowCap as part of a more complex system using multiple cues or as an initialization to a part-based model like [27].

Running time. Here we have shown a proof of concept system. Each component of FlowCap is either real-time now or could be realistically made real time (flow estimation, part prediction, Kalman filtering, and pose estimation). The optical flow method of [26] used in most of the experiments has a running time of 3 seconds in a Nvidia Quadro K4000. We also experimented with a fast version of the flow code that runs at about 30ms/frame. Despite lower quality flow, the results in Fig. 3a show that FlowCap performance degrades very little when using the real-time optical flow. Flow feature extraction and the Random Forest method are slow; currently taking on the order of ten seconds per frame in VGA images. However, these can run in super-real-time [21]. The running times of our Kalman Filter and of the regression to joint space are negligible.

Failure cases and future work. Although we have shown that our system works well in a number of situations, there is still room for improvement. Figure 3b shows that our system would benefit from improving the realism of training data, better disambiguation between front and back poses or tracking multiple subjects. An obvious drawback of using only flow is that our system only tracks body parts that have moved in the past; this could be solved by

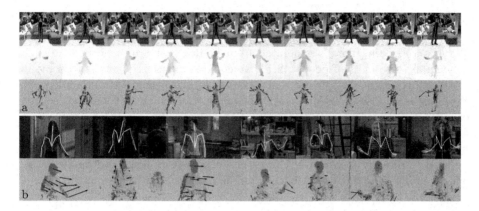

Fig. 4. a) Smartphone FlowCap. Here the video is captured using a hand-held phone camera. This results in overall flow due to rotation and translation of the camera. Despite this, part estimates remain good and pose is well estimated. **b) Archival video.** Results on archival data from series Friends and Buffy. Ground truth shown in red, [27] in yellow, FlowCap part centers in white (Colour figure online).

using image-based initialization. Other future directions include a multi-camera version [9], model-based tracking, dealing with background motions and using multi-frame optical flow features. More sophisticated flow algorithms could also be evaluated.

6 Conclusion

We have demonstrated how optical flow alone can provide information for 2D human pose estimation. Like range data, it can factor out variations in image appearance and additionally gives information about the motion of body parts. We have also demonstrated how flow can be used to detect and track human pose in monocular videos such as television shows. This demonstrates a simple proof of the concept that flow offers something like the appearance invariance of depth while being available from ordinary video. The application of the techniques from [21] to monocular flow fields is non-obvious since our system deals with vanishing flow when a body part is static by exploiting the lack of flow. Zero flow is bad for pose estimation but good for tracking and we exploit this duality. The 2D predictions are surprisingly good in a range of complex videos. Because no special hardware is required, optical flow may be a useful component in pose estimation, opening up more widespread applications.

While we only use optical flow as input, future work should include additional 2D image cues. Head, feet, and hand detectors could readily be incorporated as, for that matter, depth data from a range sensor or stereo system. Alternatively, FlowCap could be used as a complementary source of information for other pose estimation and tracking methods. For example, we could use FlowCap to initialize more precise model-based trackers. In addition to providing pose, we provide an initial segmentation of the image into regions corresponding to parts. This evidence could readily be incorporated in to existing 2D pose trackers. While our training flow is generated from bodies that are unclothed, we find it generalizes to clothed people. Still, we could simulate sequences of people in clothing (e.g. as in [14]) or use real video of clothed people with ground truth. We could train also FlowCap for specific applications such as TV shows, sports, or video games by constructing training sets with specific motions. Since we start with 3D pose, it would be interesting to directly try to estimate 3D pose, and possibly body shape, from flow (and other cues). Finally our training data could be used to directly train a CNN to estimate pose from flow (and image data). This is an exciting direction that our public dataset[2] will help support.

References

1. http://gpu4vision.icg.tugraz.at
2. Baker, S., Scharstein, D., Lewis, J.P., Roth, S., Black, M.J., Szeliski, R.: A database and evaluation methodology for optical flow. IJCV **92**(1), 1–31 (2011)
3. Bissacco, A., Yang, M.-H., Soatto, S.: Fast human pose estimation using appearance and motion via multi-dimensional boosting regression. In: CVPR, pp. 1–8 (2007)
4. Bogo, F., Romero, J., Loper, M., Black, M.J.: FAUST: dataset and evaluation for 3D mesh registration. In: CVPR, pp. 3794–3801 (2014)
5. Bradski, G.R., Davis, J.W.: Motion segmentation and pose recognition with motion history gradients. Mach. Vis. Appl. **13**(3), 174–184 (2002)
6. Bregler, C., Malik, J.: Tracking people with twists and exponential maps. In: CVPR, pp. 8–15 (1998)
7. Efros, A., Berg, A., Mori, G., Malik, J.: Recognizing action at a distance. In: ICCV, pp. 726–733 (2003)
8. Eichner, M., Marin-Jimenez, M., Zisserman, A., Ferrari, V.: 2D articulated human pose estimation and retrieval in (almost) unconstrained still images. IJCV **99**, 190–214 (2012)
9. Elhayek, A., Aguiar, E., Jain, A., Tompson, J., Pishchulin, L., Andriluka, M., Bregler, C., Schiele, B., Theobalt, C.: Efficient convnet-based marker-less motion capture in general scenes with a low number of cameras. In: CVPR, pp. 3810–3818 (2015)
10. Fablet, R., Black, M.J.: Automatic detection and tracking of human motion with a view-based representation. In: Heyden, A., Sparr, G., Nielsen, M., Johansen, P. (eds.) ECCV 2002, Part I. LNCS, vol. 2350, pp. 476–491. Springer, Heidelberg (2002)
11. Felzenszwalb, P. Girshick, R., McAllester, D.: Cascade object detection with deformable part models. In: CVPR, pp. 2241–2248 (2010)
12. Ferrari, V., Marin-Jimenez, M., Zisserman, A.: Progressive search space reduction for human pose estimation. In: CVPR, pp. 1–8 (2008)
13. Fragkiadaki, K., Hu, H., Shi, J.: Pose from flow and flow from pose estimation. In: CVPR, pp. 2059–2066 (2013)
14. Guan, P., Reiss, L., Hirshberg, D., Weiss, A., Black, M.J.: DRAPE: DRessing any PErson. SIGGRAPH **31**(4), 35:1–35:10 (2012)

---

[2] http://ps.is.tuebingen.mpg.de/project/FlowCap.

15. Hirshberg, D.A., Loper, M., Rachlin, E., Black, M.J.: Coregistration: simultaneous alignment and modeling of articulated 3D shape. In: Fitzgibbon, A., Lazebnik, S., Perona, P., Sato, Y., Schmid, C. (eds.) ECCV 2012, Part VI. LNCS, vol. 7577, pp. 242–255. Springer, Heidelberg (2012)

16. Jain, A., Tompson, J., LeCun, Y., Bregler, C.: MoDeep: a deep learning framework using motion features for human pose estimation. In: Cremers, D., Reid, I., Saito, H., Yang, M.-H. (eds.) ACCV 2014. LNCS, vol. 9004, pp. 302–315. Springer, Heidelberg (2015)

17. Ju, S., Black, M.J., Yacoob, Y.: Cardboard people: a parameterized model of articulated motion. In: Face and Gesture, pp. 38–44 (1996)

18. Pedregosa, F., Varoquaux, G., Gramfort, A., Michel, V., Thirion, B., Grisel, O., Blondel, M., Prettenhofer, P., Weiss, R., Dubourg, V., Vanderplas, J., Passos, A., Cournapeau, D., Brucher, M., Perrot, M., Duchesnay, E.: Scikit-learn: machine learning in python. JMLR **12**, 2825–2830 (2011)

19. Sapp, B., Weiss, D., Taskar, B.: Parsing human motion with stretchable models. In: CVPR, pp. 1281–1288 (2011)

20. Schwarz, L., Mkhitaryan, A., Mateus, D., Navab, N.: Estimating human 3D pose from time-of-flight images based on geodesic distances and optical flow. In: Face and Gesture, pp. 700–706 (2011)

21. Shotton, J., Girshick, R., Fitzgibbon, A., Sharp, T., Cook, M., Finocchio, M., Moore, R., Kohli, P., Criminisi, A., Kipman, A., Blake, A.: Efficient human pose estimation from single depth images. PAMI **35**(12), 2821–2840 (2013)

22. Sidenbladh, H., Black, M.J., Fleet, D.J.: Stochastic tracking of 3D human figures using 2D image motion. In: Vernon, D. (ed.) ECCV 2000. LNCS, vol. 1843, pp. 702–718. Springer, Heidelberg (2000)

23. Sigal, L., Balan, A., Black, M.J.: HumanEva: Synchronized video and motion capture dataset and baseline algorithm for evaluation of articulated human motion. IJCV **87**(1), 4–27 (2010)

24. Wachter, S., Nagel, H.: Tracking persons in monocular image sequences. CVIU **74**(3), 174–192 (1999)

25. Welch, G., Bishop, G.: An introduction to the Kalman filter. UNC, TR **95–041**, (2006)

26. Werlberger, M., Trobin, W., Pock, T., Wedel, A., Cremers, D., Bischof, H.: Anisotropic Huber-L1 optical flow. In: BMVC, pp. 108.1–108.11 (2009)

27. Yang,Y., Ramanan, D.: Articulated pose estimation using flexible mixtures of parts. In: CVPR, pp. 1385–1392 (2011)

28. Zou, H., Hastie, T.: Regularization and variable selection via the elastic net. J. R. Stat. Soc. Ser. B (Stat. Methodol.) **67**(2), 301–320 (2005)

29. Zuffi, S., Romero, J., Schmid, C., Black, M.J.: Estimating human pose with flowing puppets. In: ICCV, pp. 3312–3319 (2013)

3D Facial Landmark Detection: How to Deal with Head Rotations?

Anke Schwarz[1,2]([✉]), Esther-Sabrina Wacker[2], Manuel Martin[3],
M. Saquib Sarfraz[1], and Rainer Stiefelhagen[1]

[1] Karlsruhe Institute of Technology, Karlsruhe, Germany
Anke.Schwarz@de.bosch.com
[2] Robert Bosch GmbH, Stuttgart, Germany
[3] Fraunhofer IOSB, Karlsruhe, Germany

Abstract. 3D facial landmark detection is important for applications
like facial expression analysis and head pose estimation. However, accurate estimation of facial landmarks in 3D with head rotations is still
challenging due to perspective variations. Current state-of-the-art methods are based on random forests. These methods rely on a large amount
of training data covering the whole range of head rotations. We present
a method based on regression forests which can handle rotations even
if they are not included in the training data. To achieve this, we modify both the weak predictors of the tree and the leaf node regressors
to adapt to head rotations better. Our evaluation on two benchmark
datasets, Bosphorus and FRGC v2, shows that our method outperforms
state-of-the-art methods with respect to head rotations, if trained solely
on frontal faces.

1 Introduction

Accurate facial landmark positions are necessary for several applications. In particular facial expression analysis and head pose estimation algorithms benefit
from robust facial landmark detections. Towards this direction most facial landmark estimation approaches utilize 2D image information to locate these salient
points on the face. However, 2D methods are not robust in case of texture-less
regions and illumination changes, so considering range data offers the possibility
to overcome these problems. Facial expressions, rotations and occlusions remain
challenging for facial landmark localization from range data. Applying rotational
invariant local descriptors [1,8], such as shape index or spin image histograms,
can handle these problems to some extent. These descriptors are often computationally expensive and are therefore difficult to apply in real time applications.
Recently, random forests showed promising results to estimate facial landmark
localizations in real time [4]. In order to achieve robustness to head pose changes,
these approaches need a large amount of training data which covers the range
of possible head rotations. Generating training data covering the head rotation
space is challenging and expensive. Thus, many approaches rely on synthetic
training data. However, specific characteristics of sensors are difficult to simulate on synthetic data. To overcome the challenge of generating training data

© Springer International Publishing Switzerland 2015
J. Gall et al. (Eds.): GCPR 2015, LNCS 9358, pp. 424–434, 2015.
DOI: 10.1007/978-3-319-24947-6_35

containing all possible head rotations we present a new method. Our approach is an extension of existing random regression forests [3,5,13] but in contrast to existing methods it performs better for unseen rotated faces. We propose a rotation-normalization to counter the effect of depth changes caused by head rotations. The leaf node predictors of the regression forests are modified with a local coordinate transformation. Additionally, we extend the depth comparison feature in the internal nodes to perform rotational invariant. Experiments show the robustness of our method against unseen head rotation. The remainder of this paper is structured as follows. In Sect. 2, we discuss recent related work. Then, in Sect. 3 we present our new approach for 3D facial landmark detection with regression forests. The experimental Sect. 4 shows the performance of our method in case of head rotations. Additionally, we show the robustness against unseen individuals and facial expressions on frontal images.

2   Related Work

In general, 2D facial landmark methods can be divided into global methods and local methods. Global methods take the whole face into account whereas local methods rely on the localization of salient points by considering the local neighborhood. In recent years, combinations became popular [11,14]. However, 2D image based approaches are often sensitive to varying illumination and texture-less image regions, whereas depth based methods offer the chance to overcome these problems [15]. With the introduction of affordable depth sensors, 3D data gained interest for facial landmark detection. Similar to 2D methods, they can be divided into global and local methods.

Global methods often rely on a facial model that describes the position of the facial landmarks in relation to each other. Recent approaches [1,8] generate candidate landmarks by local shape descriptors like spin images or shape index features. Then a global model refines the candidate landmarks to establish final facial landmark positions. Due to the high computational cost of estimating the shape descriptors, it remains difficult to achieve real time performance.

Local methods do not use a model to filter outliers. Instead local information is leveraged to estimate the position of each landmark individually. One way to achieve this is to use conditional random forests [4] because of their ability to handle multi class problems and their ability to generalize well if a lot of training data is available. Random forests have the advantage of computational efficiency and therefore achieve real time performance.

Criminisi et al. summarize recent random forest approaches [2], especially for real time applications where they show promising results. Random forests are applied in several applications such as human pose estimation [13], hand gesture recognition [6] and facial landmark estimation [4]. There are mainly two types of random forests, classification forests to determine a set of discrete labels or regression forests to estimate continuous labels.

Shotton et al. [13] present an approach using classification forests to estimate joint positions in real time. Girshick et al. [5] extend this approach with

(a) Internal nodes   **(b)** Displacement vector

Fig. 1. Figure (a) shows a patch (*black*) with two subregions (*blue*). In the internal nodes the difference is compared to a threshold. In case of rotation this difference changes. Figure (b) visualizes a displacement vector (*red*) pointing from a patch towards the left outer eye. In case of rotation the oriented displacement vector to the landmark location will change (Color figure online).

regression forests to accurately locate joint positions. It was shown that in particular for joint positions with stable surroundings such as the head and shoulder regression forests outperform classification forests. In case of facial landmark estimation the surrounding is stable especially around the eye and nose region, so we use regression forests.

3 Regression Forests for Rotational Robust Facial Landmark Estimation

Establishing a dataset with all possible rotations available remains difficult. Especially in case of further variations, such as facial expressions, occlusion, person independence and illumination changes, where all combinations have to be collected. Hence, our goal is to estimate facial landmark locations of rotated faces without having rotated views in the training data set. To achieve this, we adapt the split function and the leaf regressors of the regression forests to handle rotations. We first summarize the approach of random regression forests for facial landmark detection, as presented by Fanelli et al. [4] and Girshick et al. [5]. Then we point out the drawbacks of this approach in case of unseen rotations and present our modifications which are more robust to rotations of the face.

3.1 Regression Forests for Facial Landmark Estimation

A random forest is an ensemble of decision trees. A tree is built based on a set of training samples. Each training sample consists of a rectangular patch of depth image representing a part of the face and the displacement vectors of the patch center points to the facial landmarks established from the ground-truth landmark locations. Each tree consists of internal nodes and leaf nodes. The internal nodes contain a splitting function, distributing the input samples to the child nodes. In the leaf nodes predictions are stored. These predictions are displacement vectors towards the facial landmark locations, estimated from the samples that reach the leaf node in the training phase. In the following we will describe the learning and the testing phase.

Training. The goal of the training phase is to determine the tree parameters and the leaf node predictors. The tree parameters are determined by a split function and by a quality measure which is maximized while training the tree. For each internal node in a tree, starting at the root the following steps are executed:

1. Generate a set of random splitting functions
2. Find the best splitting function with regard to the input samples and a given quality measure
3. Distribute the samples based on the best splitting function to the child nodes

In our general implementation we use the splitting function defined by Fanelli et al. [4]:

$$(|F_1|^{-1} \sum_{\mathbf{q} \in F_1} I(\mathbf{q})) - (|F_2|^{-1} \sum_{\mathbf{q} \in F_2} I(\mathbf{q})) > \tau \tag{1}$$

where F_1 and F_2 are asymmetric rectangles within a training patch $\mathcal{P}$ and τ is a threshold. $|F_1|^{-1} \sum_{\mathbf{q} \in F_1} I(\mathbf{q})$ and $|F_2|^{-1} \sum_{\mathbf{q} \in F_2} I(\mathbf{q})$ are the mean depth values inside the regions F_1 and F_2. A set of rectangles and thresholds are randomly generated when training a node. To evaluate the quality of a splitting function we use the same measure for regression forests as Girshick et al. [5].

Each internal node is split until either the maximum depth is reached or the number of examples falling into the node is smaller than a threshold. As described by Dantone et al. [3] in the leaf nodes a final predictor $v_l = \{\mu_l, \omega_l\}_{l=1,..,k}$ for each landmark l is stored by combining the training examples reaching this leaf node. μ_l is the mean of the displacement vectors and $\omega = \frac{1}{trace(\Sigma_l)}$ is a weight estimated from the variance inside the node.

Testing. Given a range scan the goal of the testing phase is to estimate the 3D location of all facial landmarks. To achieve this, patches are densely sampled from the face area and branched through the random regression forest. For each patch the trees provide displacement vectors to the facial landmark positions including a weight. Displacement vectors are only considered with a weight larger than a threshold to ignore results from leaf nodes with high variances. To obtain estimations of the facial landmark positions the displacement vector reached in the tree is added to the center of the patch. Doing this for all patches results in a density map for each landmark.

To estimate the final facial feature location from these maps, clustering based on the euclidean distance is applied. The final landmark position is then estimated by applying mean shift to the cluster with the maximum number of votes.

3.2   Rotational Robust Facial Landmark Estimation

The general decision forest approach has some limitations concerning the robustness to unseen rotations. As shown in Fig. 1a, at the internal nodes the depth values of the subregions inside a patch are compared to a threshold. In case

(a) Top view of a face   **(b)** Normalization at internal node

Fig. 2. Figure (a) shows an example patch (*black*) with two subregions (*light blue*) on a frontal face (*left*) and a rotated face (*right*). Figure (b) visualizes the normalization offsets (red) γ_1 and γ_2 dependent on the normal direction (*blue*) and the distance vectors towards the subregions d_1 and d_2 (*pink*) (Color figure online)

of rotations, the depth values change which causes a modification in their difference. Furthermore, as shown in Fig. 1b, the displacement vector learned for a specific leaf node points towards the landmark location. However, in case of rotations the displacement vector will not point towards the correct location.

To overcome these issues, we extend the regression forest in two ways:

1. *internal nodes:* We add an offset to the depth values used by the splitting function according to the normal direction
2. *leaf nodes:* We apply a rotation-normalization, both in the training and testing phase. Therefore, in the training phase we transform the input displacement vectors according to their local neighborhood. The tree training is performed with the normalized displacement vectors. Then, in the testing phase we back project the displacement vectors to obtain votes for the facial landmarks.

Internal Nodes. As shown in Fig. 1a, the difference of depth values changes in case of rotations. To overcome this issue we add an offset to the depth values of the subregions depending on the normal direction which is related to the rotation, shown in Fig. 2.

We add offsets γ_1 and γ_2 to the splitting function in Eq. (1) to achieve a rotation invariant depth comparison. The offsets are dependent on the normal direction n and the distance vectors d_j pointing towards the subregions from the center of the patch, as shown in Fig. 2b. Our test function at the internal nodes results in:

$$(|F_1|^{-1} \sum_{q \in F_1} I(q) + \gamma_1) - (|F_2|^{-1} \sum_{q \in F_2} I(q) + \gamma_2) > \tau \tag{2}$$

with:

$$\gamma_j = n^T * d_j \tag{3}$$

Since the normal vector is in world coordinates and the distance vectors are in image coordinates, we transform the distance vectors into world coordinates. To achieve this we scale the pixel distances with σ_x and σ_y, which are dependent on the focal length f and the mean distance of the face to the sensor z_{face}:

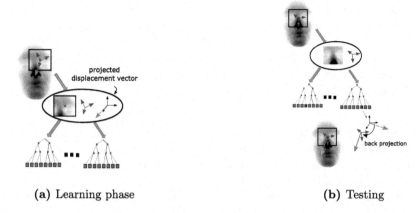

(a) Learning phase   (b) Testing

Fig. 3. Figure (a) shows the training phase, where the tree is set up with projected displacement vectors. Figure (b) shows the testing phase, votes are back projected with the transformation (*blue*) (Color figure online).

$$d_j = \begin{pmatrix} \sigma_x * x_{dj} \\ \sigma_y * y_{dj} \\ 0 \end{pmatrix} \quad , \text{ with } \sigma_x = \frac{z_{face}}{f_x}, \sigma_y = \frac{z_{face}}{f_y} \qquad (4)$$

with (x_{dj}, y_{dj}) the distance vector in pixels. The world coordinates can be achieved directly from the point cloud. But this fails in case of missing or corrupted data due to noise.

Leaf Nodes. In the leaf nodes displacement vectors are stored pointing towards the facial landmark position. To obtain a rotation invariant displacement vector we estimate a local coordinate transformation, which we apply in the training and testing phase. In the following, we first explain the estimation of the local coordinate transformation and then how we apply it in the regression trees.

The local coordinate transformation is estimated with PCA for each 3D point separately by the principal directions of the neighboring 3D points [7,10]. To obtain a unique coordinate transformation, we define the directions of the last and second axes. The last axis w, which is the normal, is projected towards the viewing direction. We project the second axis v towards the right side. The direction of the first axis u is computed from the cross product of the first and second. This is performed without loss of generalization for the reason that the head is pointing towards the viewing direction and the roll rotation is limited to 90 degrees. This results in a coordinate transformation $M = (u, v, w)^T \in SO(3)$

To overcome the problem with the displacement vector, as shown in Fig. 1b, we use the local coordinate transformation. The transformation is applied in the training phase to learn the trees in a rotational invariant way and in the testing phase to obtain the results by backprojecting from the rotational invariant space to the currently rotated space.

In the training phase we apply the coordinate transformation at each patch i as follows (see Fig. 3a): To train the tree structure patches $\mathcal{P}_i = \{\mathcal{I}_i, \mathbf{M}_i, \boldsymbol{\delta}'_i\}$ are used, containing depth values of the patch $\mathcal{I}_i \subset \mathcal{I}$, the local coordinate transformation matrix $\mathbf{M}_i \in SO(3)$ and displacement vectors to k facial landmark locations projected with the local coordinate transformation $\boldsymbol{\delta}'_i = \{\boldsymbol{\delta}'^1_i, \ldots \boldsymbol{\delta}'^k_i\}$, $\boldsymbol{\delta}'^l_i \in \mathbb{R}^3$ with $l = 1, \ldots k$:

$$\boldsymbol{\delta}'^l_i = \mathbf{M}_i * \boldsymbol{\delta}^l_i \tag{5}$$

With these input patches the trees are trained as explained in Sect. 3.1 using the transformed offsets $\boldsymbol{\delta}'_i$ in the leaf nodes. In the leaf nodes voting elements $\boldsymbol{v}'_l = \{\boldsymbol{\mu}'_l, \boldsymbol{\omega}'_l\}_{l=1,..,k}$ for each landmark l are stored by summarizing the training examples reaching this leaf node.

In the testing phase, patches of new range scan are extracted from the face region and branched through the trees as explained in Sect. 3.1. In the leaf node a patch i reaches a displacement vector $\boldsymbol{v}'_l$ pointing towards a facial landmark normalized with regard to rotations, as shown in Fig. 3b. To obtain votes $\boldsymbol{y}_i$ for facial feature locations, the displacement vector $\boldsymbol{v}'_l$ is therefore back projected with the current local rotation matrix $\mathbf{M}_i$:

$$\boldsymbol{y}_i = \boldsymbol{x}_i + \mathbf{M}_i^T * \boldsymbol{v}'_l \tag{6}$$

with $\boldsymbol{x}_i \in \mathbb{R}^3$ the current patch location. Afterwards we determine the final facial landmarks by applying the same steps as explained in Sect. 3.1: A probability map for each landmark is generated from the obtained votes. Final landmark locations are estimated by applying clustering and mean shift.

One issue of the local coordinate transformation is that, in case of flat regions the transformation is not definitely determined, but random forests can compensate this problem. By applying the transformation in the training phase patches with strongly varying local rotations will generate leaf nodes with large variances. Therefore those leaf nodes will not influence the final landmark locations since in the testing phase votes of leaf nodes with high variance are ignored.

4   Evaluation

We perform two experiments to evaluate our methods.

To demonstrate the performance of our method against unseen rotations we use the Bosphorus dataset, where both frontal faces and faces with yaw rotations are available. It consists of 105 different subjects taken with a structured-light based 3D system. To evaluate our estimations we use the ground truth labels provided with the dataset by Savran et al. [12]. For training we only use the frontal faces whereas for testing we use the rotated faces.

Furthermore we evaluate our method on a frontal face dataset, to show that our extension does not lose performance in case of training and testing on frontal faces compared to state-of-the-art methods applied on frontal faces. For this experiment we use the FRGC dataset [9], which consists of frontal range scans with different expressions. Furthermore, we show the person independence of our

Table 1. Percentage of correctly estimated landmark locations inside a radius of 10 mm. right eye outer corner (REOC), right eye inner corner (REIC), left eye inner corner (LEIC), left eye outer corner (LEOC), nose tip (NT), mouth right corner (MRC), mouth left corner (MLC), chin tip (CT)

| | YawRot20 | | YawRot30 | |
	RF	RF-Ext (Our)	RF	RF-Ext (Our)
REOC	**42.66**	13.01	**3.68**	2.40
REIC	**93.37**	76.63	43.75	**62.61**
LEIC	49.74	**82.49**	6.67	**62.14**
LEOC	4.88	**9.26**	0.00	0.00
NT	86.73	**93.49**	34.89	**66.43**
MRC	**33.42**	22.86	4.26	**7.53**
MLC	14.09	**24.21**	1.13	**4.58**
CT	2.87	**12.71**	0.00	**2.38**
MEAN	40.97	**41.5**	12.85	**25.63**

method by considering the same training and test set as Perakis et al. [8] which consists of different people in the training and test set. Here, the ground truth landmarks are the ones provided by [8].

4.1 Head Rotations

To evaluate our method against unseen head rotations we perform our first experiment on the Bosphorus database. We train on frontal faces and evaluate on rotated faces. We divided the 300 frontal faces into 250 faces to train the tree parameters and perform cross validation on the remaining 50 neutral images to optimize the weighting threshold. We choose the fixed parameters of the trees according to Fanelli et al. [4]. To train our trees we randomly choose 3000 patches on 200 frames out of the 250 training frames. The size of the patches is set to 40 × 40. We trained 10 trees with a maximum depth of 20. Each tree votes for all landmark locations in the leaf node. The threshold of the maximum displacement length is set to 60 mm. In our first experiment we evaluated the mean success rate on rotated faces of a standard regression forest versus our extended regression forest.

Table 1 shows the success rate of our method against recent regression forests. In this experiment we trained on frontal faces and evaluated on faces with yaw rotations. All evaluations are performed with a stride of 20. Our method outperforms recent regression forests in case of new rotations. For both methods, the landmarks at the borders are more noisy. In case of rotation the surrounding of the facial landmarks at the border changes significantly, unavailable features such as the ear become visible. Whereas, the surrounding of the area in the middle of the face stays similar. Regarding the results of the inner eye corners

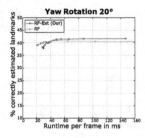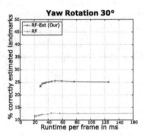

Fig. 4. Average time in ms per frame versus percentage of correctly estimated land-mark locations inside a radius of 10 mm for strides ranging from 0 to 75. Our method outperforms usual regression forests on faces rotated more than 30° while not loosing performance.

Fig. 5. Example results of our method on rotated faces [12] and frontal faces [9]. Left: Successful landmark localization results, right: failure cases

and the nose tip, our method outperforms regression forests significantly. These three landmarks are enough to estimate the head pose.

Figure 4 shows the ratio of correctly estimated landmark locations versus the time per frame in ms. The time is varied by changing the stride between the patches branched through the tree. The evaluation is performed with an unoptimized c++ code on 1 cpu core with 2.80GHz. This results in a runtime of less then 50 ms per frame fixing the stride to 20.

This experiment shows that we perform better on rotated faces while not los-ing computational time. Sample results are shown in Fig. 5. We do not compare our method to [1] since we focus on real-time applications.

4.2   Person Independence and Facial Expressions on Frontal Faces

This experiment is performed for the sake of completeness to evaluate the robust-ness of our method against facial expressions and person independence. Accord-ing to the approach of Perakis et al. [8] we use the same 300 frontal faces as training images. We divide this training set again into 250 images to set up the tree structure and perform cross validation on the remaining 50 training images. The tree parameters are chosen as explained in the previous experiments. To compare our approach to the method presented by [8] we evaluated our method on the same 975 depth images with various facial expressions.

Table 2. Comparison of mean average error estimation in mm (std. dev.) on frontal faces of FRGC v2 [9] to [8] and regression forests. Our method outperforms [8] and performs comparable to regression forests on frontal faces. However our approach generalizes better on rotated faces as shown in Table 1.

	Perakis et al. [8]	RF	RF-Ext (Our)
REOC	5.58 (3.33)	**3.44** (3.58)	4.59 (5.93)
REIC	4.15 (2.35)	**2.48** (1.73)	2.93 (1.93)
LEIC	4.41 (2.49)	**2.49** (1.83)	3.10 (2.13)
LEOC	5.83 (3.42)	**3.44** (2.20)	4.79 (6.96)
NT	4.09 (2.41)	**2.64** (1.80)	**2.64** (2.44)
MRC	5.56 (3.93)	**3.47** (2.70)	3.97 (3.27)
MLC	5.42 (3.84)	**3.54** (4.14)	4.21 (4.20)
CT	4.92 (3.74)	**3.38** (2.45)	3.62 (3.82)
Mean	5.00	**3.11**	3.74

Table 2 shows the mean average error of our method compared to the approach of [8]. Our method can handle unseen people and various facial expression robustly. It even outperforms a state-of-the-art method and performs comparable to the implementation of usual regression forest. However, on rotated faces it outperforms recent regression forest methods.

5 Conclusion

We present a new method for facial feature localization on rotated faces based on regression forests. In comparison to existing approaches we extend the forests by a rotation-normalization in order to improve the landmark localization across pose differences. Our approach generalizes better under unseen rotations for facial landmark localization. We obtain the same performance as current state-of-the-art approaches on frontal faces. Moreover, our method outperforms existing real time approaches with respect to rotated faces. The important benefit is, that rotated faces do not have to be covered by the training set. The computational cost stays low achieving real-time performance with 20 fps.

References

1. Creusot, C., Pears, N., Austin, J.: A machine-learning approach to keypoint detection and landmarking on 3D meshes. Int. J. Comput. Vis. **102**(1–3), 146–179 (2013)
2. Criminisi, A., Shotton, J.: Decision Forests for Computer Vision and Medical Image Analysis. Springer Science & Business Media, London (2013)
3. Dantone, M., Gall, J., Fanelli, G., Van Gool, L.: Real-time facial feature detection using conditional regression forests. In: IEEE Conference on Computer Vision and Pattern Recognition (CVPR), pp. 2578–2585. IEEE (2012)

4. Fanelli, G., Dantone, M., Gall, J., Fossati, A., Van Gool, L.: Random forests for real time 3D face analysis. Int. J. Comput. Vis. **101**(3), 437–458 (2013)
5. Girshick, R., Shotton, J., Kohli, P., Criminisi, A., Fitzgibbon, A.: Efficient regression of general-activity human poses from depth images. In: IEEE International Conference on Computer Vision (ICCV), pp. 415–422. IEEE (2011)
6. Keskin, C., Kıraç, F., Kara, Y.E., Akarun, L.: Real time hand pose estimation using depth sensors. In: Fossati, A., Gall, J., Grabner, H., Ren, X., Konolige, K. (eds.) Consumer Depth Cameras for Computer Vision, pp. 119–137. Springer, London (2013)
7. Pears, N., Yonghuai, L., Bunting, P.: 3D Imaging Analysis and Applications. Springer, London (2012)
8. Perakis, P., Passalis, G., Theoharis, T., Kakadiaris, I.A.: 3D facial landmark detection under large yaw and expression variations. IEEE Trans. Pattern Anal. Mach. Intell. **35**(7), 1552–1564 (2013)
9. Phillips, P.J., Flynn, P.J., Scruggs, T., Bowyer, K.W., Chang, J., Hoffman, K., Marques, J., Min, J., Worek, W.: Overview of the face recognition grand challenge. In: IEEE Computer Society Conference on Computer Vision and Pattern Recognition (CVPR), vol. 1, pp. 947–954. IEEE (2005)
10. Rusu, R.B.: Semantic 3D object maps for everyday manipulation in human living environments. Ph.D. thesis, Computer Science department, Technische Universitaet Muenchen, Germany (2009)
11. Ren, S., Cao, X., Wei, Y., Sun, J.: Face alignment at 3000 FPS via regressing local binary features. In: 2014 IEEE Conference on Computer Vision and Pattern Recognition (CVPR), pp. 1685–1692. IEEE (2014)
12. Savran, A., Alyüz, N., Dibeklioğlu, H., Çeliktutan, O., Gökberk, B., Sankur, B., Akarun, L.: Bosphorus database for 3D face analysis. In: Schouten, B., Juul, N.C., Drygajlo, A., Tistarelli, M. (eds.) BIOID 2008. LNCS, vol. 5372, pp. 47–56. Springer, Heidelberg (2008)
13. Shotton, J., Girshick, R., Fitzgibbon, A., Sharp, T., Cook, M., Finocchio, M., Moore, R., Kohli, P., Criminisi, A., Kipman, A., et al.: Efficient human pose estimation from single depth images. IEEE Trans. Pattern Anal. Mach. Intell. **35**(12), 2821–2840 (2013)
14. Xiong, X., De la Torre, F.: Supervised descent method and its applications to face alignment. In: IEEE Conference on Computer Vision and Pattern Recognition (CVPR), pp. 532–539. IEEE (2013)
15. Ye, M., Zhang, Q., Wang, L., Zhu, J., Yang, R., Gall, J.: A survey on human motion analysis from depth data. In: Grzegorzek, M., Theobalt, C., Koch, R., Kolb, A. (eds.) Time-of-Flight and Depth Imaging. LNCS, vol. 8200, pp. 149–187. Springer, Heidelberg (2013)

Enhanced GPT Correlation for 2D Projection Transformation Invariant Template Matching

Toru Wakahara[1]($^{(\boxtimes)}$) and Yukihiko Yamashita[2]

[1] Faculty of Computer and Information Sciences, Hosei University,
3-7-2 Kajino-cho, Koganei-shi, Tokyo 184-8584, Japan
wakahara@hosei.ac.jp
[2] Graduate School of Engineering and Science, Tokyo Institute of Technology,
2-12-1 O-okayama, Meguro-ku, Tokyo 152-8552, Japan
yamasita@ide.titech.ac.jp

Abstract. This paper describes a newly enhanced technique of 2D projection transformation invariant template matching, GPT (Global Projection Transformation) correlation. The key ideas are threefold. First, we show that arbitrary 2D projection transformation (PT) with a total of eight parameters can be approximated by a simpler expression. Second, using the simpler PT expression we propose an efficient computational model for determining sub-optimal eight parameters of PT that maximize a normalized cross-correlation value between a PT-superimposed input image and a template. Third, we obtain optimal eight parameters of PT via the successive iteration method. Experiments using templates and their artificially distorted images with random noise as input images demonstrate that the proposed method is far superior to the former GPT correlation method. Moreover, k-NN classification of handwritten numerals by the proposed method shows a high recognition accuracy through its distortion-tolerant template matching ability.

Keywords: Distortion-tolerant template matching · 2D projection transformation · Normalized cross-correlation

1 Introduction

Distortion-tolerant template matching has been intensively pursued over decades and is required to deal with all possible translations and a variety of image degradations [1]. Template matching in computer vision is useful for seeking a given pattern in a given image as a "whole-to-part" image matching problem. There have been such feature-based techniques as SIFT [2] and more recent ones [3–5]. Also, region-based techniques guided by Lukas-Kanade's paradigm [6,7], have been pursued so as to handle arbitrary 2D affine transformation [8].

On the other hand, template matching in the research arena of pattern recognition has been tackling a problem of distortion-tolerant "whole-to-whole" image matching. Those representative works include the tangent distance [9], the perturbation method [10], and DP-based 2D warping [11].

© Springer International Publishing Switzerland 2015
J. Gall et al. (Eds.): GCPR 2015, LNCS 9358, pp. 435–445, 2015.
DOI: 10.1007/978-3-319-24947-6_36

Wakahara et al. [12] proposed the affine-invariant GAT correlation method as one of promising techniques of distortion-tolerant template matching. Recently, they extended the GAT correlation method to the GPT (Global Projection Transformation) correlation method for absorbing 2D projection transformation [13]. They focused on the fact that arbitrary 2D projection transformation (PT) with eight parameters can be decomposed into a product of affine transformation (AT) with six parameters and partial projection transformation (PPT) with two parameters, i.e., PT = AT ∘ PPT. An efficient computational model was presented for determining sub-optimal components of AT and PPT independently or separately that maximize a normalized cross-correlation value between a template and a deformed input image by either of AT and PPT. However, how to determine a total of eight parameters of PT not separately but simultaneously remained unsolved as a fundamental problem.

In this paper, we propose an enhanced GPT correlation technique to resolve the above-mentioned problem. The key ideas are threefold.

First, we show that arbitrary 2D projection transformation (PT) with a total of eight parameters can be approximated by a simpler functional form of expression. Second, using the simpler PT expression we propose an efficient computational model for determining sub-optimal eight parameters of PT that maximize a normalized cross-correlation value between a PT-superimposed input image and a template by solving a set of simultaneous linear equations via the 0-th order approximation. Third, we obtain optimal eight parameters of PT using the successive iteration method.

Experiments using templates and their artificially distorted images with random noise as input images demonstrate that the proposed method is far superior to the former GPT correlation method. Moreover, k-NN based recognition experiments made on the handwritten numeral database IPTP CDROM1B [14] show that competitive matching techniques of the simple correlation, the tangent distance, and the enhanced GPT correlation achieve recognition rates of 97.07 %, 97.50 %, and 98.75 %, respectively.

2   Enhanced GPT Correlation

First, we outline the basic concept of Global Projection Transformation (GPT) [13]. Second, we newly introduce a computational model of enhanced GPT correlation to obtain sub-optimal eight parameters of PT simultaneously. Finally, we propose to use the successive iteration method to achieve an optimal GPT solution via a synthesis rule for updating PT components at every iteration.

2.1   Basic Formulation of Global Projection Transformation

As is well-known, 2D projection transformation (PT) has a total of eight parameters and is defined by

$$x' = \frac{Ax + b}{1 + c^{\mathrm{T}}x} ,$$

$$A = \begin{pmatrix} a_{00} & a_{01} \\ a_{10} & a_{11} \end{pmatrix}, \quad b = \begin{pmatrix} b_0 \\ b_1 \end{pmatrix}, \quad c = \begin{pmatrix} c_0 \\ c_1 \end{pmatrix}, \tag{1}$$

where all vectors are assumed to be column vectors. Also, c^{T} denotes the transpose of a column vector c, and $x = (x, y)^{\mathrm{T}}$.

In correlation-based image matching between an input image, $f(x)$, and a template, $g(x)$, Wakahara et al. [13] proposed to maximize a normalized cross-correlation value by applying optimal PT to $f(x)$. They called this technique GPT correlation.

First, by means of definite canonicalization [15] pixel values of $f(x)$ and $g(x)$ were linearly transformed to satisfy the following normalization requirements. $\mathcal{D}$ denotes the domain common to $f(x)$ and $g(x)$, and $e(x) \equiv 1$.

$$(f, e) = (g, e) = 0, \quad \| f \| = \| g \| = 1, \tag{2}$$

where

$$(f, g) \equiv \int_{\mathcal{D}} f(x) g(x) dx, \quad \| f \| \equiv \sqrt{(f, f)}.$$

As a result, a normalized cross-correlation value between $f(x)$ and $g(x)$ was obtained by means of an inner product on $f(x)$ and $g(x)$, i.e., (f, g).

Second, they defined a normalized cross-correlation value, $C^{\mathrm{GPT}}(f, g)$, of the form

$$C^{\mathrm{GPT}}(f, g) = \max_{A, b, c} J_{\mathrm{GPT}}(A, b, c),$$

$$J_{\mathrm{GPT}}(A, b, c) = \int_{\mathcal{D}} f(x) g \left(\frac{Ax + b}{1 + c^{\mathrm{T}} x} \right) dx. \tag{3}$$

Third, in order to avoid an exhaustive search for optimal parameters in (3) they introduced a new objective function, $\tilde{J}_{\mathrm{GPT}}(A, b, c)$, with a Gaussian kernel of PT components given by

$$\tilde{J}_{\mathrm{GPT}}(A, b, c) = \int_{\mathcal{D}} \int_{\mathcal{D}} G \left(\frac{Ax_1 + b}{1 + c^{\mathrm{T}} x_1} - x_2 \right) \times$$
$$\delta \left(d(\nabla f(x_1)), d(\nabla g(x_2)) \right) f(x_1) g(x_2) dx_1 dx_2,$$

$$G(x) = \exp \left(-\frac{\|x\|^2}{2W^2} \right), \tag{4}$$

where $d(\nabla f(x))$ and $d(\nabla g(x))$ stand for directions of gradients of $f(x)$ and $g(x)$ quantized with the $\frac{\pi}{4}$ interval, and take integers ranging from zero to eight. The value of zero corresponds to no gradient. Also, the $\delta(i, j)$ is a kind of the Kronecker delta of the form

$$\delta(i, j) = \begin{cases} 1, & \text{for } i = j \neq 0 \\ 0. & \text{for } i \neq j \text{ or } i = 0 \text{ or } j = 0 \end{cases} \tag{5}$$

The value of W of (4) controlled the spread of the Gaussian kernel as a function of the disparity in gradients between the input image and the template according to

$$W = \frac{1}{2} \underset{x_1}{Av} \left\{ \min_{\{x_2 | d(\nabla f(x_1)) = d(\nabla g(x_2)) \neq 0\}} \|x_1 - x_2\| \right\}$$
$$+ \frac{1}{2} \underset{x_2}{Av} \left\{ \min_{\{x_1 | d(\nabla f(x_1)) = d(\nabla g(x_2)) \neq 0\}} \|x_1 - x_2\| \right\}, \tag{6}$$

where Av stands for an averaging operation.

2.2 Computational Model of Enhanced GPT Correlation

We newly propose to approximate the exact expression of PT appearing as an argument of the Gaussian kernel of (4) to obtain its simpler functional form.

Concretely, by assuming that A is nearly equal to an identity matrix, I, and both b and c are nearly equal to zero vectors we can obtain the approximation of PT given by

$$\frac{Ax_1 + b}{1 + c^T x_1} - x_2 \approx (Ax_1 + b)(1 - c^T x_1) - x_2$$
$$\approx (Ax_1 + b) - x_1 x_1^T c - x_2.$$
$$\therefore \left\| \frac{Ax_1 + b}{1 + c^T x_1} - x_2 \right\|^2 \approx \left\| (Ax_1 + b) - x_1 x_1^T c - x_2 \right\|^2$$
$$= (a_{00}x_1 + a_{01}y_1 + b_0 - c_0 x_1^2 - c_1 x_1 y_1 - x_2)^2$$
$$+ (a_{10}x_1 + a_{11}y_1 + b_1 - c_0 x_1 y_1 - c_1 y_1^2 - y_2)^2. \tag{7}$$

After substituting the exact expression of PT with the above approximation we set the derivatives of $\tilde{J}_{GPT}(A, b, c)$ of (4) with respect to A, b, and c equal to zero. Then, we can obtain a set of simultaneous equations as a necessary condition for maximizing $\tilde{J}_{GPT}(A, b, c)$. Moreover, we adopt the 0th order approximation that sets $A = I$, $b = 0$, and $c = 0$ in the Gaussian kernel. As a result, we have

$$0 = \frac{\partial \tilde{J}_{GPT}}{\partial a_{00}} \approx -\frac{1}{W^2} \int_D \int_D G(x_1 - x_2) f(x_1) g(x_2) \delta \left(d(\nabla f(x_1)), d(\nabla g(x_2)) \right)$$
$$\times (a_{00}x_1 + a_{01}y_1 + b_0 - c_0 x_1^2 - c_1 x_1 y_1 - x_2) x_1 dx_1 dx_2,$$

$$0 = \frac{\partial \tilde{J}_{GPT}}{\partial a_{01}} \approx -\frac{1}{W^2} \int_D \int_D G(x_1 - x_2) f(x_1) g(x_2) \delta \left(d(\nabla f(x_1)), d(\nabla g(x_2)) \right)$$
$$\times (a_{00}x_1 + a_{01}y_1 + b_0 - c_0 x_1^2 - c_1 x_1 y_1 - x_2) y_1 dx_1 dx_2,$$

$$0 = \frac{\partial \tilde{J}_{GPT}}{\partial a_{10}} \approx -\frac{1}{W^2} \int_D \int_D G(x_1 - x_2) f(x_1) g(x_2) \delta \left(d(\nabla f(x_1)), d(\nabla g(x_2)) \right)$$
$$\times (a_{10}x_1 + a_{11}y_1 + b_1 - c_0 x_1 y_1 - c_1 y_1^2 - y_2) x_1 dx_1 dx_2,$$

$$0 = \frac{\partial \tilde{J}_{\text{GPT}}}{\partial a_{11}} \approx -\frac{1}{W^2} \int_D \int_D G(\boldsymbol{x}_1 - \boldsymbol{x}_2) f(\boldsymbol{x}_1) g(\boldsymbol{x}_2) \delta\left(d(\nabla f(\boldsymbol{x}_1)), d(\nabla g(\boldsymbol{x}_2))\right)$$
$$\times \, (a_{10}x_1 + a_{11}y_1 + b_1 - c_0 x_1 y_1 - c_1 y_1^2 - y_2) y_1 d\boldsymbol{x}_1 d\boldsymbol{x}_2,$$

$$0 = \frac{\partial \tilde{J}_{\text{GPT}}}{\partial b_0} \approx -\frac{1}{W^2} \int_D \int_D G(\boldsymbol{x}_1 - \boldsymbol{x}_2) f(\boldsymbol{x}_1) g(\boldsymbol{x}_2) \delta\left(d(\nabla f(\boldsymbol{x}_1)), d(\nabla g(\boldsymbol{x}_2))\right)$$
$$\times \, (a_{10}x_1 + a_{11}y_1 + b_1 - c_0 x_1 y_1 - c_1 y_1^2 - y_2) d\boldsymbol{x}_1 d\boldsymbol{x}_2,$$

$$0 = \frac{\partial \tilde{J}_{\text{GPT}}}{\partial b_1} \approx -\frac{1}{W^2} \int_D \int_D G(\boldsymbol{x}_1 - \boldsymbol{x}_2) f(\boldsymbol{x}_1) g(\boldsymbol{x}_2) \delta\left(d(\nabla f(\boldsymbol{x}_1)), d(\nabla g(\boldsymbol{x}_2))\right)$$
$$\times \, (a_{10}x_1 + a_{11}y_1 + b_1 - c_0 x_1 y_1 - c_1 y_1^2 - y_2) d\boldsymbol{x}_1 d\boldsymbol{x}_2,$$

$$0 = \frac{\partial \tilde{J}_{\text{GPT}}}{\partial c_0} \approx -\frac{1}{W^2} \int_D \int_D G(\boldsymbol{x}_1 - \boldsymbol{x}_2) f(\boldsymbol{x}_1) g(\boldsymbol{x}_2) \delta\left(d(\nabla f(\boldsymbol{x}_1)), d(\nabla g(\boldsymbol{x}_2))\right)$$
$$\times \, [(a_{00}x_1 + a_{01}y_1 + b_0 - c_0 x_1^2 - c_1 x_1 y_1 - x_2) x_1^2$$
$$+ \, (a_{10}x_1 + a_{11}y_1 + b_1 - c_0 x_1 y_1 - c_1 y_1^2 - y_2) x_1 y_1] d\boldsymbol{x}_1 d\boldsymbol{x}_2,$$

$$0 = \frac{\partial \tilde{J}_{\text{GPT}}}{\partial c_1} \approx -\frac{1}{W^2} \int_D \int_D G(\boldsymbol{x}_1 - \boldsymbol{x}_2) f(\boldsymbol{x}_1) g(\boldsymbol{x}_2) \delta\left(d(\nabla f(\boldsymbol{x}_1)), d(\nabla g(\boldsymbol{x}_2))\right)$$
$$\times \, [(a_{00}x_1 + a_{01}y_1 + b_0 - c_0 x_1^2 - c_1 x_1 y_1 - x_2) x_1 y_1$$
$$+ \, (a_{10}x_1 + a_{11}y_1 + b_1 - c_0 x_1 y_1 - c_1 y_1^2 - y_2) y_1^2] d\boldsymbol{x}_1 d\boldsymbol{x}_2. \tag{8}$$

Finally, by using the following notation:

$$\bar{v} \equiv \frac{\int_D \int_D v(\boldsymbol{x}_1, \boldsymbol{x}_2) G(\boldsymbol{x}_1 - \boldsymbol{x}_2) \delta\left(d(\nabla f(\boldsymbol{x}_1)), d(\nabla g(\boldsymbol{x}_2))\right) f(\boldsymbol{x}_1) g(\boldsymbol{x}_2) d\boldsymbol{x}_1 d\boldsymbol{x}_2}{\int_D \int_D G(\boldsymbol{x}_1 - \boldsymbol{x}_2) \delta\left(d(\nabla f(\boldsymbol{x}_1)), d(\nabla g(\boldsymbol{x}_2))\right) f(\boldsymbol{x}_1) g(\boldsymbol{x}_2) d\boldsymbol{x}_1 d\boldsymbol{x}_2}$$

we can rewrite a set of simultaneous linear equations of eight unknown parameters of (8) and find

$$\begin{pmatrix} \overline{x_1^2} & \overline{x_1 y_1} & 0 & 0 & \overline{x_1} & 0 & -\overline{x_1^3} & -\overline{x_1^2 y_1} \\ \overline{x_1 y_1} & \overline{y_1^2} & 0 & 0 & \overline{y_1} & 0 & -\overline{x_1^2 y_1} & -\overline{x_1 y_1^2} \\ 0 & 0 & \overline{x_1^2} & \overline{x_1 y_1} & 0 & \overline{x_1} & -\overline{x_1^2 y_1} & -\overline{x_1 y_1^2} \\ 0 & 0 & \overline{x_1 y_1} & \overline{y_1^2} & 0 & \overline{y_1} & -\overline{x_1 y_1^2} & -\overline{y_1^3} \\ \overline{x_1} & \overline{y_1} & 0 & 0 & 1 & 0 & -\overline{x_1^2} & -\overline{x_1 y_1} \\ 0 & 0 & \overline{x_1} & \overline{y_1} & 0 & 1 & -\overline{x_1 y_1} & -\overline{y_1^2} \\ \overline{x_1^3} & \overline{x_1^2 y_1} & \overline{x_1^2 y_1} & \overline{x_1 y_1^2} & \overline{x_1^2} & \overline{x_1 y_1} & -(\overline{x_1^4 + x_1^2 y_1^2}) & -(\overline{x_1^3 y_1 + x_1 y_1^3}) \\ \overline{x_1^2 y_1} & \overline{x_1 y_1^2} & \overline{x_1 y_1^2} & \overline{y_1^3} & \overline{x_1 y_1} & \overline{y_1^2} & -(\overline{x_1^3 y_1 + x_1 y_1^3}) & -(\overline{x_1^2 y_1^2 + y_1^4}) \end{pmatrix} \begin{pmatrix} a_{00} \\ a_{01} \\ a_{10} \\ a_{11} \\ b_0 \\ b_1 \\ c_0 \\ c_1 \end{pmatrix}$$

$$= \left(\overline{x_1 x_2}, \ \overline{y_1 x_2}, \ \overline{x_1 y_2}, \ \overline{y_1 y_2}, \ \overline{x_2}, \ \overline{y_2}, \ \overline{x_1^2 x_2 + x_1 y_1 y_2}, \ \overline{x_1 y_1 x_2 + y_1^2 y_2}\right)^{\text{T}}. \tag{9}$$

These simultaneous linear equations of (9) are easily solved. However, it is to be noted that obtained eight parameters are sub-optimal ones for maximizing $J_{\text{GPT}}(A, \boldsymbol{b}, \boldsymbol{c})$ of (3).

2.3   Iterative Solution for Optimal PT Components

We propose to update sub-optimal solutions of PT components so that they should converge into optimal ones via the successive iteration method [16].

First of all, we can obtain a synthesis rule for updating PT components at every iteration as follows.

$$x' = \frac{Ax + b}{1 + c^T x} \; ,$$

$$x'' = \frac{A'x' + b'}{1 + c'^T x'} = \frac{A'\left(\frac{Ax+b}{1+c^T x}\right) + b'}{1 + c'^T \left(\frac{Ax+b}{1+c^T x}\right)} = \frac{A'(Ax + b) + (1 + c^T x)b'}{1 + c^T x + c'^T(Ax + b)}$$

$$\equiv \frac{A''x + b''}{1 + c''^T x} \; ,$$

$$\therefore A'' = \frac{A'A + b'c^T}{1 + c'^T b} \; , \qquad b'' = \frac{A'b + b'}{1 + c'^T b} \; , \qquad c'' = \frac{c + A^T c'}{1 + c'^T b} \; . \tag{10}$$

Then, we adopt a procedure of the successive iteration method given by

Step 1 : In the initial state ($\tau = 0$), we set $A^{(0)} = I$, $b^{(0)} = 0$, $c^{(0)} = 0$ and $f^{(0)}(x) = f(x)$. We calculate $W^{(0)}$ of (6) and $J_{\mathrm{GPT}}^{(0)}$ of (3) by substituting $f^{(0)}(x)$ for $f(x)$.

Step 2 : We set $\tau = \tau + 1$. We calculate A, b, and c of (9) by substituting $f^{(\tau-1)}(x)$ for $f(x)$. If $J_{\mathrm{GPT}}^{(\tau)} \leq J_{\mathrm{GPT}}^{(\tau-1)}$, we output $C^{\mathrm{GPT}}(f, g) = J_{\mathrm{GPT}}^{(\tau-1)}$ and stop the iteration. Otherwise, we go to *Step* 3.

Step 3 : By using the synthesis rule of (10) we obtain updated $A^{(\tau)}, b^{(\tau)}$, and $c^{(\tau)}$. Also, we calculate $W^{(\tau)}$ of (6) by substituting $f^{(\tau)}(x)$ for $f(x)$, and go back to *Step* 2.

3   Experimental Results

We compare the ability of the enhanced or new GPT correlation method against that of the former or old GPT correlation method [13] in template matching using artificially distorted images subject to Gaussian random noise. Moreover, we show that k-NN classification of handwritten numerals by the proposed method achieves a high recognition accuracy.

3.1   Affine Transformation Tolerance

We take up rotation as a representative of affine transformation.

Figure 1 shows the template of "Chess board" and examples of artificially rotated images at intervals of five degrees. Here, we added random noise with a Gaussian distribution having standard deviation $\sigma = 50.0$ to those artificially rotated images, where gray values take integers in $[0, 255]$.

Figure 2 shows relations between rotation angles and correlation values obtained by matching the template of "Chess board" with its artificially rotated

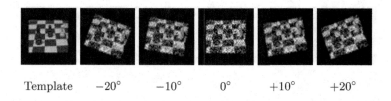

Template   −20°   −10°   0°   +10°   +20°

Fig. 1. Template of "Chess board" and examples of artificially rotated images

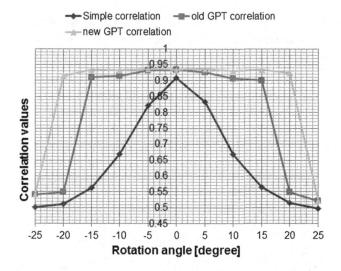

Fig. 2. Relations between rotation angles and correlation values obtained for rotated images of "Chess board" via the simple correlation, the old GPT correlation, and the new GPT correlation methods

images via the simple correlation, the old GPT correlation, and the new GPT correlation methods.

From Fig. 2, it is clear that the new GPT correlation method exhibited a higher ability of rotation tolerance than the old GPT correlation method. Also, we can point out that both of old and new GPT correlation methods realize noise tolerance inherent in correlation-based template matching techniques.

3.2   2D Projection Transformation Tolerance

We generated input images by applying 2D projection transformation of $A = I$, $b = 0$, and $c_0 = c_1 = s \times 0.001, (s = 1, 2, ..., 10)$ to the template of "Chess board". Those distorted images were also subject to Gaussian random noise.

Figure 3 shows the template of "Chess board" and examples of 2D projection transformed images with random noise.

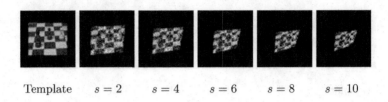

| Template | $s = 2$ | $s = 4$ | $s = 6$ | $s = 8$ | $s = 10$ |

Fig. 3. Template of "Chess board" and examples of 2D projection transformed images

Figure 4 shows correlation values for 2D projection transformed images of "Chess board" obtained by the simple correlation, the old GPT correlation, and the new GPT correlation methods.

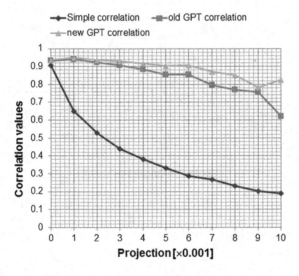

Fig. 4. Correlation values for 2D projection transformed images of "Chess board" obtained by the simple correlation, the old GPT correlation, and the new GPT correlation methods

From Fig. 4, it is found that the new GPT correlation method achieved a higher tolerance against 2D projection transformation than the old GPT correlation method.

From these results, we can say that the proposed method is very powerful in absorbing 2D projection transformation when being applied to "whole-to-whole" image matching.

Incidentally, the average matching time per iteration between two images with 64 × 64 pixels was 0.24 s on a 3.40 GHz Intel Xeon E3-1240 processor.

3.3   Recognition of Handwritten Numerals

We use the handwritten numeral database IPTP CDROM1B [14]. This database contains binary images of handwritten digits divided into two groups of 17,985 samples for training and 17,916 samples for test. Incidentally, the highest recognition rate ever reported for this database is 99.49 % [17] obtained via a pseudo-Bayes discriminant function and LBG clustering in 400-dimensional feature space reduced by KL transform.

In our experiments, position and size normalization by moments [18] is first applied to each binary image so that the center of gravity of black pixels is located at the center of the image and the average distance of black pixels from the center of the image is set at the predetermined value of ρ (= 6.0). Then, we transform all of binary images into grayscale images by Gaussian filtering and set the image size at 24×16 pixels.

In recognition experiments, we make a comparative study of k-NN classification of a total of 17,916 test samples using four kinds of matching measures: the simple correlation, the tangent distance, the GAT correlation [19], and the enhanced GPT correlation. Here, all of 17,985 training samples are used as templates.

Table 1 shows the recognition rates of the simple correlation, the tangent distance, the GAT correlation, and the enhanced GPT correlation in k-NN classification. The value of k was set at three.

Table 1. Recognition rates of the simple correlation, the tangent distance, the GAT correlation, and the enhanced GPT correlation in handwritten numeral recognition.

Matching measure	Recognition rates (%)
Simple correlation	97.07
Tangent distance	97.50
GAT correlation	98.71
Enhanced GPT correlation	98.75

From Table 1, it is found that the proposed method achieved the highest recognition rate among these k-NN based template matching techniques.

However, there is a typical problem of excessive matching common to distortion-tolerant image matching techniques.

Figure 5 shows the occurrence rates of the correlation values at intervals of 0.01 in two cases: matching against correct categories and matching against almost similar but incorrect or "rival" categories. Here, we counted only one highest correlation value obtained against a correct category's template and one highest correlation value obtained against an incorrect category's template for each test sample.

From Fig. 5 and Table 1, we can see that an excellent shape matching ability does not always exhibit a distinct improvement in shape discrimination ability.

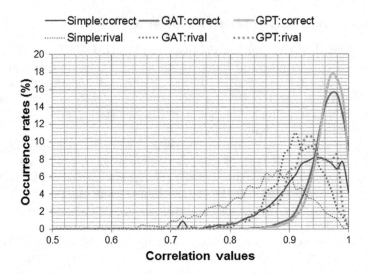

Fig. 5. Occurrences of correlation values of enhanced GPT correlation, GAT correlation, and simple correlation

4   Conclusion

This paper proposed a newly enhanced template matching technique, the enhanced GPT correlation, featuring 2D projection transformation (PT) tolerance. The key contribution of this paper to distortion-tolerant template matching is a simple but effective computational model as expressed by a set of simultaneous linear equations that determine optimal eight parameters of PT attaining a maximum cross-correlation value between a template and a PT-superimposed input image.

Experimental results showed that the proposed method exhibited a much higher tolerance for geometric distortion subject to random noise than the former GPT correlation method.

Future work is to apply the proposed method to "whole-to-part" image matching with the aim of detecting distorted objects in a complex background. Also, it is necessary to reduce the computational cost of the proposed method.

Acknowledgments. A part of this work was supported by JSPS KAKENHI Grant Numbers 26330207 and 26280054.

References

1. Ouyang, W., Tombari, F., Mattoccia, S., Stefano, L.D., Cham, W.-K.: Performance evaluation of full search equivalent pattern matching algorithms. IEEE Trans. Pattern Anal. Machine Intell. **34**(2), 127–143 (2012)
2. Lowe, D.G.: Distinctive image features from scale-invariant keypoints. Int. J. Comput. Vision **60**(2), 91–110 (2004)

3. Morel, J.M., Yu, G.: Asift: A new framework for fully affine invariant image comparison. SIAM J. Imaging Sci. **2**(2), 438–469 (2009)
4. Jiang, H., Yu, S.X.: Linear solution to scale and rotation invariant object matching. In: Proceedings of IEEE Computer Society Conference on Computer Vision and Pattern Recognition, pp. 2474–2481. IEEE Press, New York (2009)
5. Li, H., Huang, X., He, L.: Object matching using a locally affine invariant and linear programming techniques. IEEE Trans. Pattern Anal. Machine Intell. **35**(2), 411–424 (2013)
6. Lucas, B.D., Kanade, T.: An iterative image registration technique with an application to stereo vision. In: Proceedings of 7th International Joint Conference on Artificial Intelligence, pp. 674–679. IEEE Press, New York (1981)
7. Baker, S., Matthews, I.: Lucas-Kanade 20 years on: a unifying framework. Int. J. Comput. Vision **56**(3), 221–255 (2004)
8. Korman, S., Reichman, Tsur, D.G., Avidan, S.: FAsT-Match: fast affine template matching. In: Proceedings of IEEE Computer Society Conference on Computer Vision and Pattern Recognition, pp. 2331–2338. IEEE Press, New York (2013)
9. Simard, P., LeCun, Y., Denker, J.: Efficient pattern recognition using a new transformation distance. In: Proceedings of Advances in Neural Information Processing Systems 5, pp. 50–58. Morgan Kaufmann Publishers Inc., San Francisco (1992)
10. Ha, T.M., Bunke, H.: Off-line, handwritten numeral recognition by perturbation method. IEEE Trans. Pattern Anal. Machine Intell. **19**(5), 535–539 (1997)
11. Ronee, M., Uchida, S., Sakoe, H.: Handwritten character recognition using piecewise linear two-dimensional warping. In: Proceedings of Sixth International Conference on Document Analysis and Recognition, pp. 39–43. The IEEE Computer Society, Los Alamitos (2001)
12. Wakahara, T., Kimura, Y., Tomono, A.: Affine-invariant recognition of gray-scale characters using global affine transformation correlation. IEEE Trans. Pattern Anal. Machine Intell. **23**(4), 384–395 (2001)
13. Wakahara, T., Yamashita, Y.: GPT correlation for 2D projection transformation invariant template matching. In: Proceedings of 22nd International Conference on Pattern Recognition, pp. 3810–3815. The IEEE Computer Society, Los Alamitos (2014)
14. Osuga, K., Tsutsumida, T., Yamaguchi, S., Nagata, K.: IPTP survey on handwritten numeral recognition. IPTP Research and Survey Report R-96-V-02, The Ministry of Posts and Telecommunications (1996) (in Japanese)
15. Iijima, T.: Pattern Recognition. Corona, Tokyo (1973). (in Japanese)
16. The Mathematical Society of Japan, Ito, K.: Encyclopedic Dictionary of Mathematics, 2nd edn. The MIT Press, Cambridge (1987)
17. Shi, M., Fujisawa, Y., Wakabayashi, T., Kimura, F.: Handwritten numeral recognition using gradient and curvature of gray scale image. Pattern Recogn. **35**, 2051–2059 (2002)
18. Casey, R.G.: Moment normalization of handprinted characters. IBM J. Res. Develop. **14**, 548–557 (1970)
19. Wakahara, T., Yamashita, Y.: k-NN classification of handwritten characters via accelerated GAT correlation. Pattern Recogn. **47**, 994–1001 (2014)

Semantic Segmentation Based Traffic Light Detection at Day and at Night

Vladimir Haltakov[1,2]([✉]), Jakob Mayr[1,3], Christian Unger[1,2],
and Slobodan Ilic[2]

[1] BMW Group, Munich, Germany
{vladimir.haltakov,christian.unger}@bmw.de
[2] Technical University Munich, Munich, Germany
slobodan.ilic@in.tum.de
[3] Munich University of Applied Sciences, Munich, Germany
jamayr@web.de

Abstract. Traffic light detection from a moving vehicle is an important technology both for new safety driver assistance functions as well as for autonomous driving in the city. In this paper we present a machine learning framework for detection of traffic lights that can handle in real-time both day and night situations in a unified manner. A semantic segmentation method is employed to generate traffic light candidates, which are then confirmed and classified by a geometric and color features based classifier. Temporal consistency is enforced by using a tracking by detection method.

We evaluate our method on a publicly available dataset recorded at daytime in order to compare to existing methods and we show similar performance. We also present an evaluation on two additional datasets containing more than 50 intersections with multiple traffic lights recorded both at day and during nighttime and we show that our method performs consistently in those situations.

1 Introduction

In the past decade various advanced driver assistance systems (ADAS) have found their way into series production and today almost all car manufacturers offer a wide variety of comfort and safety features like for example speed limit information, adaptive cruise control and automatic emergency breaking. In addition, safety organizations like the EuroNCAP and the equivalent institutions in other countries, traditionally performing crash tests to assess passive safety, are developing and introducing new test procedures for active safety systems, which further promote the usage of ADAS in commercial vehicles. While there are multiple sensors that can be used in such systems, cameras are usually the most universal and cheapest choice, because they have the highest spatial resolution and are able to detect the highest variety of object types, e.g. traffic signals, lane markings and other road users.

The position and the current state of the traffic lights in front of the vehicle is a valuable information for many safety and comfort driver assistance functions.

© Springer International Publishing Switzerland 2015
J. Gall et al. (Eds.): GCPR 2015, LNCS 9358, pp. 446–457, 2015.
DOI: 10.1007/978-3-319-24947-6_37

Traffic lights detection is needed in order to enable autonomous and highly automated driving in cities and on country roads. Furthermore, red light running is a major safety problem, with estimated 165,000 motorists, cyclists and pedestrians injured in the USA every year, a lot of which fatal [1,15]. Similar studies in Germany [2] show that 7,356 incidents with people or property damaged happened in 2013 because of disregarding traffic signals at intersections.

In this paper, we focus on the problem of detecting the presence and the state of traffic lights from camera images both at day and at night. Day and night scenes pose fundamentally different challenges for visual traffic light recognition. At day, the structure of the traffic light is well visible, but the light source can be difficult to detect due to the presence of many other bright image regions especially in sunny weather. Furthermore, traffic lights are relatively small in width compared to traffic signs or other road users, which makes the detection at large distances difficult. In contrast, at nighttime, light sources are visible from a very high distance, but since the traffic light box is usually not visible in the camera image (or only at very short distances), there is no textural support to distinguish the traffic lights from other light sources like street lamps and advertisements. Figure 1 shows examples of such difficult situations.

Fig. 1. The same scene recorded on a sunny day and at night showing the challenges for a traffic light detection system that needs to operate in all conditions.

The method presented in this paper is based on machine learning and can handle both day and night situations in a unified manner, such that only the trained classifier parameters are different for day and night, while the whole method remains unchanged. While there is a vast amount of literature on traffic light recognition, only very few vision methods deal with both day and night situations [18,23]. A detailed overview of the related work is given in Sect. 2.

Our method consists of two main stages. First, we use a pixel-wise semantic segmentation method similar to [13] to find image regions that are potential traffic light candidates. While similar image segmentation steps, usually based on color thresholding, are used by many other systems, we show that more advanced machine learning methods like our semantic segmentation approach can provide more robust candidates. In a second step, we compute multiple color and geometric features on the regions found in the first step, which are then used by another classifier to confirm or reject the candidates and to also determine the current color of the traffic light. Additionally, a tracking algorithm is used to enforce temporal consistency.

The proposed system is evaluated on two datasets with 57 intersections recorded both at day and at night in order to show that we can handle both scenarios using the same approach. Furthermore, we also present our results on the publicly available dataset of [4], which contains only daytime recordings.

Our main contribution is a unified framework for real-time traffic light detection both at day and at night based on semantic segmentation to generate traffic lights proposals and the subsequent classifier used to confirm or reject those candidates based on geometric and color features.

2   Related Work

We divide the related methods in three groups based on the situations they operate in: at day, at night or both. While there are works that rely on high-accuracy maps as a prior for the traffic lights position in the camera image [8,10], here we focus on purely vision based systems, because they pose unique challenges.

2.1   Detection at Day

Most of the related works focus on traffic light detection at day. Many methods rely only on pure image processing by applying color segmentation followed by geometric and visual filters [3,7,11,21,22,24]. Those methods may deliver good results if the light shape is clearly visible, but it is not clear if they can scale well to various traffic light types and night conditions. The evaluation provided on those methods is also very limited and sometimes only qualitative.

The methods described in [4,26] rely on template matching in addition to image processing techniques, which increases the robustness of the system in some situations, but they work only during the day. Both methods are evaluated on the dataset or part of it that is introduced in [4], which we also use for the quantitative evaluation of our method.

More powerful machine learning methods are employed by [5,12,16,20] in order to learn the appearance of the traffic lights at day. However, at night most parts of the traffic light are not visible, so it is not clear if those methods can be extended to also work in all situations.

Most of the works above provide very limited evaluation based on short sequences of couple of minutes or done only qualitatively, which makes comparison of performance difficult.

2.2   Detection at Night

The big challenge for traffic light detection methods at night is to filter out light emitting objects that are not traffic lights. Several works exist that explicitly focus on the night detection problem either by using template matching methods

[9,19], support vector machines classification [17] or just image processing [6]. However, due to the lack of a publicly available datasets for traffic lights detection with night recordings, those methods are tested only qualitatively or on small non-public datasets.

2.3 Detection at Day and Night

The methods that are most strongly related to ours are those that are designed to deal both with day and night conditions [18,23].

The authors of [18] use a pipeline consisting of image adjustments in the RGB space, thresholding and applying a median filter to detect traffic lights in different weather and illumination conditions. However, the scenarios where this method is applied are limited, because only suspended traffic lights are detected, while at many smaller intersections, only supported traffic lights are available.

Another system designed to handle both day and night situations as well as adverse weather conditions is presented by [23]. The authors employ a color pre-processing step, followed by a fast radial symmetry transform to extract candidates and a spatio-temporal consistency check to reduce false positives. While the detection at day is quantitatively evaluated on the dataset of [4], the night detection is evaluated only qualitatively, which makes comparison of the performance in different situations impossible.

Our method is evaluated quantitatively both on the dataset of [4] and on two new datasets recorded at night and at day. In this way, we are able to analyze the performance of our method in different lighting conditions.

3   Method

The general method pipeline is illustrated in Fig. 2. A semantic segmentation algorithm is first used to label each image pixel and find potential candidate regions in the image. Those regions are then verified by a classifier based on several color and geometric features, which are also used to determine the state of the traffic light. The verification stage also includes a tracking step, which helps to enforce temporal consistency on the traffic lights.

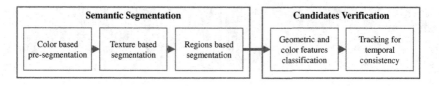

Fig. 2. Overview of the method pipeline.

3.1   Semantic Segmentation Based Candidates

The goal of this stage is to find regions in the image that are potential traffic light objects. In this stage, having false positives (e.g. candidates that are not traffic lights) is not critical, since the subsequent verification stage is designed to filter them out. The number of false negatives, on the other hand, needs to be low, because missed traffic lights will not be evaluated in the next steps. Nevertheless, a segmentation method that has few false positives is desirable since the verification stage will be both more accurate and more efficient. It is also important to note that our goal is to design a method that will be applicable both at day and at nighttime.

The semantic segmentation problem aims to divide the image into semantically meaningful regions. This is usually done by classifying each image pixel x_i with a label y_i from a predefined set of labels $\mathcal{L}$. In our case, we need only two labels: BACKGROUND or TRAFFIC LIGHT CANDIDATE. Our goal here is to label only the light spot of the traffic light and not the whole box, because in most cases the box is not visible in the camera image at night.

We employ a three-step semantic segmentation method based on the method of [13]. Each step follows the same approach: for every pixel we compute features from the image and from the result of the previous steps. Each pixel is then classified based on those features by a JointBoost [25] classifier. The three steps are described in detail below, while in Sect. 4.3 we show how they contribute to the final detection performance.

Color Segmentation. The first step is a simple color segmentation used to improve the runtime of the method. Instead of tuning the color thresholds by hand, we employ a classifier that uses only the color of the pixel in the Lab color space as input and is biased to have few false negatives on traffic light candidates by giving the traffic light pixels very high weight (see Fig. 3). Formally, the color

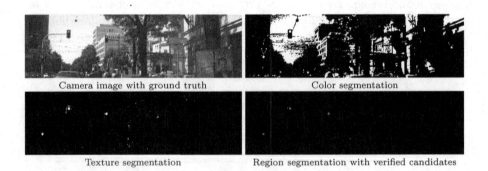

Camera image with ground truth   Color segmentation

Texture segmentation   Region segmentation with verified candidates

Fig. 3. Intermediate results of our method at the different stages of the pipeline. At every step the number of traffic light candidates (in white) is reduced. The candidate regions confirmed by the classifier in the last stage are marked in red (Color figure online).

classifier models the conditional probability distribution $P(y_i|x_i)$ of the pixel label y_i given the pixel intensities x_i. The subsequent steps ignore all pixels that were labeled as background.

Texture Segmentation. In the second step, the pixels are classified based on the texture in their surrounding area. For this we compute a feature vector $f(x_i)$ based on the 2D Walsh-Hadamard Transform [14], which is a discrete and computationally efficient approximation of the cosine transform and has successfully been used for template matching [14] and semantic segmentation [13,27]. Similarly to the other works, we compute the first 16 coefficients of the transform separately for each Lab color channel at five scales around the pixel of interest. We also add the 2D coordinates of the pixel to the feature vector to encode spatial context. The classifier operating on those features can be seen as modeling distribution $P(y_i|f(x_i))$.

While the classifier trained on texture features is already able to provide good results, the shape of the regions may not be very robust due to small pixel errors around the borders (see Fig. 3). This happens because the classifier takes the decision about the class of each pixel individually and independently of the labels of the neighboring pixels. This problem is addressed in the next step.

Region Segmentation. This step is equivalent to the neighborhood classification stage from [13]. The region classifier considers not only the pixel of interest itself, but also a set of related pixels called a neighborhood. While in [13] several alternatives are proposed that deliver highly accurate results, they are based on geodesic distance which is slow to compute. We define the neighborhood N_i of pixel i to contain all pixels in a circle of radius 3 around each pixel, because it is much more computationally efficient.

Every pixel j in the neighborhood N_i votes for its most probable class v_j based on the output of the classifier in the texture segmentation step $P(y_j = v_j|f(x_j))$. Those votes are then summarized in a normalized histogram h_i over the possible labels $c \in \mathcal{L}$. Formally, we write:

$$h_i(c) = \frac{\sum_{j \in N_i}[c = v_j]}{|N_i|}. \tag{1}$$

The normalized histogram computed in this way is used as a feature vector for the region segmentation classifier together with the response of the pixel itself, which means that the region classifier models the distribution $P(y_i|h_i, P(y_i|f(x_i)))$. This formulation allows the classifier to model local context relations, which leads to better segmentation performance and better candidate regions (see Fig. 3).

3.2 Candidates Verification

The semantic segmentation method introduced in the previous section learns texture features and label interactions that are characteristic for traffic lights.

However, since the classifiers from the segmentation stage classify each pixel individually, it is difficult to model geometric features that describe whole regions, like for example, if the region has a circular shape. Therefore, in the verification stage we train another classifier based on the region geometry and color features. The classifier does not take decisions on the pixel level anymore, but on the region level. Furthermore, we introduce a simple tracking by detection algorithm in order to enforce temporal consistency of the detections.

Traffic Lights Classifier. Each candidate region coming from the semantic segmentation method is classified in the classes BACKGROUND, GREEN, YELLOW or RED traffic light. The input to the classifier is a set of 21 geometric and color features described in Table 1. Here, we again make use of the JointBoost classifier, which now operates on regions instead of pixels. The result of the classification is shown visually in Fig. 3, where only the candidates that were classified correctly are painted in the corresponding color, while the white candidates are rejected.

Table 1. Geometric and color features used for the classification of candidate regions.

Feature	Values	Description
Mean (RGB)	3	Mean of the region pixels computed separately for each color channel.
Mean (Lab)	3	
Std. deviation (RGB)	3	Standard deviation of the region pixels computed separately for each color channel.
Std. deviation (Lab)	3	
Image position	2	The pixel coordinates of the center of the region
Area	1	Area of the region
Orientation	1	Angle between the x-axis and the major axis of the region
Aspect ratio	1	Aspect ratio of the two sides of the region's bounding box
Ratio of areas	1	Ratio of the areas of the region and its bounding box
Y-coordinate-area ratio	1	Ratio between the region's center y-coordinate and its area
Solidity	1	Ratio between the areas of the region and its convex hull
Eccentricity	1	Ratio of the distance between the foci and the major axis length of an ellipse that has the same second moment as the region

Tracking. Since the verification method described above operates on individual frames, one can often observe sporadic false detections that last only one or two frames or detected traffic lights can be missed for several frames mainly due to motion blur or due to LED traffic lights appearing too dark in some frames.

To deal with this problem we introduce a simple tracking by detection algorithm to enforce temporal consistency. The traffic lights are detected separately in each frame and then the detections from two subsequent frames are matched based on the distance between them. This allows us to determine the number of frames each traffic lights has been tracked and only traffic lights that were already seen in at least three frames are counted as detected.

4   Results

We evaluate our method on three challenging datasets in both day and night situations and present a comparison with two related works. Furthermore, we evaluate the influence of the different steps of our method and its runtime.

4.1   Datasets

We use the publicly available dataset of [4] which is recorded at day in Paris and has a length of around 17 min and manually labeled bounding boxes in each frame. Since there is no fixed training and testing split we perform a 3-fold cross-validation. In the rest of the section we refer to this dataset as *France Day*.

We also created two additional datasets in order to analyze the performance of our method at day and nighttime. We used a 1 megapixel camera taking images at 16 frames per second mounted behind the windscreen of a vehicle. We defined a city route in Germany with a length of around 17 km, which contains 57 intersections with traffic lights ranging from side streets to big multi-lane streets. The recordings were done both on a sunny day and at night. All traffic lights have been labeled with bounding boxes around the 3 lights for the day scenes and around the illuminated light only for the night scenes, if the light source is bigger than 5 pixels in the camera image. We refer to these datasets as *Germany Day* and *Germany Night* respectively. Because of the small number of yellow traffic lights in all of the datasets, they are ignored during evaluation.

4.2   Comparison to Related Methods

Two of the related methods [4,23] have published results on the complete *France Day* dataset so that we can perform a quantitative comparison.

Although the authors of [4] use precision and recall as benchmark measure, they define a computation rule based on temporal tracks instead of frames. This means that one physical traffic light is counted as correctly detected if it is detected in at least one frame during its lifetime. Since our method is able to detect 33 of the 34 traffic lights in at least one of the frames (we also consider the partially occluded ones), the recall of our method is 97.1 %, while the authors of [4, 23] report 97.7 % and 93.8 % respectively. Unfortunately, the authors of [4] do not give precise description of how they compute the precision measure. For details about the false positive detections of our method we refer to our frame based precision in the next section.

4.3 Method Analysis

Semantic Segmentation. For the training of the semantic segmentation method all bounding boxes are first converted into pixel-wise labels on the active light spot of the traffic light. The performance of the three segmentation steps is measured according to the percentage of pixels labeled correctly as BACK-GROUND or CANDIDATE. While this does not directly translate to detection rate for the traffic lights, because some traffic light regions could be only partially segmented, it is a very good indicator.

From the quantitative results shown in Fig. 6 we see that with every step in the pipeline the number of pixels labeled as traffic lights ("Coverage") decreases significantly, while our semantic segmentation method is able to retain almost all of the real traffic lights ("Traffic lights"). While the *Germany Day* dataset is more challenging for the simple color segmentation due to the big variety of traffic lights and illumination conditions because of the sunny weather, the region segmentation step achieves results similar to those of the other datasets.

Candidates Verification. The tracks based recall measure used by the authors of the *France Day* dataset [4] is not suitable for many functions that need a stable tracking of the traffic lights while approaching the intersection, like for example red light warning or autonomous breaking. Therefore, we employ a frame based measure of recall and accuracy, which are more natural for the mentioned functions.

The quantitative results on all three datasets are summarized in Table 2 with our method achieving similar performance in all scenarios. Figures 4 and 5 show some example detections. The tracker is an essential step to reduce the amount of false positives both at day and at night, because they tend to appear only for short periods of time.

System Runtime. Semantic segmentation methods can be slow in general, since they need to classify each image pixel. Our three-step semantic segmentation approach, however, filters out many of the pixels in the first step, so that the more expensive texture analysis is performed only on the relevant image parts.

The total runtime of our method is 65 ms per frame, with the semantic segmentation accounting for 92 % of it. All experiments were performed on a machine with 2 Intel Xeon X5690 processors running at 3.5 GHz. The code is written in C++ without the use of SSE instructions and is only partially parallelized.

Table 2. Quantitative results based on frame-wise recall and precision.

Stage	France Day		Germany Day		Germany Night	
	Recall	Precision	Recall	Precision	Recall	Precision
Without tracking	76.1%	63.3%	91.6%	61.3%	91.5%	57.4%
With tracking	71.7%	73.2%	84.3%	71.5%	84.4%	73.8%

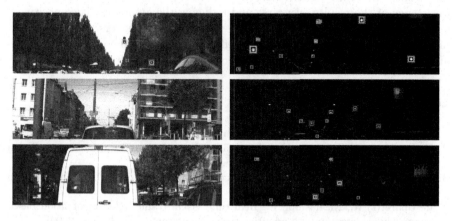

Fig. 4. Results from *Germany Day* and *Germany Night*. The candidates are shown in cyan, the confirmed detections in red or green and the ground truth with a dashed bounding box. The last row shows typical false positive detections (Color figure online).

Fig. 5. Results from *France Day* [4]. The candidates are shown in cyan, the confirmed detections in red or green and the ground truth with a dashed bounding box (Color figure online).

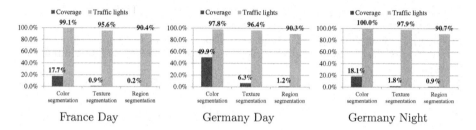

Fig. 6. Results of the 3 steps of the segmentation stage showing the percentage of all image pixels labeled as candidates and the correctly classified traffic light pixels.

5   Conclusion

In this paper, we presented a unified machine learning framework for traffic light detection at different lighting conditions. The used powerful semantic segmentation method is able to provide robust candidates both at day and at night by analyzing the image structure. We also describe several geometric and color features that are used to reject false candidates and to classify the color of the traffic light. An additional tracking by detection step is important for enforcing consistency of the results over time and reducing the amount of false positives.

We showed that our method runs in real-time and delivers good results on three challenging datasets recorded in different illumination conditions and containing data from more than 100 intersections with multiple traffic lights.

References

1. Traffic Safety Facts 2008. National Highway Traffic Safety Administration (2008)
2. Fachserie. 8, Verkehr. 7, Verkehrsunfälle. Statistisches Bundesamt Wiesbaden (2013)
3. Cai, Z., Li, Y., Gu, M.: Real-time recognition system of traffic light in urban environment. In: CISDA (2012)
4. de Charette, R., Nashashibi, F.: Real time visual traffic lights recognition based on spot light detection and adaptive traffic lights templates. In: IV (2009)
5. Chiang, C.C., Ho, M.C., Liao, H.S., Pratama, A., Syu, W.C.: Detecting and recognizing traffic lights by genetic approximate ellipse detection and spatial texture layouts. Int. J. Innovative Comput. Inf. Control 17, 6919–6934 (2011)
6. Diaz-Cabrera, M., Cerri, P.: Traffic light recognition during the night based on fuzzy logic clustering. In: Moreno-Díaz, R., Pichler, F., Quesada-Arencibia, A. (eds.) EUROCAST. LNCS, vol. 8112, pp. 93–100. Springer, Heidelberg (2013)
7. Diaz-Cabrera, M., Cerri, P., Sanchez-Medina, J.: Suspended traffic lights detection and distance estimation using color features. In: ITS (2012)
8. Fairfield, N., Urmson, C.: Traffic light mapping and detection. In: ICRA (2011)
9. Fan, B., Lin, W., Yang, X.: An efficient framework for recognizing traffic lights in night traffic images. In: CISP (2012)
10. Franke, U., Pfeiffer, D., Rabe, C., Knoeppel, C., Enzweiler, M., Stein, F., Herrtwich, R.G.: Making bertha see. In: ICCV Workshop on Computer Vision for Autonomous Driving (2013)
11. Gomez, A., Alencar, F., Prado, P., Osorio, F., Wolf, D.: Traffic lights detection and state estimation using hidden markov models. In: IV (2014)
12. Gong, J., Jiang, Y., Xiong, G., Guan, C., Tao, G., Chen, H.: The recognition and tracking of traffic lights based on color segmentation and camshift for intelligent vehicles. In: IV (2010)
13. Haltakov, V., Unger, C., Ilic, S.: Geodesic pixel neighborhoods for multi-class image segmentation. In: BMVC (2014)
14. Hel-Or, Y., Hel-Or, H.: Real time pattern matching using projection kernels. In: ICCV (2003)
15. Insurance Institute for Highway Safety (IIHS): Status Report, vol. 42, no. 1. Rep. IIHS (2007). http://www.iihs.org/externaldata/srdata/docs/sr4201.pdf

16. Jang, C., Kim, C., Kim, D., Lee, M., Sunwoo, M.: Multiple exposure images based traffic light recognition. In: IV (2014)
17. Kim, H.K., Shin, Y.N., Kuk, S.G., Park, J.H., Jung, H.Y.: Night-time traffic light detection based on SVM with geometric moment features. World Acad. Sci. Eng. Technol. **7**, 454–457 (2013)
18. Kim, Y., Kim, K., Yang, X.: Real time traffic light recognition system for color vision deficiencies. In: ICMA (2007)
19. Li, J.: An efficient night traffic light recognition method. J. Inf. Comput. Sci. **10**(9), 2773–2781 (2013)
20. Lindner, F., Kressel, U., Kaelberer, S.: Robust recognition of traffic signals. In: IV (2004)
21. Omachi, M., Omachi, S.: Traffic light detection with color and edge information. In: ICCSIT (2009)
22. Shen, Y., Ozguner, U., Redmill, K., Liu, J.: A robust video based traffic light detection algorithm for intelligent vehicles. In: IV (2009)
23. Siogkas, G., Skodras, E., Dermatas, E.: Traffic lights detection in adverse conditions using color, symmetry and spatiotemporal information. In: VISAPP 2012 (2012)
24. Tae-Hyun, H., In-Hak, J., Seong-Ik, C.: Detection of traffic lights for vision-based car navigation system. In: Chang, L.-W., Lie, W.-N. (eds.) PSIVT 2006. LNCS, vol. 4319, pp. 682–691. Springer, Heidelberg (2006)
25. Torralba, A., Murphy, K.P., Freeman, W.T.: Sharing visual features for multiclass and multiview object detection. PAMI **29**(5), 854–869 (2007)
26. Wang, C., Jin, T., Yang, M., Wang, B.: Robust and real-time traffic lights recognition in complex urban environments. Int. J. Comput. Intell. Syst. **4**(6), 1383–1390 (2011)
27. Wojek, C., Schiele, B.: A dynamic conditional random field model for joint labeling of object and scene classes. In: Forsyth, D., Torr, P., Zisserman, A. (eds.) ECCV 2008, Part IV. LNCS, vol. 5305, pp. 733–747. Springer, Heidelberg (2008)

Pose Estimation and Shape Retrieval with Hough Voting in a Continuous Voting Space

Viktor Seib[✉], Norman Link, and Dietrich Paulus

Active Vision Group (AGAS), University of Koblenz-Landau,
Universitaetsstr. 1, 56070 Koblenz, Germany
{vseib,nlink,paulus}@uni-koblenz.de
http://agas.uni-koblenz.de

Abstract. In this paper we present a method for 3D shape classification and pose estimation. Our approach is related to the recently popular adaptations of Implicit Shape Models to 3D data, but differs in some key aspects. We propose to omit the quantization of feature descriptors in favor of a better descriptiveness of training data. Additionally, a continuous voting space, in contrast to discrete Hough spaces in state of the art approaches, allows for more stable classification results under parameter variations. We evaluate and compare the performance of our approach with recently presented methods. The proposed algorithm achieves best results on three challenging datasets for 3D shape retrieval.

1 Introduction

Traditionally, 2D images form the basis for the developed algorithms in object recognition and image classification tasks. However, with the development of low-cost consumer RGB-D cameras and 3D printers 3D data can be generated and processed by anyone. It is likely that 3D shape databases will emerge in the near future, where models need to be classified or retrieved. New approaches need to take this trend into account and handle data from these new imaging modalities.

A viable way seems to be the adaption of successful approaches from 2D data. One of the most successful and widely used methods for visual categorization is the bag-of-words or bag-of-keypoints approach [6]. Several extensions of this approach to handle 3D data were proposed [16,18,24]. Algorithms based on the bag-of-words approach usually do not use the spatial relations between features. However, studies show that taking into account spatial relation between features improves results [3,22].

Apart from improving classification results, a great benefit of considering spatial relations of features lies in the ability to estimate the pose and localize objects in cluttered scenes. This is exploited by Leibe et al. in the Implicit Shape Model (ISM) formulation [14,15]. Recently, extensions of the ISM approach to 3D data have been proposed [13,19,20,27]. Inspired by these work we present a novel approach for 3D shape retrieval and classification using Hough voting that is closely related to Implicit Shape Models.

© Springer International Publishing Switzerland 2015
J. Gall et al. (Eds.): GCPR 2015, LNCS 9358, pp. 458–469, 2015.
DOI: 10.1007/978-3-319-24947-6_38

In this paper we make the following contributions: Unlike approaches in related work, we do not construct a dictionary of codewords, but rather use the features as they are to achieve higher discriminativity. We compare the obtained results with codebooks of different sizes to support our approach. Since in the proposed method no codebook is created, generalization from learned shapes is achieved by a k-NN activation strategy during classification (instead of training as in many approaches). Further, contrary to many ISM approaches we uniformly sample key points on input data instead of using a key point detector of salient points. The benefits of this strategy have been shown to improve classification rates compared to salient points [9]. Finally, we evaluate different vote weighting strategies and additionally show that weighted votes are sufficient to accurately estimate the pose of detected objects.

In the following Section we review related work on previous ISM extensions to 3D data. In Sects. 3 and 4 we present our approach in detail. An extensive evaluation on various datasets and comparison with state of the art approaches is given in Sect. 5 and a discussion in Sect. 6. Finally, Sect. 7 concludes the paper and gives an outlook to our ongoing and future work.

2 Related Work

Leibe et al. first introduced the concept of Implicit Shape Models (ISM) in [14]. They group key points into visually similar clusters, the so called *codewords*. Each codeword is associated with vectors from positions of the clustered features to the object's center. These vectors are referred to as *activation vectors*, while the set of codewords is called *codebook*. For recognition, the ISM is employed in a probabilistic framework based on a Generalized Hough Transform [1]. Each codeword that is matched with image descriptors casts a number of votes for a possible object location into a voting space. Finally, object locations are acquired by analyzing the voting space for maxima using Mean-shift mode estimation [4].

While the general scheme is the same for 3D data, feature descriptors representing the geometry of the local key point neighborhood are applied [13,26]. Knopp et al. [13] use 3D-SURF as descriptor which allows for a scale invariant feature representation. As a heuristic, the number of clusters is set to 10 % of the number of input features. To account for feature-specific variations, Knopp et al. introduced a weighted voting scheme. Votes are cast into a discrete 5D voting space (3D object position, scale and class). In a subsequent work, Knopp et al. [12] discuss approaches to implement rotation invariant object recognition.

Contrary to Knopp et al., Salti et al. [19] claim that scale invariance does not need to be taken care of, since 3D sensors provide metric data. In their approach Salti et al. use the SHOT descriptor [26] and investigate which combinations of clustering and codebook creation methods are best for 3D object classification. Salti et al. report best results when no clustering is used and all features are stored. Further, Salti et al. propose to omit vote weighting as it does not show significant benefits in their experiments. Considering this results, Tombari and Di Stefano [25] continue their work without clustering and vote weighting. In their proposed method Hough voting achieves promising results for 3D object recognition with occlusion in cluttered scenes.

A more recent approach presented by Wittrowski et al. [27] uses ray voting in Hough space. Like in other ISM adaptations to 3D a discrete voting space is used. However, in this approach bins are represented by spheres which form directional histograms towards the object's center. This voting scheme proves very efficient with an increasing number of training data.

Our previous work [20] where we use a continuous voting space confirms the results of Salti et al. that omitting feature quantization in 3D leads to better classification results. However, in [20] the quantization experiments were performed only on a small dataset. Thus, in this work we provide further analysis on a bigger dataset and employ a k-NN matching strategy which was not used in [20].

3   Learning Object Representations

The main difference between the algorithm proposed here and the Implicit Shape Model formulation from related work such as [13,20] and also bag-of-features approaches [24] is the lack of feature clustering, to allow for a more precise object representation.

In a first step, consistently oriented normals are computed on the models with the method proposed by Hoppe et al. [11]. Subsequently, key points are densely sampled and a SHOT descriptor is calculated around each key point in the determined local reference frame. The local reference frame for feature f is stored as rotation matrix R^f.

For each feature, a vector pointing from the feature to the object's centroid is stored, in the following referred to as *center vector*. First, the key point positions have to be transferred from global coordinates into an object centered coordinate frame. For this purpose a minimum volume bounding box (MVBB) of the object is calculated as described by Har-Peled [10] and Barequet and Har-Peled [2]. The estimated bounding box is determined by the direction between the two most distant points of the object, $\boldsymbol{p}_i$ and $\boldsymbol{p}_j$, and the minimum box enclosing the point set. The resulting MVBB B is given by the size $\boldsymbol{s}^B = \boldsymbol{p}_i - \boldsymbol{p}_j$ and the center position $\boldsymbol{p}^B = \boldsymbol{p}_i + \frac{\boldsymbol{s}^B}{2}$. The bounding box is stored with the training data and is used later to estimate the pose of the detected object. The object's position is now given by $\boldsymbol{p}^B$ as the center of B. The relative feature position $\boldsymbol{v}_{\text{rel}}^f$ is then given in relation to the object position $\boldsymbol{p}^B$ by

$$\boldsymbol{v}_{\text{rel}}^f = \boldsymbol{p}^B - \boldsymbol{p}^f \tag{1}$$

and represents the vector pointing from $\boldsymbol{p}^f$, the location on the object where the feature was detected, to the object's center. In order to provide rotation invariance, each feature was associated with a unique and repeatable reference frame given by a rotation matrix R^f. Transforming the vector $\boldsymbol{v}_{\text{rel}}^f$ from the global into the local reference frame is then achieved by

$$\boldsymbol{v}^f = R^f \cdot \boldsymbol{v}_{\text{rel}}^f. \tag{2}$$

We obtain $\boldsymbol{v}^f$, the translation vector from the feature location to the object center in relation to the feature-specific local reference frame. Thus, $\boldsymbol{v}^f$ provides a position and rotation independent representation of a feature f.

The final data pool after training contains all features that were computed on the training models. Along with each feature, the center vector, a bounding box B and the class c of the trained object is stored.

4   Object Classification and Pose Estimation

To classify objects, features are detected on the input point cloud in the same manner as in the training stage. Matching detected features with the previously trained data pool yields a list of feature correspondences. The distance between learned feature descriptor f_l and detected feature descriptor f_d is determined by the distance function $d(f_l, f_d) = \|f_l - f_d\|_2$. The center vectors of the created correspondences are used to create hypotheses on object center locations in a continuous voting space (Fig. 1).

Please note that we omitted the vector quantization step during training to retain a higher number of features and reduce training time, since no high-dimensional clustering needs to be performed. In the classification step, each of the detected features is associated with the k best matching features in the learned data pool. Thus, we effectively move the feature generalization step from training to detection. This procedure has the advantage of a generalized feature matching while having a broad data pool for each object class. The degree of generalization is controlled by the parameter k and can be changed without retraining. While this parameter is also applied in approaches from related work, matching is performed with a clustered codebook which has a lower descriptiveness as was shown in [19, 20].

During training, the center vector $\boldsymbol{v}^f_{\mathrm{rel}}$ of feature f has been rotated into the feature's local reference frame given by the rotation matrix R^f as shown in Eq. (2). Now the rotation is reversed by the inverse rotation matrix $R^{f-1} = R^{fT}$ computed from feature f on the scene, resulting in the back rotated vector $\hat{\boldsymbol{v}}^f_{\mathrm{rel}}$. This vector is used to create an object hypothesis at position $\boldsymbol{x}$ relative to the position $\boldsymbol{p}^f$ of the detected feature f:

$$\boldsymbol{x} = \boldsymbol{p}^f + \hat{\boldsymbol{v}}^f_{\mathrm{rel}}. \tag{3}$$

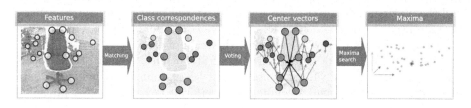

Fig. 1. Features are matched with the k closest learned features. Center vectors form hypotheses for object locations. Clusters in the voting space are detected by searching for maximum density regions.

To reduce the dimensionality of the voting space the object's rotation is ignored in this step. Further, a separate voting space for each class reduces the voting space dimensionality to three, namely the 3D position of the hypotheses.

Optionally, each point in the voting space can be assigned a weight. However, there is on open debate of whether or not vote weighting should be used [19] and different strategies are applied (e.g. two weights in [13] and three weights in [20]). In Sect. 5 we report our results on two different weighting strategies. We compare uniform weighting (i.e. no weighting) and weighting votes by their likelihood

$$w = \frac{1}{\sqrt{2\pi\sigma^2}} \exp\left(-\frac{\mathrm{d}(f_\mathrm{l}, f_\mathrm{d})^2}{2\sigma^2}\right). \tag{4}$$

Here, f_l is the learned feature descriptor and f_d the detected feature descriptor. The value σ^2 is class specific and is determined during training by the sample covariance. Given F_c, the set of features detected on all training models for a class c, the sample mean of distances is computed by

$$\mu_c = \frac{1}{M^2} \sum_{i=1}^{M} \sum_{j=1}^{M} \mathrm{d}(f_i, f_j) \tag{5}$$

over all features $f \in F_c$, where $M = \|F_c\|$ is the number of training features for class c. The final value of σ_c^2 is then computed as the sample covariance

$$\sigma_c^2 = \frac{1}{M^2 - 1} \sum_{i=1}^{M} \sum_{j=1}^{M} (\mathrm{d}(f_i, f_j) - \mu_c)^2. \tag{6}$$

4.1 Maxima Extraction

To avoid issues arising from discrete Hough spaces we implemented a continuous voting space for each object class. Each voting space can be seen as a sparse representation of a probability density function. Maxima in the probability density function are detected using the Mean-shift algorithm described by Fukunaga and Hostetler [8]. We use the Mean-shift formulation by Comaniciu and Meer [5] and account for weighted votes as proposed by Cheng [4].

Given a point $x \in \mathbb{R}^3$, the Mean-shift algorithms applies a Gaussian kernel K to all neighboring points x_i within the kernel bandwidth. Since we search for maxima in the voting space, the data points x_i are the individual votes. To find the maximum density regions, the gradient $m_{h,g}$ of the probability density function needs to be estimated. The step size is computed adaptively. Maxima are obtained by iteratively following the direction of $m_{h,g}$.

To create seed points for the Mean-shift algorithm a regular grid is superimposed on the data. Each cell containing at least a minimum number of data points creates a seed point. A pruning step performs non-maximum suppression to eliminate duplicate maxima. The final probability for the detected maximum at x_{max} is given by the kernel density estimation at the maximum position in the voting space.

4.2   Pose Estimation

When casting votes into the Hough space the associated bounding boxes are transferred back into the global coordinate system using the corresponding local reference frame for the current feature. After maxima detection yields the most likely object hypotheses all votes that contributed to a hypothesis and lie around the maximum location within the kernel bandwidth are collected.

This results in a list of bounding box hypotheses weighted with the corresponding vote weight. Estimation of the bounding box is performed by creating an average bounding box based on the collected votes. While the size can be averaged, computing an average weighted rotation is more complex. The rotation matrix is converted into a quaternion representation. Averaging quaternions is achieved by computing the 4×4 scatter matrix

$$M = \sum_{i=1}^{N} \omega_i q_i q_i^T \qquad (7)$$

over all quaternions q_i and their associated weights ω_i. After computing the eigenvalues and eigenvectors of M, the eigenvector with the highest eigenvalue corresponds to the weighted average quaternion [17]. Together with the position in the voting space, this quaternion defines the 6 DOF pose of the object.

5   Experiments and Results

In this paper we use the following datasets for evaluation (example objects from each dataset are shown in Fig. 2):

1. Aim@Shape-Watertight (ASW): This dataset consists of 400 shapes in 20 different categories. The first 10 objects of each category are used for training, the remaining 10 for testing. In [27] evaluation was performed on a partial dataset (here denoted as ASWp) that consisted of 19 different categories.
2. Princeton Shape Benchmark (PSB) [21]: This dataset consists of 1814 shapes and different levels of class granularity. For better comparison with other approaches we use the class granularity named *coarse 2* (7 classes), with half of the shapes assigned for training and the other half for testing.
3. SHREC'09 (SH) [7]: This dataset from the Partial Shape Retrieval Contest has 720 objects divided into 40 classes and used for training. Classification is performed on 20 partial query shapes.
4. Stanford 3D Scanning Repository (SSR) [23]: 6 models from this dataset were used to build up 45 scenes of 3 to 5 models in [26]. The models were randomly rotated and translated, ground truth is provided. We use this dataset to evaluate the accuracy of pose estimation of our approach.

All of these datasets are available as mesh files. We converted the meshes to point clouds and scaled each model to the unit circle for shape classification.

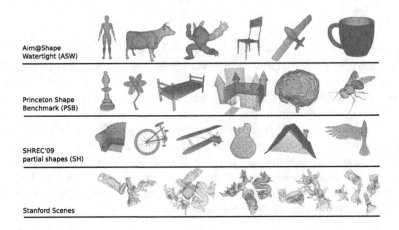

Fig. 2. Examples for the variety of different shapes in the used datasets.

5.1 Shape Classification

For shape classification, each test scene consisted of a single shape without any clutter - a typical classification task for shape retrieval as might occur if shapes need to be found in a database. Evaluation was performed on previously unseen instances with a continuous and a discrete voting space. Each detected feature was matched with the $k \in \{1,\ldots 5\}$ closest ones from the learned dataset to simulate different degrees of generalization. In all experiments a bandwidth of 0.5 m (half the object radius), a SHOT support radius of 0.3 m as well as the two vote weighting strategies were used (no weights and likelihood weights). The highest ranked hypothesis per object was taken as classification result.

Table 1. Comparison of our classification results with state of the art approaches (correct classification rate). The proposed approach outperforms previous methods on all evaluated datasets.

	Salti et al. [19]	Wittrowski et al. [27]	Seib et al. [20]	Liu et al. [16]	Toldo et al. [24]	Knopp et al. [13]	Proposed approach
ASW	79 %	-	80.5 %	-	-	-	**85.0 %**
ASWp	81 %	82 %	82.6 %	-	-	-	**86.8 %**
PSB	50.2 %	-	-	55 %	52 %	58.3 %	**61.7 %**
SH	-	-	-	-	60 %	40 %	**70.0 %**

Table 1 compares our best results with approached that use the same partitions in training and testing data as we do. The rightmost column shows that the proposed method outperforms current state of the art approaches on all tested datasets. An overview over all our results is given in Fig. 3(a)–(c). In general,

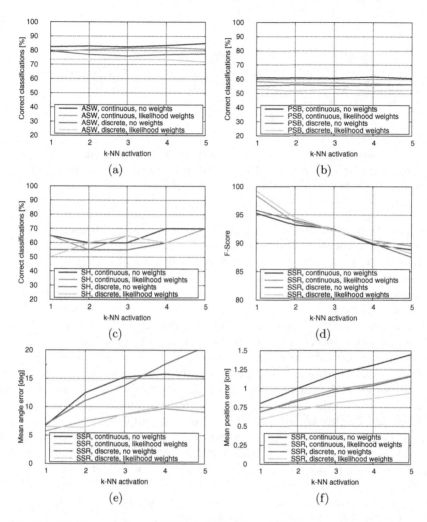

Fig. 3. Classification rates on ASW (a), PSB (b) and SH (c) datasets and the f-score (d), mean angle errors (e) and mean position errors (f) on SSR dataset are shown.

when classification is performed on full 3D models (ASW and PSB), the continuous voting space leads to better results. For both types of voting spaces, not using any vote weighting achieves higher classification rates. However, with partial shapes (SH) the results are not as clear as with full 3D models. Still, on average the continuous voting space performs better than the discrete one. Best classification rates were achieved with $k = 4$ or $k = 5$ on all datasets.

5.2   Pose Estimation

Pose estimation was tested on the SSR dataset. Additionally, we tested the ability of the algorithm to classify known objects in scenes. This is a particularly

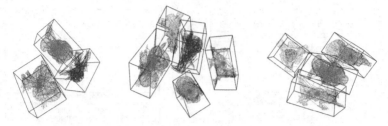

Fig. 4. Pose estimation on scenes from the SSR dataset. Object centers are shown as red dots inside the bounding box. The colored lines represent votes that contributed to the detected maximum (Color figure online).

different task than shape classification. In this case several maxima need to be considered and a meaningful threshold needs to be defined determining which maxima should be discarded. Further, if the bandwidth parameter is set too low, true maxima are split resulting in false positive object detections. Consequently, in these experiments we report the f-score instead of the true classification rate.

The complete scenes were scaled to the unit circle and we set the SHOT radius to 3 cm for these experiments. The bandwidth and bin size were set to 0.2 m and 0.4 m, respectively. The results are reported in Fig. 3(d)–(f). Example pose estimations are shown in Fig. 4.

The resulting f-score is best for $k = 1$ activation, where both voting spaces perform better with weighted votes. For all other values for k no significant differences between the voting spaces or weighting strategies are observed.

Since vote weights are used to filter out outliers, applying likelihood weights leads to lower angular and position errors than the not weighted counterparts in the corresponding voting spaces. While the continuous voting space seems to perform worse regarding the mean position error, with higher k both voting space designs have higher errors. This is also true for the angular error, however, the errors seem to stabilize around $k = 3$ for the continuous voting space, while they continue to rise for the discrete voting space.

6   Discussion

As was shown in Sect. 5, the proposed approach achieves higher classification rates on the tested datasets than the state of the art. These results stem from omitting the vector quantization and instead using k-NN feature activation during classification. Additionally, a dense key point sampling leads to a better object representation than salient key point detection as in many approaches in related work.

However, this huge amount of additional features comes at the price of higher runtime during object classification. We therefore investigated the influence of codebook creation on the classification performance and runtime of the algorithm. These experiments were performed on the Aim@Shape Watertight

dataset. Training was performed multiple times and a different number of feature clusters were created. The number of clusters was set to 100 % (no clustering), 70 %, 50 % and 30 % of the number of all extracted features. Subsequently,
classification was performed with each of these codebooks using the parameters
that led to best classification results in Sect. 5 (SHOT radius of 0.3 m and $k = 5$). The results are reported in Table 2 and clearly show that smaller codebook
sizes lead to a significant loss in the ability of the algorithm to correctly classify
objects. At the same time the runtime of the algorithm also decreases. However,
the gain in runtime is not as high as one might expect from the reduction of the
codebook size. This is due to the fact that a lot of runtime is used for feature
extraction and computation, while the feature matching is performed in a very
efficient way.

Table 2. Influence of different codebooks on the classification rate and runtime on the
Aim@Shape Watertight dataset

Clustering factor in codebook	Classification rate	Classification time per object [s]	Relative classification time per object
1.0 (no clustering)	85 %	18.4	1
0.7	77 %	14.1	0.77
0.5	70 %	13.5	0.73
0.3	60 %	14.4	0.78

7   Conclusion and Outlook

The presented approach enables us to detect and classify objects in scenes as
well as determine their classes. This is supported by the good results obtained in
our shape classification experiments. We showed that the choice of a continuous
voting space is superior to a discrete Hough space in terms of 3D object classification. The results obtained on the three challenging shape retrieval datasets
Aim@Shape Watertight, the Princeton Shape Benchmark and SHREC'09 outperform current state of the art approaches. We attribute these results to the use
of the continuous voting space without feature clustering, the dense key point
sampling and k-NN matching during classification.

In estimating the object's pose, both voting space designs perform similar.
However, when vote weighting is used to remove outliers the errors decrease
compared to not weighted votes. Specifically for the angular errors the continuous
voting space is superior to the discrete voting space for higher values of k in k-NN
activation.

It needs to be pointed out that the scenes in our evaluation consisted only
of known objects without any clutter. Our current work thus concentrates on
improving the robustness of the proposed method towards clutter and partial
models. We further plan to perform experiments with data from RGB-D cameras.

References

1. Ballard, D.H.: Generalizing the hough transform to detect arbitrary shapes. Pattern Recognit. **13**(2), 111–122 (1981)
2. Barequet, G., Har-Peled, S.: Efficiently approximating the minimum-volume bounding box of a point set in three dimensions. J. Algorithms **38**(1), 91–109 (2001)
3. Bronstein, A.M., Bronstein, M.M., Guibas, L.J., Ovsjanikov, M.: Shape google: geometric words and expressions for invariant shape retrieval. ACM Trans. Graph. (TOG) **30**(1), 1 (2011)
4. Cheng, Y.: Mean shift, mode seeking, and clustering. IEEE Trans. Pattern Anal. Mach. Intell. **17**(8), 790–799 (1995)
5. Comaniciu, D., Meer, P.: Mean shift: a robust approach toward feature space analysis. IEEE Trans. Pattern Anal. Mach. Intell. **24**(5), 603–619 (2002)
6. Csurka, G., Dance, C., Fan, L., Willamowski, J., Bray, C.: Visual categorization with bags of keypoints. In: Workshop on Statistical Learning in Computer Vision, ECCV, vol. 1, pp. 1–2 (2004)
7. Dutagaci, H., Godil, A., Axenopoulos, A., Daras, P., Furuya, T., Ohbuchi, R.: Shrec'09 track: querying with partial models. In: Proceedings of the 2nd Eurographics Conference on 3D Object Retrieval, pp. 69–76. Eurographics Association (2009)
8. Fukunaga, K., Hostetler, L.D.: The estimation of the gradient of a density function, with applications in pattern recognition. IEEE Trans. Inf. Theory **21**(1), 32–40 (1975)
9. Gall, J., Lempitsky, V.: Class-specific hough forests for object detection. In: IEEE Conference on Computer Vision and Pattern Recognition, CVPR 2009, pp. 1022–1029, June 2009
10. Har-Peled, S.: A practical approach for computing the diameter of a point set. In: Proceedings of the Seventeenth Annual Symposium on Computational Geometry, pp. 177–186 (2001)
11. Hoppe, H., DeRose, T., Duchamp, T., McDonald, J., Stuetzle, W.: Surface reconstruction from unorganized points. In: Proceedings of the 19th Annual Conference on Computer Graphics and Interactive Techniques, pp. 71–78 (1992)
12. Knopp, J., Prasad, M., Van Gool, L.: Orientation invariant 3d object classification using hough transform based methods. In: Proceedings of the ACM Workshop on 3D Object Retrieval, 3DOR 2010, pp. 15–20 (2010)
13. Knopp, J., Prasad, M., Willems, G., Timofte, R., Van Gool, L.: Hough transform and 3D SURF for robust three dimensional classification. In: Daniilidis, K., Maragos, P., Paragios, N. (eds.) ECCV 2010, Part VI. LNCS, vol. 6316, pp. 589–602. Springer, Heidelberg (2010)
14. Leibe, B., Leonardis, A., Schiele, B.: Combined object categorization and segmentation with an implicit shape model. In: Workshop on Statistical Learning in Computer Vision, ECCV 2004, pp. 17–32 (2004)
15. Leibe, B., Leonardis, A., Schiele, B.: Robust object detection with interleaved categorization and segmentation. Int. J. Comput. Vis. **77**(1–3), 259–289 (2008)
16. Liu, Y., Zha, H., Qin, H.: Shape topics: a compact representation and new algorithms for 3d partial shape retrieval. In: IEEE Computer Society Conference on Computer Vision and Pattern Recognition, 2006, vol. 2, pp. 2025–2032. IEEE (2006)

17. Markley, F.L., Cheng, Y., Crassidis, J.L., Oshman, Y.: Quaternion averaging. J. Guidance Control Dyn. **30**(4), 1193–1197 (2007)
18. Ohbuchi, R., Osada, K., Furuya, T., Banno, T.: Salient local visual features for shape-based 3d model retrieval. In: IEEE International Conference on Shape Modeling and Applications, SMI 2008, pp. 93–102. IEEE (2008)
19. Salti, S., Tombari, F., Di Stefano, L.: On the use of implicit shape models for recognition of object categories in 3D data. In: Kimmel, R., Klette, R., Sugimoto, A. (eds.) ACCV 2010, Part III. LNCS, vol. 6494, pp. 653–666. Springer, Heidelberg (2011)
20. Seib, V., Link, N., Paulus, D.: Implicit shape models for 3d shape classification with a continuous voting space. In: International Joint Conference on Computer Vision, Imaging and Computer Graphics Theory and Applications (2014)
21. Shilane, P., Min, P., Kazhdan, M., Funkhouser, T.: The princeton shape benchmark. In: Proceedings of Shape Modeling Applications, 2004, pp. 167–178. IEEE (2004)
22. Sivic, J., Zisserman, A.: Video google: a text retrieval approach to object matching in videos. In: Proceedings of Ninth IEEE International Conference on Computer Vision, 2003, pp. 1470–1477. IEEE (2003)
23. Stanford University Computer Graphics Laboratory: Stanford 3d scanning repository, November 2014. http://graphics.stanford.edu/data/3Dscanrep/
24. Toldo, R., Castellani, U., Fusiello, A.: A *Bag of Words* approach for 3D object categorization. In: Gagalowicz, A., Philips, W. (eds.) MIRAGE 2009. LNCS, vol. 5496, pp. 116–127. Springer, Heidelberg (2009)
25. Tombari, F., Di Stefano, L.: Object recognition in 3d scenes with occlusions and clutter by hough voting. In: Fourth Pacific-Rim Symposium on Image and Video Technology (PSIVT 2010), pp. 349–355. IEEE (2010)
26. Tombari, F., Salti, S., Di Stefano, L.: Unique signatures of histograms for local surface description. In: Daniilidis, K., Maragos, P., Paragios, N. (eds.) ECCV 2010, Part III. LNCS, vol. 6313, pp. 356–369. Springer, Heidelberg (2010)
27. Wittrowski, J., Ziegler, L., Swadzba, A.: 3d implicit shape models using ray based hough voting for furniture recognition. In: 2013 International Conference on 3DTV-Conference, pp. 366–373. IEEE (2013)

Fast Approximate GMM Soft-Assign for Fine-Grained Image Classification with Large Fisher Vectors

Josip Krapac[⊠] and Siniša Šegvić

Faculty of Electrical Engineering and Computing,
University of Zagreb, Zagreb, Croatia
josip.krapac@fer.hr

Abstract. We address two drawbacks of image classification with large Fisher vectors. The first drawback is the computational cost of assigning a large number of patch descriptors to a large number of GMM components. We propose to alleviate that by a generally applicable approximate soft-assignment procedure based on a balanced GMM tree. This approximation significantly reduces the computational complexity while only marginally affecting the fine-grained classification performance. The second drawback is a very high dimensionality of the image representation, which makes the classifier learning and inference computationally complex and prone to overtraining. We propose to alleviate that by regularizing the classification model with group Lasso. The resulting block-sparse models achieve better fine-grained classification performance in addition to memory savings and faster prediction. We demonstrate and evaluate our contributions on a standard fine-grained categorization benchmark.

1 Introduction

In this work we address fine-grained classification (FGC), a problem where the inter-class variance is small *w.r.t.* intra-class variance, *i.e.* the objects from different classes may be very similar. This is a challenging task since the differences between the categories can be subtle and may cover a very small part of the image. For example, a discriminating feature between two bird species can be a specific feather pattern around the eye. The more specialized the class, the less data for learning its class model we can expect, and the more challenging learning good class models becomes. In short, FGC relies on finding a few discriminative features in a very large feature pool using a small amount of images annotated only with class labels, which resembles searching for needle in a haystack.

Although large Fisher vectors have displayed state-of-the-art performance for several FGC tasks [7], their main drawback remains computational complexity. First, obtaining large Fisher vector representation involves costly assignment of a large number of patches to a large number of GMM components. Second, classifier learning and inference involves very high dimensional dense vectors. This may pose scalability problems when the number of classes is large.

© Springer International Publishing Switzerland 2015
J. Gall et al. (Eds.): GCPR 2015, LNCS 9358, pp. 470–480, 2015.
DOI: 10.1007/978-3-319-24947-6_39

Our contributions address both of these drawbacks. In practice each patch is assigned to a very small number of GMM components [18]. We exploit this to build a hierarchy over GMM components by agglomerative clustering [16]. This enables us to discard a large number of components early. GMM tree yields significant soft-assign speed up while mostly retaining classification performance. The technique is general since it does not require any labeled data, so it can be used *e.g.* in image retrieval. Second, we propose group-sparse classification models which are fast to train and evaluate, and have a small memory footprint. In addition, these models display significantly improved classification performance, especially when coupled with Fisher vector intra-normalization. We demonstrate the value of our contributions experimentally on the 14 category subset ("Birdlets") [5] of the Caltech-UCSD Birds 200-2011 dataset [22].

2   Related Work

Goldberger and Roweis [6] consider grouping of GMM components by an iterative regroup-refit procedure similar to the k-means clustering algorithm. The main idea is to find the grouping of original components into a smaller mixture model such that the KL divergence between the obtained smaller model and the original one is minimized. However, there is no guarantee that the obtained higher-level GMM will indeed speedup the soft-assign, since many lower-level components can be merged into a single higher-level component.

Simonyan *et al.* [19] used hard assignment to the closest GMM component in order to speed up Fisher vector computation. Although this procedure speeds up the computation of Fisher vector once the soft-assigns have been computed, it does not reduce the complexity of the soft-assign computation which is the most intensive part of Fisher vector computation.

Verbeek *et al.* [21] speed up the EM algorithm for large datasets by first clustering the data with a kd-tree, and then performing EM steps on the clusters instead of individual points. The combination of this approach and the one proposed here is an interesting avenue for speeding the soft-assign for a group of descriptors, since our contribution is able to speed up the soft-assign for a single descriptor.

Gosselin *et al.* [7] speed up large Fisher vector construction by discarding the patches whose SIFT descriptor norm is below a threshold. They show that this does not influence significantly the classification performance, while it reduces the computational complexity of Fisher vector computation. For the remaining SIFT descriptors they still have to perform computationally intensive soft-assign.

Approximate nearest neighbor methods (ANN) like product quantization [9] or locality-sensitive hashing [8] can be used to quickly short-list the components most responsible for generating the data point. However, in our case the number of the descriptors in the image is an order of magnitude larger than the number of the GMM components. Therefore it is difficult to obtain a good trade-off between feature coding time and quality of the recall of the GMM components. Additionally, ANN methods usually assume L_2 distance, while the GMM soft-assign requires computing the likelihood of a normal distribution, which corresponds to Mahalanobis distance.

Group-sparse classification models have been previously used for general object classification with bag-of-visual-words histograms [13], but to the best of our knowledge we are the first to report results of group-sparse classification models with Fisher vectors. We have previously used sparse classification models [11], but have not constrained them to be group-sparse. Instead, we have selected a predefined number of top components considering the norm of the corresponding part of the model vector. In this work, due to group-sparse regularizers, we are able to directly control the trade-off between the classification performance and the number of GMM components selected by the model.

The intra-component variant of Fisher vector normalization we use here is related to intra-normalization used in VLAD descriptor [1]. As noted in [1], this normalization is beneficial for reducing the influence of bursty visual elements on the image representation.

3   Fisher Vector Image Representation

We represent images with a set of densely sampled patches at a fixed grid and multiple scales [4]. This enables a good description of image content and invariance to scale changes, but it also usually results in a fairly large number N of patches per image. Each patch is described by a D-dimensional descriptor $\mathbf{x} \in \mathbb{R}^D$ invariant to local photometric and geometric transformations [14] and coded using a generative model of patch descriptors, which is usually a Gaussian mixture model (GMM):

$$p(\mathbf{x}|\Theta) = \sum_{k=1}^{K} \pi_k \mathcal{N}(\mathbf{x}|\mu_k, \boldsymbol{\Sigma}_k), \quad \pi_k = \frac{\exp(\alpha_k)}{\sum_{i=1}^{K} \exp(\alpha_i)} . \tag{1}$$

In the above equation, K is the number of components, while $\Theta = [\pi_k, \mu_k, \boldsymbol{\Sigma}_k]_{k=1}^{K}$ are GMM parameters. The parametrization of component weights $\boldsymbol{\pi} = \{\pi_k\}_{k=1}^{K}$ with $\boldsymbol{\alpha} = \{\alpha_k\}_{k=1}^{K}$ ensures that $\boldsymbol{\pi}$ sum to one. To reduce the number of GMM parameters we assume a diagonal $\boldsymbol{\Sigma}_k$ for all K components. The parameters are learned to maximize the training data likelihood using the EM algorithm. Each patch descriptor $\mathbf{x}$ is coded with a Fisher vector $\Phi(\mathbf{x})$ [18] that is a gradient of the GMM log-likelihood $w.r.t.$ the GMM parameters Θ:

$$\Phi(\mathbf{x}) = [\cdots \Phi_k(\mathbf{x}) \cdots] = [\cdots \nabla_{\alpha_k} \log p(\mathbf{x}|\Theta), \nabla_{\mu_k} \log p(\mathbf{x}|\Theta), \nabla_{\boldsymbol{\Sigma}_k^{-1}} \log p(\mathbf{x}|\Theta), \cdots]$$
$$= [\cdots \gamma_k(\mathbf{x}) - \pi_k, \gamma_k(\mathbf{x})\boldsymbol{\Sigma}_k^{-1}(\mathbf{x} - \mu_k), \gamma_k(\mathbf{x})(\boldsymbol{\Sigma}_k - (\mathbf{x} - \mu_k)^2), \cdots]. \tag{2}$$

In the Eq. (2) $\gamma_k(\mathbf{x}) = p(k|\mathbf{x})$ corresponds to the responsibility of component k for generating the descriptor $\mathbf{x}$, also known as the soft-assign of the descriptor $\mathbf{x}$ to the Gaussian component k:

$$\gamma_k(\mathbf{x}) = \frac{\pi_k \mathcal{N}(\mathbf{x}|\mu_k, \boldsymbol{\Sigma}_k)}{p(\mathbf{x}|\Theta)}. \tag{3}$$

Assuming independence of the image patches, we obtain the Fisher vector for the whole image $\mathbf{X} = \{\mathbf{x}_i\}_{i=1}^N$ as an average of patch Fisher vectors $\Phi(\mathbf{X}) = \sum_{i=1}^N \Phi(\mathbf{x}_i)/N$. The dimension of this representation is $(2D+1)K$. In the implementation we use the improved version of Fisher vector [17] which employs normalizations that significantly improve the classification performance.

To ensure that object's fine-grained class-specific parts remain identifiable even after aggregation of patch Fisher vectors into the image representation a large number of GMM components K is needed. This way a set of patch descriptors is embedded in a highly-dimensional vector space, in which a hyperplane defined by a linear classifier corresponds to a highly non-linear decision surface in the patch descriptor space. Therefore large Fisher vectors enable modeling of subtle image details, a requirement necessary for discrimination of very similar images.

4 Fast Approximated Soft-Assign Computation

Our main contribution is related to the fast computation of soft-assign Eq. (3). For each of N patches we need to compute the Mahalanobis distances to K components, required to compute the denominator of Eq. (3). Therefore the complexity of the soft-assign computation for N patches represented by D-dimensional vectors is $O(DKN)$. In practice only a small fraction of components is responsible for generation of a data point. This means that the Fisher vector encoding for each data point $\mathbf{x}$ will be block-sparse, since for many components $\Phi_k(\mathbf{x})$ will be zero.

We want to take advantage of this sparsity to speed up the soft-assign by discarding the components that are not likely to be responsible for generation of the data point. To this end we construct a hierarchy of GMM models by iteratively merging the components of the original flat GMM. This hierarchy enables us to concentrate, at each level of hierarchy, on a subset of top K_t most responsible components for generating the data point. Thus at each level of the GMM tree, the soft-assign computation for each data point requires $O(DK_t)$ operations.

GMM Tree Construction. Since our goal is to speed-up the soft-assign we concentrate on balanced binary trees. Clearly, this constraint produces a sub-optimal approximation of the considered GMM with a given number of components. However, it gives us theoretical guarantees in terms of expected speed-up, since the number of operations to compute soft-assign is the same for each data point, unlike [6]. We start from a large flat GMM whose soft-assign we want to speed up, and consider its components as the leaves of the tree. At each new level of the tree we create a new component (the parent node) by merging exactly two components at the lower level (children nodes). To determine the best two children nodes to merge, we first find the closest sibling of each child node in terms of KL divergence:

$$c(i) = \underset{j \in \{1...K\}/i}{\arg\min} \ d_{KL}(\theta_i, \theta_j) \tag{4}$$

$$d(i) = d_{KL}(\theta_i, \theta_{c(i)}). \tag{5}$$

There exists a closed-form solution for KL divergence between two normal distributions, so we can quickly determine the distances between the children nodes. We then greedily merge the closest children nodes, by first merging the child node i whose KL divergence $d(i)$ to the closest sibling $c(i)$ is the largest. Every time we merge the children nodes into the parent node we re-compute the closest siblings for the ones that are not yet merged. The main motivation for this procedure is to ensure that the newly created parent nodes do not overlap.

When merging the children nodes i and $j = c(i)$, we derive the parameters of the parent node m following [23]:

$$\pi_m = \pi_i + \pi_j \tag{6}$$

$$\pi_m \mu_m = \pi_i \mu_i + \pi_j \mu_j \tag{7}$$

$$\pi_m(\Sigma_m + \mu_m^\top \mu_m) = \pi_i(\Sigma_i + \mu_i^\top \mu_i) + \pi_j(\Sigma_j + \mu_j^\top \mu_j). \tag{8}$$

This construction does not produce optimal component pairings in the sense of minimizing the KL divergence between the GMMs at the two neighboring levels of binary tree. However, the procedure is very fast and gives very good results, as we demonstrate in the experimental section.

Fast Assignment. We use the GMM tree to perform the soft-assignment of patch descriptor $\mathbf{x}$ to the original GMM components that are the leaves of the GMM tree. Given a selected top number K_t of components we skip first $\log_2(K_t)+1$ levels of the tree, since at these levels the number of nodes is smaller than K_t. At each level we expand the K_t nodes of interest into $2K_t$ nodes at the next level. We subsequently select the top K_t nodes by considering the value of numerator in Eq. (3). We continue this procedure until we reach the bottom of the tree. The denominator of the expression Eq. (3) is then approximated by considering only K_t components selected by the tree. This way the complexity for each patch is reduced from $O(DK)$ to $O(DK_t \log_2(\frac{K}{K_t}))$, which significantly speeds up the computation of Fisher vectors. This fast assignment is illustrated in Fig. 1. The choice of K_t determines the trade-off between soft-assign speed up and the quality of the approximation.

5   Group-Sparse Models

In order to perform FGC, we learn a linear classifier $\mathbf{w}$ operating on the Fisher vector representation:

$$\mathbf{w}^* = \underset{\mathbf{w}}{\arg\min} \sum_{i=1}^{M} \ell(\mathbf{w}, \varPhi(\mathbf{X}_i), y_i) + \lambda \mathcal{R}(\mathbf{w}), \tag{9}$$

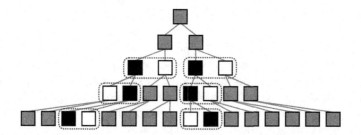

Fig. 1. The fast assignment procedure for $K = 16, K_t = 2$. The likelihood for the gray nodes is not evaluated. At each level we evaluate the likelihood of only $2K_t$ components (circled) and only top K_t components are expanded (black).

where $(\Phi(\mathbf{X}_i), y_i)_{i=1}^M$ is the training set of M image representations and class labels, ℓ is the loss function, $\mathcal{R}$ is the regularizer, while λ determines the compromise between the two. To enforce block sparsity, we employ group Lasso regularization $\mathcal{R}(\mathbf{w}) = \sum_{k=1}^K \|\mathbf{w}_k\|_2$, where $\mathbf{w}_k$ is the Fisher vector block of size $2D + 1$ corresponding to the kth GMM component. We use the logistic loss $\ell_{\log}(\mathbf{w}, \mathbf{x}, y) = \log(1 + \exp(-y\mathbf{w}^\top \mathbf{x}))$ which means that the optimization problem Eq. (9) is convex.

We assume that class-specific object parts correspond to small number of class-specific patches that lie in compact parts of the patch descriptor space. Fisher vector representation maps compact parts of the descriptor space into blocks of Fisher vector representation. The learned group-sparse discriminative model selects the GMM components corresponding to the class-specific features. Therefore these models are well suited for FGC, especially where scalability is needed, since the sparsity also enables fast model evaluation and small memory requirements.

6   Experiments

Dataset. We demonstrate our contributions on the 14-class subset [5] of Caltech-UCSD Birds 200-2011 birds dataset [22]. This subset consists of 7 classes of *Vireos* (Black-capped Vireo, Blue-headed Vireo, Philadelphia Vireo, Red-eyed Vireo, Warbling Vireo, White-eyed Vireo and Yellow-throated Vireo) and 7 classes of *Woodpeckers* (American Three-toed Woodpecker, Pileated Woodpecker, Red-bellied Woodpecker, Red-cockaded Woodpecker, Red-headed Woodpecker, Downy Woodpecker and Northern Flicker). There are 419 train and 398 test images, each split having around 30 images per class.

Parameters. We follow the standard Fisher vector classification pipeline: we use dense patch sampling at four scales following the procedure from [3] and describe the patches by SIFT [14] and color features of Perronnin et al. [17]. We used the VLFeat library [20] for computing SIFT descriptors. We reduce both SIFT and color features to 64 dimensions by PCA. For each feature type we select a random subset of 500000 features from the images in the training set and learn one GMM per feature type. We use the learned GMMs to obtain Fisher vectors, again one per feature type. We normalize the Fisher vectors using the power and metric normalizations, as suggested in [17]. We do not use spatial layout coding, although it is likely that such coding (e.g. SPM [12]) could improve classification results, especially when training data is enlarged by using mirrored images (image flips) and random crops. All our classification models are one *vs.* all logistic regression, learned with 1000 iterations of FISTA algorithm [2] implemented in SPAMS [15].

Results. Figure 2 shows the speedup and the quality of Fisher vectors with fast approximate soft-assign as we vary K_t. Increasing K_t gives a better approximation at the expense of a smaller speed-up. The speed-up is defined by the ratio of the time needed to compute the original Fisher vector and the time needed to compute its approximated version. Notice that the speedup can be very high

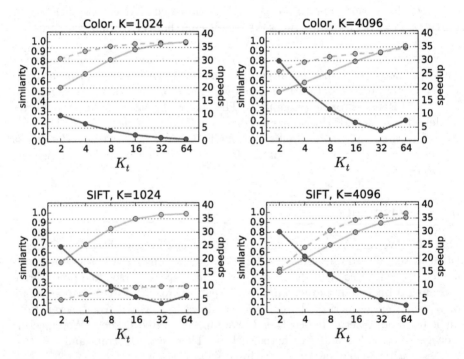

Fig. 2. Influence of the approximated soft-assign on the speedup and the approximation error measured as the dot product between the original Fisher vector and the approximated one. The magenta curves denote dot product between vectors (full: block-wise L_2 normalization, dotted: full L_2 normalization). The cyan curve displays the speedup achieved with top K_t components at each level of the GMM tree. Our approximation offers a trade-off between quality and the speed-up.

for smaller K_t because of the caching patterns employed by the CPU: the components in the higher levels of the tree that are queried more often could be kept the L1 cache. The quality of approximation is measured by the dot product between the original and the approximated Fisher vector normalized with their L_2 norm. We consider the full Fisher vector normalization and the block-wise (or intra-component [1]) normalization where we normalize Fisher vector blocks corresponding to GMM components.

The approximated Fisher vector is different from the original vector due to the errors in soft-assign approximation. The Fisher vector of the patch descriptor can "blow up" if the GMM tree does not give a correct prediction of the soft-assign. A couple of mis-assigned descriptors can significantly influence the Fisher vector of the image (*c.f.* SIFT features with $K = 1024$). Block-wise normalization ensures that the approximation errors influence only the Fisher vector blocks corresponding to the components whose responsibility is mis-predicted. This is another benefit of using blockwise normalization, in addition to reducing the influence of bursty visual elements [1]. With $K_t = 64$, for all considered cases, we obtain the Fisher vectors that are very close to original ones. Although we concentrate on image classification, these results suggest that the approximations could also be useful for image retrieval, *e.g.* for construction of the VLAD descriptor [10].

Next we show the influence of the Fisher vector approximations on classification performance measured by mean average precision (mAP). In these experiments we fix $\lambda = 10^{-4}$ to obtain sparse models, and to ensure that only the approximations influence the performance. Table 1 shows that classification performance is not significantly influenced for a wide range of approximations. For our best performing feature and vocabulary size (color features with $K = 1024$), when using only $K_t = 2$ we lose only 5.5 points of mAP compared to using Fisher vectors computed without approximations, while achieving 10x speedup. In all following experiments we report results on the approximated Fisher vec-

Table 1. Influence of approximated soft-assign on the classification performance, with metric intra-normalization and group Lasso regularization.

		Color				SIFT			
	K	1024		4096		1024		4096	
		mAP	speedup	mAP	speedup	mAP	speedup	mAP	speedup
K_t	2	51.08	9.70	46.08	29.90	37.52	24.58	32.99	30.09
	4	52.87	6.62	48.20	19.09	39.96	15.83	36.10	20.85
	8	54.50	4.03	51.25	11.88	42.60	9.83	39.28	14.06
	16	54.73	2.40	52.25	6.85	42.65	5.91	39.34	8.24
	32	55.00	1.39	54.32	3.86	43.30	3.52	40.15	4.58
	64	**56.00**	0.83	54.90	7.56	**43.44**	6.36	40.35	2.55
	Full	55.59	1	54.71	1	42.58	1	41.59	1

tors using $K_t = 16$, since this setting offers a good trade-off between obtained speedup and classification performance.

We also compare our performance to the Fisher vector baseline and show how block-wise normalization, sparsity-inducing regularization and use of approximations influence the classification performance (Table 2). Here we determine the hyper-parameter λ by two-fold cross-validation in the range of values $\log_{10}(\lambda) = [-4, -7]$. Our first experiment uses Fisher vectors obtained without approximations, with overall metric normalization and L_2 regularization. This is the standard Fisher vector representation, used also in [7]. Intra-component L_2 normalization achieves remarkable effects: the classification performance is improved by almost 10 percent points with color descriptors and 7 percent points with SIFT descriptors. The group Lasso regularization gives additional 5 percent points with color descriptors, while only marginally improving the classification performance with SIFT descriptors. When we use our approximated Fisher vectors, we obtain almost the same performance as with original Fisher vectors: marginally worse with color descriptors and marginally better with SIFT. We also tried learning the classifier on concatenation of color and SIFT Fisher vectors, but this resulted in slightly worse performance compared to using color features alone (53.54 % mAP).

Table 2. Influence of Fisher vector normalization, regularization and approximated soft-assign on the classification performance. Fast Fisher vectors were obtained with $K_t = 16$.

L_2 normalization	Regularization	Fast	Color	SIFT
full	L_2	No	41.67	35.18
intra-component	L_2	No	50.09	42.09
intra-component	group Lasso	No	55.83	42.67
intra-component	group Lasso	Yes	55.00	43.37

Finally, Table 3 shows per-class performance with a fixed $\lambda = 10^{-4}$ and when λ is cross-validated. We first notice that our performance is worse for *Vireos*, and that for these 7 classes the cross-validating λ results in non-sparse models. The classification performance for *Woodpeckers* is much better and almost all cross-validated models are sparse. When we fix λ to give more weight to the regularizer we obtain sparse models without significant drop in performance: 55.00 % mAP with cross-validated λ *vs.* 54.73 % mAP with the fixed λ. This setting is especially interesting when learning models for a large number of classes, since the obtained classification performance is almost the same, while the used modes are 2–4 times smaller. In addition to memory savings, the sparsity enables faster model learning and evaluation. When coupled with our approximations for Fisher vector computation, the group-sparsity allows skipping the computation of Fisher vectors for the descriptors generated by the GMM components discarded by the classification model.

Table 3. Per-class analysis of influence of sparsity on classification performance when using color features and $K = 1024$. The performance is measured by average precision (AP), while NNZ denotes the number of GMM components selected by the group sparse classification model. Enforcing sparsity only slightly degrades classification performance, while it yields 2-4x more compact models $w.r.t.$ to L_2 regularized models. The best results are obtained with group-sparse models (boldface).

Name	$\lambda = \lambda_{cv}$ AP	NNZ	$\lambda = 10^{-4}$ AP	NNZ	Name	$\lambda = \lambda_{cv}$ AP	NNZ	$\lambda = 10^{-4}$ AP	NNZ
BC	47.02	1024	**48.17**	403	AT	72.77	327	**72.77**	327
BH	25.83	1024	24.19	409	PW	64.56	292	**64.56**	292
P	32.90	1024	29.06	357	RB	88.89	242	**88.88**	242
RE	24.94	1020	**25.74**	374	RC	81.44	1015	80.54	311
W	21.79	1018	**22.43**	387	RH	84.74	251	**84.74**	251
WE	50.51	374	**50.51**	374	D	60.94	268	**60.94**	268
YT	46.54	252	**46.54**	252	NF	67.15	294	**67.15**	294

Vireos   Woodpeckers

7   Conclusion

We have proposed an approximate algorithm for fast soft-assignment of high-dimensional patterns to the components of a large GMM model. The proposed algorithm brings substantial speed-ups to the recovery of global image representations based on Fishers vectors, at the price of a tolerable (or even negligible) impact to the classification accuracy. Additionally, we have shown that a recent method for enforcing group sparsity may improve both the classification performance and the processing speed at the same time. Finally, we have shown that these sparse models achieve best results when the Fisher vectors are subjected to the metric intra-normalization, rather than the usual metric normalization across the whole vector.

These three contributions improve the classification performance in the fine-grained case, where only a small portion of the image allows to bring the decision about the image class. Experiments performed on the "Birdlets" dataset confirm substantial advantage over the baseline in terms of better performance classification performance and faster execution. The proposed method allows to choose a desired trade-off between the classification performance and the execution speed. Our best performing classification models achieved improvement of 14 points of mAP $w.r.t.$ the baseline while offering 2× increase in the execution speed. The most interesting direction for the future work is application of the presented contribution to more diverse classification datasets such as PASCAL VOC.

Acknowledgement. This work has been fully supported by Croatian Science Foundation under the project I-2433-2014.

References

1. Arandjelović, R., Zisserman, A.: All about VLAD. In: CVPR (2013)
2. Beck, A., Teboulle, M.: A fast iterative shrinkage-thresholding algorithm for linear inverse problems. SIAM J. Imaging Sci. **2**, 183–202 (2009)
3. Chatfield, K., Lempitsky, V., Vedaldi, A., Zisserman, A.: The devil is in the details: an evaluation of recent feature encoding methods. In: BMVC (2011)
4. Csurka, G., Dance, C.R., Fan, L., Willamowski, J., Bray, C.: Visual categorization with bags of keypoints. In: ECCV-WSLCV, pp. 1–22 (2004)
5. Farrell, R., Oza, O., Zhang, N., Morariu, V.I., Darrell, T., Davis, L.S.: Birdlets: Subordinate categorization using volumetric primitives and pose-normalized appearance. In: ICCV, pp. 161–168 (2011)
6. Goldberger, J., Roweis, S.: Hierarchical clustering of a mixture model. In: NIPS, pp. 505–512. MIT Press (2005)
7. Gosselin, P.H., Murray, N., Jégou, H., Perronnin, F.: Inria+Xerox@FGcomp: Boosting the Fisher vector for fine-grained classification. Technical report, INRIA/XRCE (2013)
8. Indyk, P., Motwani, R.: Approximate nearest neighbors: towards removing the curse of dimensionality. In: Proceedings of the 30th ACM Symposium on the Theory of Computing (STOC 1998), pp. 604–613 (1998)
9. Jégou, H., Douze, M., Schmid, C.: Product quantization for nearest neighbor search. PAMI **33**(1), 117–128 (2011)
10. Jégou, H., Douze, M., Schmid, C., Pérez, P.: Aggregating local descriptors into a compact image representation. In: CVPR (2010)
11. Krapac, J., Šegvić, S.: Weakly supervised object localization with large fisher vectors. In: VISAPP (2015)
12. Lazebnik, S., Schmid, C., Ponce, J.: Beyond bags of features: spatial pyramid matching for recognizing natural scene categories. In: CVPR (2006)
13. Liu, Y.: Image classification with group fusion sparse representation. In: ICME, pp. 568–573 (2012)
14. Lowe, D.G.: Distinctive image features from scale-invariant keypoints. IJCV **60**, 91–110 (2004)
15. Mairal, J., Jenatton, R., Bach, F.R., Obozinski, G.R.: Network flow algorithms for structured sparsity. In: NIPS (2009)
16. Murtagh, F., Contreras, P.: Algorithms for hierarchical clustering: an overview. Wiley Interdisc. Rew.: Data Min. Knowl. Disc. **2**(1), 86–97 (2012)
17. Perronnin, F., Sánchez, J., Mensink, T.: Improving the fisher kernel for large-scale image classification. In: Daniilidis, K., Maragos, P., Paragios, N. (eds.) ECCV 2010, Part IV. LNCS, vol. 6314, pp. 143–156. Springer, Heidelberg (2010)
18. Sánchez, J., Perronnin, F., Mensink, T., Verbeek, J.J.: Image classification with the fisher vector: theory and practice. IJCV **105**(3), 222–245 (2013)
19. Simonyan, K., Vedaldi, A., Zisserman, A.: Deep fisher networks for large-scale image classification. In: NIPS, pp. 163–171 (2013)
20. Vedaldi, A., Fulkerson, B.: VLFeat: An Open and Portable Library of Computer Vision Algorithms (2008). http://www.vlfeat.org
21. Verbeek, J.J., Nunnink, J., Vlassis, N.: Accelerated EM-based clustering of large data sets. Data Min. Knowl. Disc. **13**(3), 291–307 (2006)
22. Wah, C., Branson, S., Welinder, P., Perona, P., Belongie, S.: The Caltech-UCSD birds-200-2011 dataset. Technical report, California Institute of Technology (2011)
23. Zhang, Z., Chen, C., Sun, J., Chan, K.L.: EM algorithms for Gaussian mixtures with split-and-merge operation. Pattern Recognit. **36**(9), 1973–1983 (2003)

Regressor Based Estimation of the Eye Pupil Center

Necmeddin Said Karakoc$^{(\boxtimes)}$, Samil Karahan, and Yusuf Sinan Akgul

GTU Vision Lab, Gebze Technical University, 41400 Gebze, Kocaeli, Turkey
{said.karakoc, samilkarahan}@gmail.com,
akgul@gtu.edu.tr
http://vision.gyte.edu.tr

Abstract. The locations of the eye pupil centers are used in a wide range of computer vision applications. Although there are successful commercial eye gaze tracking systems, their practical employment is limited due to required specialized hardware and extra restrictions on the users. On the other hand, the precision and robustness of the off the shelf camera based systems are not at desirable levels. We propose a general purpose eye pupil center estimation method without any specialized hardware. The system trains a regressor using HoG features with the distance between the ground-truth pupil center and the center of the train patches. We found HoG features to be very useful to capture the unique gradient angle information around the eye pupils. The system uses a sliding window approach to produce a score image that contains the regressor estimated distances to the pupil center. The best center positions of two pupils among the candidate centers are selected from the produced score images. We evaluate our method on the challenging BioID and Columbia CAVE data sets. The results of the experiments are overall very promising and the system exceeds the precision of the similar state of the art methods. The performance of the proposed system is especially favorable on extreme eye gaze angles and head poses. The results of all test images are publicly available.

1 Introduction

Accurate estimation of the eye pupil center locations is crucial for many applications such as eye gaze estimation and tracking [1], human-machine interfaces [2], user attention estimation [3], and controlling devices for disabled people [4]. There are several types of methods for pupil center localization. One of these types uses specialized hardware such as head-mounted devices [5] or multiple near-infrared cameras [6]. These methods estimate the center accurately but they are expensive, uncomfortable, intrusive, and generally require a calibration stage. Furthermore, the systems based on active infrared (IR) illumination are less robust in daylight applications and outdoor scenarios.

Recently, appearance based pupil center localization methods, which need only webcam type cameras, started addressing the above problems. These techniques can roughly be divided into three categories [7]: model-based methods [8–10], feature-based methods [7, 11], and hybrid methods [7, 12]. The model based methods use the holistic appearance of the eye to estimate the centers. These approaches often

© Springer International Publishing Switzerland 2015
J. Gall et al. (Eds.): GCPR 2015, LNCS 9358, pp. 481–491, 2015.
DOI: 10.1007/978-3-319-24947-6_40

use classification or regression of a set of features or fitting of a learned model to estimate the location of the pupil centers [7]. Hamouz et al. [8] use Gabor filters to localize features, including eye corners and pupil centers. They generate face hypotheses in the affine space by using feature triplets. Finally, an appearance model is applied to pick out the best among the pre-selected face hypotheses. Markus et al. [10] describe a method for pupil location estimation based on an ensemble of randomized regression trees. This method employs the human body part segment classification method of MS Kinect [13] which uses difference of random pixels around the pupil center. Our proposed regression method, on the other hand, employs Support Vector Regressor (SVR) technique, which is known to be precise in terms of localization of structures [14]. Our employment of HoG [15] features also helps us take advantage of the rich image gradient angle information around the eye regions.

Feature based methods do not use any learning. They employ eye properties to detect candidate pupil centers from local image features (e.g. corners, edges, gradients). Timm et al. [11] propose an approach based on the analysis of image gradients. They define an objective function that expects the intersection of all the gradient vectors on the pupil center. Although, this method also uses image gradients like our method, our employment of gradient information involves model training which makes our system more robust for head pose and eye gaze changes.

The hybrid methods collect pupil center location candidates using feature based methods. Model based methods are employed to select the optimal values among the candidates. Valenti et al. [7] use the curvature of isophotes as image features to design a voting scheme for pupil localization. They later combine this information with the extracted SIFT [16] vectors for each candidate location and match it with examples in a database to obtain the final decision.

In this paper, we propose a new model based approach for accurate and robust pupil center localization on images supplied from a monocular camera system. We argue that the gradient angle information around the eye pupil region has a unique signature (see the extracted HoGs in Figs. 1 and 3) and employing HoG technique as the basic feature extraction tool should capture this information. Classically, HoG features are used with binary classifiers to detect objects such as pedestrians [15], which is not suitable for accurate pupil center detection. Instead of using binary detectors, given the HoG vector of an image patch, we feed this information to an SVR [17] to estimate the distance between the patch center and the pupil center. This approach eliminates overlapping positive patches problem of binary classifiers and each image patch contributes towards the position estimation of the pupil center. The estimated distances to the pupil center from image patches are used in a polynomial curve fitting approach to obtain an accurate pupil center estimation. The resulting pupil center estimation system is both very accurate and robust against extreme head positions and eye gaze angles. We employed the output of this work for an iterative pupil center refinement framework and presented the general architecture of the system in a paper [18]. Note that there are studies that employ HoG features to detect the eye regions on face image such as, [19, 20]. Our task of pupil detection uses similar HoG features but our system is based on regression methods that measures the distance to pupil center for each patch candidate which makes our system more precise.

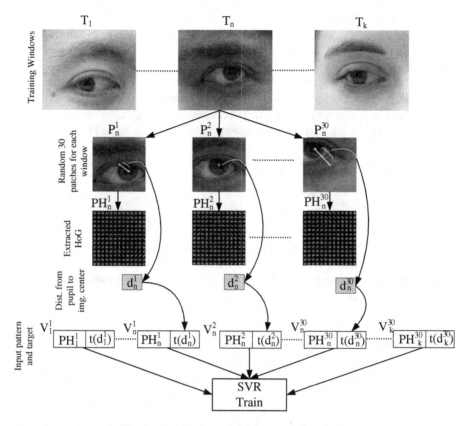

Fig. 1. Training stage of the proposed method.

The rest of the paper is organized as follows: Sect. 2 describes the proposed method; in Sect. 3 experimental results are reported and compared with the state of the art algorithms presented in the literature; Sect. 4 draws the conclusions of our work.

2 Method

The proposed system consists of two phases: training and testing. To train the model (Fig. 1), we use k training windows around the eye regions $(T_1, T_2, \ldots, T_k)$. The window sizes are chosen much larger than the eye region to make the final trained regressor robust against eye detector errors. About 30 patches $(P_1^n, P_2^n, \ldots, P_{30}^n)$ are randomly sampled from each T_n. The sizes of these patches are 96×96.

Suppose patch P_O contains the pupil center at the patch center (such as P_2^n in Fig. 1). We like to learn a function $y(.)$ such that $y(f(P_O))$ produces maximum value where f is a function for extracting feature vectors from the image patches. The value of the function y decreases proportional to the Euclidian distance between the patch center and the pupil center. For example, $y(f(P_{30}^n))$ would produce the smallest value and $y(f(P_2^n))$ would produce the largest value for the patches of Fig. 1. We propose to learn the function y using the SVR method. To train the SVR model, we need input patterns, which are the image features produced by the function f. In our case, the function f produces HoG vectors for the given patch. SVR training also needs the targets for each input pattern. To provide this target data to the SVR model, we calculate the Euclidian distance d_r^n between the center of the patch P_r^n and the pupil center. The calculated distance values are fed to an exponential function t (Eq. 1) whose values rapidly increase around the pupil centers (see the exponential function in Fig. 2), which makes the overall localization problem more accurate [14].

$$t(d_r^n) = \begin{cases} e^{a\left(1-\frac{d_r^n}{PS}\right)} - 1 & \text{if } d_r^n < PS \\ 0 & \text{otherwise}, \end{cases} \tag{1}$$

where $a > 0$ is a constant that controls the exponential increase rate. PS is taken proportional to the patch size and it is used for producing value of zero if the distance d_r^n is larger than the patch. We observed that training a polynomial SVR model with the target values from function t (instead of d_r^n) produces much better results for the task of pupil center detection.

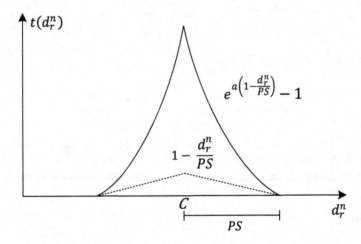

Fig. 2. The functions to generate labels against image patches.

The function f takes an image patch P_r^n and produces HoG vector $\dot{PH}_r^n$. Finally, the vector V_r^n is formed by combining the input pattern PH_r^n with the target $t(d_r^n)$. The SVR model is trained with all V_r^n vectors, where $n = 1, 2, \ldots, k$ and $r = 1, 2, \ldots, 30$. The proposed work trains only one regressor model for both eyes by flipping the left eye horizontally to make it act like the right eye. Based on our experiments, we observe that using a third degree polynomial kernel for the regressor outperforms alternative kernels.

Given a testing image I, first approximate face and eye positions are obtained (Fig. 3). There are many good face and eye detectors in the literature and our method can work with any of them such as [21]. We fix the size of the pupil center search areas (Fig. 3, E_L and E_R) proportional to the detected distance between the left and right eyes. The eye region E_L is scanned to produce sliding windows S_L^1 to S_L^m, where m is the number of sliding windows in eye region E_L. Each sliding window S_L^n is scaled to 96×96 pixels similar to the scaling process done in the training phase. We then produce the HoG vector SH_L^n for each S_L^n. The vector SH_L^n is fed to the trained SVR to produce the estimated exponential distance to the pupil center for each S_L^n. The same process is repeated for the other eye region E_R. A score image is formed by using the regressor results which visually shows where the pupil centers are located (Fig. 3).

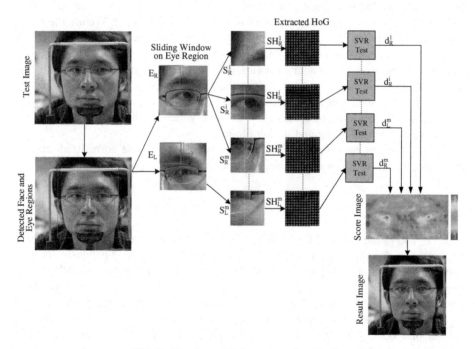

Fig. 3. Test stage of the proposed method.

We employ a two stage approach for the scanning window process. First, we start from the top-left corner and slide the window by skipping 5 pixels. The regressor response is calculated for each sliding window S. The maximal response areas are then scanned again with 1 pixel window skipping. Thus, we reduce the search time considerably. For the final estimation, our method selects the best 20 positions on the score image. Second degree polynomials are fit around these maximal points on the score image. We calculate the zero value of the first derivative of the polynomials to find the pupil center. Our task of estimating the pupil centers is for both eyes, thus we run a special algorithm that finds the pupil centers of both eyes simultaneously. Out of the best 20 positions on the score image of both eyes, we chose the best combination that produces best total score within a minimum and maximum Euclidian separation. As a result, eye centers that have too close or too far positions are eliminated.

3   Evaluation

For the first set of validation experiments, we have chosen the BioID database [21], which has a challenging set of images for pupil center estimation. It consists of more than 1500 gray level face images of 24 subjects taken in different locations and times, which cause variable illumination conditions. Additionally, several subjects are wearing glasses. The eyes of some subjects are closed and sometimes there are shadow effects around the eyes. In a few images, strong reflection on the glasses causes invisible pupils. The image resolution (286×384) is equal quality of a low-resolution camera. The centers of the both eyes are hand marked in the dataset. We use these eye centers as the eye detection results for this experiment. The experiments are performed using leave-3-person-out cross validation method, i.e., the system is trained with images of 21 persons, tested with 3 persons, and this process is repeated using different person combinations until all the images in the set are tested. This method guarantees no person is included both in the training and testing set. We also repeated the same experiment with 10-fold cross validation method, which might include very similar face images in both training and testing phases.

To measure the accuracy for the estimated pupil centers, the normalized error is evaluated. This measure was proposed by Jesorsky et al. [22] and is defined as

$$e \le \frac{max(e_L, e_R)}{d} \tag{2}$$

where e_L and e_R are the Euclidean distances between the estimated and the ground-truth pupil centers for the left and right eyes, respectively. d is the Euclidean distance between the ground-truth pupil centers. Approximately, an error of $e \le 0.25$ corresponds to distance between the pupil center and the eye corners, $e \le 0.1$ corresponds to the diameter of the iris, and $e \le 0.05$ corresponds to the diameter of the pupil [12]. We argue that more accurate pupil center localization methods should produce values smaller than 0.05. Table 1 compares our normalized results with the results of other known methods. As can be seen from the data, our method achieves best error rates for two categories and matches the best method for the third error category. Since the other methods did not report their cross validation details, we report our results for both leave-3-person-out and classical 10-fold cross validation. We should note that our search windows around the pupils are much larger than other methods to eliminate any problems due to eye region detection errors. If the employed eye region detectors are robust, then the search regions can be kept smaller to achieve better performance due to reduced search space. The first two rows of Fig. 4 show some of our results on BioID data set. The last column shows failure cases. The results of our system different data sets are available publicity at the project page [23].

For the second set of validation experiments, we evaluate our system on the Columbia gaze dataset, CAVE [24]. It contains high-resolution (5184×3456 pixels)

Table 1. Comparison of the normalized error on the BioID set.

Method	$e \leq 0.05$	$e \leq 0.1$	$e \leq 0.25$
Our Results (leave-3-person-out)	**92.2 %**	**97.7 %**	99.6 %
Our Results (10-fold validation)	**94.7 %**	**98.7 %**	**99.7 %**
Markus et al. $p = 31$ [10]	89.9 %	97.1 %	**99.7 %**
Tim et al. [11]	82.5 %	93.4 %	98.0 %
Valenti et al. [7] hybrid	86.1 %	91.7 %	97.9 %

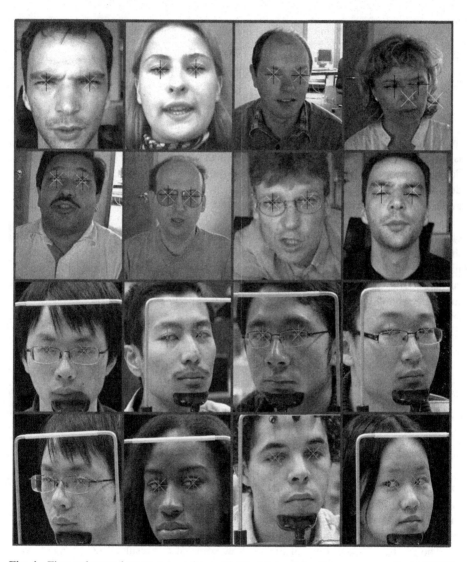

Fig. 4. First and second rows: our results on BioID, third and fourth row: our results on CAVE. The last column shows the failure cases. Plus marks show the ground truth, cross marks show the estimated pupil positions.

images of 56 subjects each looking at 21 different positions that require a wide range of eye gaze positions. In addition to different eye gaze angles, the subject heads take one of the five head poses. We manually marked the pupil centers for 300 images, which involve nominal and extreme eye gaze angles and head poses, and report our results for 10-fold cross validation. We also run the system of [11] with the publicly available code on CAVE set. Table 2 compares our results with the results of [11]. Although [11] performs worse on this dataset due to very extreme head poses and eye gaze angles, our system takes advantage of the extra resolution to produce much better results.

Table 2. Comparison of the normalized error on the CAVE set.

Method	$e \leq 0.05$	$e \leq 0.1$	$e \leq 0.25$
Our Results (10-fold validation)	**98.3 %**	**99.3 %**	**100 %**
Tim et al. [11]	74.7 %	78.0 %	83.7 %

For the third set of experiments, we employed a face and eye detector to find the initial eye positions instead of the hand marked positions provided by the datasets. This is the standard practice with the other state of the art methods. The well-known face detection algorithm Viola and Jones [25] is used for this purpose. If the face and eye detector is successful, then we find the pupil centers. Otherwise, we do not estimate the pupil center. Since the face and eye detectors fail on bad images, the success rate of pupil detectors are higher for this experiment. In test stage, leave-3-person-out and classical 10-fold cross validation is followed like the first test strategy. As can be seen the Table 3, better performance is achieved than the using the full dataset. Generally, non detected face images contain the extreme head pose, profile face, or occluded scenario. These situations mostly cause to increase detection error for the first two experiments and decrease the error for the third experiment.

Table 3. Comparison of the normalized error on the detected face images in BioID set.

Method	$e \leq 0.05$	$e \leq 0.1$	$e \leq 0.25$
Our Results (leave-3-person-out)	**97.5 %**	**99.6 %**	**99.9 %**
Markus et al. $p = 31$ [10]	89.9 %	97.1 %	99.7 %
Tim et al. [11]	82.5 %	93.4 %	98.0 %
Valenti et al. [7] hybrid	86.1 %	91.7 %	97.9 %

In order to show the characteristics of the proposed method on nominal and extreme cases, we show the normalized error versus accuracy graph of the CAVE experiments in Fig. 5. As expected our method and [11] show similar performances as the BioID set on nominal cases. However, the performance of [11] drops significantly for extreme cases while our results stays at good levels.

The third and fourth rows of Fig. 4 show some of our results on CAVE data set. The last column shows failure cases. There are two main reasons for the failures whose score images are shown in Fig. 6. First, for some cases, our score images do not produce the correct positions of the eye pupils, which may indicate a training set problem. If the training set includes more closed eye lid examples or glass subject examples, our training could reflect the real world cases better. Second, for some cases, although the score images produce the correct positions, our simultaneous pupil estimation method fails, which suggests we may need a more sophisticated combined pupil estimation method.

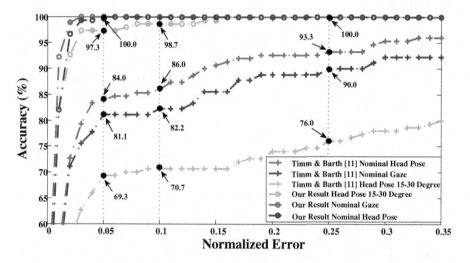

Fig. 5. Proposed method versus [11] on the CAVE set.

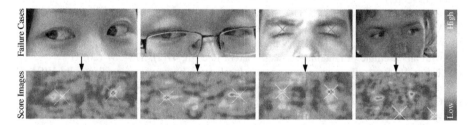

Fig. 6. First row: the failure cases, second row: score images generated from the failure cases. Cross marks show the estimated pupil positions.

4   Conclusions

We propose an appearance based approach to estimate the eye pupil centers accurately and robustly by using a Support Vector Regressor. Our method extracts HoG features from the candidate eye patches and estimates the distance of the patch center to the pupil center. The HoG features can take advantage of the gradient direction information around the eye region especially with good resolution images. As a result, our method is more suitable for pupil center localization for the eye gaze angle estimation. The experiments performed on the standard datasets show the effectiveness of the proposed method. For the future work, we plan to make our method faster by using a steepest ascent algorithm on the regressor function results that moves towards the pupil center. It is also possible to make our system faster by running parallel threads for each sliding window patch, which are independent of each other.

References

1. Duchowski, A.: Eye Tracking Methodology: Theory and Practice. Springer, London (2007)
2. Poole, A., Linden, B.J.: Eye tracking in HCI and usability research. In: Encyclopedia of Human Computer Interaction, pp. 211–219. Idea Group, Pennsylvania (2006)
3. Rayner, K., Rotello, C.M., Stewart, A.J., Keir, J., Duffy, S.A.: Integrating text and pictorial information: eye movements when looking at print advertisements. J. Exp. Psychol. Appl. **7**(3), 219–226 (2001)
4. Levine, J.: An eye-controlled computer. IBM Thomas J. Watson Research Center, Yorktown Heights, N.Y. (1982)
5. Li, D., Babcock, J., Parkhurst, D.J.: openEyes: a low-cost head-mounted eye-tracking solution. In: Proceedings of the 2006 Symposium on Eye Tracking Research & Applications (2006)
6. Ohno, T., Mukawa, N.: A free-head, simple calibration, gaze tracking system that enables gaze-based interaction. In: Proceedings of the 2004 Symposium on Eye Tracking Research & Applications (2004)
7. Valenti, R., Gevers, T.: Accurate eye center location through invariant isocentric patterns. IEEE Trans. Pattern Anal. Mach. Intell. **34**(9), 1785–1798 (2012)
8. Hamouz, M., Josef, K., Kamarainen, J.-K., Pekka, P., Heikki, K., Jiri, M.: Feature-based affine-invariant localization of faces. IEEE Trans. Pattern Anal. Mach. Intell. **27**(9), 1490–1495 (2005)
9. Wang, P., Ji, Q.: Multi-view face and eye detection using discriminant features. Comput. Vis. Image Underst. **105**(2), 99–111 (2007)
10. Markus, N., Frljak, M., Pandzic, I.S., Ahlberg, J., Forchheimer, R.: Eye pupil localization with an ensemble of randomized trees. Pattern Recogn. **47**(2), 578–587 (2014)
11. Timm, F., Barth, E.: Accurate eye centre localisation by means of gradients. In: VISAPP (2011)
12. Campadelli, P., Lanzarotti, R., Lipori, G.: Precise eye localization through a general-to-specific model definition. In: BMVC (2006)
13. Shotton, J., Fitzgibbon, A., Cook, M., Sharp, T., Finocchio, M., Moore, R., Kipman, A., Blake, A.: Real-time human pose recognition in parts from single depth images. Commun. ACM **56**(1), 116–124 (2013)
14. Sironi, A., Lepetit, V., Fua, P.: Multiscale centerline detection by learning a scale-space distance transform. In: Conference on Computer Vision and Pattern Recognition (CVPR) (2014)
15. Dalal, N., Triggs, B.: Histograms of oriented gradients for human detection. In: Conference on Computer Vision and Pattern Recognition (CVPR) (2005)
16. Lowe, D.G.: Distinctive image features from scale-invariant keypoints. Int. J. Comput. Vis. **60**(2), 91–110 (2004)
17. Drucker, H., Burges, C.J., Kaufman, L., Smola, A., Vapnik, V.: Machines, support vector regression. In: Advances in Neural Information Processing Systems, pp. 155–161 (1997)

18. Karakoc, N.S., Karahan, S., Akgul, Y.S.: Iterative estimation of the eye pupil center. In: Signal Processing and Communications Applications Conference (SIU), Turkey, In Turkish (2015)
19. Chen, S., Liu, C.: Precise eye detection using discriminating HOG features. In: Real, P., Diaz-Pernil, D., Molina-Abril, H., Berciano, A., Kropatsch, W. (eds.) CAIP 2011, Part I. LNCS, vol. 6854, pp. 443–450. Springer, Heidelberg (2011)
20. Monzo, D., Albiol, A., Sastre, J., Albiol, A.A.: Precise eye localization using HOG descriptors. Mach. Vis. Appl. 22(3), 471–480 (2011)
21. BioID Image Dataset. https://www.bioid.com/About/BioID-Face-Database. Accessed May 2015
22. Oliver, J., Kirchberg, K.J., Frischholz, R.W.: Robust face detection using the hausdorff distance. In: Audio-and video-Based Biometric Person Authentication, pp. 90–95 (2001)
23. Estimation of The Eye Gaze Direction. http://vision.gyte.edu.tr/projects.php?id=14. Accessed July 2015
24. Smith, B.A., Yin, Q., Feiner, S.K., Nayar, S.K.: Gaze locking: passive eye contact detection for human-object interaction. In: Proceedings of the 26th Annual ACM Symposium on User Interface Software and Technology (2013)
25. Viola, P., Jones, M.J.: Robust real-time face detection. Int. J. Comput. Vis. 57(2), 137–154 (2004)

Patch-Level Spatial Layout for Classification and Weakly Supervised Localization

Valentina Zadrija[1]([✉]), Josip Krapac[1], Jakob Verbeek[2], and Siniša Šegvić[1]

[1] Faculty of Electrical Engineering and Computing,
University of Zagreb, Zagreb, Croatia
valentina.zadrija@gmail.com
[2] INRIA Rhone-Alpes, Grenoble, France

Abstract. We propose a discriminative patch-level model which combines appearance and spatial layout cues. We start from a block-sparse model of patch appearance based on the normalized Fisher vector representation. The appearance model is responsible for (i) selecting a discriminative subset of visual words, and (ii) identifying distinctive patches assigned to the selected subset. These patches are further filtered by a sparse spatial model operating on a novel representation of pairwise patch layout. We have evaluated the proposed pipeline in image classification and weakly supervised localization experiments on a public traffic sign dataset. The results show significant advantage of the combined model over state of the art appearance models.

1 Introduction

Detecting the presence and precise locations of objects in images is a fundamental problem in computer vision. Best results are achieved with strongly supervised training [6,10,15,23] where object locations have to be annotated with bounding boxes. However, the annotation process is difficult, time-consuming and error-prone, especially when the objects are small. These problems are alleviated in weakly supervised localization which learns from image-wide labels only.

Most previous work on weakly supervised learning for object localization follows the multiple instance learning [2,26] approach (MIL) in order to account for the missing ground truth locations [7,8,11,30,35]. MIL iteratively trains an instance classifier on bags of instances. A positive bag contains at least one positive instance, while negative bags contain only negative instances. Bags correspond to images, while instances in the bags are tentative object locations.

However, the localization problem can also be expressed as a search for patches which contribute most to the image classification score. We have previously shown [21] that traffic signs can be localized by a sparse linear model trained on non-normalized Fisher vectors (FV) of entire images. In this paper we present two contributions which further improve these results. First, we propose to approximate the patch contribution to the normalized FV score with the first-order Taylor expansion. This allows to improve the patch appearance model by training it on the normalized FVs. Second, we propose a novel spatial

© Springer International Publishing Switzerland 2015
J. Gall et al. (Eds.): GCPR 2015, LNCS 9358, pp. 492–503, 2015.
DOI: 10.1007/978-3-319-24947-6_41

Fig. 1. The appearance model identifies distinctive patches (enclosed in yellow rectangles) assigned to selected visual words (shown in colors). The spatial model learns consistent spatial configurations between pairs of selected visual words, e.g. between a_1 (purple) and a_2 (cyan), a_1 (purple) and a_3 (green) and so on (Colour figure online).

representation of the pairwise patch layout. This representation captures distinctive spatial configurations between the visual words selected by the appearance model. The interplay between the two models is illustrated in Fig. 1.

2   Related Work

Most of the existing weakly-supervised localization approaches mitigate the computational complexity by relying on bottom-up location proposals. Unfortunately, this risks to overlook true object patches, which is especially pertinent in traffic scenes with small objects and rich backgrounds. In our preliminary experiments, a popular objectness algorithm [1] failed to produce accurate traffic sign locations in top 2000 proposals. Due to recent success of cascaded classifiers [27,38], strongly supervised traffic sign localization is considered solved today. However, due to greedy training, these approaches have a limited feature sharing potential, and none of them is able to detect all kinds of traffic signs at once. Thus, current research and commercial products typically disregard important classes such as the stop sign, priority road, no entry etc.

Modeling co-occurrence of visual words has been of interest ever since the introduction of the bag-of-words (BoW) image classification paradigm [9]. Most previous research considered unordered co-occurrence patterns of particular visual words. The discovery of such patterns can be cast as a frequent pattern mining problem, where BoW histograms are viewed as transactions while co-occurring tuples of visual words correspond to frequent patterns [39] or itemsets [16,41]. Many approaches attempt to discover co-occurrence patterns in an unsupervised setting, and to use these patterns to augment the BoW representation [16,41] or to supply weak classifiers for boosting [39]. Recent work suggests that better performance can be obtained in a supervised discriminative context, by employing so called jumping emerging patterns [37]. This relation between frequent and discriminative patterns in data mining is similar to the generative-discriminative dichotomy in computer vision classification models.

The second line of research goes beyond simple co-occurrence and attempts to model spatial constellations of visual words. The approach by Lin et al. [24]

uses histograms to represent the spatial layout of pairs of visual words. A major problem with this approach is stability. Many pairs of features may be needed to represent a given trait of an object class, since several visual words typically fire in any discriminative image region. Due to use of histograms, this approach may require large training datasets in order to properly model discretization issues. The approach by Yang et al. [40] deals with these problems by choosing a small dictionary of 100 visual words, and by considering crude spatial predicates of proximity and orientation. Singh et al. [34] present an interesting iterative approach for selection of discriminative visual words. In each round of learning and for each visual word, a discriminative classifier is trained on the first fold of training data. The classifiers are subsequently applied to the second fold, and the positive responses are clustered to define the visual words for the next round (this procedure is similar to the multi-fold multiple-instance learning for weakly supervised localization [7]). Pairs of spatially correlated visual words (doublets) are greedily discovered in the postprocessing phase, which provides a slight increase in classification performance.

In this work, we present an approach for learning the spatial layout of visual word pairs, which is suitable for classification and weakly supervised localization. In contrast with [24,34,40], we perform a globally optimal selection of visual words from a large dictionary. The selection procedure is optimal in the sense of image classification performance over the Fisher vector representation. Our approach does not rely on bottom-up location proposals such as segmentation [6,7,17] or objectness [11,35]. Due to generative front-end, we have a better sharing potential than pure discriminative approaches used in [27]. In contrast with [21], we use block-sparsity [20], the normalized score gradient and the spatial model of the pairwise layout.

Our appearance model is able to provide two-fold filtering of patches from the test image. The filtering procedure discards (i) patches which are not assigned to the selected set of visual words, and (ii) patches with a negative contribution to the classification score. The filtered patches are further tested by the spatial model based on [22], which improves the performance by considering pairwise spatial relations in a local neighbourhood. Our approach is non-iterative and therefore provides potential for combining with other approaches [16,34].

3   Selecting Discriminative Visual Words

We regard images as bags of visual words and represent them with a normalized FV embedding built atop the generative Gaussian mixture model (GMM) of patch appearance. Two types of FV normalizations are widely used to improve the performance in this setup [31]. The power normalization is applied to each dimension X_d of the FV as $s(X_d) = \text{sign}(X_d)|X_d|^\rho$, with $0 < \rho < 1$. This "un-sparsifies" the vector $\mathbf{X}$ and makes it more suitable for comparison with the dot product. The metric normalization projects the FV onto the unit hyper-sphere by dividing it by its ℓ_2 norm. This accounts for the fact that different images contain different amounts of background information. The ℓ_2 normalization is applied by dividing the power-normalized FV $s(\mathbf{X})$ with $\sqrt{n(\mathbf{X})}$ where $n(\mathbf{X}) = \sum_d s(X_d)^2$.

In our work, we use the intra-component normalization [3] where the ℓ_2 normalization is separately applied to the components of the FV corresponding to different visual words. This accounts for the effect of "burstiness" [18] where a few large components of the FV can dominate the similarity computed towards another FV. In order to formally define the intra-normalized FV of the image, we use $\mathbf{X_k}$ to denote the part of the FV corresponding to the k-th visual word and write the corresponding ℓ_2 norm as $n(\mathbf{X_k})$.

We train our appearance model from image-wide training labels y_i as a linear classifier $\mathbf{w}$ which minimizes the following regularized logistic loss function:

$$\ell(\mathbf{w}, \mathbf{X}, \mathbf{y}) = \sum_{i=1}^{N} \log \left(1 + \exp(y_i \cdot \mathbf{w}^\top \mathbf{X}_i)\right) + \lambda \cdot \mathcal{R}(\mathbf{w}). \qquad (1)$$

In the above equation, N denotes the number of the training examples, $\mathcal{R}$ denotes the regularizer, while the parameter λ represents a trade-off between the loss and the regularization. We prefer a sparse regularizer because it (i) alleviates the high dimensionality of the FV and (ii) performs a globally optimal feature selection within the learning algorithm. The most commonly used choice for this purpose is the ℓ_1 norm [29]. However this would ignore the specific FV structure induced by the blocks that correspond to different visual words. In order to provide better regularization, we capture this structure by using the $\ell_{2,1}$ norm [19,42]: $\mathcal{R}(w) = \lambda \sum_k \|\mathbf{w}_k\|$, where k denotes visual words. This acts like the lasso at the group level: depending on the choice of λ, all coefficients corresponding to the particular visual word are set to zero. Note that block sparsity favours the selection of discriminative visual words, which is especially helpful in weakly supervised localization and fine-grained classification [20]. The main benefits include faster execution (many patches can be discarded without applying the model) and better performance due to reduced overfitting.

4   Gradient of the Classification Score

For the purpose of image classification, we denote the score of the full-image FV descriptor as $f(\mathbf{X})$, and the contribution of the patch $\mathbf{x}$ as $f(\mathbf{X}) - f(\mathbf{X} - \mathbf{x})$. In the case of un-normalized FV representation, the contribution of local features to the final classification score can be easily derived. The linearity of the classifier and the sum-pooling of the encoding of the local features makes that the scoring and pooling can be reversed, i.e. $\mathbf{w}^T \cdot \mathbf{X} = \sum_i \mathbf{w}^T \cdot \mathbf{x}_i$. As a result, we obtain the patch contribution using a simple dot product with the model [21].

On the other hand, the score of the normalized image FV corresponds to[1] $f(\mathbf{X}) = \mathbf{w}^\top \cdot s(\mathbf{X})/\sqrt{n(\mathbf{X})}$. Due to the non-linear normalizations, the above linear decomposition of the image score into patch scores is no longer possible. The patch contribution could be computed directly as $f(\mathbf{X}) - f(\mathbf{X} - \mathbf{x})$. However, that would require for each patch $\mathbf{x}$ to subtract it from $\mathbf{X}$, apply power and

---

[1] For the sake of simplicity, we assume the global ℓ_2 normalization $n(X)$. We later show the proposed reasoning also holds in the case of the intra- ℓ_2 normalization.

ℓ_2 normalizations to the $\mathbf{X} - \mathbf{x}$, and finally to score it with the classifier and subtract it from $f(\mathbf{X})$. A computationally more efficient approach is to approximate the contribution to the score by using the gradient $\nabla_{\mathbf{x}} f(\mathbf{X})$ of the score w.r.t. the unnormalized FV $\mathbf{x}$. The dot-product of the local FV with this gradient $\langle \mathbf{x}, \nabla_{\mathbf{x}} f(\mathbf{X}) \rangle$ then approximates the impact of a local descriptor on the final classification score. Let us now derive the gradient of the classification score w.r.t. the non-normalized FV. The partial derivative of the score w.r.t. an element of the non-normalized patch x_d is given by $\partial f(\mathbf{X})/\partial x_d = \partial f(\mathbf{X})/\partial \mathbf{X} \cdot \partial \mathbf{X}/\partial x_d$. The derivative of the non-normalized image FV w.r.t. the d-th element of the patch FV corresponds to the vector with all zero elements except the d-th, which is equal to one. Hence, the gradient w.r.t. the patch element x_d is equal to the gradient w.r.t. an image element X_d:

$$\frac{\partial f(\mathbf{X})}{\partial x_d} = \frac{\partial f(\mathbf{X})}{\partial X_d} = \frac{\rho |X_d|^{\rho-1}}{\sqrt{n(\mathbf{X})}} \left(w_d - \frac{s(X_d)f(X)}{\sqrt{n(\mathbf{X})}} \right). \tag{2}$$

Please note that this derivative is undefined for $X_d = 0$. In practice, we set the derivative to zero in this case, to ignore the impact of such dimensions.

In the case of per-component intra-normalization, the classification score is a sum of per-component classification scores: $f(\mathbf{X}) = \sum_k f_k(\mathbf{X}_k)$. Since the $f_k(\mathbf{X}_k)$ have precisely the same form as $f(\mathbf{X})$ above, we can compute the gradients in the same manner, per block. Note that the gradient of the intra-normalized FV preserves the sparsity (i.e. the zero elements) of the original model 1. This is not the case for the global ℓ_2 normalization, where the gradient sparsity depends on the difference between the model $\mathbf{w}$ and the normalized FV multiplied with the score. A fixed set of visual words makes the gradient of the intra-normalized FV more suitable for the construction of the spatial layout.

5   Spatial Layout Model

The proposed patch appearance model reduces the number of possible object locations by an order of magnitude (e.g. from 100000 to 7000). Still, some of the difficult background patches are scored positively and as such generate false alarms (see Fig. 1). One way to address this problem is to learn a distinctive spatial layout between the patches corresponding to different visual words. We assume that the *soft-assign* distribution is sharply peaked, i.e. each local feature is assigned to a single GMM component (see Fig. 2) [32,33]. The appearance model identifies K_w discriminative components $\{a_i\}_{i=1}^{K_w}$ from the GMM vocabulary of the size K, where $K_w \ll K$. For each positively scored patch p assigned to some visual word a_i, we consider a square neighbourhood upon which we construct the spatial descriptors. The spatial features are based on displacement vectors $\mathbf{d}(p,q)$ between the central patch p and neighbouring patches q. We aggregate the spatial descriptors over the whole image and train an ℓ_1 regularized model using image-wide labels. In the evaluation stage, the spatial model is applied only to patches which are positively scored by the appearance model.

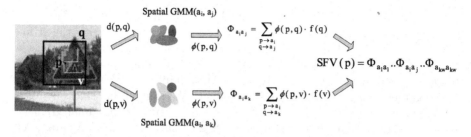

Fig. 2. SFV derivation for the local neighbourhood around the patch p (black rectangle) with $K_s = 4$. Patches assigned to different visual words are shown in different colors. The patches p, q and v are assigned to visual words a_i, a_j, a_k. The SFV contribution $\phi(p,q)$ is determined as the gradient of the log likelihood of the displacement $\mathbf{d}(p,q)$ with respect to the spatial GMM component (a_i, a_j).

We experiment with two types of descriptors: (i) spatial histograms (SH) [24], and (ii) spatial Fisher vectors (SFV) [22]. The SHs are constructed as follows. For each pair of the visual words, we construct a 2D histogram by discretizing the local neighbourhood into b bins over both axes. The displacement vectors $\mathbf{d}(p,q)$ are assigned to the appropriate bins, to which they contribute with the appearance score of the patch q. The dimensionality of the 2D histogram is b^2, and since there are K_w^2 possible pairs, the size of the final SH is $K_w^2 \cdot b^2$.

We construct the SFVs as follows (cf. Fig. 2). For each visual word pair (a_i, a_j) we assume a distinct spatial GMM with K_s components and diagonal covariance. For each patch p assigned to a_i we aggregate the weighted contributions $\phi(p,q)$ of all neighbouring patches q assigned to a_j into the SFV component $\boldsymbol{\Phi}_{a_i, a_j}$. We incorporate the appearance information by weighting the contributions $\phi(p,q)$ with the appearance score $f(q)$. This is similar to [6] where the segmentation masks are used to weight the Fisher vectors of the candidate windows. The final SFV is obtained by concatenating the $\boldsymbol{\Phi}_{a_i, a_j}$ for all (a_i, a_j). Each of the $\boldsymbol{\Phi}_{a_i, a_j}$ is of dimension $5K_s$, since for each of the K_s spatial Gaussians it concatenates 2D gradients for its mean and variance, as well as one dimension for its mixing weight. The SFV dimensionality is $K_w^2 \cdot K_s \cdot (2D + 1) = K_w^2 \cdot K_s \cdot 5$.

6   Experiments

Dataset. We evaluate the proposed approach on a public traffic sign dataset [5]. The dataset contains 3296 images acquired from the driver's perspective along local countryside roads. We focus on triangular warning signs (30 different types). We train our classifiers using image-wide labels on the training split with 453 positive and 1252 negative images. The train and test splits are disjoint: images containing the same physical traffic sign are assigned to the same split. In general, the dataset contains very small objects taking approximately 1% of the image area making the classification and weakly supervised localization difficult. We perform the bounding box evaluation as proposed in [14] and use the average precision (AP) as the performance measure.

Implementation Details. We extract dense 128-dimensional SIFT descriptors over square patches being 16, 24, 32 and 40 pixels wide, with the stride of $1/8$ patch width. The descriptors are ℓ_2 normalized and projected onto a 80-dimensional PCA subspace. We train a GMM vocabulary with $K = 1024$ components and diagonal covariance with EM, as implemented in Yael [13]. The resulting appearance FV is 164864-dimensional. We train our classifiers by optimizing the logistic loss with block sparse regularization by proximal gradient descent (FISTA), as implemented in SPAMS [25]. The regularization parameter λ is determined using 10-fold cross-validation for all presented experiments.

We build local spatial layout descriptors by considering a neighbourhood 4 times larger than the corresponding reference patch. We construct the spatial 2D histograms by discretizing the patch neighbourhood into 8 bins per each axis. As a result, for each pair of visual words, we obtain a 64 dimensional descriptor. We construct the spatial Fisher vectors over a fixed GMM with $K_s = 4$ components shared across all visual word pairs. The mean and the variances of the components match the first and second order moments of the uniform distribution over the four quadrants of the unit square [22]. The dimensionality of the SFV descriptor is $K_s \cdot (2 \cdot 2 + 1) = 20$ per each pair of visual words.

Classification. We apply the proposed spatial layout model through the following stages: (1) extract the dense SIFT descriptors and determine their Fisher vectors, (2) apply the power normalization and ℓ_2 intra-component normalization, (3) identify positive patches by employing the gradient of the appearance-based classification score, and (4) aggregate the spatial layout descriptor and score it with the spatial model. We present the obtained results in Table 1.

In the first set of experiments (rows 1–3) we consider Fisher vectors without non-linear normalizations and evaluate models trained with different regularizers. The results show that the group-sparse model outperforms the ℓ_2 regularized model for 7 % points (pp). In comparison with the ℓ_1 regularized model [21], the group-sparse model is 17 times more sparse and achieves comparable AP. This implies substantial performance advantage in terms of execution time.

In the next set of experiments (rows 4–5), we evaluate the effect of non-linear normalizations to the performance of the group-sparse model (note that here the power normalization is always on). The ℓ_2 global and ℓ_2-intra normalizations produce comparable results and improve the performance for approximately 6 pp w.r.t. model without normalizations (row 3). We further observe that intra-component normalization obtains a sparser model (7 vs. 10 components) without any performance hit. The next two experiments (rows 6–7) explore the gradient approximation presented in Sect. 4. Here we (i) compute the gradient of the normalized classification score w.r.t. the raw Fisher vector, and (ii) score that gradient with the raw Fisher vector of the image. We observe almost no penalty of the approximation. However, we note that the global ℓ_2 normalization (row 7) does not preserve the number of non-zero visual words in the gradient of the classification score. As a consequence, it is not suitable for constructing a spatial layout model where we require a fixed set of selected model components.

Table 1. Classification performance with different configurations (M: appearance model, G: gradient of the appearance model, SH: spatial histogram, SFV: spatial Fisher vector), FV normalizations (p: power, ℓ_2 intra: metric per component, ℓ_2 global: metric across the entire vector) and regularizations (ℓ_1, ℓ_2, group: ℓ_2 inside component, ℓ_1 between components). K_w denotes the number of non-zero components of the appearance model (out of 1024 total), where each component corresponds to a visual word.

Nr.	Configuration	FV normalization	Penalty	K_w	AP train	AP test
1	M	-	ℓ_2	1024	100	64
2	M [21]	-	ℓ_1	185	98	71.9
3	M	-	group	11	80	71.1
4	M	p, ℓ_2 global	group	10	83	76.9
5	M	p, ℓ_2 intra	group	7	81	76.8
6	G	p, ℓ_2 global	group	*	83	76.9
7	G	p, ℓ_2 intra	group	7	81	76.7
8	G + SH	p, ℓ_2 intra	group	7	92	**81.8**
9	G + SFV	p, ℓ_2 intra	group	7	94	81.2

Finally, we evaluate the spatial layout model (rows 8–9). Here we require the classification score gradient in order to be able to identify the positive patches. We observe that the combination of the group-sparsity and spatial layout model achieves the best classification AP (around 81 %), which is 4 pp better than the appearance-based counterpart (row 7) and more than 9 pp better than [21] (row 2). The group-sparse model identifies only 7 visual words, so there are only 49 possible pairs to consider in the spatial model. The spatial histograms (SH) and spatial Fisher vectors (SFV) achieve comparable AP. However, the SFV descriptor is more than 3 times smaller than the SH (20 vs 64 dimensions per visual word pair), which makes it more efficient in terms of execution time.

Localization. The localization results are shown in Table 2. We first provide a strongly supervised baseline [10] which employs HOG features in the sliding window[2]. In comparison to our best weakly supervised result (row 7), the supervised HOG obtains a higher AP by 7 pp. However, the HOG implementation scans the image at 64 scales, while we only extract the SIFT descriptors at 4 scales. The second set of experiments (rows 2–5) concerns the weakly supervised appearance-only models. We identify the bounding boxes by looking at T=100 top scored patches. We construct the spatial connectivity graph according to the patch overlap and identify the connected components. The results stress out the importance of non-linear normalizations (rows 4 and 5) as they increase the AP by 5 pp w.r.t. the weakly supervised baseline [21] (row 2). Further, by

---

[2] These results are worse than [21] since here we do not use additional negative images for training, i.e. the training dataset is the same as in other experiments.

Table 2. Localization performance. T denotes the number of patches used to compute the object bounding box. K_w denotes the number of non-zero model components. p_{miss} denotes the miss frequency at the rightmost data point of the PR curve.

Nr.	Configuration	FV normalization	Penalty	K_w	T	AP test	p_{miss}
1	S HOG [10]	-	l_2	-	-	**88**	**0.05**
2	M [21]	-	l_1	64	100	72	0.13
3	M	-	group	11	100	74	0.25
4	M	p, ℓ_2 intra	group	7	100	77	0.11
5	G	p, ℓ_2 intra	group	7	100	77	0.16
6	G + SH	p, ℓ_2 intra	group	7	all	75	0.14
7	G + SFV	p, ℓ_2 intra	group	7	all	**81**	**0.11**

using the gradient approximation (row 5) instead of the direct patch contribution $f(\mathbf{X}) - f(\mathbf{X} - \mathbf{x})$ (row 4), we obtain a comparable AP but increase the p_{miss} for 5 pp. However, we shall show that the gradient requires less execution time.

In the third set of experiments (rows 6–7), we evaluate the localization performance of the spatial layout models. We construct the bounding boxes by taking a union of *all* patches which are positively scored by the spatial layout model. The SH achieves somewhat worse results w.r.t. appearance-only counterpart (row 5), but reduces the number of parameters (we do not have to choose T). The best performance is achieved with the SFV (row 7), where we increase the AP by 9 pp in comparison to the baseline (row 2) and by 4 pp in comparison to the appearance model (row 5). Thus the SFV model outperforms the SH model which is unable to take into account intra-bin distribution.

Figure 3 shows some localization examples. We are quite successful in detecting very small (distant) objects. Most of our false alarms are caused by multiple detections on objects which are very close to the camera.

Fig. 3. Localization results: first two images depict the successful operation of our approach. The positively scored patches corresponding to different visual words are shown in different colors. The second two images show examples of false alarms (Color figure online).

Execution Speed. All experiments have been performed on a 3.4 GHz Intel Core i7-3770 CPU. Our Python + numpy implementation takes on average 7.4 s per image for G + SFV (7.2 s for G and 0.2 s for SFV), which is 3 s faster than the HOG baseline. We are currently unable to match the cascaded approaches [12,36], but we think that our approach might scale better in the multi-class case due to feature sharing. Significant speed-ups could be achieved by approximate soft assign [20] or by using random decision forests as a generative model [4]. Preliminary experiments have shown that additional speed-up could be achieved by an optimized soft-assign implementation in C. We further discuss our two main contributions in terms of execution speed.

The gradient-based evaluation of a single patch is almost twice as fast than the direct computation $f(\mathbf{X}) - f(\mathbf{X} - \mathbf{x})$ (70 μs vs. 160 μs). The effects of this speed-up are especially important when the appearance model is not so sparse and the number of patches assigned to the selected components is large. An interesting application area is the traffic sign localization in the multi-class case. To the best of our knowledge, prominent commercial real-time systems still detect only a single type of sign at a time [28] (typically the prohibition signs).

As for the choice of the spatial model, both SFV and SH take approximately 0.2 s per image. In comparison to SH, the SFV includes the computation of the gradient w.r.t. spatial GMM. However, the SFVs can be precomputed due to (i) the known size of the local neighbourhood, and (ii) fixed GMM shared across all component pairs. Thus, by using SFV we improve the classification performance while retaining the execution speed.

7 Conclusion

We have presented an approach to learn discriminative spatial relations between pairs of visual words selected by a block-sparse appearance classifier trained on the FV of entire images. The local spatial layout between the visual word pairs is represented by a suitable spatial descriptor and aggregated across the image. The recovered spatial descriptors are used to train a spatial classification model suitable for image classification and weakly supervised object localization.

Our first contribution concerns the applicability of power and metric normalizations in patch-level appearance models. Although these normalizations invalidate the additivity of Fisher vectors, we show that excellent results can be achieved by considering the gradient of the normalized Fisher vector score instead of the raw linear model. Our second contribution enriches the sparse patch-level classification model with spatial information. We show that the second-level descriptors can be formulated as spatial Fisher vectors corresponding to the pairs of selected visual words. We have evaluated the presented contributions on a public traffic sign dataset. The experimental results clearly show advantages of the normalized FV score gradient and the proposed pairwise spatial layout model in image classification and weakly supervised localization.

The obtained results suggest that sparse patch-level models may be strong enough to support weakly supervised learning of rich visual representations.

Our future work shall explore further applications of the proposed spatial layout representation in the multi-class scenario.

Acknowledgement. This work has been fully supported by Croatian Science Foundation under the project I-2433-2014.

References

1. Alexe, B., Deselaers, T., Ferrari, V.: Measuring the objectness of image windows. IEEE Trans. Pattern Anal. Mach. Intell. **34**(11), 2189–2202 (2012)
2. Andrews, S., Tsochantaridis, I., Hofmann, T.: Support vector machines for multiple-instance learning. In: NIPS (2003)
3. Arandjelović, R., Zisserman, A.: All about VLAD. In: CVPR (2013)
4. Baecchi, C., Turchini, F., Seidenari, L., Bagdanov, A.D., Bimbo, A.D.: Fisher vectors over random density forests for object recognition. In: ICPR (2014)
5. Brkić, K., Pinz, A., Šegvić, S., Kalafatić, Z.: Histogram-based description of local space-time appearance. In: Heyden, A., Kahl, F. (eds.) SCIA 2011. LNCS, vol. 6688, pp. 206–217. Springer, Heidelberg (2011)
6. Cinbis, R., Verbeek, J., Schmid, C.: Segmentation driven object detection with Fisher vectors. In: ICCV (2013)
7. Cinbis, R., Verbeek, J., Schmid, C.: Multi-fold MIL training for weakly supervised object localization. In: CVPR (2014)
8. Crowley, E.J., Zisserman, A.: Of gods and goats: weakly supervised learning of figurative art. In: BMVC (2013)
9. Csurka, G., Bray, C., Dance, C., Fan, L.: Visual categorization with bags of keypoints. In: Workshop on Statistical Learning in Computer Vision, ECCV (2004)
10. Dalal, N., Triggs, B.: Histograms of oriented gradients for human detection. In: CVPR (2005)
11. Deselaers, T., Alexe, B., Ferrari, V.: Weakly supervised localization and learning with generic knowledge. Int. J. Comput. Vis. **100**(3), 275–293 (2012)
12. Dollár, P., Belongie, S., Perona, P.: The fastest pedestrian detector in the west. In: BMVC (2010)
13. Douze, M., Jégou, H.: The Yael library. In: Proceedings of the ACM International Conference on Multimedia (2014)
14. Everingham, M., Gool, L., Williams, C.K., Winn, J., Zisserman, A.: The Pascal visual object classes (VOC) challenge. Int. J. Comput. Vis. **88**(2), 303–338 (2010)
15. Felzenszwalb, P., Girshick, R., McAllester, D., Ramanan, D.: Object detection with discriminatively trained part-based models. IEEE Trans. Pattern Anal. Mach. Intell. **32**(9), 1627–1645 (2010)
16. Fernando, B., Fromont, E., Tuytelaars, T.: Mining mid-level features for image classification. Int. J. Comput. Vis. **108**(3), 186–203 (2014)
17. Galleguillos, C., Babenko, B., Rabinovich, A., Belongie, S.: Weakly supervised object localization with stable segmentations. In: Forsyth, D., Torr, P., Zisserman, A. (eds.) ECCV 2008, Part I. LNCS, vol. 5302, pp. 193–207. Springer, Heidelberg (2008)
18. Jégou, H., Douze, M., Schmid, C.: On the burstiness of visual elements. In: CVPR (2009)
19. Jenatton, R., Mairal, J., Obozinski, G., Bach, F.R.: Proximal methods for hierarchical sparse coding. J. Mach. Learn. Res. **12**, 2297–2334 (2011)

20. Krapac, J., Šegvić, S.: Fast approximate GMM soft-assign for fine-grained image classification with large Fisher vectors. In: GCPR (2015)
21. Krapac, J., Šegvić, S.: Weakly supervised object localization with large Fisher vectors. In: VISAPP (2015)
22. Krapac, J., Verbeek, J., Jurie, F.: Modeling spatial layout with Fisher vectors for image categorization. In: ICCV (2011)
23. Lampert, C.H., Blaschko, M.B., Hofmann, T.: Efficient subwindow search: a branch and bound framework for object localization. IEEE Trans. Pattern Anal. Mach. Intell. **31**, 2129–2142 (2009)
24. Liu, D., Hua, G., Viola, P.A., Chen, T.: Integrated feature selection and higher-order spatial feature extraction for object categorization. In: CVPR (2008)
25. Mairal, J., Bach, F., Ponce, J., Sapiro, G.: Online learning for matrix factorization and sparse coding. J. Mach. Learn. Res. **11**, 19–60 (2010)
26. Maron, O., Lozano-Pérez, T.: A framework for multiple-instance learning. In: NIPS, pp. 570–576 (1997)
27. Mathias, M., Timofte, R., Benenson, R., Gool, L.J.V.: Traffic sign recognition - how far are we from the solution? In: IJCNN, pp. 1–8 (2013)
28. Mobileye: Traffic Sign Detection. http://www.mobileye.com. Accessed 22 July 2015
29. Murphy, K.: Machine learning a probabilistic perspective. MIT Press, Cambridge (2012)
30. Nguyen, M.H., Torresani, L., De la Torre, F., Rother, C.: Learning discriminative localization from weakly labeled data. Pattern Recogn. **47**(3), 1523–1534 (2014)
31. Perronnin, F., Sánchez, J., Mensink, T.: Improving the Fisher Kernel for large-scale image classification. In: Daniilidis, K., Maragos, P., Paragios, N. (eds.) ECCV 2010, Part IV. LNCS, vol. 6314, pp. 143–156. Springer, Heidelberg (2010)
32. Sánchez, J., Perronnin, F., Mensink, T., Verbeek, J.: Image classification with the Fisher vector: theory and practice. Int. J. Comput. Vis. **105**(3), 222–245 (2013)
33. Simonyan, K., Vedaldi, A., Zisserman, A.: Deep Fisher networks for large-scale image classification. In: NIPS, pp. 163–171 (2013)
34. Singh, S., Gupta, A., Efros, A.A.: Unsupervised discovery of mid-level discriminative patches. In: Fitzgibbon, A., Lazebnik, S., Perona, P., Sato, Y., Schmid, C. (eds.) ECCV 2012, Part II. LNCS, vol. 7573, pp. 73–86. Springer, Heidelberg (2012)
35. Siva, P., Xiang, T.: Weakly supervised object detector learning with model drift detection. In: ICCV (2011)
36. Viola, P.A., Jones, M.J.: Robust real-time face detection. Int. J. Comput. Vis. **57**(2), 137–154 (2004). http://dx.doi.org/10.1023/B:VISI.0000013087.49260.fb
37. Voravuthikunchai, W., Cremilleux, B., Jurie, F.: Histograms of pattern sets for image classification and object recognition. In: CVPR (2014)
38. Šegvić, S., Brkic, K., Kalafatic, Z., Pinz, A.: Exploiting temporal and spatial constraints in traffic sign detection from a moving vehicle. Mach. Vis. Appl. **25**(3), 649–665 (2014)
39. Weng, C., Yuan, J.: Efficient mining of optimal AND/OR patterns for visual recognition. IEEE Trans. Multimedia **17**(5), 626–635 (2015)
40. Yang, Y., Newsam, S.: Spatial pyramid co-occurrence for image classification. In: ICCV (2011)
41. Yuan, J., Wu, Y., Yang, M.: Discovery of collocation patterns: from visual words to visual phrases. In: CVPR (2007)
42. Yuan, M., Lin, Y.: Model selection and estimation in regression with grouped variables. J. Roy. Stat. Soc.: Ser. B (Stat. Methodol.) **68**(1), 49–67 (2006)

A Deeper Look at Dataset Bias

Tatiana Tommasi[1]([✉]), Novi Patricia[2,3], Barbara Caputo[4],
and Tinne Tuytelaars[5]

[1] Department of Computer Science, University of North Carolina, Chapel Hill, USA
ttommasi@cs.unc.edu
[2] Idiap Research Institute, Martigny, Switzerland
[3] EPFL, Lausanne, Switzerland
[4] La Sapienza University of Rome, Rome, Italy
[5] KU Leuven, ESAT-PSI, iMinds, Leuven, Belgium

Abstract. The presence of a bias in each image data collection has recently attracted a lot of attention in the computer vision community showing the limits in generalization of any learning method trained on a specific dataset. At the same time, with the rapid development of deep learning architectures, the activation values of Convolutional Neural Networks (CNN) are emerging as reliable and robust image descriptors. In this paper we propose to verify the potential of the DeCAF features when facing the dataset bias problem. We conduct a series of analyses looking at how existing datasets differ among each other and verifying the performance of existing debiasing methods under different representations. We learn important lessons on which part of the dataset bias problem can be considered solved and which open questions still need to be tackled.

1 Introduction

Since its spectacular success in the 2012 edition of the Imagenet Large Scale Visual Recognition Challenge (ILSVRC, [28]), deep learning has dramatically changed the research landscape in visual recognition [20]. By training a Convolutional Neural Network (CNN) over millions of data it is possible to get impressively high quality object annotations [1] and detections [38]. A large number of studies have recently proposed improvements over the CNN architecture of Krizhevsky *et al.* [20] with the aim to better suit an ever increasing typology of visual applications [16,30,38]. At the same time, the activation values of the final hidden layers have quickly gained the status of off-the-shelf state of the art features [27]. Indeed, several works demonstrated that DeCAF (as well as Caffe [6],

T. Tommasi—Work done mainly while at KU Leuven, Belgium.

T. Tuytelaars—T. Tommasi and T. Tuytelaars acknowledge the support of the FP7 EC project AXES and of the FP7 ERC Starting Grant 240530 COGNIMUND.

Electronic supplementary material The online version of this chapter (doi:10. 1007/978-3-319-24947-6_42) contains supplementary material, which is available to authorized users.

© Springer International Publishing Switzerland 2015
J. Gall et al. (Eds.): GCPR 2015, LNCS 9358, pp. 504–516, 2015.
DOI: 10.1007/978-3-319-24947-6_42

Overfeat [32], VGG-CNN [3] and other implementations) can be used as powerful image descriptors [3,14]. The improvements obtained over previous methods are so impressive that one might wonder whether they can be considered as a sort of "universal features", *i.e.* image descriptors that can be helpful in any possible visual recognition problem. The aim of this paper is to contribute to answering this question when focusing on the bias of existing computer vision datasets.

The main causes and consequences of the *dataset bias* have been pointed out and named in [34]. The *capture bias* is related to how the images are acquired both in terms of the used device and of the collector preferences for point of view, lighting conditions, etc. The *category or label bias* is due to a poor definition of the visual semantic categories and to the in-class variability: similar images may be annotated with different names and the same name can be assigned to visually different images. Finally, each collection may contain a distinct set of categories and this causes the *negative bias*. If we focus only on the classes shared among them, the rest of the world will be defined differently depending on the collection. All these bias aspects induce a generalization problem when training and testing a learning algorithm on images extracted from different collections. Previous work seemed to imply that this issue was solved, or on the way to be solved, by using CNN features [6,37]. However, the evaluation is generally restricted to controlled cases limited to specific visual domain shift [6,18] or with images extracted from the testing collection available at training time [26,37].

In this work we revisit and scale up the dataset bias analysis, making two contributions:

1. we asses the performance of the DeCAF CNN features on the most comprehensive experimental setup existing for dataset bias. We build on the setting proposed in [33], consisting of a cross-dataset testbed over twelve different databases.
2. we propose a new measure to quantify the ability of a given algorithm to address the dataset bias. As opposed to what was proposed in [34], our measure takes into account both the performance obtained on the in-dataset task and the percentage drop in performance across datasets.

Our experiments evaluate the suitability of CNN features for attacking the dataset bias problem, pointing out that: (1) the capture bias is class-dependent and can be enhanced by the CNN representation due to the influence of the classes on which the neural network was originally trained; (2) the negative bias persists regardless of the representation; (3) attempts of undoing the dataset bias with existing ad-hoc learning algorithms do not help, while some previously discarded adaptive strategies appear effective; (4) fine-tuning the CNN network does not fit in the dataset bias setting and if naïvely forced does not seem beneficial.

The picture emerging from these findings is that of a problem open for research and in need for new directions, able to accommodate at the same time the potential of deep learning and the difficulties of large scale cross-database generalization.

2   Evaluation Protocol

We describe here the setup adopted for the experiments and we introduce the measures used to evaluate the cross-dataset generalization performance.

Datasets and Features. We focus on twelve datasets, created and used before for object categorization, that have been recently organized in a cross-dataset testbed with the definition of two data setups [33]:

- **sparse set**. It contains 105 Imagenet classes [5] aligned to 95 classes of Caltech256 [15] and Bing [35], 89 classes of SUN [36], 35 classes of Caltech101 [10], 17 classes of Office [31], 18 classes of RGB-D [21], 16 classes of Animals with Attributes (AwA) [22] and Pascal VOC07 [8], 13 classes of MSRCORID [25], 7 classes of ETH80 [23], and 4 classes of a-Yahoo [9].
- **dense set**. It contains 40 classes shared by Bing, Caltech256, Imagenet and SUN.

The testbed has been released together with three feature representations:

- **BOWsift**: dense SIFT descriptors [24] extracted with the protocol defined for the ILSVRC2010 contest [29] and quantized into a BOW representation based on a vocabulary of 1000 visual words;
- **DeCAF6, DeCAF7**: the mean-centered raw RGB pixel intensity values of all the collection images (warped to 256×256) are given as input to the CNN architecture of Krizhevsky *et al.* by using the DeCAF implementation [6]. The activation values of the 4096 neurons in the 6-th and 7-th layers of the network are considered as image descriptors.

In our experiments we use the L2-normalized version of the feature vectors and adopt the z-score normalization for the BOWsift features when testing domain adaptation methods. We mostly focus on the results obtained with the DeCAF features and use the BOWsift representation as a reference baseline.

Evaluation Measures. We analyze both the *in-dataset* (training and testing on samples extracted from the same dataset) and the *cross-dataset* (training and testing samples belonging to different collections) performance. We use *Self* to specify the in-dataset performance and *Mean Other* for the average cross-dataset performance over multiple test collections.

In [34] cross dataset generalization was evaluated through the percentage drop (% *Drop*) between *Self* and *Mean Others*. However, being a relative measure, it loses the information on the value of *Self* which is important if we want to compare the effect of different learning methods or different representations. For instance a 75 % drop w.r.t. a 100 % self average precision has a different meaning than a 75 % drop w.r.t. a 25 % self average precision. To overcome this drawback, we propose here a different *Cross-Dataset (CD)* measure defined as

$$CD = \frac{1}{1 + exp^{-\{(Self - Mean\ Others)/100\}}}.$$

CD uses directly the difference ($Self - Mean\ Others$) while the sigmoid function rescales this value between 0 and 1. This allows for the comparison among the results of experiments with different setups. Specifically CD values over 0.5 indicate a presence of a bias, which becomes more significant as CD gets close to 1. On the other hand, CD values below 0.5 correspond to cases where either $Mean\ Other \geq Self$ or the $Self$ result is very low. Both these conditions indicate that the learned model is not reliable on the data of its own collection and it is difficult to draw any conclusion from its cross-dataset performance.

3   Studying the Sparse Set

Dataset Recognition. One of the effect of the capture bias is that it makes any dataset easily recognizable. We want to evaluate whether this effect is enhanced or decreased by the use of the CNN features. To do it we run the *name the dataset* test [34] on the sparse data setup. We extract randomly 1000 images from each of the 12 collections and we train a 12-way linear SVM classifier that we then test on a disjoint set of 300 images. The experiment is repeated 10 times with different data splits and we report the obtained average results in Fig. 1. The plot on the left indicates that DeCAF allows for a much better separation among the collections than what is obtained with BOWsift. In particular DeCAF7 shows an advantage over DeCAF6 for large number of training samples. From the confusion matrices (middle and right in Fig. 1) we see that it is easy to distinguish ETH80, Office and RGB-D datasets from all the others regardless of the used representation, given the specific lab-nature of these collections. DeCAF captures better than BOWsift the characteristics of A-Yahoo, MSRCORID, Pascal VOC07 and SUN, improving the recognition results on them. Finally, Bing, Caltech256 and Imagenet are the datasets with the highest confusion level, an effect mainly due to the large number of classes and images per class. Still, this confusion decreases when using DeCAF.

These experiments show that the idiosyncrasies of each data collection become more evident when using a highly accurate representation. However, the dataset recognition performance does not provide an insight on how the classes in each collection are related among each other, nor how a specific class model will generalize to other datasets. We look into this problem in the following paragraph.

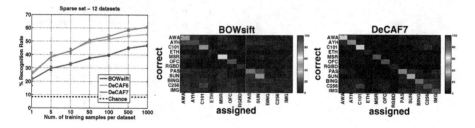

Fig. 1. Name the dataset experiment over the sparse setup with 12 datasets. The title of each confusion matrix indicates the feature used for the corresponding experiments.

Class-Specific cross-dataset generalization test. We study the effect of the CNN features on the cross-dataset performance of two object class models: *car* and *cow*. Four collections in the sparse set contain images labeled with these object classes: PascalVOC07 (P), SUN (S), ETH80 (E), and MSRCORID (M). For the class car we selected randomly from each dataset two groups of 50 positive/1000 negative examples respectively for training and testing. For the class cow we considered 30 positive/1000 negative examples in training and 18 positive/1000 negative examples in testing. We repeat the sample selection 10 times and the average precision results obtained by linear SVM are presented in Table 1.

Coherently with what deduced over all the classes from the *name the dataset* experiment, scene-centric (P,S) and object-centric (E,M) collections appear separated among each other. For the first ones, the low in-dataset results are mainly due to their multi-label nature: an image labeled as people may still contain a car and this creates confusion both at training and at test time. The final effect is a cross-dataset performance higher than the respective in-dataset one. This behavior becomes even more evident when using DeCAF than with BOWsift.

Although the *name the dataset* experiment indicated almost no overall confusion between E and M, the per-class results on car and cow show different trends. Learning a *car* model from images of toys (E) or of real objects (M)

Table 1. Binary cross-dataset generalization for two example categories, car and cow. Each matrix contains the object classification performance (AP) when training on one dataset (rows) and testing on another (columns). The diagonal elements correspond to the self results, *i.e.* training and testing on the same dataset. We report in bold the CD values higher than 0.5.

	BOWsift	% Drop	CD	DeCAF6	% Drop	CD	DeCAF7	% Drop	CD
Car	P 28.6 26.4 26.7 29.2	3.9	0.50	P 26.2 19.2 44.3 42.6	-35.1	0.47	P 14.5 11.8 28.9 28.3	-59.1	0.47
	S 25.4 26.8 25.7 25.7	4.3	0.50	S 15.4 15.6 19.9 17.9	-13.9	0.49	S 27.1 27.4 32.8 28.1	-6.8	0.49
	E 14.7 9.1 98.5 25.2	83.4	**0.69**	E 27.3 18.7 100.0 93.5	53.5	**0.63**	E 31.0 24.0 100.0 90.9	51.3	**0.62**
	M 17.4 8.7 9.7 90.5	86.8	**0.69**	M 41.6 12.8 95.8 99.7	49.8	**0.62**	M 43.8 14.9 93.8 99.7	49.0	**0.62**
	P S E M			P S E M			P S E M		
Cow	P 14.1 18.8 11.9 17.9	-15.1	0.49	P 35.3 34.4 20.2 29.7	11.4	**0.51**	P 46.5 44.6 31.3 47.3	12.3	**0.51**
	S 16.1 38.3 12.5 27.1	51.4	**0.54**	S 18.6 62.7 10.7 33.8	66.7	**0.60**	S 12.8 40.1 12.1 23.6	59.7	**0.56**
	E 2.3 2.3 29.8 2.0	92.6	**0.57**	E 4.4 8.3 91.9 4.1	93.9	**0.70**	E 7.2 7.7 90.1 5.3	92.5	**0.70**
	M 8.6 17.4 2.4 52.5	82.0	**0.61**	M 13.8 46.7 9.3 97.2	76.0	**0.68**	M 14.1 39.4 10.4 97.7	78.2	**0.68**
	P S E M			P S E M			P S E M		
Cow - fixed negatives	P 14.1 16.2 12.0 18.6	-10.7	0.49	P 35.3 32.7 16.9 46.6	9.1	0.50	P 46.6 38.1 26.4 48.9	18.2	**0.52**
	S 18.7 38.3 17.0 35.8	-37.8	**0.53**	S 36.6 53.7 21.0 69.5	31.4	**0.54**	S 25.7 40.1 12.8 43.3	31.9	**0.53**
	E 23.5 22.2 29.8 14.0	33.3	**0.52**	E 6.1 7.9 91.9 4.6	93.2	**0.70**	E 11.2 9.0 90.1 11.0	88.4	**0.69**
	M 8.9 9.4 2.0 52.5	87.1	**0.61**	M 66.2 62.6 51.5 97.2	38.5	**0.59**	M 69.4 55.1 47.4 97.7	41.3	**0.59**
	P S E M			P S E M			P S E M		

does not seem so different in terms of the final testing performance when using DeCAF. The diagonal matrix values prominent with BOWsift are surrounded by high average precision results for DeCAF. On the other hand, recognizing a living non-rigid object like a *cow* is more challenging. An important factor that may influence these results is the high level nature of the DeCAF representation: they are obtained as a byproduct of a training process over 1000 object classes [6] which cover several vehicles and animal categories. The class *car* is in this set, but *cow* is not. This intrinsically induce a category-specific bias effect, which may augment the image collection differences. Overall the DeCAF features provide a high performance inside each collection, but the difference between the in-dataset and cross-dataset results remains large almost as with BOWsift.

We also re-run the experiments on the class cow by using a fixed negative set in the test always extracted from the training collection. The visible increase in the cross-dataset results indicate that the negative set bias maintain its effect regardless of the used representation.

From the values of *%Drop* and *CD* we see that these two measures may have a different behavior: for the class cow with BOWsift, the *%Drop* value for E (92.6) is higher than the corresponding value for M (82.0), but the opposite happens for *CD* (respectively 0.57 and 0.61). The reason is that *CD* integrates the information on the in-dataset recognition which is higher and more reliable for M. Passing from BOWsift to DeCAF the *CD* value increases in some cases indicating a more significant bias.

On the basis of the presented results we can state that the DeCAF features are not fully solving the dataset bias. Although similar conclusions have been mentioned in a previous publication [18], our more extensive analysis provides a reliable measure to evaluate the bias and explicitly indicate some of the main causes of the observed effect: (1) the capture bias appears class-dependent and may be influenced by the original classes on which the CNN features have been trained; (2) the negative bias persists regardless of the feature used to represent the data.

Undoing the Dataset Bias. We focus here on the method proposed in [19] to overcome the dataset bias. Our aim is to verify its effect when using the DeCAF features. The *Unbias* approach has a formulation similar to multi-task learning: the available images of multiple datasets are kept separated as belonging to different tasks and a max-margin model is learned from the information shared over all of them. We run the experiments focusing on the classes *car, cow, dog* and *chair*, reproducing a similar setup to what previously used in [19] and using the original implementation of the *Unbias* method provided by the authors. For the class car we consider two settings with three and five datasets, while we use five datasets for cow and chair and six datasets for dog. One of the datasets is left out in round for testing while all the others are used as sources of training samples[1].

---

[1] More details about the method and the experimental setup can be found in the supplementary material.

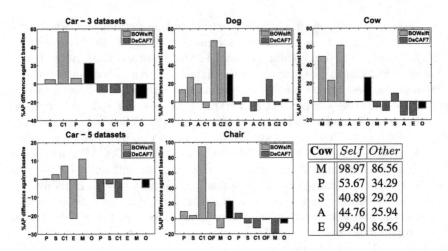

Fig. 2. Percentage difference in average precision between the results of *Unbias* and the baseline *All* over each target dataset. P,S,E,M,A,C1,C2,OF stand respectively for Pascal VOC07, SUN, ETH80, MSRCORID, AwA, Caltech101, Caltech256 and Office. With O (in black) we indicate the overall value: average percentage difference over all the considered datasets.

We compare the obtained results against those produced by a linear SVM when *All* the training images of the source datasets are considered together. We show the percentage relative difference in terms of average precision for these two learning strategies in Fig. 2. The results indicate that, in most cases when using BOWsift the *Unbias* method improves over the plain *All* SVM, while the opposite happens when using DeCAF7. As already suggested by the results of the cross-dataset generalization test, the DeCAF features, by capturing the image details, may enhance the differences among the same object category in different collections. As a consequence, the amount of shared information among the collections decreases, together with the effectiveness of the methods that leverage over it. On the other hand, removing the dataset separation and considering all the images together provides a better coverage of the object variability and allows for a higher cross-dataset performance.

In the last column of Fig. 2 we present the results obtained with the class *cow* together with the average precision per dataset when using DeCAF7. The table allows to compare the performance of training and testing on the same dataset (*Self*) against the best result between *Unbias* and *All* (indicated as *Other*). Despite the good performance obtained by directly learning on other datasets, the obtained results are still lower than what can be expected having access to training samples of each collection. This suggests that an adaptation process from generic to specific is still necessary to close the gap. Similar trends can be observed for the other categories.

4   Studying the Dense Set

Dataset Recognition. A second group of experiments on the dense setup allows us to analyze the differences among the datasets avoiding the negative set bias. We run again the *name the dataset* test maintaining the balance among the 40 classes shared by Caltech256, Bing, SUN and Imagenet. We consider a set of 5 samples per object class in testing and an increasing amount of training samples per class from 1 to 15. The results in Fig. 3 indicate again the better performance of DeCAF7 over DeCAF6 and BOWsift. From the confusion matrices it is clear that the separation between object- (Bing, Caltech256, Imagenet) and scene-centric (SUN) datasets is quite easy regardless of the representation, while the differences among the object-centric collections become more evident when passing from BOW to DeCAF.

Since all the datasets contain the same object classes, we are in fact reproducing a setup generally adopted for domain adaptation [11,13]. By identifying each dataset with a domain, we can interpret the results of this experiment as an indication of the domain divergence [2] and deduce that a model trained on SUN will perform poorly on the object-centric collections and vice versa. On the other hand, a better cross dataset generalization should be observed among Imagenet, Caltech256 and Bing. We verify it in the following sections.

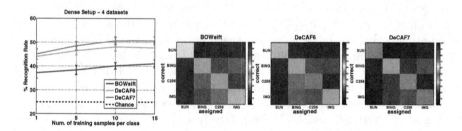

Fig. 3. Name the dataset experiment over the dense setup with 4 datasets. The title of each confusion matrix indicates the feature used for the corresponding experiments.

Cross-dataset generalization test. We consider the same setup used before with 15 samples per class from each collection in training and 5 samples per class in test. However, now we train a one-vs-all multiclass SVM per dataset. Due to its noisy nature we exclude Bing here and we dedicate more attention to it in the next paragraph.

The average recognition rate results over 10 data splits are reported in Table 2. By comparing the values of %*Drop* and *CD* we observe that they provide opposite messages. The first suggests that we get a better generalization when passing from BOWsift to DeCAF7. However, considering the higher *Self* result, *CD* evaluates the dataset bias as more significant when using DeCAF7. The expectation indicated before on the cross-dataset performance are confirmed here:

Table 2. Multiclass cross-dataset generalization performance (recognition rate). The percentage difference between the self results and the average of the other results per row correspond to the value indicated in the column % *Drop*. CD is our newly proposed cross-dataset measure.

	BOWsift			% Drop	CD		DeCAF7			% Drop	CD
C256	25.15	15.05	9.35	51.5	0.53	C256	73.15	56.05	20.20	47.9	0.58
IMG	14.50	17.85	9.05	34.0	0.52	IMG	64.10	64.90	22.65	33.2	0.55
SUN	7.70	8.00	13.55	42.1	0.51	SUN	21.35	23.15	30.05	25.9	0.52
	C256	IMG	SUN				C256	IMG	SUN		
		test						test			

the classification models learned on Caltech256 and Imagenet have low recognition rate on SUN. Generalizing between Caltech256 and Imagenet, instead, appears easier and the results show a particular behavior: although the classifier on Caltech256 tends to fail more on Imagenet than on itself, when training on Imagenet the in-dataset and cross-dataset performance are almost the same. Of course we have to remind that the DeCAF features were defined over Imagenet samples and this can be part of the cause of the observed asymmetric results.

Noisy Source Data and Domain Adaptation. Until now we have discussed and demonstrated empirically that the difference among two data collections can originate from multiple and often co-occurring causes. However the standard assumption is that the label assigned to each image is correct. In some practical cases this condition does not hold, as in learning from web data [4]. Some state-of-art domain adaptation methods seem perfectly suited for this task (see Fig. 4 top part) and we use them here to evaluate the cross-dataset generalization performance when training on Bing (noisy object-centric source domain) and testing on Caltech256 and SUN (respectively an object-centric and a scene-centric target domain).

The obtained results go in the same direction of what was observed previously with the *Unbias* method. Despite the presence of noisy data, selecting them (landmark) or grouping the samples (reshape+SA, reshape+DAM) do not seem to work better than just using all the source data at once. On the other hand, keeping all the source data together and augmenting them with target samples by *self-labeling* [33] consistently improves the original results. One well known drawback of this strategy is that progressively accumulated errors in the target annotations may lead to significant drift from the correct solution. However, when working with DeCAF features this risk appears highly reduced as can be appreciated by looking at the recognition rate obtained over ten iterations of the target selection procedure and considering the comparison against BOWsift (small plots in Fig. 4).

Fine-Tuning. As indicated in Sect. 2 the DeCAF CNN features were obtained from an initial pre-trained network whose parameters remain untouched. Fine-tuning the network before using it for recognition on a new task is an alternative

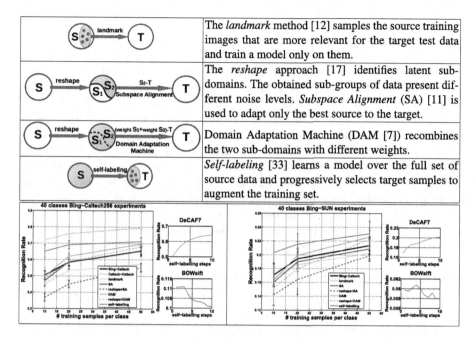

Fig. 4. Top: schematic description of the used domain adaptation methods. Bottom: Results of the Bing-Caltech256 and Bing-SUN experiments with DeCAF7. We report the performance of different domain adaptation methods (big plots) together with the recognition rate obtained in 10 subsequent steps of the self-labeling procedure (small plots). For the last ones we show the performance obtained both with DeCAF7 and with BOWsift when having originally 10 samples per class from Bing.

strategy which demonstrated good results in transfer learning [26,37]. To complete our analysis we clarify here that this fine-tuning process does not fit in the dataset bias setting.

A network pre-trained on a dataset D is generally fine-tuned on a new dataset D' when the final task is also tested on D'. Thus the scheme (train, fine-tune, test) corresponds to (D, D', D'). For dataset bias, the condition is instead (D, D', D''): here D' and D'' are different collection and no labeled data from D'' is available at training time. The advantage of fine-tuning consists in making the network specific for D' [3], which in our setting can worsen the bias with respect to D''. By using the Caffe CNN implementation we fine-tuned the Imagenet (D) pre-trained network on the dense set, specifically on Caltech256 (5046 train images) and SUN (3015 train images), reserving respectively 1500 and 1300 images as test samples. The in-dataset and cross-dataset experimental results are: $(Caltech256(D'), Caltech256(D')) = 86.4\%$; $(Caltech256(D'), SUN(D'')) = 25.7\%$; $(SUN(D'), Caltech256(D'')) = 37.5\%$; $(SUN(D'), SUN(D')) = 41.1\%$. Compared with what presented in Table 2 these results show the advantage of fine-tuning in terms of in-dataset recognition rate. However they also indicate that the fine-tuning process does not remove the cross-dataset bias ($86.4\% > 25.7\%; 41.1\% > 37.5\%$) and that using the wrong dataset to refine the network can be detrimental ($86.4\% > 37.5\%; 41.1\% > 25.7\%$).

5   Conclusions

In this paper we attempted at positioning the dataset bias problem in the CNN-based features arena with an extensive experimental evaluation. At the same time, we pushed the envelope in terms of the scale and complexity of the evaluation protocol, so to be able to analyze all the different nuances of the problem. We focused on DeCAF features, as they are popular CNN-learned descriptors, and for the impressive results obtained so far in several visual recognition domains.

A first main result of our analysis is that DeCAF not only does not solve the dataset bias problem in general, but in some cases (both class- and dataset-dependent) they capture specific information that, although otherwise useful, induce a low performance in the cross-dataset object categorization task. The high level nature of the CNN features add a further hidden bias that needs to be considered when comparing the experimental results against standard hand-crafted representations. Moreover, the negative bias remains, as it cannot intrinsically be removed (or alleviated) by changing feature representation. A second result concerns the effectiveness of learning methods applied over the chosen features: nor a method specifically designed to undo the dataset bias, neither algorithms successfully used in the domain adaptation setting seem to work when applied over DeCAF features. It appears as if the highly descriptive power of the features, that determined much of their successes so far, in the particular dataset-bias setting backfires, as it makes the task of learning how to extract general information across different data collection more difficult. Interestingly, a simple selection procedure based on target self-labeling leads to a significant increase in performance. Finally, a third outcome derives from the fine-tuning experiments. Although standardly used for transfer learning, fine-tuning does seem beneficial to remove the dataset bias. Together with the failure of existing adaptive approaches, this questions whether methods effectively used in transfer and domain adaptation settings should be considered automatically as suitable for dataset bias, and vice versa.

How to leverage over the power of deep learning methods to attack the dataset bias problem in all its complexity, well represented by our proposed experimental setup, is open for research in future work.

References

1. Agrawal, P., Girshick, R., Malik, J.: Analyzing the performance of multilayer neural networks for object recognition. In: Fleet, D., Pajdla, T., Schiele, B., Tuytelaars, T. (eds.) ECCV 2014, Part VII. LNCS, vol. 8695, pp. 329–344. Springer, Heidelberg (2014)
2. Ben-David, S., Blitzer, J., Crammer, K., Pereira, F.: Analysis of representations for domain adaptation. In: NIPS (2007)
3. Chatfield, K., Simonyan, K., Vedaldi, A., Zisserman, A.: Return of the devil in the details: delving deep into convolutional nets. In: BMVC (2014)
4. Chatfield, K., Simonyan, K., Zisserman, A.: Efficient on-the-fly category retrieval using ConvNets and GPUs. In: Cremers, D., Reid, I., Saito, H., Yang, M.-H. (eds.) ACCV 2014. LNCS, vol. 9003, pp. 129–145. Springer, Heidelberg (2015)

5. Deng, J., Dong, W., Socher, R., Li, L., Li, K., Fei-Fei, L.: ImageNet: a large-scale hierarchical image database. In: CVPR (2009)
6. Donahue, J., Jia, Y., Vinyals, O., Hoffman, J., Zhang, N., Tzeng, E., Darrell, T.: Decaf: a deep convolutional activation feature for generic visual recognition. In: ICML (2014). https://github.com/UCB-ICSI-Vision-Group/decaf-release/
7. Duan, L., Tsang, I.W., Xu, D., Chua, T.S.: Domain adaptation from multiple sources via auxiliary classifiers. In: ICML (2009)
8. Everingham, M., Gool, L.V., Williams, C.K., Winn, J., Zisserman, A.: The pascal visual object classes (VOC) challenge. IJCV **88**(2), 303–338 (2010)
9. Farhadi, A., Endres, I., Hoiem, D., Forsyth, D.: Describing objects by their attributes. In: CVPR (2009)
10. Fei-Fei, L., Fergus, R., Perona, P.: Learning generative visual models from few training examples: an incremental bayesian approach tested on 101 object categories. Comput. Vis. Image Underst. **106**(1), 59–70 (2007)
11. Fernando, B., Habrard, A., Sebban, M., Tuytelaars, T.: Unsupervised visual domain adaptation using subspace alignment. In: ICCV (2013)
12. Gong, B., Grauman, K., Sha, F.: Connecting the dots with landmarks: discriminatively learning domain-invariant features for unsupervised domain adaptation. In: ICML (2013)
13. Gong, B., Shi, Y., Sha, F., Grauman, K.: Geodesic flow kernel for unsupervised domain adaptation. In: CVPR (2012)
14. Gong, Y., Wang, L., Guo, R., Lazebnik, S.: Multi-scale orderless pooling of deep convolutional activation features. In: Fleet, D., Pajdla, T., Schiele, B., Tuytelaars, T. (eds.) ECCV 2014, Part VII. LNCS, vol. 8695, pp. 392–407. Springer, Heidelberg (2014)
15. Griffin, G., Holub, A., Perona, P.: Caltech 256 object category dataset. Technical report UCB/CSD-04-1366, California Institue of Technology (2007)
16. Hoffman, J., Guadarrama, S., Tzeng, E., Hu, R., Donahue, J., Girshick, R., Darrell, T., Saenko, K.: LSDA: Large scale detection through adaptation. In: NIPS (2014)
17. Hoffman, J., Kulis, B., Darrell, T., Saenko, K.: Discovering latent domains for multisource domain adaptation. In: Fitzgibbon, A., Lazebnik, S., Perona, P., Sato, Y., Schmid, C. (eds.) ECCV 2012, Part II. LNCS, vol. 7573, pp. 702–715. Springer, Heidelberg (2012)
18. Hoffman, J., Tzeng, E., Donahue, J., Jia, Y., Saenko, K., Darrell, T.: One-shot adaptation of supervised deep convolutional models (2014)
19. Khosla, A., Zhou, T., Malisiewicz, T., Efros, A.A., Torralba, A.: Undoing the damage of dataset bias. In: Fitzgibbon, A., Lazebnik, S., Perona, P., Sato, Y., Schmid, C. (eds.) ECCV 2012, Part I. LNCS, vol. 7572, pp. 158–171. Springer, Heidelberg (2012)
20. Krizhevsky, A., Sutskever, I., Hinton, G.E.: ImageNet classification with deep convolutional neural networks. In: NIPS (2012)
21. Lai, K., Bo, L., Ren, X., Fox, D.: A large-scale hierarchical multi-view rgb-d object dataset. In: ICRA (2011)
22. Lampert, C.H., Nickisch, H., Harmeling, S.: Learning to detect unseen object classes by between class attribute transfer. In: CVPR (2009)
23. Leibe, B., Schiele, B.: Analyzing appearance and contour based methods for object categorization. In: CVPR (2003)
24. Lowe, D.G.: Object recognition from local scale-invariant features. In: ICCV (1999)
25. Microsoft.: Microsoft Research Cambridge Object Recognition Image Database (2005). http://research.microsoft.com/en-us/downloads/b94de342-60dc-45d0-830b-9f6eff91b301/default.aspx

26. Oquab, M., Bottou, L., Laptev, I., Sivic, J.: Learning and transferring mid-level image representations using convolutional neural networks. In: CVPR (2014)

27. Razavian, A.S., Azizpour, H., Sullivan, J., Carlsson, S.: CNN Features off-the-shelf: an Astounding Baseline for Recognition (2014). arXiv:1403.6382

28. Russakovsky, O., Deng, J., Su, H., Krause, J., Satheesh, S., Ma, S., Huang, Z., Karpathy, A., Khosla, A., Bernstein, M., Berg, A.C., Fei-Fei, L.: ImageNet large scale visual recognition challenge (2014). arXiv:1409.0575

29. Russakovsky, O., Deng, J., Su, H., Krause, J., Satheesh, S., Ma, S., Huang, Z., Karpathy, A., Khosla, A., Bernstein, M., Berg, A.C., Fei-Fei, L.: ImageNet Large Scale Visual Recognition Challenge. Int. J. Comput. Vis. (IJCV), 1–42 (2015). doi:10.1007/s11263-015-0816-y

30. Chopra, S., Balakrishnan, S., Gopalan, R.: DLID: deep learning for domain adaptation by interpolating between domains. In: ICML Workshop on Challenges in Representation Learning (2013)

31. Saenko, K., Kulis, B., Fritz, M., Darrell, T.: Adapting visual category models to new domains. In: Daniilidis, K., Maragos, P., Paragios, N. (eds.) ECCV 2010, Part IV. LNCS, vol. 6314, pp. 213–226. Springer, Heidelberg (2010)

32. Sermanet, P., Eigen, D., Zhang, X., Mathieu, M., Fergus, R., LeCun, Y.: Overfeat: integrated recognition, localization and detection using convolutional networks. In: ICLR (2014)

33. Tommasi, T., Tuytelaars, T.: A testbed for cross-dataset analysis. In: Agapito, L., Bronstein, M.M., Rother, C. (eds.) ECCV 2014 Workshops. LNCS, vol. 8927, pp. 18–31. Springer, Heidelberg (2015)

34. Torralba, A., Efros, A.A.: Unbiased look at dataset bias. In: CVPR (2011)

35. Torresani, L., Szummer, M., Fitzgibbon, A.: Efficient object category recognition using classemes. In: Daniilidis, K., Maragos, P., Paragios, N. (eds.) ECCV 2010, Part I. LNCS, vol. 6311, pp. 776–789. Springer, Heidelberg (2010)

36. Xiao, J., Hays, J., Ehinger, K.A., Oliva, A., Torralba, A.: Sun database: large-scale scene recognition from abbey to zoo. In: CVPR (2010)

37. Zeiler, M.D., Fergus, R.: Visualizing and understanding convolutional networks. In: Fleet, D., Pajdla, T., Schiele, B., Tuytelaars, T. (eds.) ECCV 2014, Part I. LNCS, vol. 8689, pp. 818–833. Springer, Heidelberg (2014)

38. Zhang, N., Donahue, J., Girshick, R., Darrell, T.: Part-based R-CNNs for fine-grained category detection. In: Fleet, D., Pajdla, T., Schiele, B., Tuytelaars, T. (eds.) ECCV 2014, Part I. LNCS, vol. 8689, pp. 834–849. Springer, Heidelberg (2014)

What Is Holding Back Convnets for Detection?

Bojan Pepik[(✉)], Rodrigo Benenson, Tobias Ritschel,
and Bernt Schiele

Max-Planck Institute for Informatics, Saarbrücken, Germany
bojan@mpi-inf.mpg.de

Abstract. Convolutional neural networks have recently shown excellent
results in general object detection and many other tasks. Albeit very
effective, they involve many user-defined design choices. In this paper we
want to better understand these choices by inspecting two key aspects
"what did the network learn?", and "what can the network learn?". We
exploit new annotations (Pascal3D+), to enable a new empirical analysis
of the R-CNN detector. Despite common belief, our results indicate that
existing state-of-the-art convnets are not invariant to various appearance
factors. In fact, all considered networks have similar weak points which
cannot be mitigated by simply increasing the training data (architectural
changes are needed). We show that overall performance can improve
when using image renderings as data augmentation. We report the best
known results on Pascal3D+ detection and view-point estimation tasks.

1 Introduction

In the last years convolutional neural networks (convnets) have become "the
hammer that pounds many nails" of computer vision. Classical problems such as
general image classification [17], object detection [12], pose estimation [4], face
recognition [28], object tracking [20], keypoint matching [10], stereo matching
[40], optical flow [9], boundary estimation [38], and semantic labelling [21], have
now all top performing results based on a direct usage of convnets. The price
to pay for such versatility and good results is a limited understanding of why
convnets work so well, and how to build & train them to reach better results.

In this paper we focus on convnets for object detection. For many object
categories convnets have almost doubled over previous detection quality. Yet, it
is unclear what exactly enables such good performance, and critically, how to
further improve it. The usual word of wisdom for better detection with convnets
is "larger networks and more data". But: how should the network grow; which
kind of additional data will be most helpful; what follows after fine-tuning an
ImageNet pre-trained model on the classes of interest? We aim at addressing
such questions in the context of the R-CNN detection pipeline [12] (Sect. 2).

Previous work aiming to analyse convnets have either focused on theoretical aspects [2], visualising some specific patterns emerging inside the network
[18,22,29,31], or doing ablation studies of working systems [1,3,12]. However, it
remains unclear what is withholding the detection capabilities of convnets.

© Springer International Publishing Switzerland 2015
J. Gall et al. (Eds.): GCPR 2015, LNCS 9358, pp. 517–528, 2015.
DOI: 10.1007/978-3-319-24947-6_43

Contributions. This paper contributes a novel empirical exploration of R-CNNs for detection. We use the recently available Pascal3D+ [37] dataset, as well as rendered images to analyze R-CNNs capabilities at a more detailed level than previous work. In a new set of experiments we explore which appearance factors are well captured by a trained R-CNN, and which ones are not. We consider factors such as rotation (azimuth, elevation), size, category, and instance shape. We want to know which aspects can be improved by simply increasing the training data, and which ones require changing the network. We want to answer both "what did the network learn?" (Sect. 5) and "what can the network learn?" (Sects. 6 and 7). Our results indicate that current convnets (AlexNet [17], GoogleNet [33], VGG16 [30]) struggle to model small objects, truncation, and occlusion and are not invariant to these factors. Simply increasing the training data does solve these issues. On the other hand, properly designed synthetic training data can help pushing forward the overall detection performance.

1.1 Related Work

Understanding Convnets. The tremendous success of convnets coupled with their black-box nature has drawn much attention towards understanding them better. Previous analyses have either focused on highlighting the versatility of its features [26,27], learning equivariant mappings [19], training issues [5,16], theoretical arguments for its expressive power [2], discussing the brittleness of the decision boundary [14,34], visualising specific patterns emerging inside the network [18,22,29,31], or doing ablation studies of working systems [1,3,12].

We leverage the recent Pascal3D+ annotations [37] to do a new analysis complementary to previous ones. Rather than aiming to explain how does the network work, we aim at identifying in which cases the network does not work well, and if training data is sufficient to improve these issues. While previous work has shown that convnets are increasingly invariant with depth, here we show that current architectures are still not overall invariant to many appearance factors.

Synthetic Data. The idea of using rendered images to train detectors has been visited multiple times. Previous works include photo-realistic video game renderings [39], wire-frame renderings [24,32] focusing on object boundaries, or augmenting the data by subtle deformations of the positive samples [7,25]. Most of these works focused on DPM-like detectors, which can only make limited use of large training sets [41]. In this paper we investigate how different types of renderings (wire-frame, materials, and textures) impact the performance of a convnet. A priori convnets are more suitable to ingest larger volumes of data.

2 The R-CNN Detector

The remarkable convnet results in the ImageNet 2012 classification competition [17] ignited a new wave of neural networks for computer vision. R-CNN [12] adapts such convnets for the task of object detection, and has become the de-facto architecture for state-of-the-art object detection (with top results on Pascal

VOC [8] and ImageNet [6]) and is thus the focus of attention in this paper. The R-CNN detector is a three stage pipeline: object proposal generation [36], convnet feature extraction, and one-vs-all SVM classification with bounding box regression. We refer to the original paper for details of the training procedure [12]. Different networks can be used for feature extraction (AlexNet [17], VGG [3], GoogleNet [33]), all pre-trained on ImageNet and fine-tuned for detection. The larger the network, the better the performance. The SVM gains a couple of final mAP points compared to logistic regression used during fine-tuning (and larger networks benefit less from it [11]).

In this work we primarily focus on the core ingredient: convnet fine-tuning for object detection. We consider fine-tuning with various training distributions, and analyse the performance under various appearance factors. Unless otherwise specified reported numbers do not include the bounding box regression.

3   Pascal3D+ Dataset

Our experiments are enabled by the recently introduced Pascal3D+ [37] dataset. It enriches PASCAL VOC 2012 with 3D annotations in the form of aligned 3D CAD models for 11 classes (*aeroplane, bicycle, boat, bus, car, chair, diningtable, motorbike, sofa, train,* and *tv monitor*) of the *train* and *val* subsets. The alignments are obtained through human supervision, by first selecting the visually most similar CAD model for each instance, and specifying the correspondences between a set of 3D CAD model keypoints and their image projections, which are used to compute the 3D pose of the instance in the image. The rich object annotations include object pose and shape, and we use them as a test bed for our analysis. Unless otherwise stated all presented models are trained on the Pascal3D+ *train* set and evaluated on its test set (Pascal VOC 2012 *val*).

4   Synthetic Images

Convnets reach high classification/detection quality by using a large parametric model (e.g. in the order of 10^7 parameters). The price to pay is that convnets need a large training set to reach top performance. We want to explore whether the performance scales as we increase the amount of training data. To that end, we explore two possible directions to increase the data volume: data augmentation and synthetic data generation.

Data augmentation consists of creating new training samples by simple transformations of the original ones (such as scaling, cropping, blurring, subtle colour shifts, etc.), and it is a common practice during training on large convnets [3,17]. To generate synthetic images we rely on CAD models of the object classes of interest. Rendering synthetic data has the advantage that we can generate large amounts of training data in a controlled setup, allowing for arbitrary appearance factor distributions. For our synthetic data experiments we use an extended set of CAD models, and consider multiple types of renderings (Sect. 4.1).

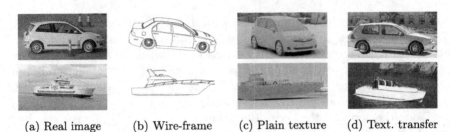

| (a) Real image | (b) Wire-frame | (c) Plain texture | (d) Text. transfer |

Fig. 1. Example training samples for different type of synthetic rendering.

Extended Pascal3D+ CAD Models. Although the Pascal3D+ dataset [37] comes with its own set of CAD models, this set is rather small and it comes without material information (only polygonal mesh). Thus the Pascal3D+ models alone are not sufficient for our analysis. We extend this set with models collected from internet resources. We use an initial set of ~ 40 models per class. For each Pascal3D+ training sample we generate one synthetic version per model using a "plain texture" rendering (see next section) with the same camera-to-object pose. We select suitable CAD models by evaluating the R-CNN (trained on Pascal 2007 train set) on the rendered images, and we keep a model if it generates the highest scoring response (across CAD models) for at least one training sample. This procedure makes sure we only use CAD models that generate somewhat realistic images close to the original training data distribution, and makes it easy to prune unsuitable models. Out of ~ 440 initial models, ~ 275 models pass the selection process (~ 25 models per class).

4.1 Rendering Types

A priori it is unclear which type of rendering will be most effective to build or augment a convnet training set. We consider multiple options using the same set of CAD models. Note that all rendering strategies exploit the Pascal3D+ data to generate training samples with a distribution similar to the real data (similar size and orientation of the objects). See Fig. 1 for example renderings.

Wire-Frame. Using a white background, shape boundaries of a CAD model are rendered as black lines. This rendering reflects the shape (not the mesh) of the object, abstracting its texture or material properties and might help the detector to focus on the shape aspects of the object.

Plain Texture. A somewhat more photo-realistic rendering considers the material properties (but not the textures), so that shadows are present. We considered using a blank background, or an environment model to generate plausible backgrounds. We obtain slightly improved results using the plausible backgrounds, and thus only report these results. This rendering provides "toy car" type images, that can be considered as middle ground between "wire frame" and "texture transfer" rendering.

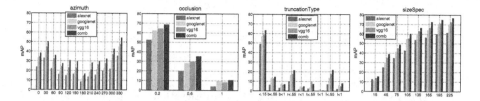

Fig. 2. mAP of R-CNN over appearance factors. Pascal3D+.

Texture Transfer. All datasets suffer from bias [35], and it is hard to identify it by hand. Ideally, synthetic renderings should have the same bias as the real data, while injecting additional diversity. We aim at solving this by generating new training samples via texture transfer. For a given annotated object on the Pascal3D+ dataset, we have both the image it belongs to and an aligned 3D CAD model. We create a new training image by replacing the object with a new 3D CAD model, and by applying over it a texture coming from a different image. This approach allows to generate objects with slightly different shapes, and with different textures, while still adequately positioned in a realistic background context (for now, our texture transfer approach ignores occlusions). This type of rendering is close to photo-realistic, using real background context, while increasing the diversity by injecting new object shapes and textures.

As we will see in Sect. 7, any of our renderings can be used to improve detection performance. Still the level of realism affects how much improvement is obtained.

5 What Did the Network Learn from Real Data?

In this section we analyze R-CNNs detection performance in an attempt to understand what have the models actually learned. We first explore models performance across different appearance factors (Sect. 5.1), going beyond the usual per-class detection performance. Second, we dive deeper and aim at understanding what have the network layers actually learned (Sect. 5.2).

5.1 Detection Performance Across Appearance Factors

To analyze the performance across appearance factors we split each factor into equi-spaced bins. We present a new evaluation protocol where for each bin only the data falling in it are actually considered in the evaluation and the rest are ignored. This allows to dissect the detection performance across different aspects of an appearance factor. The original R-CNN [12] work includes a similar analysis based on the toolkit from [15]. Pascal3D+ however enables a more fine-grained analysis. Our experiments report results for AlexNet (51.2 mAP) [17], GoogleNet (56.6 mAP) [33], VGG16 (58.8 mAP) [30] and their combination (62.4 mAP).

Appearance Factors. We focus the evaluation on the following appearance factors: rotation (azimuth, elevation), size, occlusion and truncation as these

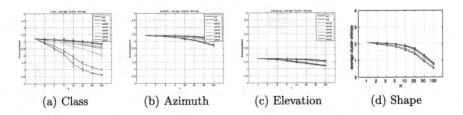

(a) Class	(b) Azimuth	(c) Elevation	(d) Shape

Fig. 3. Average cluster entropy versus number of clusters K; at different layers, for different appearance factors. Pascal3D+ test data.

factors have strong impact on objects appearance. Azimuth and elevation refer to the angular camera position w.r.t. the object. Size refers to the bounding box height. Although the Pascal3D+ dataset comes with binary occlusion and truncation states, using the aligned CAD models and segmentation masks we compute level of occlusion as well as level and type of truncation. While occlusion and truncation levels are expressed as object area percentage, we distinguish between 4 truncation types: bottom (b), top (t), left (l) and right (r) truncation.

Analysis. Figure 2 reports performance across the factors. The results point to multiple general observations. First, there is a clear ordering among the models. VGG16 is better than GoogleNet on all factor bins, which in turn consistently outperforms AlexNet. The combination of the three models (SVM trained on concatenated features) consistently outperforms all of them suggesting there is underlying complementarity among the networks. Second, the relative strengths and weaknesses across the factors remain the same across models. All networks struggle with occlusions, truncations, and objects below 120 pixels in height. Third, for each factor the performance is not homogeneous across bins, suggesting the networks are not invariant w.r.t. the appearance factors.

It should be noted that there are a few confounding factors in the results. First such factor is the image support (pixel area) of the object, which is strongly correlated with performance. Whenever the support is smaller e.g. small sizes, large occlusions/truncations or frontal views the performance is lower. Second confounding factor is the training data distribution. For a network with a finite number of parameters, it needs to decide to which cases it will allocate resources. The loss used during training will push the network to handle well the most common cases, and disregard the rare cases. Typical example is the elevation, where the models learn to handle well the near 0° cases (well represented), while they fail on the outliers: upper (90°)and lower (−90°) cases. We explore this aspect in Sect. 6 by investigating performance under different training distributions.

Conclusion. There is a clear performance ordering among the convnets which all have similar weaknesses, tightly related to data distribution and object area. Occlusion, truncation, and small objects are clearly weak points of the R-CNN detectors (arguably harder problems by themselves). Given similar tendencies next sections focus on AlexNet.

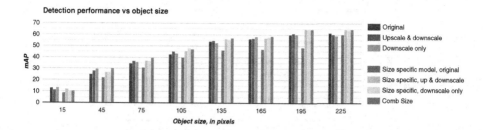

Fig. 4. Training with varying object size distribution.

5.2 Appearance Vector Disentanglement

Other than just the raw detection quality, we are interested in understanding what did the network learn internally. While previous work focused on specific neuron activations [13], we aim at analyzing the feature representations of individual layers. Given a trained network, we apply it over positive test samples, and cluster the feature vectors at a given layer. We then inspect the cluster entropy with respect to different appearance factors, as we increase the number of clusters. The resulting curves are shown in Fig. 3. Lower average entropy indicates that at the given layer the network is able to disentangle the considered appearance factor. Disentanglement relates to discriminative power, invariance, and equivariance. (Related entropy based metric is reported in [1], however they focus on individual neurons).

Analysis. From Fig. 3a we see that classes are well disentangled. As we go from the lowest conv1 layer to the highest fc7 layer the disentanglement increases, showing that with depth the network layers become more variant w.r.t. category. This is not surprising as the network has been trained to distinguish classes. On the other hand for azimuth, elevation and shape (class-specific disentanglement) the disentanglement across layers and across cluster number stays relatively constant, pointing out that the layers are not as variant to these factors.

Conclusion. We make two observations. First, convnet representations at higher layers disentangle object categories well, explaining its strong recognition performance. Second, network layers are to some extent invariant to different factors.

6 What Could the Network Learn with More Data?

Section 5 inspected what the network learned when trained with the original training set. In this section we explore what the network could learn if additional data is available. We will focus on size (Sect. 6.1), truncations and occlusions (Sect. 6.2) since these are aspects that R-CNNs struggle to handle. For each case we consider two general approaches: changing the training data distribution, or using additional supervision during training. For the former we use data augmentation to generate additional samples for specific size, occlusion, or truncation bins. Augmenting the training data distribution helps us realize if adding

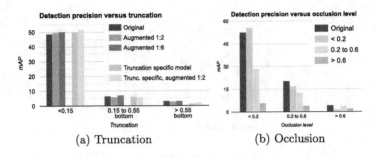

(a) Truncation   (b) Occlusion

Fig. 5. Varying truncated and occluded training data distribution

extra data for a specific factor bin helps improving the performance on that particular bin. When using additional supervision, we leverage the annotations to train a separate model for each bin. Providing an explicit signal during training forces the network to distinguish among specific factor bins. The experiments involve fine-tuning the R-CNN only as we are interested in convnet modelling capabilities.

6.1 Size Handling

More Data. Figure 4 shows the results with different object size training distributions. The "original" bars correspond to the results in Fig. 2. "Up & downscale" corresponds to training with a uniform size distribution across bins by up/downscaling all samples to all bins. As upscaled images are blurry, "downscale only" avoids such blur, resulting in a distribution with more small size samples than larger sizes. Results in Fig. 4 indicate that data augmentation can provide a few mAP points gain for small objects, however the network still struggles with small size, thus it is not invariant w.r.t. size despite the uniform training distribution.

Bin-Specific Models. The right side bars of Fig. 4 show results for bin-specific networks. Each bar corresponds to a model trained and tested on that size range. Both augmentation methods outperform the original data distribution on all size bins (e.g. at 195 pixels, "up & downscale" improves by 5.2 mAP). In "comb size" we combine the "up & downscale" size specific models via an SVM trained on their concatenated features. This results in superior overall performance (54.0 mAP) w.r.t. the original data (51.2 mAP with SVM).

Conclusion. These results indicate that (a) adding data uniformly across sizes provides mild gains for small objects and does not result in size invariant models, suggesting that the models suffer from limited capacity and (b) training bin-specific models results in better per bin and overall performance.

6.2 Truncation and Occlusion Handling

More Data. Figure 5a shows that generating truncated samples from non-truncated ones, respecting the original data distribution, help improve (1.5 mAP

Table 1. Pascal3D+ results

Synthetic type	Ratio Real:Synth.	mAP
-	1:0	47.6
Wire-frame	0:1	21.8
Plain texture	0:1	23.5
Texture transfer	0:1	38.4
Wire-frame	1:2	48.3
Plain texture	1:2	49.9
Texture transfer	1:2	**51.5**

(a) Different synthetic data types

Data	CNN	mAP	AAVP
Pascal3D+	AlexNet	51.2	35.3[23]
	GoogleNet	56.6	-
	VGG16	58.8	-
	comb	62.6	-
Pascal3D+	AlexNet	54.6	-
&	GoogleNet	59.1	-
Texture	VGG16	61.9	-
transfer	comb	64.1	**43.8**
	comb+size	64.7	-
	comb+bb	66.3	-
	comb+size+bb	**67.2**	-

(b) Combining convnets

points) handling objects with minimal truncation; but does not improve medium or large truncation handling (trends for top, left and right are similar).

Bin-Specific Models. Similar to the "more data" case, training a convnet for each truncation case only helps for the low truncation cases, but is ineffective for medium/large truncations. Similar to truncations, Fig. 5b shows that specialising a network for each occlusion case is only effective for the low occlusions. Medium/high occlusions are a "distraction" for training non-occluded detectors.

Conclusion. These results are a clear indication that training data do not help per-se handling these cases. Simply adding data or focusing the network on subtasks seems insufficient. Architectural changes to the detector seem required to obtain a meaningful improvement.

7 Does Synthetic Data Help?

We have seen that convnets have weak spots for object detection, and adding data results in limited gains. As convnets are data hungry methods, the question remains what happens when more data from the same distribution is introduced. Obtaining additional annotated data is expensive, thus we consider the option of using renderings. The results are summarised in Table 1a. Again we focus on fine-tuning convnets only. All renderings are done using a similar data distribution as the original one, aiming to improve on common cases.

Analysis. From Table 1a we observe that using synthetic data alone (0:1 ratio) under-performs compared to using real data, showing there is still room for improvement on the synthetic data itself. That being said, we observe that even the arguably weak wire-frame renderings do help improve detections when used as an extension of the real data. We empirically chose data ratio of 1:2 between real and synthetic as that seemed to strike good balance among the two data sources. As expected, the detection improvement is directly proportional to the photo-realism (see Table 1a). This indicates that further gains can be expected as photo-realism is improved. Our texture transfer approach is quite effective, with a 4 mAP points improvement. Wire-frame renderings inject information from the extended CAD models. The plain texture renderings additionally inject material and background information. The texture transfer renderings use Pascal3D+ data, which include ImageNet images too. If we add these images directly to the training set (instead of doing texture transfer) we obtain 50.6 mAP (original to ImageNet images ratio is 1:3). This shows that the increased diversity of our synthetic samples further improve results. Plain textures provide 2 mAP points improvement, and texture transfer 4 mAP points. In comparison, [11] reports 3 mAP points gain (on Pascal VOC 2012 test set) when using the Pascal VOC 2007 and the 2012 data. Our gains are quite comparable despite relying on synthetic renderings.

Conclusion. Synthetic renderings are an effective mean to increase the overall detection quality. Even simple wire-frame renderings can be of help.

8   All-in-One

In Table 1b we show results when training the SVM on top of the concatenated features of the convnets fine-tuned with real and mixed data. We also report joint object localization and viewpoint estimation results (AAVP [23] measure). As in [23], for viewpoint prediction we rely on a regressor trained on convnet features fine-tuned for detection.

We observe that the texture renderings improve performance on all models (e.g. VGG16 58.8 to 61.9 mAP). Combining the three models further improves detection performance achieving state-of-the-art viewpoint estimation. Adding size specific VGG16 models (like in Sect. 6.1) further pushes the results, improving up to 5 mAP on small/medium sized objects. Adding bounding box regression, our final combination achieves 67.2 mAP, the best reported result on Pascal3D+.

9   Conclusion

We presented new results regarding the performance and potential of the R-CNN architecture. Although higher overall performance can be reached with deeper convnets (VGG16), the considered state-of-the-art networks have similar weaknesses; they underperform for truncated, occluded and small objects (Sect. 6). Additional data does not solve these weak points, hinting that structural changes are needed. Despite common belief, our results suggest these models are not invariant to various appearance factors. Increased training data, however, does improve overall performance, even when using synthetic image renderings (Sect. 7).

In future work, we would like to extend the CAD model set in order to cover more categories. Understanding which architectural changes will be most effective to handle truncation, occlusion, or small objects remains an open question.

References

1. Agrawal, P., Girshick, R., Malik, J.: Analyzing the performance of multilayer neural networks for object recognition. In: Fleet, D., Pajdla, T., Schiele, B., Tuytelaars, T. (eds.) ECCV 2014, Part VII. LNCS, vol. 8695, pp. 329–344. Springer, Heidelberg (2014)
2. Bengio, Y., Delalleau, O.: On the expressive power of deep architectures. In: Kivinen, J., Szepesvári, C., Ukkonen, E., Zeugmann, T. (eds.) ALT 2011. LNCS, vol. 6925, pp. 18–36. Springer, Heidelberg (2011)
3. Chatfield, K., Simonyan, K., Vedaldi, A., Zisserman, A.: Return of the devil in the details: delving deep into convolutional nets. In: BMVC (2014)
4. Chen, X., Yuille, A.: Articulated pose estimation by a graphical model with image dependent pairwise relations. In: NIPS (2014)
5. Dauphin, Y.N., Pascanu, R., Gulcehre, C., Cho, K., Ganguli, S., Bengio, Y.: Identifying and attacking the saddle point problem in high-dimensional non-convex optimization. In: NIPS, pp. 2933–2941 (2014)
6. Deng, J., Dong, W., Socher, R., Li, L.J., Li, K., Fei-Fei, L.: ImageNet: a large-scale hierarchical image database. In: CVPR (2009)
7. Enzweiler, M., Gavrila, D.M.: A mixed generative-discriminative framework for pedestrian classification. In: CVPR, pp. 1–8. IEEE (2008)
8. Everingham, M., Zisserman, A., Williams, C.K.I., Van Gool, L.: The 2007 Pascal Visual Object Classes Challenge. Springer-Verlag, Berlin (2007)
9. Fischer, P., Dosovitskiy, A., Ilg, E., Häusser, P., Hazirbas, C., Golkov, V., van der Smagt, P., Cremers, D., Brox, T.: Flownet: learning optical flow with convolutional networks. Arxiv. No. 1405.5769 (2015). http://lmb.informatik.uni-freiburg. de//Publications/2015/FDIB15
10. Fischer, P., Dosovitskiy, A., Brox, T.: Descriptor matching with convolutional neural networks: a comparison to sift (2014). arXiv:1405.5769
11. Girshick, R.: Fast R-CNN (2015). arXiv:1504.08083
12. Girshick, R., Donahue, J., Darrell, T., Malik, J.: Rich feature hierarchies for accurate object detection and semantic segmentation. arXiv (2014)
13. Goodfellow, I., Le, Q., Saxe, A., Ng, A.Y.: Measuring invariances in deep networks. In: NIPS (2009)
14. Goodfellow, I.J., Shlens, J., Szegedy, C.: Explaining and harnessing adversarial examples. In: ICLR (2015)
15. Hoiem, D., Chodpathumwan, Y., Dai, Q.: Diagnosing error in object detectors. In: Fitzgibbon, A., Lazebnik, S., Perona, P., Sato, Y., Schmid, C. (eds.) ECCV 2012, Part III. LNCS, vol. 7574, pp. 340–353. Springer, Heidelberg (2012)
16. Ioffe, S., Szegedy, C.: Batch normalization: accelerating deep network training by reducing internal covariate shift (2015). arXiv:1502.03167
17. Krizhevsky, A., Sutskever, I., Hinton, G.E.: Imagenet classification with deep convolutional neural networks. In: NIPS (2012)
18. Le, Q.V., Monga, R., Devin, M., Chen, K., Corrado, G.S., Dean, J., Ng, A.Y.: Building high-level features using large scale unsupervised learning. In: ICML (2012)
19. Lenc, K., Vedaldi, A.: Understanding image representations by measuring their equivariance and equivalence. In: CVPR (2015)
20. Li, H., Li, Y., Porikli, F.: Robust online visual tracking with a single convolutional neural network. In: Cremers, D., Reid, I., Saito, H., Yang, M.-H. (eds.) ACCV 2014. LNCS, vol. 9007, pp. 194–209. Springer, Heidelberg (2015)

21. Long, J., Shelhamer, E., Darrell, T.: Fully convolutional networks for semantic segmentation. In: CVPR, November 2015
22. Mahendran, A., Vedaldi, A.: Understanding deep image representations by inverting them. In: CVPR, June 2015
23. Pepik, B., Stark, M., Gehler, P., Ritschel, T., Schiele, B.: 3D object class detection in the wild. In: 3DSI in Conjunction with CVPR (2015)
24. Pepik, B., Stark, M., Gehler, P., Schiele, B.: Multi-view and 3D deformable part models. TPAMI (2015)
25. Pishchulin, L., Jain, A., Andriluka, M., Thormaehlen, T., Schiele, B.: Articulated people detection and pose estimation: reshaping the future. In: CVPR, June 2012
26. Razavian, A.S., Azizpour, H., Maki, A., Sullivan, J., Ek, C.H., Carlsson, S.: Persistent evidence of local image properties in generic convnets (2014). arXiv:1411.6509
27. Razavian, A.S., Azizpour, H., Sullivan, J., Carlsson, S.: CNN features off-the-shelf: an astounding baseline for recognition. In: CVPR Workshops, pp. 512–519. IEEE (2014)
28. Schroff, F., Kalenichenko, D., Philbin, J.: Facenet: A unified embedding for face recognition and clustering (2015). arXiv:1503.03832
29. Simonyan, K., Vedaldi, A., Zisserman, A.: Deep inside convolutional networks: visualising image classification models and saliency maps. In: ICLR Workshop (2014)
30. Simonyan, K., Zisserman, A.: Very deep convolutional networks for large-scale image recognition. In: ICLR (2015)
31. Springenberg, J.T., Dosovitskiy, A., Brox, T., Riedmiller, M.: Striving for simplicity: the all convolutional net. In: ICLR (2015)
32. Stark, M., Goesele, M., Schiele, B.: Back to the future: learning shape models from 3D CAD data. In: BMVC, vol. 2, p. 5 (2010)
33. Szegedy, C., Liu, W., Jia, Y., Sermanet, P., Reed, S., Anguelov, D., Erhan, D., Vanhoucke, V., Rabinovich, A.: Going deeper with convolutions (2014). arXiv preprint arXiv:1409.4842
34. Szegedy, C., Zaremba, W., Sutskever, I., Bruna, J., Erhan, D., Goodfellow, I., Fergus, R.: Intriguing properties of neural networks. In: ICLR (2014)
35. Torralba, A., Efros, A.A.: Unbiased look at dataset bias. In: CVPR, pp. 1521–1528. IEEE (2011)
36. Uijlings, J., van de Sande, K., Gevers, T., Smeulders, A.: Selective search for object recognition. In: IJCV (2013)
37. Xiang, Y., Mottaghi, R., Savarese, S.: Beyond pascal: a benchmark for 3D object detection in the wild. In: WACV (2014)
38. Xie, S., Tu, Z.: Holistically-nested edge detection (2015). arXiv:1504.06375
39. Xu, J., Vazquez, D., Lopez, A.M., Marin, J., Ponsa, D.: Learning a part-based pedestrian detector in a virtual world. IEEE Trans. Intell. Transp. Syst. **15**(5), 2121–2131 (2014)
40. Zbontar, J., LeCun, Y.: Computing the stereo matching cost with a convolutional neural network. In: CVPR, June 2015
41. Zhu, X., Vondrick, C., Ramanan, D., Fowlkes, C.: Do we need more training data or better models for object detection? In: BMVC (2012)

A Modified Isomap Approach to Manifold Learning in Word Spotting

Sebastian Sudholt[(✉)] and Gernot A. Fink

Technische Universität Dortmund, Dortmund, Germany
{sebastian.sudholt,gernot.fink}@tu-dortmund.de

Abstract. Word spotting is an effective paradigm for indexing document images with minimal human effort. Here, the use of the Bag-of-Features principle has been shown to achieve competitive results on different benchmarks. Recently, a spatial pyramid approach was used as a word image representation to improve the retrieval results even further. The high dimensionality of the spatial pyramids was attempted to be countered by applying Latent Semantic Analysis. However, this leads to increasingly worse results when reducing to lower dimensions. In this paper, we propose a new approach to reducing the dimensionality of word image descriptors which is based on a modified version of the Isomap Manifold Learning algorithm. This approach is able to not only outperform Latent Semantic Analysis but also to reduce a word image descriptor to up to 0.12 % of its original size without losing retrieval precision. We evaluate our approach on two different datasets.

Keywords: Word spotting · Manifold learning · Isomap · Multidimensional scaling · Bray Curtis distance · Document image analysis

1 Introduction

The automatic transcription of handwritten documents is a challenging task for automated systems. In contrast to machine printed character recognition, it is still considered an unsolved problem and has attracted major interest in the research community. Standard OCR methods perform poorly on these kinds of documents as the variability in characters is much higher than in a machine printed context. Additionally, a large number of handwritten documents are from ancient times thus exhibiting different kinds of degradation such as fading ink or noise.

In order to overcome the limitations of OCR systems, different approaches have been proposed with *Keyword spotting* or simply *word spotting* being one of the most prominent for automatic document indexing. In *Query-by-Example (QbE)* word spotting the user supplies a query word image to the system and a list of potentially relevant word images is returned from the document collection. The major advantage here is that only a very small amount of annotated query word images is needed thus reducing manual labeling work.

© Springer International Publishing Switzerland 2015
J. Gall et al. (Eds.): GCPR 2015, LNCS 9358, pp. 529–539, 2015.
DOI: 10.1007/978-3-319-24947-6_44

As QbE word spotting is essentially a form of image retrieval, most word spotting approaches have made use of well established computer vision techniques. Here, the use of local descriptors in a Bag-of-Features approach has been proven to be well suited for this task. As the visual words used here exploit no spatial knowledge, spatial pyramids and Fisher vectors were used to regain a certain amount of spatial information [4, 10]. As the visual vocabulary is generally much bigger in word spotting than in other image retrieval applications, the resulting spatial pyramids and Fisher vectors are very high dimensional [2, 4, 10]. This fact has been accounted for by using *Latent Semantic Analysis (LSA)* to embed the word image descriptors into a lower dimensional space [10]. However, the resulting representations almost always lead to a loss in retrieval precision. Moreover, satisfying results were only achieved when projecting into still high-dimensional spaces (roughly 1500 dimensions).

Based on a metric evaluation to find the dissimilarity measure best suited for comparing spatial pyramid representations of word images, we present a new approach for reducing their dimensionality by modifying the well known Isomap algorithm. This algorithm belongs to the family of manifold learning techniques. It uses a non-linear function to obtain the low-dimensional data thus allowing for more complex projections than LSA. The modified version is able to deal with high-dimensional histograms in a sparsely sampled space. We evaluate the presented method on two different datasets.

2   Manifold Learning

The objective for dimension reduction techniques is to find a low-dimensional representation of the original data. The main assumption in manifold learning is that the original data lies on or close to a manifold which is embedded in a high-dimensional space and has a lower intrinsic dimensionality. When applying dimensionality reduction by manifold learning, the projected data is referred to as the *embedding*.

There exists a vast amount of different unsupervised manifold learning algorithms which can be classified into two classes. Local techniques, such as *Locally Linear Embedding (LLE)* [9] and *Local Tangient Space Alignment (LTSA)* [13], find the embedding by preserving local neighborhood structures of the supplied data. Global techniques, such as *Isomap* [12], aim at keeping global structures of the data thus keeping geometrically close points together while maintaining a bigger distance between geometrically distant data points. In the following, we will concentrate on the Isomap algorithm as it can be exploited in numerous ways in the context of word spotting. It is an unsupervised paradigm thus posing no need for annotated word images. Additionally, there exists an extension for Isomap called *Landmark Isomap* [11] which allows for a computationally efficient approximation of the Isomap embedding when faced with a large amount of data.

The backbone of the Isomap algorithm is the use of *Multidimensional Scaling (MDS)*. MDS solves the inverse distance problem: given a set of pairwise distances between unknown points in a d-dimensional space, find the location of the points. Given a matrix $\mathbf{D}$ of pairwise distances between n data samples, MDS starts by double centering the matrix of squared distances $\mathbf{D}^2$:

$$\mathbf{B} = -\frac{1}{2}\mathbf{H}\mathbf{D}^2\mathbf{H}, \tag{1}$$

$$\mathbf{H} = I_n - \frac{1}{n}\mathbf{1}_n\mathbf{1}_n^T, \tag{2}$$

where I_n is the $n \times n$ identity matrix and $\mathbf{1}_n\mathbf{1}_n^T$ the $n \times n$ matrix of all ones. Essentially, the double centering removes the column and row mean of $\mathbf{D}^2$.

Afterwards, the eigenvalues λ_i and their corresponding eigenvectors $\mathbf{v}_i$ are extracted from $\mathbf{B}$. The eigenvalues are then sorted in descending order. With λ_1 being the biggest eigenvalue and λ_d being the smallest, the embedding $\mathbf{E}$ is then generated as follows:

$$\mathbf{E} = \begin{pmatrix} \sqrt{\lambda_1} \cdot \mathbf{v}_1^T \\ \sqrt{\lambda_2} \cdot \mathbf{v}_2^T \\ \vdots \\ \sqrt{\lambda_d} \cdot \mathbf{v}_d^T \end{pmatrix}. \tag{3}$$

$\mathbf{E}$ is of shape $d \times n$ and each column represents the d-dimensional embedding for a specific data point.

In classical MDS the pairwise dissimilarities are Euclidean distances. In Isomap these distances are replaced by an approximation of the geodesic distances along the manifold: for each data sample the k nearest neighbors are calculated and connected to form a neighborhood graph. The distance between two data samples is now its shortest path distance along the graph.

Data samples that have not been used for the initial embedding computation can easily be projected into the embedding space for MDS as well as Isomap. This process is referred to as *out-of-sample embedding* [5]. Let $\mathbf{d}$ denote the column vector of distances from a new data sample $\mathbf{x}$ to all samples used for embedding (geodesic distances in the case of Isomap) and $\mathbf{m}$ the mean of each column in $\mathbf{D}^2$, then the embedding $\mathbf{e}$ for $\mathbf{x}$ is obtained by computing

$$\mathbf{e} = \frac{1}{2}\mathbf{E}^\# \left(\mathbf{m} - \mathbf{d}^2\right), \tag{4}$$

where

$$\mathbf{E}^\# = \begin{pmatrix} \lambda_1^{-\frac{1}{2}} \cdot \mathbf{v}_1^T \\ \lambda_2^{-\frac{1}{2}} \cdot \mathbf{v}_2^T \\ \vdots \\ \lambda_d^{-\frac{1}{2}} \cdot \mathbf{v}_d^T \end{pmatrix}. \tag{5}$$

3   Method

Using LSA leads to noticable performance drops when applied in a word spotting scenario. We believe the main reason for this to be that the singular value decomposition used in LSA assumes an Euclidean metric on the input data. This distance measure has already been shown to not perform well on histogram representations [6].

Based on this observation, we propose the use of a dimensionality reduction technique that does not assume an Euclidean metric on the input data. While the use of a manifold learning approach appears to be a well suited solution here, we will show that it performs poorly on this task as well. The main reason for this is that the standard manifold algorithms expect real valued data. We will show that treating the histogram representations as residing in $\mathbb{R}^n$ leads to an insufficient approximation of the geodesic distances and subsequently to bad embeddings. Thus, we propose to combine Isomap and a local metric which is suitable for spatial pyramid representations.

The standard metric for histogram comparison in word spotting has been the Cosine distance [2,3,10]. For other image retrieval tasks, such as [6], the L1 and L2 norms are used. Other discrete distributions, i.e. *Local Binary Pattern (LBP) histograms* [1], are often times compared by the χ^2 distance. Given two histograms $\mathbf{a}$ and $\mathbf{b}$ the χ^2 distance is obtained by

$$\chi^2(\mathbf{a}, \mathbf{b}) = \sum_i \frac{(\mathbf{a}_i - \mathbf{b}_i)^2}{\mathbf{a}_i + \mathbf{b}_i} \tag{6}$$

where $\mathbf{a}_i$ and $\mathbf{b}_i$ are the i-th elements of the respective histograms.

Though the χ^2 distance leads to good results, this metric is not well suited for spatial pyramid comparison in a word spotting scenario. Opposed to LBP histograms, spatial pyramids are very sparse quite frequently which leads to multiple zero-divisions when applying the χ^2 distance metric. This problem is accounted for by the Bray Curtis distance:

$$BC(\mathbf{a}, \mathbf{b}) = \frac{\sum_i |\mathbf{a}_i - \mathbf{b}_i|}{\sum_i \mathbf{a}_i + \mathbf{b}_i}. \tag{7}$$

Here, no zero-division occurs when assuming that one of the histograms compared contains at least one non-zero entry. To the best of our knowledge, the BC distance has not been used in a computer vision context before.

As will be shown in the following section, the Bray Curtis distance emerges as most suitable metric for spatial pyramid comparisons on the tested benchmarks. Thus, we use this metric instead of the Euclidean distance to compute nearest neighbors and their approximate geodesic distance. Subsequently, we will term our approach *Bray Curtis Isomap (BC-Isomap)*.

The pipeline for our method is outlined in Fig. 1. First, a spatial pyramid is extracted for each word image. Afterwards, a nearest neighbor graph is extracted

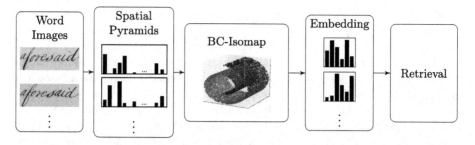

Fig. 1. The figure displays the pipeline of our BC-Isomap method.

from the spatial pyramids where the nearest neighbor distance is calculated with the Bray Curtis distance metric. MDS is used on the geodesic distances computed from the graph to find an embedding that preserves these distances. The embedded representations are then used to perform word spotting. Please note that after embedding the word image representations reside in an Euclidean space. Thus the Euclidean distance has to be used in order to perform word spotting.

4   Experiments

4.1   Datasets and Implementation Details

For the following experiments we are going to use two datasets. The first is the *George Washington dataset (GW)* [7]. It consists of a 20 page excerpt from a bigger collection of letters by George Washington and his associates. The corresponding ground truth contains 4860 words. As the writing style does not exhibit large variations, it is widely considered a single writer scenario [4,8]. Sample word images from the George Washington database can be seen in Fig. 2a. We follow the evaluation protocol used in [3] and [4] with minor modifications: each segmented word image is used once as a query to retrieve a ranked list of the

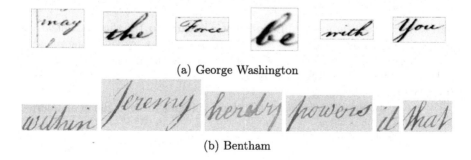

(a) George Washington

(b) Bentham

Fig. 2. Sample word images for the (a) George Washington dataset and (b) Bentham validation dataset.

remaining word images. Words which appear only once in the dataset are not used as queries. In order to generate a spatial pyramid representation for each word, SIFT descriptors are extracted in a dense grid with a step size of 5 pixels and a descriptor size of 40 × 40 pixels. The descriptors are then clustered into a visual vocabulary of size 4096. This descriptor and quantization parametrization has already been shown to produce competitive results [8,10]. A two level spatial pyramid is then constructed from the quantized descriptors with a global Bag-of-Features histogram in the first level and a left and right partition in the second level as is done in [10]. While in [10] each partition is weighted by the amount of partitions on the corresponding level, we found that weighting by the square of partitions gives slightly better results. This way, the spatial pyramid's bins with finer resolution are weighted higher than those with a coarser resolution.

The second dataset is the validation subset of the Bentham benchmark used in the 2015 Keyword Spotting for Handwritten Documents competition which was conducted as part of the 2015 International Conference on Document Analysis and Recognition[1]. It consists of 95 dedicated query word images and 3234 test word images. A subsample of the test words can be seen in Fig. 2b. Just as with the GW dataset, we densely extract SIFT descriptors at a single scale and pool them into spatial pyramids. In a preliminary experiment we found descriptor sizes of 24 × 24 at a step size of 2 pixels to work well. Additionally, smaller visual vocabularies generally performed better than larger ones. Here, we found codebooks of size 1024 to work the best. The spatial pyramid itself has two levels with the first level being split into a 2 × 3 grid and the second level into a 2 × 9 grid.

As a baseline, we extract the spatial pyramids from the word images of each dataset, perform a tf-idf transform and reduce the dimensionality of the resulting representation with LSA. The resulting lower dimensional representations are then compared using the Cosine distance metric. For each query q the *Average Precision (AP)* is calculated by

$$AP(q) = \frac{\sum\limits_{i=1}^{s} P(q,i) \cdot rel(q,i)}{\sum\limits_{i=1}^{s} rel(q,i)}, \tag{8}$$

where $rel(q,i)$ is an indicator function that evaluates to 1 if the element at i is relevant w.r.t. q and 0 otherwise, $P(q,i)$ represents the precision of the retrieval list for query q when cut off at i elements and s is the length of the retrieval list. Please note that the retrieval list is not cut off at any point which leads to a recall of 100 %.

The *mean Average Precision (mAP)* then evaluates to the mean of all queries.

---

[1] http://transcriptorium.eu/~icdar15kws/data.html.

4.2   Standard Isomap

The first experiment evaluates the practicability of the standard Isomap to reduce the dimensionality of the spatial pyramids. Figure 3 shows the results for this approach with an exemplary parametrization compared to reducing the dimensionality with LSA. As already hinted at in Sect. 3, this manifold learning approach performs poorly compared to LSA which holds true for all parametrizations tested (please refer to the supplemental material for a complete evaluation). The major reason for this is the nature of the data: using a 12 288 dimensional spatial pyramid for the GW dataset and a 24 756 spatial pyramid for the Bentham dataset, both input spaces are sparsely sampled. The path lengths along the nearest neighbor graphs appear not to be a good approximation of the geodesic distance as the underlying manifold is not sampled densely enough.

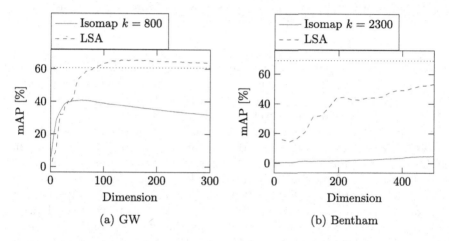

(a) GW   (b) Bentham

Fig. 3. The figure displays the different mAP values when applying standard Isomap and LSA to the two datasets. The dotted black line indicates the mAP without any dimension reduction.

4.3   Distance Metric Evaluation

In the second experiment, we will provide evidence for our claim that the BC distance is the metric best suited for word spotting on our benchmarks.

Figure 4 shows the mAP for the two datasets when applying no dimension reduction and sorting the retrieval list according to the individual metrics. As expected, the L1 and L2 norm fall short of the results obtained by the Cosine distance on both datasets. However, the BC distance is able to outperform all other metrics which were evaluated.

4.4   Bray Curtis Isomap

In the third experiment, we apply the proposed BC-Isomap to the spatial pyramid representations and conduct word spotting on the embedding representations. Additionally, we use the BC distance metric in combination with MDS to

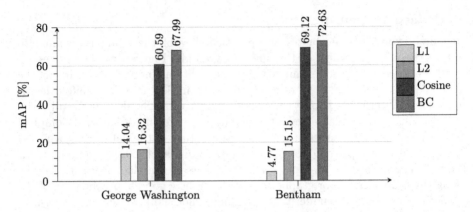

Fig. 4. The figure displays the mAP values when sorting the retrieval lists by the specified metrics for the two datasets (no dimension reduction is applied).

embed the word image descriptors. We will dub this combination *Bray Curtis MDS (BC-MDS)*. In order to give a fair comparison between the baseline and the proposed method, we will compare the representations obtained with LSA with the BC distance metric as well.

Figure 5 compares the retrieval results of the low-dimensional representations obtained from LSA, BC-MDS and BC-Isomap. As can be seen in the figure, the LSA results are the worst on both datasets for smaller dimensions. LSA is only able to outperform the BC-Isomap results on the GW dataset when the dimensionality gets higher. For the Bentham dataset it can only outperform the manifold learning approach when the parameter k is set to very small values. LSA is not able to achieve better results on either dataset when compared to BC-MDS for any embedding dimension. On both datasets BC-Isomap is able to obtain higher mAP values when the dimensionality is low but gets outperformed by BC-MDS with a rising number of dimensions. Please note that the plots for BC-Isomap in Fig. 5b stop at dimension 450. This is due to the eigenvalue decomposition yielding negative results after the first 450 eigenvalues (see Eq. 3).

Table 1 lists the mAP results for LSA, BC-MDS and different BC-Isomap parametrizations when setting the dimensionality of the embedding to 0.4 % of the original spatial pyramid dimension. For the George Washington benchmark, the mAP is improved by an absolute value of 18.29 % when comparing BC-Isomap to LSA and still 4.86 % compared to no dimension reduction. While for the Bentham validation dataset the retrieval precision of the standard spatial pyramid could not be surpassed, the LSA results were improved by 41.29 %.

4.5 Discussion

The results presented in the previous section show that both BC-MDS and BC-Isomap are superior to LSA when applied to spatial pyramids in a word spotting scenario. For the George Washington dataset, the modified Isomap algorithm is

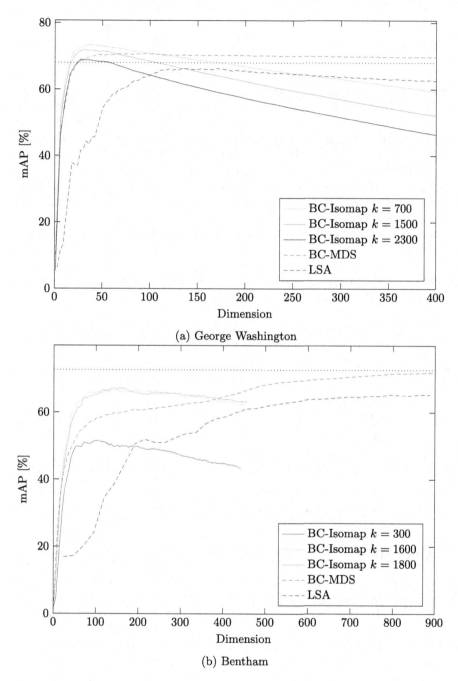

(a) George Washington

(b) Bentham

Fig. 5. The figure displays the different mAP values for different neighborhood sizes k when reducing to a certain dimension for (a) the George Washington dataset and (b) the Bentham validation dataset. The dotted black line indicates the mAP without any dimension reduction. Please note that the BC-Isomap plots in (b) stop at 450 dimensions as this was the maximum dimension for embedding (the eigenvalue decomposition yielded negative eigenvalues for larger dimensions).

able to achieve the same mAP values compared to no dimension reduction at an embedding dimensionality of 16. This is 0.12 % of the original representation size. The manifold learning approach is also fairly robust with respect to its parameters (Fig. 5a, please refer to the supplemental material for a complete evaluation of $k = 300$ to $k = 2300$).

For the Bentham dataset, the retrieval precision of BC-MDS converges to the mAP value of the plain spatial pyramids with increasing dimensionality (Fig. 5b). When reducing to smaller dimensions, BC-Isomap outperforms the other two approaches. As with the George Washington benchmark, the parameters are fairly stable to even a medium amount of change (Table 1, Fig. 5b). While neither dimension reduction technique is able to achieve the same mAP value compared to using no dimension reduction, it should be noted that using a 24 576-dimensional word image representation to obtain the best mAP possible is more of an academic than a practically applicable solution. The Bentham validation set contains merely 3234 segmented word images and is only a small subset of the overall Bentham collection which contains 60 000 manuscripts and an estimated 30 000 000 words. Performing word spotting with the standard spatial pyramid would become virtually impossible on this task.

Table 1. mAP values when reducing to 0.4 % of the original size

Method	GW	Bentham
	mAP @ dim. 50	mAP @ dim. 100
No Dim. Reduction	67.99	72.63
LSA	54.56	24.23
BC-MDS	70.22	58.19
BC-Isomap $k = 500$	**72.85**	61.07
BC-Isomap $k = 900$	72.64	57.50
BC-Isomap $k = 1300$	71.92	61.82
BC-Isomap $k = 1700$	70.97	**65.52**

5   Conclusion

In this paper, we presented Bray Curtis Isomap which is an extension of the Isomap manifold learning algorithm. This extension is able to deal will high-dimensional histogram representations in a sparsely sampled input space such as spatial pyramids. These representations occur quite frequently in a word spotting context. The resulting low-dimensional embedding is able to outperform the commonly used Latent Semantic Analysis on the George Washington and Bentham datasets. We contribute this improvement to the use of the Bray Curtis distance metric. Opposed to the Euclidean distance metric used in LSA, BC-Isomap bases its embedding on the BC distance which is a metric specifically designed for histogram representations. Additionally, the non-linear projection is able to uncover more complex structures than its linear counterpart.

References

1. Ahonen, T., Hadid, A., Pietik, M., Pietikäinen, M.: Face recognition with local binary patterns. In: European Conference on Computer Vision, pp. 469–481 (2004)
2. Aldavert, D., Rusinol, M., Toledo, R., Llados, J.: Integrating visual and textual cues for query-by-string word spotting. In: Proceedings of the International Conference on Document Analysis and Recognition, ICDAR, pp. 511–515 (2013)
3. Almazan, J., Fornes, A., Valveny, E.: Deformable HOG-based shape descriptor. In: Proceedings of the International Conference on Document Analysis and Recognition, ICDAR, pp. 1022–1026 (2013)
4. Almazan, J., Gordo, A., Fornes, A., Valveny, E.: Word spotting and recognition with embedded attributes. IEEE Trans. Pattern Anal. Mach. Intell. **36**(12), 2552–2566 (2014)
5. Bengio, Y., Paiement, J.F., Vincent, P., Delalllaux, O., Le Roux, N., Ouimet, M.: Out-of-sample extensions for LLE, Isomap, MDS, eigenmaps and spectral clustering. In: Advances in Neural Information Processing Systems, vol. 16, pp. 177–184 (2004)
6. Perronnin, F., Sánchez, J., Mensink, T.: Improving the Fisher kernel for large-scale image classification. In: Daniilidis, K., Maragos, P., Paragios, N. (eds.) ECCV 2010, Part IV. LNCS, vol. 6314, pp. 143–156. Springer, Heidelberg (2010)
7. Rath, T.M., Manmatha, R.: Word spotting for historical documents. Int. J. Doc. Anal. Recogn. **9**, 139–152 (2007)
8. Rothacker, L., Rusinol, M., Fink, G.A.: Bag-of-features HMMs for segmentation-free word spotting in handwritten documents. In: Proceedings of the International Conference on Document Analysis and Recognition, ICDAR, pp. 1305–1309 (2013)
9. Roweis, S.T., Saul, L.K.: Nonlinear dimensionality reduction by locally linear embedding. Science **290**, 2323–2326 (2000)
10. Rusiñol, M., Aldavert, D., Toledo, R., Lladós, J.: Efficient segmentation-free keyword spotting in historical document collections. Pattern Recognit. **48**(2), 545–555 (2015)
11. Silva, V.D., Tenenbaum, J.B.: Global versus local methods in nonlinear dimensionality reduction. In: Advances in Neural Information Processing Systems, vol. 15, pp. 705–712 (2003)
12. Tenenbaum, J.B., de Silva, V., Langford, J.C.: A global geometric framework for nonlinear dimensionality reduction. Science **290**(5500), 2319–2323 (2000)
13. Zhang, Z.Y., Zha, H.Y.: Principal manifolds and nonlinear dimensionality reduction via tangent space alignment. SIAM J. Sci. Comput. **26**(1), 313–338 (2005)

Offline Writer Identification Using Convolutional Neural Network Activation Features

Vincent Christlein[✉], David Bernecker, Andreas Maier, and Elli Angelopoulou

Pattern Recognition Lab, Friedrich-Alexander-Universität Erlangen-Nürnberg, Erlangen, Germany
{vincent.christlein,david.bernecker, andreas.maier,elli.angelopoulou}@fau.de

Abstract. Convolutional neural networks (CNNs) have recently become the state-of-the-art tool for large-scale image classification. In this work we propose the use of activation features from CNNs as local descriptors for writer identification. A global descriptor is then formed by means of GMM supervector encoding, which is further improved by normalization with the KL-Kernel. We evaluate our method on two publicly available datasets: the ICDAR 2013 benchmark database and the CVL dataset. While we perform comparably to the state of the art on CVL, our proposed method yields about 0.21 absolute improvement in terms of mAP on the challenging bilingual ICDAR dataset.

1 Introduction

In contrast to physiological biometric identifiers like fingerprints or iris scans, handwriting can be seen as a behavioral identifier [31]. It is influenced by factors like schooling or aging. Finding an individual writer in a large data corpus is formally defined as *writer identification*. Typical applications lie in the fields of forensics or security. However, writer identification recently also raised interest in the analysis of historical texts [3,10].

The task can be categorized into (a) *online* writer identification, for which temporal information of the text formation can be used, and (b) *offline* writer identification which relies solely on the handwritten text. The latter can be further categorized into *allograph*-based and *textural*-based methods [4]. Allograph-based methods rely on local descriptors computed from small letter parts (allographs). Subsequently, a global document descriptor is computed by means of statistics using a pretrained vocabulary [5,9,10,15,28]. In contrast, textural-based methods rely on global statistics computed from the handwritten text, e. g., the ink width or angle distribution [3,8,12,21,28]. Both methods can be combined to form a stronger global descriptor [4,25,29].

In this work we propose an allograph-based method for offline writer identification. In contrast to expert-designed features like SIFT, we use activation

© Springer International Publishing Switzerland 2015
J. Gall et al. (Eds.): GCPR 2015, LNCS 9358, pp. 540–552, 2015.
DOI: 10.1007/978-3-319-24947-6_45

features learned by a convolutional neural network (CNN). This has the advantage of obtaining features guided by the data. In each additional CNN layer the script is indirectly analyzed on a higher level of abstraction. CNNs have been widely used in image retrieval and object classification, and are among the top contenders on challenges like the Pascal-VOC or ImageNet [19]. However, to the best of our knowledge CNNs have not been used for writer identification so far. A reason might be that typically the training and test sets of current writer identification datasets are disjoint making it impossible to train a CNN for classification. Thus, we propose to use CNNs not for the classification task but to learn local activation features. Subsequently, the local descriptors are encoded to form global feature vectors by means of GMM supervector encoding [5]. We also propose to use the Kullback-Leibler kernel, instead of the Hellinger kernel, on top of mean-only adapted GMM parameters. We show that this combination of activation features and encoding method performs at least as well as the current state of the art on two public datasets ICDAR13 and CVL.

2   Related Work

Allograph-based methods rely on a dictionary trained from local descriptors. This dictionary is subsequently used to collect statistics from the local descriptors of the query document. These statistics are then aggregated to form the global descriptor that is used to classify the document. Jain and Doerman proposed the use of vector quantization [14] as encoding method. More recent work concentrates on using Fisher vectors for aggregation [9,15]. While Fiel and Sablatnig [9] propose to use solely SIFT descriptors as the local descriptor, Jain and Doermann [15] suggest to fuse multiple Fisher vectors computed from different descriptors. In contrast, we will rely on the findings of Christlein et al. [5]. They showed that a very well known approach in speaker recognition, namely GMM supervector encoding, performs better than both Fisher vectors and VLAD encoding.

CNNs have been widely used in the field of image classification and object recognition. In the ImageNet Large Scale Visual Recognition Challenge for example, CNNs are among the top contenders [19]. In document analysis, CNNs have been used for word spotting by Jaderberg et al. [13], and for handwritten text recognition by Bluche et al. [2]. However, to the best of our knowledge, they have not been used in the context of writer identification.

Compared to regular feed forward neural networks, convolutional neural networks have fewer parameters that need to be trained due to sharing the weights of their filters across the whole input patch. This makes them easier to train, while not sacrificing classification performance for a smaller sized network. Instead of using a CNN for direct classification, one can choose to use a CNN to extract local features by interpreting the activations of the last hidden layer as the feature vector. Bluche et al. [2] propose to use features learned by a CNN for word recognition in conjunction with HMMs, and show that the learned features outperform previous representations. Gong et al. [11] employ a similar approach for image classification. Their local activation features are computed by calculating the activation of a pretrained CNN on the image itself, and on patches of various scales extracted from the image. The activations for each scale are then aggregated using VLAD encoding. The final image descriptor is formed by concatenating the resulting feature vectors from each scale.

3   Writer Identification Pipeline

Our proposed pipeline (cf. Fig. 1) consists of three main steps: the feature extraction from image patches using a CNN; the aggregation of all the local features from one document into one global descriptor; and the successive normalization of this descriptor. A pretrained CNN and a pretrained GMM are required for feature extraction and encoding, respectively.

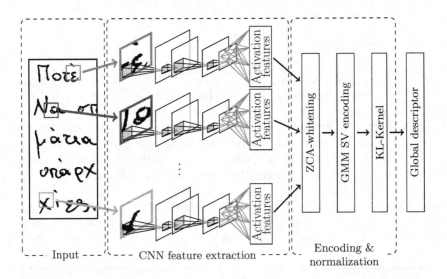

Fig. 1. Overview of the encoding process. The two main steps are the feature extraction using a pretrained CNN, and the encoding step, where the local features are agreggated using a pretrained GMM.

3.1   Convolutional Neural Networks

In our pipeline the CNN is only used to calculate a feature representation of a small image patch, but not for directly identifying the writer. The training of the CNN, however, has to be performed by backpropagation, which requires labels for the individual patches. Therefore, during the training phase, the last layer of our network consists of 100 SoftMax nodes, representing the writer IDs of the ICDAR13 training set. After the training, this last layer is discarded and the remaining layers are used to generate the feature representation for the image

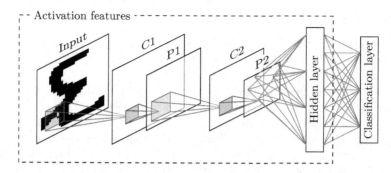

Fig. 2. Schematic representation of the used CNN. C1 and C2 are convolutional layers (red connections). P1 and P2 are max pooling layers (blue connections). The last three layers are fully connected (gray connections). After training only the part of the net inside the dashed box (activation features) is kept. The activations of the hidden layer become the local descriptor for the image patch (Colour figure online).

patches. The architecture of the CNN we use is shown in Fig. 2, where the dashed box marks the part of the CNN that is kept after the training procedure.

The CNN consists of 6 layers in total. The first layer is a convolutional layer, followed by a pooling layer. In the convolutional layer, the input patch is convolved with 16 filters. The pooling layer is then used to reduce the dimensions of the filter responses by performing a max pooling over regions of size 2×2 or 3×3. The two subsequent layers follow the same principle: a convolutional layer with 256 filters is followed by a pooling layer. These first four layers constitute the convolutional part of the network. The output of the second pooling layer is next transformed into a 1-D vector which is fed into a layer of hidden nodes. For all of these layers rectified linear units (ReLU) are used as nodes. The last layer then consists of 100 nodes with a SoftMax activation function. They are used for classification during the training.

The training set consists of patches extracted from the ICDAR13 training set that are centered on the contour of the writing. For each of the 100 writers, ICDAR13 contains four images, two of Greek handwritten text and two of English handwritten text. We further divided this set into a training and test set, by using patches from the first English and Greek text for training, and patches from the second English and Greek text for testing the trained convolutional network. The training and test set consist independently of 4 million image patches of size 32×32. The image patches are not preprocessed in any manner.

The training is performed by using the CUDA capabilities of the neural network library Torch [6]. All the CNNs are trained using the Torch implementation of stochastic gradient descent (SGD) with a learning rate of 0.01 for 20 epochs. For the first five epochs of training a Nesterov momentum $m = 0.9$ is used to speed up the training process.

3.2   GMM Supervector Encoding

Given the local activation features, we need to aggregate them to form one global descriptor for each document. For this task we use a variant of the GMM supervector approach of Christlein et al. [5].

In the training step a Gaussian mixture model (GMM) is trained as the dictionary from a set of ZCA-whitened activation features. This dictionary is subsequently used to encode the local descriptors by calculating their statistics with regard to the dictionary. The K-component GMM is denoted by $\lambda = \{w_k, \boldsymbol{\mu}_k, \boldsymbol{\Sigma}_k \,| k = 1, \ldots, K\}$, where w_k, $\boldsymbol{\mu}_k$ and $\boldsymbol{\Sigma}_k$ are the mixture weight, mean vector and diagonal covariance matrix for mixture k, respectively. The parameters λ are estimated with the expectation-maximization (EM) algorithm [7].

Given the pretrained GMM and one document, the parameters λ are first adapted to all activation features extracted from the document by means of a maximum-a-posteriori (MAP) step. Using a data-dependent mixing coefficient they are coupled with the parameters of the pretrained GMM. This leads to different mixtures being adapted depending on the current set of activation features [23]. Given the descriptors $\mathbf{X} = \{\mathbf{x}_t, \mathbf{x}_t \in \mathcal{R}^D, t = 1, \ldots T\}$ of a document, first the posterior probabilities $\gamma_t(k)$ for each $\mathbf{x}_t$ and Gaussian mixture $g_k(\mathbf{x})$ are computed as:

$$\gamma_t(k) = \frac{w_k g_k(\mathbf{x}_t)}{\sum_{j=1}^{K} w_j g_j(\mathbf{x}_t)}. \tag{1}$$

Since the covariances and weights give only a slight improvement in accuracy [5], we chose to adapt only the means of the mixtures, thus, reducing the size of the output supervector and lowering the computational effort. The first order statistics are computed as:

$$\hat{\boldsymbol{\mu}}_k = \frac{1}{n_k} \sum_{i=1}^{T} \gamma_t(k) \mathbf{x}_t, \tag{2}$$

where $n_k = \sum_{t=1}^{T} \gamma_t(k)$. Then, these new means are mixed with the original GMM means:

$$\tilde{\boldsymbol{\mu}}_k = \alpha_k \hat{\boldsymbol{\mu}}_k + (1 - \alpha_k) \boldsymbol{\mu}_k, \tag{3}$$

where α_k denotes a data dependent adaptation coefficient. It is computed by $\alpha_k = \frac{n_k}{n_k + \tau}$, where τ is a relevance factor. The new parameters of the mixed GMM are then concatenated forming the GMM supervector: $\mathbf{s} = \left(\tilde{\boldsymbol{\mu}}_1^\top, \ldots, \tilde{\boldsymbol{\mu}}_K^\top\right)^\top$. This global descriptor $\mathbf{s}$ is a KD dimensional vector which is eventually used for nearest neighbor search using the cosine-distance as metric.

3.3   Normalization

While contrast-normalization is an often used intermediate step in CNN training [1], we employ ZCA whitening to decorrelate the activation features followed by a global L_2 normalization. We will show that the accuracy of the GMM supervector benefits greatly from this normalization step.

Additionally, our GMM supervector is normalized, too. Christlein et al. suggested to normalize the full GMM supervector (consisting of the adapted weight, mean and covariance parameters) using power normalization with a power of 0.5 prior to a L_2 normalization [5]. Effectively this results in applying the Hellinger kernel. In contrast, we employ a kernel derived from the symmetrized Kullback-Leibler divergence [30] to normalize the adapted components:

$$\mathring{\boldsymbol{\mu}}_k = \sqrt{w_k}\boldsymbol{\sigma}_k^{-\frac{1}{2}}\tilde{\boldsymbol{\mu}}_k\,, \tag{4}$$

where $\boldsymbol{\sigma}_k$ is the vector of the diagonal elements of the covariance matrix $\boldsymbol{\Sigma}$ of the trained Gaussian mixture k. This implicitly encodes information contained in the variances and weights of the GMM, although only the means were adapted in the main encoding step. The normalized supervector becomes $\mathring{\mathbf{s}} = \left(\mathring{\boldsymbol{\mu}}_1^{\top}, \ldots, \mathring{\boldsymbol{\mu}}_K^{\top}\right)^{\top}$.

3.4   Implementation Notes

For the computation of the posteriors, we set all but the ten highest posterior probabilities computed from each descriptor to zero. Consequently, we compute the adaptation only for the data having non-zero posteriors. This has the effect of reducing the computational cost with nearly no loss in accuracy. Similar to the work of Christlein et al. [5], we used 100 Gaussian mixtures, but raised the relevance factor τ to 68 which was found to slightly improve the results.

4   Evaluation

4.1   Datasets

We use two different datasets for evaluation: the ICDAR13 benchmark set [20] and the CVL dataset [18]. Both are publicly available and have been used in many recent publications [5,9,15].

ICDAR13 [20]. The ICDAR13 benchmark set is separated into a training set consisting of documents from 100 writers and a writer independent test set consisting of documents from 250 writers. Each writer contributed four documents. Two are written in Greek, and two are written in English. This provides for a challenging cross-language writer identification.

CVL [18]. The CVL dataset consists of 310 writers. The dataset is split in a training set and a test set without overlap of the writers. The training set contains 27 writers contributing seven documents each. The test set consists of 283 writers who contributed five documents each. One document out of the five (seven) documents is written in German, the others in English. Note that we binarized the documents using Otsu's method.

4.2 Metrics

To evaluate our experiments we use the mean average precision (mAP) and the hard TOP-k scores. Both are common metrics in information retrieval tasks. Given a query document from one writer, an ordered list of documents is returned, where the first returned document is regarded as being the closest to the query document. The mAP then is the mean of the average precision (aP) over all queries. aP is defined as

$$\text{aP} = \frac{\sum_{k=1}^{n} P(k) \cdot \text{rel}(k)}{\#\text{relevant documents}} . \tag{5}$$

Given the ordered list of documents for a query document, the aP averages over $P(k)$, the precision at rank k, that is given by the number of documents from the same writer in the query up to rank k divided by k. $\text{rel}(k)$ is an indicator function that is one if the document retrieved at rank k is from the same writer and zero otherwise.

The hard TOP-k scores are determined by calculating the percentage of queries, where the k highest ranked documents were from the same writer, e.g., the hard TOP-3 denotes the probability that the three best ranked documents stem from the correct writer.

4.3 Convolutional Neural Network Parameters

With the CNN architecture fixed to two convolutional and one hidden layer there are two main parameters that are essential for the performance of the trained activation features: the filter size, and the number of hidden nodes in the last layer, i.e., the size of the output descriptor. We conducted some preliminary experiments using the ICDAR13 training set to determine the optimal parameters for the chosen network architecture. We evaluated two different setups of the filter and pooling sizes for the convolutional layers. The values for the two configurations **A** and **B** are shown in Table 1a. Comparing the two configurations shows that, **B** uses larger filters and pooling sizes and should therefore be more insensitive to translations of the patches. For both filter sizes we also evaluated the effect of the output feature size by using three different numbers of hidden nodes in the last layer: 64, 128, and 256.

For these preliminary experiments we used VLAD encoding [17] instead of GMM supervectors due to its faster computation time. VLAD is a non-probabilistic version of Fisher vectors which hard-encodes the first order statistics, i.e., $\mathbf{s}_k = \sum_{\mathbf{x}_t \in \tilde{\mathbf{X}}} (\mathbf{x}_t - \boldsymbol{\mu}_k)$, where $\tilde{\mathbf{X}}$ refers to the set of descriptors for which the cluster center $\boldsymbol{\mu}_k$ is the closest one. The dictionary can be efficiently computed by using a mini-batch version of k-means [26]. We report the average mAP over the results of 10 VLAD-encoding runs.

Besides the network configurations, Table 1 shows the classification accuracy obtained with the CNN including the classification layer on the test set after 20 epochs of training in part (b) and the averaged mAP of 10 runs of VLAD encoding in part (c). Interestingly, the results for both evaluation approaches are almost complementary. The CNN alone reaches the best results for smaller

Table 1. Evaluation of different CNN configurations on the ICDAR13 training set

Filter configuration	C1	P1	C2	P2
A	5×5	2×2	5×5	2×2
B	7×7	2×2	5×5	3×3

(a) Convolutional and pooling layer configurations of the CNN

Filter size	No. hidden nodes		
	64	128	256
A	38.18%	49.25%	54.99%
B	40.26%	45.57%	53.53%

Filter size	No. hidden nodes		
	64	128	256
A	0.937	0.926	0.895
B	0.948	0.929	0.910

(b) Classification accuracy using the classification layer of the CNN

(c) Averaged mAP of VLAD encoding

filters and a large number of hidden nodes, while the VLAD encoding prefers larger filters and a smaller size of the activation features vector (i. e., number of hidden nodes). A possible explanation might be that, for a larger number of hidden nodes the activations of the hidden layer are less descriptive for discerning between writers because the connections between the hidden and the classification layer take over that part. In contrast, for a small number of hidden nodes, the descriptiveness of the activations of the hidden layer seems to be higher, making them more suitable for use as features independent from the classification layer of the CNN. It should also be noted that the classification accuracy of the CNN is already quite impressive considering that the classification is performed using only a single patch of size 32×32 for 100 different writers/classes. Since configuration **B** shows the highest mAP, this configuration of the CNN is used for all of the following experiments.

4.4   Performance Analysis

We now investigate the influence of the individual steps in our pipeline. We replace the CNN activation features by other local descriptors. We also examine the influence of applying ZCA- and PCA-whitening to the CNN activation features. Lastly, we evaluate the replacement of the GMM supervectors with other encoding methods.

Table 2a compares the learned activation features with SURF and RootSIFT. Both have been used successfully for offline writer identification by Jain and Doermann [15] and Christlein et al. [5], respectively. Interestingly, SURF performs better than RootSIFT. However, our proposed activation features outperform both descriptors by 0.14 and 0.18 mAP, respectively.

Table 2b shows the effect of decorrelating the activation features using PCA and ZCA whitening (CNN-AF$_{pwh}$ + SV$_{m,kl}$ vs. CNN-AF$_{zwh}$ + SV$_{m,kl}$) and the comparison with the other encoding methods. CNN-AF$_{zwh}$+SV$_{wmc,ssr+l2}$ is using

Table 2. The influence of different parts of the pipeline on the ICDAR13 test set

Method	mAP
RootSIFT + $SV_{wmc,ssr+l2}$ [5]	0.671
RootSIFT + $SV_{m,kl}$	0.680
SURF + $SV_{m,kl}$	0.718
CNN-AF + $SV_{m,kl}$	0.860

Method	mAP
CNN-AF_{pwh} + $SV_{m,kl}$	0.880
CNN-AF_{zwh} + $SV_{m,kl}$	0.886
CNN-AF_{zwh} + $SV_{wmc,ssr+l2}$	0.877
CNN-AF_{zwh} + FV	0.866

(a) Comparison of different local descriptors

(b) Influence of different whitening and encoding methods

GMM supervectors as proposed by Christlein et al. [5] and CNN-AF_{zwh} + FV uses Fisher vectors as proposed by Sanchez et al. [24]. The SV encoding by Christlein et al. adapts all components (weights, means, covariances) while the FV encoding uses the means and covariances. Both methods use power normalization (power of 0.5) followed by l_2 normalization instead of the KL-kernel normalization.

The decorrelation of the features brings an improvement of 0.02 mAP, with ZCA giving slightly better results than PCA. The decorrelated score with the proposed method also outperforms the two other encoding methods.

4.5   Comparison with the State of the Art

Tables 3a and 4 show the results achieved with the complete pipeline on the ICDAR13 and CVL test sets, respectively. We compare with the state of the art[1] and SURF descriptors encoded with GMM supervectors, cf. Table 2. Since the CVL training set is too small to compute a comparable GMM, we used the GMM and ZCA transformation matrix estimated on the ICDAR13 training set for evaluating the pipeline on the CVL dataset. On both datasets the proposed pipeline using CNN activation features outperforms the previous methods in terms of mAP. The increase in performance is particularly evident on the complete ICDAR13 test set, where our method achieves an absolute improvement of 0.21 mAP. This is significantly better than the state of the art [5] (permutation test: $p \ll 0.05$). On the CVL dataset we achieve comparable results to the state of the art (permutation test: $p = 0.11$). However note that a) the ICDAR13 dataset is much more challenging due to its bilingual nature, and b) that we have not trained explicitly for the CVL dataset. Thus, our results show that the features learned from the ICDAR training set can generally be used for other datasets, too. We believe that the results could be further improved if the CVL training set would be incorporated into the training of the CNN activation features.

Table 3b shows the results for evaluating the Greek and English subsets of the ICDAR13 test set independently. Again, the proposed method further improves the already high scores of the previous methods.

---

[1] The methods [12,15] did not provide results on the full ICDAR13 dataset.

Table 3. Hard criterion TOP-k scores and mAP evaluated on ICDAR13 (test set)

	TOP-1	TOP-2	TOP-3	mAP
CS [14]	0.951	0.196	0.071	NA
SV [5]	0.971	0.428	0.238	0.671
SURF	0.967	0.551	0.273	0.718
Proposed	**0.989**	**0.832**	**0.613**	**0.886**

(a) Complete ICDAR13 test set

	Greek TOP-1	Greek mAP	English TOP-1	English mAP
Δ-n H. [12]	0.960	NA	0.934	NA
Comb. [15]	0.992	0.995	0.974	0.979
SURF	0.950	0.965	0.956	0.964
Proposed	**0.996**	**0.998**	**0.976**	**0.981**

(b) ICDAR13 language subsets

Table 4. Hard criterion and mAP evaluated on CVL

	TOP-1	TOP-2	TOP-3	TOP-4	mAP
FV [9]	0.978	0.956	0.894	0.758	NA
Comb [15]	**0.994**	0.983	0.948	0.829	0.969
SV [5]	0.992	0.981	0.958	0.887	0.971
SURF	0.986	0.973	0.948	0.836	0.958
Proposed	**0.994**	**0.988**	**0.973**	**0.926**	**0.978**

5 Conclusion

The writer identification method proposed in this paper exploits activation features learned by a deep CNN, which in comparison to traditional local descriptors like SIFT or SURF yield higher mAP scores on the ICDAR13 and CVL datasets. On the ICDAR13 test set, an increase of about 0.21 mAP is achieved with this new set of features. We show in our experiments that the retrieval rate is strongly influenced by the design choices of the CNN architecture. The local activation features are encoded using a modified variant of the GMM supervectors approach. However, we adapt only the means of the Gaussian mixtures in the aggregation step. Subsequently, the supervector is normalized using the KL-kernel. By implicitly adding information contained in the weights and covariances of the mixtures in the normalization step, the performance is increased while at the same time halving the dimensionality of the global descriptor.

For future work, we would like to explore larger and more complex CNN architectures and recent discoveries like the benefit of L_p-pooling [27] instead of max pooling and normalization of activations after convolutional layers of the network. There is also still room for improvement in the encoding step of the local descriptors, where democratic aggregation [16] or higher order VLAD [22] could further improve the writer identification rates.

Acknowledgments. This work has been supported by the German Federal Ministry of Education and Research (BMBF), grant-nr. 01UG1236a. The contents of this publication are the sole responsibility of the authors.

References

1. Bengio, Y.: Deep learning of representations for unsupervised and transfer learning. In: Unsupervised and Transfer Learning, Challenges in Machine Learning, vol. 7, pp. 19–41. Bellevue, Jun 2011

2. Bluche, T., Ney, H., Kermorvant, C.: Feature extraction with convolutional neural networks for handwritten word recognition. In: 2013 12th International Conference on Document Analysis and Recognition, pp. 285–289. Buffalo, August 2013. http://ieeexplore.ieee.org/lpdocs/epic03/wrapper.htm?arnumber=6628629

3. Brink, A., Smit, J., Bulacu, M., Schomaker, L.: Writer identification using directional ink-trace width measurements. Pattern Recogn. **45**(1), 162–171 (2012). http://linkinghub.elsevier.com/retrieve/pii/S0031320311002810

4. Bulacu, M., Schomaker, L.: Text-independent writer identification and verification using textural and allographic features. IEEE Trans. Pattern Anal. Mach. Intell. **29**(4), 701–717 (2007). http://www.ncbi.nlm.nih.gov/pubmed/17299226

5. Christlein, V., Bernecker, D., Hönig, F., Angelopoulou, E.: Writer identification and verification using GMM supervectors. In: 2014 IEEE Winter Conference on Applications of Computer Vision (WACV), pp. 998–1005, March 2014

6. Collobert, R., Kavukcuoglu, K., Farabet, C.: Torch7: a Matlab-like environment for machine learning. In: Big Learning, Workshop on Advances in Neural Information Processing Systems 24 (NIPS 2011), Granada, December 2011

7. Dempster, A., Laird, N., Rubin, D.: Maximum likelihood from incomplete data via the EM algorithm. J. Roy. Stat. Soc. Ser. B (Methodol.) **39**(1), 1–38 (1977). http://www.jstor.org/stable/10.2307/2984875

8. Djeddi, C., Meslati, L.S., Siddiqi, I., Ennaji, A., Abed, H.E., Gattal, A.: Evaluation of texture features for offline arabic writer identification. In: 2014 11th IAPR International Workshop on Document Analysis Systems (DAS), pp. 8–12, Tours, April 2014

9. Fiel, S., Sablatnig, R.: Writer identification and writer retrieval using the Fisher vector on visual vocabularies. In: 2013 12th International Conference on Document Analysis and Recognition (ICDAR), pp. 545–549, Washington, D.C., August 2013. http://ieeexplore.ieee.org/xpls/abs_all.jsp?arnumber=6628679

10. Gilliam, T., Wilson, R., Clark, J.: Scribe identification in medieval English manuscripts. In: 2010 20th International Conference on Pattern Recognition (ICPR), pp. 1880–1883, Istanbul, August 2010. http://ieeexplore.ieee.org/lpdocs/epic03/wrapper.htm?arnumber=5597227

11. Gong, Y., Wang, L., Guo, R., Lazebnik, S.: Multi-scale orderless pooling of deep convolutional activation features. In: Fleet, D., Pajdla, T., Schiele, B., Tuytelaars, T. (eds.) ECCV 2014, Part VII. LNCS, vol. 8695, pp. 392–407. Springer, Heidelberg (2014). doi:10.1007/978-3-319-10584-0_26

12. He, S., Schomaker, L.: Delta-n Hinge: rotation-invariant features for writer identification. In: 2014 22nd International Conference on Pattern Recognition (ICPR), pp. 2023–2028, Stockholm, August 2014. http://ieeexplore.ieee.org/lpdocs/epic03/wrapper.htm?arnumber=6977065

13. Jaderberg, M., Vedaldi, A., Zisserman, A.: Deep Features for text spotting. In: Fleet, D., Pajdla, T., Schiele, B., Tuytelaars, T. (eds.) ECCV 2014. LNCS, vol. 8692, pp. 512–528. Springer, Zurich (2014). http://link.springer.com/chapter/10.1007/978-3-319-10593-2_34

14. Jain, R., Doermann, D.: Writer identification using an alphabet of contour gradient descriptors. In: International Conference on Document Analysis and Recognition (ICDAR), pp. 550–554, Buffalo, August 2013. http://ieeexplore.ieee.org/xpls/abs_all.jsp?arnumber=6628680

15. Jain, R., Doermann, D.: Combining local features for offline writer identification. In: 2014 14th International Conference on Frontiers in Handwriting Recognition (ICFHR), pp. 583–588, Heraklion, September 2014

16. Jégou, H., Zisserman, A.: Triangulation embedding and democratic aggregation for image search. In: 2014 IEEE Conference on Computer Vision and Pattern Recognition (CVPR), pp. 3310–3317, Columbus, June 2014. http://hal.inria.fr/hal-00977321/

17. Jégou, H., Perronnin, F., Douze, M., Sánchez, J., Pérez, P., Schmid, C.: Aggregating local image descriptors into compact codes. IEEE Trans. Pattern Anal. Mach. Intell. **34**(9), 1704–1716 (2012). http://www.ncbi.nlm.nih.gov/pubmed/22156101

18. Kleber, F., Fiel, S., Diem, M., Sablatnig, R.: CVL-DataBase: An off-line database for writer retrieval, writer identification and word spotting. In: 2013 12th International Conference on Document Analysis and Recognition (ICDAR), pp. 560–564, Washington, D.C., August 2013. http://ieeexplore.ieee.org/xpls/abs_all.jsp?arnumber=6628682

19. Krizhevsky, A., Sutskever, I., Hinton, G.E.: ImageNet classification with deep convolutional neural networks. In: Advances in Neural Information Processing Systems 25, pp. 1097–1105. Curran Associates, Inc., (2012)

20. Louloudis, G., Gatos, B., Stamatopoulos, N., Papandreou, A.: ICDAR 2013 competition on writer identification. In: 2013 12th International Conference on Document Analysis and Recognition (ICDAR), pp. 1397–1401, Washington, D.C., August 2013

21. Newell, A.J.A., Griffin, L.D.L.: Writer identification using oriented basic image features and the delta encoding. Pattern Recogn. **47**(6), 2255–2265 (2014). http://linkinghub.elsevier.com/retrieve/pii/S0031320313005153, http://www.sciencedirect.com/science/article/pii/S0031320313005153

22. Peng, X., Wang, L., Qiao, Y., Peng, Q.: Boosting VLAD with supervised dictionary learning and high-order statistics. In: Fleet, D., Pajdla, T., Schiele, B., Tuytelaars, T. (eds.) ECCV 2014. LNCS, vol. 8691, pp. 660–674. Springer, Zurich (2014)

23. Reynolds, D.A., Quatieri, T.F., Dunn, R.B.: Speaker verification using adapted gaussian mixture models. Digit. Sig. Process. **10**(1–3), 19–41 (2000)

24. Sánchez, J., Perronnin, F., Mensink, T., Verbeek, J.: Image classification with the Fisher vector: theory and practice. Int. J. Comput. Vis. **105**(3), 222–245 (2013). http://link.springer.com/10.1007/s11263-013-0636-x

25. Schomaker, L., Bulacu, M.: Automatic writer identification using connected-component contours and edge-based features of uppercase western script. IEEE Trans. Pattern Anal. Mach. Intell. **26**(6), 787–798 (2004). http://ieeexplore.ieee.org/xpls/abs_all.jsp?arnumber=1288527

26. Sculley, D.: Web-scale K-means clustering. In: 19th International Conference on World Wide Web, WWW 2010, pp. 1177–1178. ACM, New York, April 2010. http://doi.acm.org/10.1145/1772690.1772862

27. Sermanet, P., Chintala, S., LeCun, Y.: Convolutional neural networks applied to house numbers digit classification. In: 2012 21st International Conference on Pattern Recognition (ICPR), pp. 3288–3291. IEEE, Tsukuba, November 2012. http://ieeexplore.ieee.org/xpls/abs_all.jsp?arnumber=6460867

28. Siddiqi, I., Vincent, N.: Text independent writer recognition using redundant writing patterns with contour-based orientation and curvature features. Pattern Recogn. **43**(11), 3853–3865 (2010). http://linkinghub.elsevier.com/retrieve/pii/S0031320310002438

29. Wu, X., Tang, Y., Bu, W.: Offline text-independent writer identification based on scale invariant feature transform. IEEE Trans. Inf. forensics Secur. **9**(3), 526–536 (2014). http://ieeexplore.ieee.org/lpdocs/epic03/wrapper.htm?arnumber=6716030

30. Xu, M., Zhou, X., Li, Z., Dai, B., Huang, T.S.: Extended hierarchical Gaussianization for scene classification. In: 2010 17th IEEE International Conference on Image Processing (ICIP), pp. 1837–1840, Hong Kong, September 2010

31. Zhu, Y.Z.Y., Tan, T.T.T., Wang, Y.W.Y.: Biometric personal identification based on handwriting. In: 15th International Conference on Pattern Recognition (ICPR), vol. 2, pp. 2–5, Barcelona, September 2000

Young Researchers Forum

Superpixel Segmentation: An Evaluation

David Stutz[(✉)]

Computer Vision Group, RWTH Aachen University, Aachen, Germany
david.stutz@rwth-aachen.de

Abstract. In recent years, superpixel algorithms have become a standard tool in computer vision and many approaches have been proposed. However, different evaluation methodologies make direct comparison difficult. We address this shortcoming with a thorough and fair comparison of thirteen state-of-the-art superpixel algorithms. To include algorithms utilizing depth information we present results on both the Berkeley Segmentation Dataset [3] and the NYU Depth Dataset [19]. Based on qualitative and quantitative aspects, our work allows to guide algorithm selection by identifying important quality characteristics.

1 Introduction

The term superpixel was introduced by Ren and Malik in 2003 [16] and is used to describe a group of pixels similar in color or other low-level properties. The concept of superpixels is motivated by two important aspects [16]: firstly, pixels do not represent natural entities but are merely a result of discretization; and secondly, the high number of pixels in large images prevents many algorithms from being computationally feasible.

Superpixels have actively been used for a wide range of applications such as classical segmentation [16,17], semantic segmentation [6], stereo matching [30] or tracking [26] and numerous superpixel algorithms have been proposed. However, keeping an overview of the different approaches and their suitability for specific applications is difficult. This is caused by varying experimental setups and metrics used for evaluation [12]. Furthermore, only few publications are devoted to a thorough comparison of existing algorithms.

In this paper, we address this shortcoming and present an extensive comparison of thirteen state-of-the-art superpixel algorithms. In Sect. 2 we discuss important related work regarding the comparison of superpixel algorithms and subsequently we survey existing superpixel algorithms. In Sect. 3 we discuss relevant datasets and introduce our benchmark in Sect. 4. Finally, in Sect. 5, we present a qualitative and quantitative comparison of the superpixel algorithms, before concluding in Sect. 6.

Recommended for submission to YRF2015 by Prof. Dr. Bastian Leibe.

© Springer International Publishing Switzerland 2015
J. Gall et al. (Eds.): GCPR 2015, LNCS 9358, pp. 555–562, 2015.
DOI: 10.1007/978-3-319-24947-6_46

2   Related Work

There are only few publications devoted to the comparison of existing superpixel algorithms in a consistent framework: to the best of our knowledge these are [2,12,18]. However, these publications cannot include several recent algorithms (for example [13,23,27]). Meanwhile, authors tend to include a brief evaluation intended to show superiority of their proposed superpixel algorithm over selected existing approaches (for example [8,13,23,23,25,27]). However, these results are not comparable across publications.

2.1   Superpixel Algorithms

Table 1 gives an overview of all evaluated superpixel algorithms. We categorize the algorithms according to criteria we find important for evaluation and algorithm selection. Roughly, the algorithms can be categorized as either graph-based approaches or gradient ascent approaches [2]. Furthermore, we distinguish algorithms offering direct control over the number of superpixels as well as algorithms providing a compactness parameter. Overall, we evaluated thirteen state-of-the-art superpixel algorithms including three algorithms utilizing depth information. We also note that there are additional superpixel algorithms [4,11,14,17,20,28] for which evaluation was not possible due to the lack of open source code.

Table 1. Overview of all evaluated superpixel algorithms ordered by year of publication. In Row 3, we categorize the algorithms in either graph-based approaches (gb) or gradient ascent approaches (ga) [2]. Furthermore, in Row 4, we note the programming language of the evaluated implementations as it may influence the runtime reported in Sect. 5.2 (M refers to MatLab). We distinguish algorithms offering direct control over the number of superpixels (Row 5), algorithms providing a compactness parameter (Row 6) and algorithms using depth information (Row 7).

	NC	FH	QS	TP	SLIC	CIS	ERS	PB	CRS	SEEDS	TPS	DASP	VCCS
Ref	[16]	[5]	[24]	[7]	[1]	[25]	[8]	[29]	[10]	[23]	[22]	[27]	[13]
Year	2003	2004	2008	2009	2010	2010	2011	2011	2011	2012	2012	2012	2013
Cat	gb	gb	ga	ga	ga	gb	gb	gb	ga	ga	gb	ga	ga
Impl	C/M	C++	C/M	C/M	C++	C++	C++	C++	C++	C++	C/M	C++	C++
Sup	✓	✗	✗	✓	✓	✓	✓	✓	✓	✓	✓	✓	✗
Comp	✗	✗	✗	✗	✓	✗	✗	✗	✓	✗	✗	✓	✓
Depth	✗	✗	✗	✗	✗	✗	✗	✗	✗	✗	✓	✓	✓

3   Datasets

As popular dataset for image segmentation and contour detection, the Berkeley Segmentation Dataset [3], referred to as BSDS500, consists of 500 natural images of size 482×321 (200 training images, 100 validation images, 200 test images). The provided ground truth segmentations, at least five per image, have been obtained from different persons and reflect the difficult nature of image segmentation.

In contrast to the natural images of the BSDS500, The NYU Depth Dataset [19], referred to as NYUV2, comprises 1449 images of different indoor scenes (we chose 200 validation images and 400 test images including most of the scenes). For all images, pre-processed depth images are provided. As these images have been undistorted and aligned with the color images, we crop the original images of size 640×480 to 608×448 pixels. In addition, following Ren and Bo [15], we remove small unlabeled regions and combine class and instance labels to guarantee connected ground truth segments. Overall, difficult lighting conditions and cluttered scenes contribute to the difficulty of the NYUV2.

4   Benchmark

We use an extended version of the Berkeley Segmentation Benchmark, introduced by Arbeláez et al. [3], to evaluate superpixel algorithms. Among other metrics, the benchmark includes Boundary Recall (Rec) and Undersegmentation Error (UE) [7,12] as primary metrics to assess superpixel algorithms.

Boundary Recall is part of the Precision-Recall Framework [9] originally used to evaluate contour detectors. Treating region boundaries of a superpixel segmentation as contours, Boundary Recall represents the fraction of boundary pixels correctly detected by the superpixel algorithm. As superpixels are expected to adhere to boundaries, high Boundary Recall is desirable.

Undersegmentation Error, as originally proposed by Levinshtein et al. [7], measures the "bleeding" of superpixels with respect to a ground truth segmentation. We implemented the corrected formulation proposed by Neubert and Protzel [12] computing an error in the range of $[0, 1]$. Low Undersegmentation Error is preferable as each superpixel is expected to cover at most one ground truth segment.

5   Evaluation and Comparison

In addition to the superpixel algorithms introduced in Sect. 2.1, we include a 2D and 3D re-implementation of *SEEDS*, called *reSEEDS* and *reSEEDS3D*, respectively. Further details can be found in [21].

Our comparison is split into a qualitative part, examining the visual quality of the generated superpixels, and a quantitative part based on Boundary Recall, Undersegmentation Error and runtime. To ensure a fair comparison, the parameters have been chosen to jointly optimize Boundary Recall and Undersegmentation Error using discrete grid search. Parameter optimization was performed on the validation sets while comparison is performed on the test sets.

5.1 Qualitative

The visual appearance of superpixels is determined by compactness and regularity – properties that may also have strong influence on possible applications. Figures 1 and 2 present results on the BSDS500 and NYUV2, respectively, obtained after parameter optimization. We note that these images are intended to be as representative as possible, however, generated superpixel segmentations may vary across different images.

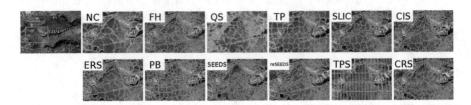

Fig. 1. Superpixel segmentations obtained for an example image from the BSDS500. From left to right, top to bottom: original image, *NC, FH, QS, TP, SLIC, CIS, ERS, PB, SEEDS, reSEEDS, TPS* and *CRS*. Approximately 600 superpixels have been generated for the whole image.

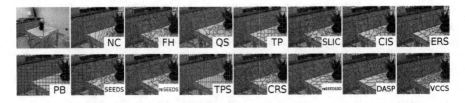

Fig. 2. Superpixel segmentations obtained for an example image from the NYUV2. From left to right, top to bottom: original image, *NC, FH, QS, TP, SLIC, CIS, ERS, PB, SEEDS, reSEEDS, TPS, CRS, reSEEDS3D, DASP, VCCS*. Note that *reSEEDS3D, DASP* and *VCCS* use depth information for superpixel segmentation. Approximately 840 superpixels have been computed for the whole image.

Both *FH* and *QS* produce highly irregular superpixels. However, they are able to capture small details and all important boundaries. Furthermore, note that *QS* produces more superpixels in highly textured areas. In contrast, *TP* generates highly compact superpixels at the expense of missing several boundaries. *CRS* and *ERS* produce irregular superpixels with good boundary adherence and are more visually appealing than superpixels generated by *FH* or *QS*. While *PB* shows reasonable results on the BSDS500, producing irregular and small superpixels, results on the NYUV2 appear to be unfinished and of poor quality. Similarly, *TPS* produces unfinished superpixel segmentations on both datasets. Both *SLIC* and *CRS* provide a compactness parameter which has been traded off for boundary adherence during parameter optimization. Thus, the generated superpixels are irregular and not compact, especially on the NYUV2. The original implementation of *SEEDS* produces highly irregular superpixels capturing the majority of boundaries. Our implementation, *reSEEDS*, shows similar behavior.

Intuitively, depth information allows to adapt superpixels to the underlying three-dimensional structure. While *DASP* is able to resemble this structure at least in parts, *VCCS* produces highly irregular superpixels. This may be due to the fact that *DASP* adapts the number of superpixels according to depth, whereas *VCCS* directly operates within the point cloud and merely the back projection is shown. As result, the generated superpixels occur irregular and voxelization (see [13]) is still visible. Compared to *DASP*, *reSEEDS3D* generates slightly less irregular superpixels with better boundary adherence.

5.2   Quantitative

The quantitative comparison is based on Boundary Recall and Undersegmentation Error, averaged over the test sets, as a function of the number of superpixels. As shown in Fig. 3, *FH* performs excellent on both datasets and is only outperformed by *VCCS*. However, as *VCCS* operates within point clouds, these results are hardly comparable. In addition, *FH* is closely followed by approaches such as *QS, SLIC, CRS* and *ERS*. Our implementation of *SEEDS, reSEEDS*, is able to keep up with *FH*, while consistently outperforming the original implementation. Unfortunately, as shown by *reSEEDS3D*, depth information may not necessarily improve performance. This is supported by the poor performance of *DASP*. In addition, our implementation of *SEEDS* demonstrates that any ranking extracted from Fig. 3 is possibly challenged by revising existing implementations. This also justifies a qualitative comparison as performed in Sect. 5.1.

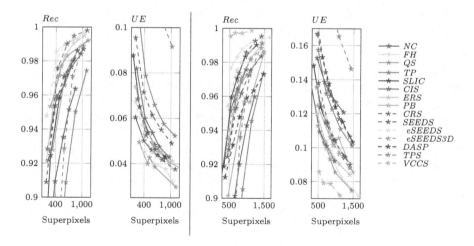

Fig. 3. Comparison of thirteen superpixel algorithms with respect to Boundary Recall (*Rec*) and Undersegmentation Error (*UE*) on the test sets of the BSDS500 (left) and the NYUV2 (right). Note that for visualization purposes only a small part of the range of both metrics is shown.

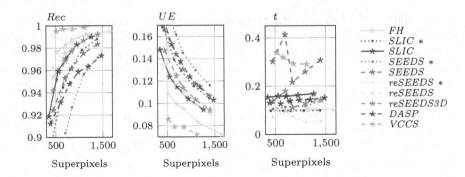

Fig. 4. Comparison of the runtime t in seconds of superpixel algorithms requiring less than 0.5 s per image on the NYUV2. *SLIC*, *SEEDS* and *reSEEDS* may be optimized with respect to runtime by decreasing the number of iterations. These optimized versions are indicated by an *.

Another important aspect of superpixel algorithms is runtime (measured using a 64bit machine with Intel Core i7-3770@3.4GHz, 16GB RAM and without GPU acceleration or multi-threading). Iterative algorithms such as *SLIC* and *SEEDS* may be optimized with respect to runtime by decreasing the number of iterations. Figure 4 compares these optimized versions to algorithms requiring less than 0.5 s on the NYUV2 (images of size 608 × 448). The optimized versions of *SLIC*, *SEEDS* and *reSEEDS*, indicated by an *, show significantly reduced runtime while providing similar performance in terms of Boundary Recall and Undersegmentation Error. The drop in performance is lowest for *reSEEDS* – Boundary Recall even increases – which simultaneously shows the lowest runtime with ∼0.05 s per image. We also observe low runtimes for *FH* and *DASP*.

6   Conclusion

Several algorithms provide both excellent performance and low runtime. Furthermore, including additional information such as depth may not necessarily improve performance. Therefore, additional criteria are necessary to asses superpixel algorithms. In particular, we find that visual quality, runtime and the provided parameters are among these criteria. Clearly, visual appearance is difficult to measure appropriately, however, it may have serious impact on possible applications. Furthermore, low runtime is desirable when using superpixel algorithms as pre-processing step, especially in real-time settings. Finally, parameters should be interpretable and easy to tune and algorithms providing a compactness parameter are preferable. In addition, as the number of superpixels can be understood as a lower bound on performance, we prefer algorithms offering direct control over the number of superpixels.

In conclusion, while many algorithms provide excellent performance with respect to Undersegmentation Error [7,12] and Boundary Recall [9], they lack control over the number of superpixels or a compactness parameter. Furthermore, these impressive results with respect to Boundary Recall and Undersegmentation Error do not necessarily reflect the perceived visual quality of the generated superpixel segmentations.

References

1. Achanta, R., Shaji, A., Smith, K., Lucchi, A., Fua, P., Süsstrunk, S.: SLIC superpixels. Technical report, École Polytechnique Fédérale de Lausanne, Lusanne, Switzerland, June 2010
2. Achanta, R., Shaji, A., Smith, K., Lucchi, A., Fua, P., Süsstrunk, S.: SLIC superpixels compared to state-of-the-art superpixel methods. IEEE Trans. Pattern Anal. Mach. Intell. **34**(11), 2274–2281 (2012)
3. Arbeláez, P., Maire, M., Fowlkes, C., Malik, J.: Contour detection and hierarchical image segmentation. IEEE Trans. Pattern Anal. Mach. Intell. **33**(5), 898–916 (2011)
4. Drucker, F., MacCormick, J.: Fast superpixels for video analysis. In: WMVC, pp. 1–8. IEEE Computer Society, Snowbird, Utah, December 2009
5. Felzenswalb, P.F., Huttenlocher, D.P.: Efficient graph-based image segmentation. Int. J. Comput. Vis. **59**(2), 167–181 (2004)
6. Gupta, S., Arbeláez, P., Malik, J.: Perceptual organization and recognition of indoor scenes from RGB-D images. In: CVPR, pp. 564–571. IEEE Computer Society, Portland, Oregon, June 2013
7. Levinshtein, A., Stere, A., Kutulakos, K.N., Fleet, D.J., Dickinson, S.J., Siddiqi, K.: TurboPixels: fast superpixels using geometric flows. IEEE Trans. Pattern Anal. Mach. Intell. **31**(12), 2290–2297 (2009)
8. Lui, M.Y., Tuzel, O., Ramalingam, S., Chellappa, R.: Entropy rate superpixel segmentation. In: CVPR, pp. 2097–2104. IEEE Computer Society, Providence, RI, June 2011
9. Martin, D., Fowlkes, C., Malik, J.: Learning to detect natural image boundaries using local brightness, color, and texture cues. IEEE Trans. Pattern Anal. Mach. Intell. **26**(5), 530–549 (2004)
10. Mester, R., Conrad, C., Guevara, A.: Multichannel segmentation using contour relaxation: fast super-pixels and temporal propagation. In: Heyden, A., Kahl, F. (eds.) SCIA 2011. LNCS, vol. 6688, pp. 250–261. Springer, Heidelberg (2011)
11. Moore, A.P., Prince, S.J.D., Warrell, J., Mohammed, U., Jones, G.: Superpixel lattices. In: CVPR, pp. 1–8. IEEE Computer Society, Anchorage, AK, June 2008
12. Neubert, P., Protzel, P.: Superpixel benchmark and comparison. In: Forum Bildverarbeitung, Regensburg, Germany, November 2012
13. Papon, J., Abramov, A., Schoeler, M., Wörgötter, F.: Voxel cloud connectivity segmentation - supervoxels for point clouds. In: CVPR, pp. 2027–2034. IEEE Computer Society, Portland, Oregon, June 2013
14. Perbet, F., Maki, A.: Homogeneous superpixels from random walks. In: (IAPR) MVA, pp. 26–30. Nara, Japan, June 2011
15. Ren, X., Bo, L.: Discriminatively trained sparse code gradients for contour detection. In: Bartlett, P.L., Pereira, F.C.N., Burges, C.J.C., Bottou, L., Weinberger, K.Q. (eds.) NIPS, vol. 25, pp. 584–592. Curran Associates, Red Hook, New York (2012)

16. Ren, X., Malik, J.: Learning a classification model for segmentation. In: ICCV, pp. 10–17. IEEE Computer Society, Nice, France, October 2003

17. Rohkohl, C., Engel, K.: Efficient image segmentation using pairwise pixel similarities. In: Hamprecht, F.A., Schnörr, C., Jähne, B. (eds.) DAGM 2007. LNCS, vol. 4713, pp. 254–263. Springer, Heidelberg (2007)

18. Schick, A., Fischer, M., Stiefelhagen, R.: Measuring and evaluating the compactness of superpixels. In: ICPR, pp. 930–934. IEEE Computer Society, Tsukuba, Japan, November 2012

19. Silberman, N., Hoiem, D., Kohli, P., Fergus, R.: Indoor segmentation and support inference from RGBD images. In: Fitzgibbon, A., Lazebnik, S., Perona, P., Sato, Y., Schmid, C. (eds.) ECCV 2012, Part V. LNCS, vol. 7576, pp. 746–760. Springer, Heidelberg (2012)

20. Siva, P., Wong, A.: Grid seams: A fast superpixel algorithm for real-time applications. In: CRV, pp. 127–134. IEEE Computer Society, Montreal, Canada, May 2014

21. Stutz, D.: Superpixel segmentation using depth information. B.Sc. thesis, Computer Vision Group, RWTH Aachen University, Aachen, Germany, September 2014. http://davidstutz.de/projects/superpixelsseeds/

22. Tang, D., Fu, H., Cao, X.: Topology preserved regular superpixel. In: ICME, pp. 765–768. IEEE Computer Society, Melbourne, Australia, July 2012

23. Van den Bergh, M., Boix, X., Roig, G., de Capitani, B., Van Gool, L.: SEEDS: superpixels extracted via energy-driven sampling. In: Fitzgibbon, A., Lazebnik, S., Perona, P., Sato, Y., Schmid, C. (eds.) ECCV 2012, Part VII. LNCS, vol. 7578, pp. 13–26. Springer, Heidelberg (2012)

24. Vedaldi, A., Soatto, S.: Quick shift and Kernel methods for mode seeking. In: Forsyth, D., Torr, P., Zisserman, A. (eds.) ECCV 2008, Part IV. LNCS, vol. 5305, pp. 705–718. Springer, Heidelberg (2008)

25. Veksler, O., Boykov, Y., Mehrani, P.: Superpixels and supervoxels in an energy optimization framework. In: Daniilidis, K., Maragos, P., Paragios, N. (eds.) ECCV 2010, Part V. LNCS, vol. 6315, pp. 211–224. Springer, Heidelberg (2010)

26. Wang, S., Lu, H., Yang, F., Yang, M.H.: Superpixel tracking. In: ICCV, pp. 1323–1330. IEEE Computer Society, Barcelona, Spain, November 2011

27. Weikersdorfer, D., Gossow, D., Beetz, M.: Depth-adaptive superpixels. In: ICPR. pp. 2087–2090. IEEE Computer Society, Tsukuba, Japan, November 2012

28. Zeng, G., Wang, P., Wang, J., Gan, R., Zha, H.: Structure-sensitive superpixels via geodesic distance. In: ICCV, pp. 447–454. IEEE Computer Society, Barcelona, Spain, November 2011

29. Zhang, Y., Hartley, R., Mashford, J., Burn, S.: Superpixels via pseudo-boolean optimization. In: ICCV, pp. 1387–1394. IEEE Computer Society, Barcelona, Spain, November 2011

30. Zhang, Y., Hartley, R., Mashford, J., Burn, S.: Superpixels, occlusion and stereo. In: DICTA, pp. 84–91. IEEE Computer Society, Noosa, Australia, December 2011

Author Index

Printed in the United States
by Baker & Taylor Publisher Services